Troubleshootin

A Practical Guide to Understanding and Troubleshooting BGP

Vinit Jain, CCIE No. 22854

Brad Edgeworth, CCIE No. 31574

Cisco Press

800 East 96th Street

Indianapolis, Indiana 46240 USA

Troubleshooting BGP

Vinit Jain, Brad Edgeworth

Copyright© 2017 Cisco Systems, Inc.

Published by:

Cisco Press
800 East 96th Street
Indianapolis, IN 46240 USA

Printed in the United States of America

1   16

Library of Congress Control Number: 2016958006

ISBN-13: 978-1-58714-464-6

ISBN-10: 1-58714-464-6

Warning and Disclaimer

Trademark Acknowledgments

Special Sales

For information about buying this title in bulk quantities, or for special sales opportunities (which may include electronic versions; custom cover designs; and content particular to your business, training goals, marketing focus, or branding interests), please contact our corporate sales department at corpsales@pearsoned.com or (800) 382-3419.

For government sales inquiries, please contact governmentsales@pearsoned.com.

For questions about sales outside the U.S., please contact intlcs@pearson.com.

Feedback Information

At Cisco Press, our goal is to create in-depth technical books of the highest quality and value. Each book is crafted with care and precision, undergoing rigorous development that involves the unique expertise of members from the professional technical community.

Readers' feedback is a natural continuation of this process. If you have any comments regarding how we could improve the quality of this book, or otherwise alter it to better suit your needs, you can contact us through email at feedback@ciscopress.com. Please make sure to include the book title and ISBN in your message.

We greatly appreciate your assistance.

Editor-in-Chief: Mark Taub

Alliances Manager, Cisco Press: Ron Fligge

Product Line Manager: Brett Bartow

Managing Editor: Sandra Schroeder

Development Editor: Marianne Bartow

Senior Project Editor: Tonya Simpson

Copy Editor: Barbara Hacha

Technical Editors: Richard Furr, Ramiro Garza Rios

Editorial Assistant: Vanessa Evans

Cover Designer: Chuti Prasertsith

Composition: codeMantra

Indexer: Cheryl Lenser

Proofreader: Deepa Ramesh

Americas Headquarters	**Asia Pacific Headquarters**	**Europe Headquarters**
Cisco Systems, Inc.	Cisco Systems (USA) Pte. Ltd.	Cisco Systems International BV
San Jose, CA	Singapore	Amsterdam, The Netherlands

Cisco has more than 200 offices worldwide. Addresses, phone numbers, and fax numbers are listed on the Cisco Website at **www.cisco.com/go/offices.**

CCDE, CCENT, Cisco Eos, Cisco HealthPresence, the Cisco logo, Cisco Lumin, Cisco Nexus, Cisco StadiumVision, Cisco TelePresence, Cisco WebEx, DCE, and Welcome to the Human Network are trademarks; Changing the Way We Work, Live, Play, and Learn and Cisco Store are service marks; and Access Registrar, Aironet, AsyncOS, Bringing the Meeting To You, Catalyst, CCDA, CCDP, CCIE, CCIP, CCNA, CCNP, CCSP, CCVP, Cisco, the Cisco Certified Internetwork Expert logo, Cisco IOS, Cisco Press, Cisco Systems, Cisco Systems Capital, the Cisco Systems logo, Cisco Unity, Collaboration Without Limitation, EtherFast, EtherSwitch, Event Center, Fast Step, Follow Me Browsing, FormShare, GigaDrive, HomeLink, Internet Quotient, IOS, iPhone, iQuick Study, IronPort, the IronPort logo, LightStream, Linksys, MediaTone, MeetingPlace, MeetingPlace Chime Sound, MGX, Networkers, Networking Academy, Network Registrar, PCNow, PIX, PowerPanels, ProConnect, ScriptShare, SenderBase, SMARTnet, Spectrum Expert, StackWise, The Fastest Way to Increase Your Internet Quotient, TransPath, WebEx, and the WebEx logo are registered trademarks of Cisco Systems, Inc. and/or its affiliates in the United States and certain other countries.

All other trademarks mentioned in this document or website are the property of their respective owners. The use of the word partner does not imply a partnership relationship between Cisco and any other company. (0812R)

About the Authors

Vinit Jain, CCIE No. 22854 (R&S, SP, Security & DC), is a High Touch Technical Support (HTTS) engineer with Cisco providing support to premium customers of Cisco on complex routing technologies. Before joining Cisco, Vinit worked as a CCIE trainer and a network consultant. In addition to his expertise in networks, he has experience with software development, with which he began his career.

Vinit holds certifications for multiple vendors, such as Cisco, Microsoft, Sun Microsystems, VMware, and Oracle, and also is a Certified Ethical Hacker. Vinit is a speaker at Cisco Live and various other forums, including NANOG. Vinit pursued his graduation from Delhi University in Mathematics and earned his Masters in Information Technology from Kuvempu University in India. Vinit is married and is presently based out of RTP, North Carolina. Vinit can be found on Twitter @vinugenie.

Brad Edgeworth, CCIE No. 31574 (R&S & SP), has been with Cisco working as a systems engineer and a technical leader. Brad is a distinguished speaker at Cisco Live, where he has presented on multiple topics. Before joining Cisco, Brad worked as a network architect and consulted for various Fortune 500 companies. Brad's other certifications include Cisco Certified Design Professional (CCDP) and Microsoft Certified Systems Engineer (MCSE). Brad has been working in the IT field with an emphasis on enterprise and service provider environments from an architectural and operational perspective. Brad holds a Bachelor of Arts degree in Computer Systems Management from St. Edward's University in Austin, Texas. Brad can be found on Twitter @BradEdgeworth.

About the Technical Reviewers

Richard Furr, CCIE No. 9173 (R&S & SP), is a technical leader with the Cisco Technical Assistance Center (TAC). For the past 15 years, Richard has worked for Cisco TAC and high touch technical support (HTTS) organizations, supporting service providers and large enterprise environments with a focus on troubleshooting routing protocols, MPLS, IP Multicast, and QoS.

Ramiro Garza Rios, CCIE No. 15469 (R&S, SP, and Security), is a solutions integration architect with Cisco Advanced Services, where he plans, designs, implements, and optimizes IP NGN service provider networks. Before joining Cisco in 2005, he was a network consulting and presales engineer for a Cisco Gold Partner in Mexico, where he planned, designed, and implemented both enterprise and service provider networks.

Dedications

I would like to dedicate this book to my brother, Lalit, who is the inspiration and driving force behind everything I have achieved.

—*Vinit*

This book is dedicated to my family. Thank you both for letting me sleep in after a late-night writing session. To my wife, Tanya, "The Queen of Catan," thank you for bringing joy to my life. To my daughter, Teagan, listen to your mother. She is *almost* always right, and way better with her grammar than I am.

—*Brad*

Acknowledgments

Vinit Jain:

I would like to thank Russ White, Carlos Pignataro, Richard Furr, Pete Lumbis, Alejandro Eguiarte, and Brett Bartow for making this book possible.

I'd like to give special recognition to Alvaro Retana, Xander Thujis, and Steven Cheung for providing expert technical knowledge and advice on various topics, making this book more useful and close to real-life troubleshooting scenarios.

To our technical editors, Richard and Ramiro. In addition to your technical accuracy, your insight into the technologies needed versus and different perspective has kept the size of the book manageable.

Many people within Cisco have provided feedback and suggestions to make this a great book. Thanks to all who have helped in the process, especially to my managers, Ruwani Biggers and Chip Little, who have helped me with this adventurous and fun-filled project.

Brad Edgeworth:

A debt of gratitude goes toward my co-author, Vinit. Thank you for allowing me to work on this book with you, although we spent way too many nights on the phone at 1 a.m. Your knowledge and input made this a better book.

To our technical editors, Richard and Ramiro. Thank you for finding all of our mistakes. Not that we had many, but you still saved us a couple times. I won't tell if you won't.

A special thank you goes to Brett Bartow and the Cisco Press team. You are the "magicians" that make this book look as good as it does!

A special thanks goes to Craig Smith. "*You are so money, and you don't even know it!*" To my co-workers Rob, John, and Gregg. Yes, this means I probably will need to go on another "book signing tour." If anything breaks while I'm gone, order a queso and chips!

Contents at a Glance

Contents

Icons Used in This Book

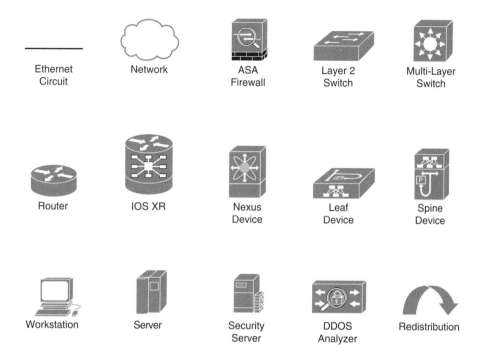

Ethernet Circuit	Network	ASA Firewall	Layer 2 Switch	Multi-Layer Switch
Router	IOS XR	Nexus Device	Leaf Device	Spine Device
Workstation	Server	Security Server	DDOS Analyzer	Redistribution

Command Syntax Conventions

The conventions used to present command syntax in this book are the same conventions used in the IOS Command Reference. The Command Reference describes these conventions as follows:

- **Boldface** indicates commands and keywords that are entered literally as shown. In actual configuration examples and output (not general command syntax), boldface indicates commands that are manually input by the user (such as a **show** command).

- *Italic* indicates arguments for which you supply actual values.

- Vertical bars (|) separate alternative, mutually exclusive elements.

- Square brackets ([ ]) indicate an optional element.

- Braces ({ }) indicate a required choice.

- Braces within brackets ([{ }]) indicate a required choice within an optional element.

Foreword

The Internet has revolutionized the world by providing an unlimited supply of information to a user's fingertips in a matter of seconds, or connecting people halfway around the world with voice and video calls. More people are using the Internet in ways unimaginable when it was first conceived. The size of the Internet routing prohibits the use of almost any routing protocol except for BGP.

More and more organizations continue to deploy BGP across every vertical, segment, and corner of the Earth because there have been so many new features and technologies introduced to BGP. BGP is not only used by the service providers but has become a fundamental technology in enterprises and data centers.

As the leader of Cisco's technical services for more than 25 years, I have the benefit of working with the best network professionals in the industry. This book is written by Vinit and Brad, two "Network Rock Stars," who have been in my organization for years supporting multiple Cisco customers. Vinit continues to provide dedicated service to Cisco's premium customers, with an emphasis on network routing protocols.

With any network deployment, it becomes important to understand and learn how to troubleshoot the network and the technologies the network uses. Organizations strive to achieve five 9s (that is, 99.999%) availability of their network. This makes it more important that the network engineers attain the skills to troubleshoot such complex network environments. BGP has features that provide such a highly available network that some large hosting companies use only BGP. This book delivers a convenient reference for troubleshooting, deployment of best practices, and advanced protocol theory of BGP.

Joseph Pinto

SVP, Technical Services

Cisco, San Jose

Introduction

BGP is a standardized routing protocol that provides scalability, flexibility, and network stability for a variety of functions. Originally, BGP was developed to support large IP routing tables. It is the de facto protocol for routers connecting to the Internet, which provides connectivity to more than 600,000 networks and continues to grow.

Although BGP provides scalability and unique routing policy, the architecture can be intimidating or create complexity, too. Over the years, BGP has had significant increases in functionality and feature enhancements. BGP has expanded from being an Internet routing protocol to other aspects of the network, including the data center. BGP provides a scalable control plane for IPv6, MPLS VPNs (L2 and L3), Multicast, VPLS, and Ethernet VPN (EVPN).

Although most network engineers understand how to configure BGP, they lack the understanding to effectively troubleshoot BGP issues. This book is the single source for mastering techniques to troubleshoot all BGP issues for the following Cisco operating systems: Cisco IOS, IOS XR, and NX-OS. Bringing together content previously spread across multiple sources and Cisco Press titles, it covers updated various BGP design implementations found in blended service providers and enterprise environments and how to troubleshoot them.

Who Should Read This Book?

This book is for network engineers, architects, or consultants who want to learn more about BGP and learn how to troubleshoot all the various capabilities and features that it provides. Readers should have a fundamental understanding of IP routing.

How This Book Is Organized

Although this book could be read cover to cover, it is designed to be flexible and allow you to easily move between chapters and sections of chapters to cover just the material that you need more work with.

Part I, "BGP Fundamentals," provides an overview of BGP fundamentals—its various attributes and features.

- **Chapter 1, "BGP Fundamentals"**: This chapter provides a brief overview of the BGP protocols, configuration, and some of the most commonly used features. Additional information is provided on how BGP's behavior is different between an internal and an external BGP neighbor.

Part II, "Common BGP Troubleshooting," provides the basic building blocks for troubleshooting BGP. These concepts are then carried over into other sections of the book.

- **Chapter 2, "Generic Troubleshooting Methodologies":** This chapter discusses the various basic troubleshooting methodologies and tools that are used for troubleshooting generic network problems. It also discusses how to approach a problem and how the problem can be replicated to identify the root cause.

- **Chapter 3, "Troubleshooting Peering Issues":** This chapter discusses the common issues seen with BGP peering. It provides detailed troubleshooting methods that can be used when investigating BGP peering issues, such as peer down and peer flapping. The chapter finally concludes by discussing dynamic BGP peering functionality.

- **Chapter 4, "Troubleshooting Route Advertisement and BGP Policies":** This chapter covers the BGP path selection mechanism and troubleshooting complex BGP path selection or missing route issues, which are commonly seen in BGP deployments.

- **Chapter 5, "Troubleshooting BGP Convergence":** This chapter examines various scenarios and conditions that could cause convergence issues. It provides a detailed explanation of how the BGP messages are formatted for the update and the complete update generation process on all the platforms.

Part III, "BGP Scalability Issues," explains how specific problems can arise in a scaled BGP network.

- **Chapter 6, "Troubleshooting Platform Issues Due to BGP":** This chapter examines various platform issues that are usually seen in a production environment caused by BGP. It examines conditions such as high CPU conditions, high memory utilization, and memory leak conditions caused by BGP.

- **Chapter 7, "Scaling BGP":** This chapter walks you through various features in BGP that can be implemented to scale the BGP environment. It explains in detail how to scale BGP using route reflectors and other advanced features, such as BGP diverse paths.

- **Chapter 8, "Troubleshooting BGP Edge Architectures":** This chapter discusses BGP multihoming, which is mostly deployed in enterprise networks. It also discusses problems faced with the multihomed deployments. This chapter also explains how to achieve load balancing with BGP and how to troubleshoot any problems faced with such deployments.

Part IV, "Securing BGP," discusses how BGP can be secured and how BGP can be used to prevent attacks in the network.

- **Chapter 9, "Securing BGP":** This chapter explains various features that help to secure Internet routing and thus prevent outages due to security breaches. It explains and differentiates between S-BGP and SO-BGP. The chapter then explains the SIDR solution using RPKI. Then we talk about DDoS attacks and mitigating them through RTBH and the BGP Flowspec feature.

Part V, "Multiprotocol BGP," discusses Multiprotocol BGP and how other address families provide connectivity outside traditional IP routing.

- **Chapter 10, "MPLS Layer 3 VPN (L3VPN)":** This chapter discusses and explains various BGP use cases of Multi-Protocol BGP deployment in Layer 3 MPLS VPN services and how to troubleshoot them. It also describes how to scale the network in the service provider environment for L3 VPN services.

- **Chapter 11, "BGP for MPLS L2VPN Services":** This chapter discusses and explains various BGP use cases of Multi-Protocol BGP deployment in Layer 2 MPLS VPN services and how to troubleshoot them. It talks about features such as BGP autodiscovery for VPLS and EVPN.

- **Chapter 12, "IPv6 BGP for Service Providers":** This chapter covers various IPv6 services for service providers, such as 6PE, 6VPE, and methods for how to troubleshoot the problems with such deployments.

- **Chapter 13, "VxLAN BGP EVPN":** This chapter covers implementation of BGP in data-center deployments by providing VxLAN Overlay using BGP. The chapter also explains how the VxLAN BGP EVPN control-plane learning mechanism works and how to troubleshoot various issues faced with the VxLAN EVPN feature.

Part VI, "High Availability," explains the techniques to increase the availability of BGP in the network.

- **Chapter 14, "BGP High Availability":** High availability is one of the primary concerns in almost all network deployments. This chapter discusses in detail the various high-availability features such as GR, NSR, BFD, and so on that can be implemented in BGP.

Part VII, "BGP: Looking Forward," provides an overview of the recent enhancements to BGP and insight into future applications of BGP.

- **Chapter 15, "Enhancements in BGP":** This chapter discusses new enhancements in BGP, such as BGP for Link-State distribution, BGP for tunnel setup, and EVPN.

Learning in a Lab Environment

This book may contain new features and functions that do not match your current environment. As with any new technology, it is best to test in advance of actual deployment of new features.

Cisco Virtual Internet Routing Lab (VIRL) provides a scalable, extensible network design and simulation environment. Many customers use VIRL for a variety of testing before deployment of features or verification of the techniques explained in this book. VIRL includes several Cisco Network Operating System virtual machines (IOSv, IOS-XRv, CSR1000v, NX-OSv, IOSvL2, and ASAv) and has the capability to integrate with third-party vendor virtual machines or external network devices. It includes many unique capabilities, such as live visualization, that provide the capability to create protocol diagrams in real-time from your running simulation. More information about VIRL can be found at http://virl.cisco.com.

Additional Reading

The authors tried to keep the size of the book manageable while providing only necessary information for the topics involved.

Some readers may require additional reference material around the design concepts using BGP and may find the following books a great supplementary resource for the topics in this book:

Edgeworth, Brad, Aaron Foss, and Ramiro Garza Rios. *IP Routing on Cisco IOS, IOS XE, and IOS XR*. Indianapolis: Cisco Press, 2014.

Halabi, Sam. *Internet Routing Architectures*. Indianapolis: Cisco Press, 2000.

White, Russ, Alvaro Retana, and Don Slice. *Optimal Routing Design*. Indianapolis: Cisco Press, 2005.

Doyle, Jeff. *Routing TCP/IP, Volume 2*, Second Edition. Indianapolis: Cisco Press, 2016.

Chapter 1

BGP Fundamentals

The following topics are covered in this chapter:

- BGP Messages and Inter-Router Communication

- Basic BGP Configuration for IOS, IOS XR, and NX-OS

- IBGP Rules

- EBGP Rules

- BGP Route Aggregation

A router's primary function is to move packets from one network to a different network. A router learns about unattached networks through static configuration or through dynamic routing protocols that distribute network topology information between routers. Routers try to select the best loop-free path in a network based on the destination network. Link flaps, router crashes, and other unexpected events could impact the best path, so the routers must exchange information with each other so that the network topology updates during these types of events.

Routing protocols are classified as either an Interior Gateway Protocol (IGP) or an Exterior Gateway Protocol (EGP), which indicates whether the protocol is designed for exchanging routes within an organization or between organizations. In IGP protocols, all routers use a common logic within the routing domain to find the shortest path to reach a destination. EGP protocols may require a unique routing policy for every external organization that it exchanges routes.

Border Gateway Protocol

RFC 1654 defines Border Gateway Protocol (BGP) as an EGP standardized path-vector routing protocol that provides scalability, flexibility, and network stability. When BGP was created, the primary design consideration was for IPv4 inter-organization connectivity on public networks, such as the Internet, or private dedicated networks. BGP is the only protocol used to exchange networks on the Internet, which has more than 600,000 IPv4 routes and continues to grow. BGP does not advertise incremental updates or refresh network advertisements like OSPF or ISIS. BGP prefers stability within the network, because a link flap could result in route computation for thousands of routes.

From the perspective of BGP, an autonomous system (AS) is a collection of routers under a single organization's control, using one or more IGPs, and common metrics to route packets within the AS. If multiple IGPs or metrics are used within an AS, the AS must appear consistent to external ASs in routing policy. An IGP is not required within an AS, and could use BGP as the only routing protocol in it, too.

Autonomous System Numbers

Organizations requiring connectivity to the Internet must obtain an Autonomous System Number (ASN). ASNs were originally 2 bytes (16 bit) providing 65,535 ASNs. Due to exhaustion, RFC 4893 expands the ASN field to accommodate 4 bytes (32 bit). This allows for 4,294,967,295 unique ASNs, providing quite a leap from the original 65,535 ASNs.

Two blocks of private ASNs are available for any organization to use as long as they are never exchanged publicly on the Internet. ASNs 64,512–65,535 are private ASNs within the 16-bit ASN range, and 4,200,000,000–4,294,967,294 are private ASNs within the extended 32-bit range.

The Internet Assigned Numbers Authority (IANA) is responsible for assigning all public ASNs to ensure that they are globally unique. IANA requires the following items when requesting a public ASN:

- Proof of a publicly allocated network range
- Proof that Internet connectivity is provided through multiple connections
- Need for a unique route policy from your providers

In the event that an organization does not meet those guidelines, it should use the ASN provided by its service provider.

Note   It is imperative that you use only the ASN assigned by IANA, the ASN assigned by your service provider, or private ASNs. Using another organization's ASN without permission could result in traffic loss and cause havoc on the Internet.

Path Attributes

BGP attaches path attributes (PA) associated with each network path. The PAs provide BGP with granularity and control of routing policies within BGP. The BGP prefix PAs are classified as follows:

- Well-known mandatory
- Well-known discretionary
- Optional transitive
- Optional nontransitive

Per RFC 4271, well-known attributes must be recognized by all BGP implementations. Well-known mandatory attributes must be included with every prefix advertisement, whereas well-known discretionary attributes may or may not be included with the prefix advertisement.

Optional attributes do not have to be recognized by all BGP implementations. Optional attributes can be set so that they are *transitive* and stay with the route advertisement from AS to AS. Other PAs are nontransitive and cannot be shared from AS to AS. In BGP, the Network Layer Reachability Information (NLRI) is the routing update that consists of the network prefix, prefix length, and any BGP PAs for that specific route.

Loop Prevention

BGP is a path vector routing protocol and does not contain a complete topology of the network-like link state routing protocols. BGP behaves similar to distance vector protocols to ensure a path is loop free.

The BGP attribute AS_PATH is a well-known mandatory attribute and includes a complete listing of all the ASNs that the prefix advertisement has traversed from its source AS. The AS_PATH is used as a loop prevention mechanism in the BGP protocol. If a BGP router receives a prefix advertisement with its AS listed in the AS_PATH, it discards the prefix because the router thinks the advertisement forms a loop.

Address Families

Originally, BGP was intended for routing of IPv4 prefixes between organizations, but RFC 2858 added Multi-Protocol BGP (MP-BGP) capability by adding extensions called address-family identifier (AFI). An address-family correlates to a specific network protocol, such as IPv4, IPv6, and the like, and additional granularity through a subsequent address-family identifier (SAFI), such as unicast and multicast. MBGP achieves this separation by using the BGP path attributes (PAs) MP_REACH_NLRI and MP_UNREACH_NLRI. These attributes are carried inside BGP update messages and are used to carry network reachability information for different address families.

Note   Some network engineers refer to Multi-Protocol BGP as MP-BGP, and other network engineers use the term MBGP. Both terms are the same thing.

Network engineers and vendors continue to add functionality and feature enhancements to BGP. BGP now provides a scalable control plane for signaling for overlay technologies like MPLS VPNs, IPsec Security Associations, and Virtual Extensible LAN (VXLAN). These overlays can provide Layer 3 connectivity via MPLS L3VPNs, or Layer 2 connectivity via MPLS L2VPNs (L2VPN), such as Virtual Private LAN Service (VPLS) or Ethernet VPNs (EVPNs).

Every address-family maintains a separate database and configuration for each protocol (address-family + subaddress family) in BGP. This allows for a routing policy in one address-family to be different from a routing policy in a different address family even though the router uses the same BGP session to the other router. BGP includes an AFI and a SAFI with every route advertisement to differentiate between the AFI and SAFI databases. Table 1-1 provides a small list of common AFI and SAFIs.

Table 1-1   *Common BGP Address Families and Subaddress Families*

AFI	SAFI	Network Layer Information
1	1	IPv4 Unicast
1	2	IPv4 Multicast
1	4	IPv4 Unicast with MPLS Label
1	128	MPLS L3VPN IPv4
2	1	IPv6 Unicast
2	4	IPv6 Unicast with MPLS Label
2	128	MPLS L3VPN IPv6
25	65	Virtual Private LAN Service (VPLS)
		Virtual Private Wire Service (VPWS)
25	70	Ethernet VPN (EVPN)

BGP Sessions

A BGP session refers to the established adjacency between two BGP routers. BGP sessions are always point-to-point and are categorized into two types:

- **Internal BGP (IBGP):** Sessions established with an IBGP router that are in the same AS or participate in the same BGP confederation. IBGP sessions are considered more secure, and some of BGP's security measures are lowered in comparison to EBGP sessions. IBGP prefixes are assigned an administrative distance (AD) of 200 upon installing into the router's routing information base (RIB).

■ **External BPG (EBGP):** Sessions established with a BGP router that are in a different AS. EBGP prefixes are assigned an AD of 20 upon installing into the router's RIB.

Note   Administrative distance (AD) is a rating of the trustworthiness of a routing information source. If a router learns about a route to a destination from more than one routing protocol, and they all have the same prefix length, AD is compared. The preference is given to the route with the lower AD.

Inter-Router Communication

BGP does not use hello packets to discover neighbors like IGP protocols and cannot discover neighbors dynamically. BGP was designed as an interautonomous routing protocol, implying that neighbor adjacencies should not change frequently and are coordinated. BGP neighbors are defined by an IP address.

BGP uses TCP port 179 to communicate with other routers. TCP allows for handling of fragmentation, sequencing, and reliability (acknowledgement and retransmission) of communication packets.

IGP protocols follow the physical topology because the sessions are formed with hellos that cannot cross network boundaries (that is, single hop only). BGP uses TCP, which is capable of crossing network boundaries (that is, multihop capable). While BGP can form neighbor adjacencies that are directly connected, it can also form adjacencies that are multiple hops away. Multihop sessions require that the router use an underlying route installed in the RIB (static or from any routing protocol) to establish the TCP session with the remote endpoint.

In Figure 1-1, R1 is able to establish a direct BGP session with R2. In addition, R2 is able to form a BGP session with R4, even though it passes through R3. R1 and R2 use a directly connected route to locate each other. R2 uses a static route to reach the 10.1.34.0/24 network, and R4 has a static route to reach the 10.1.23.0/24 network. R3 is unaware that R2 and R4 have established a BGP session, even though the packets flow through R3.

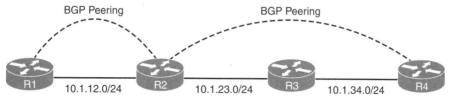

Figure 1-1   *BGP Direct and Multihop Sessions*

> **Note**   BGP neighbors connected via the same network use the ARP table to locate the Layer 2 address of the peer. Multihop BGP sessions require route table information for finding the IP address of the peer. It is common to have a static route or IGP running between IBGP neighbors for providing the topology path information for establishing the BGP TCP session. A default route is not sufficient to form a multihop BGP session.

BGP can be thought of as a control plane routing protocol or as an application, because it allows for the exchanging of routes with peers multiple hops away. BGP routers do not have to be in the data plane (path) to exchange prefixes, but all routers in the data path need to know all the routes that will be forwarded through them.

BGP Messages

BGP communication uses four message types, as shown in Table 1-2.

Table 1-2   *BGP Packet Types*

Type	Name	Functional Overview
1	OPEN	Sets up and establishes BGP adjacency
2	UPDATE	Advertises, updates, or withdraws routes
3	NOTIFICATION	Indicates an error condition to a BGP neighbor
4	KEEPALIVE	Ensures that BGP neighbors are still alive

OPEN

The OPEN message is used to establish a BGP adjacency. Both sides negotiate session capabilities before a BGP peering establishes. The OPEN message contains the BGP version number, ASN of the originating router, Hold Time, BGP Identifier, and other optional parameters that establish the session capabilities.

Hold Time

The Hold Time attribute sets the Hold Timer in seconds for each BGP neighbor. Upon receipt of an UPDATE or KEEPALIVE, the Hold Timer resets to the initial value. If the Hold Timer reaches zero, the BGP session is torn down, routes from that neighbor are removed, and an appropriate update route withdraw message is sent to other BGP neighbors for the impacted prefixes. The Hold Time is a heartbeat mechanism for BGP neighbors to ensure that the neighbor is healthy and alive.

When establishing a BGP session, the routers use the smaller Hold Time value contained in the two router's OPEN messages. The Hold Time value must be at least three seconds, or zero. For Cisco routers the default hold timer is 180 seconds.

BGP Identifier

The BGP Router-ID (RID) is a 32-bit unique number that identifies the BGP router in the advertised prefixes as the BGP Identifier. The RID can be used as a loop prevention mechanism for routers advertised within an autonomous system. The RID can be set manually or dynamically for BGP. A nonzero value must be set for routers to become neighbors. The dynamic RID allocation logic varies between the following operating systems.

- **IOS:** IOS nodes use the highest IP address of the any *up* loopback interfaces. If there is not an *up* loopback interface, then the highest IP address of any active *up* interfaces becomes the RID when the BGP process initializes.

- **IOS XR:** IOS XR nodes use the IP address of the lowest *up* loopback interface. If there is not any *up* loopback interfaces, then a value of zero (0.0.0.0) is used and prevents any BGP adjacencies from forming.

- **NX-OS:** NX-OS nodes use the IP address of the lowest *up* loopback interface. If there is not any *up* loopback interfaces, then the IP address of the lowest active *up* interface becomes the RID when the BGP process initializes.

Router-IDs typically represent an IPv4 address that resides on the router, such as a loopback address. Any IPv4 address can be used, including IP addresses not configured on the router. For IOS and IOS XR, the command **bgp router-id** *router-id* is used, and NX-OS uses the command **router-id** *router-id* under the BGP router configuration to statically assign the BGP RID. Upon changing the router-id, all BGP sessions reset and need to be reestablished.

Note   Setting a static BGP RID is a best practice.

KEEPALIVE

BGP does not rely on the TCP connection state to ensure that the neighbors are still alive. Keepalive messages are exchanged every one-third of the Hold Timer agreed upon between the two BGP routers. Cisco devices have a default Hold Time of 180 seconds, so the default Keepalive interval is 60 seconds. If the Hold Time is set for zero, no Keepalive messages are sent between the BGP neighbors.

UPDATE

The Update message advertises any feasible routes, withdraws previously advertised routes, or can do both. The Update message includes the Network Layer Reachability Information (NLRI) that includes the prefix and associated BGP PAs when advertising prefixes. Withdrawn NLRIs include only the prefix. An UPDATE message can act as a Keepalive to reduce unnecessary traffic.

NOTIFICATION Message

A Notification message is sent when an error is detected with the BGP session, such as a hold timer expiring, neighbor capabilities change, or a BGP session reset is requested. This causes the BGP connection to close.

BGP Neighbor States

BGP forms a TCP session with neighbor routers called peers. BGP uses the Finite State Machine (FSM) to maintain a table of all BGP peers and their operational status. The BGP session may report in the following states:

- Idle

- Connect

- Active

- OpenSent

- OpenConfirm

- Established

Figure 1-2 displays the BGP FSM and the states in order of establishing a BGP session.

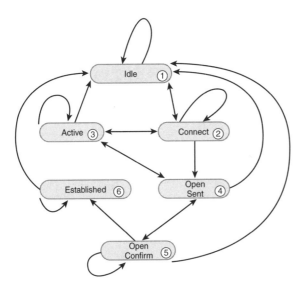

Figure 1-2   *BGP Finite State Machine*

Idle

This is the first stage of the BGP FSM. BGP detects a start event, tries to initiate a TCP connection to the BGP peer, and also listens for a new connect from a peer router.

If an error causes BGP to go back to the Idle state for a second time, the ConnectRetryTimer is set to 60 seconds and must decrement to zero before the connection is initiated again. Further failures to leave the Idle state result in the ConnectRetryTimer doubling in length from the previous time.

Connect

In this state, BGP initiates the TCP connection. If the 3-way TCP handshake completes, the established BGP Session BGP process resets the ConnectRetryTimer and sends the Open message to the neighbor, and then changes to the OpenSent State.

If the ConnectRetry timer depletes before this stage is complete, a new TCP connection is attempted, the ConnectRetry timer is reset, and the state is moved to Active. If any other input is received, the state is changed to Idle.

During this stage, the neighbor with the higher IP address manages the connection. The router initiating the request uses a dynamic source port, but the destination port is always 179.

Example 1-1 shows an established BGP session using the command **show tcp brief** to display the active TCP sessions between routers. Notice that the TCP source port is 179 and the destination port is 59884 on R1, and the ports are opposite on R2.

Example 1-1 *Established BGP Session*

```
RP/0/0/CPU0:R1# show tcp brief | exc "LISTEN|CLOSED"
  PCB       VRF-ID     Recv-Q Send-Q Local Address      Foreign Address      State
 0x088bcbb8 0x60000000    0      0   10.1.12.1:179      10.1.12.2:59884      ESTAB


R2# show tcp brief
TCB       Local Address          Foreign Address           (state)
EF153B88  10.1.12.2.59884        10.1.12.1.179             ESTAB
```

Note   Service providers consistently assign their customers the higher or lower IP address for their networks. This helps the service provider create proper instructions for access control lists (ACL) or firewall rules, or for troubleshooting them.

Active

In this state, BGP starts a new 3-way TCP handshake. If a connection is established, an Open message is sent, the Hold Timer is set to 4 minutes, and the state moves to OpenSent. If this attempt for TCP connection fails, the state moves back to the Connect state and resets the ConnectRetryTimer.

OpenSent

In this state, an Open message has been sent from the originating router and is awaiting an Open message from the other router. After the originating router receives the OPEN message from the other router, both OPEN messages are checked for errors. The following items are being compared:

- BGP Versions must match.
- The source IP address of the OPEN message must match the IP address that is configured for the neighbor.
- The AS number in the OPEN message must match what is configured for the neighbor.
- BGP Identifiers (RID) must be unique. If a RID does not exist, this condition is not met.
- Security Parameters (Password, TTL, and the like).

If the Open messages do not have any errors, the Hold Time is negotiated (using the lower value), and a KEEPALIVE message is sent (assuming the value is not set to zero). The connection state is then moved to OpenConfirm. If an error is found in the OPEN message, a Notification message is sent, and the state is moved back to Idle.

If TCP receives a disconnect message, BGP closes the connection, resets the ConnectRetryTimer, and sets the state to Active. Any other input in this process results in the state moving to Idle.

OpenConfirm

In this state, BGP waits for a Keepalive or Notification message. Upon receipt of a neighbor's Keepalive, the state is moved to Established. If the hold timer expires, a stop event occurs, or a Notification message is received, and the state is moved to Idle.

Established

In this state, the BGP session is established. BGP neighbors exchange routes via Update messages. As Update and Keepalive messages are received, the Hold Timer is reset. If the Hold Timer expires, an error is detected and BGP moves the neighbor back to the Idle state.

Basic BGP Configuration

When configuring BGP, it is best to think of the configuration from a modular perspective. BGP router configuration requires the following components:

- **BGP Session Parameters:** BGP session parameters provide settings that involve establishing communication to the remote BGP neighbor. Session settings include the ASN of the BGP peer, authentication, and keepalive timers.

- **Address-Family Initialization:** The address-family is initialized under the BGP router configuration mode. Networks advertisement and summarization occur within the address-family.

- **Activate the Address-Family on the BGP Peer:** Activate the address-family on the BGP peer. For a session to initiate, one address-family for that neighbor must be activated. The router's IP address is added to the neighbor table, and BGP attempts to establish a BGP session or accepts a BGP session initiated from the peer router.

For the remainder of this chapter, the BGP context is directed toward IPv4 routing. Other address families are throughout the book.

IOS

The steps for configuring BGP on an IOS router are as follows:

Step 1. Create the BGP Routing Process. Initialize the BGP process with the global command **router bgp** *as-number*.

Step 2. Identify the BGP Neighbor's IP address and Autonomous System Number. Identify the BGP neighbor's IP address and autonomous system number with the BGP router configuration command **neighbor** *ip-address* **remote-as** *as-number*.

> **Note** IOS activates the IPv4 address-family by default. This can simplify the configuration in an IPv4 environment because Steps 3 and 4 are optional, but may cause confusion when working with other address families. The BGP router configuration command **no bgp default ip4-unicast** disables the automatic activation of the IPv4 AFI so that Steps 3 and 4 are required.

Step 3. Initialize the address-family with the BGP router configuration command **address-family** *afi safi*.

Step 4. Activate the address-family for the BGP neighbor with the BGP address-family configuration command **neighbor** *ip-address* **activate**.

> **Note** On IOS routers, the default address-family modifier for the IPv4 and IPv6 address families is unicast and is optional. The address-family modifier is required on IOS XR nodes.

Example 1-2 demonstrates how to configure R1 and R2 using the IOS default and optional IPv4 AFI modifier CLI syntax. R1 is configured using the default IPv4 address-family enabled, and R2 disables IOS's default IPv4 address-family and manually activates it for the specific neighbor 10.1.12.1.

Example 1-2 *IOS Basic BGP Configuration*

```
R1 (Default IPv4 Address-Family Enabled)
router bgp 65100
 neighbor 10.1.12.2 remote-as 65100
```

```
R2 (Default IPv4 Address-Family Disabled)
router bgp 65100
 no bgp default ipv4-unicast
 neighbor 10.1.12.1 remote-as 65100
 !
 address-family ipv4
  neighbor 10.1.12.1 activate
 exit-address-family
```

IOS XR

The steps for configuring BGP on an IOS XR router are as follows:

Step 1. Create the BGP routing process. Initialize the BGP process with the global configuration command **router bgp** *as-number*.

Step 2. Initialize the address-family with the BGP router configuration command **address-family** *afi safi* so it can be associated to a BGP neighbor.

Step 3. Identify the BGP neighbor's IP address with the BGP router configuration command **neighbor** *ip-address*.

Step 4. Identify the BGP neighbor's autonomous system number with the BGP neighbor configuration command **remote-as** *as-number*.

Step 5. Activate the address-family for the BGP neighbor with the BGP neighbor configuration command **address-family** *afi safi*.

Step 6. Associate a route policy for EBGP Peers. IOS XR requires a routing policy to be associated to an EBGP peer as a security measure to ensure that routes are not accidentally accepted or advertised. If a route policy is not configured in the appropriate address-family, then NLRIs are discarded upon receipt and no NLRIs are advertised to EBGP peers.

An inbound and outbound route policy is configured with the command **route-policy** *policy-name* {**in** | **out**} under the BGP neighbor address-family configuration.

> **Note** IOS XR nodes do not establish a BGP session if the RID is set to zero, because the dynamic RID allocation did not find any *up* loopback interfaces. The RID needs to be set manually with the BGP router configuration command **bgp router-id.**

Example 1-3 displays the BGP configuration for R1 if it was running IOS XR. The RID is set on R1 because that router does not have any loopback interfaces.

Example 1-3 *IOS XR BGP Configuration*

```
IOS XR
router bgp 65100
 bgp router-id 192.168.1.1
 address-family ipv4 unicast
 !
 neighbor 10.1.12.2
  remote-as 65100
  address-family ipv4 unicast
```

NX-OS

The steps for configuring BGP on an NX-OS device are as follows:

Step 1.   Create the BGP routing process. Initialize the BGP process with the global configuration command **router bgp** *as-number*.

Step 2.   Initialize the address-family with the BGP router configuration command **address-family** *afi safi* so it can be associated to a BGP neighbor.

Step 3.   Identify the BGP neighbor's IP address and autonomous system number with the BGP router configuration command **neighbor** *ip-address* **remote-as** *as-number*.

Step 4.   Activate the address-family for the BGP neighbor with the BGP neighbor configuration command **address-family** *afi safi*.

Example 1-4 displays the BGP configuration for R1 if it was running NX-OS.

Example 1-4   *NX-OS BGP Configuration*

```
NX-OS
router bgp 65100
 address-family ipv4 unicast
 neighbor 10.1.12.2 remote-as 65100
  address-family ipv4 unicast
```

Verification of BGP Sessions

The BGP session is verified with the command **show bgp** *afi safi* **summary** on IOS, IOS XR, and NX-OS devices. Example 1-5 displays the IPv4 BGP unicast summary. Notice that the BGP RID and table versions are the first components shown. The Up/Down column reflects that the BGP session is up for over 5 minutes.

Example 1-5   *BGP IPv4 Session Summary Verification*

```
R1-IOS# show bgp ipv4 unicast summary
BGP router identifier 192.168.2.2, local AS number 65100
BGP table version is 1, main routing table version 1


Neighbor        V    AS MsgRcvd MsgSent   TblVer  InQ OutQ Up/Down   State/PfxRcd
10.1.12.2       4 65100       8       9        1    0    0 00:05:23            0
```
```
RP/0/0/CPU0:R1-XR# show bgp ipv4 unicast summary
! Output omitted for brevity
BGP router identifier 192.168.1.1, local AS number 65100
BGP main routing table version 4


Process    RcvTblVer   bRIB/RIB   LabelVer   ImportVer   SendTblVer   StandbyVer
Speaker            4          4          4           4            4            4


Neighbor      Spk    AS MsgRcvd MsgSent   TblVer  InQ OutQ  Up/Down   St/PfxRcd
10.1.12.2       0 65100       8       7        4    0    0 00:05:23           0
```
```
R1-NXOS# show bgp ipv4 unicast summary
! Output omitted for brevity
BGP router identifier 192.168.1.1, local AS number 65100
BGP table version is 5, IPv4 Unicast config peers 2, capable peers 1
Neighbor        V    AS MsgRcvd MsgSent   TblVer  InQ OutQ  Up/Down   State/PfxRcd
10.1.12.2       4 65100      32      37        5    0    0 00:05:24             0
```

Table 1-3 explains the fields of output when displaying the BGP Table.

Table 1-3   *BGP Summary Fields*

Field	Description
Neighbor	IP address of the BGP peer
V	BGP Version spoken by BGP peer (IOS and NX-OS only)
AS	Autonomous system number of BGP peer
MsgRcvd	Count of messages received from the BGP peer
MsgSent	Count of messages sent to the BGP peer
TblVer	Last version of the BGP database sent to the peer
InQ	Number of messages queued to be processed from the peer
OutQ	Number of messages queued to be sent to the peer
Up/Down	Length of time the BGP session is established, or the current status if the session is not in established state
State/PfxRcd	Current state of BGP peer or the number of prefixes received from the peer

> **Note**   Earlier commands like **show ip bgp summary** came out before MBGP and do not provide a structure for the current multiprotocol capabilities within BGP. Using the AFI and SAFI syntax ensures consistency for the commands regardless of information exchanged by BGP.

BGP neighbor session state, timers, and other essential peering information is shown with the command **show bgp** *afi safi* **neighbors** *ip-address*, as shown in Example 1-6.

Example 1-6   *BGP IPv4 Neighbor Output*

```
R2# show bgp ipv4 unicast neighbors 10.1.12.1
! Output ommitted for brevity

! The first section provides the neighbor's IP address, remote-as, indicates if
! the neighbor is 'internal' or 'external', the neighbor's BGP version, RID,
! session state, and timers.
BGP neighbor is 10.1.12.1, remote AS100, internal link
  BGP version 4, remote router ID 192.168.1.1
  BGP state = Established, up for 00:01:04
  Last read 00:00:10, last write 00:00:09, hold is 180, keepalive is 60 seconds
  Neighbor sessions:
    1 active, is not multisession capable (disabled)
```

```
! This second section indicates the capabilities of the BGP neighbor and
! address-families configured on the neighbor.
  Neighbor capabilities:
    Route refresh: advertised and received(new)
    Four-octets ASN Capability: advertised and received
    Address family IPv4 Unicast: advertised and received
    Enhanced Refresh Capability: advertised
    Multisession Capability:
    Stateful switchover support enabled: NO for session 1
  Message statistics:
    InQ depth is 0
    OutQ depth is 0
! This section provides a list of the BGP packet types that have been received
! or sent to the neighbor router.
                        Sent       Rcvd
    Opens:               1          1
    Notifications:       0          0
    Updates:             0          0
    Keepalives:          2          2
    Route Refresh:       0          0
    Total:               4          3
  Default minimum time between advertisement runs is 0 seconds
! This section provides the BGP table version of the IPv4 Unicast address-
! family. The table version is not a 1-to-1 correlation with routes as multiple
! route change can occur during a revision change. Notice the Prefix Activity
! columns in this section.
For address family: IPv4 Unicast
  Session: 10.1.12.1
  BGP table version 1, neighbor version 1/0
  Output queue size : 0
  Index 1, Advertise bit 0
                            Sent       Rcvd
  Prefix activity:         ----       ----
    Prefixes Current:       0          0
    Prefixes Total:         0          0
    Implicit Withdraw:      0          0
    Explicit Withdraw:      0          0
    Used as bestpath:      n/a         0
    Used as multipath:     n/a         0

                          Outbound    Inbound
  Local Policy Denied Prefixes:    --------    -------
    Total:                    0          0
  Number of NLRIs in the update sent: max 0, min 0
```

```
! This section indicates that a valid route exists in the RIB to the BGP peer IP
! address, provides the number of times that the connection has established and
! time dropped, since the last reset, the reason for the reset, if path-mtu-
! discovery is enabled, and ports used for the BGP session.
  Address tracking is enabled, the RIB does have a route to 10.1.12.1
  Connections established 2; dropped 1
  Last reset 00:01:40, due to Peer closed the session
  Transport(tcp) path-mtu-discovery is enabled
Connection state is ESTAB, I/O status: 1, unread input bytes: 0
Mininum incoming TTL 0, Outgoing TTL 255
Local host: 10.1.12.2, Local port: 179
Foreign host: 10.1.12.1, Foreign port: 56824
```

Prefix Advertisement

BGP uses three tables for maintaining the network prefix and path attributes (PA) for a route. The BGP tables are as follows:

- **Adj-RIB-in:** Contains the NLRIs in original form before inbound route policies are processed. The table is purged after all route policies are processed to save memory.

- **Loc-RIB:** Contains all the NLRIs that originated locally or were received from other BGP peers. After NLRIs pass the validity and next-hop reachability check, the BGP best path algorithm selects the best NLRI for a specific prefix. The Loc-RIB table is the table used for presenting routes to the ip routing table.

- **Adj-RIB-out:** Contains the NLRIs after outbound route policies have processed.

BGP **network** statements do not enable BGP for a specific interface. Instead they identify a specific network prefix to be installed into the BGP table, known as the *Loc-RIB table*.

After configuring a BGP network statement, the BGP process searches the global RIB for an exact network prefix match. The network prefix can be a connected network, secondary connected network, or any route from a routing protocol. After verifying that the network statement matches a prefix in the global RIB, the prefix installs into the BGP Loc-RIB table. As the BGP prefix installs into the Loc-RIB, the following BGP PA are set depending on the RIB prefix type:

- **Connected Network:** The next-hop BGP attribute is set to 0.0.0.0, the origin attribute is set to *i* (IGP), and the BGP weight is set to 32,768.

- **Static Route or Routing Protocol:** The next-hop BGP attribute is set to the next-hop IP address in the RIB, the origin attribute is set to *i* (IGP), the BGP weight is set to 32,768; and the MED is set to the IGP metric.

The network statement resides under the appropriate address-family within the BGP router configuration. The command **network** *network* **mask** *subnet-mask* [**route-map** *route-map-name*] is used for advertising IPv4 networks on IOS and NX-OS devices.

NX-OS devices also support prefix-length notation with the command **network** *network /prefix-length* [**route-map** *route-map-name*]. IOS XR routers use the command **network** *network/prefix-length* [**route-policy** *route-policy-name*] for installing routes into the BGP table. The optional **route-map** or **route-policy** parameter provides a method to set specific BGP PAs when the prefix installs into the Loc-RIB.

The command **show bgp** *afi safi* displays the contents of the BGP database (Loc-RIB) on IOS, IOS XR, and NX-OS devices. Every entry in the BGP Loc-RIB table contains at least one route, but could contain multiple routes for the same network prefix.

Note   By default, BGP advertises only the best path to other BGP peers regardless of the number of routes (NLRIs) in the BGP Loc-RIB. The BGP best path executes individually per address-family. The best path selection of one address-family cannot impact the best path calculation on a different address-family.

Example 1-7 displays the BGP table for IOS, IOS XR, and NX-OS. The BGP table contains received routes and locally generated routes.

Example 1-7   *Display of BGP Table*

```
R1-IOS# show bgp ipv4 unicast
BGP table version is 5, local router ID is 192.168.1.1
Status codes: s suppressed, d damped, h history, * valid, > best, i - internal,
              r RIB-failure, S Stale, m multipath, b backup-path, f RT-Filter,
              x best-external, a additional-path, c RIB-compressed,
Origin codes: i - IGP, e - EGP, ? - incomplete
RPKI validation codes: V valid, I invalid, N Not found

     Network          Next Hop          Metric LocPrf Weight Path
 *>  192.168.1.1/32   0.0.0.0                0        32768 i
 *   192.168.2.2/32   10.1.13.3                          0 65300 65200 i
 *>                   10.1.12.2              0            0 65200 i
 *>  192.168.3.3/32   10.1.13.3                          0 65300 i
 *                    10.1.12.2                           0 65200 65300 i


RP/0/0/CPU0:R2-XR# show bgp ipv4 unicast
! Output omitted for brevity
BGP router identifier 192.168.2.2, local AS number 65200
Status codes: s suppressed, d damped, h history, * valid, > best
              i - internal, r RIB-failure, S stale, N Nexthop-discard
Origin codes: i - IGP, e - EGP, ? - incomplete
   Network          Next Hop          Metric LocPrf Weight Path
 *> 192.168.1.1/32   10.1.12.1              0            0 65100 i
 *                   10.1.23.3                           0 65300 65100 i
```

```
*> 192.168.2.2/32      0.0.0.0                0        32768 i
*  192.168.3.3/32      10.1.12.1                       0 65100 65300 i
*>                     10.1.23.3                        0 65300 i
Processed 3 prefixes, 5 paths
```

```
R3-NXOS# show bgp ipv4 unicast
! Output omitted for brevity
Status: s-suppressed, x-deleted, S-stale, d-dampened, h-history, *-valid, >-best
Path type: i-internal, e-external, c-confed, l-local, a-aggregate, r-redist,
  I-injected
Origin codes: i - IGP, e - EGP, ? - incomplete, | - multipath, & - backup

   Network             Next Hop         Metric      LocPrf      Weight Path
*>e192.168.1.1/32      10.1.13.1           0                      0 65100 i
* e                    10.1.23.2                                  0 65200 65100 i
*>e192.168.2.2/32      10.1.23.2           0                      0 65200 i
* e                    10.1.13.1                                  0 65100 65200 i
*>l192.168.3.3/32      0.0.0.0                         100      32768 i
```

Note   NX-OS devices place *e* beside external learned BGP routes and *l* beside locally advertised BGP routes. IOS and IOS XR devices do not have this behavior.

Table 1-4 explains the fields of output when displaying the BGP table.

Table 1-4   *BGP Table Fields*

Field	Description
Network	List of the network prefixes installed in BGP. If multiple NLRIs exist for the same prefix, only the first prefix is identified, and others leave a blank space.
	Valid NLRIs are indicated by the *.
	The NLRI selected as the best path is indicated by an angle bracket (>).
Next Hop	*Next Hop*: A well-known mandatory BGP path attribute that defines the IP address for the next-hop for that specific NLRI.
Metric	*Multiple-Exit Discriminator (MED)*: An optional nontransitive BGP path attribute used in BGP algorithm for that specific NLRI.
LocPrf	*Local Preference*: A well-known discretionary BGP path attribute used in the BGP best path algorithm for that specific NLRI.
Weight	Locally significant Cisco defined attribute used in the BGP best path algorithm for that specific NLRI.

Field	Description
Path and Origin	*AS_PATH*: A well-known mandatory BGP path attribute used for loop prevention and in the BGP best path algorithm for that specific NLRI.
	Origin: A well-known mandatory BGP path attribute used in the BGP best path algorithm. A value of *i* represents an IGP, *e* for EGP, and *?* for a route that was redistributed into BGP.

BGP Best-Path Calculation

In BGP, route advertisements consist of the Network Layer Reachability Information (NLRI) and the path attributes (PAs). The NLRI composes the network prefix and prefix-length, and the BGP attributes such as AS-Path, Origin, and the like are stored in the path attributes. A BGP route may contain multiple paths to the same destination network. Every path's attributes impact the desirability of the route when a router selects the best path. A BGP router advertises only the best path to the neighboring routers.

Inside the BGP Loc-RIB table, all the routes and their path attributes are maintained with the best path calculated. The best path is then installed in the RIB of the router. In the event the best path is no longer available, the router can use the existing paths to quickly identify a new best path. BGP recalculates the best path for a prefix upon four possible events:

- BGP next-hop reachability change
- Failure of an interface connected to an EBGP peer
- Redistribution change
- Reception of new paths for a route

The BGP best path selection algorithm influences how traffic enters or leaves an autonomous system (AS). BGP does not use metrics to identify the best path in a network. BGP uses path attributes to identify its best path.

Some router configurations modify the BGP attributes to influence inbound traffic, outbound traffic, or inbound and outbound traffic depending on the network design requirements. BGP path attributes can be modified upon receipt or advertisement to influence routing in the local AS or neighboring AS. A basic rule for traffic engineering with BGP is that modifications in outbound routing policies influence inbound traffic, and modifications to inbound routing policies influence outbound traffic.

BGP installs the first received path as the best path automatically. When additional paths are received, the newer paths are compared against the current best path. If there is a tie, then processing continues onto the next step, until a best path winner is identified.

The following list provides the attributes that the BGP best path algorithm uses for the best route selection process. These attributes are processed in the order listed:

1. Weight

2. Local Preference

3. Local originated (network statement, redistribution, aggregation)

4. AIGP

5. Shortest-AS Path

6. Origin Type

7. Lowest MED

8. EBGP over IBGP

9. Lowest IGP Next-Hop

10. If both paths are external (EBGP), prefer the first (oldest)

11. Prefer the route that comes from the BGP peer with the lower RID

12. Prefer the route with the minimum cluster list length

13. Prefer the path that comes from the lowest neighbor address

The best path algorithm can be used to manipulate network traffic patterns for a specific route by modifying various path attributes on BGP routers. Changing of BGP PA can influence traffic flow into, out of, and around an AS.

BGP supports three types of equal cost multipath (ECMP): EBGP multipath, IBGP multipath, or eIBGP multipath. EBGP multipath requires that the weight, local preference, AS-Path length, AS-Path content, Origin, and MED match for a second route to install into the RIB. Chapter 8, "Troubleshooting BGP Edge Architectures," explains BGP ECMP in more detail.

Route Filtering and Manipulation

Route filtering is a method for selectively identifying routes that are advertised or received from neighbor routers. Route filtering may be used to manipulate traffic flows, reduce memory utilization, or to improve security. For example, it is common for ISPs to deploy route filters on BGP peerings to customers. Ensuring that only the customer routes are allowed over the peering link prevents the customer from accidentally becoming a transit AS on the Internet.

Filtering of routes within BGP is accomplished with filter-lists, prefix-lists, or route-maps on IOS and NX-OS devices. IOS XR uses route policies for filtering of routes. Route-filtering is explained in more detail in Chapter 4, "Troubleshooting Route Advertisement and BGP Policies."

Depending on the change to the BGP route manipulation technique, the BGP session may need to be refreshed to take effect. BGP supports two methods of clearing a BGP session: The first method is a hard reset, which tears down the BGP session, removes BGP routes from the peer, and is the most disruptive. The second method is a soft reset, which invalidates the BGP cache and requests a full advertisement from its BGP peer.

IOS and NX-OS devices initiate a hard reset with the command **clear ip bgp** *ip-address* [**soft**], and the command **clear bgp** *ip-address* [**graceful**] is used on IOS XR nodes. Soft reset on IOS and NX-OS devices use the optional **soft** keyword, whereas IOS XR nodes use the optional **graceful** keyword. Sessions can be cleared with all BGP neighbors by using an asterisk * in lieu of the peer's IP address.

When a BGP policy changes, the BGP table must be processed again so that the neighbors can be notified accordingly. Routes received by a BGP peer must be processed again. If the BGP session supports route refresh capability, then the peer readvertises (refreshes) the prefixes to the requesting router, allowing for the inbound policy to process using the new policy changes. The route refresh capability is negotiated for each address-family when the session is established.

Performing a soft reset on sessions that support route refresh capability actually initiates a route refresh. Soft resets can be performed for a specific address-family with the command **clear bgp** *address-family address-family modifier ip-address* **soft** [**in** | **out**]. Soft resets reduce the amount of routes that must be exchanged if multiple address families are configured with a single BGP peer. Changes to the outbound routing policies use the optional **out** keyword, and changes to inbound routing policies use the optional **in** keyword.

Older IOS versions that do not support route refresh capability require the usage of inbound soft reconfiguration so that updates to inbound route policies can be applied without performing a hard reset. Inbound soft reconfiguration does not purge the Adj-RIB-In table after routes process into the Loc-RIB table. The Adj-RIB-In maintains only the raw unedited routes (NLRIs) that were received from the neighbors and thereby allows the inbound route policies to be processed again.

Enabling this feature can consume a significant amount of memory because the Adj-RIB-In table stays in memory. Inbound soft reconfiguration uses the address-family command **neighbor** *ip-address* **soft-reconfiguration inbound** for IOS nodes. IOS XR and NX-OS devices use the neighbor specific address-family command **soft-reconfiguration inbound**.

IBGP

The need for BGP within an AS typically occurs when the multiple routing policies exist, or when transit connectivity is provided between autonomous systems. In Figure 1-3, AS65200 provides transit connectivity to AS65100 and AS65300. AS65100 connects at R2, and AS65300 connects at R4.

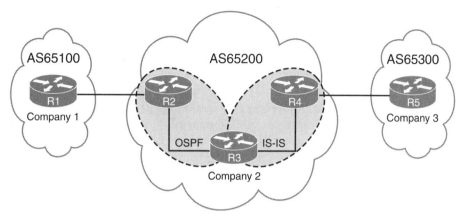

Figure 1-3 *AS65200 Provides Transit Connectivity*

R2 could form a BGP session directly with R4, but R3 would not know where to route traffic from AS65100 or AS65300 when traffic from either AS reaches R3, as shown in Figure 1-4, because R3 would not have the appropriate route forwarding information for the destination traffic.

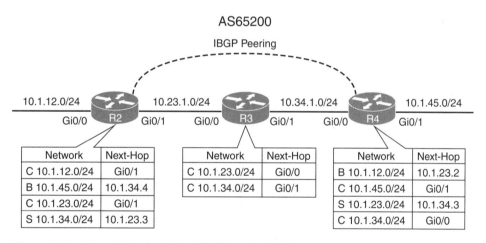

Figure 1-4 *Transit Devices Need Full Routing Table*

Advertising the full BGP table into an IGP is not a viable solution for the following reasons:

- **Scalability:** The Internet at the time of this writing has 600,000+ IPv4 networks and continues to increase in size. IGPs cannot scale to that level of routes.

- **Custom Routing:** Link state protocols and distance vector routing protocols use metric as the primary method for route selection. IGP protocols always use this routing pattern for path selection. BGP uses multiple steps to identify the best path and allows for BGP path attributes to manipulate the path for a specific prefix (NLRI). The path could be longer, which would normally be deemed suboptimal from an IGP protocol's perspective.

■ **Path Attributes:** All the BGP path attributes cannot be maintained within IGP proto-cols. Only BGP is capable of maintaining the path attribute as the prefix is advertised from one edge of the AS to the other edge.

IBGP Full Mesh Requirement

It was explained earlier in this chapter how BGP uses the AS_PATH as a loop detection and prevention mechanism because the ASN is prepended when advertising to an EBGP neighbor. IBGP peers do not prepend their ASN to the AS_PATH, because the NLRIs would fail the validity check and would not install the prefix into the IP routing table.

No other method exists to detect loops with IBGP sessions, and RFC 4271 prohibits the advertisement of a NLRI received from an IBGP peer to another IBGP peer. RFC 4271 states that all BGP routers within a single AS must be fully meshed to provide a complete loop-free routing table and prevent traffic blackholing.

In Figure 1-5, R1, R2, and R3 are all within AS65100. R1 has an IBGP session with R2, and R2 has an IBGP session with R3. R1 advertises the 10.1.1.0/24 prefix to R2, which is processed and inserted into R2's BGP table. R2 does not advertise the 10.1.1.0/24 NLRI to R3 because it received the prefix from an IBGP peer. To resolve this issue, R1 must form a multihop IBGP session so that R3 can receive the 10.1.1.0/24 prefix directly from R1. R1 connects to R3's 10.1.23.3 IP address, and R3 connects to R1's 10.1.12.1 IP address. R1 and R3 need a static route to the remote peering link, or R2 must advertise the 10.1.12.0/24 and 10.1.23.0/24 network into BGP.

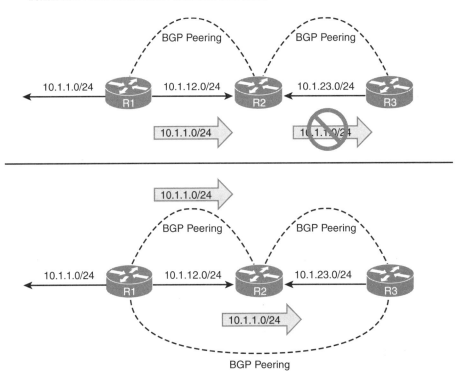

Figure 1-5 *IBGP Prefix Advertisement Behavior*

Peering via Loopback Addresses

BGP sessions are sourced by the outbound interface toward the BGP peers IP address by default. Imagine three routers connected via a full mesh. In the event of a link failure on the R1-R3 link, R3's BGP session with R1 times out and terminates. R3 loses connectivity to R1's networks even though R1 and R3 could communicate through R2 (multihop path). The loss of connectivity occurs because IBGP does not advertise routes learned from another IBGP peer as in the previous section.

Two solutions exist to overcome the link failure:

■ Add a second link between all routers (3 links will become 6 links) and establish two BGP sessions between each router.

■ Configure an IGP protocol on the routers' transit links, advertise loopback interfaces into the IGP, and then configure the BGP neighbors to establish a session to the remote router's loopback address.

Of the two methods, the second is more efficient and preferable.

The loopback interface is virtual and always stays up. In the event of link failure, the session remains intact while the IGP finds another path to the loopback address and, in essence, turns a single-hop IBGP session into a multihop IBGP session.

Updating the BGP configuration to set the destination of the BGP session to the remote router's loopback IP address is not enough. The source IP address of the BGP packets will still reflect the IP address of the outbound interface. When a BGP packet is received, the router correlates the source IP address of the packet to the BGP neighbor table. If the BGP packet source does not match an entry in the neighbor table, the packet cannot be associated to a neighbor and is discarded.

The source of BGP packets can be set statically to an interface's primary IP address with the BGP session configuration command **neighbor** *ip-address* **update-source** *interface-type interface-number* on IOS nodes. IOS XR and NX-OS devices use the command **update-source** *interface-type interface-number* under the neighbor session within the BGP router configuration.

Figure 1-6 illustrates the concept of peering using loopback addresses after the 10.1.13.0/24 network link fails. R1 and R3 still maintain BGP session connectivity while routes learned from OSPF allow BGP communication traffic between the loopbacks via R2. R1 can still forward packets to R3 via R2 because R1 performs a recursive lookup to identify R2 as the next-hop address.

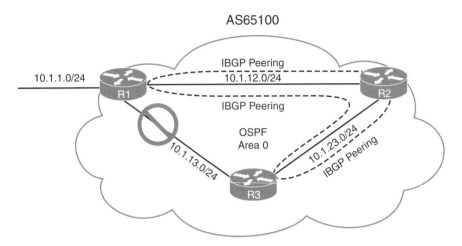

Figure 1-6   *Link Failure with IBGP Sessions on Loopback Interfaces*

Note   Sourcing BGP sessions from loopback interfaces eliminates the need to recompute the BGP best path algorithm if a peering link fails as shown in Figure 1-6. It also provides automatic load balancing if there are multiple equal cost paths via IGP to the loopback address.

EBGP

EBGP peerings are the core component of the BGP protocol on the Internet. EBGP is the exchange of network prefixes between autonomous systems. The following behaviors are different on EBGP sessions when compared to IBGP sessions:

- Time to Live (TTL) on BGP packets is set to one. BGP packets drop in transit if a multihop BGP session is attempted (TTL on IBGP packets is set to 255, which allows for multihop sessions).

- The advertising router modifies the BGP next-hop to the IP address sourcing the BGP connection.

- The advertising router prepends its ASN to the existing AS_PATH.

- The receiving router verifies that the AS_PATH does not contain an ASN that matches the local routers. BGP discards the NLRI if it fails the AS_PATH loop prevention check.

The configuration for EBGP and IBGP sessions are fundamentally the same on IOS, IOS XR, and NX-OS devices, except that the ASN in the **remote-as** statement is different from the ASN defined in the BGP process.

> **Note**   Different outbound (or inbound) route policies may be different from neighbor-to-neighbor, which allows for a dynamic routing-policy within an AS.

EBGP learned paths always have at least one ASN in the AS_PATH. If multiple ASs are listed in the AS_PATH, the most recent AS is always prepended (the furthest to the left). The BGP attributes for all paths to a specific network prefix can be shown with the command **show bgp ipv4 unicast** *network* on IOS, IOS XR, and NX-OS devices.

Example 1-8 displays the BGP path attributes for the remote prefix (192.168.3.3/32).

Example 1-8   *BGP Prefix Attributes for Remote Prefix*

```
R1-IOS# show bgp ipv4 unicast 192.168.3.3
BGP routing table entry for 192.168.3.3/32, version 11
Paths: (1 available, best #1, table default)
  Not advertised to any peer
  Refresh Epoch 1
  65200 65300
    10.1.12.2 from 10.1.12.2 (192.168.2.2)
      Origin IGP, localpref 100, valid, external, best
```

Table 1-5 explains the output provided in Example 1-8 and its correlation to BGP. Some of the BGP path attributes may change depending on the BGP features used.

Table 1-5   *BGP Prefix Attributes*

Output	Description
Paths: (1 available, best #1)	Provides a count of BGP paths in the BGP Loc-RIB and identifies the path selected as the BGP best path.
	All the paths and BGP attributes are listed after this.
Not advertised to any peer	Identifies whether the prefix was advertised to a BGP peer or not.
	BGP neighbors are consolidated into BGP update-groups. Explicit neighbors can be seen with the command **show bgp ipv4 unicast update-group** on IOS or IOS XR nodes.
65200 65300	This is the AS_PATH for the NLRI as it was received.

Output	Description
10.1.12.2 from 10.1.12.2 (192.168.2.2)	The first entry lists the IP address of the EBGP edge peer.
	The *from* field lists the IP address of the IBGP router that received this route from the EBGP edge peer. (In this case, the route was learned from an EBGP edge peer, so the address will be the EBGP edge peer.) Expect this field to change when an external route is learned from an IBGP peer. The number in parentheses is the BGP Identifier (RID) for that node.
Origin IGP	The Origin is the BGP well-known mandatory attribute that states the mechanism for advertising this route. In this instance, it is an Internal route
metric 0	Displays the optional nontransitive BGP attribute *Multiple-Exit Discriminator (MED)*, also known as BGP metric.
localpref 100	Displays the well-known discretionary BGP attribute Local Preference.
valid	Displays the validity of this path.
External	Displays how the route was learned. It will be internal, external, or local.

EBGP and IBGP Topologies

Combining EBGP sessions with IBGP sessions can cause confusion in terminology and concepts. Figure 1-6 provides a reference topology for clarification of concepts. R1 and R2 form an EBGP session, R3 and R4 form an EBGP session as well, and R2 and R3 form an IBGP session. R2 and R3 are IBGP peers and follow the rules of IBGP advertisement, even if the routes are learned from an EBGP peer.

As an EBGP prefix is advertised to an IBGP neighbor, issues may arise with the NLRI passing the validity check and the next-hop reachability check preventing advertisements to other BGP peers. The most common issue involves the failure of the next-hop accessibility. IBGP peers do not modify the next-hop address if the NLRI has a next-hop address other than 0.0.0.0. The next-hop address must be resolvable in the global RIB for it to be valid and advertised to other BGP peers.

To demonstrate this concept, only R1 and R4 have advertised their loopback interfaces into BGP, 192.168.1.1/32, and 192.168.4.4/32. Figure 1-7, displays the BGP table for all four routers. Notice that the BGP best path symbol (>) is missing for the 192.168.4.4/32 prefix on R2, and for the 192.168.1.1/32 on R3.

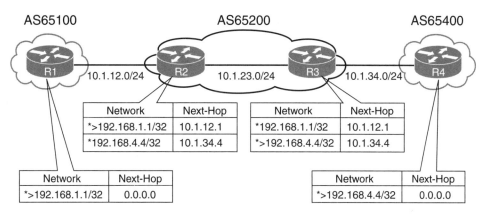

Figure 1-7 *EBGP and IBGP Topology*

R1's BGP table is missing the 192.168.4.4/32 prefix because the prefix did not pass R2's next-hop accessibility check preventing the execution of the BGP best path algorithm. R4 advertised the prefix to R3 with the next-hop address of 10.1.34.4, and R3 advertised the prefix to R2 with a next-hop address of 10.1.34.4. R2 does not have a route for the 10.1.34.4 IP address and deems the next-hop inaccessible. The same logic applies to R1's 192.168.1.1/32 prefix when advertised toward R4.

Example 1-9 shows the BGP attributes on R3 for the 192.168.1.1/32 prefix. Notice that the prefix is not advertised to any peer because the next-hop is *inaccessible.*

Example 1-9 *BGP Path Attributes for 192.168.1.1/32*

```
R3-IOS# show bgp ipv4 unicast 192.168.1.1
BGP routing table entry for 192.168.1.1/32, version 2
Paths: (1 available, no best path)
  Not advertised to any peer
  Refresh Epoch 1
  65100
    10.1.12.1 (inaccessible) from 10.1.23.2 (192.168.2.2.2)
      Origin IGP, metric 0, localpref 100, valid, internal
```

To correct the issue, the peering links, 10.1.12.0/24 and 10.1.34.0/24, need to be in both R2's and R3's routing table via either technique:

■ IGP advertisement. Remember to use the passive interface to prevent an accidental adjacency from forming. Most IGPs do not provide the filtering capability like BGP.

■ Advertising the networks into BGP.

Both techniques allow the prefixes to pass the next-hop accessibility test.

Figure 1-8 displays the topology with both transit links advertised into BGP. Notice that this time all four prefixes are valid with a BGP best path selected.

AS65100　　　　　AS65200　　　　　AS65400

R1　10.1.12.0/24　R2　10.1.23.0/24　R3　10.1.34.0/24　R4

R2:

Network	Next-Hop
*>192.168.1.1/32	10.1.12.1
*>192.168.4.4/32	10.1.34.4
*>10.1.12.0/24	0.0.0.0
*>10.1.34.0/24	10.1.23.3

R3:

Network	Next-Hop
*>192.168.1.1/32	10.1.12.1
*>192.168.4.4/32	10.1.34.4
*>10.1.12.0/24	10.1.23.2
*>10.1.34.0/24	0.0.0.0

R1:

Network	Next-Hop
*>192.168.1.1/32	0.0.0.0
*>192.168.4.4/32	10.1.12.2
*>10.1.12.0/24	0.0.0.0
*>10.1.34.0/24	10.1.12.2

R4:

Network	Next-Hop
*>192.168.1.1/32	10.1.34.3
*>192.168.4.4/32	0.0.0.0
*>10.1.12.0/24	10.1.34.3
*>10.1.34.0/24	0.0.0.0

Figure 1-8　*EBGP and IBGP Topology After Advertising Peering Links*

Next-Hop Manipulation

Imagine a service provider network with 500 routers and every router containing 200 EBGP peering links. To ensure that the next-hop address is reachable to the IBGP peers requires the advertisement of 100,000 peering networks in BGP or an IGP consuming router resources.

Another technique to ensure that the next-hop address check passes without advertising peering networks into a routing protocol involves the modification of the next-hop address in the BGP advertisement. The next-hop IP address can be modified on inbound or outbound neighbor routing policies. Managing IP addresses in a route policy can be a complicated task. Configuring the **next-hop-self** address-family feature modifies the next-hop address in all external NLRIs using the IP address of the BGP neighbor.

The command **neighbor** *ip-address* **next-hop-self** [**all**] is used for each neighbor under the address-family configuration on IOS nodes, and the command **next-hop-self** is applied under the neighbor address-family configuration for IOS XR and NX-OS devices.

Figure 1-9 shows the topology and BGP routing table for all four routers. Notice that R2 and R3 advertised the EBGP routes to each other with the next-hop address as the BGP session IP address, allowing the NLRIs to pass the next-hop accessibility check.

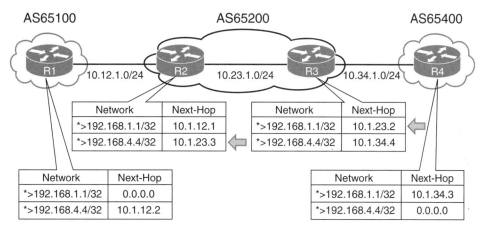

Figure 1-9 *EBGP and IBGP Topology with Next-Hop-Self*

> **Note** The **next-hop-self** feature does not modify the next-hop address for IBGP prefixes by default. IOS nodes can append the optional **all** keyword, which modifies the next-hop address on IBGP prefixes, too. IOS XR provides the BGP configuration command **IBGP policy out enforce-modifications** that will modify IBGP NLRIs in the same manner as EBGP NLRIs. NX-OS devices need to modify the next-hop address in a route-map to overcome this behavior for IBGP routes.

IBGP Scalability

The inability for BGP to advertise a prefix learned from one IBGP peer to another IBGP peer can lead to scalability issues within an AS. The formula *n(n-1)/2* provides the number of sessions required where *n* represents the number of routers. A full mesh topology of 5 routers requires 10 sessions, and a topology of 10 routers requires 45 sessions. IBGP scalability becomes an issue for large networks.

Route Reflectors

RFC 1966 introduces the concept that an IBGP peering can be configured so that it reflects routes to another IBGP peer. The router reflecting routes is known as a *route reflector (RR)*, and the router receiving reflected routes is a *route reflector client*. Three basic rules involve route reflectors and route reflection:

Rule #1: If a RR receives a NLRI from a non-RR client, the RR advertises the NLRI to a RR client. It does not advertise the NLRI to a non-route-reflector client.

Rule #2: If a RR receives a NLRI from a RR client, it advertises the NLRI to RR client(s) and non-RR client(s). Even the RR client that sent the advertisement receives a copy of the route, but it discards the NLRI because it sees itself as the route originator.

Rule #3:   If a RR receives a route from an EBGP peer, it advertises the route to RR client(s) and non-RR client(s).

Figure 1-10 demonstrates the route reflector rules.

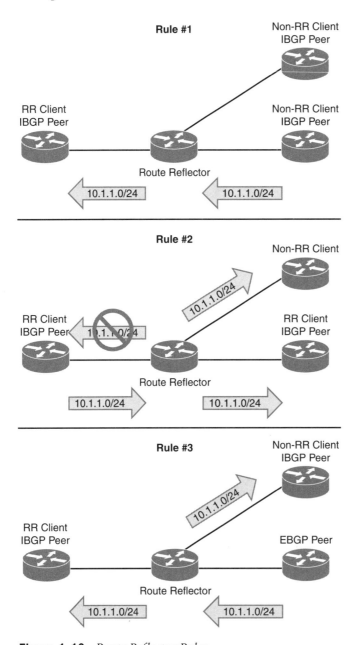

Figure 1-10   *Route Reflector Rules*

Only route reflectors are aware of this change in behavior because no additional BGP configuration is performed on route-reflector clients. BGP route reflection is specific to each address-family. The command **neighbor** *ip-address* **route-reflector-client** is used on IOS nodes, and the command **route-reflector-client** is used on IOS XR and NX-OS devices under the neighbor address-family configuration.

Loop Prevention in Route Reflectors

Removing the full mesh requirements in an IBGP topology introduces the potential for routing loops. When RFC 1966 was drafted, two other BGP route reflector specific attributes were added to prevent loops.

ORIGINATOR_ID, an optional nontransitive BGP attribute is created by the first route reflector and sets the value to the RID of the router that injected/advertised the route into the AS. If the ORIGINATOR_ID is already populated on an NLRI, it should not be overwritten.

If a router receives a NLRI with its RID in the Originator attribute, the NLRI is discarded.

CLUSTER_LIST, a nontransitive BGP attribute, is updated by the route reflector. This attribute is appended (not overwritten) by the route reflector with its cluster-id. By default this is the BGP identifier. The cluster-id can be set with the BGP configuration command **bgp cluster-id** *cluster-id* on IOS and IOS XR nodes. NX-OS devices use the command **cluster-id** *cluster-id*.

If a route reflector receives a NLRI with its cluster-id in the Cluster List attribute, the NLRI is discarded.

Example 1-10 provides sample output prefix output from a route that was reflected. Notice that the originator ID is the advertising router and that the cluster list contains two route-reflector IDs listed in the order of the last route reflector that advertised the route.

Example 1-10 *Route Reflector Originator ID and Cluster List Attributes*

```
RP/0/0/CPU0:R1-XR# show bgp ipv4 unicast 10.4.4.0/24
! Output omitted for brevity
Paths: (1 available, best #1)
  Local
    10.1.34.4 from 10.1.12.2 (192.168.4.4)
      Origin IGP, metric 0, localpref 100, valid, internal, best, group-best
      Received Path ID 0, Local Path ID 1, version 7
      Originator: 192.168.4.4, Cluster list: 192.168.2.2, 192.168.3.3
```

Out-of-Band Route Reflectors

As explained earlier, BGP can establish multihop BGP sessions and does not change the next-hop path attribute when routes are advertised to IBGP neighbors. Some large network topologies use dedicated BGP routers for route reflection that are outside of the data path.

These out-of-band route reflectors provide control plane programming for the BGP routers that are in the data path and only require sufficient memory and processing power for the BGP routing table. Out-of-band route reflectors should not use the **next-hop-self**, or it will place the route reflector into the data path. Organizations that use MPLS L2VPNs, L3VPNs, and so on will use multiple out-of-band route reflectors for exchanging BGP path information.

Confederations

RFC 3065 introduced the concept of BGP confederations as an alternative solution to IBGP full mesh scalability issues shown earlier. A confederation consists of sub-ASs known as a Member-AS that combine into a larger AS known as an AS Confederation. Member ASs normally use ASNs from the private ASN range (64512-65535). EBGP peers from the confederation have no knowledge that they are peering with a confederation, and they reference the confederation identifier in their configuration.

Figure 1-11 demonstrates a BGP confederation with the confederation identifier of AS200. The Member-ASs are AS65100 and AS65200. R3 provides route reflection in Member-AS 65100.

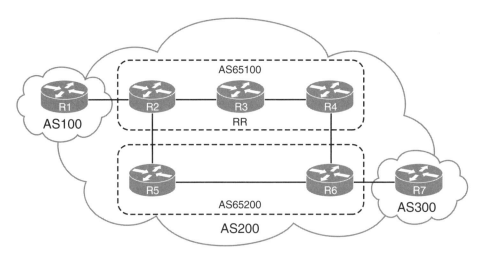

Figure 1-11 *Sample BGP Confederation Topology*

Confederations share behaviors from both IBGP sessions and EBGP sessions. The changes are as follows:

■ The AS_PATH attribute contains a subfield called AS_CONFED_SEQUENCE. The AS_CONFED_SEQUENCE is displayed in parentheses before any external ASNs in the AS_PATH. As the route passes from Member-AS to Member-AS, the AS_CONFED_SEQUENCE is appended to contain the Member-AS ASNs. The

AS_CONFED_SEQUENCE attribute is used to prevent loops, but it is not used (counted) when choosing shortest AS_PATH.

■ Route reflectors can be used within the Member-AS like normal IBGP peerings.

■ The BGP MED attribute is transitive to all other Member-ASs, but does not leave the confederation.

■ The LOCAL_PREF attribute is transitive to all other Member-ASs, but does not leave the confederation.

■ IOS XR nodes do not require a route policy when peering with a different Member-AS, even though the **remote-as** is different.

■ The next-hop address for external confederation routes does not change as the route is exchanged between Member-AS to Member-AS.

■ The AS_CONFED_SEQUENCE is removed from the AS_PATH when the route is advertised outside of the confederation.

Configuring a BGP confederation is shown in the following steps:

Step 1.   Create the BGP Routing Process. Initialize the BGP process with the global command **router bgp** *member-asn*.

Step 2.   Set the BGP Confederation Identifier. Identify the BGP confederations with the command **bgp confederation identifier** *as-number*. The *as-number* is the BGP confederation ASN.

Step 3.   Identify Peer Member-ASs. On routers that directly peer with another Member-AS, identify the peering Member-AS with the command **bgp confederation peers** *member-asn*.

Step 4.   Configure BGP confederation members as normal; the remaining configuration follows normal BGP configuration guidelines.

Example 1-11 displays R1's and R2's BGP table. R1 resides in AS100 and does not see any of the BGP subconfederation information. R1 is not aware the AS200 is subdivided into a BGP confederation.

R2's BGP table participates in the Member-AS 65100. Notice the next-hop address is not modified for the 10.67.1.0/24 (Network between R6 and R7) even though a Member-AS. The AS_CONFED_SEQUENCE is listed in parentheses to indicate it passed through Sub-AS 65200 in the AS200 confederation.

Example 1-11 *R1's and R2's BGP Table*

```
R1-IOS# show bgp ipv4 unicast
! Output omitted for brevity
     Network          Next Hop          Metric LocPrf Weight Path
 r>  10.1.12.0/24     10.1.12.2              0             0 200 i
 *>  10.1.23.0/24     10.1.12.2              0             0 200 i
 *>  10.1.25.0/24     10.1.12.2              0             0 200 i
 *>  10.1.34.0/24     10.1.12.2                            0 200 i
 *>  10.1.46.0/24     10.1.12.2                            0 200 i
 *>  10.1.56.0/24     10.1.12.2                            0 200 i
 *>  10.1.67.0/24     10.1.12.2                            0 200 i
R2-IOS# show bgp ipv4 unicast
```

```
! Output omitted for brevity
     Network          Next Hop          Metric LocPrf Weight Path
 *>  10.1.12.0/24     0.0.0.0                0         32768 i
 *  i 10.1.23.0/24    10.1.23.3             0   100       0 i
 *>                   0.0.0.0                0         32768 i
 *   10.1.25.0/24     10.1.25.5             0   100       0 (65200) i
 *>                   0.0.0.0                0         32768 i
 *>i 10.1.34.0/24     10.1.23.3             0   100       0 i
 *>i 10.1.46.0/24     10.1.34.4             0   100       0 i
 *>  10.1.56.0/24     10.1.25.5             0   100       0 (65200) i
 *   10.1.67.0/24     10.1.56.6             0   100       0 (65200) i
 *>i                  10.1.46.6             0   100       0 (652000) i
```

Example 1-12 displays the NLRI information for 10.67.1.0/24 from the perspective of R2. Notice that the NLRI from within a confederation includes the option of *confed-internal* and *confed-external* for sources.

Example 1-12 *Confederation NLRI*

```
R2-IOS# show bgp ipv4 unicast 10.67.1.0/24
! Output omitted for brevity
BGP routing table entry for 10.1.67.0/24, version 8
Paths: (2 available, best #2, table default)
  Advertised to update-groups:
     1        3
  Refresh Epoch 1
  (65200)
    10.56.1.6 from 10.1.25.5 (10.1.56.5)
      Origin IGP, metric 0, localpref 100, valid, confed-external
      rx pathid: 0, tx pathid: 0
```

```
Refresh Epoch 1
(65200)
  10.46.1.6 from 10.1.23.3 (10.1.23.3)
    Origin IGP, metric 0, localpref 100, valid, confed-internal, best
    Originator: 10.1.34.4, Cluster list: 10.1.23.3
    rx pathid: 0, tx pathid: 0x0
```

BGP Communities

BGP communities provide additional capability for tagging routes and for modifying BGP routing policy on upstream and downstream routers. BGP communities can be appended, removed, or modified selectively on each attribute as the route travels from router to router.

BGP communities are an optional transitive BGP attribute that can traverse from *autonomous system* to *autonomous system*. A BGP community is a 32-bit number that can be included with a route. A BGP community can be displayed as a full 32-bit number (0-4,294,967,295) or as two 16-bit numbers (0-65535):(0-65535) commonly referred to as *new-format*.

Private BGP communities follow the convention that the first 16-bits represent the AS of the community origination, and the second 16-bits represent a pattern defined by the originating AS. The private BGP community pattern could vary from organization to organization, do not need to be registered, and could signify geographic locations for one AS while signifying a method of route advertisement in another AS. Some organizations publish their private BGP community patterns on websites, such as http://www.onesc.net/communities/.

In 2006, RFC 4360 expanded BGP communities' capabilities by providing an extended format. *Extended BGP communities* provide structure for various classes of information and are commonly used for VPN Services.

IOS XR and NX-OS devices display BGP communities in new-format by default, and IOS nodes display communities in decimal format by default. IOS nodes can display communities in new-format with the global configuration command **ip bgp-community new-format**.

Example 1-13 displays the BGP community in decimal format on top, and in new-format on bottom.

Example 1-13 *BGP Community Formats*

```
! DECIMAL FORMAT
R3# show bgp 192.168.1.1
! Output omitted for brevity
BGP routing table entry for 192.168.1.1/32, version 6
Community: 6553602 6577023


! New-Format
R3# show bgp 192.168.1.1
! Output omitted for brevity
BGP routing table entry for 192.168.1.1/32, version 6
Community: 100:2 100:23423
```

IOS and NX-OS devices do not advertise BGP communities to peers by default. Communities are enabled on a neighbor-by-neighbor basis with the BGP address-family configuration command **neighbor** *ip-address* **send-community** [standard | extended | both], and NX-OS devices use the command **send-community** [standard | extended | both] under the neighbor address-family configuration. Standard communities are sent by default, unless the optional **extended** or **both** keywords are used.

IOS XR advertises BGP communities to IBGP peers by default, but EBGP peers require the neighbor address-family configuration command **send-community-ebgp** for advertising standard BGP communities, and the command **send-extended-community-ebgp** to advertise extended BGP communities. Both commands are required if both community formats are to be sent to an EBGP peer.

Route Summarization

Summarizing prefixes conserves router resource(s) and accelerates best path calculation by reducing the size of the table. Summarization also provides the benefit(s) of stability by reducing routing churn by hiding route flaps from downstream routers. Although most ISPs do not accept prefixes larger than /24 for IPv4 (/25-/32), the Internet, at the time of this writing, still has more than 600,000 routes and continues to grow toward a million routes. Route summarization is required to reduce the size of the BGP table for Internet routers.

BGP route summarization on EBGP routers for nontransitive ASs reduce route computation on routers in the core of the nontransitive AS. In Figure 1-12, R3 summarizes all the EBGP routes received from AS65100 and AS65200 to reduce route computation on R4 during link flaps. In the event of a link flap on the 10.1.13.0/24 network, R3 removes all AS65100 routes learned directly from R1 and identifies the same networks via R2 with a different (longer AS_PATH). R4 processes the same changes that R3 processes and is a waste of CPU cycles because R4 receives connectivity only from R3. If R3 summarized the network range, instead of running the best-path algorithm against multiple routes, the best-path algorithm would execute only once.

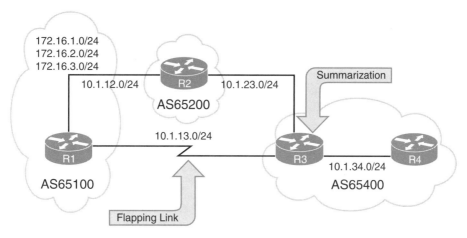

Figure 1-12 *BGP Route Summarization*

The two techniques for BGP summarization are the following:

- **Static:** Create a static route to Null 0 for the prefix, and then advertise the network via a network statement. The downfall to this technique is that the summary route will always be advertised even if the networks are not available.

- **Dynamic:** Configure an aggregation network range. When viable routes that match the network range enter the BGP table, an aggregate route is created. On the originating router, the aggregated prefix sets the next-hop to Null 0. The route to Null 0 is automatically created by BGP as a loop-prevention mechanism.

In both methods of route aggregation, a new network prefix with a shorter prefix length is advertised into BGP. Because the aggregated prefix is a new route, the summarizing router is the originator for the new aggregate route.

Aggregate-Address

Dynamic route summarization is accomplished with the BGP address-family configuration commands identified in Table 1-6.

Table 1-6 *BGP Route-Aggregation Commands*

OS	Command
IOS	**aggregate-address** *network subnet-mask* [**summary-only** | **suppress-map** *route-map-name*] [**as-set**] [**advertise-map** *route-map-name*]
IOS XR	**aggregate-address** *network/prefix-length* [**summary-only** | **route-policy** *route-policy-name*] [**as-set**] [**advertise-map** *route-policy-name*]
NX-OS	**aggregate-address** {*network subnet-mask network/prefix-length*}[**summary-only** | **suppress-map** *route-map-name*] [**as-set**] [**advertise-map** *route-map-name*]

The aggregate-address command advertises the aggregated route in addition to the original networks. Using the optional **no-summary** keyword suppresses the networks in the summarized network range. BGP considers aggregated addresses as local routes.

Note Aggregate addresses are local BGP routes when modifying BGP AD.

Flexible Route Suppression

Some traffic engineering designs require "leaking" routes, which is the advertisement of a subset of more specific routes in addition to performing the summary. Leaking routes can be done at the process by explicitly stating the prefixes to suppress, or on a neighbor level by indicating which prefixes should not be suppressed.

Selective Prefix Suppression

Selective prefix suppression explicitly lists the networks that should not be advertised along with the summary route to neighbor routers.

IOS and NX-OS uses a *suppress-map*, which uses the keyword **suppress-map** *route-map-name* instead of using the **no-summary** keyword. In the referenced route-map, only the prefixes that should be suppressed are permitted. IOS XR routers use the keyword **route-policy** *route-policy-name* in lieu of the **no-summary** keyword. In the route policy, the action command **suppress** is used after conditionally matching the prefixes that should be suppressed.

Leaking Suppressed Routes

The **summary-only** keyword suppresses all the more specific routes of an aggregate address from being advertised. After a route is suppressed, it is still possible to advertise the suppressed route to a specific neighbor.

IOS devices use an *unsuppress-map* with the BGP neighbor address-family configuration command **neighbor** *ip-address* **unsuppress-map** *route-map-name*. In the referenced route-map, only the prefixes that should be leaked are permitted. IOS XR routers use an outbound route policy with the action command **unsuppress** to indicate which prefixes should be leaked.

Atomic Aggregate

Aggregated routes act like new BGP routes with a shorter prefix length. When a BGP router summarizes a route, it does not advertise the AS path information from before the aggregation. BGP path attributes such as AS-Path, MED, and BGP communities are not included in the new BGP advertisement. The Atomic Aggregate attribute indicates that a loss of path information has occurred.

For example:

- R1 and R2 are advertising the 172.16.1.0/24 and 172.16.2.0/24 networks.

- R3 is aggregating the routes into the 172.16.0.0/22 network range, which is advertised to all of R3's peers

Example 1-14 displays R3's BGP table. R1's BGP prefix 172.16.1.0/24 advertised to R3. Notice the AS-Path of 65100 and BGP Community of 100:100.

Example 1-14 *172.16.1.0/24 BGP Path Information*

```
R3-IOS# show bgp ipv4 unicast 172.16.1.0
BGP routing table entry for 172.16.1.0/24, version 13
Paths: (1 available, best #1, table default, Advertisements suppressed by an aggre-
  gate.)
  Not advertised to any peer
  Refresh Epoch 1
  65100
    10.1.13.1 from 10.1.13.1 (192.168.1.1)
      Origin IGP, metric 0, localpref 100, valid, external, best
    Community: 100:100
```

R3's aggregate route (summary) does not include the BGP communities (including AS-Path history) for the routes in the summarization range. R3 advertises the aggregate route to R1 and R2, and those routers install the 172.16.0.0/22 summary route because their AS-Path is not listed in the AS-Path attribute and passes the AS-Path loop check.

Example 1-15 displays the BGP path information for the 172.16.0.0/22 summary network on R1. The AS-Path of the aggregated route displays only the aggregating router, but does not include the AS-Path of the routes being summarized (AS65100 or AS65200), nor is the BGP community included in the routes being summarized. The BGP path information indicates that this is an aggregated prefix and was aggregated by R3 (192.168.3.3). The *Atomic-Aggregate* in the route indicates a loss of information occurred during aggregation on the aggregating router.

Example 1-15 *172.16.0.0/22 BGP Path Information*

```
R1-IOS# show bgp ipv4 unicast 172.16.0.0
BGP routing table entry for 172.16.0.0/21, version 5
Paths: (1 available, best #1, table default)
  Not advertised to any peer
  Refresh Epoch 1
  300, (aggregated by 300 192.168.3.3)
    10.1.13.3 from 10.1.13.3 (192.168.3.3)
      Origin IGP, metric 0, localpref 100, valid, external, atomic-aggregate, best
```

Route Aggregation with AS_SET

To keep the BGP path information history, the optional **as-set** keyword may be used with the **aggregate-address** command. As the router generates the aggregate route, BGP attributes from the summarized routes are copied over to it. The AS-Path settings from the original prefixes are stored in the AS_SET portion of the AS-Path. (The AS_SET is displayed within brackets, and counts only as one hop, even if multiple ASs are listed.)

Route Aggregation with Selective Advertisement of AS-SET

Using the AS-SET feature with network aggregation combines all the attributes of the original prefixes into the aggregated prefixes. This might cause issues with your routing policy. For example, if one of the prefixes contains the No-Export BGP community, the aggregate address will not be exported. To resolve these types of problems, selectively choose the routes that the path attributes will copy to the aggregate route. The use of the **advertise-map** option allows for conditionally matching and denying attributes that should be permitted or denied in the aggregated route.

Default Route Advertisement

Advertising a default route into the BGP table requires the default route to exist in the RIB and the BGP configuration command **default-information originate** to be used. The redistribution of a default route or use of a network 0.0.0.0/0 does not work without the **default-information originate** command.

Default Route Advertisement per Neighbor

Some network topologies restrict the size of the BGP advertisements to a neighbor because the remote router does not have enough processing power or memory for the full BGP routing table. Connectivity is still required, so the peering routers only advertise the default route to the remote router.

A default route is advertised to a BGP peer with the BGP address-family configuration command **neighbor** *ip-address* **default-originate** for IOS nodes or with the BGP neighbor address-family configuration command **default-originate** for IOS XR and NX-OS devices. Default route advertisement to a specific neighbor does not require a default route to be present in the RIB or BGP Loc-RIB table.

> **Note**   A behavior difference between IOS and IOS XR occurs when a default route is already present in the BGP table. IOS nodes advertise the route as if it was the originating router. (None of the existing attributes are passed to the peer.) IOS XR nodes advertise the network to the peer as it exists in the BGP table with the entire default route attributes (AS-Path, and so on).

Remove Private AS

Some organizations might not be able to meet the qualifications for obtaining their own ASN but still want to receive Internet routing tables from their service provider. In these situations, the service provider may assign the organization a private ASN for peering. Private ASNs should not be advertised by the service provider to other ISPs on the Internet.

The feature *remove private AS* removes the private AS of routes that are advertised to the configured peer. The router performs the following path analysis with the remove private AS feature:

- Removes only private ASNs on routes advertised to EBGP peers.

- If the AS-Path for the route has only private ASNs, the private ASNs are removed.

- If the AS-Path for the route has a private ASN between public ASNs, it is assumed that this is a design choice, and the private ASN is not removed

- If the AS-Path contains confederations (AS_CONFED_SEQ), BGP removes the private AS numbers only if they are included after the AS_CONFED_SEQ (Confederation AS-Path) of the path.

The remove private AS feature is configured on IOS nodes with the BGP address-family configuration command **neighbor** *ip-address* **remove-private-as**. IOS XR and NX-OS devices use the BGP neighbor address-family configuration command **remove-private-as**.

Allow AS

The *Allow AS* feature allows for routes to be received and processed even if the router detects its own ASN in the AS-Path. A router discards BGP network prefixes if it sees its ASN in the AS-Path as a loop prevention mechanism. Some network designs use a transit AS to provide connectivity to two different locations. BGP detects the network advertisements from the remote site as a loop and discards the route. The AS-Path loop check feature needs to be disabled to maintain connectivity in scenarios such as these.

On IOS nodes, the command **neighbor** *ip-address* **allowas-in** is placed under the address-family. IOS XR and NX-OS nodes use the BGP neighbor address-family configuration command **allowas-in**.

LocalAS

When two companies merge, one of the ASNs is usually returned to the regional Internet registry (RIR). During the migration, each company needs to maintain its own ASN while changes are made with its peering neighbors to update their configuration.

The *LocalAS* feature is configured on a per peer basis, and allows for BGP sessions to establish using an alternate ASN than the ASN that the BGP process is running on. The LocalAS feature works only with EBGP peerings.

IOS nodes use the BGP address-family neighbor configuration command **neighbor** *ip-address* **local-as** *alternate-as-number* [**no-prepend** [**replace-as** [**dual-as**]]]. IOS XR and NX-OS devices use the equivalent command **local-as** *alternate-as-number* [**no-prepend** [**replace-as** [**dual-as**]]] under the neighbor. By default, the alternate ASN is added to the AS-Path for routes that are sent and received between these two peers.

One problem with the alternate ASN being prepended when receiving the routes is that other IBGP peers drop the network prefixes as part of a routing loop detection.

- To stop the alternate ASN from being prepended when *receiving routes*, the optional keyword **no-prepend** is used.

- To stop the alternate ASN from being prepended when *sending routes*, the optional keywords **no-prepend replace-as** is used.

- If both **no-prepend replace-as** keywords are used, all routers see the BGP advertisements as if they were running the original AS in the BGP process.

After the remote peer changes the remote-as setting on the BGP configuration, the **local-as** commands should be removed. If the coordination of maintenance windows cannot occur during the same time, the **no-prepend replace-as dual-as** optional keywords allow the remote peer to user either ASN for the BGP session. The remote BGP router peers with the ASN in the router process statement, or the alternate ASN in the **local-as** configuration.

Summary

BGP is a powerful path vector routing protocol that provides scalability and flexibility that cannot be compared to any other routing protocol. BGP uses TCP port 179 for all BGP communication between peers, which allows BGP to establish sessions with directly attached routers or with routers that are multiple hops away.

Originally, BGP was intended for the routing of IPv4 prefixes between organizations, but over the years has had significant increase in functionality and feature enhancements. BGP has expanded from being an Internet routing protocol to other aspects of the network, including the data center.

BGP provides a scalable control-plane signaling for overlay topologies, including MPLS VPNs, IPsec SAs, and VXLAN. These overlays can provide Layer 3 services, such as L3VPNs, or Layer 2 services, such as eVPNs, across a widely used scalable control plane for everything from provider-based services to data center overlays. Every AFI / SAFI combination maintains an independent BGP table and routing policy, which makes BGP the perfect control plane application.

This chapter provided a fundamental overview of BGP from a session perspective, as well as route advertisement behaviors for IPv4 and IPv6 protocols. Networking vendors continue to use BGP for new features, and having the ability to effectively troubleshoot BGP is becoming more and more necessary.

This book provides emphasis on various BGP-related problems that are encountered in real-life deployments, which have caused major outages to the network over the years.

References

RFC 1654: *A Border Gateway Protocol 4 (BGP-4)*, Y. Rekhter, T. Li, http://tools.ietf.org/html/rfc1654, July 1994.

RFC 1966: *BGP Route Reflection, An alternative to full mesh IBGP*, T. Bates, R. Chandra, http://www.ietf.org/rfc/rfc1966.txt, June 1996.

RFC 3065: *Autonomous System Confederations for BGP*, P. Traina et al., http://www.ietf.org/rfc/rfc3065.txt, February 2001.

RFC 4271: *A Border Gateway Protocol 4 (BGP-4)*, Y. Rekhter et al., http://www.ietf.org/rfc/rfc4271.txt, January 2006.

RFC 4360: *BGP Extended Communities Attribute*, Srihari Sangli, Dan Tappan, Yakov Rekhter, IETF, http://www.ietf.org/rfc/rfc4360.txt, February 2006.

RFC 4451: *BGP MULTI_EXIST_DISC (MED) Considerations*, D. McPherson, V. Gill, http://www.ietf.org/rfc/rfc4451.txt, March 2006.

RFC 4893: *BGP Support for Four-octet AS Number Space*, Q. Vohra, E. Chen, http://www.ietf.org/rfc/rfc4893.txt, May 2007.

Edgeworth, Brad, Foss, Aaron, Garz Rios, Ramiro. *IP Routing on Cisco IOS, IOS XE, and IOS XR*. Indianapolis: Cisco Press: 2014.

Cisco. Cisco IOS Software Configuration Guides. http://www.cisco.com

Cisco. Cisco IOS XR Software Configuration Guides. http://www.cisco.com

Cisco. Cisco NX-OS Software Configuration Guides. http://www.cisco.com

## Chapter 2

Generic Troubleshooting Methodologies

The following topics are covered in this chapter:

- Identifying problems
- Understanding variables
- Reproducing the problem
- Platform-specific packet capture tools
- Event monitoring/tracing

Finding and narrowing down a problem is not so easy. For this reason, troubleshooting is considered to be an art. Every issue can be quickly resolved when approached logically and examined thoroughly. Most network problems are not as complex as they look. Even simpler network problems can appear to be complex because either the issue is not defined clearly or is not properly understood. A few basic questions help clarify the problem and further help with troubleshooting:

1. What is the problem description?
2. What caused the problem?
3. Is the problem reproducible?

These questions are discussed in detail throughout this chapter.

Identifying the Problem

The most important information required during troubleshooting is defining the problem description, which should be done first. A vague or generic description can be misleading.

A common example for an Internet connection not working properly is a generic statement such as "the Internet is down" or "the Internet is broken." From the initial reading of the problem description, you might start thinking, How could the Internet break? Is the Internet down for everyone or just one user? The problem could be that users are unable to access certain websites, which can possibly indicate a problem with the DNS server, or that a company's Internet gateway could have problems. If the DNS server is not able to resolve the website name to an IP address, the websites are not accessible.

If the problem description is not clearly defined, a network engineer might start investigating the state of the network rather than focusing on the actual problem, which in the above stated example could be a DNS server. After the issue is defined, it should be documented. Documentation plays a vital role in every network deployment as it helps in forensic investigation, analysis of network outages, and mitigating future outages due to similar problems. It is rightly said that "unless it is documented, it never happened."

In most cases, the focus is on solving a problem instead of understanding it. Proper troubleshooting is crucial for a timely resolution. Therefore, defining, documenting, and understanding a problem is very important in minimizing the outage.

Understanding Variables

The famous Newton's law of physics says, "For every action, there is an equal and opposite reaction." In context of a computer network, "Every event (reaction) is the result of some action." The statement means that every network event (expected or unexpected) is the consequence of one or more triggers, such as configuration changes or software or hardware changes. This rule applies for any major or minor network outage. For every network incident, there has to be a trigger, and the trigger could be a manual trigger or due to a network event or any external tool-generated trigger. These triggers are obvious triggers. There are also other non-obvious triggers, such as inter-process communication (IPC) failure or Finite State Machine (FSM) errors. These non-obvious triggers may not have an obvious signature, such as syslog messages, and may be called defects, or bugs.

For example, a router in a network crashes and goes down. The crash could occur due to a hardware or software failure. Hardware failure like Dynamic Random Access Memory (DRAM) on the router might have gone bad, or the motherboard itself may have failed, causing the router to be completely down. Software failure could be due to a new configuration change or a software defect. Similarly, high CPU utilization on a router could be due to a flapping link on one of the remote end devices. Along with the trigger, there are other variables that require serious consideration. Some of the examples of such variables are traffic pattern, traffic load, number of paths, and so on. These variables are as important as the trigger of the problem. It may so happen that the problem occurs only if a certain type of traffic is passing through the router, or the problem might occur only during business hours when the traffic load on the device is high. For instance, a router experiences a crash and goes down when there is Transmission Control Protocol (TCP) stream coming to the router sourced from a particular IP address and for a defined destination port number and when such traffic hits an ACL entry. In this situation, the traffic hitting the ACL entry is the trigger, but the variables are the TCP stream with a particular IP address and destination port number.

A problem can be identified and temporarily mitigated using workarounds, but those are not permanent fixes. If the exact trigger of the problem is not known, such as the event that primarily triggered the problem, the *root cause analysis (RCA)* cannot be done nor a proper fix be prepared. For example, a user reports management access to the router is lost after a recent configuration change. Unless the exact configuration change is known and verified, it is still possible that the user can repeat the same mistake, even if the problem was resolved after rebooting the router. The configuration change should be verified as to whether it is a valid configuration. An incorrect configuration, such as an incorrectly configured ACL, can block the legitimate traffic as well and cause a network outage.

As mentioned before, documentation plays a vital role during investigation of network outages. Documenting the trigger of the problem is as important as noting the description of the problem. The next time that a similar problem occurs, it will not take long to understand if it is a known problem or a new one.

Reproducing the Problem

It is now clear how important it is to document the detailed problem description, the variables attached to the problem, and the trigger that led to that problem. But if the documented event is just a one-time event that caused the problem, then RCA for that problem could not be validated and would merely be a hypothesis based on assumptions. For a successful documentation of a problem and its resolution, the problem should be reproducible all the time using the same trigger. Different triggers can exhibit same or different behaviors. For example, two different triggers can cause a same problem, or the same trigger can exhibit two different problems. Therefore, consistency is required for a problem to be successfully documented and fixed. If there are different behaviors, the problems may not be the same.

Simulating a problem is not an easy task either. It takes a lot of effort to set up the lab, put up the configuration, and simulate multiple triggers. And yes, sometimes it includes a bit of luck. The first three points are crucial for reproducing a problem. The problem might get reproduced in single attempt. It might take multiple tries.

If the problem is not replicated in a lab environment, sometimes it is worth taking a downtime in the production environment to investigate the problem. When scheduling such windows, it is advised to move the traffic to backup devices to minimize any outage for end users; or if the problem is related to traffic or occurs only when the traffic is present on the box, then downtime is the way to go so that users are aware of the outage.

Setting Up the Lab

Lab environments have fewer resources as compared to the production environments. The production environment has hundreds of routers and switches and other devices that cannot be accommodated in a lab environment. Based on the problem, only a relevant part of the topology should be focused on, and the lab environment should be built and set up using the same.

The relevant part of the topology is based on the assumption and understanding of the problem. This does not imply that the minimum setup will always help replicate the problem. Sometimes the lab environment has to be scaled up to make it closer to the production deployment.

Figure 2-1 shows a topology for Multiprotocol Label Switching (MPLS) Virtual Private Networks (VPN) deployment of a service provider for Customer A and Customer B. The service provider is using MPLS and MPLS Traffic Engineering (TE) in its core network. In this topology, Customer A faces reachability issues between two sites after the MPLS TE tunnel flapped between R1 and R14 caused by a link failure between R7 and R14.

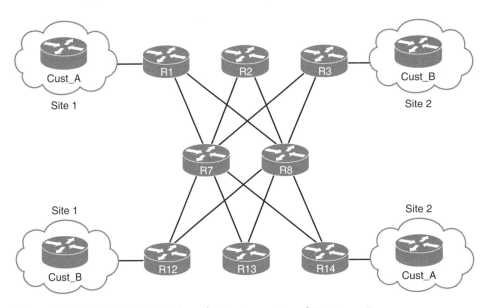

Figure 2-1   *MPLS VPN Topology for Customer A and Customer B*

Though the topology in Figure 2-1 is not large, it is hard to allocate this many routers in the lab to simulate this problem. So how can the lab be setup? Before setting up the lab, the most crucial step is to understand and list the requirements for the lab topology. There are two Provider Edge (PE) routers and two Customer Edge (CE) routers required at minimum. Because TE is the variable in this problem, it should be provisioned as well. Now the TE tunnel can be configured directly between the two PE routers, but in the preceding topology there are multiple paths from R1 to reach R14. Thus, a minimum of two distinct paths should be set up. Therefore, two more routers should be added in the core to simulate two distinct paths. This concludes the topology requirements to replicate the problem. Figure 2-2 shows the topology that can be used to set up the lab to replicate this problem.

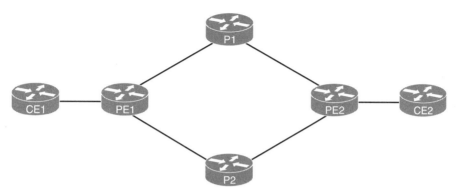

Figure 2-2 *MPLS VPN Lab Topology for Customer A*

After the lab topology is finalized, the next task is to determine the hardware and software requirements to replicate the problem. It is necessary to use the exact software version, because the similar problem may not exist in another software version or might have been fixed.

Choosing the hardware depends on various factors. For example, the problem might exist on a particular kind of hardware, but the same feature and configuration might run smoothly on a different hardware. In modern world network technologies, lots of features get programmed in hardware based on the instructions from software. This is because hardware-based packet switching is faster than software-based switching. Those processed at a hardware level are called Platform Dependent (PD) features and those processed at the software level are called the Platform Independent (PI) features. For instance, most of the control-plane functions are PI features, whereas most data plane functions are PD features on platforms such as Cisco ASR1000 or ASR9000 or even Nexus 7000 / 9000 series.

If the problem is related to a PI feature, real hardware equipment is not required. PI problems can be simulated in virtual environment using tools such as GNS3 or Cisco Virtual Internet Routing Labs (VIRL) by using the same version of software.

Note There are multiple simulators available, but Cisco VIRL provides a scalable, extensible network design and simulation environment. VIRL includes several Cisco Network Operating System virtual machines (IOSv, IOS-XRv, CSR1000v, NX-OSv, IOSvL2, and ASAv) and has the capability to integrate with third-party vendor virtual machines. It includes many unique capabilities, such as "live visualization," that provide the capability to create protocol diagrams in real-time from a running simulation. More information about VIRL can be found at http://virl.cisco.com.

For simulating PD problems, the exact hardware and software is required. The reason is that different line cards on a router have different architecture and different registers and asics, which are used to program the hardware. So based on the problem and the components involved in a feature, a choice has to be made between a physical hardware or a virtual environment.

Configuring Lab Devices

After the lab is set up with relevant software and hardware components, the next step is to configure the lab devices. It should be a close match to what is present in the production environment from the perspective of features being used.

In the topology shown in Figure 2-1, the ISP has Open Shortest Path First (OSPF) as its IGP, MPLS Label Distribution Protocol (LDP), MPLS Traffic Engineering (TE), and BGP vpnv4 address-family, along with Virtual Routing and Forwarding (VRF); all these features should be configured on the lab devices to match as closely as possible with the production devices. Whenever possible, using the exact configuration is preferred. Though you may need to change interface numbering to apply the configuration to the specific lab, but using the exact configuration sometimes catches problems associated with specific network addressing, especially for features such as BGP route-policy, access-lists, NAT, and so on. This also saves time by not having to reengineer the entire configuration in the lab.

These are the minimum features required to set up the lab. But sometimes just having the minimum configuration to bring up the lab devices is not enough. There may be other features configured on the router globally or in interface configuration mode that could add to the trigger of the problem. For example, a QoS policy configuration, though having no correlation with MPLS functionality, might add to the trigger of the problem. Whenever possible, using the exact configuration as that of the production is recommended.

It is also possible that in order to trigger the problem, the box needs to be loaded with configuration. Configuring various features on the device consumes more system resources, which can also play a vital role in triggering the problem. Another important factor that sometimes helps replicate the problem is by simulating traffic using traffic generator devices or software, such as Cisco's TREX, which is used for application simulation or from a third-party vendor like IXIA and Spirent that are highly capable of generating traffic. In addition, these devices help scale the environment because they can also simulate Layer 2 and Layer 3 protocols.

> **Note**   You can find more details about TREX Traffic Generator at http://trex-tgn.cisco.com.

Not everyone can afford IXIA or Spirent type of devices in their testing environment. Other alternative tools and applications are available online that can be used to generate traffic. One such application is Iperf. Iperf is commonly used to measure throughput of a network and is capable of creating TCP and User Datagram Protocol (UDP) streams. Some Cisco devices have a built-in tool, Test TCP (TTCP) utility, that helps simulate TCP streams in a client/server (Transmit/Receive) mode. Example 2-1 demonstrates how to use TTCP to simulate a TCP stream from router R1 to router R6. R6 is configured as the receive side, and R1 is configured as the transmit side.

Example 2-1 *TTCP on Cisco 7600 / ASR1000 Router*

```
! TTCP on Receive side
R6# ttcp
transmit or receive [receive]:
receive packets asynchronously [n]:
perform tcp half close [n]:
receive buflen [32768]:
bufalign [16384]:
bufoffset [0]:
port [5001]:
sinkmode [y]:
rcvwndsize [32768]:
ack frequency [0]:
delayed ACK [y]:
show tcp information at end [n]: y

ttcp-r: buflen=32768, align=16384/0, port=5001
rcvwndsize=32768, delayedack=yes  tcp
ttcp-r: accept from 12.12.12.1
ttcp-r: 23658496 bytes in 155593 ms (155.593 real seconds) (~148 kB/s) +++
ttcp-r: 7197 I/O calls
ttcp-r: 0 sleeps (0 ms total) (0 ms average)
Connection state is CLOSEWAIT, I/O status: 1, unread input bytes: 1
Connection is ECN Disabled
Mininum incoming TTL 0, Outgoing TTL 255
Local host: 6.6.6.6, Local port: 5001
Foreign host: 12.12.12.1, Foreign port: 58747
Connection tableid (VRF): 0


Enqueued packets for retransmit: 0, input: 0  mis-ordered: 0 (0 bytes)


Event Timers (current time is 0x31E05897):
Timer         Starts    Wakeups          Next
Retrans            1         0           0x0
TimeWait           0         0           0x0
AckHold         7198        27           0x0
SendWnd            0         0           0x0
KeepAlive       8273         0           0x31E142E8
GiveUp             0         0           0x0
PmtuAger           0         0           0x0
DeadWait           0         0           0x0
Linger             0         0           0x0
```

```
iss: 3992454486  snduna: 3992454487  sndnxt: 3992454487     sndwnd:   4128
irs: 1163586071  rcvnxt: 1187244569  rcvwnd:      32696  delrcvwnd:     72


SRTT: 37 ms, RTTO: 1837 ms, RTV: 1800 ms, KRTT: 0 ms
minRTT: 1 ms, maxRTT: 300 ms, ACK hold: 200 ms
Status Flags: passive open, retransmission timeout, gen tcbs
Option Flags: none


Datagrams (max data segment is 536 bytes):
Rcvd: 44795 (out of order: 7177), with data: 44764, total data bytes: 23658496
Sent: 51276 (retransmit: 0 fastretransmit: 0),with data: 0, total data bytes: 0
```

```
! TTCP on Transmit side
R1# ttcp
transmit or receive [receive]: transmit
Target IP address: 6.6.6.6
calculate checksum during buffer write [y]:
perform tcp half close [n]:
send buflen [32768]:
send nbuf [2048]:
bufalign [16384]:
bufoffset [0]:
port [5001]:
sinkmode [y]:
buffering on writes [y]:
show tcp information at end [n]: y


ttcp-t: buflen=32768, nbuf=2048, align=16384/0, port=5001  tcp  -> 6.6.6.6
ttcp-t: connect
ttcp-t: 23625728 bytes in 155584 ms (155.584 real seconds) (~147 kB/s) +++
ttcp-t: 722 I/O calls
ttcp-t: 0 sleeps (0 ms total) (0 ms average)
Connection state is ESTAB, I/O status: 1, unread input bytes: 0
Connection is ECN Disabled
Mininum incoming TTL 0, Outgoing TTL 255
Local host: 12.12.12.1, Local port: 58747
Foreign host: 6.6.6.6, Foreign port: 5001
Connection tableid (VRF): 0


Enqueued packets for retransmit: 24, input: 0  mis-ordered: 0 (0 bytes)


Event Timers (current time is 0x31E05892):
Timer         Starts    Wakeups        Next
Retrans         9470      1748      0x31E059BA
```

```
TimeWait           0          0           0x0
AckHold            0          0           0x0
SendWnd            0          0           0x0
KeepAlive          0          0           0x0
GiveUp             0          0           0x0
PmtuAger           0          0           0x0
DeadWait           0          0           0x0
Linger             0          0           0x0


iss: 1163586071  snduna: 1187232168  sndnxt: 1187244568     sndwnd:   32768
irs: 3992454486  rcvnxt: 3992454487  rcvwnd:        4128  delrcvwnd:      0


SRTT: 300 ms, RTTO: 303 ms, RTV: 3 ms, KRTT: 0 ms
minRTT: 0 ms, maxRTT: 843 ms, ACK hold: 200 ms
Status Flags: retransmission timeout
Option Flags: higher precendence


Datagrams (max data segment is 536 bytes):
Rcvd: 51252 (out of order: 0), with data: 0, total data bytes: 0
Sent: 45270 (retransmit: 1769 fastretransmit: 525),with data: 45268,
      total data bytes: 23926320
```

Note The receive node should always be configured first so that when the transmit direction is set up, the destination device is ready and listening on the port specified (in this case, port number 5001—the default port for ttcp).

This feature is also available on IOS XR but not on NX-OS. Example 2-2 demonstrates the use of **ttcp** cli on the IOS XR platform.

Example 2-2 *TTCP on IOS XR*

```
RP/0/0/CPU0:XR_R1# ttcp ?
  align        Align the start of buffers to this modulus (default 16384)
  buflen       Length of bufs read from or written to network (default 8192)
  debug        Enable socket debug mode(cisco-support)
  format       Format for rate: k,K = kilo{bit,byte}; m,M = mega; g,G = giga
  fullblocks   (Receiver) Only output full blocks as specified by buflen
  host         Host name or Ip address(cisco-support)
  multi        Number of connections(cisco-support)
  nbufs        (Transmitter) Number of source bufs written to network
               (default 2048)
  nobuffering  (Tranmitter) Don't buffer TCP writes (sets TCP_NODELAY socket
               option)(cisco-support)
```

```
    nofilter     Don't filter icmp errors(cisco-support)

    nonblock     Use non-blocking sockets(cisco-support)

    offset       Start buffers at this offset from the modulus (default 0)

    password     MD5 Password to be used for tcp connection(cisco-support)

    port         Port number to send to or listen at (default 5001)

    receive      Receive mode(cisco-support)

    sockbuf      Socket buffer size(cisco-support)

    source       Source/Sink a pattern to/from network(cisco-support)

    timeout      Stop listening after timeout seconds(cisco-support)

    touch        (Receiver) "touch": access each byte as it's read

    transmit     Transmit mode(cisco-support)

    udp          Use UDP instead of TCP(cisco-support)

    verbose      Verbose: print more statistics(cisco-support)

    vrfid        Use this VRF to connect(cisco-support)


RP/0/0/CPU0:XR_R1# ttcp receive

ttcp-r: thread = 1, buflen=8192, nbuf=2048, align=16384/0, port=5001  tcp

 ttcp-r: socket

! Output omitted for brevity
```

```
RP/0/0/CPU0:XR_R6# ttcp transmit verbose host 1.1.1.1

ttcp-t: thread = 1, buflen=8192, nbuf=2048, align=16384/0, port=5001  tcp  ->
   1.1.1.1

ttcp-t: socket

! Output omitted for brevity
```

The difference between the IOS and IOS XR command-line interface (CLI) is that in IOS XR there is no step-by-step method, but options are part of the command itself. If no options are specified, default values are taken. The TTCP cli on IOS XR has more options. For example, there is an option to specify the format of the transmit or received rate, MD5 password for the TCP connection, Source of TCP stream, and so on. In IOS XR, TTCP can be used to send a UDP stream as well, which is not possible with Cisco IOS.

All the previously discussed factors increase the chances of successful reproduction of the problem.

Triggering Events

The fun part actually begins after the lab is set up and configured. Based on the documentation of the series of events that occurred before the problem started, various triggers are tried in lab.

In Figure 2-1, a link flap appears to be the trigger of the problem. In any network, a link flap can occur every now and then. Therefore, it should not be assumed that triggering just one link flap would reproduce the problem in a lab environment. The problem can be due to a timing condition, and the trigger has to be tried multiple times before the device runs into a problem state.

For example, one of the most complex problems to replicate in a lab could be simulating a memory leak problem. The triggers (if known) have to be tried multiple times to replicate the problem in a lab. Repetitive attempts of the same trigger or a combination of different triggers have to be tried, which is a tedious task. For such situations, it is better to make use of automation, which could trigger the event continuously or at a certain time interval. Various scripting languages can be used for automation purposes—for example Perl, Expect, TCL, and the like.

If the trigger is required to be instantiated based on an event, it is a better option to use Cisco's Embedded Event Manager (EEM). With EEM, certain actions are configured, which get triggered based on an event. For example, an EEM script can be configured to capture a set of commands and save it in a file on bootflash wherever the router experiences a BGP session flap or a high CPU condition.

Note   EEM is explained in Chapter 6, "Troubleshooting Platform Issues due to BGP."

Sniffer-Packet Capture

Troubleshooting at the packet level is complex, and it becomes more difficult when it is unknown what kind of packet is being received or transmitted. It is important to know if the packet is actually reaching the device. There are three perspectives:

- Transmitting router

- Receiving router

- Transmission media

This is where the concept of *sniffing* comes in. Sniffing is the technique of intercepting the traffic passing over the transmission media for protocol or packet analysis. A sniffing technique is not used just for network troubleshooting purposes but also by network security experts for analysis for any security loopholes. In sniffing, a packet capture tool such as Wireshark is installed on a PC that can be attached to a network device such as a switch. The switch, in most cases, is capable of mirroring the packets coming in on a switch interface and sending it to the PC connected to the switch. Figure 2-3 shows how a sniffer capture is set up on a switch.

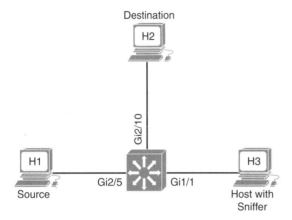

Figure 2-3 *Sniffer Setup on Switch*

On Cisco devices, the sniffing capability is called a Switched Port Analyzer (SPAN) feature. The source port is called a monitored port, and the destination port is called the monitoring port. SPAN functionality has variations in different platforms that are discussed in the following section.

SPAN on Cisco IOS

Almost all Cisco Catalyst switches, including multilayer switches/routers such as the Cisco 6500 or Cisco 7600 series, support the SPAN feature. Before configuring SPAN, the source and the destination interface should be identified. There could be one or more source interfaces from which the traffic can be spanned, but there can be only one destination interface. The SPAN can be configured using the command **monitor session** *session-number* [**source** | **destination**] **interface** *interface-id*.

Example 2-3 demonstrates setting up a SPAN session on Cisco 7600 series router. The same configuration applies to catalyst switches as well. The SPAN session 1 uses a source interface of GigabitEthernet2/5 and a destination interface as GigabitEthernet1/1. Thus, all the traffic coming on the interface GigabitEthernet2/5 is mirrored and sent to interface GigabitEthernet1/1, where a PC connected with the *Wireshark* software installed on it captures the packets received on the interfaces. Optionally, the direction of the packet that needs to be captured on the incoming interface can also be specified just after the interface name using option [**both** | **rx** | **tx**]. In this example, the source interface is a physical interface. The source interface can also be configured as a VLAN interface. Therefore, all traffic coming on the SVI is mirrored and sent to the configured destination interface.

Example 2-3 *SPAN Configuration*

```
R1# configure terminal
R1(config)# monitor session 1 source interface GigabitEthernet2/5 both
R1(config)# monitor session 1 destination interface GigabitEthernet1/1
```

The SPAN sessions can also be configured to capture the traffic based on the filter, such as VLAN or an access control list (ACL), by using the command **monitor session session-id filter** [**vlan** *vlan-id* | **ip access-group** *acl*]. This is useful in cases when it is required to capture specific traffic.

To verify the SPAN session, use the command **show monitor session** *session-number*. Example 2-4 displays the configured span session. Remember that after the destination interface is specified for the SPAN, no protocol will work on that port. The port will be working in promiscuous mode. Notice that the **show interface GigabitEthernet1/1** command's output displays that the port is in "monitoring" status.

Example 2-4 *Verifying SPAN Session*

```
R1# show monitor session 1
Session 1
---------
Type                    : Local Session
Source Ports            :
    Both                : Gi2/5
Destination Ports       : Gi1/1
MTU                     : 1464


Egress SPAN Replication State:
Operational mode        : Distributed
Configured mode         : Distributed
```

```
R1# show interface GigabitEthernet1/1
GigabitEthernet1/0/7 is up, line protocol is down (monitoring)
  Hardware is Gigabit Ethernet, address is 2c54.2d68.1207 (bia 2c54.2d68.1207)
  MTU 1998 bytes, BW 1000000 Kbit/sec, DLY 10 usec,
     reliability 255/255, txload 1/255, rxload 18/255
  Encapsulation ARPA, loopback not set
  Keepalive not set
  Full-duplex, 1000Mb/s, link type is auto, media type is 10/100/1000BaseTX SFP
! Output omitted for brevity
```

SPAN on Cisco IOS XR

The SPAN feature is not available on all IOS XR platforms. Traffic mirroring or SPAN capability is available only on ASR9000 and CRS routers. This feature was introduced on the Cisco Carrier Routing System (CRS) platform in XR 4.3.0 release and was introduced on the Aggregation Services Routers 9000 (ASR9000) series platform, starting with the XR 3.9.1 release, with some enhancements made in the 4.0.1 release. Cisco 12000 series— that is, the Gigabit Switch Router (GSR) router running IOS XR, does not have traffic mirroring capabilities. IOS XR supports two types of traffic mirroring methods:

- Layer 3 traffic mirroring

- ACL-based traffic mirroring

In Layer 3 traffic mirroring, the destination port is identified by an IP Address and not by an interface, because routing decides which interface the mirrored packets are actually sent over.

Note   Layer 2 SPAN is not supported on Cisco Carrier Routing Services (CRS) routers.

Example 2-5 displays how to configure Layer 3 traffic mirroring configuration. In this example, a SPAN session named test is configured with the destination IP of 10.1.1.1. On the source port, which is interface GigabitEthernet0/1/3/1, the span session named TEST is applied with the direction set to capture ingress only packets; that is, **rx-only**. It is optional to specify how many bytes to mirror, and it is also optional to specify if the mirroring has to be done just for IPv4 or IPv6 packets.

Example 2-5   *Configuring Layer 3 Traffic Mirroring*

```
RP/0/RP0/CPU0:CRS(config)# monitor-session TEST ipv4
RP/0/RP0/CPU0:CRS(config-mon)# destination next-hop 10.1.1.1
RP/0/RP0/CPU0:CRS(config-mon)# exit
RP/0/RP0/CPU0:CRS(config)# interface gigabitEthernet0/1/3/1
RP/0/RP0/CPU0:CRS(config)# ip address 192.168.10.1 255.255.255.0
RP/0/RP0/CPU0:CRS(config-if)# monitor-session test ipv4 direction rx-only
RP/0/RP0/CPU0:CRS(config-if)# exit
RP/0/RP0/CPU0:CRS(config)# commit
```

To verify the status of the configured monitor-session, the **show monitor-session** *name* **status detail** command can be used. Example 2-6 displays the status of the monitor-session test with the command **show monitor-session** *name* **status detail errors**. The status should always be in Operational state, but if there is an error on the monitor-session, it is displayed in the command output.

Example 2-6 *Verifying Configured Traffic Mirroring Status*

```
RP/0/RP0/CPU0:CRS# show monitor-session test status detail
Monitor-session TEST (IPv4)
  Destination next-hop IPv4 address 10.1.1.1
  Source Interfaces
  ----------------
  GigabitEthernet0/1/3/0
    Direction: Rx-only
    ACL match: Enabled
    Portion:   Full packet
    Status:    Operational
```

ACL-based traffic mirroring adds an interesting flavor to IOS XR SPAN capabilities. The permit and deny statements determine the behavior of the regular traffic being forwarded or dropped. The **capture** keyword determines whether the packet is mirrored to the destination. But the main behavior lies on which direction the ACL is applied. If the ACL is on ingress direction, SPAN mirrors all traffic, including traffic dropped by an ACL. In other words, it always mirrors the traffic. If the ACL is on egress direction, it mirrors traffic if the regular traffic is forwarded via the **permit** statement and does not mirror if the regular traffic is dropped via the **deny** statement.

Example 2-7 displays how to configure ACL-based traffic mirroring. In this example, SPAN session TEST is created with the destination interface as GigabitEthernet0/1/0/2. Note that the destination interface can also be an ipv4 or ipv6 address. Next, an ACL named **SPAN_ACL** is created which allows traffic from any source, destined to host 1.1.1.10 address and denies the rest of the traffic.

Example 2-7 *Configuring Layer 3 ACL-Based Traffic Mirroring*

```
RP/0/RP0/CPU0:CRS(config)# monitor-session TEST
RP/0/RP0/CPU0:CRS(config-mon)# destination interface GigabitEthernet0/1/0/2
RP/0/RP0/CPU0:CRS(config-mon)# exit
RP/0/RP0/CPU0:CRS(config)# ipv4 access-list SPAN_ACL
RP/0/RP0/CPU0:CRS(config)# permit ipv4 any host 1.1.1.10 capture
RP/0/RP0/CPU0:CRS(config)# deny ipv4 any any
RP/0/RP0/CPU0:CRS(config)# interface gigabitEthernet0/1/3/0
RP/0/RP0/CPU0:CRS(config-if)# ip address 192.168.10.1 255.255.255.0
RP/0/RP0/CPU0:CRS(config-if)# monitor-session TEST
RP/0/RP0/CPU0:CRS(config-if)# acl
RP/0/RP0/CPU0:CRS(config-if)# ipv4 access-group SPAN_ACL ingress
RP/0/RP0/CPU0:CRS(config-if)# exit
RP/0/RP0/CPU0:CRS(config)# commit
```

Notice that there is a **capture** keyword at the end of the first ACL entry. It means that this traffic will be captured. Any other traffic mapped to the ACL entry that does not have the **capture** keyword at the end is not sent to the sniffer. SPAN session **TEST** is then assigned under the source interface GigabitEthernet0/1/3/0 along with the **acl** subcommand. This command specifies that the mirrored traffic is according to the defined global interface ACL. Along with assigning the SPAN session TEST to the interface, ACL is also bound to the ingress direction of the interface.

ASR9000 also supports traffic mirroring for pseudowire and Layer 2–based traffic mirroring. Other XR platforms do not support this feature.

SPAN on Cisco NX-OS

The SPAN feature on Cisco Nexus OS (NX-OS) is not different from Cisco IOS. Depending on the hardware platform, NX-OS may run differently from IOS platforms for the number of interfaces per monitor session. For example, there can be 128 source interfaces and 32 destination interfaces configured per session. Two active sessions are supported for all virtual device contexts (VDC).

Note The number of active sessions, sources interfaces and destination interfaces supported per session can vary on different Nexus platforms. Platform documentation should be referenced before using the feature for any such limitations.

Example 2-8 shows the SPAN configuration on Cisco NX-OS. In Example 2-8, the **switchport monitor** command is configured on the destination interface. SPAN session is configured using the **monitor session** *session-number* command with the subcommands to configure source and destination interfaces.

Example 2-8 *SPAN Configuration on Cisco NX-OS*

```
N7k-1(config)# interface Ethernet4/3
N7k-1(config-if)# switchport
N7k-1(config-if)# switchport monitor
N7k-1(config-if)# no shut
N7k-1(config)# monitor session 1
N7k-1(config-monitor)# source interface Ethernet4/1
N7k-1(config-monitor)# destination interface Ethernet4/3
N7k-1(config-monitor)# no shut
N7k-1(config-monitor)# exit
```

Note The source interface can also be a range of interfaces or a range of VLANs.

Notice that under the monitor session configuration, the **no shutdown** command is configured. By default, the monitor session is in shutdown state and has to be manually unshut for SPAN session to function using the **no shut** command.

Example 2-9 displays the monitor session status. In this example, the rx, tx, and both fields are seen as interface Eth4/1. Direction of the source interface can be manually specified in configuration, but it will be set to both if not specified. There is also an option to filter VLANs under the monitor session using the **filter vlan** command.

Example 2-9 *Verifying SPAN Session*

```
N7k-1# show monitor session 1
   session 1
---------------
type               : local
state              : up
source intf        :
   rx              : Eth4/1
   tx              : Eth4/1
   both            : Eth4/1
source VLANs       :
   rx              :
   tx              :
   both            :
filter VLANs       : filter not specified
destination ports  : Eth4/3
```

Note   For more details on using SPAN on Cisco IOS, IOS XR, and NX-OS platforms, refer to the documentation at cisco.com.

Remote SPAN

Remote SPAN (RSPAN) is an extension of SPAN with a difference that the destination port where the host is attached to capture traffic is on a remote switch a few hops away. In Figure 2-4, the topology demonstrates a remote SPAN setup across multiple switches. Switch SW1 is the source switch, whereas SW3 is the destination switch.

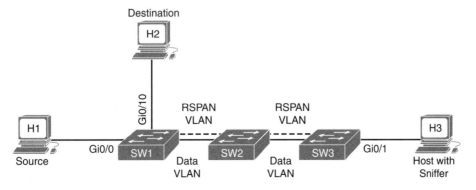

Figure 2-4 *Remote SPAN*

The VLAN used between the two switches to carry the SPAN traffic is called the RSPAN VLAN and is configured using the **remote-span** command under the vlan-config mode. The actual traffic flow is between the hosts connected on SW1, such as H1 and H2. The interface being spanned is GigabitEthernet0/0. On the source switch SW1, the destination interface is set to the RSPAN VLAN, whereas on the destination switch, the source interface is specified as the RSPAN VLAN. The reason is that when the packet arrives to the destination switch, the packet is being traversed across the RSPAN VLAN, and therefore the mirrored packets are received on that VLAN.

The RSPAN VLAN should be enabled on all the trunk ports on the switch in the middle. If the Layer 2 network has pruning enabled, then the RSPAN VLAN should be excluded from pruning using the command **switchport trunk pruning vlan remove** *rspan-vlan-id*.

Example 2-10 demonstrates the configuration of remote SPAN session on the source switch and the remote destination switch. In this example, the SW1 is attached to the monitored host on port GigabitEthernet0/0, with RSPAN VLAN 30, which spans across SW2 to reach SW3 where the host H3 is attached on port GigabitEthernet0/1 to capture the traffic.

Example 2-10 *RSPAN Configuration*

```
SW1# configure terminal
SW1(config)# vlan 30
SW1(config-vlan)# name RSPAN_Vlan
SW1(config-vlan)# remote-span
SW1(config-vlan)# exit
SW1(config)# monitor session 1 source interface GigabitEthernet0/0 rx
SW1(config)# monitor session 1 destination remote vlan 30
SW1(config)# end

SW3# configure terminal
SW3(config)# vlan 30
SW3(config-vlan)# name RSPAN_Vlan
SW3(config-vlan)# remote-span
SW3(config-vlan)# exit
SW3(config)# monitor session 1 destination interface GigabitEthernet0/1
SW3(config)# monitor session 1 source remote vlan 30
SW3(config)# end
```

The only problem that may arise with RSPAN is when the trunk between the two switches is not configured to allow the RSPAN VLAN. In that case, it will not function properly, and there could be a possible impact on the switch, because the CPU will keep dropping the spanned traffic.

Platform-Specific Packet Capture Tools

Most high-end routers and switches have in-built tools that are capable of capturing a packet at different ASIC levels within the router. These tools are capable of capturing either traffic destined to the devices or the transit traffic, which can be very useful during troubleshooting. With the use of the packet capture capability within the platform, it is easy to figure the actions being taken on a packet by each platform at various ASIC levels. These tools help figure out up to which hop the packet has reached in the network, and if a particular router/switch is dropping a packet, figure out where (on the ingress or egress line card or on the route processor) it is dropping it. These tools are helpful while troubleshooting complete packet loss, hardware programming issues, various routing protocol and QoS issues, as well as in situations where an external sniffer is not possible.

The following is a list of a few packet capture tools on various Cisco platforms:

- IOS/IOS XE
  - 7600/6500
    - ☐ ELAM
    - ☐ Mini Protocol Analyzer (MPA)
    - ☐ Netdr
  - ASR1K and other IOS and IOS XE platforms
    - ☐ Embedded Packet Capture
    - ☐ Packet Tracker (ASR1k)
- IOS XR
  - ASR9k
    - ☐ Network Processor Capture
  - CRS
    - ☐ Show captured packets
- NX-OS
  - Nexus 7K, 5K, 3K
    - ☐ Ethanalyzer
    - ☐ ELAM

Note   Discussing all the packet capture tools is outside the scope of this book because many of these captures require deep platform architecture knowledge.

Netdr Capture

Netdr capture is a very handy tool to use on 6500 or 7600 Multilayer Switching (MLS) platforms. This tool is available starting with the 12.2(18)SXF release. Netdr capture can be run on the Route Processor (RP) and the Switch Processor (SP) of various supervisor cards, such as SUP720/RSP720/SUP2T, or on line cards with the Distributed Forwarding Card (DFC) installed on them, such as ES+, ES20, or WS-67XX cards with DFC module.

The DFC cards are similar to the supervisor card where all the Cisco Express Forwarding (CEF) and MLS information is downloaded to the line card. So all the lookups for the packets occur on the line card itself rather than punting the packet to the supervisor card for lookup on where to forward the packet.

The Netdr capture allows up to 4096 packets, after which the captured packets are over-written. This tool is helpful in cases where there is a high CPU condition on the router due to traffic interrupts, and multiple packets are hitting the CPU. It can also be useful to capture the incoming or outgoing packets that are destined to the CPU, such as control plane packets. In other words, netdr is helpful only for capturing packets to or from Route Processor (RP) or Switch Processor (SP). For example, Netdr capture can help confirm that BGP packets are being received or sent out, and when received by the line card, whether they are being sent toward the Supervisor card.

Example 2-11 illustrates the use of netdr capture in rx direction on the RP to capture BGP packets coming from peer IP address 10.1.13.1. After waiting for few seconds (based on the packet rate hitting the CPU), use the **show netdr captured-packets** command to view the captured packets hitting the CPU.

In Example 2-11, the two captured packets are BGP packets based on the highlighted information. VLAN information is also valuable. On Cisco 6500 / 7600 platforms, every physical interface is allocated on an internal VLAN, which can be viewed using the **show vlan internal usage** command. This information locates the interface the packet is destined to. In this case, the destination index is *0x380*, which indicates that the packet is destined to CPU. The source VLAN is 1016, which resolves to interface TenGig1/4.

Example 2-11   *Netdr Capture on Cisco 7600 Platform*

```
7600_RTR# debug netdr capture ?
  acl                     (11) Capture packets matching an acl
  and-filter              (3) Apply filters in an and function: all must match
  continuous              (1) Capture packets continuously: cyclic overwrite
  destination-ip-address  (10) Capture all packets matching ip dst address
  dstindex                (7) Capture all packets matching destination index
  ethertype               (8) Capture all packets matching ethertype
  interface               (4) Capture packets related to this interface
  or-filter               (3) Apply filters in an or function: only one must
                          match
  rx                      (2) Capture incoming packets only
  source-ip-address       (9) Capture all packets matching ip src address
  srcindex                (6) Capture all packets matching source index
  tx                      (2) Capture outgoing packets only
```

```
vlan                        (5) Capture packets matching this vlan number
  <cr>
7600_RTR# debug netdr capture source-ip-address 10.1.13.1
```

```
7600-RTR# show netdr captured-packets
A total of 2 packets have been captured
The capture buffer wrapped 0 times
Total capture capacity: 4096 packets
------- dump of incoming inband packet -------
interface Te1/4, routine process_rx_packet_inline, timestamp 15:20:07.111
dbus info: src_vlan 0x3F8(1016), src_indx 0x3(3), len 0x4F(79)
  bpdu 0, index_dir 0, flood 0, dont_lrn 0, dest_indx 0x380(896)
  48020400 03F80400 00030000 4F000000 00060408 0E000008 00000000 0380E753
destmac 00.1E.F7.F7.16.80, srcmac 84.78.AC.0F.76.C2, protocol 0800
protocol ip: version 0x04, hlen 0x05, tos 0xC0, totlen 61, identifier 7630
  df 1, mf 0, fo 0, ttl 1, src 10.1.13.1, dst 10.1.13.3
  tcp src 179, dst 11655, seq 788085885, ack 4134684341, win 17520 off 5 checksum
0x5F4E ack psh

------- dump of incoming inband packet -------
interface Te1/4, routine process_rx_packet_inline, timestamp 15:20:07.111
dbus info: src_vlan 0x3F8(1016), src_indx 0x3(3), len 0x40(64)
  bpdu 0, index_dir 0, flood 0, dont_lrn 0, dest_indx 0x380(896)
  50020400 03F80400 00030000 40000000 00060408 0E000008 00000000 0380639F
destmac 00.1E.F7.F7.16.80, srcmac 84.78.AC.0F.76.C2, protocol 0800
protocol ip: version 0x04, hlen 0x05, tos 0xC0, totlen 40, identifier 7631
  df 1, mf 0, fo 0, ttl 1, src 10.1.13.1, dst 10.1.13.3
  tcp src 179, dst 11655, seq 788085906, ack 4134684342, win 17520 off 5 checksum
0x6670 ack
```

```
7600-RTR# show vlan internal usage | in 1016
1016 TenGigabitEthernet1/4
```

To determine the packets hitting the CPU, use the command **show ibc | in rate** on Cisco 7600 platform which displays the ingress (rx) and egress (tx) packet rate. The rx packets are the ones punted to the CPU for processing, whereas the tx packets are processed or generated from the CPU.

Note   Rx mode captures packets coming from ingress line card toward the supervisor card, and the tx mode captures packets leaving the supervisor card (from the supervisor card toward egress line card).

Embedded Packet Capture

SPAN is not supported on all the routers and switches. Even if supported, it may not be possible to run it in live production environments because of a company's security policies. It may take time to arrange for a sniffing device. Cisco created the Embedded Packet Capture (EPC) tool, which is capable of capturing packets on a router's buffer and later exporting the packets in PCAP format, which is suitable for analysis using Wireshark. Therefore, the packets captured can be later analyzed using Wireshark.

EPC allows for packet data to be captured at various points in the CEF packet-processing path—flowing through, to, and from a Cisco router. It is supported on various Cisco Routers, such as Cisco 800, 1900, 3900, 7200, and ASR 1000. The rate at which the packets are captured can be throttled by specifying a sampling interval, maximum packet capture rate, and even limiting the capture to interested packets by using an access control list (ACL). You can use EPC in five simple steps:

Step 1.   Define capture buffer

Step 2.   Define capture point

Step 3.   Associate capture buffer and capture point

Step 4.   Start and stop capture

Step 5.   Display/export the data

Note   In Step 3, associating the capture buffer and capture point depends on the platform and OS version. This step is not really required on the ASR1k platform.

Example 2-12 demonstrates EPC on the ASR1k platform and on 7200 series routers for capturing BGP packets. In this example, the buffer is set up to capture the packets matching the ACL named MYACL. This ACL is configured to capture BGP packets. If the size is not specified, the default value is taken by the base IOS.

Example 2-12   *Embedded Packet Capture*

```
ASR1k(config)# ip access-list extended MYACL
ASR1k(config-acl)# permit tcp any eq bgp any
ASR1k(config-acl)# permit tcp any any eq bgp
ASR1k# monitor capture CAP1 buffer circular packets 1000
ASR1k# monitor capture CAP1 buffer size 10
ASR1k# monitor capture CAP1 interface GigabitEthernet0/0/0 in
ASR1k# monitor capture CAP1 access-list MYACL
ASR1k# monitor capture CAP1 start
```

```
ASR1k# monitor capture CAP1 stop
ASR1k# monitor capture CAP1 export bootflash:cap1.pcap
```

```
7200_RTR(config)# ip access-list extended MYACL
7200_RTR(config-acl)# permit tcp any eq bgp any
7200_RTR(config-acl)# permit tcp any any eq bgp
7200_RTR# monitor capture buffer CAP1 circular
7200_RTR# monitor capture buffer CAP1 size 1024
7200_RTR# monitor capture buffer CAP1 filter access-list MYACL
7200_RTR# monitor capture point ip cef CPT1 GigabitEthernet0/0 in
7200_RTR# monitor capture associate CPT1 CAP1
7200_RTR# monitor capture point start CPT1
7200_RTR# monitor capture point stop CPT1
7200_RTR# monitor capture buffer CAP1 export tftp://10.1.1.1/cap1.pcap
```

The capture can be stopped either by setting the duration or the limit of the number of packets or by stopping the capture manually if the packet is captured. The buffer can then be exported to a bootflash: or an external tftp: / ftp: server. Saving the buffer capture to bootflash: is not available on all platforms and IOS versions.

The packet can be viewed on the terminal as well using the **show monitor capture buffer** *name* **dump** (**show monitor capture** *name* **buffer dump** for ASR1k) command, but it is in raw format and therefore needs to be decoded from a hex value to an understandable format. Example 2-13 displays the packet on the terminal session. In this example, **AABBCC00 0800** is the destination MAC, **AABBCC00 0700** is the source MAC, **0707 0707 (7.7.7.7)** in the third row is the source IP, and **0808 0808 (8.8.8.8)** is the destination IP. **0800** in the second row means that it is an IPv4 packet. **4A07** (18951) is the Source port, whereas **00B3** (179) is the destination port. From 9372 in the third row until 0000 in the fourth row are the various TCP fields, such as SEQ number, ACK number, Window size, and so on. **FFFF FFFFFFFF FFFFFFFF FFFFFFFF** at the end is the BGP marker.

Example 2-13 *BGP Packet Captured Using EPC*

```
7200_RTR# show monitor capture buffer CAP1 dump
16:25:44.938 JST Aug 21 2015 : IPv4 LES CEF    : Gig0/0 None

F19495B0:                    AABBCC00 0800AABB          *;L...*;
F19495C0: CC000700 08004540 003B1C5D 4000FE06  L.....E@.;.]@.~.
F19495D0: 42020707 07070808 08084A07 00B39372  B.........J..3.r
F19495E0: FFE37CDC E3D35018 3D671161 0000FFFF  .c|\cSP.=g.a....
F19495F0: FFFFFFFF FFFFFFFF FFFFFFFF FD          ............}
```

Note The easiest method to analyze the EPC capture is by exporting it a remote server and reading the .pcap file using Wireshark.

Ethanalyzer

Ethanalyzer is a NX-OS implementation of TShark. TShark is a terminal version of Wireshark. It is capable of capturing inband and management traffic on all Nexus platforms. Ethanalyzer can be simply configured in three simple steps, as shown:

Step 1.   Define Capture Interface.

Step 2.   Define Filters. Set Capture Filter. Set Display Filter.

Step 3.   Define Stop Criteria.

Starting with the capture interface, there are three kinds of capture interfaces:

- **Mgmt:** Captures traffic on Mgmt0 interface of the switch

- **Inbound-Hi:** Captures high-priority control packets on the inband, such as Spanning Tree Protocol (STP), Link Aggregation Control Protocol (LACP), Cisco Discovery Protocol (CDP), Data Center Bridging Exchange (DCBX), Fibre Channel, and Fibre Channel over Ethernet (FCOE)

- **Inbound-Lo:** Captures low-priority control packets on the inband, such as IGMP, TCP, UDP, IP, and ARP traffic.

The next step is setting the filters. With a working knowledge of Wireshark, it is fairly simple to configure filters for Ethanalyzer. There are two kinds of filters that can be set up for configuring Ethanalyzer: capture filter and display filter. As the name suggests, when capture filter is set, only frames matching the filter are captured. The display filter is used to display the packets matching the filter from the captured set of packets. That means Ethanalyzer captures other frames that are not matching the display filter but are not displayed in the output.

Ethanalyzer, by default, stops after capturing 10 frames. This value can be changed by setting the **limit-captured-frames** option where 0 means no limit. Example 2-14 illustrates how to configure Ethanalyzer for capturing BGP packets. In the Ethanalyzer output, various captured BGP packets can be seen, such as the BGP OPEN message, KEEPALIVE message, and UPDATE message.

Example 2-14 *Ethanalyzer on NX-OS*

```
N3K-1# ethanalyzer local interface inbound-hi display-filter "bgp"
limit-captured-frames 0

Capturing on 'eth4'
1 wireshark-cisco-mtc-dissector: ethertype=0xde09, devicetype=0x0
wireshark-broadcom-rcpu-dissector: ethertype=0xde08, devicetype=0x0
<snip>
2   81 2015-09-01 04:50:34.115833 192.168.10.2 -> 192.168.10.1 BGP 236 OPEN Message
5   86 2015-09-01 04:50:34.259108 192.168.10.1 -> 192.168.10.2 BGP 200 OPEN Message
   87 2015-09-01 04:50:34.259440 192.168.10.1 -> 192.168.10.2 BGP 149 KEEPALIVE Me
ssage
   88 2015-09-01 04:50:34.271319 192.168.10.2 -> 192.168.10.1 BGP 185 KEEPALIVE Me
ssage
6   92 2015-09-01 04:50:35.272488 192.168.10.1 -> 192.168.10.2 BGP 178 UPDATE Messa
ge, KEEPALIVE Message
8   93 2015-09-01 04:50:35.288438 192.168.10.2 -> 192.168.10.1 BGP 214 UPDATE Messa
ge, KEEPALIVE Message
   94 2015-09-01 04:50:35.288813 192.168.10.2 -> 192.168.10.1 BGP 214 UPDATE Messa
ge, KEEPALIVE Message
```

Example 2-14 displayed various packets with a brief description of the packet. To view the detailed view of the packet, use the **detail** keyword as shown in Example 2-15. The Ethanalyzer capture with the **detail** keyword has a similar view of Wireshark but on a terminal. The example shows the packet view, such as the source and destination mac and source and destination IP. Because this is a BGP control plane packet, the Differentiated Services Code Point (DSCP) value is seen as CS6, and at the end of the captured packet is a BGP KEEPALIVE Message.

Example 2-15 *Detailed Ethanalyzer Output*

```
N3K-1# ethanalyzer local interface inbound-hi display-filter "bgp"
limit-captured-frames 0 detail

Capturing on 'eth4'
wireshark-cisco-mtc-dissector: ethertype=0xde09, devicetype=0x0
wireshark-broadcom-rcpu-dissector: ethertype=0xde08, devicetype=0x0
Frame 8: 149 bytes on wire (1192 bits), 149 bytes captured (1192 bits) on interf
ace 0
    Interface id: 0
    Encapsulation type: Ethernet (1)
    Arrival Time: Sep  1, 2015 04:51:35.283124000 UTC
    [Time shift for this packet: 0.000000000 seconds]
```

```
    Epoch Time: 1441083095.283124000 seconds
    [Time delta from previous captured frame: 0.150360000 seconds]
    [Time delta from previous displayed frame: 0.000000000 seconds]
    [Time since reference or first frame: 1.440361000 seconds]
    Frame Number: 8
    Frame Length: 149 bytes (1192 bits)
    Capture Length: 149 bytes (1192 bits)
    [Frame is marked: False]
    [Frame is ignored: False]
    [Protocols in frame: eth:vlan:rcpu:eth:ip:tcp:bgp]
Ethernet II, Src: 02:10:18:97:3f:21 (02:10:18:97:3f:21), Dst: c0:8c:60:a8:ac:42
(c0:8c:60:a8:ac:42)
    Destination: c0:8c:60:a8:ac:42 (c0:8c:60:a8:ac:42)
        Address: c0:8c:60:a8:ac:42 (c0:8c:60:a8:ac:42)
        .... ..0. .... .... .... .... = LG bit: Globally unique address (factory
 default)
        .... ...0 .... .... .... .... = IG bit: Individual address (unicast)
    Source: 02:10:18:97:3f:21 (02:10:18:97:3f:21)
        Address: 02:10:18:97:3f:21 (02:10:18:97:3f:21)
        .... ..1. .... .... .... .... = LG bit: Locally administered address (th
is is NOT the factory default)
        .... ...0 .... .... .... .... = IG bit: Individual address (unicast)
    Type: 802.1Q Virtual LAN (0x8100)
802.1Q Virtual LAN, PRI: 0, CFI: 0, ID: 4048
    000. .... .... .... = Priority: Best Effort (default) (0)
    ...0 .... .... .... = CFI: Canonical (0)
    .... 1111 1101 0000 = ID: 4048
    Type: Unknown (0xde08)
! Output omitted for brevity
Ethernet II, Src: c0:8c:60:a8:ac:41 (c0:8c:60:a8:ac:41), Dst: c0:8c:60:a8:68:01
(c0:8c:60:a8:68:01)
    Destination: c0:8c:60:a8:68:01 (c0:8c:60:a8:68:01)
        Address: c0:8c:60:a8:68:01 (c0:8c:60:a8:68:01)
        .... ..0. .... .... .... .... = LG bit: Globally unique address (factory
 default)
        .... ...0 .... .... .... .... = IG bit: Individual address (unicast)
    Source: c0:8c:60:a8:ac:41 (c0:8c:60:a8:ac:41)
        Address: c0:8c:60:a8:ac:41 (c0:8c:60:a8:ac:41)
        .... ..0. .... .... .... .... = LG bit: Globally unique address (factory
 default)
        .... ...0 .... .... .... .... = IG bit: Individual address (unicast)
    Type: IP (0x0800)
Internet Protocol Version 4, Src: 192.168.10.1 (192.168.10.1), Dst: 192.168.10.2
 (192.168.10.2)
```

```
    Version: 4
    Header length: 20 bytes
    Differentiated Services Field: 0xc0 (DSCP 0x30: Class Selector 6; ECN: 0x00:
 Not-ECT (Not ECN-Capable Transport))
        1100 00.. = Differentiated Services Codepoint: Class Selector 6 (0x30)
        .... ..00 = Explicit Congestion Notification: Not-ECT (Not ECN-Capable T
ransport) (0x00)
    Total Length: 71
    Identification: 0x356e (13678)
    Flags: 0x00
        0... .... = Reserved bit: Not set
        .0.. .... = Don't fragment: Not set
        ..0. .... = More fragments: Not set
    Fragment offset: 0
    Time to live: 64
    Protocol: TCP (6)
    Header checksum: 0xaf2f [correct]
        [Good: True]
        [Bad: False]
    Source: 192.168.10.1 (192.168.10.1)
    Destination: 192.168.10.2 (192.168.10.2)
Transmission Control Protocol, Src Port: 64176 (64176), Dst Port: 179 (179), Seq
: 1, Ack: 1, Len: 19
    Source port: 64176 (64176)
    Destination port: 179 (179)
    [Stream index: 0]
    Sequence number: 1     (relative sequence number)
    [Next sequence number: 20    (relative sequence number)]
    Acknowledgment number: 1    (relative ack number)
    Header length: 32 bytes
    Flags: 0x018 (PSH, ACK)
        000. .... .... = Reserved: Not set
        ...0 .... .... = Nonce: Not set
        .... 0... .... = Congestion Window Reduced (CWR): Not set
        .... .0.. .... = ECN-Echo: Not set
        .... ..0. .... = Urgent: Not set
        .... ...1 .... = Acknowledgment: Set
        .... .... 1... = Push: Set
        .... .... .0.. = Reset: Not set
        .... .... ..0. = Syn: Not set
        .... .... ...0 = Fin: Not set
    Window size value: 17376
    [Calculated window size: 17376]
    [Window size scaling factor: -1 (unknown)]
```

```
    Checksum: 0x0139 [validation disabled]
        [Good Checksum: False]
        [Bad Checksum: False]
! Output omitted for brevity
            Kind: Timestamp (8)
            Length: 10
            Timestamp value: 10033933
            Timestamp echo reply: 13878630
    [SEQ/ACK analysis]
        [Bytes in flight: 19]
Border Gateway Protocol - KEEPALIVE Message
    Marker: ffffffffffffffffffffffffffffffff
    Length: 19
    Type: KEEPALIVE Message (4)
! Output omitted due to brevity
```

Logging

Network issues are hard to troubleshoot and investigate if there is not any information found on the device. For instance, if an OSPF adjacency goes down and there is not a correlating alert, it will be hard to find out what caused the problem and when it happened. For these reasons, logging is very important. All Cisco routers and switches support logging functionality. Logging capabilities are also available for specific features and protocols. For example, logging can be enabled for BGP neighborship state changes or OSPF neighborship state changes.

Table 2-1 lists the various logging levels that can be configured.

Table 2-1 *Logging Levels*

Level Number	Level Name
0	Emergency
1	Alert
2	Critical
3	Errors
4	Warnings
5	Notifications
6	Informational
7	Debugging

When the higher value is set; the lower logging level is enabled by default. That means if the logging level is set to 5, Notifications, it implies that all events falling under the category from 0 to 5—that is, from Emergency to Notifications—are logged. For troubleshooting purpose, it is always good to set the logging level to 7, which is debugging.

There are multiple logging options available on Cisco devices:

- Console logging
- Buffered logging
- Logging to syslog server

Console logging is important in conditions where the device is experiencing crashes or a high CPU condition. Access to the terminal session via Telnet or SSH is not available, but it is not a good practice to have it enabled when running debugs. Some debug outputs are chatty and can flood the device console. As a best practice, console logging should always be disabled when running debugs. Example 2-16 illustrates how to enable console logging on various Cisco platforms.

Example 2-16 *Configuring Console Logging*

```
IOS_R2(config)# logging console informational
```

```
RP/0/0/CPU0:XR_R3(config)# logging console informational
RP/0/0/CPU0:XR_R3(config)# commit
```

```
Nexus-R1(config)# logging console ?
  <CR>
  <0-7>   0-emerg;1-alert;2-crit;3-err;4-warn;5-notif;6-inform;7-debug
 Nexus-R1(config)# logging console 6
```

Buffered logging, on the other hand, is useful while running debugs and for more persistent logging as compared to console logging. The default buffer size is 4096 bytes, which gets filled very quickly, and the logs become overridden when the value is exceeded. The buffer size can be increased to a higher value, such as 1000000. Example 2-17 demonstrates how to configure buffered logging with the logging level as debugging.

Example 2-17 *Configuring Buffered Logging*

```
IOS_R2(config)# logging buffered debugging 1000000
```

```
RP/0/0/CPU0:XR_R3(config)# logging buffered 1000000 severity debugging
RP/0/0/CPU0:XR_R3(config)# commit
```

```
Nexus-R1(config)# logging buffered 7
Nexus-R1(config)# logging buffered 1000000
```

Although increasing the buffer size always helps, it is better to limit the number of messages to be logged in the buffer. This should be done when running chatty debugs such as **debug ip packet.** It is very important to understand the impact of a debug command and should be tested before any of the debug commands are run in a production environment. If chatty debugs are enabled on the router, they can lead to a high CPU condition on the router, which may in turn cause loss of management access to the router and other critical services getting impacted. In such situations, reloading the device is the only option to recover and gain back the management access. If there are dual route processors (RP) present on the router running in stateful switchover (SSO) mode, an RP switchover would help as well.

The rate-limit value can be set for all messages or for the messages sent to the console. This can be achieved using the **logging rate-limit** command. Setting the rate-limiter for the logs may cause some of the crucial messages to be missed but can be helpful when chatty debugs are enabled, which can flood the console or the terminal session (vty session). Example 2-18 demonstrates setting the logging rate limiter using the **logging rate-limit** command. In this example, the logging messages are rate limited to 100 messages, except for debug messages. Similarly, console messages can be rate limited using the **console** keyword with the command.

Example 2-18   *Logging Rate Limiter*

```
IOS_R2(config)# logging rate-limit ?
  <1-10000>  Messages per second
  all        Rate limit all messages, including debug messages
  console    Rate limit only console messages
IOS_R2(config)# logging rate-limit 100 except debugging
```

The most persistent form of logging is using a syslog server to log all the device logs. A syslog server can be anything from a text file to a custom application that actively stores device logging information in a database. Unless there is a packet loss that occurs in the network, or the device is continuously experiencing a high CPU condition, such as 99% or 100% for a long period of time, the device keeps logging the information to the syslog server. During the packet loss or high CPU conditions, there are chances of the syslog server logging or SNMP traps getting disrupted.

Example 2-19 illustrates syslog logging configuration. Before configuring syslog-based logging on Cisco IOS, enable the **service timestamps [log | debug] [datetime | uptime] [localtime] [show-timezone]** command for the logging messages. This ensures that all log messages have timestamps and helps in performing an investigation of the log messages. The timestamp can be set for a log message or a debug log. The log can either be viewed in Date-Time format or just-in-time format starting from system uptime. The CLI also provides an option to use the local time zone using the **localtime** keyword and also to display the time zone using the **show-timezone** keyword. If there is a separate interface for management traffic, enable the syslog server logging using that interface as the source interface, as shown in Example 2-19.

Example 2-19   *Syslog Logging Configuration*

```
IOS_R2(config)# service timestamps log datetime
IOS_R2(config)# logging host 10.1.1.1
IOS_R2(config)# logging trap 7
IOS_R2(config)# logging source-interface GiabitEthernet0/1

RP/0/0/CPU0:XR_R3(config)# logging 10.1.1.1
RP/0/0/CPU0:XR_R3(config)# logging trap
RP/0/0/CPU0:XR_R3(config)# logging hostnameprefix 100.1.1.1
RP/0/0/CPU0:XR_R3(config)# logging source-interface MgmtEth0/RSP0/CPU0/0
RP/0/0/CPU0:XR_R3(config)# commit

Nexus-R1(config)# logging server 10.1.1.1 7
Nexus-R1(config)# logging timestamp [microseconds | milliseconds | seconds]
```

Generally, the management interfaces are configured with a management **vrf**. In such
cases, the syslog host has to be specified using the **logging host vrf** *vrf-name ip-address*
command on IOS or **logging hostnameprefix** *ip-address* **use-vrf** *vrf-name* command on
NX-OS, so that the router knows from which VRF routing table the server is reachable.
If the vrf option is not specified, the system does a lookup in the default vrf; that is, the
global routing table.

In Nexus platforms, there is another option to redirect debug output in a file, which is
useful when running debugs and segregating the debug outputs with regular log messages. This feature can be used using the **debug logfile** *file-name* **size** *size* command.
Example 2-20 demonstrates the use of the **debug logfile** command for capturing debugs
in a log file. In this example, a debug log file named *bgp_dbg* is created with size of
10000 bytes. The size of the log file can range from 4096 bytes to 4194304 bytes. After
the log file is created, all the debugs that are enabled are logged under the log file.

Example 2-20   *Capturing Debug in a Logfile on NX-OS*

```
Nexus-R1# debug logfile bgp_dbg size 100000
Nexus-R1# debug ip bgp update
```

The NX-OS software creates the logfile in the log: file system root directory and therefore
all the created logfiles can be viewed using **dir log:**. After the debug logfile is created, the
respective debugs can be enabled, and all the debug outputs are redirected to the debug
logfile. To view the contents of the logfile, use the **show debug logfile** *file-name* command.

Event Monitoring/Tracing

Event tracing is an important feature that helps collect event-related information for various protocols. Event traces generate debug-like messages based on the events without
enabling debugs and is stored in the memory of the router. There is no debug output

or syslog message generated for the event traces. These traces run in the background, therefore having the least impact on the router. There are no specific event traces or event history logs for BGP in IOS, but they are available in XR and NX-OS platforms.

Adjacency and CEF-related event traces can be collected on IOS devices, which are useful while troubleshooting forwarding issues or failed peering issues due to missing adjacency. Example 2-21 displays the various configuration options for event traces on Cisco IOS. In this example, adjacency related event trace is enabled.

Example 2-21 *Adjacency Event Trace Configuration*

```
IOS_R2(config)# monitor event-trace ?
  ac              AC traces
  adjacency       Adjacency Events
  all-traces      Configure merged event traces
  arp             ARP Events
  atom            AToM traces
  c3pl            Group traces
  cce             Group traces
  cef             CEF traces
! Output omitted for brevity
IOS_R2(config)# monitor event-trace adjacency
```

The event trace for adjacency can start logging an event whenever there is a change in any adjacency on the router. For example, bringing up a subinterface on the router, such as GigabitEthernet0/1.100, and then trying to form adjacency over that interface can trigger the logging for the adjacency in event traces. Example 2-22 demonstrates adjacency event traces generated for a subinterface. In this example, when the ping test is performed and the adjacency event traces show that router requests to add ARP, after the ARP is learned, it forms the adjacency for IP address 100.1.1.12 over the subinterface GigabitEthernet0/1.100.

Example 2-22 *Event Traces Showing Adjacency Formation*

```
IOS_R2# show run int GigabitEthernet0/1.100
interface GigabitEthernet0/1.100
  encapsulation dot1Q 100
  ip address 100.1.1.1 255.255.255.252

IOS_R2# ping 100.1.1.2
Type escape sequence to abort.
Sending 5, 100-byte ICMP Echos to 100.1.1.2, timeout is 2 seconds:
.!!!!
Success rate is 80 percent (4/5), round-trip min/avg/max = 7/10/14 ms
```

```
IOS_R2# show monitor event-trace adjacency all
! Output omitted for brevity
05:19:12.964: GLOBAL: adj mgr notified of fibidb state change int
                      GigabitEthernet0/1 to up [Ignr]
05:19:16.906: GLOBAL: adj mgr notified of fibidb state change int
                      GigabitEthernet0/1.100 to up [Ignr]
05:23:04.952: ADJ: IP 100.1.1.2 GigabitEthernet0/1.100: request to add ARP [OK]
05:23:04.952: ADJ: IP 100.1.1.2 GigabitEthernet0/1.100: update oce
                      bundle,  IPv4 incomplete adj oce [OK]
05:23:04.952: ADJ: IP 100.1.1.2 GigabitEthernet0/1.100: allocate [OK]
05:23:04.952: ADJ: IP 100.1.1.2 GigabitEthernet0/1.100: add source ARP [OK]
05:23:04.952: ADJ: IP 100.1.1.2 GigabitEthernet0/1.100: incomplete
                      behaviour change to drop [OK]
05:23:04.952: ADJ: IP 100.1.1.2 GigabitEthernet0/1.100: request to
                      update [OK]
05:23:04.952: ADJ: IP 100.1.1.2 GigabitEthernet0/1.100: update oce
                      bundle,  IPv4 no fixup, no redirect adj oce [OK]
05:23:04.953: ADJ: IP 100.1.1.2 GigabitEthernet0/1.100: update [OK]
```

If the adjacency is not formed or an incomplete ARP is seen in the **show ip arp** command output, no events for the adjacency getting completed will be seen in the event traces. This indicates that there is either a Layer 1 issue or a misconfiguration, such as VLAN Id not allowed on the switch in the middle. Similarly, event traces can be enabled for other features and protocols like EIGRP, MPLS, and ATOM, although it is not necessary to enable all the traces. The event traces for specific features and protocols can be turned on when a problem is seen on the device with respect to those features. In Cisco IOS, the size of the event traces is limited by default and thus, if the traces are captured after a certain time of the problem, they might not be of much use because the logs get rolled over. The size of the event traces can be increased, but the maximum number of entries supported is 1 million entries. Alternatively, if the problem is occurring frequently for features for which event traces are available, the event trace should be enabled for that feature just before the problem occurs and can be disabled after relevant logs have been captured. This will save system resources as well.

In IOS XR, traces are available for respective protocols and are very useful during troubleshooting. For example, in IOS XR, BGP traces can be verified when troubleshooting a peering issue for neighbor. Example 2-23 displays the BGP trace for a neighborship coming up. The **show bgp trace** command available for BGP captures all the activities taking place in BGP. At the beginning, the trace shows an OPEN message being sent out for peer IP 192.168.200.1. At the end, the trace log shows the neighborship being established.

Example 2-23 *BGP Neighborship Event Trace on IOS XR*

```
RP/0/0/CPU0:XR_R3# show bgp trace
! Output omitted for brevity
17:55:22.373 default-bgp/spkr-tr2-err 0/0/CPU0 t14 [ERR][GEN]:1300: OPEN from
  '192.168.200.1' has unrecognized cap code/len 70/0 - Ignored
17:55:22.373 default-bgp/spkr-tr2-upd 0/0/CPU0 t14 [UPD]:1820: Updgrp change
 scheduled after open processing: nbr=192.168.200.1, nbrfl=0x8310000
17:55:22.373 default-bgp/spkr-tr2-gen 0/0/CPU0 t14 [GEN]:546: nbr 192.168.200.1,
 old state 4, new state 5, fd type 1, fd 124
17:55:22.373 default-bgp/spkr-tr2-gen 0/0/CPU0 t14 [GEN]:2295: calling bgp_send_kee-
  palive, nbr 192.168.200.1, loc 1, data 0,0
17:55:22.373 default-bgp/spkr-tr2-gen 0/0/CPU0 t14 [GEN]:546: nbr 192.168.200.1,
 old state 5, new state 6, fd type 1, fd 124
17:55:22.373 default-bgp/spkr-tr2-gen 0/0/CPU0 t14 [GEN]:549: Nbr '192.168.200.1'
 established
```

The trace output can be filtered using the various keyword options available after the
show bgp trace command, such as **show bgp trace error** or **show bgp trace update**,
which helps in viewing the specific error and the BGP update, respectively.

Similarly in NX-OS, an **event-history** keyword option is available for various features
under the respective feature command line. Example 2-24 displays the event-history cli
option for BGP. In this example, the event history log displays an event with **clear_ip_
bgp_cmd**, which tells that there was an execution of the **clear ip bgp** command on the
router.

Example 2-24 *BGP Event History CLI*

```
Nexus_R1# show bgp event-history msgs
! Output omitted for brevity
46) Event:E_DEBUG, length:66, at 35995 usecs after Fri Aug 28 18:25:48 2015
     [100] [28046]: comp-mts-rx opc - from sap 9530 cmd clear_ip_bgp_cmd
47) Event:E_DEBUG, length:42, at 245222 usecs after Fri Aug 28 18:25:43 2015
     [100] [28046]: nvdb: terminate transaction
```

NX-OS not only maintains the event-history logs but also allows the user to define the
size of the event-trace buffer per feature. Different sizes that can be set, such as small,
medium, large, and so on.

Other event-history cli options are available for BGP, such as events, errors, logs, and so
on. These are discussed and used in various chapters in this book.

Summary

This chapter explained various methodologies for troubleshooting network events. This chapter lays down a foundation of how to approach a network problem in few simple steps:

Step 1.   Define the problem.

Step 2.   Collect data.

Step 3.   Refine the problem statement.

Step 4.   Build a theory.

Step 5.   Test the theory.

Step 6.   Conclusion.

Step 7.   Document the conclusion.

The chapter stressed the importance of documentation and reproducing the problem in a lab environment. Logging and event tracing options are essential tools for identifying what happened, when it happened, and where it happened. This information is vital for isolating a problem in the network.

Just as there are three sides to a story: yours, mine, and the truth, there are three sides to an event: sending router, receiving router, and the wire. Packet capture tools are available to verify what is happening from every perspective of the network.

Reference

BRKARC-2011, *Overview of Packet Capturing Tools*, Cisco Live.

## Chapter 3

Troubleshooting Peering Issues

The following topics are covered in this chapter:

- BGP peering down issues

- BGP peer flapping issues

- Dynamic BGP peering

Border Gateway Protocol (BGP) is a complex protocol that requires proficient troubleshooting skills. To troubleshoot BGP issues, you should have a deep understanding of BGP protocol, its attributes, and its features. Some of these have already been discussed in Chapter 1, "BGP Fundamentals" and are discussed further in upcoming chapters. The most common problem with BGP is establishing and maintaining a BGP session that can occur when a new BGP neighbor is configured or can occur for an existing peer after a network event.

This chapter explains various techniques and commands that are helpful during the investigation of many BGP peering issues.

BGP Peering Down Issues

When a configured BGP neighbor is not in an established state, network engineers refer to this scenario as *BGP peering down*. The peering down issue occurs because of one of the following circumstances:

- During establishment of BGP sessions because of misconfiguration

- Triggered by network migration or event, or software or hardware upgrades

- Failure to maintain BGP keepalives due to transmission problems

- High CPU

- Blocked or stuck processes

- Firewall or ACL misconfiguration

- Software defects

A down BGP peer state is in either an Idle or Active state. From the peer state standpoint, these states would mean following possible problems:

- Idle state

  - No connected route to peer

- Active state

  - No route to peer address (IP connectivity not present)

  - Configuration error, such as update-source missing or wrongly configured

- Idle/Active state

  - Transmission Control Protocol (TCP) establishes but BGP negotiation fails; for example, misconfigured AS

  - Router did not agree on the peering parameters

Figure 3-1 provides a topology to demonstrate the logic and steps followed for trouble-shooting BGP peering issues. In this topology, R1 and R2 are internal BGP (IBGP) neighbors, and R2 and R3 are external BGP (EBGP) neighbors. R1 is running NX-OS, R2 is running Cisco IOS, and R3 is running IOS XR.

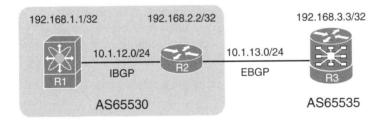

Figure 3-1 *IBGP and EBGP Topology*

Verifying Configuration

The first step for troubleshooting should be verifying the configuration and understanding the design. A lot of times, a basic configuration mistake can cause a BGP session not to come up. Example 3-1 displays working configurations of IBGP and EBGP sessions for the topology shown in Figure 3-1.

Note Nexus platforms require the BGP feature to be enabled using the command **feature bgp** to configure BGP. The **configuration** and **show** commands for BGP are not available on NX-OS until it is enabled.

Example 3-1 *BGP Configuration on All Routers*

```
R1# show running-config bgp
feature bgp

 router bgp 65530
   router-id 192.168.1.1
   address-family ipv4 unicast
     network 192.168.1.1/32
   neighbor 192.168.2.2
     remote-as 65530
     update-source loopback0
     address-family ipv4 unicast
```

```
R2# show running-config | section router bgp
 router bgp 65530
  bgp router-id 192.168.2.2
  bgp log-neighbor-changes
  no bgp default ipv4-unicast
  neighbor 10.1.13.2 remote-as 65535
  neighbor 192.168.1.1 remote-as 65530
  neighbor 192.168.1.1 update-source Loopback0
  !
  address-family ipv4
   network 192.168.2.2 mask 255.255.255.255
   neighbor 10.1.13.2 activate
   neighbor 192.168.1.1 activate
   neighbor 192.168.1.1 next-hop-self
```

```
RP/0/0/CPU0:R3# show running-config router bgp
router bgp 65535
  bgp router-id 192.168.3.3
  address-family ipv4 unicast
   network 192.168.3.3/32
   !
  neighbor 10.1.13.1
   remote-as 65530
   address-family ipv4 unicast
```

The following items should be checked when a new BGP neighbor is configured:

- Local autonomous system (AS) number

- Remote AS number

- Reachability between the peering addresses

- Verifying the network topology and other documentations

- Route policy planning, though not required for BGP neighborship to establish.

It is important to understand the traffic flow of BGP packets between peers. The source IP address of the BGP packets still reflects the IP address of the outbound interface. When a BGP packet is received, the router correlates the source IP address of the packet to the BGP neighbor table. If the BGP packet source does not match an entry in the neighbor table, the packet cannot be associated to a neighbor and is discarded.

In most of the deployments, the IBGP peering is configured over the loopback interface of the router. For the IBGP peering session to come up, the loopback interface should be explicitly defined as the source. The explicit sourcing of BGP packets from an interface can be verified by ensuring that the **neighbor** *ip-address* **update-source** *interface-id* command is correctly configured for the peer.

If there are multiple hops between the EBGP peers, then a proper hop count is required. Ensure the **neighbor** *ip-address* **ebgp-multihop** [*hop-count*] is configured with the correct hop count. If the *hop-count* is not specified, the default TTL value for IBGP sessions is 255, and the default TTL value for EBGP sessions is 1. The time to live (TTL) value can be viewed only on IOS routers, as shown in Example 3-2. Notice that the TTL value changes between IBGP and EBGP sessions. The TTL information is not displayed on IOS XR or NX-OS command output.

Example 3-2   *TTL Values for IBGP and EBGP Sessions*

```
R2# show bgp ipv4 unicast neighbor 192.168.1.1 | in TTL
 Connection is ECN Disabled, Mininum incoming TTL 0, Outgoing TTL 255
```

```
R2# show bgp ipv4 unicast 10.1.13.2 | in TTL
 Connection is ECN Disabled, Mininum incoming TTL 0, Outgoing TTL 1
```

Note   With the **neighbor** *ip-address* **ttl-security** command, the **ebgp-multihop** command is not required. TTL security is discussed in more detail in Chapter 9, "Securing BGP."

Use the **neighbor** *ip-address* **disable-connected-check** command for an EBGP peer session that is single-hop away but peering over loopback interface. This command disables the connection verification mechanism, which by default prevents the session from getting established when the EBGP peer is not in the directly connected segment.

Another configuration that is important, although optional, for successful establishment of the BGP session is peer authentication. Misconfiguration or typo errors in authentication passwords can cause the BGP session to fail.

Verifying Reachability

After the configuration has been verified, the connectivity between the peering IPs must be confirmed as well. If the peering is being established between loopback interfaces, a loopback-to-loopback ping test should be performed. If a ping test is performed without specifying loopback as the source interface, the outgoing physical interface IP address will be used as the packet's source IP address instead of the router's loopback IP address.

Example 3-3 displays a loopback-to-loopback ping test between R1 and R2

Example 3-3 *Ping with Source Interface as Loopback*

```
NX-OS
R1# ping 192.168.2.2 source 192.168.1.1
PING 192.168.2.2 (192.168.2.2) from 192.168.1.1: 56 data bytes
64 bytes from 192.168.2.2: icmp_seq=0 ttl=254 time=4.809 ms
64 bytes from 192.168.2.2: icmp_seq=1 ttl=254 time=5.524 ms
64 bytes from 192.168.2.2: icmp_seq=2 ttl=254 time=8.882 ms
64 bytes from 192.168.2.2: icmp_seq=3 ttl=254 time=4.643 ms
64 bytes from 192.168.2.2: icmp_seq=4 ttl=254 time=6.091 ms
--- 192.168.2.2 ping statistics ---
5 packets transmitted, 5 packets received, 0.00% packet loss
round-trip min/avg/max = 4.643/5.989/8.882 ms
```

```
IOS
R2# ping 192.168.1.1 source loopback0
Sending 5, 100-byte ICMP Echos to 192.168.1.1, timeout is 2 seconds:
Packet sent with a source address of 192.168.2.2
!!!!!
Success rate is 100 percent (5/5), round-trip min/avg/max = 3/5/8 ms
```

Reachability has to be verified for all IBGP and EBGP sessions. Example 3-3 shows that connectivity exists between the peering IP addresses. But if connectivity cannot be verified, refer to the upcoming subsections that explain how to isolate the issue in order to better understand if the connectivity problem is in the forwarding path or the return path. The following conditions are explained in more detail:

- Find the location and direction of packet loss.

- Verify whether packets are being transmitted.

- Use access control lists (ACL) to verify that packets are received.

- Check ACLs and firewalls in path.

- Verify TCP sessions.

- Simulate a BGP session.

Find the Location and Direction of Packet Loss

The **show ip traffic** command output is helpful to understand the direction of the packet loss. This command's output has a section for Internet Control Message Protocol (ICMP) packets, which shows the received and sent counters for both Echo-Request and Echo-Reply. First, ensure that the sent and receive counters are stable on both the source and the destination devices. If the counters keep incrementing, it will be difficult to correlate if the ICMP echo packet actually made it to the other end or if the other end sent an echo reply or not. In such cases, ACLs or packet capture tools can be used to verify whether the packets have been received and if the ICMP echo reply has been sent. If the counters are not incrementing, by using the source IP, such as loopback interface, perform a ping test to the destination IP. After the ping is completed (with or without success), verify the output of **show ip traffic | include echo**. The value by which echo (echo request) sent counters incremented on the source should match the value of echo received counters incremented on the destination device. The same value should be incremented for echo reply sent on the destination device and echo reply received on the source device.

Example 3-4 demonstrates the use of the **show ip traffic** command to understand the direction of the packet loss from R2 to R1. The echo reply sent counter is not incrementing where the echo received counter has incremented on R2.

Example 3-4   show ip traffic *Command Output*

```
NX-OS
R1# show ip traffic | include echo
   Redirect: 0, unreachable: 0, echo request: 10, echo reply: 5,
   Redirect: 0, unreachable: 0, echo request: 5, echo reply: 5,
! This is the Source Router
R1# ping 192.168.2.2 source 192.168.1.1
PING 192.168.2.2 (192.168.2.2) from 192.168.1.1: 56 data bytes
Request timed out
Request timed out
Request timed out
Request timed out
Request timed out
--- 192.168.2.2 ping statistics ---
5 packets transmitted, 0 packets received, 100.00% packet loss
round-trip min/avg/max = 3.482/3.696/3.904 ms
```

```
R1# show ip traffic | include echo
    Redirect: 0, unreachable: 0, echo request: 15, echo reply: 5,
    Redirect: 0, unreachable: 0, echo request: 5, echo reply: 5,
```

```
IOS
R2# show ip traffic | include echo
        10 echo, 14 echo reply, 0 mask requests, 0 mask replies, 0 quench
    Sent: 0 redirects, 0 unreachable, 55 echo, 10 echo reply
! Notice the below echo reply counter is not incrementing in the Sent section.
R2# show ip traffic | include echo
        15 echo, 14 echo reply, 0 mask requests, 0 mask replies, 0 quench
    Sent: 0 redirects, 0 unreachable, 55 echo, 10 echo reply
```

Note   On IOS XR, use the command **show ipv4 traffic** to verify the ICMP packet counters.

To understand why R2 is not sending ICMP echo replies to R1, routing and the CEF table on R2 can be checked. Interface configurations on R2 should also be checked for ACLs that could be dropping the ICMP echo replies. If you are still unable to figure out the cause, one of the packet capture tools, as shown in Chapter 2, "Generic Troubleshooting Methodologies," can be used to further troubleshoot the problem.

Verify Whether Packets Are Being Transmitted

If there is complete packet loss on the link, perform a ping connectivity test with the timeout set to 0 to confirm if the packet is actually leaving the router or if the other side is receiving the packets. The purpose of this test is to send the packets out and ensure that the counters are incrementing and not really waiting for a reply from the other endpoint.

When the ping with timeout value 0 is performed, the output packets counter should be incremented by the amount of ping packets sent in the **show interface** command output. The router sends out ping packets without waiting for any response.

Example 3-5 displays the use of ping with timeout 0. It can be seen from the output that R2's Gi0/1 interface output counter is incrementing while the input counter is not. Notice that on the Nexus platform, **show ip interface** *interface-id* displays the packets sent and received counters, rather than the **show interface** *interface-id* command.

Example 3-5 *Ping with Timeout 0*

```
IOS
R2# show interface Gi0/1 | in packets
   5 minute input rate 0 bits/sec, 0 packets/sec
   5 minute output rate 0 bits/sec, 0 packets/sec
      26540 packets input, 2129461 bytes, 0 no buffer
      37292 packets output, 2870820 bytes, 0 underruns
R2# ping 10.1.12.1 timeout 0 repeat 10
Type escape sequence to abort.
Sending 10, 100-byte ICMP Echos to 10.1.12.1, timeout is 0 seconds:
..........
Success rate is 0 percent (0/10)
R2# show interface Gi0/1 | in packets
   5 minute input rate 1000 bits/sec, 0 packets/sec
   5 minute output rate 1000 bits/sec, 1 packets/sec
      26540 packets input, 2129461 bytes, 0 no buffer
      37306 packets output, 2872281 bytes, 0 underruns


NX-OS
R1# show ip interface E2/1 | include packets
      Unicast packets    : 6602/6611/0/6602/7753
      Multicast packets  : 19846/15636/0/19846/31272
      Broadcast packets  : 0/2/0/0/2
      Labeled packets    : 0/0/0/0/0
! Sent and Received packet counts after the ping test on R1
R1# show ip interface E2/1 | include packets
      Unicast packets    : 6602/6611/0/6602/7753
      Multicast packets  : 19846/15637/0/19846/31274
      Broadcast packets  : 0/2/0/0/2
      Labeled packets    : 0/0/0/0/0
```

Use Access Control Lists to Verify Whether Packets Are Received

ACLs prove to be really useful when troubleshooting packet loss or reachability issues. Configuring an ACL matching the source and the destination IP can help confirm whether the packet has reached the destination router. As a best practice, specific protocol packets with specific source and destination addresses should be used as part of the ACL. For example, if the troubleshooting is being performed for ICMP traffic and BGP packets between routers R1 and R2, the ACL entry should match for just the ICMP traffic and TCP traffic on port 179 with the source and destination of R1 and R2 address. The only caution that needs to be taken is that while configuring ACL, **permit ip any any** should be configured at the end, or else it will trigger all the other packets to get dropped and cause a service impact.

Check ACLs and Firewalls in Path

In most of the deployments, the edge routers or Internet Gateway (IGW) routers are configured with ACLs to limit the traffic allowed in the network. If the BGP session is being established across those links where the ACL is configured, ensure that BGP packets (TCP port 179) are not getting dropped because of those ACLs.

Example 3-6 shows how the ACL configuration should look if BGP is passing through that link. The example shows the configuration for both IPv4 as well as ipv6 access-list in case of IPv6 BGP sessions. For applying IPv4 ACL on interface, the **ip access-group** *access-list-name* {in|out} command is used on all platforms. For IPv6 ACL, the **ipv6 traffic-filter** *access-list-name* {in|out} interface command is used on NX-OS and IOS, whereas **ipv6 access-group** *access-list-name* {in|out} interface config is used on IOS XR.

Example 3-6 *ACL for Permitting BGP Traffic*

```
NX-OS
R1(config)# ip access-list v4_BGP_ACL
R1(config-acl)# permit tcp any eq bgp any
R1(config-acl)# permit tcp any any eq bgp
! Output omitted for brevity
R1(config)# ipv6 access-list v6_BGP_ACL
R1(config-ipv6-acl)# permit tcp any eq bgp any
R1(config-ipv6-acl)# permit tcp any any eq bgp
! Output omitted for brevity
R1(config)# interface Ethernet2/1
R1(config-if)# ip access-group v4_BGP_ACL in
R1(config-if)# ipv6 traffic-filter v6_BGP_ACL in


IOS
R2(config)# ip access-list v4_BGP_ACL
R2(config-acl)# permit tcp any eq bgp any
R2(config-acl)# permit tcp any any eq bgp
! Output omitted for brevity
R2(config)# ipv6 access-list v6_BGP_ACL
R2(config-ipv6-acl)# permit tcp any eq bgp any
R2(config-ipv6-acl)# permit tcp any any eq bgp
! Output omitted for brevity
R2(config)# interface Gi0/1
R2(config-if)# ip access-group v4_BGP_ACL in
R1(config-if)# ipv6 traffic-filter v6_BGP_ACL in


IOS XR
RP/0/0/CPU0:R3(config)# ipv4 access-list v4_BGP_ACL
RP/0/0/CPU0:R3(config-ipv4-acl)# permit tcp any eq bgp any
RP/0/0/CPU0:R3(config-ipv4-acl)# permit tcp any any eq bgp
! Output omitted for brevity
```

```
RP/0/0/CPU0:R3(config)# ipv6 access-list v6_BGP_ACL
RP/0/0/CPU0:R3(config-ipv4-acl)# permit tcp any eq bgp any
RP/0/0/CPU0:R3(config-ipv4-acl)# permit tcp any any eq bgp
! Output omitted for brevity
RP/0/0/CPU0:R3(config)# interface Gi0/0/0/0
RP/0/0/CPU0:R3(config-if)# ipv4 access-group v4_BGP_ACL in
RP/0/0/CPU0:R3(config-if)# ipv6 access-group v6_BGP_ACL in
RP/0/0/CPU0:R3(config-if)# commit
```

Having two ACL entries for BGP ensures that the BGP packet is not dropped if the TCP session is initiated from either the local or the remote router or if the ACL is on a device that is in transit.

Other than having ACLs configured on the edge devices, many deployments have firewalls to protect the network from unwanted and malicious traffic. It is a better option to have a firewall installed than to have a huge ACL configured on the routers and switches. Firewalls can be configured in two modes:

■ Routed mode

■ Transparent mode

In Routed mode, the firewall has routing capabilities and is considered to be a routed hop in the network. In Transparent mode, the firewall is not considered as a router hop to the connected device but merely acts like a "bump in the wire." Therefore, if an EBGP session is being established across a transparent firewall, then **ebgp-multihop** might not be required. Even if it is required to configure **ebgp-multihop** because of multiple devices in the path, the firewall is not counted as another routed hop.

In some deployments, network operators add NAT on the routed firewalls. In cases where NAT is configured on the router or on the firewall, the BGP peering should be configured with the translated IP address rather than the remote IP. If the peering is configured with the remote IP address and there is a NAT device in transit, the packet on the remote router will be received with the source address of the translated IP and not sourcing the IP address of the source router. This will cause the remote router to reset the TCP connection and send a reset (RST) and acknowledgment (ACK) in response to the synchronize (SYN) packet received for the TCP connection. This is because the receiving router is configured for BGP connection with the IP address of the source router but is receiving a different IP address than the configured peer.

In Figure 3-2, a transparent firewall is added between router R2 and R3 of our topology. There is no need to configure the **neighbor** *ip-address* **ebgp-multihop** [*hop-count*] command for the EBGP neighborship.

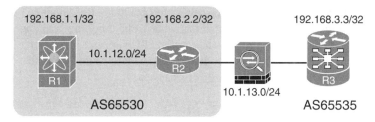

192.168.1.1/32   192.168.2.2/32   192.168.3.3/32

10.1.12.0/24

R1   R2   R3

AS65530   10.1.13.0/24   AS65535

Figure 3-2 *IBGP and EBGP Topology with Firewall*

Firewalls implement various security levels for the interfaces. For example, on Cisco's Adaptive Security Appliance (ASA) firewall, the inside interface is assigned a security level of 100 (highest security level) and the outside interface is assigned a security level of 0 (lowest security level). An ACL needs to be configured to permit the relevant traffic from the least secure interface going toward a higher security interface. This rule applies for both Routed and Transparent mode firewalls.

Bridge groups are configured in Transparent mode firewall for each network to help minimize the overhead on security contexts. The interfaces become part of a bridge group and a bridge virtual interface (BVI) interface is configured with a management IP address.

Example 3-7 displays an ASA ACL configuration that allows ICMP as well as BGP packets to traverse across the firewall. It also demonstrates how to assign the ACL to the interface. Any traffic that is not part of the ACL gets dropped.

Example 3-7 *ASA Transparent Mode Firewall Configuration for Permitting BGP*

```
interface GigabitEthernet0/0
  nameif Inside
  bridge-group 200
  security-level 100
!
interface GigabitEthernet0/1
  nameif Outside
  bridge-group 200
  security-level 0
!
! Creating BVI with Management IP and should be the same subnet
! as the connected interface subnet
interface BVI200
  ip address 10.1.13.10 255.255.255.0
!
access-list Out extended permit icmp any any
access-list Out extended permit tcp any eq bgp any
access-list Out extended permit tcp any any eq bgp
!
access-group Out in interface Outside
```

In the ACL named Out, both ACL entries permitting BGP are not required, although it is good practice to have both. It is important to note that while troubleshooting flapping BGP peers, firewall MTUs could also play a part while sending BGP updates across the firewall. This concept is explained in detail for troubleshooting BGP flapping issues later in this chapter.

Verify TCP Sessions

A BGP session is a TCP session. Therefore, it is very important to verify if the TCP session is getting established to ensure successful BGP session establishment. Example 3-8 shows TCP sessions on port 179 on all the routers. Notice that the routers are listening on port 179. On R3 (IOS XR), there are two VRF-IDs. VRF-ID 0x60000000 indicates default VRF, whereas 0x00000000 indicates that it is a Multi Virtual Routing and Forwarding (VRF) TCP protocol control block (pcb) under which specific VRF pcbs are created by applications using TCP. The application can be BGP, Label Discovery Protocol (LDP), and so on.

Note   The TCP session is allowed to be established only for a specific VRF pcb.

Example 3-8   *Output Showing TCP in Listening State*

```
R1# show sockets connection tcp
! Output omitted for brevity
 Total number of tcp sockets: 6
 Active connections (including servers)
 Protocol State/        Recv-Q/    Local Address(port)/
          Context       Send-Q     Remote Address(port)
   tcp    LISTEN         0          *(179)
          Wildcard       0          *(*)

   tcp6   LISTEN         0          *(179)
          Wildcard       0          *(*)

   tcp    ESTABLISHED    0          192.168.1.1(179)
          default        0          192.168.2.2(15529)


R2# show tcp brief all
   TCB        Local Address          Foreign Address           (state)
   0DFE19B0   192.168.2.2.15529      192.168.1.1.179           ESTAB
   0F7D44F8   10.1.13.1.179          10.1.13.2.52005           ESTAB
   0BB8FC40   0.0.0.0.179            10.1.13.2.*               LISTEN
   0D911608   0.0.0.0.179            192.168.1.1.*             LISTEN


RP/0/0/CPU0:R3# show tcp brief
! Output omitted for brevity
```

```
    PCB       VRF-ID     Recv-Q Send-Q Local Address    Foreign Address      State
0x101ad27c 0x60000000     0      0     :::179           :::0                LISTEN
0x101a521c 0x00000000     0      0     :::179           :::0                LISTEN
0x101ad62c 0x60000000     0      0     10.1.13.2:52005  10.1.13.1:179       ESTAB
0x10158cd0 0x60000000     0      0     0.0.0.0:179      0.0.0.0:0           LISTEN
0x101a5e30 0x00000000     0      0     0.0.0.0:179      0.0.0.0:0           LISTEN
```

If BGP is not getting established and there is a stale entry noticed in the TCP table in established state, clear the TCP session using the TCP control block (tcb) entry by issuing the **clear tcp tcb** *value* on IOS or **clear tcp pcb** *value* command on IOS XR. Such stale entry problems would cause stopping of BGP keepalives, and TCP would move to a closing state.

Note   The **clear** command is not available on NX-OS for TCP sessions. The **clear** command is available only to clear statistics.

Simulate a BGP Session

A good troubleshooting technique for BGP peers that are down is using Telnet on TCP port 179 toward the destination peer IP and implementing local peering IP as the source. This technique helps ensure that the TCP is not getting blocked or dropped between the two BGP peering devices. This test is useful for verifying any TCP issues on the destination router and also helps define any ACL or firewall that could possibly block the BGP packets.

Example 3-9 shows the use of Telnet on port 179 to verify the BGP session. When this test is performed, the BGP TCP session is established, but the BGP remains in *OpenSent* state.

Example 3-9   *Using Telnet to Port 179*

```
NX-OS
R1# telnet 192.168.2.2 179 source loopback 0
 Trying 192.168.2.2...
 Connected to 192.168.2.2.
 Escape character is '^]'.


ÿÿÿÿ9
 Connection closed by foreign host.


IOS
R2# show bgp ipv4 unicast summary
! Output omitted for brevity
 Neighbor        AS    MsgRcvd MsgSent   TblVer  InQ OutQ Up/Down  State/PfxRcd
 10.1.13.2    4  65535    1409    1329       5    0    0 20:00:13        0
 192.168.1.1  4  65530       0       1       1    0    0 00:01:40    OpenSent
```

```
R2# show tcp brief
TCB        Local Address              Foreign Address            (state)
0FE84118   192.168.2.2.179            192.168.1.1.5282           ESTAB
0FEE0558   10.1.13.1.62644            10.1.13.2.179              ESTAB
```

> **Note**   The preceding Telnet method will not work if BGP authentication has been configured. This test is primarily useful when there is any ACL configured in the path or a firewall is involved.

If the Telnet is not sourced from the interface or IP that the remote device is configured to form a BGP neighborship with, the Telnet request will be refused. This is another way to confirm that the peering device is configured as dictated by the network requirements.

Demystifying BGP Notifications

BGP notifications play a crucial role in understanding and troubleshooting failed BGP peering or flapping peer issues. A BGP notification is sent from a BGP speaker to a peer when an error is detected. The notification can be sent either before the BGP session has been established or afterward based on the type of error. Each message has a fixed-size header. There may or may not be a data portion following the header, depending on the message type. The layout of these fields is as follows:

```
 0                   1                   2                   3
 0 1 2 3 4 5 6 7 8 9 0 1 2 3 4 5 6 7 8 9 0 1 2 3 4 5 6 7 8 9 0 1
+-+-+-+-+-+-+-+-+-+-+-+-+-+-+-+-+-+-+-+-+-+-+-+-+-+-+-+-+-+-+-+-+
|                                                               |
                             Marker
|                                                               |
+-+-+-+-+-+-+-+-+-+-+-+-+-+-+-+-+-+-+-+-+-+-+-+-+-+-+-+-+-+-+-+-+
|          Length                 |          Type         |
+-+-+-+-+-+-+-+-+-+-+-+-+-+-+-+-+-+-+-+-+-+-+-+-+-+
```

In addition to the fixed-size BGP message header, a notification contains the following fields:

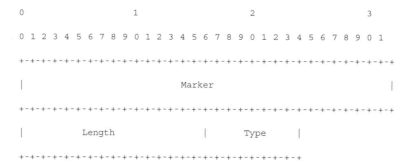

```
 0                   1                   2                   3
 0 1 2 3 4 5 6 7 8 9 0 1 2 3 4 5 6 7 8 9 0 1 2 3 4 5 6 7 8 9 0 1
+-+-+-+-+-+-+-+-+-+-+-+-+-+-+-+-+-+-+-+-+-+-+-+-+-+-+-+-+-+-+-+-+
| Error code    | Error subcode   |    Data (variable)          |
+-+-+-+-+-+-+-+-+-+-+-+-+-+-+-+-+-+-+-+-+-+-+-+-+-+-+-+-+-+-+-+-+
```

The Error code and Error-Subcode values are defined in RFC 4271. Table 3-1 shows all the Error codes, Error-Subcodes and their interpretation.

Table 3-1 *BGP Notification Error and Error-Subcode*

Error Code	Subcode	Description
01	00	Message Header Error
01	01	Message Header Error—Connection Not Synchronized
01	02	Message Header Error—Bad Message Length
01	03	Message Header Error—Bad Message Type
02	00	OPEN Message Error
02	01	OPEN Message Error—Unsupported Version Number
02	02	OPEN Message Error—Bad Peer AS
02	03	OPEN Message Error—Bad BGP Identifier
02	04	OPEN Message Error—Unsupported Optional Parameter
02	05	OPEN Message Error—Deprecated
02	06	OPEN Message Error—Unacceptable Hold Time
03	00	Update Message Error
03	01	Update Message Error—Malformed Attribute List
03	02	Update Message Error—Unrecognized Well-known Attribute
03	03	Update Message Error—Missing Well-Known Attribute
03	04	Update Message Error—Attribute Flags Error
03	05	Update Message Error—Attribute Length Error
03	06	Update Message Error—Invalid Origin Attribute
03	07	(Deprecated)
03	08	Update Message Error—Invalid NEXT_HOP Attribute
03	09	Update Message Error—Optional Attribute Error
03	0A	Update Message Error—Invalid Network Field
03	0B	Update Message Error—Malformed AS_PATH
04	00	Hold Timer Expired
05	00	Finite State Machine Error
06	00	Cease
06	01	Cease—Maximum Number of Prefixes Reached
06	02	Cease—Administrative Shutdown

Error Code	Subcode	Description
06	03	Cease—Peer Deconfigured
06	04	Cease—Administrative Reset
06	05	Cease—Connection Rejected
06	06	Cease—Other Configuration Change
06	07	Cease—Connection Collision Resolution
06	08	Cease—Out of Resources

Whenever a notification is generated, the error code and the subcode are always printed in the message. These notification messages are helpful when troubleshooting down peering issues or flapping peer issues.

Example 3-10 demonstrates a BGP notification being sent to the peer device when the peer is in the wrong autonomous system. The notification received by R2 displays the neighbor from which the notification was received, and the error code '2/2'—which is the Error/Error-Subcode format. From the preceding table, the error code 2 represents an OPEN error message, and the subcode 2 represents that the peer is in the wrong AS. The other important thing is the notification data, which is seen at the end (4 bytes 0000FFFA). The hex value in the data section helps to understand the problem and also gives the correct value in this case. The data section tells that the AS number should be 65530 rather than 65531.

Example 3-10 *BGP Notification*

```
IOS XR
RP/0/0/CPU0:R3# configure terminal
RP/0/0/CPU0:R3(config)# router bgp 65535
RP/0/0/CPU0:R3(config-bgp)# neighbor 10.1.13.1
RP/0/0/CPU0:R3(config-bgp-nbr)# remote-as 65531
RP/0/0/CPU0:R3(config-bgp-nbr)# commit
Sep 19 15:57:52.153 : bgp[1046]: %ROUTING-BGP-5-ADJCHANGE : neighbor 10.1.13.1
    Down - Remote AS configuration changed (VRF: default) (AS: 65531)
RP/0/0/CPU0:Sep 19 15:57:52.153 : bgp[1046]: %ROUTING-BGP-5-NSR_STATE_CHANGE :
    Changed state to NSR-Ready


IOS
R2#
*Sep 19 15:55:34.859: %BGP-3-NOTIFICATION: received from neighbor 10.1.13.2 active
  2/2 (peer in wrong AS) 4 bytes 0000FFFA
15:55:34.860: %BGP-5-NBR_RESET: Neighbor 10.1.13.2 active reset (BGP Notification
  received)
15:55:34.866: %BGP-5-ADJCHANGE: neighbor 10.1.13.2 active Down BGP Notification
received
15:55:34.867: %BGP_SESSION-5-ADJCHANGE: neighbor 10.1.13.2 IPv4 Unicast topology
base removed from session  BGP Notification received
```

Note that in Example 3-10, the notification message has a 4-byte data field with a value of 0000FFFA, which resolves to AS number 65530. But if the similar testing is done from the Cisco IOS router R2 toward R3, which is an IOS XR router, the notification data sent out from R2 with the 2-byte data field displays the AS number of 65535 (FFFF). Therefore, it is important to remember that for a wrong AS notification message, an IOS XR router will send a 4-byte data field, whereas the Cisco IOS router sends a 2-byte data field.

Sometimes, the BGP notifications can be confusing on the IOS devices. For example, the notification might contain the Error/Subcode as 2/8, but as per RFC 4271, Subcode 8 is not defined. IOS has some newer Error-Subcodes, as defined in Table 3-2.

Table 3-2 *Special BGP Error-Subcode in IOS*

Error Code	Subcode	Description
02	07	OPEN Message Error—No Supported Capability Value
02	08	OPEN Message Error—No Supported AFI/SAFI
02	09	OPEN Message Error—Grouping Conflict
02	0A	OPEN Message Error—Grouping Required

These special error codes and subcodes may not be applicable on other platforms and other vendors. They are specific to Cisco IOS platforms.

Decode BGP Messages

Various BGP notifications contain a huge data section that has a lot of information regarding the notification itself. This information is not understood from the notification Error/Subcode. If a peer sends any message, and the receiver of the message detects an error in that message or does not recognizes the message, BGP generates a hex dump of the message. These hex dumps can then be analyzed to understand why the BGP router was unable to process the message.

Because all the data is in hexadecimal format, it becomes an extremely difficult and time-consuming process to decode those messages. Yet without doing so, it is not possible to get to root of the problem and fix it.

Examine the notification message shown in Example 3-11. The example shows a notification message generated in the logs along with huge notification data. The notification sent before the message dump was generated shows that the peer is in the wrong AS and also shows that the AS number is 65535 (FFFF). Therefore, the main value that needs to be checked in the message dump is the AS value, which is 0xFFFF as highlighted.

Example 3-11   *BGP Message Dump*

```
BGP-3-NOTIFICATION: sent to neighbor 10.1.13.2 active 2/2 (peer in wrong AS)
    2 bytes FFFF
%BGP-4-MSGDUMP: unsupported or mal-formatted message received from 10.1.13.2:
FFFF FFFF FFFF FFFF FFFF FFFF FFFF FFFF 003B 0104 FFFF 00B4 C0A8 0303 1E02 0601
 0400 0100 0102 0280 0002 0202 0002 0641 0400 00FF FB02 0440 0280 78
BGP Message Decode:

BGP Marker:    0xFFFFFFFFFFFFFFFFFFFFFFFFFFFFFFFF
BGP Length:    0x003B    - 59 bytes
BGP Type:    0x01    - OPEN Message
OPEN Message
VERSION:    0x04    - 4
AS:        0xFFFF    - 65535
HOLD TIME:    0x00B4    - 180
ROUTER ID:    0xC0A80303    - 192.168.3.3
OPTIONAL PARAMETERS LENGTH:    0x1E    - 30 bytes
Opt Length:    28
Param Type:    2 - Optional Parameter
Param Length:    6
Cap Type:    0x01    - 1
            Multi Protocol Capability
Cap Length:    0x04    - 4 bytes
    AFI:    0x0001    - 1
      Reserved Bits:    0x00    - 0
     SAFI:    0x01    - 1
Opt Length:    20
Param Type:    2 - Optional Parameter
Param Length:    2
Cap Type:    0x80    - 128
       Route Refresh Capability (old)
Cap Length:    0x00    - 0 bytes
Opt Length:    16
Param Type:    2 - Optional Parameter
Param Length:    2
Cap Type:    0x02    - 2
        Route Refresh Capability (new)
Cap Length:    0x00    - 0 bytes
Opt Length:    12
Param Type:    2 - Optional Parameter
Param Length:    6
Cap Type:    0x41    - 65
         4-byte AS Capability
```

```
Cap Length:    0x04    - 4 bytes
AS Number:     0.65531 (0x0000.0xFFFB)
Opt Length:    4
Param Type:    2 - Optional Parameter
Param Length:    4


Cap Type:    0x40    - 64
        Graceful Restart Capability
Cap Length:    0x02    - 2 bytes
Restart flag:        0x8078    - 32888
```

Note   There are external websites that help decode BGP messages; for example, http://bgpaste.convergence.cx.

IOS XR makes it easy to understand what value to look for and where to locate the problem in the message data. The command **show bgp update in error neighbor** *ip-address* **detail** provides more information about the malformed update.

Example 3-12 demonstrates a malformed update received on R3 and the use of the **show bgp update in error neighbor** *ip-address* **detail** command to further understand where the problem is present in the BGP message. Notice that the problem is in the Attribute 2 field of the update and also a missing attribute in Attribute 2 of the update. The process of decoding the BGP message remains the same, as shown in Example 3-11.

Example 3-12   *Malformed BGP Update on IOS XR*

```
RP/0/0/CPU0:R3# show logging | in MALFORM
bgp[1046]: %ROUTING-BGP-3-MALFORM_UPDATE : Malformed UPDATE message received
from neighbor 10.1.13.1 - message length 126 bytes, error flags 0x00000a00,
action taken "TreatAsWithdraw". Error details: "Error 0x00000800,
Field "Attr-missing", Attribute 2 (Flags 0x00, Length 0), Data []"


RP/0/0/CPU0:R3# show bgp update in error neighbor 10.1.13.1 detail
! Output omitted for brevity
VRF "default"

 Neighbor 10.1.13.1
   Update error-handling: Allow session reset

   Malformed messages stored: 5 (current index: 0)
     Malformed message #1
       Received: Sep 20 02:53:02.269
```

```
Error flags: 0x00000a00

Discarded attributes: 0

Final action: TreatAsWithdraw

Error elements: 2

  [1] Error 0x00000200, Field "Attr-data", Attribute 2 (Flags 0x40, Length 10)
      Error data&colon; [40020a02020000272a00005d7a] (13 bytes)
        Action: TreatAsWithdraw

  [2] Error 0x00000800, Field "Attr-missing", Attribute 2 (Flags 0x00, Length 0)
      Error data&colon; [] (0 bytes)
        Action: TreatAsWithdraw

  Reset/notification information:
    Reason "None", Postit type "Update malformed"
    Notification code 3, sub-code 3
      Notification data [02] (1 bytes)

  Message data&colon; 81 bytes
    FFFFFFFF FFFFFFFF FFFFFFFF FFFFFFFF
    00510200 00003640 01010040 020A0202
    0000272A 00005D7A 400304CE 7EEC28C0
      07080000 5D7A797F 0040C008 10272A10
    68272A7E 58272A9C A65E3327 2A18745D
    30
```

On NX-OS, the BGP messages are not dumped on logs but have to be collected using debugs. The command **debug bgp packets** helps view what BGP messages are being received and can be decoded. Example 3-13 demonstrates how to capture a BGP packet on NX-OS using the **debug bgp packet** command. The BGP packet shown in the output is a BGP OPEN message between R1 and R2. The initial hexdump of the data contains the BGP marker. The second line begins with 00460104. 0046 is the BGP Length field followed by 01, which tells that the message is a BGP OPEN message.

Example 3-13 debug bgp packet *on NX-OS*

```
R1# debug logfile bgp
R1# debug bgp packets
! Below debug output shows the Hexdump of the BGP packet received.
R1# show debug logfile bgp
! Output omitted for brevity
18:24:04.560109 bgp: 65530 [8480] Hexdump at 0x84bc64c, 70 bytes:
18:24:04.560631 bgp: 65530 [8480]     FFFFFFFF FFFFFFFF FFFFFFFF FFFFFFFF
18:24:04.560743 bgp: 65530 [8480]     00460104 FFFA00B4 C0A80101 29022742
 18:24:04.560853 bgp: 65530 [8480]      00430302 01408000 02000104 00010001
18:24:04.560953 bgp: 65530 [8480]     40060078 00010100 41040000 FFFA0506
18:24:04.561051 bgp: 65530 [8480]     00010001 0002
! Output omitted for brevity
R1# undebug all
```

If too many BGP updates and messages are being exchanged on the NX-OS devices, it is better to perform an Ethanalyzer or Switched Port Analyzer (SPAN) to capture a malformed BGP update packet to further analyze it.

Troubleshoot Blocked Process in IOS XR

IOS XR is a distributed operating system, and every component (feature) runs as a separate process with its own set of threads that manages various tasks of the component. Unlike traditional IOS, if a process crashes on the router, IOS XR does not reboot the whole system. Rather, the process is restarted without affecting other running processes. Because it's a multithreaded environment, threads keep changing their states. Some are for a short span of time and some for longer. An essential low-level process such as a kernel thread may block a high-level process thread so it can perform the tasks at a higher priority. Blocked processes can cause various features to malfunction or not function at all on the system.

In IOS XR, the BGP Process Manager (BPM) and BGP processes create the BGP protocol functionality. The primary tasks of a BPM process is to spawn the speaker process, such as the BGP process and verify and apply all BGP-related configurations. When BGP runs in multi-instance mode, it works with a placed process to distribute the different BGP speaker processes to appropriate nodes.

The BPM process also has the responsibility to calculate the router-id if one is not explicitly configured. It interacts with NETIO, TCP, and a few other processes internally to perform the necessary tasks in the system and finally installs the routes in the Routing Information Base (RIB). Figure 3-3 displays the interaction between these processes on a route processor (RP).

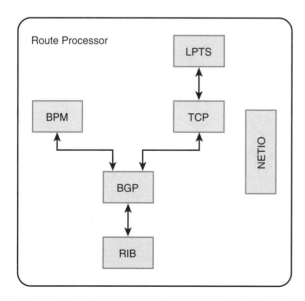

Figure 3-3 *Interaction of Processes with BGP in IOS XR*

Note There are other processes that are not shown in Figure 3-3. The discussion of those processes is outside the scope of this book.

Therefore, if any these processes are blocked on the RP or line card (LC) for a longer period of time, it could severely impact BGP services on the router. The following sections show how to troubleshoot the BGP processes on IOS XR platforms.

Verify BGP and BPM Process State

Verify that the BGP and BPM processes are in Run state by using the command **show process** *process-name* [**detail** | **location** {LC/RP *location* | **all**}] where *process-name* can be either *bgp* or *bpm* or any other process. The location option is helpful when the process state and information has to be checked on the line card or standby route processor card. Example 3-14 shows the use of the **show process** command for verifying the state of the *bgp* process. In this output, the most important fields to look at are the Job Id, PID, Respawn count, Process state, and the state of the threads under the process. In Example 3-14, the Respawn count is seen as 6. This number can be incremented if the *bgp* process keeps crashing or is unconfigured and reconfigured.

Example 3-14 show process bgp *Command Output*

```
RP/0/0/CPU0:R3# show process bgp
            Job Id: 1046
               PID: 827666
   Executable path: /disk0/iosxr-routing-5.3.0/bin/bgp
        Instance #: 1
        Version ID: 00.00.0000
           Respawn: ON
     Respawn count: 6
      Last started: Sun Sep 13 05:18:54 2015
     Process state: Run
     Package state: Normal
 Started on config: default
      Feature name: ON
               Tag : default
     Process group: v4-routing
              core: MAINMEM
         Max. core: 0
         Placement: Placeable
      startup_path: /pkg/startup/bgp.startup
             Ready: 1.229s
         Available: 7.849s
  Process cpu time: 1.470 user, 0.610 kernel, 2.080 total
```

```
JID     TID    Stack pri state         TimeInState      HR:MM:SS:MSEC NAME
1046    1      392K  10 Receive         0:00:00:0099     0:00:00:0136 bgp
1046    2      392K  10 Receive        50:56:47:0715     0:00:00:0019 bgp
1046    3      392K  10 Receive        84:33:28:0736  '  0:00:00:0000 bgp
1046    4      392K  10 Receive        84:33:27:0646     0:00:00:0000 bgp
1046    5      392K  10 Receive        84:33:23:0086     0:00:00:0000 bgp
1046    6      392K  10 Sigwaitinfo    84:33:28:0606     0:00:00:0000 bgp
1046    7      392K  10 Receive        83:59:49:0874     0:00:00:0009 bgp
1046    8      392K  10 Receive         0:00:01:0529     0:00:00:0000 bgp
1046    9      392K  10 Receive        36:49:17:0309     0:00:00:0000 bgp
1046    10     392K  10 Receive         0:00:01:0689     0:00:00:0010 bgp
1046    11     392K  10 Receive        12:37:51:0414     0:00:00:0000 bgp
1046    12     392K  10 Nanosleep       0:00:00:0899     0:00:00:0030 bgp
1046    13     392K  10 Receive        84:21:24:0516     0:00:00:0000 bgp
! Output omitted for brevity
```

If the BGP processes are crashing, it is important to understand what really triggered them. Verifying the last event or change before the crash will help stabilize the *bgp* process.

Verify Blocked Processes

Execute **show process blocked [location {RP/LC}]** to verify whether there are any blocked processes, which could cause an impact on the BGP process. Primarily the *bgp*, *bpm*, *tcp*, and *netio* processes are the ones that are critical. Example 3-15 demonstrates how to verify any blocked processes and the amount of time that they have been in that state. There are always some processes, which will be in blocked state like *ksh*, or *lpts_fm* process in the output. You can ignore those processes.

Example 3-15   show process blocked *Command Output*

```
RP/0/0/CPU0:R3# show processes blocked
Thu Sep 17 06:25:11.639 UTC
  Jid      Pid Tid           Name State   TimeInState     Blocked-on
65542   200710  1            ksh Reply   121:14:38:0413        2  devc-ser8250
65555   217107  1            ksh Reply   121:14:28:0649   217106  devc-conaux
65692   680092  1           exec Reply    0:00:00:0079        1  kernel
  289   643248  2        lpts_fm Reply   11:30:09:0743   331870  lpts_pa
65734   975046  1  show_processes Reply    0:00:00:0000        1  kernel
```

Restarting a Process

If for some reason a process is in blocked state for a long period of time, restart the process using **process restart** [*job-id* | *process-name*]. However, there can be processes that might be blocked for very long time and might not be related, such as *devc-conaux* process. This process is for the console access. Based on what problem is being troubleshot, related processes to the problem, and when the problem actually started, the time of the blocked process could be analyzed and the process could then be restarted. For example, if the TCP process got stuck 10 hours ago, which was about the same time BGP peering went down and never came back up, the blocked TCP process would make more sense to have restarted.

BGP Traces in IOS XR

The IOS XR BGP tracing facility has been implemented to help track BGP issues. BGP traces allow the user to see some level of history concerning what BGP has been doing when the problem occurred. In general, BGP trace messages fall into two categories:

- Nonfatal error conditions
- Informational messages

Nonfatal error conditions can recover automatically. Informational messages are used for logging data regarding the events that occurred in context to the error message. But they do not provide a complete log on what BGP is doing. Fatal error always logs an unsolicited message in the system log and therefore is not included in the trace output.

Because logging trace messages is a slow process and the trace buffer is stored in memory, tracing of successful events or detailed tracing about particular events is not supported. Traces stored in memory have limited size. So when the buffer memory is full, the trace logs are overridden. For this reason, error traces are written in different buffer than informational traces.

Each BGP trace message used for debugging BGP issues belongs to one of the categories shown in Table 3-3.

Table 3-3   *BGP Trace Categories*

Category	Debugging Problem
bgp	Router-id, neighbor resets, and state changes, OPEN messages, and the like
update	Inbound and outbound update messages
event	Process startup/shutdown and mode, general failures, and so on
io	TCP socket level failures
rib	RIB install and redistribution
brib	bRIB events and bRIB/speaker communication
policy	Routing Policy Language (RPL)

An easy way to find all the BGP-related trace commands is by using the command **show parser dump | include (.*bgp.*trace)**. This command prints all the **show** commands available for BGP trace.

Example 3-16 shows BGP trace using **show bgp trace** command for a BGP session coming up. Each trace entry starts with a timestamp, followed by the trace buffer name. The buffer name identifies the process that recorded the trace and whether it is an informational or an error trace. Distributed speaker processes and BGP RIB (bRIB) processes also include the process ID in the name. For error traces, the name ends with err. Example 3-16 shows both the error and informational messages.

Example 3-16 show bgp trace *Output*

```
RP/0/0/CPU0:R3# show bgp trace
! Output omitted for brevity
04:58:19.822 default-bgp/spkr-tr2-gen 0/0/CPU0 t21 [GEN]:546: nbr 10.1.13.1,
    old state 7, new state 1, fd type 0, fd 0
04:58:33.871 default-bgp/spkr-tr2-sync 0/0/CPU0 t1  [SYNC]:8104: Nbr '10.1.13.1'
: Loc 2: Determined lport/fport 179/38338
04:58:33.871 default-bgp/spkr-tr2-gen 0/0/CPU0 t1  [GEN]:546: nbr 10.1.13.1,
old state 1, new state 2, fd type 1, fd 125
04:58:33.901 default-bgp/spkr-tr2-err 0/0/CPU0 t14 [ERR][GEN]:1300: OPEN
from '10.1.13.1' has unrecognized cap code/len 70/0 - Ignored
04:58:33.901 default-bgp/spkr-tr2-upd 0/0/CPU0 t14 [UPD]:1818: Updgrp change not
  scheduled after open processing: nbr=10.1.13.1, nbrfl=0x8010000
04:58:33.901 default-bgp/spkr-tr2-gen 0/0/CPU0 t14 [GEN]:2222: calling
bgp_send_open, nbr 10.1.13.1, loc 4, data 0,0
04:58:33.901 default-bgp/spkr-tr2-gen 0/0/CPU0 t14 [GEN]:546: nbr 10.1.13.1,
old state 2, new state 4, fd type 1, fd 125
04:58:33.901 default-bgp/spkr-tr2-gen 0/0/CPU0 t14 [GEN]:546: nbr 10.1.13.1,
old state 4, new state 5, fd type 1, fd 125
04:58:33.901 default-bgp/spkr-tr2-gen 0/0/CPU0 t14 [GEN]:2295: calling bgp_send_
  keepalive, nbr 10.1.13.1, loc 1, data 0,0
04:58:33.961 default-bgp/spkr-tr2-sync 0/0/CPU0 t19 [SYNC]:5610: Sent
NSR-Not-Ready notif to Rmf
04:58:33.961 default-bgp/spkr-tr2-upd 0/0/CPU0 t18 [UPD]:1376: Filter-group op
(Alloc) Tbl/Nbr(TBL:default (1/1)) fgrp idx 0.2 subgrp idx 0.1 updgrp 0.0 rtset 0
04:58:33.961 default-bgp/spkr-tr2-upd 0/0/CPU0 t18 [UPD]:2640: Filter-group op
(Filter-group Add Nbr new) Tbl/Nbr(Afi:IPv4 Unicast:Nbr:10.1.13.1)
    fgrp idx 0.2 subgrp idx 0.1 updgrp 0.2 rtset 0
04:58:33.961 default-bgp/spkr-tr2-upd 0/0/CPU0 t18 [UPD]:2662: Created filtergrp 2
for nbr 10.1.13.1, afi 0. Subgrp version 0
04:58:33.961 default-bgp/spkr-tr2-upd 0/0/CPU0 t18 [UPD]:4213: Created  subgrp 1
for nbr 10.1.13.1, afi 0 with version 0
```

```
04:58:33.961 default-bgp/spkr-tr2-ev 0/0/CPU0 t14 [EV]:1952: Inside scan_adjust_
  estab_outstanding for nbr 10.1.13.1, nbr-down 0, state 2,
evt-in-nbrwait 0
04:58:33.961 default-bgp/spkr-tr2-gen 0/0/CPU0 t14 [GEN]:546: nbr 10.1.13.1,
old state 5, new state 6, fd type 1, fd 125
04:58:33.961 default-bgp/spkr-tr2-gen 0/0/CPU0 t14 [GEN]:549: Nbr '10.1.13.1'
established
! Output omitted for brevity
```

To filter just the error messages or any other messages, such as update or event, use the **show bgp trace** *trace-option* command, where *trace-option* value can be error, event, or other supported BGP trace filters.

Example 3-17 demonstrates the use of the **show bgp trace error** command to view BGP errors. The error trace demonstrates that the router ignores the capability code value 70, which refers to Enhanced Route Refresh Capability.

> **Note**   The Enhanced Route Refresh Capability is explained in detail in Chapter 7, "Scaling BGP."

Example 3-17   show bgp trace *error Command*

```
RP/0/0/CPU0:R3# show bgp trace error
 6 wrapping entries (1826304 possible, 3840 allocated, 643 filtered, 649 total)
21:14:28.248 default-bgp/spkr-tr2-err 0/0/CPU0 t1  [ERR][SYNC]:284: pid 0 : Got my
  local_node as 0x0
21:14:35.638 default-bgp/spkr-tr2-err 0/0/CPU0 t14 [ERR][GEN]:1300: OPEN from
'10.1.13.1' has unrecognized cap code/len 70/0 - Ignored

! Output omitted for brevity
```

BGP Traces in NX-OS

In NX-OS, all the traces related to all the events and errors are stored as event-history. A few event-history traces are enabled by default, such as for BGP events or errors, but more detailed event-history logging must be enabled using the **event-history** [cli | **detail** | **events** | **periodic**] [**size** {*size_in_text* | *bytes*}] under **router bgp**. This command is also used to set the size of the buffer for the event-history. Example 3-18 shows the BGP event-history configuration under router bgp configuration, how to enable detailed event-history event logging and event-history logging generated for syslog.

Example 3-18 *BGP Event-History on NX-OS*

```
R1(config)# router bgp 65530
R1(config-router)# event-history ?
   cli       CLI event history buffer
   detail    Detailed event history buffer
   events    Events history buffer
   periodic  Periodic events history buffer

R1(config-router)# event-history detail size ?
   disable  Disabled the buffer
            *Default value is disble
   large    Large buffer
   medium   Medium buffer
   small    Small buffer

 R1(config-router)# event-history detail size medium
 R1(config-router)# end

R1# show bgp event-history logs
 bgp-65530 logs events
19:37:15.618509 bgp 65530 [8556]: [8566]: (default) neighbor 192.168.2.2 Up
19:37:07.425970 bgp 65530 [8556]: [8567]: (default) neighbor
192.168.2.2 Down - session cleared
```

Table 3-4 displays the use of various **show bgp event-history** command options.

Table 3-4 *BGP event-history Options*

Option	Description
cli	Event-history for cli commands executed
detail	Show detail event logs
errors	Show error logs for BGP
events	Show event logs for BGP
logs	Show messages logged by Syslog
msgs	Show various message logs of BGP
periodic	Show periodic event logs

When troubleshooting BGP peering issues, it is also important to check the event-history logs for a netstack process. Netstack is an implementation of a Layer 2 to Layer 4 stack on NX-OS. It is one of the critical components involved in the control plane on NX-OS. If there is a problem with establishing a TCP session on a Nexus device, it could be an issue with the netstack process. The **show sockets internal event-history events** command helps determine the TCP state transitions that occurred for the BGP peer IP.

Example 3-19 demonstrates the use of the **show sockets internal event-history events** command to see the TCP session getting closed for BGP peer IP 192.168.2.2 but does not show any TCP request coming in for establishing a new session.

Example 3-19   show sockets internal event-history events *Command*

```
R1# show sockets internal event-history event
 1) Event:E_DEBUG, length:67, at 24439 usecs after Tue Sep 22 20:36:01 2015
    [138] [3767]: Marking desc 22 in mts_open for client 15195, sotype 2
! Output omitted for brevity
60) Event:E_DEBUG, length:91, at 471283 usecs after Tue Sep 22 19:37:12 2015
    [138] [3730]: PCB: Removing pcb from hash list L: 192.168.1.1.179, F:
192.168.2.2.29051 C: 1
61) Event:E_DEBUG, length:62, at 471234 usecs after Tue Sep 22 19:37:12 2015
    [138] [3730]: PCB: Detach L 192.168.1.1.179 F 192.168.2.2.29051
62) Event:E_DEBUG, length:77, at 471174 usecs after Tue Sep 22 19:37:12 2015
    [138] [3730]: TCP: Closing connection L: 192.168.1.1.179, F: 192.168.2.2.29051
```

For more detailed troubleshooting on netstack, the **show tech netstack [detail]** command can be collected to investigate the problem.

Debugs for BGP

Running debugs should always be the last resort for troubleshooting any network problem. Debugs can sometimes cause an impact in the network if not used carefully. But sometimes they are the only options when other troubleshooting techniques cannot repair the problem.

Note   A lot of debugs are chatty, which means that a huge amount of log messages are printed in the debug output. If console logging is enabled along with such debugs, it can result in high CPU condition on the router and may lead to the loss of management connectivity, traffic loss, or even router or process crash. In such situations, sometimes the only alternative to recover the service is reloading the router. But when run cautiously, the debugs can remedy the problem and achieve a faster resolution.

When the BGP peers are down, and all the other troubleshooting steps cannot resolve the problem or are unable to capture the BGP packets, debugs can be enabled. They detect if the router is generating and sending the necessary BGP packets and if it is receiving the relevant packets.

On IOS devices, use the **debug ip bgp** *ip-address* or **debug bgp ipv4 unicast** *ip-address* command to run the debugs for a particular neighbor that is down. **debug** is not required on NX-OS because the traces in BGP have sufficient information to debug the problem. **debug bgp ipv4 unicast events** return almost the same output as **show bgp event-history periodic** output.

Example 3-20 displays that router R2 is going into an Active state because the remote host is not responding. The session goes from Idle to Active state but from Active it doesn't go to Established state.

Example 3-20   debug bgp ipv4 unicast *ip-address Command*

```
R2# debug bgp ipv4 unicast 192.168.1.1
BGP debugging is on for neighbor 192.168.1.1 for address family: IPv4 Unicast
19:44:10.859: BGP: 192.168.1.1 active went from Idle to Active
19:44:10.860: BGP: 192.168.1.1 open active, local address 192.168.2.2
19:44:21.831: BGP: topo global:IPv4 Unicast:base Scanning routing tables
19:44:40.866: BGP: 192.168.1.1 open failed: Connection timed out;
    remote host not responding
19:44:40.866: BGP: 192.168.1.1 Active open failed - tcb is not available,
 open active delayed 10240ms (35000ms max, 60% jitter)
19:44:40.867: BGP: ses global 192.168.1.1 (0xF63BD98:0) act Reset
     (Active open failed).
19:44:40.872: BGP: 192.168.1.1 active went from Active to Idle
```

The output also shows that the tcb is not available for the session. This indicates that the TCP session is not getting established. On an IOS device, if the TCP session is not getting established, the **debug ip tcp transaction** [**address** *src-or-dst-addr*] [**port** *port-num*] command can be enabled to check why the TCP session is not getting established.

On IOS XR devices, **debug tcp packet** [**v4-access-list** *acl-name*] can be used to limit the debugs to just the packets matching the ACL. On Nexus, **debug sockets tcp** can be employed. Although there is no option to filter the output in Cisco IOS or IOS XR, the outputs can be captured in a log file. Example 3-21 demonstrates the use of debugs on both R1 and R2 to check the TCP negotiations between them. The debug output shows that R2 is sending a SYN packet to R1, which is received at R1, but R2 does not receive any SYN-ACK in return for the SYN packet. This indicates that the TCP packet is being lost in the direction from R1 to R2.

Example 3-21   *TCP Debugs on IOS and NX-OS*

```
NX-OS
R1# debug sockets tcp
20:22:18.687624 netstack: syncache_insert: SYN added for
    L:192.168.2.2.42829 F:192.168.1.1.179, tp:0x8740cd4 inp:0x8740c0c
20:22:48.790993 netstack: tcp_connect: Originating Connections
    with ports (Src 60250, Dst 179)
20:22:48.793718 netstack: tcp_notify: TCP: Notify
    L: 192.168.1.1.60250, F: 192.168.2.2.179 of error Connection refused
```

```
20:22:51.813236 netstack: tcp_notify: TCP: Notify L: 192.168.1.1.60250, F:
  192.168.2.2.179 of error Connection refused
```

```
IOS
R2# debug ip tcp transaction 192.168.1.1
20:18:27.194: TCP0: RETRANS timeout timer expired
20:18:27.195: 192.168.2.2:15033 <---> 192.168.1.1:179   congestion window changes
20:18:27.195: cwnd from 1460 to 1460, ssthresh from 65535 to 2920
20:18:27.196: TCP0: timeout #1 - timeout is 4000 ms, seq 2704785302
20:18:27.196: TCP: (15033) -> 192.168.1.1(179)
20:18:31.194: TCP0: RETRANS timeout timer expired
20:18:31.196: TCP0: timeout #2 - timeout is 8000 ms, seq 2704785302
20:18:31.196: TCP: (15033) -> 192.168.1.1(179)
20:18:39.194: TCP0: RETRANS timeout timer expired
20:18:39.196: TCP0: timeout #3 - timeout is 15999 ms, seq 2704785302
! Output omitted for brevity
*Oct  4 20:18:55.194: TCP0: state was SYNSENT -> CLOSED [15033 -> 192.168.1.1(179)]
20:18:55.198: TCB 0xD770800 destroyed
```

Based on the debug logs, the path or interfaces between R1 and R2 can be checked for any blocking ACLs.

Troubleshooting IPv6 Peers

With the depletion of IPv4 routes, the IPv6 addresses have caught up pace. Most of the service providers have already upgraded or are planning to upgrade their infrastructure to dual stack for supporting both IPv4 and IPv6 traffic and are offering IPv6 ready services to their customers. Even the new applications are being developed with IPv6 compatibility or completely running on IPv6. With such a pace, there is also a need to have appropriate techniques for troubleshooting IPv6 BGP neighbors.

The methodology for troubleshooting IPv6 BGP peers is same as that of IPv4 BGP peers. The following steps can be used to troubleshoot BGP peering down issues for IPv6 BGP neighbors:

Step 1.   Verify the configuration for correct peering IPv6 addresses, AS numbers, **update-source** *interface-id*, authentication passwords, **ebgp-multihop** configuration.

Step 2.   The reachability is verified using **ping ipv6** *ipv6-neighbor-address* [**source** *interface-id* | *ipv6-address*].

Step 3.   The TCP connections is verified using **show tcp brief** on IOS and IOS XR or **show socket connection tcp** on NX-OS. In the case of IPv6, check for TCP connections for source and destination IPv6 addresses and one of the ports as port 179.

Step 4.   Like IPv4, the IPv6 ACLs in the path should permit for TCP connections on port 179 and ICMPv6 packets that help in verifying reachability.

Step 5.   On IOS routers, use the **debug bgp ipv6 unicast** *ipv6-neighbor-address* command to capture IPv6 BGP packets. The debugs on NX-OS and IOS XR remain the same, with the exception that the ACLs when matched for debugs are IPv6 ACLs.

Case Study—Single Session Versus Multisession

Company A is having a merger with Company B. As part of the merger, both companies are exchanging their network information using EBGP at each location. Company A has a multivendor network environment, whereas Company B has all Cisco devices. At one location, the EBGP session between two routers is not establishing. Customer A opens a service request with Cisco Technical Assistance Center (TAC), and the following troubleshooting steps are performed:

Step 1.   Customer verified that the configuration on both sides (A and B) are correct.

Step 2.   Verified reachability.

Step 3.   Performed TCP tests on port 179, which also worked fine.

Even after all the verifications, the BGP session was not establishing. On Company A's router, a BGP notification for unsupported/disjoint capability was noticed, as shown in Example 3-22.

Example 3-22 *BGP Notification on Company A Router*

```
*Oct  5 06:06:58.557: %BGP-3-NOTIFICATION: sent to neighbor 10.1.12.2
       active 2/7 (unsupported/disjoint capability) 0 bytes
*Oct  5 06:06:58.557: %BGP-4-MSGDUMP: unsupported or mal-formatted message
       received from 10.1.12.2:
FFFF FFFF FFFF FFFF FFFF FFFF FFFF FFFF 0039 0104 FDE9 00B4 0A01 0C02 1C02 0601
0400 0100 0102 0280 0002 0202 0002 0246 0002 0641 0400 00FD E9
```

The preceding notification clarified that there is a capability being exchanged by one of the peers that is not supported by the other. With the help of the **show bgp ipv4 unicast neighbor** *ip-address* command, it was noticed that one side is multisession capable, whereas the other side is not. Example 3-23 shows the difference between both BGP neighbors.

Example 3-23   show bgp ipv4 unicast neighbor *ip-address Command Output*

```
Comp_A_R1# show bgp ipv4 unicast neighbor 10.1.12.2
BGP neighbor is 10.1.12.2,  remote AS 65001, external link
  BGP version 4, remote router ID 10.1.12.2
  BGP state = Idle
  Neighbor sessions:
    0 active, is multisession capable
    Stateful switchover support enabled: NO for session 0
! Output omitted for brevity

Comp_B_R2# show bgp ipv4 unicast neighbor 10.1.12.1
BGP neighbor is 10.1.12.1,  remote AS 65000, external link
  BGP version 4, remote router ID 0.0.0.0
  BGP state = Idle
  Neighbor sessions:
    0 active, is not multisession capable (disabled)
    Stateful switchover support enabled: NO
! Output omitted for brevity
```

This means that one side is trying to establish a BGP session in single-session mode when the other side is trying to use multisession mode. This causes the BGP session not to come up. To resolve this problem, the session capabilities should match by either configuring the **transport multisession** command on side B or the **transport single-session** command on side A.

The following sections provide a brief description of BGP single-session and multisession capabilities.

Multisession Capability

Multisession capability is available on all the latest Cisco IOS software but is not enabled by default. With this capability, multiple sessions are established for a particular neighbor for each address-family. Multisession mode can be used for MP-BGP sessions where multiple BGP sessions are used between peers instead of a single session that exchanges updates for all address-families. For example, if a neighbor is establishing a session in IPv4 address-family and vpnv4 address-family, there are two BGP sessions established on the router. This capability provides more granularity for managing BGP sessions. One important benefit is that multiple address-families can be added in an incremental way without affecting neighborship in previously configured address-families. If multisession is disabled on the router, it can be enabled using the **neighbor** *ip-address* **transport multisession** configuration. This command forces the OPEN message to contain only one address-family while establishing the BGP neighbor relationship and therefore one session per address-family.

Single-Session Capability

In single-session mode, BGP adds multiple address-families together in a single OPEN message. In single-session mode, updates for all address-families are exchanged over a single BGP session. All the later IOS releases have this command deprecated, and therefore it is hidden. This is the default mode for forming neighbor relationships. If the router is running multisession in default mode, it can be changed into single-session mode using the **neighbor** *ip-address* **transport single-session** command.

BGP Peer Flapping Issues

A BGP peering down issue is when the BGP neighbor establishment keeps toggling between the Idle and Active states and never goes into the Established state. But when the BGP peer is flapping, it means it is changing state after the session is established. In this case the BGP state keeps flapping between Idle and Established states. Following are the two flapping states in BGP:

- Idle/Active: Discussed in the previous section.

- Idle/Established: Bad Update, TCP Problem (MSS size in multi-hop deployment).

Flapping BGP peers could be due to one of several reasons:

- Bad BGP update

- Hold timer expired

- MTU mismatch

- High CPU

- Interface and platform drops

- Improper control-plane policing

Bad BGP Update

A bad BGP update refers to a corrupted update packet received from a peer. This condition is not normal. It can be caused by one of the following reasons:

- Bad link carrying the update; bad hardware

- Problem with BGP update packaging

- Malicious update by an attacker (hacker)

Whenever a BGP update is corrupted, a BGP notification is generated with the error code of 3, as shown in Table 3-1.

Example 3-24 shows a sample malformed update that caused the BGP session to flap. It shows that one of the attribute length fields has a length higher than the update length itself and is therefore a corrupted update. The BGP message when decoded shows that the BGP update packet length is 93 bytes (0x005D) and the Attribute Type 17 (0x11) the Attribute Length equals to 53572 bytes (0xD144) which is not possible because an individual attribute length cannot exceed a total length of 93 bytes. Therefore the notification of 3/1 was generated, which points to Malformed Attribute List.

Example 3-24 *Malformed BGP Update*

```
Nov 17 09:36:06.990 CET: %BGP-3-NOTIFICATION: sent to neighbor 10.1.13.2 3/1 (update
  malformed) 47 bytes D011D144 02030000 32E60000 12830000 B0
Nov 17 09:36:06.990 CET: BGP: 10.1.13.2 Bad attributes FFFF FFFF FFFF FFFF FFFF FFFF
  FFFF FFFF 005D 0200 0000 4240 0101 0240 020C 0203 32E6 1283 B066 0101 5BA0 D011
  D144 0203 0000 32E6 0000 1283 0000 B066 0101 0001 0049 4003 04D5 9080 C580 0404
  0000 0001 C007 06FF 77AC 11F1 0815 781D F0
Nov 17 09:36:21.518 CET: %BGP-5-ADJCHANGE: neighbor 10.1.13.2 Up
```

Hold Timer Expired

Hold timer expiry is a very common cause for flapping BGP peers. It means that the router didn't receive or process a keepalive message or any update message before the hold timer expired. So it sends a notification message (4/0) and closes the session. On IOS, the keepalive messages are sent by the BGP I/O process, and the BGP Router process interprets the incoming keepalive messages. BGP flaps due to hold timer expiry can be caused by one of the following reasons:

- Interface issues
  - Physical connectivity
  - Physical interface
  - Input hold queue
- TCP receive queue and BGP InQ
- BGP InQ
- Mismatch MTU

Interface Issues

Various interface issues, such as a physical layer concern or drops on the interface, can lead to a BGP session flapping because of hold timer expiry. The sections that follow examine a few interface related problems and various ways to resolve them.

Physical Connectivity

If the problem is with the physical connectivity, packets are not transmitted correctly through the wire, or sometimes it affects only a given pattern of packet. In such a scenario, try to ping between the peering IPs and with different packet sizes and patterns. Setting a different value than 0 for the Type of Service (TOS) field or changing the data pattern itself by setting the value of 0xaabb rather than using the default value of 0xabcd. If the problem is with the physical media, then cyclic redundancy check (CRC) errors and reliability on the interface using the **show interface** command need to be checked. Typically, this problem can be solved by replacing the cable, small form-factor pluggable (SFP), line card, or the chassis, based on the location of the problem.

Physical Interface

Sometimes a packet received via an interface is dropped at the driver level. The most common reason could be that the interface was unable to process the packet because it was receiving traffic at an excessive rate. Check the **show interface** output for *overrun* or *ignore* counters. If there is excessive traffic, that needs to be controlled.

Input Hold Queue

Packets arrive to the router but are dropped in the input hold queue of the incoming interface. These packets are intended to be processed by the router's CPU or are being process switched (processed by software). The hold-queue size is a finite size. On most of Cisco's platforms, the default input hold queue size value is 75 packets and can be configured to a max value of 4096. A good value to be configured on the interface for input hold queue size is between 1500 and 2000. Check the input queue drops on the interface using the **show interface** command. The input queue size can be changed using the **hold-queue** *size* **in** command.

Typically, any router acting as a BGP speaker has the processing capability to process all BGP messages it receives, without having to drop them at the input hold queue. If the drops are seen, the problem is not usually with the BGP packets but with the other process switched traffic or traffic destined to the router received on the interface. Use Selective Packet Discard (SPD), which gives congestion precedence to high-priority traffic like BGP. Because BGP packets are sent with IP Precedence value of 6, they are considered inside the SPD headroom, such as an extra queuing space beyond input hold queue size. To configure SPD, use **spd enable**, and to set the SPD headroom size, use the **spd headroom** *headroom-size* global config commands. The SPD configuration is a hidden configuration, but the values can be checked using the **show ip spd** command output.

Note   The headroom size should be enough to hold at least two packets per neighbor.

Example 3-25 shows the various fields to check in the show interface output and also how to configure the interface hold queue and SPD.

Example 3-25   show interface *and Configuring* hold-queue *and* spd *Commands*

```
R2# show interface gigabitEthernet 0/1
GigabitEthernet0/1 is up, line protocol is up
  Hardware is iGbE, address is fa16.3e86.6c2b (bia fa16.3e86.6c2b)
  Internet address is 10.1.12.2/30
  MTU 1500 bytes, BW 1000000 Kbit/sec, DLY 10 usec,
     reliability 255/255, txload 1/255, rxload 1/255
  Encapsulation ARPA, loopback not set
  Keepalive set (10 sec)
  Auto Duplex, Auto Speed, link type is auto, media type is RJ45
  output flow-control is unsupported, input flow-control is unsupported
  ARP type: ARPA, ARP Timeout 04:00:00
  Last input 00:00:00, output 00:00:04, output hang never
  Last clearing of "show interface" counters never
  Input queue: 0/75/0/0 (size/max/drops/flushes); Total output drops: 0
  Queueing strategy: fifo
  Output queue: 0/40 (size/max)
  5 minute input rate 0 bits/sec, 0 packets/sec
  5 minute output rate 0 bits/sec, 0 packets/sec
     355 packets input, 32292 bytes, 0 no buffer
     Received 0 broadcasts (0 IP multicasts)
     0 runts, 0 giants, 0 throttles
     0 input errors, 0 CRC, 0 frame, 0 overrun, 0 ignored
     0 watchdog, 0 multicast, 0 pause input
     876 packets output, 151705 bytes, 0 underruns
     0 output errors, 0 collisions, 2 interface resets
     0 unknown protocol drops
     0 babbles, 0 late collision, 0 deferred
     1 lost carrier, 0 no carrier, 0 pause output
     0 output buffer failures, 0 output buffers swapped out

! Configuring Input Hold Queue
R2(config)# interface GigabitEthernet 0/1
R2(config-if)# hold-queue 1500 in

R2# show ip spd
Current mode: disabled.
Queue min/max thresholds: 73/74, Headroom: 100, Extended Headroom: 75
IP normal queue: 0, priority queue: 0.
SPD special drop mode: none
```

```
! Configuring and verifying SPD

R2# configure terminal
R2(config)# spd enable
R2(config)# spd headroom 1000
R2(config)# end

R2# show ip spd
Current mode: init.
Queue min/max thresholds: 73/74, Headroom: 1000, Extended Headroom: 75
IP normal queue: 0, priority queue: 0.
SPD special drop mode: none
```

Note   The SPD feature is available only on Cisco IOS/IOS XE platforms and not on IOS XR or NX-OS platforms.

TCP Receive Queue

Sometimes, BGP keepalives arrive at the TCP receiving queue but are not being processed and moved to the BGP InQ. When a non-zero value is seen for the BGP neighbor in the **show bgp** *afi safi* **summary** command, it indicates that the TCP messages are waiting in queue to be processed. The BGP InQ queues are empty when a BGP neighbor expires. It is possible that the BGP I/O process did not get a chance to run. BGP I/O process is in charge of putting messages from the TCP receiving queue into the BGP InQ. This often occurs if the BGP hold timer values are very low, there are many neighbors, and the CPU is running high.

Another possible reason for this issue could be that just one TCP packet was missed during a transient failure. Although there are some other packets in the TCP receiving queue, the router is still waiting for the first one (TCP has to deliver the packets in order or will not deliver them at all). The sending speaker waits for a transmission timeout and then again sends the first packet. If the BGP hold timer is small, the retransmission may not arrive on time. The only solution is to increase the BGP hold timer. Also Fast Retransmit can help in this scenario. The BGP Fast Retransmit feature resends the first packet after receiving three duplicate ACKs. Therefore, a better workaround is to increase the BGP hold timer and then enable BGP Fast Retransmit.

Finally, the TCP packets can also be dropped because of a CoPP policy. If the CoPP policy does have enough bandwidth allocated for the TCP packets, specifically for BGP, the packets can be dropped. CoPP policy issues are discussed later in this chapter.

MTU Mismatch Issues

Generally MTU is not a big concern when bringing up a BGP neighborship, but maximum transmission unit (MTU) mismatch issues cause BGP sessions to flap. MTU settings vary in different devices in the network because of various factors, such as the following:

- Improper planning and network design

- Device not supporting Jumbo MTU or certain MTU values

- Unknown transport circuits such as EoMPLS (may not support Jumbo MTU end to end)

- Change due to application requirement

- Change due to end customer requirement

BGP sends updates based on the maximum segment size (MSS) value calculated by TCP. If Path-MTU-Discovery (PMTUD) is not enabled and the destination is remote (not on same interface/subnet), the BGP MSS value defaults to 536 bytes as defined in RFC 879. So if there are a huge number of updates getting exchanged between the two routers at the MSS value of 536 bytes, convergence issues are detected, which cause inefficient use of the network. The reason is that the interface is capable of sending three times the MSS value, but it has to break down the updates in chunks of 536 bytes. If the TCP destination is on the same interface (case of non-multihop EBGP), the MSS value will be calculated based on the outgoing interface IP MTU settings.

Defined in RFC 1191, PMTUD is introduced to reduce the chances of IP packets getting fragmented along the path and to help with faster convergence. Using PMTUD, the source identifies the lowest MTU along the path to destination and then decides what packet size to send.

How does PMTUD work? When the source generates a packet, it sets the MTU size equal to the outgoing interface with a DF (Do-Not-Fragment) bit set. Any intermittent device that receives the packet and has an MTU value of its egress interface lower than the packet it received, the device drops the packet and sends an ICMP error message with Type 3 (Destination Unreachable) and Code 4 (Fragmentation needed and DF bit set) along with the MTU information of the outgoing interface in the Next-Hop MTU field back toward the source. When the source receives the ICMP unreachable error message, it modifies the MTU size of the outgoing packet to the value specified in the Next-Hop MTU field above. This process continues until the packet successfully reaches the final destination.

BGP also has support for PMTUD. PMTUD allows a BGP router to discover the best MTU size along the path to the neighbor to ensure efficient usage of exchanging packets. With Path MTU discovery enabled, the initial TCP negotiation between two neighbors has MSS value equal to (IP MTU – 20 byte IP Header – 20 byte TCP Header) and DF bit set. So the IP MTU value is 1500 (equal to the interface MTU) and the MSS value is

1460. If the device in the path has a lower MTU, or even if the destination router has a lower MTU, say 1400, then the MSS value is negotiated based on 1400-40 bytes = 1360 bytes. To derive MSS calculation, use one of the following formulas:

- **MSS without MPLS** = MTU – IP Header (20 bytes) – TCP Header (20 bytes)

- **MSS over MPLS** = MTU – IP Header – TCP Header – n*4 bytes (where n is the number of labels in the label stack)

- **MSS across GRE Tunnel** = MTU – IP Header (Inner) – TCP Header – [IP Header (Outer) + GRE Header (4 bytes)]

Note   MPLS VPN Providers should increase the MPLS MTU to at least 1508 (assuming minimum of two labels) or MPLS MTU of 1516 (to accommodate up to four labels).

Example 3-26 demonstrates MSS negotiation with and without PMTUD enabled. Use the **ip tcp path-mtu-discovery** command to enable PMTUD. This command is applicable for IOS and NX-OS. For IOS XR, use the **tcp path-mtu-discovery** command.

Example 3-26   *TCP MSS Negotiation*

```
! Test without PMTUD enabled on Nexus R1 (192.168.1.1)
R2# debug ip tcp transaction
TCP special event debugging is on
R2# clear ip bgp 192.168.1.1
R2#
! Output omitted for brevity
*Sep 27 02:05:48.996: Reserved port 25222 in Transport Port Agent for TCP IP type 1
*Sep 27 02:05:48.996: TCB0F54AA18 getting property TCP_STRICT_ADDR_BIND (19)
*Sep 27 02:05:48.997: TCP: pmtu enabled,mss is now set to 1460
*Sep 27 02:05:48.998: TCP: sending SYN, seq 342586080, ack 0
*Sep 27 02:05:48.998: TCP0: Connection to 192.168.1.1:179, advertising MSS 1460
*Sep 27 02:05:48.999: TCP0: state was CLOSED -> SYNSENT [25222 -> 192.168.1.1(179)]
*Sep 27 02:05:49.002: TCP0: state was SYNSENT -> ESTAB [25222 -> 192.168.1.1(179)]
*Sep 27 02:05:49.002: TCP: tcb F54AA18 connection to 192.168.1.1:179, peer MSS 536,
    MSS is 536
! Output omitted for brevity
*Sep 27 02:05:57.952: %BGP-5-ADJCHANGE: neighbor 192.168.1.1 Up

R2# show bgp ipv4 unicast neighbor 192.168.1.1 | include max
  Number of NLRIs in the update sent: max 6, min 0
sndwnd:  16616  scale:       0  maxrcvwnd:  16384
minRTT: 8 ms, maxRTT: 1000 ms, ACK hold: 200 ms
Datagrams (max data segment is 536 bytes):
```

```
! Enabling PMTUD on Nexus R1 (192.168.1.1)
R1(config)# ip tcp path-mtu-discovery
Path-mtu-discovery enabled
```

```
! Test without PMTUD enabled on Nexus R1 (192.168.1.1)
R2# clear bgp ipv4 unicast 192.168.1.1
! Output omitted for brevity
02:11:56.653: TCP: pmtu enabled,mss is now set to 1460
02:11:56.653: TCP: sending SYN, seq 2163041542, ack 0
02:11:56.653: TCP0: Connection to 192.168.1.1:179, advertising MSS 1460
02:11:56.655: TCP0: state was CLOSED -> SYNSENT [50640 -> 192.168.1.1(179)]
02:11:56.659: TCP0: state was SYNSENT -> ESTAB [50640 -> 192.168.1.1(179)]
02:11:56.660: TCP: tcb FB9C638 connection to 192.168.1.1:179, peer MSS 1444,
    MSS is 1444
! Output omitted for brevity
*Sep 27 02:11:56.895: %BGP-5-ADJCHANGE: neighbor 192.168.1.1 Up
R2# show bgp ipv4 unicast neighbor 192.168.1.1 | include max
  Number of NLRIs in the update sent: max 6, min 0
sndwnd:  17328  scale:      0  maxrcvwnd:  16384
minRTT: 8 ms, maxRTT: 1000 ms, ACK hold: 200 ms
Datagrams (max data segment is 1444 bytes):
```

On IOS and IOS XR routers, PMTUD is enabled by default, whereas on Nexus, it is disabled by default.

Based on Example 3-26 and with an understanding of PMTUD, how can an MTU mismatch cause BGP flapping issues? If there are MTU discrepancies in the path, and if ICMP messages are blocked in the path from source to destination, PMTUD does not function and may result in session flap. After the configuration is done between the source and the destination router for BGP, TCP negotiation are successful, and BGP moves to an Established state. Now when BGP starts sending the update with the negotiated MSS value, it sends it with a DF bit set. If a device in the path or even the destination is not able to accept the packets with higher MTU, it sends an ICMP error message back to BGP speaker. The destination router either waits for the BGP keepalive or BGP update packet to update its hold down timer. After 180 seconds, the destination router sends a notification back to source with a *Hold time expired* error message.

Note   When a BGP router sends an update to a BGP neighbor, it does not send a BGP keepalive; instead, the keepalive timer is restarted for that neighbor.

In Figure 3-4, R2 and R4 have a default MTU setting of 1500 where R1 has configured MTU of 1400 with ACL blocking ICMP packets. Now when the TCP session is being instantiated for BGP, both sides send the initial MSS value of 1460. Because R1 has a lower MTU value for its outgoing interface, it tries to send an ICMP unreachable error message back toward both the routers. But because ICMP messages are blocked, none of the devices receive the ICMP error message. Therefore, both routers R2 and R4 have their TCP session established with the MSS value of 1460. When the router R2 exchanges its BGP table with the router R4, two things can happen:

1. If BGP is advertising only a few prefixes and the BGP Update packet is less than 1360 bytes, the session does not expire.

2. If the number of advertised prefixes is high and the BGP Update packet size is more than 1360 bytes, the BGP session keeps flapping around at the expiry time of the BGP Hold Timer.

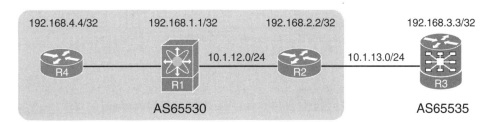

Figure 3-4 *Topology with MTU Mismatch Settings*

Example 3-27 demonstrates BGP flapping due to an MTU mismatch, as previously explained. R2 is having an IBGP neighborship with R4 and EBGP session with R3. R3 is advertising 10,000 prefixes toward R2. The BGP session starts flapping when R2 tries to send updates toward R4.

Example 3-27 *BGP Flapping due to MTU Mismatch*

```
NX-OS
! Blocking ICMP packets and setting MTU value of 1400
R1(config)# ip access-list BlockICMP
R1(config-acl)# deny icmp any any
R1(config-acl)# permit ip any any
R1(config-acl)# exit
R1(config)# interface Ethernet 2/1-2
R1(config-if-range)# mtu 1400
R1(config-if-range)# ip access-group BlockICMP in
R1(config-if-range)# ip access-group BlockICMP out


IOS
R2# show bgp ipv4 unicast summary
```

```
! Output omitted for brevity
Neighbor      V      AS MsgRcvd MsgSent   TblVer   InQ OutQ Up/Down   State/PfxRcd
10.1.13.2     4   65535    1006       8    10005     0    0 00:02:21    10001
192.168.1.1   4   65530       5    1006    10005     0    0 00:00:41        1
192.168.4.4   4   65530       4      14    10005     0  992 00:00:15        0
```

```
IOS
R4# show bgp ipv4 unicast summary
BGP router identifier 192.168.4.4, local AS number 65530
BGP table version is 1, main routing table version 1


Neighbor      V      AS MsgRcvd MsgSent   TblVer   InQ OutQ Up/Down   State/PfxRcd
192.168.2.2   4   65530       3       5        1     0    0 00:01:16        0
R4# show bgp ipv4 unicast summary
BGP router identifier 192.168.4.4, local AS number 65530
BGP table version is 1, main routing table version 1


Neighbor      V      AS MsgRcvd MsgSent   TblVer   InQ OutQ Up/Down   State/PfxRcd
192.168.2.2   4   65530       3       7        1     0    0 00:02:59        0
R4#
07:35:26.950: %BGP-3-NOTIFICATION: sent to neighbor 192.168.2.2 4/0
(hold time expired) 0 bytes
*Sep 27 07:35:26.952: %BGP-5-NBR_RESET: Neighbor 192.168.2.2 reset
(BGP Notification sent)
07:35:26.955: %BGP-5-ADJCHANGE: neighbor 192.168.2.2 Down BGP Notification sent
07:35:26.955: %BGP_SESSION-5-ADJCHANGE: neighbor 192.168.2.2 IPv4 Unicast topology
base removed from session  BGP Notification sent
07:35:38.229: %BGP-5-ADJCHANGE: neighbor 192.168.2.2 Up
```

The following are a few possible causes of BGP session flapping due to an MTU mismatch:

- The interface MTU on both the peering routers do not match.

- The Layer 2 path between the two peering routers do not have consistent MTU settings.

- PMTUD didn't calculate correct MSS for the TCP BGP session.

- BGP PMTUD could be failing because of blocked ICMP messages by a router or a firewall in path.

To verify there are MTU mismatch issues in the path, perform extended **ping** tests by setting the size of the packet as the outgoing interface MTU value along with DF bit set. Also, ensure that ICMP messages are not being blocked in the path to have PMTUD function properly. An accurate review of the configuration should be done to ensure that the MTU values are consistent throughout the network.

High CPU Causing Control-Plane Flaps

The CPU on a router is continuously performing several tasks. Some tasks are low level, such as scheduling or other kernel-related tasks, and some are high level. But the CPU is capable of performing most of the tasks on a router. Problems arise when a process takes more CPU cycles than anticipated or the CPU has to process the packets, such as process switching of packets. High CPU conditions are caused by one of the following reasons:

- CPU process issues
- Interrupt (traffic processing)

Because all the control plane packets are processed by the CPU and are not switched in the hardware, a high CPU condition can cause control plane packets to get dropped or get delayed. This can be Bidirectional Failure Detection (BFD) or BGP or any other control plane packets. Note that the packets destined to the CPU are called the *for-us* packets.

Example 3-28 shows the output of **show process cpu sorted** to verify the CPU utilization on the router. The value 99% shows the total CPU utilization percentage, the value 7% indicates the CPU utilization due to interrupt, and the SNMP ENGINE process is consuming the most CPU cycles. The output also shows a 1-minute and 5-minute average CPU utilization.

Example 3-28   show process cpu sorted *Output*

```
Rtr# show process cpu sorted | exclude 0.0
CPU utilization for five seconds: 99%/7%; one minute: 84%; five minutes: 38%
PID Runtime(ms)    Invoked    uSecs   5Sec   1Min   5Min TTY Process
212  7157624761849980789       386 82.71% 70.16% 25.65%   0 SNMP ENGINE
  8  9190575241399458158       656  1.51%  1.47%  1.47%   0 ARP Input
318    76225596 348324353      218  1.11%  0.43%  0.16%   0 OSPF Router 220
! Output omitted for brevity
```

It is also good to check the CPU history using the **show processes cpu history** command, which shows the CPU utilization graphs for last 72 hours. This helps identify when the problem actually started, and events that occurred around that time can be investigated to troubleshoot the problem.

If the CPU is high due to process, it is important to understand the role of the process on the router. For example, the CPU is reportedly high in the output shown in Example 2-28 because of the SNMP Engine process. So it's clear that the SNMP process is busy doing something on the router. The **show snmp** command output shows how many packets the SNMP process is processing. If the SNMP process is receiving or sending too many packets, the SNMP process can consume lot of CPU cycles.

If the CPU is high due to interrupts, it could be due to one of the following problems:

- Excess process switched packets
- Packets with TTL value of 1
- Excess control plane packets

Excess process switching can happen because of Cisco Express Forwarding (CEF) not being enabled on the router or CEF not having forwarding information for the packet. If **ip cef** is configured globally but **no ip route-cache cef** is configured under the interface (some features require CEF to be disabled on the interface), this makes the traffic being received on the interface to be process switched. Also, insufficient memory on the router can lead to CEF/Forwarding Information Base (FIB) getting disabled on the router or line card. Therefore, it is important to verify CEF as well as memory on the router to troubleshoot excess process switching packets.

Every IP packet has a TTL value. The TTL value ensures that the packet doesn't go into a loop and create problems in a Layer 3 network. But packets with TTL size 1 can cause an impact on the CPU utilization of the router. Regular control plane packets like OSPF hello or BGP keepalive packets for EBGP session have a TTL value of 1, but those are expected packets. A normal IP packet that is not destined to any of the router interfaces but is destined for devices behind the router and has a TTL value of 1 gets punted to the router CPU to get processed. Because the router is not the final destination of the packet, the CPU drops those packets and consumes some CPU cycles. Another example is a configuration of a multicast application that has been set with a wrong TTL value, therefore causing the multicast packets to get punted to the CPU.

The CPU on the route processor processes the control plane packets, but if those packets are excessive and aggressive in nature, they can overwhelm the CPU. For example, 500 BGP neighbors configured with aggressive timers on the router can have a huge number of keepalive packets hitting the CPU to get processed or hundreds of IP service-level agreement (SLA) probes configured toward the router from various sources can send too many ICMP packets and spike up the CPU a bit. Most router CPUs are capable of handling that many packets. The challenge comes when an outside attacker sends thousands of BGP packets or a bad virtual host sends an enormous amount of ARP request packets toward the router. These situations can overwhelm the CPU on the router and impact services running on the router.

The following methods help mitigate the problems caused by packets hitting the CPU:

- Configuring an ACL to block the packets once identified
- Configuring rate limiters
- Using Control Plane Policing (CoPP)

After the packets hitting the CPU are identified and their source and destination are known, use the tools described in Chapter 2, "Generic Troubleshooting Methodologies," to block the packets by using an ACL on the interface.

Configuring rate limiters is another option to limit certain traffic from hitting the CPU. After the configured threshold value is reached, the packets are dropped by the hardware or software based on the platform. For example, 6500 and 7600 platform is Multi-Layer Switch (MLS)–based architecture. There are various MLS rate limiters available on this platform. For example an MLS rate limiter can be configured for ICMP redirect or multicast traffic using the **mls rate-limit** command to protect the CPU.

On NX-OS platforms, there are various platform-specific rate limiters that can be configured using the command **platform rate-limit [access-log-list | layer-2 port-security | layer-2 storm-control | layer-3 control | layer-3 glean | layer-3 mtu | layer-3 multicast {directly-connected | local-groups | rpf-leak} | layer-3 ttl | receive]** *packets*. The **show hardware rate-limit** can be used to display the configured rate limiters. XR platform takes care of rate limiting the packets using Local Packet Transport Services (LPTS). LPTS is not just used for rate limiting but also performs Control Plane Policing.

Control Plane Policing

Denial-of-Service (DoS) attacks can take on many forms, affecting both servers and infrastructure. Attacks targeted at infrastructure devices can generate IP traffic streams at very high data rates. These IP data streams contain packets that are destined for processing by the control plane of the Route Processor (RP). Based on the high rate of rogue packets presented to the RP, the control plane is forced to spend an inordinate amount of time, processing this DoS traffic. This scenario can result in one of the following issues:

- Loss of line protocol keepalives, which can cause a line to go down and lead to route flaps and major network transitions.

- Loss of routing protocol updates, which can lead to route flaps and major network transitions.

- Near 100% CPU utilization can lock up the router and prevent it from completing high-priority processing, resulting in other negative side effects.

- When the RP is near 100% utilization, the response time at the user command line interface (CLI) is very slow or the CLI is locked out. This prevents the user from taking corrective action to respond to the attack.

- Resources including memory, buffers, and data structures can be consumed causing negative side effects.

- Packet queues back up leading to indiscriminate drops of important packets.

- Router crashes.

The *Control Plane Policing (CoPP)* feature increases the device security by protecting its CPU (Route Processor) from unwanted and excess traffic or Denial of Service (DoS) attacks and gives priority to relevant traffic destined to the CPU. Different types of traffic can be organized in different classes and policed under the policy-maps. If a

violate-action is set to drop, the excess packets drop. If they are marked to forward, those packets are forwarded. The service-policy is then attached to the control plane using the **service-policy input** *policy-name* command under the **control-plane** configuration. Example 3-29 shows a sample CoPP policy on an IOS router to protect BGP packets. Any other traffic that is not classified in one of the classes defined under policy-map falls under the default class.

Example 3-29 *CoPP Configuration on IOS*

```
R2(config)# ip access-list extended CPP_BGP
R2(config-ext-nacl)# permit tcp any eq bgp any
R2(config-ext-nacl)# permit tcp any any eq bgp
R2(config-ext-nacl)# exit
R2(config)# class-map Protect_BGP
R2(config-cmap)# match access-group name CPP_BGP
! Define other class-maps for matching other traffic
R2(config)# policy-map CPP_Protection
R2(config-pmap)# class Protect_BGP
R2(config-pmap-c)# police cir 36000 3000 conform-action transmit violate action drop
! Configure Policing for other defined classes
R2(config-pmap-c)# control-plane
R2(config-cp)# service-policy input CPP_Protection

19:27:30.292: %CP-5-FEATURE: Control-plane Policing feature enabled on
       Control plane aggregate path
```

Once the CoPP policy has been defined, use the **show policy-map control-plane** command to see the traffic hitting various classes and verify any violated packets in those classes. Example 3-30 shows the output of show policy-map control-plane command.

Example 3-30   show policy-map control-plane *Output*

```
R2# show policy-map control-plane
 Control Plane

  Service-policy input: CPP_Protection

    Class-map: Protect_BGP (match-all)
     215 packets, 15983 bytes
       5 minute offered rate 0000 bps, drop rate 0000 bps
       Match: access-group name CPP_Protocols
       police:
           cir 36000 bps, bc 3000 bytes, be 3000 bytes
         conformed 215 packets, 15983 bytes; actions:
           transmit
```

```
        exceeded 0 packets, 0 bytes; actions:
          transmit
        violated 0 packets, 0 bytes; actions:
          drop
        conformed 0000 bps, exceeded 0000 bps, violated 0000 bps


! Output for other defined classes follows


! Output omitted for brevity

    Class-map: class-default (match-any)
      69 packets, 19610 bytes
      5 minute offered rate 0000 bps, drop rate 0000 bps
      Match: any
```

Example 3-30 demonstrates manual configuration of CoPP policy on Cisco IOS routers.

CoPP on NX-OS

On Nexus platforms, the NX-OS installs a default *copp-system-policy* policy to protect the device from DoS attacks and excessing packet processing. Various profiles that have different protection levels provided for NX-OS default CoPP policy include the following:

■ **Strict:** This policy defines the BC value of 250 ms for regular classes, and for important classes it's set to 1000 ms.

■ **Moderate:** This policy defines the BC value of 310 ms for regular classes, and for important classes it's set to 1250 ms.

■ **Lenient:** This policy defines the BC value of 375 ms for regular classes, and for important classes it's set to 1500 ms.

■ **Dense:** Introduced in 6.0(1) release.

If one of the policies is not selected during initial setup, NX-OS attaches the Strict profile to the control plane. The user can choose not to use one of these profiles and create a custom policy to be used for CoPP. The NX-OS default CoPP policy categorizes policy into various predefined classes, such as the following:

■ **Critical:** Routing protocol packets with IP Precedence value 6

■ **Important:** Redundancy protocols like GLBP, VRRP, HSRP, etc.

■ **Management:** All management traffic, such as Telnet, SSH, FTP, NTP, Radius, and so on

■ **Monitoring:** Ping and Traceroute traffic

■ **Exception:** ICMP Unreachables and IP Options

■ **Undesirable:** All unwanted traffic

Because the ICMP messages are also rate-limited, a few ICMP packets are dropped when performing a ping from and to the Nexus device. Example 3-31 shows a Sample Strict CoPP policy when the system comes up for the first time.

Example 3-31 *CoPP Strict Policy on Nexus*

```
class-map type control-plane match-any copp-system-p-class-critical
  match access-group name copp-system-p-acl-bgp
  match access-group name copp-system-p-acl-rip
  match access-group name copp-system-p-acl-vpc
  match access-group name copp-system-p-acl-bgp6
  match access-group name copp-system-p-acl-lisp
  match access-group name copp-system-p-acl-ospf
  ! Output omitted for brevity
class-map type control-plane match-any copp-system-p-class-exception
  match exception ip option
  match exception ip icmp unreachable
  match exception ipv6 option
  match exception ipv6 icmp unreachable
class-map type control-plane match-any copp-system-p-class-important
  match access-group name copp-system-p-acl-cts
  match access-group name copp-system-p-acl-glbp
  match access-group name copp-system-p-acl-hsrp
  match access-group name copp-system-p-acl-vrrp
  match access-group name copp-system-p-acl-wccp
! Output omitted for brevity
class-map type control-plane match-any copp-system-p-class-management
  match access-group name copp-system-p-acl-ftp
  match access-group name copp-system-p-acl-ntp
  match access-group name copp-system-p-acl-ssh
  match access-group name copp-system-p-acl-ntp6
  match access-group name copp-system-p-acl-sftp
  match access-group name copp-system-p-acl-snmp
  match access-group name copp-system-p-acl-ssh6
! Output omitted for brevity
class-map type control-plane match-any copp-system-p-class-monitoring
  match access-group name copp-system-p-acl-icmp
  match access-group name copp-system-p-acl-icmp6
  match access-group name copp-system-p-acl-mpls-oam
  match access-group name copp-system-p-acl-traceroute
  match access-group name copp-system-p-acl-http-response
! Output omitted for brevity
class-map type control-plane match-any copp-system-p-class-normal
  match access-group name copp-system-p-acl-mac-dot1x
```

```
    match exception ip multicast directly-connected-sources
    match exception ipv6 multicast directly-connected-sources
    match protocol arp
class-map type control-plane match-any copp-system-p-class-undesirable
    match access-group name copp-system-p-acl-undesirable
    match exception fcoe-fib-miss

policy-map type control-plane copp-system-p-policy-strict
   class copp-system-p-class-critical
     set cos 7
     police cir 36000 kbps bc 250 ms conform transmit violate drop
   class copp-system-p-class-important
     set cos 6
     police cir 1400 kbps bc 1500 ms conform transmit violate drop
   class copp-system-p-class-management
     set cos 2
     police cir 10000 kbps bc 250 ms conform transmit violate drop
   class copp-system-p-class-normal
     set cos 1
     police cir 680 kbps bc 250 ms conform transmit violate drop
   class copp-system-p-class-exception
     set cos 1
     police cir 360 kbps bc 250 ms conform transmit violate drop
   class copp-system-p-class-monitoring
     set cos 1
     police cir 130 kbps bc 1000 ms conform transmit violate drop
   class class-default
     set cos 0
     police cir 100 kbps bc 250 ms conform transmit violate drop
```

There are a few more classes added into the latest releases for traffic related to multicast and L2 traffic, but the configuration is all available automatically. Keep in mind that the CoPP policy should not be too aggressive and should be designed based on the network design and configuration. For example, if the rate at which routing protocol packets are hitting the CoPP policy is more than the policed rate, then even the legitimate sessions are dropped and protocol flaps are detected. If the predefined CoPP policies have to be modified, a custom CoPP policy can be created by copying a preclassified CoPP policy and then editing the new custom policy. Any of the predefined CoPP profiles cannot be edited. Also, the CoPP policies are hidden from the **show running-config** output. View the CoPP policies from the **show running-config all** or **show running-config copp all** command. Example 3-32 shows how to view the CoPP policy configuration and create a custom strict policy.

Example 3-32   *Viewing CoPP Policy and Creating Custom CoPP Policy*

```
R1# show running-config copp
copp profile strict
R1# show running-config copp all
class-map type control-plane match-any copp-system-p-class-critical
  match access-group name copp-system-p-acl-bgp
  match access-group name copp-system-p-acl-rip
  match access-group name copp-system-p-acl-vpc
  match access-group name copp-system-p-acl-bgp6
! Output omitted for brevity


R1# copp copy profile strict ?
  prefix  Prefix for the copied policy
  suffix  Suffix for the copied policy
R1# copp copy profile strict prefix custom
R1# configure terminal
R1(config)# control-plane
R1(config-cp)# service-policy input custom-copp-policy-strict
```

The command **show policy-map interface control-plane** displays the counters of the CoPP policy. For an aggregated view, use this command with the **include "class|conform|violated"** filter to see how many packets have been conformed and how many have been violated and dropped, as shown in Example 3-33.

Example 3-33   show policy-map interface control-plane *Output*

```
R1# show policy-map interface control-plane | include "class|conform|violated"
    class-map custom-copp-class-critical (match-any)
        conformed 123126534 bytes; action: transmit
        violated 0 bytes; action: drop
        conformed 0 bytes; action: transmit

        violated 0 bytes; action: drop
        conformed 107272597 bytes; action: transmit
        violated 0 bytes; action: drop
        conformed 0 bytes; action: transmit
        violated 0 bytes; action: drop
    class-map custom-copp-class-important (match-any)
        conformed 0 bytes; action: transmit
        violated 0 bytes; action: drop
        conformed 0 bytes; action: transmit
        violated 0 bytes; action: drop
```

```
        conformed 0 bytes; action: transmit
        violated 0 bytes; action: drop
        conformed 0 bytes; action: transmit
        violated 0 bytes; action: drop
! Output omitted for brevity
```

As a best practice, the **copp profile strict** command should be used after each NX-OS upgrade, or at least after each major NX-OS upgrade. If a CoPP policy modification was previously done, it must be reapplied.

Starting with NX-OS release 5.1, the threshold value can be configured to generate a syslog message for the drops enforced by the CoPP policy on a particular class. The syslog messages are generated when the drops within a traffic class exceed the user-configured threshold value. Configure the threshold by using the logging **drop threshold** *dropped-bytes-count* [**level** *logging-level*] command. Example 3-34 demonstrates how to configure the logging threshold value to be set for 100 drops and logging level 7. It also shows how the syslog message is generated in the event of the drop threshold being exceeded.

Example 3-34   *Drop Threshold for Syslog Logging*

```
R1(config)# policy-map type control-plane custom-copp-policy-strict
R1(config-pmap)# class custom-copp-class-critical
R1(config-pmap-c)# logging drop threshold ?
  <1-80000000000>  Dropped byte count

R1(config-pmap-c)# logging drop threshold 100 ?
  <CR>
  level  Syslog level

R1(config-pmap-c)# logging drop threshold 100 level ?
  <1-7>  Specify the logging level between 1-7

R1(config-pmap-c)# logging drop threshold 100 level 7
%COPP-5-COPP_DROPS5: CoPP drops exceed threshold in class:
custom-copp-class-critical,
check show policy-map interface control-plane for more info.
```

Here are a few best practices for NX-OS CoPP policy configuration:

- Use strict CoPP mode by default.

- Dense CoPP profile is recommended when the chassis is fully loaded with F2 Series Modules or loaded with more F2 Series Modules than any other I/O modules.

- It is not recommended to disable CoPP. Tune the default CoPP, as needed.

- Monitor unintended drops, and add or modify the default CoPP policy in accordance to the expected traffic.

- The CoPP policy must be periodically evaluated and adjusted as network conditions change over time.

Local Packet Transport Services

Like IOS and NX-OS, IOS XR doesn't have CoPP. Instead, it uses a comprehensive and powerful feature called Local Packet Transport Services (LPTS). LPTS is an integral component of IOS-XR, which provides firewall and policing functionality. It also decides which of the for-us packets needs to be punted to the CPU or dropped. LPTS provides hardware policers on the line card that limits traffic sent to the RP.

LPTS is based on the concept of Reflexive ACLs and punt policers. It also has an Internal FIB (IFIB) that takes care of directing packets to certain nodes. Figure 3-5 shows a 1000-foot view of how LPTS functions on IOS XR.

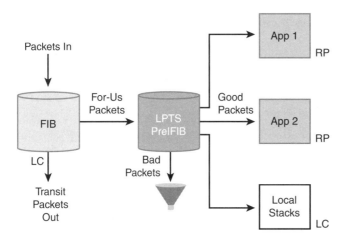

Figure 3-5 *LPTS on IOS XR*

LPTS performs a firewall function by allowing only *for-us* protocol packets into the router for only the configured application/server processes. LPTS also rate limits the *for-us* packets entering the line card (LC) so that nonconfirming packets are dropped on the ingress LC itself. LPTS installs dynamic flow entries for certain protocol packets on demand. For example, for an ICMP echo request sent out from the local router to peer router, LPTS creates flow entry in pre-IFIB (condensed version of IFIB) so that an ICMP echo reply received from the peer router will be matched against it.

Should any *for-us* packets arrive at the LC fragmented, packet lookup can be performed to determine where to deliver only upon reassembling the fragments. LPTS provides the reassembly function for fragmented *for-us* packets.

One of the most important functionalities of LPTS is dynamic ACL creation. This is configuration driven, based on the feature or service configured, so no user intervention is required. The stats indicated in Example 3-30 are from the line card in location 0/1/CPU0. If the location option is not specified, the stats shown are from the active RP.

There are various tables in LPTS at different locations maintained by hardware and software. This is very important to understand because the drops can happen in any of those tables based on the forwarding and punt path. The various tables are as follows:

- **Pre-IFIB (PIFIB):** Maintained at Ingress PSE (Packet Switching Engine) TCAM Hardware of the line card.

- **Software Pre-IFIB:** Maintained on line card as well as RP. The Software PIFIB takes care of more complex inspection and operations, such as fragmentation reassembly.

- **IFIB "Slices":** These are distributed across the RP. These act as secondary lookup tables when the PIFIB is incomplete. The IFIB table is distributed in slices, such as TCP Slice, UDP Slice, ISIS Slice, and so on.

The following steps illustrate how the bindings occur for various tables in LPTS:

Step 1.   At boot, the IFIB is empty, the bindings, PIFIB software and hardware tables have default entries.

Step 2.   As the box is configured, the LPTS IFIB populates, and the bindings and pifib are updated.

Step 3.   The first message for a configured entity (for example, BGP), hits the *any.any* entry (Unknown State) in the PIFIB hardware.

Step 4.   Subsequent matches hit more granular entries.

Step 5.   When peers oscillate, entries are added and deleted.

LPTS also maintains different flow categories based on the protocol state. For instance, BGP has three states:

- **Unknown:** Traffic flow with TCP port 179 but no neighbor is configured for that source. This resolves to *BGP-default* flow type.

- **Configured:** Flow with source address of the peer but the session is not established yet. This resolves to *BGP-cfg-peer* flow type. The neighbor statement configured under the **router bgp** section drives these entries.

- **Established:** Flow with an established state with relevant L3 and L4 information. This flow is policed lightly and the flow resolves to *BGP-known* flow type.

Example 3-35 shows the output of the **show lpts pifib hardware police** [location *location-id*] and **show lpts pifib hardware entry brief** [location *location-id*] commands. All the preceding BGP states can be seen with the use of these commands.

Example 3-35   *BGP States in LPTS*

```
RP/0/0/CPU0:R3# show lpts pifib hardware police location 0/1/CPU0
------------------------------------------------------------
              Node 0/1/CPU0:
------------------------------------------------------------
 Burst = 100ms for all flow types
------------------------------------------------------------
FlowType       Policer Type    Cur. Rate  Def. Rate  Accepted   Dropped   TOS Value
------------   ------- ------   ---------  ---------  ---------  -------   ---------
BGP-known      106     Static   2500       2500       200        0         01234567
BGP-cfg-peer   107     Static   2000       2000       0          0         01234567
BGP-default    108     Static   1500       1500       5          0         01234567
! Output omitted for brevity


RP/0/0/CPU0:R3# show lpts pifib hardware entry brief location 0/1/CPU0
          Node: 0/1/CPU0:
------------------------------------------------------------
Offset L3   VRF id      L4     Intf   Dest       laddr,Port raddr,Port
------ ---- ----------- ------ ------ ---------  ----------------------
! Below entry shows Configured state
22     IPV4 default     TCP    any    LU(30)     any,179 10.1.13.1,any
! Below entry show Established State
24     IPV4 default     TCP    any    LU(30)     10.1.13.2,57286 10.1.13.1,179
! Below entry shows Unknown State
142    IPV4 *           TCP    any    LU(30)     any,any any,179
! Output omitted for brevity
```

Example 3-36 shows the use of the **show lpts ifib all brief** command to display various entries under different slices. For example, the BGP entry for neighbor 10.1.13.1 is under BGP4 slice. Also, the use of the **statistics** keyword at the end of the command is used to verify packets that have been accepted and dropped counters to correlate the drops happening in Internal Forwarding Information Base (IFIB).

Example 3-36   show lpts ifib all brief *[statistics] Command Output*

```
RP/0/0/CPU0:R3# show lpts ifib all brief
Slice    VRF-ID   L4     Interface Dlvr       laddr,Port raddr,Port
-------- -------- ------ --------- ----------  --------------------------------
RAWIP4   default  L2TPV3 any       0/0/CPU0    any any
RAWIP6   default  ICMP6  any       0/0/CPU0    any,MLDLQUERY any
RAWIP6   default  ICMP6  any       0/0/CPU0    any,LSTNRREPORT any
RAWIP6   default  ICMP6  any       0/0/CPU0    any,MLDLSTNRDN any
RAWIP6   default  ICMP6  any       0/0/CPU0    any,LSTNRREPORT any
```

```
BGP4      default  TCP    any      0/0/CPU0    10.1.13.2,179 10.1.13.1
BGP4      default  TCP    any      0/0/CPU0    10.1.13.2,57286 10.1.13.1,179


RP/0/0/CPU0:R3# show lpts ifib all brief statistics
Slice  VRF-ID  L4      Interface Accept/Drop  laddr,Port raddr,Port
------ ------- ------  ---------- -----------  -----------------------------------
RAWIP4 default L2TPV3 any         0/0          any any
RAWIP6 default ICMP6  any         0/0          any,MLDLQUERY any
RAWIP6 default ICMP6  any         0/0          any,LSTNRREPORT any
RAWIP6 default ICMP6  any         0/0          any,MLDLSTNRDN any
RAWIP6 default ICMP6  any         0/0          any,LSTNRREPORT any
BGP4   default TCP    any         0/0          10.1.13.2,179 10.1.13.1
BGP4   default TCP    any         6/0          10.1.13.2,57286 10.1.13.1,179


 Slice    Num. Entries Accepts/Drops
 -------- ------------ -------------
 RAWIP4   1            0/0
 RAWIP6   4            0/0
 BGP4     2            6/0
 Total    7            6/0
```

The Pre-Internal Forwarding Information Base (PIFIB) software table is viewed by using the command **show lpts pifib brief [statistics]**, where the statistics displays the *Accept* and *Drop* counters. With the use of the hardware keyword, as shown in Example 3-35, the hardware-based PIFIB counters are seen. Example 3-37 demonstrates the software PIFIB table showing there were 100 packets accepted for the BGP session established between 10.1.13.1 and 10.1.13.2. Also, it shows cumulative statistics for various types of packets.

Example 3-37 *Software PIFIB Table*

```
RP/0/0/CPU0:R3# show lpts pifib brief statistics
* - Any VRF;
Type       VRF-ID   L4     Interface Accepts/Drops laddr,Port raddr,Port
---------- -------- ------ -------  -------------  --------------------------------
! Output omitted for brevity
IPv4       default  TCP    any      100/0          10.1.13.2,57286 10.1.13.1,179
IPv4       default  TCP    any      0/0            10.1.13.2,179 10.1.13.1
IPv4       *        TCP    any      6/0            any any,179
IPv4       *        TCP    any      1/0            any,179 any
! Output omitted for brevity
----------------------
```

```
statistics:
Type            Num. Entries        Accepts/Drops
------          ------------        ------------
ISIS            1                   0/0
IPv4_frag       1                   0/0
IPv4_echo       1                   174/0
IPv4            15                  182/0
IPv6_frag       1                   0/0
IPv6_echo       1                   0/0
IPv6_ND         5                   0/0
IPv6            13                  0/0
BFD_any         0                   0/0
Total           38
Packets into Pre-IFIB: 361
Lookups: 361
Packets delivered locally: 361
Packets delivered remotely: 0
```

All these commands can be used with the location keyword, which allows you to look at the counters on a particular line card or RP.

Dynamic BGP Peering

Configuring BGP neighbors is not so complex. But manually configuring a large number of peers (100 BGP neighbors, for example) could be tedious. One way to minimize the configuration is by using BGP peer groups. If there are multiple neighbors that will share the same **remote-as** number or the same outbound policies, peer groups make it very easy to manage the configuration for those neighbors. But again, those 100 BGP peers have to be manually configured and added to the peer group. With the BGP dynamic neighbors feature, BGP peering can be established with a group of remote neighbors that are defined by an IPv4 address range. This feature is not available for IPv6 addresses.

Note   At the time of writing, dynamic BGP neighbor feature is not available on IOS XR and NX-OS.

The BGP dynamic neighbor concept is helpful in a hub-spoke topology where only the spoke router needs to have the peering configuration toward the hub. The spoke routers can be part of the same subnet. The hub router only needs to know the subnet. It can also be useful in topologies where RR is configured and there are huge numbers of RR clients. Similarly, a dynamic BGP peering concept can be used with confederations.

How does BGP dynamic neighbor work? For every peer group, an IP subnet range is configured, and the router starts listening in passive mode for incoming TCP sessions for that subnet. A BGP peer tries to establish a BGP neighborship with the passively listening router and initiates a TCP session. If the IP and the AS number matches with any of the configured IP subnets, a BGP session is dynamically created on the router.

Dynamic BGP Peer Configuration

The dynamic BGP neighbor configuration is a one-time configuration. A router can be configured to dynamically form neighborship in few simple steps, as shown:

Step 1.   Define the peer group by using Rtr(config-router)# **neighbor** *peer-group-name* **peer-group**.

Step 2.   Create a global limit of BGP dynamic subnet range neighbors. The value ranges from 1 to 5000. Rtr(config-router)# **bgp listen limit** *value*.

Step 3.   Configure an IP Subnet Range and associate it with a peer group. Multiple subnets can be added to the same peer group. Rtr(config-router)# **bgp listen range** *subnet* **peer-group** *peer-group-name*.

Step 4.   Define the remote-as for the peer group. Optionally, define the list of AS numbers that can be accepted to form neighborship with. The max limit of alternate-as numbers is 5. Rtr(config-router)# **neighbor** *peer-group-name* **remote-as** *asn* [**alternate-as** [*asn*] [*asn*] [*asn*] [*asn*] [*asn*]].

Step 5.   Activate the peer group under ipv4 address-family by using Rtr(config-router-af)# **neighbor** *peer-group-name* **activate**.

A few things to note from the configuration steps are as follows:

■ The maximum number of dynamic BGP neighbors that can be configured is 5000.

■ The defined IP subnet range can form a BGP neighbor relationship with peers in six different AS numbers. The first is defined as part of **remote-as** configuration, and optional AS numbers are defined as part of **alternate-as** configuration.

Note   The alternate-as option is not available when configuring IBGP sessions.

Figure 3-6 shows a sample topology for dynamic BGP peering. In this figure, R1 forms a dynamic neighborship with routers from R2, R3, and R4.

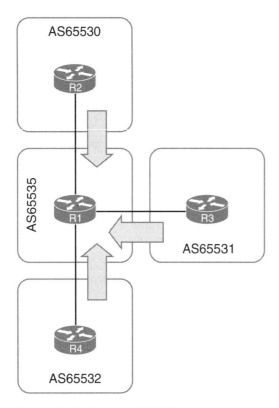

Figure 3-6   *Dynamic BGP Peering*

Example 3-38 demonstrates a dynamic BGP neighbor configuration. It shows the configuration from router R1 and R2. R3 and R4 have a similar configuration as R2.

Example 3-38   *Dynamic BGP Neighbor Configuration*

```
R1# show running-config | section router bgp
 router bgp 65535
  bgp log-neighbor-changes
  bgp listen range 10.1.0.0/16 peer-group DYNAMIC-BGP
  bgp listen limit 200
  neighbor DYNAMIC-BGP peer-group
  neighbor DYNAMIC-BGP remote-as 65530 alternate-as 65531 65532 65533
  !
  address-family ipv4
! Loopback Advertisement
   network 192.168.1.1 mask 255.255.255.255
! peer group activated
```

```
    neighbor DYNAMIC-BGP activate
  exit-address-family
```

```
R2# show running-config | section router bgp
 router bgp 65530
  bgp router-id 192.168.2.2
  bgp log-neighbor-changes
  no bgp default ipv4-unicast
  neighbor 10.1.12.1 remote-as 65535
  !
  address-family ipv4
   network 192.168.2.2 mask 255.255.255.255
   neighbor 10.1.12.1 activate
  exit-address-family
```

With dynamic BGP neighbor configuration, the **show tcp brief all** output illustrates that the router is listening on port 179 but with foreign address of *.*. Also, all the dynamically established BGP peerings have an * marked in the **show bgp ipv4 unicast summary** output, as shown in Example 3-39.

Example 3-39   *Verifying Dynamic BGP Peers*

```
R1# show tcp brief all
TCB        Local Address              Foreign Address            (state)
0C89CDD0   10.1.14.1.179              10.1.14.2.22059            ESTAB
0E4CC190   10.1.12.1.179              10.1.12.2.62747            ESTAB
0C88F3A0   10.1.13.1.179              10.1.13.2.58756            ESTAB
0D8B3B08   0.0.0.0.179                *.*                        LISTEN
```

```
R1# show bgp ipv4 unicast summary
BGP router identifier 10.1.12.1, local AS number 65535
BGP table version is 7, main routing table version 7
4 network entries using 576 bytes of memory
4 path entries using 320 bytes of memory
4/4 BGP path/bestpath attribute entries using 608 bytes of memory
3 BGP AS-PATH entries using 72 bytes of memory
0 BGP route-map cache entries using 0 bytes of memory
0 BGP filter-list cache entries using 0 bytes of memory
BGP using 1576 total bytes of memory
BGP activity 5/1 prefixes, 5/1 paths, scan interval 60 secs
```

```
Neighbor      V       AS MsgRcvd MsgSent     TblVer  InQ OutQ Up/Down  State/PfxRcd
*10.1.12.2    4    65530     377     377          7    0    0 05:38:22           1
*10.1.13.2    4    65531     376     378          7    0    0 05:37:37           1
*10.1.14.2    4    65532      80      84          7    0    0 01:08:03           1
* Dynamically created based on a listen range command
Dynamically created neighbors: 3, Subnet ranges: 1
BGP peergroup DYNCMIC-BGP listen range group members:
  10.1.0.0/16
Total dynamically created neighbors: 3/(200 max), Subnet ranges: 1
```

Dynamic BGP Challenges

With dynamic BGP features, additional challenges are present, such as

- Misconfigured MD5 password

- Resource issues in a scaled environment

- TCP starvation

Misconfigured MD5 Password

This problem is very common and is generally caused by human error due to typo mistakes. You have to be careful when configuring passwords on the router configured for dynamically establishing a BGP neighbor relationship.

Resource Issues in a Scaled Environment

Because up to 5000 neighbors can form peering dynamically, the IP subnet range in the **bgp listen** command must be configured carefully. If there are too many neighbors allowed to form peering than the router can handle, it could lead to a severe impact on the network. At some point the resource limit will be hit, and the router will not have any resources to serve any request coming to it. So proper planning must be done to determine how many neighbors can dynamically form BGP neighbor relationships on the router.

TCP Starvation

Because of the TCP slow start capability and non-availability of this for UDP traffic, a router can run into a TCP starvation condition. TCP tries to back off on bandwidth when there is traffic loss in the network, but UDP does not. As a result, UDP occupies all the queues and makes TCP starve for bandwidth. Therefore, it is good to limit the number of BGP neighbors and be cautious during removal/addition of new IP subnet ranges.

Summary

This chapter explained various techniques and commands that are used to troubleshoot BGP peering issues, such as completely down peers or flapping peers. This chapter provides multiple techniques to identify and overcome peering issues which results in a higher uptime for the BGP neighbors and make the network more stable. The chapter explains various factors like MTU issues, High CPU conditions, or misconfigured CoPP policies that could lead to unstable BGP sessions and cause them to continuously flap. At the end of the chapter, Dynamic BGP peering feature was introduced, which provides the capability to dynamically establish BGP neighbors without having to configure all of them.

References

RFC 4271, *A Border Gateway Protocol 4 (BGP-4)*, Y. Rekhter, T. Li, S. Hares, IETF, https://tools.ietf.org/html/rfc4271, January 2006.

RFC 879, *The TCP Maximum Segment Size and Related Topics*, J. Postel, IETF, https://tools.ietf.org/html/rfc879, November 1983.

RFC 1191, *Path MTU Discovery*, J. Mogul, S. Deering, IETF, https://tools.ietf.org/html/rfc1191, November 1990.

## Chapter 4

Troubleshooting Route Advertisement and BGP Policies

The following topics are covered in this chapter:

- BGP Route Advertisement Process
- BGP Best Path Selection
- Troubleshooting Missing BGP Routes
- Conditional Matching Techniques
- Troubleshooting BGP Router Policies

Chapter 3, "Troubleshooting Peering Issues," focuses on the establishment of a Border Gateway Protocol (BGP) session. Now that the BGP session has been established, network prefixes and the path attributes can be exchanged between routers. Unlike Interior Gateway Protocols (IGP) routing protocols, BGP allows a routing policy to be different from router to router in an autonomous system (AS).

BGP routers can influence path selection by intentionally blocking longer matching (more specific) routes, or the modification of BGP attributes to influence best path selection. Those behaviors should be intentional, but this chapter focuses on troubleshooting unintentional problems with BGP route advertisement.

Troubleshooting BGP Route Advertisement

BGP route advertisement is often misunderstood and is the first concept that this chapter demonstrates how to troubleshoot.

Local Route Advertisement Issues

Imagine a single router that wants to install networks 10.1.0.0/16 and 10.0.0.0/8 into BGP so that those prefixes could be advertised to other routers. Example 4-1 provides a basic configuration.

Example 4-1   *Basic 10.1.0.0/16 Network Advertisement and 10.0.0.0/8 Aggregation*

```
R1# show run | s router bgp
router bgp 100
 no bgp log-neighbor-changes
 !
 address-family ipv4
  network 10.0.0.0
  network 10.1.0.0 mask 255.255.0.0
 exit-address-family
```

Upon examination of the BGP table in Example 4-2, neither route was installed into the BGP table.

Example 4-2   *Confirmation of Missing BGP Routes*

```
R1# show bgp ipv4 unicast
R1#
```

Reviewing the router's local routing table, note that the router has a directly connected route for the 10.1.1.0/24 network, as shown in Example 4-3. Performing an explicit route lookup in the router's global routing table, routing information base (RIB), for the two configured networks reveals that neither subnet exists in the table.

Example 4-3   *Verification That Routes Are in RIB*

```
R1# show ip route | b Gateway
Gateway of last resort is not set
      10.0.0.0/8 is variably subnetted, 2 subnets, 2 masks
C        10.1.1.0/24 is directly connected, Ethernet0/1
L        10.1.1.1/32 is directly connected, Ethernet0/1
      192.168.1.0/32 is subnetted, 1 subnets
C        192.168.1.1 is directly connected, Loopback0

R1# show ip route 10.1.0.0 255.255.0.0
% Subnet not in table
R1# show ip route 10.0.0.0 255.0.0.0
% Subnet not in table
```

An exact route must exist in the router's RIB (routing table) for the route to be installed into the BGP table so that it can be advertised to BGP neighbors. There are two solutions: modify the BGP configuration to match the local networks that already exist in the RIB or create a static route for the network in the BGP configuration. Example 4-4 demonstrates the new configuration.

Example 4-4 *R1's Correct Configuration for Route Advertisement and Aggregation*

```
R1# show run | section  route
router bgp 100
!
 address-family ipv4
  network 10.0.0.0
  network 10.1.1.0 mask 255.255.255.0
 exit-address-family
ip route 10.0.0.0 255.0.0.0 Null0
```

Note   The static route uses the Null 0 interface as a safety mechanism to prevent routing loops. If R1 has a more explicit route (longer match), it can forward the packet to that direction. If it does not have a more explicit route, the packet is dropped.

After making the appropriate changes, Example 4-5 demonstrates that the 10.0.0.0/8 and 10.1.1.0/24 networks have installed into the BGP table.

Example 4-5 *Verification of BGP Routes on R1*

```
R1# show bgp ipv4 unicast
! Output omitted for brevity
     Network          Next Hop            Metric LocPrf Weight Path
 *>  10.0.0.0         0.0.0.0                  0         32768 i
 *>  10.1.1.0/24      0.0.0.0                  0         32768 i
```

Route Aggregation Issues

Another common problem occurs with BGP route aggregation. As shown in Example 4-6, R1 has multiple RIB routes in the 10.1.0.0/16 range that it would like to have aggregated to a single 10.1.0.0/16 address in BGP. Notice that the BGP configuration has been reconfigured, and only the 10.1.0.0/16 network is defined as the aggregate prefix.

Example 4-6 *R1's Global RIB Table*

```
R1# show ip route
! Output omitted for brevity
Gateway of last resort is not set
      10.0.0.0/8 is variably subnetted, 6 subnets, 2 masks
C        10.1.12.0/24 is directly connected, Ethernet0/0
```

```
C        10.1.13.0/24 is directly connected, Ethernet0/1
C        10.1.14.0/24 is directly connected, Ethernet0/2
```

```
R1# show run | s router bgp
router bgp 100
 bgp log-neighbor-changes
 !
 address-family ipv4
  aggregate-address 10.1.0.0 255.255.0.0
 exit-address-family
```

Example 4-7 displays the BGP table on R1. The 10.1.0.0/16 aggregate route is not present because there are not any prefixes within the summary aggregate prefix range in the BGP table.

Example 4-7 *BGP Table on R1*

```
R1# show bgp ipv4 unicast
R1#
```

By adding the smaller network prefixes (10.1.12.0/24, 10.1.13.0/24, and 10.1.14.0/24) into the BGP table, the 10.1.0.0/16 aggregate route can be created. Example 4-8 provides the new configuration and verifies that the BGP table has populated properly with all three smaller prefixes and the aggregate route. Notice that the smaller prefixes (10.1.12.0/24, 10.1.13.0/24, and 10.1.14.0/24) are not suppressed and are advertised with the aggregate route.

Example 4-8 *R1's Configuration for Smaller and Aggregate Prefixes*

```
R1# show run | section router bgp
router bgp 100
 bgp log-neighbor-changes
 !
 address-family ipv4
  network 10.1.12.0 mask 255.255.255.0
  network 10.1.13.0 mask 255.255.255.0
  network 10.1.14.0 mask 255.255.255.0
  aggregate-address 10.1.0.0 255.255.0.0
 exit-address-family
```

```
R1# show bgp ipv4 unicast
BGP table version is 31, local router ID is 192.168.1.1
Status codes: s suppressed, d damped, h history, * valid, > best, i - internal,
              r RIB-failure, S Stale, m multipath, b backup-path, f RT-Filter,
              x best-external, a additional-path, c RIB-compressed,
```

```
Origin codes: i - IGP, e - EGP, ? - incomplete
RPKI validation codes: V valid, I invalid, N Not found

      Network          Next Hop          Metric LocPrf Weight Path
 *>   10.1.0.0/16      0.0.0.0                          32768 i
 *>   10.1.12.0/24     0.0.0.0                0          32768 i
 *>   10.1.13.0/24     0.0.0.0                0          32768 i
 *>   10.1.14.0/24     0.0.0.0                0          32768 i
```

To keep the smaller prefixes from being advertised, they can be filtered with the router's outbound BGP policy or through the suppression locally by appending the keyword **summary-only** to the **aggregate-address** command.

Example 4-9 demonstrates the new configuration and the BGP table. Notice that the smaller prefixes are suppressed, which is indicated by the *s* in the output.

Example 4-9 *R1's BGP Configuration for Suppression of Smaller Prefixes*

```
R1# show run | section router bgp
router bgp 100
 bgp log-neighbor-changes
 !
 address-family ipv4
  network 10.1.12.0 mask 255.255.255.0
  network 10.1.13.0 mask 255.255.255.0
  network 10.1.14.0 mask 255.255.255.0
  aggregate-address 10.1.0.0 255.255.0.0 summary-only
 exit-address-family
```

```
R1# show bgp ipv4 unicast
! Output omitted for brevity
BGP table version is 34, local router ID is 192.168.1.1
Status codes: s suppressed, d damped, h history, * valid, > best, i - internal,
              r RIB-failure, S Stale, m multipath, b backup-path, f RT-Filter,
              x best-external, a additional-path, c RIB-compressed,
Origin codes: i - IGP, e - EGP, ? - incomplete
RPKI validation codes: V valid, I invalid, N Not found

      Network          Next Hop          Metric LocPrf Weight Path
 *>   10.1.0.0/16      0.0.0.0                          32768 i
 s>   10.1.12.0/24     0.0.0.0                0          32768 i
 s>   10.1.13.0/24     0.0.0.0                0          32768 i
 s>   10.1.14.0/24     0.0.0.0                0          32768 i
```

Route Redistribution Issues

Redistributing routes into BGP is a common method of populating the BGP table. Figure 4-1 provides a simple drawing where R1 connects to R2, R3, and R4.

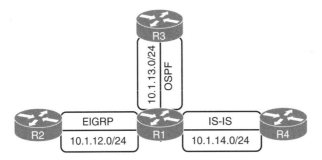

Figure 4-1   *Route Redistribution Topology*

R1 wants to redistribute all the prefixes that it has in the routing table, which includes prefixes learned via Enhanced Interior Gateway Routing Protocol (EIGRP), Open Shortest Path First (OSPF), and Intermediate System to Intermediate System (IS-IS). R1's BGP configuration and RIB has been displayed in Example 4-10. Notice that R1 has routes from all three routing protocols in the 192.168.0.0 range, and all three routing protocols should redistribute into BGP.

Example 4-10   *R1's Routing Table for Route Redistribution*

```
R1# show ip route | exclude subnetted
! Output omitted for brevity
Gateway of last resort is not set


C       10.1.12.0/24 is directly connected, Ethernet0/0
C       10.1.13.0/24 is directly connected, Ethernet0/1
C       10.1.14.0/24 is directly connected, Ethernet0/2
D EX    192.168.2.2 [170/409600] via 10.1.12.2, 00:06:30, Ethernet0/0
O E2    192.168.3.3 [110/20] via 10.1.13.3, 00:02:12, Ethernet0/1
i L2    192.168.4.4 [115/10] via 10.1.14.4, 00:06:30, Ethernet0/2
```

```
R1# show run | section router bgp
router bgp 100
!
 address-family ipv4
  redistribute isis level-2
  redistribute eigrp 1
  redistribute ospf 1
 exit-address-family
```

Example 4-11 displays R1's BGP table after redistribution. The 192.168.3.3/32 prefix learned from OSPF and the 10.1.14.0/24 network from the IS-IS routing table did not get redistributed into BGP. Notice that for the networks that are not directly connected, the BGP next-hop IP address matches the next-hop IP address from the routing protocol, as shown in Example 4-10.

Example 4-11 *R1's BGP Table After Redistribution*

```
R1# show bgp ipv4 unicast | begin Network
     Network          Next Hop          Metric LocPrf Weight Path
 *>  10.1.12.0/24     0.0.0.0                0          32768 ?
 *>  10.1.13.0/24     0.0.0.0                0          32768 ?
 *>  192.168.2.2/32   10.1.12.2         409600         32768 ?
 *>  192.168.4.4/32   10.1.14.4             10          32768 ?
```

Some of the OSPF and IS-IS routes were not redistributed into BGP for the following reasons:

- **OSPF:** When redistributing OSPF into BGP, the default behavior includes only routes that are internal to OSPF (O or O IA). The redistribution of external OSPF routes requires a conditional match in the redistribution statement and/or an optional redistribution route-map.

- **IS-IS:** IS-IS does not include directly connected subnets for any destination routing protocol. This behavior is overcome by redistributing the connected networks into BGP.

Note If the **internal** keyword is omitted on a conditional match, the internal OSPF routes are not redistributed.

Example 4-12 provides the proper configuration where the conditional match has been added to the OSPF redistribution statement and the connected networks are being redistributed to overcome the IS-IS limitation.

Example 4-12 *Corrected R1's Configuration to Redistribute All Networks into BGP*

```
R1# show run | section router bgp
router bgp 100
 !
 address-family ipv4
  redistribute connected
  redistribute isis level-2
```

```
   redistribute eigrp 1
   redistribute ospf 1 match internal external 1 external 2
 exit-address-familyR1#
```

```
R1# show bgp ipv4 unicast | begin Network
     Network           Next Hop          Metric LocPrf Weight Path
 *>  10.1.12.0/24      0.0.0.0                0           32768 ?
 *>  10.1.13.0/24      0.0.0.0                0           32768 ?
 *>  10.1.14.0/24      0.0.0.0                0           32768 ?
 *>  192.168.2.2/32    10.1.12.2         409600          32768 ?
 *>  192.168.3.3/32    10.1.13.3             20          32768 ?
 *>  192.168.4.4/32    10.1.14.4             10          32768 ?
```

Note   Although not directly related to the advertisement of routes into BGP, issues can arise when redistributing routes from BGP to an IGP protocol. By default, BGP does not redistribute internal routes (routes learned via an IBGP peer) into an IGP protocol (that is, OSPF) as a safety mechanism. The command **bgp redistribute-internal** allows IBGP routes to be redistributed into an IGP routing protocol.

BGP Tables

BGP uses three tables for maintaining a network prefix and the path attributes (PA) associated with each path for a prefix. The BGP tables are as follows:

- **Adj-RIB-in:** Contains the Network Layer Reachability Information (NLRI) (network prefix and prefix-length) and BGP PAs in the original form that they are received from a BGP peer. The Adj-RIB-in table is purged after all route policies are processed to save memory.

- **Loc-RIB:** Contains all the NLRIs that originate locally or that came from the Adj-RIB-in table after passing any inbound route policy processing. Note that BGP PAs in the Loc-RIB might have been modified by the router's inbound route policies for a specific neighbor.

  After NLRIs pass the validity and next-hop reachability check, the BGP best path algorithm selects the best NLRI for a specific prefix. The Loc-RIB table is the table used for presenting routes to the IP routing table and is the BGP table commonly referred to as "The BGP table."

- **Adj-RIB-out:** Contains the NLRIs after outbound route policies have processed. Different outbound route policies could exist between neighbors, so the Adj-RIB-out keeps track of the neighbors and the NLRIs for each neighbor. Outbound route policies could modify PAs for a specific neighbor.

The BGP **network** statements do not enable BGP for a specific interface; instead, they identify a specific network prefix to be installed into the Loc-RIB table. After configuring a BGP network statement, the BGP process searches the global RIB for an exact network prefix match. The network prefix can be a connected network, secondary connected network, or any route from a routing protocol. After verifying that the network statement matches a prefix in the global RIB, the prefix installs into the BGP Loc-RIB table.

Not every route in the Loc-RIB is advertised to a BGP peer. All routes in the Loc-RIB use the following steps for advertisement to BGP peers:

Step 1.   **Verify next-hop reachability.** Confirm that the next-hop address is resolvable in the global RIB. If the next-hop address is not resolvable in the RIB, the NLRI remains but does not process after Step 2. The next-hop address must be resolvable for the BGP best path process to occur in Step 3.

Step 2.   **Set BGP path attributes.** The following BGP PAs are set dependent upon the location of the route in the local RIB:

■ **Connected Network:** The next-hop BGP attribute is set to 0.0.0.0; the origin attribute is set to *i* (IGP); and the BGP weight is set to 32,768.

■ **Static Route or Routing Protocol:** The next-hop BGP attribute is set to the next-hop IP address in the RIB; the origin attribute is set to *i* (IGP); the BGP weight is set to 32,768; and the Multiple Exit Discriminator (MED) is set to the IGP metric.

■ **Redistribution:** The next-hop BGP attribute is set to the next-hop IP address in the RIB; the origin attribute is set to *?* (incomplete); the BGP weight is set to 32,768; and the MED is set to the IGP metric.

Step 3.   **Identify the BGP best path.** In BGP, route advertisements consist of the NLRI and the path attributes (PAs). A BGP route may contain multiple paths to the same destination network. Every path's attributes impact the desirability of the route when a router selects the best path. A BGP router only advertises the best path to the neighboring routers.

Inside the BGP Loc-RIB table, all the routes and their path attributes are maintained with the best path calculated. The best path is then installed in the RIB of the router. In the event the best path is no longer available, the router can use the existing paths to quickly identify a new best path. BGP recalculates the best path for a prefix upon four possible events:

■ BGP next-hop reachability change

■ Failure of an interface connected to an External Border Gateway Protocol (EBGP) peer

■ Redistribution change

■ Reception of new paths for a route

The BGP best path selection algorithm influences how traffic enters or leaves an AS. Changing of BGP PA can influence traffic flow into, out of, and around an AS.

Step 4.   **Process outbound neighbor route policies.** The NLRI is processed through any specific outbound neighbor route policies. After processing, if the route was not denied by the outbound policies, the route is stored in the Adj-RIB-Out table for later reference.

Step 5.   **Advertise the NLRI to BGP peers.** The router advertises the NLRI to BGP peers. If the NLRI's next-hop BGP PA is 0.0.0.0, then the next-hop address is changed to the IP address of the BGP session.

Figure 4-2 illustrates the concept of installing the network prefix from localized BGP network advertisements into the BGP table.

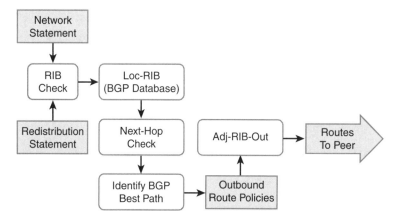

Figure 4-2 *Localized BGP Network Advertisement*

Receiving and Viewing Routes

The complete BGP route advertisement process must take into account routes that are advertised locally and routes that are received from other BGP neighbors. Not every prefix in the Loc-RIB is advertised to a BGP peer or installed into the Global RIB when received from a BGP peer. BGP performs the following route-processing steps:

Step 1.   **Perform a quick validity check.** This is performed on the route to ensure that a routing loop is not occurring. If the router recognizes its autonomous system number (ASN) in the AS-Path or its router-ID (RID) in the Internal Border Gateway Protocol (IBGP) path attributes (Originator/Cluster-ID). If no duplicates are found, the NLRI passes the validity check and moves on to the next stage.

Step 2.   **Store the route in Adj-RIB-In and process inbound route policies.** The NLRI is stored in the Adj-RIB-In table in its original state. The inbound route policy is applied based on the neighbor the route was received.

Step 3.   **Update the Loc-RIB.** The BGP Loc-RIB database is updated with the NLRI after inbound route-policy processing has occurred. The Adj-RIB-in is cleared to save memory.

Step 4.   **Verify next-hop reachability.** Confirm that the next-hop address is resolvable in the global RIB. If the next-hop address is not resolvable in the RIB, the NLRI remains but does not process further.

Step 5.   **Compute the BGP best path.** Multiple NLRIs (paths) can exist for the same network prefix in the Loc-RIB table. BGP only advertises the best path to its neighbors. The router must identify the BGP best path and pass only the best path and its path attributes to Step 6. The BGP Best Path selection process was explained in Chapter 1, "BGP Fundamentals."

Step 6.   **Install the BGP best path into the global RIB and advertise to peers.** Install the prefix into the Global RIB using the next-hop IP address from the BGP Loc-RIB table.

In some occurrences, the route cannot be installed into the Global RIB (a static route that has a lower administrative distance than BGP), which results in a RIB failure. A RIB failure does not prevent the advertisement of the NLRI to other BGP neighbors. The exact reason for a RIB failure is seen with the command **show ip bgp rib-failure**.

Step 7.   **Process outbound neighbor route policies.** The NLRI is processed through any specific outbound neighbor route policies. After processing, if the route was not denied by the outbound policies, the route is stored in the Adj-RIB-Out table for later reference.

Step 8.   **Advertise the NLRI to BGP peers.** Advertise the NLRI to BGP peers. If the NLRI's next-hop BGP PA is 0.0.0.0, then the next-hop address is changed to the IP address of the BGP session.

Figure 4-3 shows the complete BGP route-processing logic. It now includes the receipt of a route from a BGP peer and the BGP best path algorithm.

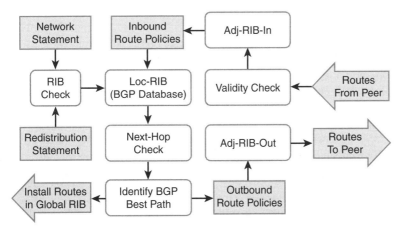

Figure 4-3   *Complete BGP Network Advertisement*

Troubleshooting Missing BGP Routes

The complete process for receiving routes from BGP peers and the advertisement to other peers has been fully explained. This knowledge provides a systematic process for trouble-shooting the advertisement of routes between peers. Reasons that route advertisement fails between BGP peers are as follows:

- Next-Hop Check Failure

- Bad Network Design

- Validity Check Failure

- BGP Communities

- Mandatory EBGP Route Policy for IOS XR

- Route filtering

Most of these issues can be found by using the following:

- **BGP Loc-RIB:** Just because a route is missing from the Global RIB, it does not mean the route did not make it into the router's BGP table. Examine the BGP Loc-RIB to see if the prefix exists in the BGP table. It is possible that the route installed in the BGP table but did not install into the RIB. Viewing the local BGP table is the first step in troubleshooting any missing route.

  The BGP Loc-RIB is viewed with the command **show bgp** *afi safi [prefix/prefix-length]*. Examining a specific prefix provides the reason a route was not installed into the RIB.

- **BGP Adj-RIB-in:** The BGP Loc-RIB table contains only valid routes that passed the router's inbound route policies. Examining the BGP Adj-RIB-in table verifies whether the peer received the NLRI. If the peer received it, the local inbound route policy prevents the route from installing into the Loc-RIB table. Inbound Soft Configuration is required to view the BGP Adj-RIB-in table, because the table is purged by default after all inbound route-policy processing has occurred.

- **BGP Adj-RIB-out:** Viewing the BGP Adj-RIB-out table on the advertising router verifies that the route was advertised and provides a list of the BGP PAs that were included with the route. In the event that the route is not present in the advertising router's BGP Adj-RIB-out table, check the advertising router's BGP Loc-RIB table to verify the prefix exists there. Assuming the prefix is in the Loc-RIB table, but not in the Adj-RIB-out table, then the outbound route policies are preventing the advertise-ment of the route. Contents of the BGP Adj-RIB-out are viewed with the command **show bgp** *afi safi* **neighbor** *ip-address [prefix/prefix-length]* **advertised-routes**.

- **Viewing BGP Neighbor Sessions:** The information contained in the BGP neighbor session varies from platform to platform, but still provides a lot of useful informa-tion, such as the number of prefixes advertised, session and address-family options, the route maps/route filters/route policy applied specifically for that neighbor. The BGP neighbor session is displayed with the command **show bgp** *afi safi* **neighbor** *ip-address*.

■ **NX-OS Event History:** NX-OS contains a form of logging that runs in the background and is not as intensive as running a debug. Event history provides visibility as to what happened and when it happened. Knowing when certain events happen can correlate to other events that occur in the network at the same time.

Increase the size of the event history with the command **event-history detail size large** under the BGP process on NX-OS devices. Event history is displayed with the command **show bgp event-history detail.**

■ **Debug Commands:** Debug commands provide the most amount of information about BGP. On IOS nodes, BGP update debugs are enabled with the command **debug bgp** *afi safi* **updates** [**in** | **out**] [**detail**]. On IOS XR nodes, BGP update debugs are enabled with the command **debug bgp update**[**afi** *afi safi*] [**in** | **out**]. On NX-OS nodes, BGP update debugs are enabled with the command **debug bgp updates** [**in** | **out**].

Figure 4-4 provides a sample topology that connects five routers in a point-to-point line. R1 is in AS100, R5 is in AS300, and R2, R3, and R4 are in AS200. This topology is used to demonstrate how to troubleshoot the various reasons a route could be missing from the routing table. All BGP sessions are established by using the directly connected interfaces (that is, peer-link IP address) and do not contain multi-hop sessions. The following routes are being advertised:

■ R1 is advertising the 10.0.0.0/8 aggregate prefix.

■ R1 is advertising the 10.1.1.0/24 prefix.

■ R2 is advertising the 10.2.2.0/24 prefix.

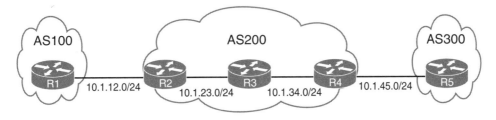

Figure 4-4 *BGP Troubleshooting Sample Topology*

Next-Hop Check Failures

R3 is missing the 10.0.0.0/8 network and the 10.1.1.0/24 network from the RIB, as shown in Example 4-13. Only the 10.2.2.0/24 network that is advertised by R2 is present.

Example 4-13 *Examination of R3's Global RIB*

```
R3# show ip route
! Output omitted for brevity
Gateway of last resort is not set
      10.0.0.0/8 is variably subnetted, 5 subnets, 2 masks
C        10.1.23.0/24 is directly connected, Ethernet0/2
C        10.1.34.0/24 is directly connected, Ethernet0/1
B        10.2.2.0/24 [200/0] via 10.1.23.2, 00:07:08
      192.168.3.0/32 is subnetted, 1 subnets
C        192.168.3.3 is directly connected, Loopback0
```

Both of the missing routes are advertised from R1. The first step is to check the R3's Loc-RIB BGP table, as shown in Example 4-14. The 10.0.0.0/8 network and the 10.1.1.0/24 network are present, but notice that both entries are missing the best path marker >.

Example 4-14 *Examination of R3's BGP Loc-RIB Table*

```
R3# show bgp ipv4 unicast
! Output omitted for brevity
BGP table version is 2, local router ID is 192.168.3.3
Status codes: s suppressed, d damped, h history, * valid, > best, i - internal,
              r RIB-failure, S Stale, m multipath, b backup-path, f RT-Filter,
              x best-external, a additional-path, c RIB-compressed,
Origin codes: i - IGP, e - EGP, ? - incomplete
RPKI validation codes: V valid, I invalid, N Not found

     Network          Next Hop          Metric LocPrf Weight Path
 * i 10.0.0.0         10.1.12.1              0    100      0 100 i
 * i 10.1.1.0/24      10.1.12.1              0    100      0 100 i
 *>i 10.2.2.0/24      10.1.23.2              0    100      0 ?
```

Displaying an explicit network prefix with the command **show bgp** *afi safi prefix/ prefix-length*, as shown in Example 4-15, provides some clarity for why the NLRI was not selected as a best path.

Example 4-15 *Examination of NLRI Without Best Path*

```
R3# show bgp ipv4 unicast 10.1.1.0/24
BGP routing table entry for 10.1.1.0/24, version 0
Paths: (1 available, no best path)
  Not advertised to any peer
  Refresh Epoch 1
  100, (received & used)
    10.1.12.1 (inaccessible) from 10.1.23.2 (192.168.2.2)
      Origin IGP, metric 0, localpref 100, valid, internal
      rx pathid: 0, tx pathid: 0
```

In the output, the next-hop 10.1.12.1 is inaccessible. Let's verify that the next-hop exists on the router with the command **show ip route** *next-hop-IP-address*, as shown in Example 4-16.

Example 4-16   *Examination of RIB for Next-Hop IP Address*

```
R3# show ip route 10.1.12.1
% Subnet not in table
```

The next-hop IP address is not available in the RIB. There are multiple solutions to this issue that include the following:

- R2 advertises the peering link (10.1.12.0/24) into BGP. R3 is adjacent to R2 and receives the route with a next-hop of 10.1.23.2, which is in R3's RIB as a directly connected route. The 10.1.12.1 next-hop IP address would then be resolvable through a recursive lookup.

- Establish an IGP routing protocol within AS200 (R2, R3, and R4) and advertise the peering link (R1–R2) in OSPF, but make the peering link interface passive in OSPF.

- On R2 configure the **next-hop-self** feature in the address-family for the BGP peering with R3. All EBGP routes (that is, routes learned from R1) would then use R2 as their next-hop for any routes learned from R2.

Note   Assuming that R3 is a route-reflector, the same scenario impacts R4 as well. As R4 learns the route from R3, the same fixes must be implemented on R3 because R4 will not know how to reach the 10.1.23.0/24 network. Most places use an IGP for advertising the internal networks among themselves. Then they choose to use either the **next-hop-self** feature or advertise the peering link's network (passive interface) into the IGP.

OSPF was enabled on R2, R3, and R4, and the **next-hop-self** feature was enabled on R2 toward R3 to address routes advertised from AS100 and on R4 toward R3 in case AS300 advertised any routes. Example 4-17 verifies that the BGP best path computation has completed and that 10.0.0.0/8 and 10.1.1.0/24 networks have been inserted into the RIB by BGP.

Example 4-17   *R3's BGP Table and Global RIB*

```
R3# show bgp ipv4 unicast
! Output omitted for brevity
     Network          Next Hop            Metric LocPrf Weight Path
*>i 10.0.0.0          10.1.23.2                0    100      0 100 i
*>i 10.1.1.0/24       10.1.23.2                0    100      0 100 i
*>i 10.2.2.0/24       10.1.23.2                0    100      0 ?

R3# show ip route
! Output omitted for brevity
```

```
Gateway of last resort is not set
      10.0.0.0/8 is variably subnetted, 7 subnets, 3 masks
B        10.0.0.0/8 [200/0] via 10.1.23.2, 00:02:33
B        10.1.1.0/24 [200/0] via 10.1.23.2, 00:02:33
C        10.1.23.0/24 is directly connected, Ethernet0/2
C        10.1.34.0/24 is directly connected, Ethernet0/1
B        10.2.2.0/24 [200/0] via 10.1.23.2, 00:15:17
      192.168.3.0/32 is subnetted, 1 subnets
C        192.168.3.3 is directly connected, Loopback0
```

Bad Network Design

Networks that use BGP are more sensitive to design flaws than networks that use only IGP routing protocols. An improperly design BGP network can result in an inconsistent routing policy, missing routes, or worse. In Figure 4-4, R4 is missing all the routes 10.0.0.0/8, 10.1.1.0/24, and 10.2.2.0/24. OSPF has been deployed between R2, R3, and R4. R2 and R4 are now using next-hop-self for their BGP session toward R3.

The first step of troubleshooting is to check the Loc-RIB table, as shown in Example 4-18. This verifies that the NLRIs were never installed into the Loc-RIB table on R4. The next step is to see if any routes were received and exist in R4's Adj-RIB-in BGP table. (This assumes that soft-configuration inbound was configured for R4's session with R3.)

Example 4-18 *Display of R4's Adj-RIB-in Table*

```
R4# show bgp ipv4 unicast
R4#
```

```
R4# show bgp ipv4 unicast neighbors 10.1.34.3 received-routes

Total number of prefixes 0
R4#
```

After examining R4's BGP neighbor session details with R3, as shown in Example 4-19, no prefixes were received or denied from R3. Notice that the BGP session is an IBGP session.

Example 4-19 *Display of R3's BGP Neighborship with R4*

```
R4# show bgp ipv4 unicast neighbors 10.1.34.3
! Output omitted for brevity
BGP neighbor is 10.1.34.3,  remote AS 200, internal link
  BGP version 4, remote router ID 192.168.3.3
  BGP state = Established, up for 4d07h
```

```
For address family: IPv4 Unicast
  Session: 10.1.34.3
  BGP table version 1, neighbor version 1/0
  Inbound soft reconfiguration allowed
  NEXT_HOP is always this router for EBGP paths
  Slow-peer split-update-group dynamic is disabled
                                  Sent        Rcvd
  Prefix activity:                ----        ----
    Prefixes Current:               0           0
    Prefixes Total:                 0           0
    Implicit Withdraw:              0           0
    Explicit Withdraw:              0           0
    Used as bestpath:             n/a           0
    Used as multipath:            n/a           0

                              Outbound    Inbound
  Local Policy Denied Prefixes: --------    -------
    Total:                          0           0
```

The next step is to see whether the routes are present on R3's Loc-RIB table and that a best path has been selected. In Example 4-20, all three prefixes have a best path and were learned internally from the IBGP peer R2.

Example 4-20 *Display of R3's BGP Table*

```
R3# show bgp ipv4 unicast
BGP table version is 12, local router ID is 192.168.3.3
Status codes: s suppressed, d damped, h history, * valid, > best, i - internal,
              r RIB-failure, S Stale, m multipath, b backup-path, f RT-Filter,
              x best-external, a additional-path, c RIB-compressed,
Origin codes: i - IGP, e - EGP, ? - incomplete
RPKI validation codes: V valid, I invalid, N Not found
     Network          Next Hop            Metric LocPrf Weight Path
 *>i 10.0.0.0         10.1.23.2                0    100      0 100 i
 *>i 10.1.1.0/24      10.1.23.2                0    100      0 100 i
 *>i 10.2.2.0/24      10.1.23.2                0    100      0 ?
```

After reviewing the topology, R2, R3, and R4 are all in the same BGP autonomous system. An IBGP learned route is not advertised to another IBGP peer as part of a loop prevention mechanism. Full route advertisement for IBGP learned routes occurs if a full mesh of IBGP sessions between R2, R3, and R4 is formed, or if R3 becomes a route-reflector to R2 and R4.

After configuring R3 as a route-reflector to R2 and R4, the routes are seen on R4, as shown in Example 4-21.

Example 4-21   *Display of R4's BGP Table After R3 Becomes a Route-Reflector*

```
R4# show bgp ipv4 unicast
! Output omitted for brevity
     Network          Next Hop          Metric LocPrf Weight Path
 *>i 10.0.0.0         10.1.23.2              0    100      0 100 i
 *>i 10.1.1.0/24      10.1.23.2              0    100      0 100 i
 *>i 10.2.2.0/24      10.1.23.2              0    100      0 ?
```

Validity Check Failure

BGP performs a validity check upon receipt of prefixes. Specifically, BGP is looking for indicators of a loop, such as

- Identifying the router's ASN in the AS-Path

- Identifying the router's RID in as the Route-Originator ID

- Identifying the router's RID as the Cluster ID

AS-Path

The AS-Path (BGP attribute AS_PATH) is used as a loop prevention mechanism. The AS-Path is not prepended as a NLRI is advertised to other IBGP peers. Some common scenarios for a router to identify its ASN in an NLRI's AS-Path are as follows:

- **AS-Prepending:** Industry standards dictate that the AS being prepended should be owned by your organization. However, some organizations may prepend a route with an ASN that they do not own. This is done for malicious purposes or unintentionally.

- **Route Aggregation:** Default behavior for route aggregation is to not include any BGP attributes of the smaller routes that are being aggregated, which adds the atomic aggregate BGP attribute. The loss of path visibility could result in route feedback when an organization advertises an aggregate route that includes a smaller network that is advertised from your network. If the **as-set** keyword is used with the aggregation command, all the BGP attributes of the routes being summarized are included. This includes the AS-Path.

After configuring the **as-set** keyword on R1, R1 includes the PAs from the smaller aggregate routes. For example, the 10.2.2.0/24 network that is being learned on R1 from AS200 would be aggregated into the 10.0.0.0/8 aggregate with the AS200 as part of the AS-Path.

Detecting a router's ASN in a route that is received from a peer can be accomplished by the following:

- Viewing the BGP session on IOS routers.

- Viewing the network routes that are advertised to the router.

- Enabling debugging for BGP updates, which will indicate the AS-Path loop.

In Example 4-22, R2 displays the BGP neighbor session details for R1. After examining the IPv4 address-family, routes were denied for an AS_PATH loop. It is important to note that the count of routes is a cumulative count of route advertisements throughout the life of that BGP session.

Example 4-22 *Verification of Denied Routes from AS-Path Check*

```
R2# show bgp ipv4 unicast neighbors 10.1.12.1
! Output omitted for brevity
BGP neighbor is 10.1.12.1,  remote AS 100, external link
  BGP version 4, remote router ID 192.168.1.1
For address family: IPv4 Unicast
!
                                    Outbound    Inbound
  Local Policy Denied Prefixes:     --------    -------
    AS_PATH loop:                        n/a          1
    Bestpath from this peer:               3        n/a
    Total:                                 3          1
```

NX-OS and IOS XR devices require additional techniques (explained later in the chapter) to identify the loss of routes. The second method is to list the routes on R1 that were advertised to R2 that include the ASN of R2 (200). As shown in Example 4-23, the 10.0.0.0/8 route includes the AS-Path of 200.

Example 4-23 *Verification of Route Advertisement of Route with AS-Path Loop*

```
R1# show bgp ipv4 unicast neighbors 10.1.12.2 advertised-routes | i Network|200
     Network          Next Hop          Metric LocPrf Weight Path
  *>  10.0.0.0         0.0.0.0                  100  32768 200 ?
```

The third method is to enable BGP debugging on R2 and initiate an inbound BGP soft-refresh as shown in Example 4-24.

Example 4-24 *Identification of AS-Path Loops with BGP Debugs*

```
R2# debug bgp ipv4 unicast updates in detail
R2# clear bgp ipv4 unicast 10.1.12.1
! Output omitted for brevity
4d07h: BGP(0): 10.1.12.1 rcv UPDATE w/ attr: nexthop 10.1.12.1, origin ?, metric 0,
   aggregated by 100 192.168.1.1, originator 0.0.0.0, merged path 100 200, AS_PATH ,
   community , extended community , SSA attribute
4d07h: BGPSSA ssacount is 0
4d07h: BGP(0): 10.1.12.1 rcv UPDATE about 10.0.0.0/8 -- DENIED due to: AS-PATH
   contains our own AS;
4d07h: BGP(0): no valid path for 10.0.0.0/8
4d07h: BGP: topo global:IPv4 Unicast:base Remove_fwdroute for 10.0.0.0/8
```

```
4d07h: BGP(0): (base) 10.1.23.3 send unreachable (format) 10.0.0.0/8
4d07h: BGP(0): 10.1.23.3 rcv UPDATE about 10.0.0.0/8 - withdrawn
```

```
RP/0/0/CPU0:XR2# debug bgp update in
RP/0/0/CPU0:XR2# clear bgp ipv4 unicast 10.1.12.1
! Output omitted for brevity
RP/0/0/CPU0: 04:55:57: bgp[1053]: (ip4u): UPDATE from 10.1.12.1, prefix 10.0.0.0/8
  (path ID: none) DENIED due to:
RP/0/0/CPU0: 04:55:57: bgp[1053]: (ip4u): as-path contains our own AS, or 0;
RP/0/0/CPU0: 04:55:57: bgp[1053]: : Received UPDATE from 10.1.12.1 (length incl.
  header = 60)
RP/0/0/CPU0: 04:55:57: bgp[1053]: Receive message dump for 10.1.12.1:
```

```
NXOS2# debug bgp updates in
NXOS2# clear bgp ipv4 unicast 10.1.12.1
! Output omitted for brevity
04:47:06 bgp: 200 [8463]) UPD: Received UPDATE message from 10.1.12.3
04:47:06 bgp: 200 [8463] UPD: 10.1.12.3 parsed UPDATE message from peer, len 66 ,
  withdraw len 0, attr len 43, nlri len 0
04:47:06 bgp: 200 [8463] UPD: Attr code 1, length 1, Origin: IGP
04:47:06 bgp: 200 [8463] UPD: Attr code 7, length 8, Aggregator: (100,10.1.1.1)
04:47:06 bgp: 200 [8463] UPD: Peer 10.1.12.3 nexthop length in MP reach: 4
04:47:06 bgp: 200 [8463] UPD: Recvd NEXTHOP 10.1.12.3
04:47:06 bgp: 200 [8463] UPD: Attr code 14, length 11, Mp-reach
04:47:06 bgp: 200 [8463] UPD: 10.1.12.3 Received attr code 2, length 10, AS-Path:
  <100 200 >
04:47:06 bgp: 200 [8463] UPD: Received AS-Path attr with own ASN from 10.1.12.3
04:47:06 bgp: 200 [8463] UPD: [IPv4 Unicast] Received prefix 10.0.0.0/8 from peer
  10.1.12.3, origin 0, next hop 10.1.12.3, localpref 0, med 0
04:47:06 bgp: 200 [8463] UPD: [IPv4 Unicast] Dropping prefix 10.0.0.0/8 from peer
  10.1.12.3, due to attribute error
```

The 10.0.0.0/8 network prefix is accepted by asking the administrator of R1 to remove the **as-set** keyword on their route aggregation, or to selectively add BGP PAs from the network prefixes that are advertised only from their AS.

Another alternative is to add the **allow-as** functionality for that neighbor. This feature disables the ASN check on a neighbor-by-neighbor basis. Enabling the command may resolve the issues for R2, but the problem will still exist for other routers in that BGP AS (that is, R3 and R4).

Note   IOS XR and NX-OS devices perform an ASN loop check as part of the advertisement process to avoid sending updates to peers that would fail the AS-Path loop check. This is done to reduce bandwidth and CPU processing on the downstream router.

This feature can be disabled globally on IOS XR routers with the BGP address-family configuration command **as-path-loopcheck out disable** and can be disabled per neighbor on NX-OS routers with the command **disable-peer-as-check**.

Originator-ID/Cluster-ID

Another potential reason a NLRI fails the validity check is if the Originator-ID or Cluster-ID matches the receiving router's RID. The Originator-ID is populated by a route-reflector (RR) with the advertising router's RID, and the Cluster-ID is populated by the RR. The default Cluster-ID setting is the RR's RID, unless it is specifically set, which is done for certain design scenarios. Checking the Originator-ID or Cluster-ID is considered a loop prevention mechanism.

Assume that in the sample topology, that R4's BGP RID was configured to 192.168.2.2, which unknowingly matches R2's BGP RID. The steps for troubleshooting are similar as before. On IOS routers, viewing the BGP neighbor session displays that some routes were dropped because of an Originator loop, as shown in Example 4-25.

Example 4-25 *Detection of Originator Loop with IOS BGP Neighbor Session*

```
R4# show bgp ipv4 unicast neighbors 10.1.34.3
! Output omitted for brevity
BGP neighbor is 10.1.34.3,  remote AS 200, internal link
  BGP version 4, remote router ID 192.168.3.3
  BGP state = Established, up for 00:01:24
  For address family: IPv4 Unicast
!

                                Outbound    Inbound
  Local Policy Denied Prefixes:    --------    -------
    ORIGINATOR loop:               n/a          3
   Total:                          0            3
  Number of NLRIs in the update sent: max
```

Just as before, IOS XR and NX-OS devices require BGP debugs to discover the reason a BGP update is denied. Example 4-26 displays the BGP updates for all three platforms with the appropriate message that indicates the Originator ID conflict.

Example 4-26 *Detection of Originator Loop via BGP Update Debugs*

```
R4# debug ip bgp updates in
BGP updates debugging is on (inbound) for address family: IPv4 Unicast
R4# clear bgp ipv4 unicast 10.1.34.3
! Output omitted for brevity
1w0d: BGP(0): 10.1.34.3 rcv UPDATE about 10.1.1.0/24 -- DENIED due to: ORIGINATOR
  is us;
1w0d: BGP: 10.1.34.3 Local router is the Originator; Discard update
1w0d: BGP(0): 10.1.34.3 rcv UPDATE w/ attr: nexthop 10.1.23.2, origin ?, localpref
  100, metric 0, originator 192.168.2.2, clusterlist 192.168.3.3, merged path ,
  AS_PATH , community , extended community , SSA attribute
1w0d: BGPSSA ssacount is 0
```

```
RP/0/0/CPU0:XR4# debug bgp update in
RP/0/0/CPU0:XR4# clear bgp 10.1.34.3
! Output omitted for brevity
RP/0/0/CPU0: 03:05:48: bgp[1053]: : UPDATE from 10.1.34.3 contains nh 10.1.23.2/32,
  gw_afi 0, flags 0x0, nlri_afi 0
RP/0/0/CPU0: 03:05:48: bgp[1053]: : NH-Validate-Create: addr=10.1.23.2/32, len=4,
  nlriafi=0, nbr=10.1.34.3, gwafi=0, gwlen=4, gwaddrlen=32::: nhout=0x10beae60,
  validity=1, attrwdrflags=0x00000000
RP/0/0/CPU0: 03:05:48: bgp[1053]: : UPDATE from 10.1.34.3 discarded: local router is
  the ORIGINATOR (192.168.2.2)
RP/0/0/CPU0: 03:05:48: bgp[1053]: : --bgp4_rcv_attributes--: END: nbr=10.1.34.3::
  msg=0x10037ddc/75, updlen=56, attrbl=0x10037df3/48, ipv4reachlen=4,
  msginpath=0x3df0bd0, asloopcheck=1, attrwdrfl=0x00002000:: samecluster=0, local_
  as_prepended=0, attr_wdr_flags 0x00002000, myascount=0:: rcvdata=0x10037e23/0,
  errptr=0x10037e1c/7
RP/0/0/CPU0: 03:05:48: bgp[1053]: (ip4u): Received unreachables from 10.1.34.3:
  attrcode=0, attrwdrflags=0x00002000
RP/0/0/CPU0: 03:05:48: bgp[1053]: (ip4u): UPDATE from 10.1.34.3 with attributes:
RP/0/0/CPU0: 03:05:48: bgp[1053]: (ip4u): nexthop 10.1.23.2/32, origin i, localpref
  100, metric 0, originator 192.168.2.2, clusterlist 3.3.168.192, path 100
RP/0/0/CPU0: 03:05:48: bgp[1053]: (ip4u): UPDATE from 10.1.34.3, prefix 10.1.1.0/24
  (path ID: none) DENIED due to:
RP/0/0/CPU0: 03:05:48: bgp[1053]: (ip4u):  originator is us;
```

```
NXOS4# debug bgp updates in
NXOS4# clear bgp ipv4 unicast 10.1.34.3
! Output omitted for brevity
04:55:38 bgp: 200 [8431]  UPD: Received UPDATE message from 10.1.34.3
04:55:38 bgp: 200 [8431]  UPD: 10.1.34.3 parsed UPDATE message from peer, len 68 ,
  withdraw len 0, attr len 45, nlri len 0
04:55:38 bgp: 200 [8431]  UPD: Attr code 1, length 1, Origin: IGP
04:55:38 bgp: 200 [8431]  UPD: Attr code 5, length 4, Local-pref: 100
04:55:38 bgp: 200 [8431]  UPD: Originator is us, dropping update from 10.1.34.3
04:55:38 bgp: 200 [8431]  UPD: Attr code 9, length 4, Originator: 192.168.2.2
04:55:38 bgp: 200 [8431]  UPD: Attr code 10, length 4, Cluster-list
04:55:38 bgp: 200 [8431]  UPD: Peer 10.1.34.3 nexthop length in MP reach: 4
04:55:38 bgp: 200 [8431]  UPD: Recvd NEXTHOP 10.1.23.2
04:55:38 bgp: 200 [8431]  UPD: Attr code 14, length 13, Mp-reach
04:55:38 bgp: 200 [8431]  UPD: [IPv4 Unicast] Received prefix 10.2.2.0/24 from peer
  10.1.34.3, origin 0, next hop 10.1.23.2, localpref 100, med 0
04:55:38 bgp: 200 [8431]  UPD: [IPv4 Unicast] Dropping prefix 10.2.2.0/24 from peer
  10.1.34.3, due to attribute error
```

Now that the issue has been isolated to the Originator-ID, it is time to identify the root cause. Example 4-27 demonstrates R3's BGP session with R2 and R4. Notice that R2 and R4 have the same RID of 192.168.2.2. By changing the RID on R4 to something unique, R4 can then process the routes.

Example 4-27 *Detection of Duplicate RID on R3*

```
R3# show bgp ipv4 unicast neighbors | i neighbor|ID
BGP neighbor is 10.1.23.2,  remote AS 200, internal link
  BGP version 4, remote router ID 192.168.2.2
  Do log neighbor state changes (via global configuration)
  BGP table version 35, neighbor version 35/0
BGP neighbor is 10.1.34.4,  remote AS 200, internal link
  BGP version 4, remote router ID 192.168.2.2
  Do log neighbor state changes (via global configuration)
  BGP table version 35, neighbor version 35/0
```

BGP Communities

BGP communities provide additional capability for tagging routes and are considered either *well-known* or *private* BGP communities. Private BGP communities are used for conditional matching for a router's route policy, which could influence routes during inbound or outbound route-policy processing. There are three well-known communities that affect only outbound route advertisement: No-Advertise, No-Export, and Local-As. Routes that contain these communities can be displayed with the command **show bgp** *afi safi* [**community** {**local-AS** | **no-advertise** | **no-export**}] on IOS, IOS XR, and NX-OS devices.

This section focuses on explaining the behavior of each of these communities and how to identify them. Conditionally matching private communities for filtering is demonstrated later in Example 4-66.

BGP Communities: No-Advertise

The No_Advertise community (0xFFFFFF02 or 4,294,967,042) specifies that routes with this community should not be advertised to any BGP peer. The No-Advertise BGP community can be advertised from an upstream BGP peer or locally with an inbound BGP policy. In either method, the No-Advertise community is set in the BGP Loc-RIB table that affects outbound route advertisement.

Figure 4-5 demonstrates that R1 is advertising the 10.1.1.0/24 network to R2, and R3 does not have the 10.1.1.0/24 network in its BGP table.

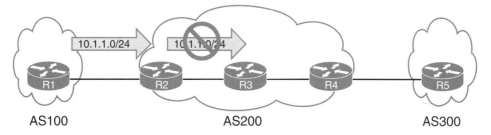

Figure 4-5 *BGP No-Advertise Community Topology*

R3 cannot see the route in its Adj-RIB-in table because the route was never advertised to it from R2. Example 4-28 displays the NLRI information for the 10.1.1.0/24 network prefix. Notice that the NLRI was "not advertised to any peer" and has the BGP community No-Advertise set.

Example 4-28 *BGP Attributes for No-Advertise Routes*

```
R2# show bgp 10.1.1.0/24
! Output omitted for brevity
BGP routing table entry for 10.1.1.0/24, version 18
Paths: (1 available, best #1, table default, not advertised to any peer)
  Not advertised to any peer
  Refresh Epoch 1
  100, (received & used)
    10.1.12.1 from 10.1.12.1 (192.168.1.1)
      Origin IGP, metric 0, localpref 100, valid, external, best
      Community: no-advertise
      rx pathid: 0, tx pathid: 0x0
```

BGP routes that are set with the No-Advertise community are quickly seen with the command **show bgp** *afi safi* **community no-advertise** on IOS, IOS XR, and NX-OS, as shown in Example 4-29.

Example 4-29 *Display of Prefixes with No-Advertise Community*

```
R2# show bgp ipv4 unicast community no-advertise
! Output omitted for brevity
     Network          Next Hop            Metric LocPrf Weight Path
 *>  10.1.1.0/24      10.1.12.1                0         0 100 i
```

On IOS routers, the count of prefixes that were denied due to any well-known BGP communities are seen by viewing the BGP neighbor sessions, as shown in Example 4-30.

Example 4-30 *Denied Prefix Advertisement Displayed on BGP Neighbor Session*

```
R2# show bgp ipv4 unicast neighbors 10.1.23.3
! Output omitted for brevity
For address family: IPv4 Unicast
!
                                 Outbound    Inbound
  Local Policy Denied Prefixes:   --------    -------
    Well-known Community:               1        n/a
    Total:                             1         0
```

BGP Communities: No-Export

The No_Export community (0xFFFFFF01 or 4,294,967,041) specifies that when a route is received with this community, the route is not advertised to any EBGP peer. If the router receiving the No-Export route is a confederation member, the route can be advertised to other sub-ASs in the confederation.

Figure 4-6 demonstrates that R1 is advertising the 10.1.1.0/24 network to R2, which advertises to R3, and then on to R4. R4 does not advertise the prefix on to R5, so R5 does not have the 10.1.1.0/24 network in its BGP table.

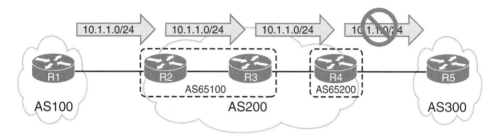

Figure 4-6 *BGP No-Export Community Topology*

Example 4-31 displays the BGP path attributes (PA) for the 10.1.1.10/24 network. Notice that the R3 and R4 displays "not advertised to EBGP peer." R3 is able to advertise the network to R4 (via Update Group #3) because they are members of the same confederation, even though their ASNs are different.

Example 4-31 *BGP Attributes for No-Export Routes*

```
R4# show bgp ipv4 unicast 10.1.1.0/24
! Output omitted for brevity
BGP routing table entry for 10.1.1.0/24, version 4
Paths: (1 available, best #1, table default, not advertised to EBGP peer)
  Not advertised to any peer
  Refresh Epoch 1
  (65100) 100, (received & used)
    10.1.23.2 (metric 20) from 10.1.34.3 (192.168.3.3)
      Origin IGP, metric 0, localpref 100, valid, confed-external, best
      Community: no-export
      rx pathid: 0, tx pathid: 0x0
```

```
R3# show bgp ipv4 unicast 10.1.1.0/24
BGP routing table entry for 10.1.1.0/24, version 6
Paths: (1 available, best #1, table default, not advertised to EBGP peer)
  Advertised to update-groups:
    3
```

```
  Refresh Epoch 1
  100, (Received from a RR-client), (received & used)
    10.1.23.2 from 10.1.23.2 (192.168.2.2)
      Origin IGP, metric 0, localpref 100, valid, confed-internal, best
      Community: no-export
      rx pathid: 0, tx pathid: 0x0

R3# show bgp ipv4 unicast update-group 3 | b member
  Has 1 member:
    10.1.34.4
```

Example 4-32 verifies that R2 and R4 both detect the No-Export community in the 10.1.1.0/24 network. This is the reason that R4 did not advertise the route to R5.

Example 4-32 *Viewing of BGP Routes with No-Export Community*

```
R4# show bgp ipv4 unicast community no-export | b Network
    Network          Next Hop          Metric LocPrf Weight Path
  *> 10.1.1.0/24     10.1.23.2              0    100      0 (65100) 100 i
```

```
R2# show bgp ipv4 unicast community no-export | b Network
    Network          Next Hop          Metric LocPrf Weight Path
  *> 10.1.1.0/24     10.1.12.1              0              0 100 i
```

Example 4-33 displays R4's neighbor session to R5. Notice that only the Well-known Community is shown for denied prefixes but does not differentiate between the No-Advertise and No-Export community.

Example 4-33 *Verification of Blocked Routes Due to Well-Known Communities*

```
R4# show bgp ipv4 unicast neighbors 10.1.45.5
! Output omitted for brevity
For address family: IPv4 Unicast
!
                                    Outbound    Inbound
  Local Policy Denied Prefixes:    --------    -------
    Well-known Community:                 1        n/a
    Total:                               1          0
```

BGP Communities: Local-AS (No Export SubConfed)

The No_Export_SubConfed community (0xFFFFFF03 or 4,294,967,043) known as the Local-AS community specifies that a route with this community is not advertised outside of the local AS. If the router receiving a route with the Local-AS community is a confederation member, the route can be advertised only within the sub-AS (Member-AS) and is not advertised between Member-ASs.

Figure 4-7 demonstrates that R1 is advertising the 10.1.1.0/24 network to R2, which advertises to R3. R3 does not advertise the prefix on to R4, so R4 does not have the 10.1.1.0/24 network in its BGP table.

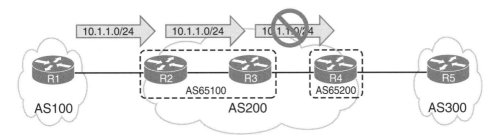

Figure 4-7   *BGP Local-AS Community Topology*

Example 4-34 confirms that the routes are set for "not advertised outside local AS" and that the routes are not advertised to any peer.

Example 4-34   *BGP Attributes for Local-AS Routes*

```
R3# show bgp ipv4 unicast 10.1.1.0/24
BGP routing table entry for 10.1.1.0/24, version 8
Paths: (1 available, best #1, table default, not advertised outside local AS)
  Not advertised to any peer
  Refresh Epoch 1
  100, (Received from a RR-client), (received & used)
    10.1.23.2 from 10.1.23.2 (192.168.2.2)
      Origin IGP, metric 0, localpref 100, valid, confed-internal, best
      Community: local-AS
      rx pathid: 0, tx pathid: 0x0
```

Example 4-35 displays how all of a router's prefixes with the Local-AS community are shown with the command **show bgp** *afi safi* **community local-as**.

Example 4-35   *Viewing of BGP Routes with Local-AS Community*

```
R3# show bgp ipv4 unicast community local-AS | b Network
     Network          Next Hop            Metric LocPrf Weight Path
 *>i 10.1.1.0/24      10.1.23.2                0    100      0 100 i


R2# show bgp ipv4 unicast community local-AS | b Network
     Network          Next Hop            Metric LocPrf Weight Path
 *>  10.1.1.0/24      10.1.12.1                0             0 100 i
```

Mandatory EBGP Route Policy for IOS XR

IOS XR does not advertise or receive prefixes from an EBGP peer by default. This is considered a safety mechanism to ensure that an organization is aware of the routes that it is receiving and advertising externally.

In Example 4-36, XR1 is configuring the initial BGP session for XR2 (10.1.12.2). Upon committing the configuration change, XR1 provides a warning message that explains that no prefixes will be accepted or advertised to the XR2.

Example 4-36   *No EBGP Route Policy for XR2*

```
RP/0/0/CPU0:XR1# config t
RP/0/0/CPU0:XR1(config)# router bgp 100
RP/0/0/CPU0:XR1(config-bgp)# neighbor 10.1.12.2
RP/0/0/CPU0:XR1(config-bgp-nbr)# remote-as 200
RP/0/0/CPU0:XR1(config-bgp-nbr)# address-family ipv4 unicast
RP/0/0/CPU0:XR1(config-bgp-nbr-af)# commit
RP/0/0/CPU0: 16:28:05.171 : config[67824]: %MGBL-CONFIG-6-DB_COMMIT : Configuration
  committed by user 'ChuckRobbins'. Use 'show configuration commit
    changes 1000000056' to view the changes.
RP/0/0/CPU0: 16:28:06.171 : bgp[1047]: %ROUTING-BGP-5-ADJCHANGE :
    neighbor 10.1.12.2 Up (VRF: default) (AS: 200)
RP/0/0/CPU0: 16:28:06.171 : bgp[1047]: %ROUTING-BGP-6-NBR_NOPOLICY :
    No inbound IPv4 Unicast policy is configured for EBGP neighbor 10.1.12.2
    No IPv4 Unicast prefixes will be accepted from the neighbor until inbound
    policy is configured.
RP/0/0/CPU0: 16:28:06.171 : bgp[1047]: %ROUTING-BGP-6-NBR_NOPOLICY :
    No outbound IPv4 Unicast policy is configured for EBGP neighbor 10.1.12..2
    No IPv4 Unicast prefixes will be sent to the neighbor until outbound policy
    is configured.
```

When you examine the BGP neighbor summary in Example 4-37, the ! is displayed next to the BGP State/Prefix Received column. In both the BGP neighbor summary and explicit BGP neighbor session output, a warning message is reiterated that routes will not be exchanged between XR1 and XR2.

Example 4-37   *IOS XR Summary with Indicator of Missing Route Policy*

```
RP/0/0/CPU0:XR1# show bgp ipv4 unicast summary
! Output omitted for brevity
BGP router identifier 192.168.1.1, local AS number 100


Some configured EBGP neighbors (under default or non-default vrfs)
do not have both inbound and outbound policies configured for IPv4 Unicast
address family. These neighbors will default to sending and/or
receiving no routes and are marked with '!' in the output below.
```

```
Use the 'show bgp neighbor <nbr_address>' command for details.

Neighbor        Spk    AS MsgRcvd MsgSent    TblVer  InQ OutQ  Up/Down  St/PfxRcd
10.1.12.2         0  1100       6       3         6    0    0 00:00:40         0!

RP/0/0/CPU0:XR1# show bgp ipv4 unicast neighbor 100.64.1.1
! Output omitted for brevity
BGP neighbor is 10.1.12.2

 For Address Family: IPv4 Unicast
  BGP neighbor version 6
  Update group: 0.3 Filter-group: 0.2  No Refresh request being processed
  EBGP neighbor with no inbound or outbound policy; defaults to 'drop'
  Route refresh request: received 0, sent 0
  0 accepted prefixes, 0 are bestpaths
```

Example 4-38 displays a simple PASS-ALL route policy that is associated to the EBGP peering between XR1 and XR2. This allows XR1 to advertise and receive all prefixes between the two routers.

Example 4-38 *Addition of Simple Route Policy for EBGP Neighbors*

```
XR1
route-policy PASS-ALL
  pass
end-policy

router bgp 100
  neighbor 10.1.12.2
    remote-as 200
    address-family ipv4 unicast
      route-policy PASS-ALL in
      route-policy PASS-ALL out
```

Filtering of Prefixes by Route Policy

The last component for finding missing BGP routes is through the examination of the BGP routing policies. As stated before, BGP route policies are applied before routes are inserted into the Loc-RIB table and as prefixes leave the Loc-RIB before they are advertised to a BGP peer.

IOS and NX-OS devices provide three methods of filtering routes inbound or outbound for a specific BGP peer. Each method could be used individually or simultaneously with other methods. The three methods are as follows:

- **Prefix-list:** A list of prefix matching specifications that permit or deny network prefixes in a top-down fashion similar to an ACL. An implicit deny is associated for any prefix that is not permitted.

- **AS-Path ACL/Filtering:** A list of regex commands that allows for the permit or deny of a network prefix based on the current AS-Path values. An implicit deny is associated for any prefix that is not permitted.

- **Route-maps:** Route-maps provide a method of conditional matching on a variety of prefix attributes and taking a variety of actions. Actions could be a simple permit or deny or could include the modification of BGP path attributes. An implicit deny is associated for any prefix that is not permitted.

IOS XR does not use any of the methods used by IOS and NX-OS routers. IOS XR uses routing policy language (RPL), which uses the fundamental concepts of route-maps and provides a more powerful method of filtering and manipulation of routes. RPL provides clarity by using a common conditional if-then-else programming structure, removing sequence numbers, and the complexities of using concurrent filtering methods.

Conditional Matching

Prefix-lists, AS-Path filtering, route-maps, and route-policy language typically use some form of conditional matching so that only certain BGP prefixes are blocked or accepted. BGP prefixes can be conditionally matched by a variety of path attributes, but the following sections explain the most common techniques for conditionally matching a BGP prefix.

Access Control Lists (ACL)

Originally, ACLs were intended to provide filtering of packets flowing into or out of a network interface, similar to the functionality of a basic firewall. Today, ACLs provide a method of identifying networks within a route-map that are then used in routing protocols for filtering or manipulating.

ACLs are composed of access control entries (ACEs), which are entries in the ACL that identify the action to be taken (**permit** or **deny**) and the relevant packet classification. Packet classification starts at the top (lowest sequence) and proceeds down (higher sequence) until a matching pattern is identified. When a match is found, the appropriate action (**permit** or **deny**) is taken and processing stops. At the end of every ACL is an implicit **deny** ACE, which denies all packets that did not match an earlier ACE in the ACL.

Extended ACLs react differently when matching BGP routes than when matching IGP routes. The source fields match against the network portion of the route, and the destination fields match against the network mask, as shown in Figure 4-8. Extended ACLs were originally the only match criteria used by IOS with BGP before the introduction of prefix-lists.

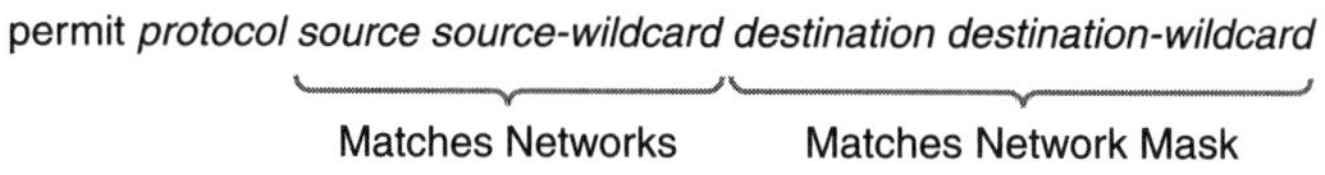

permit *protocol source source-wildcard destination destination-wildcard*

Matches Networks   Matches Network Mask

Figure 4-8 *BGP Extended ACL Matches*

Table 4-1 demonstrates the concept of the wildcard for the network and subnet mask.

Table 4-1 *Extended ACL for BGP Route Selection*

Extended ACL	Matches These Networks
permit ip 10.0.0.0 0.0.0.0 255.255.0.0 0.0.0.0	Permits only the 10.0.0.0/16 network
permit ip 10.0.0.0 0.0.255.0 255.255.255.0 0.0.0.0	Permits any 10.0.x.0 network with a /24 prefix length
permit ip 172.16.0.0 0.0.255.255 255.255.255.0 0.0.0.255	Permits any 172.16.x.x network with a /24 – /32 prefix length
permit ip 172.16.0.0 0.0.255.255 255.255.255.128 0.0.0.127	Permits any 172.16.x.x network with a /25 – /32 prefix length

Prefix Matching

Prefix lists (IOS and NX-OS) and prefix sets (IOS XR) provide another method of identifying networks in a routing protocol. They identify a specific IP address, network, or network range and allow for the selection of multiple networks with a variety of prefix lengths (subnet masks) by using a *prefix match specification*. This technique is preferred over the ACLs network selection method because it is easier to understand.

The structure for a prefix match specification contains two parts: high-order bit pattern and high-order bit count, which determines the high order bits in the bit pattern that are to be matched. Some documentation refers to the high-order bit pattern as the address or network, and the high-order bit count as length or mask length.

In Figure 4-9, the prefix match specification has the high-order bit pattern of 192.168.0.0 and a high-order bit count of 16. The high-order bit pattern has been converted to binary to demonstrate where the high-order bit count lays. Because there is not any additional matching length parameters included, the high-order bit count is an exact match.

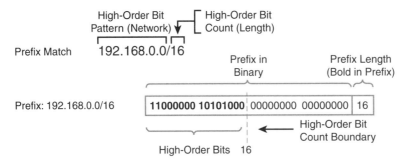

Figure 4-9 *Basic Prefix Match Pattern*

The prefix match specification logic might look identical to the functionality of an access-list. The true power and flexibility comes by using matching length parameters to identify multiple networks with specific prefix lengths with one statement. The matching length parameter options are as follows:

- **le** (less than or equal to <=)

- **ge** (greater than or equal to >=) or both.

Figure 4-10 demonstrates the prefix match specification with a high-order bit pattern of 10.168.0.0, high-order bit count of 13, and the matching length of the prefix must be greater than or equal to 24.

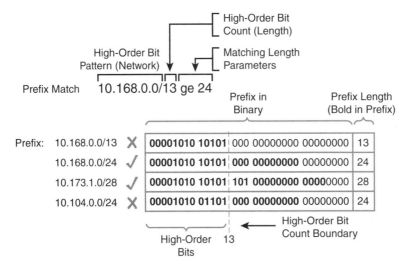

Figure 4-10 *Prefix Match Pattern with Matching Length Parameters*

The 10.168.0.0/13 prefix does not qualify because the prefix length is less than the minimum of 24 bits, whereas the 10.168.0.0/24 prefix does meet the matching length parameter. The 10.173.1.0/28 prefix qualifies because the first 13 bits match the high-order bit pattern, and the prefix length is within the matching length parameter. The 10.104.0.0/24 prefix does not qualify because the high-order bit-pattern does not match within the high-order bit count.

Figure 4-11 demonstrates a prefix match specification with a high-order bit pattern of 10.0.0.0, a high-order bit count of 8, and the matching length must be between 22 and 26.

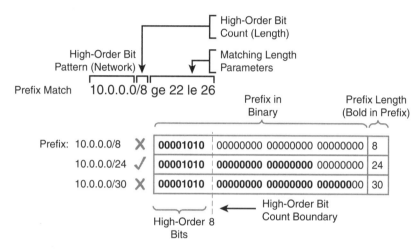

Figure 4-11   *Prefix Match with Ineligible Matched Prefixes*

The 10.0.0.0/8 prefix does not match because the prefix length is too short. The 10.0.0.0/24 qualifies because the bit pattern matches and the prefix length is between 22 and 26. The 10.0.0.0/30 prefix does not match because the bit pattern is too long. Any prefix that starts with 10 in the first octet and has a prefix length between 22 and 26 matches.

Note   Matching to a specific prefix length that is higher than the high-order bit count requires that the *ge-value* and *le-value* match.

Regular Expressions (Regex)

There may be times when conditionally matching off of network prefixes may be too complicated, and identifying all routes from a specific organization is preferred. In this manner, path selection can be made off of the BGP AS-Path.

To parse through the large amount of available ASNs (4,294,967,295), regular expressions (regex) are used. Regular expressions are based on query modifiers to select the appropriate content. The BGP table is parsed with regex using the command **show bgp** *afi safi* **regexp** *regex-pattern*. NX-OS devices require the regex-pattern to be placed within a pair of double quotes "".

Table 4-2 provides a brief list and description of the common regex query modifiers.

Table 4-2   *Regex Query Modifiers*

Modifier	Description
_ (Underscore)	Matches a space
^ (Caret)	Indicates the start of the string
$ (Dollar Sign)	Indicates the end of the string
[] (Brackets)	Matches a single character or nesting within a range
- (Hyphen)	Indicates a range of numbers in brackets
[^] (Caret in Brackets)	Excludes the characters listed in brackets
() (Parentheses)	Used for nesting of search patterns
| (Pipe)	Provides *or* functionality to the query
. (Period)	Matches a single character, including a space
* (Asterisk)	Matches zero or more characters or patterns
+ (Plus Sign)	One or more instances of the character or pattern
? (Question Mark)	Matches one or no instances of the character or pattern

Note   The.^$*+()[]? characters are special control characters that cannot be used without using the backslash (\) escape character. For example, to match on the * in the output you would use the * syntax.

The following section provides a variety of common tasks to help demonstrate each of the regex modifiers. Example 4-39 provides a reference BGP table for displaying scenarios of each regex query modifier for querying the prefixes as they are illustrated in Figure 4-12.

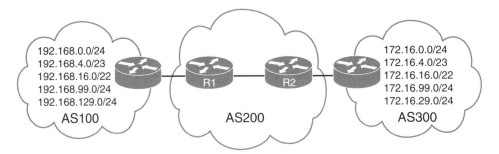

Figure 4-12   *BGP Regex Reference Topology*

Example 4-39 *BGP Table for Regex Queries*

```
R2# show bgp ipv4 unicast
! Output omitted for brevity
     Network          Next Hop       Metric LocPrf Weight Path
*>  172.16.0.0/24    192.168.200.3       0              0 300 80 90 21003 2100 i
*>  172.16.4.0/23    192.168.200.3       0              0 300 1080 1090 1100 1110 i
*>  172.16.16.0/22   192.168.200.3       0              0 300 11234 21234 31234 i
*>  172.16.99.0/24   192.168.200.3       0              0 300 40 i
*>  172.16.129.0/24  192.168.200.3       0              0 300 10010 300 30010 30050 i
*>i192.168.0.0       10.12.1.1           0    100       0 100 80 90 21003 2100 i
*>i192.168.4.0/23    10.12.1.1           0    100       0 100 1080 1090 1100 1110 i
*>i192.168.16.0/22   10.12.1.1           0    100       0 100 11234 21234 31234 i
*>i192.168.99.0      10.12.1.1           0    100       0 100 40 i
*>i192.168.129.0     10.12.1.1           0    100       0 100 10010 300 30010 30050 i
```

Note The AS-Path for the prefix 172.16.129.0/24 has the AS 300 twice nonconsecutively for a specific purpose. This is not seen in real life because it would indicate a routing loop.

UnderScore _

Query Modifier Function: Matches a space.

Scenario: Display only ASs that passed through AS 100. The first assumption is that the syntax **show bgp ipv4 unicast regex 100**, as shown in Example 4-40, would be ideal. The regex query includes the following unwanted ASNs 1100, 2100, 21003, and 10010.

Example 4-40 *BGP Regex Query for AS 100*

```
R2# show bgp ipv4 unicast regex 100
! Output omitted for brevity
     Network          Next Hop       Metric LocPrf Weight Path
*>  172.16.0.0/24    192.168.200.3       0              0 300 80 90 21003 455 i
*>  172.16.4.0/23    192.168.200.3       0              0 300 878 1190 1100 1010 i
*>  172.16.129.0/24  192.168.200.3       0              0 300 10010 300 1010 40 50 i
*>i192.168.0.0       10.12.1.1           0    100       0 100 80 90 21003 455 i
*>i192.168.4.0/23    10.12.1.1           0    100       0 100 878 1190 1100 1010 i
*>i192.168.16.0/22   10.12.1.1           0    100       0 100 779 21234 45 i
*>i192.168.99.0      10.12.1.1           0    100       0 100 145 40 i
*>i192.168.129.0     10.12.1.1           0    100       0 100 10010 300 1010 40 50 i
```

Example 4-41 uses the underscore ( ) to imply a space left of the 100 to remove the unwanted ASNs. The regex query includes the following unwanted ASNs 10010.

Example 4-41   *BGP Regex Query for AS _100*

```
R2# show bgp ipv4 unicast regexp _100
! Output omitted for brevity
     Network          Next Hop     Metric LocPrf Weight Path
*>  172.16.129.0/24  192.168.200.3      0                 0 300 10010 300 1010 40 50 i
*>i192.168.0.0       10.12.1.1          0    100          0 100 80 90 21003 455 i
*>i192.168.4.0/23    10.12.1.1          0    100          0 100 878 1190 1100 1010 i
*>i192.168.16.0/22   10.12.1.1          0    100          0 100 779 21234 45 i
*>i192.168.99.0      10.12.1.1          0    100          0 100 145 40 i
*>i192.168.129.0     10.12.1.1          0    100          0 100 10010 300 1010 40 50 i
```

Example 4-42 provides the final query by using the underscore (_) before and after the ASN (100) to finalize the query for routes that pass through AS 100.

Example 4-42   *BGP Regex Query for AS _100_*

```
R2# show bgp ipv4 unicast regexp _100_
! Output omitted for brevity
     Network          Next Hop     Metric LocPrf Weight Path
*>i192.168.0.0       10.12.1.1          0    100          0 100 80 90 21003 455 i
*>i192.168.4.0/23    10.12.1.1          0    100          0 100 878 1190 1100 1010 i
*>i192.168.16.0/22   10.12.1.1          0    100          0 100 779 21234 45 i
*>i192.168.99.0      10.12.1.1          0    100          0 100 145 40 i
*>i192.168.129.0     10.12.1.1          0    100          0 100 10010 300 1010 40 50 i
```

Caret ^

Query Modifier Function: Indicates the start of the string.

Scenario: Display only routes that were advertised from AS 300. At first glance, the command **show bgp ipv4 unicast regex _300_** might be acceptable for use, but in Example 4-43, the route 192.168.129.0/24 is also included.

Example 4-43   *BGP Regex Query for AS 300*

```
R2# show bgp ipv4 unicast regexp _300_
! Output omitted for brevity
     Network          Next Hop     Metric LocPrf Weight Path
*>  172.16.0.0/24    192.168.200.3      0                 0 300 80 90 21003 455 i
*>  172.16.4.0/23    192.168.200.3      0                 0 300 878 1190 1100 1010 i
*>  172.16.16.0/22   192.168.200.3      0                 0 300 779 21234 45 i
*>  172.16.99.0/24   192.168.200.3      0                 0 300 145 40 i
*>  172.16.129.0/24  192.168.200.3      0                 0 300 10010 300 1010 40 50 i
*>i192.168.129.0     10.12.1.1          0    100          0 100 10010 300 1010 40 50 i
```

Because AS 300 is directly connected, it is more efficient to ensure that AS 300 was the first AS listed. Example 4-44 shows the caret (^) in the regex pattern.

Example 4-44 *BGP Regex Query with Caret*

```
R2# show bgp ipv4 unicast regexp ^300_
! Output omitted for brevity
      Network        Next Hop      Metric LocPrf Weight Path
 *> 172.16.0.0/24    192.168.200.3      0           0 300 80 90 21003 455 i
 *> 172.16.4.0/23    192.168.200.3      0           0 300 878 1190 1100 1010 i
 *> 172.16.16.0/22   192.168.200.3      0           0 300 779 21234 45 i
 *> 172.16.99.0/24   192.168.200.3      0           0 300 145 40 i
 *> 172.16.129.0/24  192.168.200.3      0           0 300 10010 300 1010 40 50 i
```

Dollar Sign $

Query Modifier Function: Indicates the end of the string.

Scenario: Display only routes that originated in AS 40. In Example 4-45, the regex pattern _40_ was used. Unfortunately, this also includes routes that originated in AS 50.

Example 4-45 *BGP Regex Query with AS 40*

```
R2# show bgp ipv4 unicast regexp _40_
! Output omitted for brevity
      Network        Next Hop      Metric LocPrf Weight Path
 *> 172.16.99.0/24   192.168.200.3      0           0 300 145 40 i
 *> 172.16.129.0/24  192.168.200.3      0           0 300 10010 300 1010 40 50 i
 *>i192.168.99.0     10.12.1.1          0    100    0 100 145 40 i
 *>i192.168.129.0    10.12.1.1          0    100    0 100 10010 300 1010 40 50 i
```

Example 4-46 provides the solution using the $ for the regex pattern _40$.

Example 4-46 *BGP Regex Query with Dollar Sign*

```
R2# show bgp ipv4 unicast regexp _40$
! Output omitted for brevity
      Network        Next Hop      Metric LocPrf Weight Path
 *> 172.16.99.0/24   192.168.200.3      0           0 300 145 40 i
 *>i192.168.99.0     10.12.1.1          0    100    0 100 145 40 i
```

Brackets [ ]

Query Modifier Function: Matches a single character or nesting within a range.

Scenario: Display only routes with an AS that contains 11 or 14 in it. The regex filter 1[14] can be used as shown in Example 4-47.

Example 4-47 *BGP Regex Query with Brackets*

```
R2# show bgp ipv4 unicast regexp 1[14]
! Output omitted for brevity
     Network          Next Hop      Metric LocPrf Weight Path
*>  172.16.4.0/23    192.168.200.3      0              0 300 878 1190 1100 1010 i
*>  172.16.99.0/24   192.168.200.3      0              0 300 145 40 i
*>i192.168.4.0/23    10.12.1.1          0      100     0 100 878 1190 1100 1010 i
*>i192.168.99.0      10.12.1.1          0      100     0 100 145 40 i
```

Hyphen -

Query Modifier Function: Indicates a range of numbers in brackets.

Scenario: Display only routes with the last two digits of the AS of 40, 50, 60, 70, or 80. To achieve this scenario, the regex query [4-8]0_ can be used, as shown in Example 4-48.

Example 4-48 *BGP Regex Query with Hyphen*

```
R2# show bgp ipv4 unicast regexp [4-8]0_
! Output omitted for brevity
     Network          Next Hop      Metric LocPrf Weight Path
*>  172.16.0.0/24    192.168.200.3      0              0 300 80 90 21003 455 i
*>  172.16.99.0/24   192.168.200.3      0              0 300 145 40 i
*>  172.16.129.0/24  192.168.200.3      0              0 300 10010 300 1010 40 50 i
*>i192.168.0.0       10.12.1.1          0      100     0 100 80 90 21003 455 i
*>i192.168.99.0      10.12.1.1          0      100     0 100 145 40 i
*>i192.168.129.0     10.12.1.1          0      100     0 100 10010 300 1010 40 50 i
```

Caret in Brackets [^]

Query Modifier Function: Excludes the character listed in brackets.

Scenario: Display only routes where the second AS from AS 100 or AS 300 does not start with 3, 4, 5, 6, 7, or 8. The first component of the regex query restricts the AS to the AS 100 or 300 with the regex query ^[13]00_, and the second component filters out ASs starting with 3-8 with the regex filter _[^3-8]. The complete regex query is ^[13]00_[^3-8], as shown in Example 4-49.

Example 4-49 *BGP Regex Query with Caret in Brackets*

```
R2# show bgp ipv4 unicast regexp ^[13]00_[^3-8]
! Output omitted for brevity
     Network          Next Hop      Metric LocPrf Weight Path
*>  172.16.99.0/24   192.168.200.3      0              0 300 145 40 i
*>  172.16.129.0/24  192.168.200.3      0              0 300 10010 300 1010 40 50 i
*>i192.168.99.0      10.12.1.1          0      100     0 100 145 40 i
*>i192.168.129.0     10.12.1.1          0      100     0 100 10010 300 1010 40 50 i
```

Parentheses ( ) and Pipe |

Query Modifier Function: Nesting of search patterns and provides *or* functionality.

Scenario: Display only routes where the AS_PATH ends with AS 40 or 45 in it. The regex filter _4(5|0)$ is show in Example 4-50.

Example 4-50 *BGP Regex Query with Parentheses*

```
R2# show bgp ipv4 unicast regexp _4(5|0)$
! Output omitted for brevity
      Network          Next Hop      Metric LocPrf Weight Path
 *>  172.16.16.0/22   192.168.200.3     0              0 300 779 21234 45 i
 *>  172.16.99.0/24   192.168.200.3     0              0 300 145 40 i
 *>i192.168.16.0/22   10.12.1.1         0     100      0 100 779 21234 45 i
 *>i192.168.99.0      10.12.1.1         0     100      0 100 145 40 i
```

Period .

Query Modifier Function: Matches a single character, including a space.

Scenario: Display only routes with an originating AS of 1-99. In Example 4-51, the regex query _..$ requires a space, and then any character after that (including other spaces).

Example 4-51 *BGP Regex Query with Period*

```
R2# show bgp ipv4 unicast regexp _..$
! Output omitted for brevity
      Network          Next Hop      Metric LocPrf Weight Path
 *>  172.16.16.0/22   192.168.200.3     0              0 300 779 21234 45 i
 *>  172.16.99.0/24   192.168.200.3     0              0 300 145 40 i
 *>  172.16.129.0/24  192.168.200.3     0              0 300 10010 300 1010 40 50 i
 *>i192.168.16.0/22   10.12.1.1         0     100      0 100 779 21234 45 i
 *>i192.168.99.0      10.12.1.1         0     100      0 100 145 40 i
 *>i192.168.129.0     10.12.1.1         0     100      0 100 10010 300 1010 40 50 i
```

Plus Sign +

Query Modifier Function: One or more instances of the character or pattern.

Scenario: Display only routes where they contain at least one 10 in the AS path, but the pattern 100 should not be used in matching. When building this regex expression, the first portion is building the matching pattern of (10)+, and then add the restriction portion of the query of [^(100)]. The combined regex pattern is (10)+[^(100)], as shown in Example 4-52.

Example 4-52 *BGP Regex Query with Plus Sign*

```
R2# show bgp ipv4 unicast regexp (10)+[^(100)]
! Output omitted for brevity
     Network          Next Hop       Metric LocPrf Weight Path
*> 172.16.4.0/23    192.168.200.3        0             0 300 1080 1090 1100 1110 i
*> 172.16.129.0/24  192.168.200.3        0             0 300 10010 300 30010 30050 i
*>i192.168.4.0/23   10.12.1.1            0    100      0 100 1080 1090 1100 1110 i
*>i192.168.129.0    10.12.1.1            0    100      0 100 10010 300 30010 30050 i
```

Question Mark ?

Query Modifier Function: Matches one or no instances of the character or pattern.

Scenario: Display only routes from the neighboring AS or its directly connected AS (that is, restrict to two ASs away). This query is more complicated and requires you to define an initial query for identifying the AS, which is [0-9]+. The second component includes the space and an optional second AS. The ? limits the AS match to one or two ASs, as shown in Example 4-53.

Note The CTRL+V escape sequence must be used before entering the ?.

Example 4-53 *BGP Regex Query with Dollar Sign*

```
R1# show bgp ipv4 unicast regexp ^[0-9]+ ([0-9]+)?$
! Output omitted for brevity
     Network          Next Hop       Metric LocPrf Weight Path
*> 172.16.99.0/24   192.168.200.3        0             0 300 40 i
*>i192.168.99.0     10.12.1.1            0    100      0 100 40 i
```

Asterisk *

Query Modifier Function: Matches zero or more characters or patterns.

Scenario: Display all routes from any AS. This may seem like a useless task but may be a valid requirement when using AS-Path access lists, which are explained later in this chapter. Example 4-54 shows the regex query.

Example 4-54 *BGP Regex Query with Asterisk*

```
R1# show bgp ipv4 unicast regexp .*
! Output omitted for brevity
     Network          Next Hop      Metric LocPrf Weight Path
*> 172.16.0.0/24    192.168.200.3       0            0 300 80 90 21003 2100 i
*> 172.16.4.0/23    192.168.200.3       0            0 300 1080 1090 1100 1110 i
```

```
*>  172.16.16.0/22    192.168.200.3    0              0 300 11234 21234 31234 i
*>  172.16.99.0/24    192.168.200.3    0              0 300 40 i
*>  172.16.129.0/24   192.168.200.3    0              0 300 10010 300 30010 30050 i
*>i192.168.0.0        10.12.1.1        0      100      0 100 80 90 21003 2100 i
*>i192.168.4.0/23     10.12.1.1        0      100      0 100 1080 1090 1100 1110 i
*>i192.168.16.0/22    10.12.1.1        0      100      0 100 11234 21234 31234 i
*>i192.168.99.0       10.12.1.1        0      100      0 100 40 i
*>i192.168.129.0      10.12.1.1        0      100      0 100 10010 300 30010 30050 i
```

Looking Glass and Route Servers

Hands-on experience is helpful when learning technologies such as regex. There are public devices called *Looking Glass* or *Route Servers* that allow users to log in and view BGP tables. Most of these devices are Cisco routers, but there are other vendors as well. These servers allow network engineers to see if they are advertising their routes to the Internet, as they had intended, and provide a great method to try out regular expressions on the Internet BGP table. A quick search on the Internet provides website listings of looking glass and route servers.

Note   The authors suggest http://www.bgp4.net or http://www.traceroute.org.

Conditionally Matching BGP Communities

Conditionally matching BGP communities allows for selection of routes based upon the BGP communities within the route's path attributes so that selective processing can occur in IOS route-map or IOS XR route policies. Conditionally matching on IOS and NX-OS devices requires the creation of a community list. A community list shares a similar structure to an ACL, can be standard or expanded, and can be referenced via number or name. Standard community lists are numbered 1-99 and match either well-known communities or a private community number (as-number:16-bit-number). Expanded community lists are numbered 100-500 and use regex patterns.

Troubleshooting BGP Router Policies

Now that all the conditional matching techniques have been explained, this section illustrates how to troubleshoot missing network prefixes due to BGP router policies. It is important to note that although this is the last section in the chapter, it does not mean that these steps could not be used earlier in the troubleshooting process.

This following sections revisit Figure 4-4, which has five routers in a point-to-point line. R1 is in AS100, R5 is in AS300, and R2, R3, and R4 are in AS200. Example 4-55 displays the BGP table on R4 from Figure 4-4. Network prefixes are missing on R5, and the following sections walk through some of the troubleshooting techniques.

Example 4-55 *Reference BGP Table*

```
R4# show bgp ipv4 unicast | b Network
     Network          Next Hop          Metric LocPrf Weight Path
 *>i 10.1.1.1/32      10.1.23.2              0   100      0 100 ?
 *>i 10.1.12.0/24     10.1.23.2              0   100      0 100 500 ?
 *>i 10.2.2.0/24      10.1.23.2              0   100      0 i
 *>i 100.64.1.0/24    10.1.23.2              0   100      0 100 600 ?
 *>i 100.64.11.11/32  10.1.23.2              0   100      0 100 ?
 *>i 172.16.1.0/24    10.1.23.2              0   100      0 100 ?
 *>i 172.16.2.0/24    10.1.23.2              0   100      0 100 ?
 *>i 172.20.1.1/32    10.1.23.2              0   100      0 100 700 ?
```

IOS and NX-OS Prefix-Lists

R5 is missing the 172.20.1.1/32 network prefix. As stated earlier, the BGP tables can be used to identify where the prefix is being advertised from. The route could be coming from the original advertising router or another router along the path as a starting point for troubleshooting. Example 4-55 displays that the route is present in R4's BGP Loc-RIB table. This means that the problem is either in the advertisement from R4 or the inbound processing on R5. The first step is to examine the BGP Adj-RIB-in table on R5.

Example 4-56 displays the missing prefix on the router, which infers that the problem is related to an inbound route-policy problem on R5. If the route is not present, it infers an outbound route-policy problem on R4.

Example 4-56 *Verification of Route Presence in the BGP Adj-RIB-in*

```
R5# show bgp ipv4 unicast neighbors 10.1.45.4 received-routes
BGP table version is 53, local router ID is 192.168.5.5
Status codes: s suppressed, d damped, h history, * valid, > best, i - internal,
              r RIB-failure, S Stale, m multipath, b backup-path, f RT-Filter,
              x best-external, a additional-path, c RIB-compressed,
Origin codes: i - IGP, e - EGP, ? - incomplete
RPKI validation codes: V valid, I invalid, N Not found


     Network          Next Hop          Metric LocPrf Weight Path
 *>  10.1.1.1/32      10.1.45.4                              0 200 100 ?
 *>  10.1.12.0/24     10.1.45.4                              0 200 100 500 ?
 *>  10.2.2.0/24      10.1.45.4                              0 200 i
 *>  100.64.1.0/24    10.1.45.4                              0 200 100 600 ?
 *>  100.64.11.11/32  10.1.45.4                              0 200 100 ?
 *>  172.16.1.0/24    10.1.45.4                              0 200 100 ?
 *>  172.16.2.0/24    10.1.45.4                              0 200 100 ?
 *   172.20.1.1/32    10.1.45.4                              0 200 100 700 ?

Total number of prefixes 8
```

Next, examine the BGP neighbor session to look at the filtering techniques that are applied to the BGP session. Example 4-57 demonstrates that only an inbound prefix-list named PREFIX was configured for inbound filtering on R5. Notice that only the IOS router displays that one prefix was blocked inbound by a prefix-list, whereas if it was a NX-OS device (NXOS5), a count of blocked prefixes is not provided.

Example 4-57 *Identification of Prefix-List for a Specific Neighbor*

```
R5# show bgp ipv4 unicast neighbors 10.1.45.4
! Output omitted for brevity
For address family: IPv4 Unicast
  Inbound soft reconfiguration allowed
  Incoming update prefix filter list is PREFIX


                                 Outbound    Inbound
                                 --------    -------
  Local Policy Denied Prefixes:
    prefix-list                         0          1
  Bestpath from this peer:             19        n/a
  Total:                               19          1


NXOS5# show bgp ipv4 unicast neighbor 10.1.45.4
! Output omitted for brevity
  For address family: IPv4 Unicast
  BGP table version 29, neighbor version 29
  7 accepted paths consume 616 bytes of memory
  0 sent paths
  Inbound soft reconfiguration allowed
  Inbound ip prefix-list configured is PREFIX, handle obtained
```

In this scenario, only one route has been identified as missing, whereas there is a potential to have other routes dropped, too. The next step is to either review the IP prefix-list and try to find the flaw, or to turn on BGP debugs or examine the BGP event-history (NX-OS only). Example 4-58 demonstrates the output of both of these tasks and confirms that the 172.20.1.1/32 prefix was rejected by the prefix list.

Example 4-58 *Debug BGP Updates by Prefix-List*

```
R5# debug ip bgp updates in
BGP updates debugging is on (inbound) for address family: IPv4 Unicast
R5# clear bgp ipv4 unicast 10.1.45.4 soft in
! Output omitted for brevity
*05:26:21: BGP(0): Prefix 172.20.1.1/32 rejected by inbound distribute/prefix
  -list.
```

```
*Apr  8 05:26:21.730: BGP(0): update denied
```

```
NXOS5# show bgp event-history detail | i 172.20.1.1
2016 Apr  8 05:20:48.732273 bgp 300 [8449]: [8455]: (default) UPD: [IPv4 Unicast]
  Dropping prefix 172.20.1.1/32 from peer 10.1.45.4, due to prefix policy rejected
```

Note It is important to realize the BGP debugs and event-history do not provide any information on why a route is not permitted (discarded) as it processes between the Loc-RIB and the Adj-RIB-out for a specific table. Debugging outbound BGP updates only displays routes as they are advertised from the Adj-RIB-out to a neighbor. The network prefix has already been discarded before that part of the debug process occurs.

This complicates the troubleshooting process and requires manual calculations to identify differences between the Loc-RIB and Adj-RIB-Out tables for a specific peer.

Because all other options have been exhausted, it is time to examine the IP prefix-list manually to identify the problem, as shown in Example 4-59. The problem is that sequence 15 has an **le** value of 24, which prohibits the /32 subnet mask. Changing the **le 24** to **le 32** allows the prefix to be accepted.

Example 4-59 *Problematic and Corrective Prefix List*

```
! Problematic Prefix List
R5# show ip prefix-list PREFIX
ip prefix-list PREFIX: 3 entries
   seq 5 permit 10.0.0.0/8 le 32
   seq 10 permit 100.64.0.0/12 le 32
   seq 15 permit 172.16.0.0/12 le 24
```

```
! Correct Prefix List
R5# show ip prefix-list PREFIX
ip prefix-list PREFIX: 3 entries
   seq 5 permit 10.0.0.0/8 le 32
   seq 10 permit 100.64.0.0/12 le 32
   seq 15 permit 172.16.0.0/12 le 32
```

IOS and NX-OS AS-Path ACLs

The previous issue was remediated, and now R5 is missing the 10.1.12.0/24 network prefix. The first step is to check the Adj-RIB-in on R5 to see whether the route was received before any inbound route-policy processing has occurred. Just as before, in Example 4-56, the Adj-RIB-in table shows that the 10.1.12.0/24 network is present and infers a problem with the inbound route policy on R5.

The next step is to examine the BGP neighbor session details to identify what could be filtering network prefixes. Example 4-60 displays the neighbor session for R5/NXOS5.

As a secondary confirmation, the Adj-RIB-out can be checked on R4, which looks identical to R5's Adj-RIB-in table, inferring that the problem occurred during outbound route-policy processing.

Example 4-60 *Identification of AS-Path ACLS by Viewing Neighbor Session*

```
R5# show bgp ipv4 unicast neighbors 10.1.45.4
! Output omitted for brevity
 For address family: IPv4 Unicast
  Session: 10.1.45.4
  BGP table version 111, neighbor version 111/0
  Output queue size : 0
  Index 11, Advertise bit 0
  11 update-group member
  Inbound soft reconfiguration allowed
  Inbound path policy configured
  Incoming update AS path filter list is 1

                                  Outbound    Inbound
  Local Policy Denied Prefixes:    --------    -------
    filter-list:                          0          1
    Bestpath from this peer:              7        n/a
    Total:                                7          1
```

```
NXOS5# show bgp ipv4 unicast neighbors 10.1.45.4
! Output omitted for brevity

  For address family: IPv4 Unicast
  BGP table version 41, neighbor version 0
  0 accepted paths consume 0 bytes of memory
  0 sent paths
  Inbound soft reconfiguration allowed
  Inbound as-path-list configured is 1, handle obtained
```

The next step is to either review the AS-filter or enable the BGP debugs/event-history to verify the root cause of the dropped packet. Example 4-61 demonstrates the process.

Example 4-61   *BGP Update Debugs to View AS-Path Loops*

```
R5# debug bgp ipv4 unicast updates in
BGP updates debugging is on (inbound) for address family: IPv4 Unicast
R5# clear bgp ipv4 unicast 10.1.45.4 soft in
! Output omitted for brevity
* 18:59:42.515: BGP(0): process 10.1.12.0/24, next hop 10.1.45.4, metric 0 from
  10.1.45.4
* 18:59:42.515: BGP(0): Prefix 10.1.12.0/24 rejected by inbound filter-list.
* 18:59:42.515: BGP(0): update denied
```

```
NXOS5# debug bgp updates
NXOS5# clear bgp ipv4 unicast 10.1.45.4 soft in
! Output omitted for brevity
19:02:54 bgp: 300 [8449] UPD: [IPv4 Unicast] 10.1.45.4 Inbound as-path-list 1,
  action permit
 19:02:54 bgp: 300 [8449] UPD: [IPv4 Unicast] 10.1.45.4 Inbound as-path-list 1,
  action deny
 19:02:54 bgp: 300 [8449]  UPD: [IPv4 Unicast] Dropping prefix 10.1.12.0/24 from
  peer 10.1.45.4, due to attribute policy rejected
```

Because all other options have been exhausted, it is time to examine the AS-Path ACL to identify the problem, as shown in Example 4-62. After comparing the AS-Path of the router that is being discarded and the AS-Path ACL, the problem should become apparent. The AS-Path ACL accepts prefixes that have originated locally ^$ (IBGP), from AS100 _100$, and that come from AS200, AS600, or AS700 _(2|[6-7])00$. AS500 is missing from the AS-Path ACL, and after adding that the 10.1.12.0/24 prefix is received.

Example 4-62   *Verification of BGP-AS-Path ACLs*

```
R5# show run | inc as-path access-list 1
ip as-path access-list 1 permit ^$
ip as-path access-list 1 permit _100$
ip as-path access-list 1 permit _(2|[6-7])00$
```

```
R5# show bgp ipv4 unicast neighbors 10.1.45.4 received-routes | i 10.1.12.0
 *    10.1.12.0/24    10.1.45.4                    0 200 100 500 ?
```

Note   A common problem is to review the AS-Path ACL by looking at the configuration. Hidden characters that are inserted by copy/paste buffer problems are not shown. Sometimes the AS-Path ACL must be verified with the command **show bgp** *afi safi regex-pattern* as shown earlier in the "Conditional Matching" section. If it passes by manually typing the regex expression, then the AS-Path ACL needs to be rebuilt because it has extra invisible characters (for example, spaces).

Route-Map Processing

Route-maps provide many features to a variety of routing protocols. At the simplest level, route-maps can filter networks similar to an AS-Path filter/prefix-list, but also provide additional capability by adding or modifying a network attribute. Route-maps are referenced to a specific route-advertisement or BGP neighbor and require specifying the direction of the advertisement (inbound/outbound). Route-maps are a critical component of BGP because it allows for a unique routing policy on a neighbor-by-neighbor basis.

Route-maps are composed of four components:

- **Sequence Number:** Dictates the processing order of the route-map.
- **Conditional Matching Criteria:** Identifies prefix characteristics (network, BGP path attribute, next-hop, and so on) for a specific sequence. Conditional matching can match multiple items of the same type (for example, prefix-list PREFIX1 and prefix-list PREFIX2) or of different types (for example, prefix-list PREFIX1 and AS-Path ACL 1).
- **Processing Action:** Permits or denies the prefix.
- **Optional Action:** Allows for manipulations dependent upon how the route-map is referenced on the router. Actions include modification, addition, or removal of route characteristics.

Note   It is important to note that if you are conditional matching on multiple objects of the same type, a Boolean "or" is performed. When matching on multiple objects of a different type, a Boolean "and" is performed.

Route-map uses the command syntax **route-map** *route-map-name* [**permit** | **deny**] [*sequence-number*]. The following rules apply to route-map statements:

- If a processing action is not provided, the default value of **permit** is used.
- If a sequence number is not provided, IOS uses a default sequence of 10 but does not increment upon repeat entries.
- If a matching statement is not included, an implied *all prefixes* is associated to the statement.
- Processing within a route-map stops after all optional actions have processed (if configured) after matching a matching criteria.

Network engineers are often confused and do not know what happens to a network prefix when a route-map contains the following:

- A conditional matching component (ACL/prefix-list) that contains a **deny** statement when the route-map sequence action is a **permit**.
- A conditional matching component (ACL/prefix-list) that contains a **permit** statement when the route-map sequence action is a **deny**.

It is essential to remember that the route-map sequence is looked at first. Then the conditional matching is checked. Only when a network prefix passes the conditional check does the processing action (**permit/deny**) execute. If a network prefix does not meet the conditional check, processing moves on to the next route-map sequence.

Example 4-63 provides a sample route-map to demonstrate the four components of a route-map shown earlier. The conditional matching criteria in this route-map are based on network ranges specified in an ACL. Comments have been added to explain the behavior of the route-map in each sequence.

Example 4-63   *Sample Route-Map*

```
route-map EXAMPLE permit 10
 match ip address ACL-ONE
! Prefixes that match ACL-ONE are permitted. Route-map completes processing upon a
  match

route-map EXAMPLE deny 20
 match ip address ACL-TWO
! Prefixes that match ACL-TWO are denied. Route-map completes processing upon a
  match

route-map EXAMPLE permit 30
 match ip address ACL-THREE
 set metric 20
! Prefixes that match ACL-THREE are permitted and modify the metric. Route-map
  completes
! processing upon a match

route-map EXAMPLE permit 40
! Because a matching criteria was not specified, all other prefixes are permitted
! If this sequence was not configured, all other prefixes would drop because of the
! implicit deny  for all route-maps
```

IOS and NX-OS Route-Maps

Now let's walk through the process of troubleshooting a route-map. R5 is missing the 172.20.1.1/32 network prefix. First check the BGP Adj-RIB-in table to see if the route is present. The same output as in Example 4-56 is present, which means that the route was advertised from R4.

Next check the BGP neighbor session as shown to see what type of route filtering is being performed on the box. After examining the output in Example 4-64, the route-map R4-IN is detected. Notice that IOS nodes indicate that the route-map was the cause for the loss of a prefix.

Example 4-64 *Identification of Route-Map on BGP Session*

```
R5# show bgp ipv4 unicast neighbors 10.1.45.4
! Output omitted for brevity
 For address family: IPv4 Unicast
  Session: 10.1.45.4
  BGP table version 8, neighbor version 8/0
  Output queue size : 0
  Index 15, Advertise bit 0
  15 update-group member
  Inbound soft reconfiguration allowed
  Community attribute sent to this neighbor
  Inbound path policy configured
  Route map for incoming advertisements is R4-IN
  Slow-peer detection is disabled
  Slow-peer split-update-group dynamic is disabled


                                 Outbound    Inbound
  Local Policy Denied Prefixes:   --------    -------
    route-map:                          0          1
    Bestpath from this peer:            7        n/a
    Total:                              7          1
```

```
NXOS5# show bgp ipv4 unicast neighbors 10.1.45.4
! Output omitted for brevity
  For address family: IPv4 Unicast
  BGP table version 97, neighbor version 97
  7 accepted paths consume 616 bytes of memory
  0 sent paths
  Inbound soft reconfiguration allowed
  Community attribute sent to this neighbor
  Inbound route-map configured is R4-IN, handle obtained
  Last End-of-RIB received 00:00:01 after session start
```

Example 4-65 displays the route-map R4-IN. The first sequence performs a conditional match on the prefix-list PREFIX-LIST. Upon examining the prefix-list PREFIX-LIST, the 172.20.1.1/32 route does not match any of the prefix-list sequence numbers. If sequence #10 used a value of **le 32**, the missing prefix conditionally matches the first route-map sequence and is then permitted.

The second route-map statement is trying to conditionally match on what appears to be BGP community 700:700. Recall earlier in the "Conditional Matching" section, BGP communities must be matched through the use of a BGP community list, which is not currently being used in the route-map R4-IN. A community list needs to be created, and the route-map needs to refer to the BGP community list number.

Example 4-65 *Verification of Conditional Matching in a Route Map*

```
R5# show run | s ^route-map
route-map R4-IN permit 10
 match ip address prefix-list PREFIX-LIST
route-map R4-IN permit 20
 match community 700:700
route-map R4-IN deny 30
```

```
R5# show run | i ip prefix-list PREFIX-LIST
ip prefix-list PREFIX-LIST seq 5 permit 100.64.0.0/12 le 32
ip prefix-list PREFIX-LIST seq 10 permit 172.16.0.0/12 le 24
ip prefix-list PREFIX-LIST seq 15 permit 10.0.0.0/8 le 32
```

Example 4-66 provides verification of the creation of the BGP community list and its association to the R4-IN route-map sequence 20 statement. But even after the configuration change, the 172.20.1.1/32 network prefix is still missing.

Example 4-66 *Verification of Route-Map with Conditional Match of BGP Community*

```
R5# show run | s ^route-map|ip community
ip community-list 1 permit 700:700
route-map R4-IN permit 10
 match ip address prefix-list PREFIX-LIST
route-map R4-IN permit 20
 match community 1
route-map R4-IN deny 30
```

```
R5# show bgp ipv4 unicast
     Network          Next Hop          Metric LocPrf Weight Path
 *>  10.1.1.1/32      10.1.45.4                       0 200 100 ?
 *>  10.1.12.0/24     10.1.45.4                       0 200 100 500 ?
 *>  10.2.2.0/24      10.1.45.4                       0 200 i
 *>  100.64.1.0/24    10.1.45.4                       0 200 100 600 ?
 *>  100.64.11.11/32  10.1.45.4                       0 200 100 ?
 *>  172.16.1.0/24    10.1.45.4                       0 200 100 ?
 *>  172.16.2.0/24    10.1.45.4                       0 200 100 ?
```

Let's verify that the 700:700 community has been set properly. The BGP Adj-RIB-in table does not display any of the extended BGP path-attributes like BGP communities. So the next step is to verify that the community exists on the network prefix on R4, as shown in Example 4-67.

Example 4-67 *Confirmation of BGP Community on Network Prefix*

```
R4# show bgp ipv4 unicast 172.20.1.1/32
BGP routing table entry for 172.20.1.1/32, version 10
Paths: (1 available, best #1, table default)
  Advertised to update-groups:
     20
  Refresh Epoch 2
  100 700, (received & used)
    10.1.23.2 (metric 20) from 10.1.34.3 (192.168.3.3)
      Origin incomplete, metric 0, localpref 100, valid, internal, best
      Community: 700:700
      Originator: 192.168.2.2, Cluster list: 192.168.3.3
      rx pathid: 0, tx pathid: 0x0
```

The community has been verified on R4, but appears to be missing on R5 during the inbound route-map processing. What could be the cause of the problem? IOS and NX-OS devices do not advertise BGP communities by default. Check the BGP neighbor session to see if community support was enabled. The BGP neighbor session for R5 from R4's perspective is shown in Example 4-68.

Example 4-68 *Verification of BGP Communities on an IOS and NX-OS Device*

```
R4# show bgp ipv4 unicast neighbors 10.1.45.5
! Output omitted for brevity
For address family: IPv4 Unicast
  Session: 10.1.45.5
  BGP table version 12, neighbor version 12/0
  Output queue size : 0
  Index 20, Advertise bit 1
  20 update-group member
  Inbound soft reconfiguration allowed
  Slow-peer detection is disabled
```

```
NXOS4# show bgp ipv4 unicast neighbor 10.1.45.5
! Output omitted for brevity
  For address family: IPv4 Unicast
  BGP table version 114, neighbor version 114
  0 accepted paths consume 0 bytes of memory
  8 sent paths
  Inbound soft reconfiguration allowed
  Last End-of-RIB received 00:10:13 after session start
```

Upon comparing the output from Example 4-68 (R4's session with R5) with Example 4-64 (R5's session with R4) the community support is not enabled on R4 toward R5. R4 has been advertising the network prefixes without BGP communities.

BGP communities are not enabled by default on IOS and NX-OS devices and must be explicitly configured with the command **neighbor** *ip-address* **send-community** for all IBGP and EBGP peers. After enabling the BGP community on R4 toward R5, the routes have processed properly.

Identifying missing network prefixes with the use of a route-map requires stepping through the route-map in a sequence-by-sequence basis to find the first conditional match. After the intended conditional match is found, the issues involving that match must be identified and then resolved.

IOS XR Route-Policy Language

RPL expands upon the fundamental concepts of route-maps and provides a more powerful method of filtering and manipulating routes. RPL provides a common tool for IOS XR applications that commonly interact with BGP.

Every route sent to a route policy for processing passes through the route-policy structure. To ensure that every route has been examined, a *ticket* is required for the route to pass the default drop at the end of the route policy.

Route policies consist of four primary actions:

- **Pass:** The route is assigned a ticket to pass the default drop. Processing continues through additional RPL statements.

- **Done:** The route is assigned a ticket to pass the default drop. Processing stops for the specific route.

- **Set:** The route is assigned a ticket to pass the default drop. The specific route attribute is modified to the value set, and processing continues.

- **Drop:** The route is discarded and processing stops.

To demonstrate the process of troubleshooting a missing route on an IOS XR platform, imagine that XR5 does not have the 100.64.1.0/24 network in the BGP table. Check the BGP Adj-RIB-in table to see if the route is present. The route is present, which infers that the route was dropped during inbound route-policy processing. The route policy is identified by looking at XR5's neighbor session with XR4, as shown in Example 4-69.

XR5 is using an inbound route policy R4-IN, which is then examined with the command **show run rpl**. The structure of the RPL is easier to read and troubleshoot because of the programmatic if-then-else structure. The 100.64.1.0/24 does not pass the first match condition, nor the second condition. The prefix was never assigned a ticket to exit the RPL and is then dropped.

Example 4-69 *XR5's BGP Neighbor Session with XR4*

```
RP/0/0/CPU0:XR5# show bgp ipv4 unicast neighbors 10.1.45.4


 For Address Family: IPv4 Unicast
  BGP neighbor version 80
  Update group: 0.2 Filter-group: 0.2  No Refresh request being processed
  Inbound soft reconfiguration allowed
  Route refresh request: received 0, sent 18
  Policy for incoming advertisements is R4-IN
  Policy for outgoing advertisements is PASS-ALL
  6 accepted prefixes, 6 are bestpaths
  Cumulative no. of prefixes denied: 12.
    No policy: 0, Failed RT match: 0
    By ORF policy: 0, By policy: 12
```

```
RP/0/0/CPU0:XR5# show run rpl
route-policy R4-IN
  if destination in (10.0.0.0/8 le 32) then
    pass
  endif
  if destination in (172.16.0.0/12 le 32) then
    set med 20
  endif
end-policy
```

A third conditional match needs to be added to include the prefix 100.64.1.0/24 with a **pass**, **set**, or **done** action. After the route policy has included that logic, the missing route appears in the BGP table.

Assuming that the RPL was too difficult to troubleshoot or read through, BGP debugs are enabled for route-policy processing on IOS XR with the command **debug bgp policy-execution events**, as shown in Example 4-70. A key benefit is that the debug shows all the network prefixes path attributes, and then indicates if a conditional match is TRUE or FALSE and the outcome.

Example 4-70 *Debugging IOS XR Route-Policy Execution*

```
RP/0/0/CPU0:XR5# debug bgp policy-execution events
RP/0/0/CPU0:XR5# clear bgp ipv4 unicast 10.1.45.4 soft
RP/0/0/CPU0: 06:19:10.000 : bgp[1053]: --Running policy 'R4-IN':---
RP/0/0/CPU0: 06:19:10.000 : bgp[1053]:   Attach pt='neighbor-in-dflt'
RP/0/0/CPU0: 06:19:10.000 : bgp[1053]:   Attach pt inst='default-IPv4-Uni-10.1.45.4'
```

```
RP/0/0/CPU0: 06:19:10.000 : bgp[1053]: Input route attributes:
RP/0/0/CPU0: 06:19:10.000 : bgp[1053]:   as-path: 200 100 600
RP/0/0/CPU0: 06:19:10.000 : bgp[1053]:   as-path-length: 3
RP/0/0/CPU0: 06:19:10.000 : bgp[1053]:   as-path-unique-length: 3
RP/0/0/CPU0: 06:19:10.000 : bgp[1053]:   community: No Community Information
RP/0/0/CPU0: 06:19:10.000 : bgp[1053]:   destination: 100.64.1.0/24
RP/0/0/CPU0: 06:19:10.000 : bgp[1053]:   local-preference: <<no local preference>>
RP/0/0/CPU0: 06:19:10.000 : bgp[1053]:   med: 0
RP/0/0/CPU0: 06:19:10.000 : bgp[1053]:   nexthop: 10.1.45.4/32
RP/0/0/CPU0: 06:19:10.000 : bgp[1053]:   next-hop: 10.1.45.4
RP/0/0/CPU0: 06:19:10.000 : bgp[1053]:   origin: ?
RP/0/0/CPU0: 06:19:10.000 : bgp[1053]:   source: 10.1.45.4/32
RP/0/0/CPU0: 06:19:10.000 : bgp[1053]:   source-prefix: <<no prefix>>
RP/0/0/CPU0: 06:19:10.000 : bgp[1053]:   weight: 0
RP/0/0/CPU0: 06:19:10.000 : bgp[1053]:   rd: No route-distinguisher Information
RP/0/0/CPU0: 06:19:10.000 : bgp[1053]:   route-aggregate: Non-Aggregated Route
RP/0/0/CPU0: 06:19:10.000 : bgp[1053]:   path-type: ebgp
RP/0/0/CPU0: 06:19:10.000 : bgp[1053]:   aigp-metric: 0
RP/0/0/CPU0: 06:19:10.000 : bgp[1053]:   validation-state: not-found
RP/0/0/CPU0: 06:19:10.000 : bgp[1053]: Policy execution trace:
RP/0/0/CPU0: 06:19:10.000 : bgp[1053]:   Condition: destination in (10.0.0.0/8 ...)
RP/0/0/CPU0: 06:19:10.000 : bgp[1053]:   Condition evaluated to FALSE
RP/0/0/CPU0: 06:19:10.000 : bgp[1053]:   Condition: destination in (172.16.0.0/
   12 ...)
RP/0/0/CPU0: 06:19:10.000 : bgp[1053]:   Condition evaluated to FALSE
RP/0/0/CPU0: 06:19:10.000 : bgp[1053]:   End policy: result=DROP
! Output omitted for brevity
RP/0/0/CPU0: 06:19:10.000 : bgp[1053]:   destination: 172.20.1.1/32
RP/0/0/CPU0: 06:19:10.000 : bgp[1053]: Policy execution trace:
RP/0/0/CPU0: 06:19:10.000 : bgp[1053]:   Condition: destination in (10.0.0.0/8 ...)
RP/0/0/CPU0: 06:19:10.000 : bgp[1053]:   Condition evaluated to FALSE
RP/0/0/CPU0: 06:19:10.000 : bgp[1053]:   Condition: destination in (172.16.0.0/
   12 ...)
RP/0/0/CPU0: 06:19:10.000 : bgp[1053]:   Condition evaluated to TRUE
RP/0/0/CPU0: 06:19:10.000 : bgp[1053]:   Action: set med 20
RP/0/0/CPU0: 06:19:10.000 : bgp[1053]:   End policy: result=PASS
```

Incomplete Configuration of Routing Policies

Another common issue with route policies is the partial configuration of route-maps, specifically the conditional matching that refers to an ACL, prefix-list, AS-Path ACL, BGP community list, and that entity is not defined. In some instances all paths are accepted, and in other instances, no paths are accepted. This problem exists regardless of whether the route-map is used directly with a BGP neighbor or during route redistribution.

Verifying that all components of a route-map are defined should be a vital component of troubleshooting.

IOS XR identifies any missing dependencies in a route policy, when the change is committed as part of the validity check.

Conditional BGP Debugs

Debug commands are generally the least preferred method for finding root cause because of the amount of processing load and data that are generated while the debug is running. Processing occurs for every BGP path, and at the time of writing, there are more than 600,000 IPv4 routes on the Internet. If debug messages are enabled on the console, it could lock out access to the router.

As a preventative measure, IOS and IOS XR platforms allow for debug messages to be restricted to certain network prefixes through the use of a standard or extended ACL.

Example 4-71 displays a BGP routing table from R5's perspective. There are eight routes in total, but in the following examples, the debug is restricted to three prefixes (172.16.1.0/24, 172.16.2.0/24, and 172.20.1.1/32).

Example 4-71 *Sample BGP Table for Conditional Debugs*

```
R5# show bgp ipv4 unicast
BGP table version is 9, local router ID is 192.168.5.5
Status codes: s suppressed, d damped, h history, * valid, > best, i - internal,
              r RIB-failure, S Stale, m multipath, b backup-path, f RT-Filter,
              x best-external, a additional-path, c RIB-compressed,
Origin codes: i - IGP, e - EGP, ? - incomplete
RPKI validation codes: V valid, I invalid, N Not found

     Network          Next Hop            Metric LocPrf Weight Path
 *>  10.1.1.1/32      10.1.45.4                          0 200 100 ?
 *>  10.1.12.0/24     10.1.45.4                          0 200 100 500 ?
 *>  10.2.2.0/24      10.1.45.4                          0 200 i
 *>  100.64.1.0/24    10.1.45.4                          0 200 100 600 ?
 *>  100.64.11.11/32  10.1.45.4                          0 200 100 ?
 *>  172.16.1.0/24    10.1.45.4                          0 200 100 ?
 *>  172.16.2.0/24    10.1.45.4                          0 200 100 ?
 *>  172.20.1.1/32    10.1.45.4                          0 200 100 700 ?
```

On IOS nodes, BGP update debugs are turned on with the command **debug bgp** *afi safi* **updates** [*acl-number*] [**in** | **out**] [**detail**]. Specifying an ACL restricts the BGP debugs to the prefixes that fall into the defined network range. The **detail** keyword does not show up in context-sensitive help with the usage of an ACL, but the option still works.

Example 4-72 demonstrates the usage of the conditional debug on the IOS device. Notice that only three routes are displayed.

Example 4-72   *IOS Conditional BGP Debug*

```
R5# configuration t
Enter configuration commands, one per line. End with CNTL/Z.
R5(config)# access-list 1 permit 172.0.0.0 0.255.255.255
R5(config)# end
R5# debug ip bgp updates 1 in
BGP updates debugging is on for access list 1 (inbound) for address family: IPv4
  Unicast
R5# clear bgp ipv4 uni * sof
04:57:55.435: BGP(0): start inbound soft reconfiguration for
04:57:55.435: BGP(0): process 172.16.1.0/24, next hop 10.1.45.4, metric 0 from
  10.1.45.4
04:57:55.435: BGP(0): No inbound policy. Prefix 172.16.1.0/24 accepted
  unconditionally
04:57:55.435: BGP(0): process 172.16.2.0/24, next hop 10.1.45.4, metric 0 from
  10.1.45.4
04:57:55.435: BGP(0): No inbound policy. Prefix 172.16.2.0/24 accepted
  unconditionally
04:57:55.435: BGP(0): process 172.20.1.1/32, next hop 10.1.45.4, metric 0 from
  10.1.45.4
04:57:55.435: BGP(0): No inbound policy. Prefix 172.20.1.1/32 accepted
  unconditionally
04:57:55.435: BGP(0): complete inbound soft reconfiguration, ran for 0ms
R5# show debug
IP routing:
  BGP updates debugging is on (inbound) for access list 1 for address family: IPv4
  Unicast
```

IOS XR routers can add conditional debug capabilities by associating a route policy to the debug statement. After defining the route policy, the command **debug bgp update** [**afi** *afi safi*] [**in** | **out**] [**route-policy** *route-policy-name*] restricts the output. Example 4-73 displays the conditional BGP debug on IOS XR.

Example 4-73   *IOS XR Conditional BGP Debug*

```
RP/0/0/CPU0:XR5# configuration t
RP/0/0/CPU0:XR5(config)# route-policy DEBUG
RP/0/0/CPU0:XR5(config-rpl)# if destination in (172.0.0.0/8 le 32) then pass endif
RP/0/0/CPU0:XR5(config-rpl)# end-policy
```

```
RP/0/0/CPU0:XR5(config)# commit
RP/0/0/CPU0:XR5(config)# end
```

```
RP/0/0/CPU0:XR5# debug bgp update route-policy DEBUG in
RP/0/0/CPU0:XR5# clear bgp ipv4 unicast * soft
RP/0/0/CPU0:XR5#RP/0/0/CPU0:May 13 05:21:35.074 : bgp[1053]: [default-rtr] (ip4u):
  172.16.1.0/24: duplicate path (200 100) ignored
RP/0/0/CPU0:May 13 05:21:35.074 : bgp[1053]: [default-rtr] (ip4u): 172.16.2.0/24:
  duplicate path (200 100) ignored
RP/0/0/CPU0:May 13 05:21:35.074 : bgp[1053]: [default-rtr] (ip4u): 172.20.1.1/32:
  duplicate path (200 100 700) ignored
```

NX-OS provides a method of conditional debugging with a feature called debug-filter. The BGP debug-filter supports the restriction of BGP debugs by using the following logic:

- **Specific neighbors:** The command **debug-filter bgp neighbor** *ip-address* restricts the debugs to that specific neighbor.

- **Address-family:** The command **debug-filter bgp address-family [ipv4 | ipv6 {multicast | mvpn | unicast}]** restricts the debugs to that specific AFI and SAFI.

- **Route Policy:** The command **debug-filter bgp policy** *policy-name* restricts the debugs to network prefixes that match that specific route policy. If troubleshooting a specific BGP route policy, the debug-filter route policy will be different from the one associated to the BGP peer.

- **Prefix Range:** The command **debug-filter bgp prefix** *network/prefix-length* restricts the debugs to networks that match the specified prefix.

In addition, NX-OS supports the redirection of debugs to a logfile in lieu of outputting directly to a session with the command **debug logfile bgp** *logfile-name*. The logfile can then be viewed with the command **show debug logfile** *logfile-name*. Example 4-74 demonstrates the use of both techniques.

Example 4-74   *NX-OS Conditional BGP Debug*

```
NXOS5# debug logfile CONSOLE-REDIRECT.TXT
NXOS5# debug-filter bgp prefix 172.20.1.1/32
NXOS5# debug bgp updates
NXOS5# clear bgp ipv4 unicast * soft
NXOS5# show debug logfile CONSOLE-REDIRECT.TXT
! Output omitted for brevity
21:04:56.174484 bgp:   (default) UPD: Received UPDATE message from 10.1.45.4
21:04:56.174512 bgp:   (default) UPD: 10.1.45.4 parsed UPDATE message from peer, len
  53 , withdraw len 0, attr len 30, nlri len 0
21:04:56.174528 bgp:   (default) UPD: Attr code 1, length 1, Origin: IGP
```

```
21:04:56.174544 bgp:  (default) UPD: Peer 10.1.45.4 nexthop length in MP reach: 4
21:04:56.174581 bgp:  (default) UPD: Recvd NEXTHOP 10.1.45.4
21:04:56.174596 bgp:  (default) UPD: Attr code 14, length 13, Mp-reach
21:04:56.174629 bgp:  (default) UPD: 10.1.45.4 Received attr code 2, length 6, AS-
   Path: <200 >
21:04:56.174660 bgp:  (default) UPD: [IPv4 Unicast] 10.1.45.4 Inbound route-map
   R4-IN, action permit
21:04:56.174694 bgp:  (default) UPD: Received UPDATE message from 10.1.45.4
21:04:56.174727 bgp:  (default) UPD: 10.1.45.4 parsed UPDATE message from peer, len
   71 , withdraw len 0, attr len 48, nlri len 0
21:04:56.174740 bgp:  (default) UPD: Attr code 1, length 1, Origin: Incomplete
21:04:56.174767 bgp:  (default) UPD: Peer 10.1.45.4 nexthop length in MP reach: 4
21:04:56.174785 bgp:  (default) UPD: Recvd NEXTHOP 10.1.45.4
21:04:56.174798 bgp:  (default) UPD: Attr code 14, length 27, Mp-reach
21:04:56.174813 bgp:  (default) UPD: 10.1.45.4 Received attr code 2, length 10,
   AS-Path: <200 100 >
21:04:56.174834 bgp:  (default) UPD: [IPv4 Unicast] 10.1.45.4 Inbound route-map
   R4-IN, action permit
21:04:56.174880 bgp:  (default) UPD: [IPv4 Unicast] 10.1.45.4 Inbound route-map
   R4-IN, action permit
21:04:56.174924 bgp:  (default) UPD: [IPv4 Unicast] 10.1.45.4 Inbound route-map
   R4-IN, action permit
21:04:56.174953 bgp:  (default) UPD: [IPv4 Unicast] 10.1.45.4 Inbound route-map
   R4-IN, action permit
21:04:56.174992 bgp:  (default) UPD: Received UPDATE message from 10.1.45.4
21:04:56.175006 bgp:  (default) UPD: 10.1.45.4 parsed UPDATE message from peer,
   len 61 , withdraw len 0, attr len 38, nlri len 0
21:04:56.175018 bgp:  (default) UPD: Attr code 1, length 1, Origin: Incomplete
21:04:56.175030 bgp:  (default) UPD: Peer 10.1.45.4 nexthop length in MP reach: 4
21:04:56.175047 bgp:  (default) UPD: Recvd NEXTHOP 10.1.45.4
21:04:56.175060 bgp:  (default) UPD: Attr code 14, length 13, Mp-reach
21:04:56.175088 bgp:  (default) UPD: 10.1.45.4 Received attr code 2, length 14,
   AS-Path: <200 100 500 >
21:04:56.175107 bgp:  (default) UPD: [IPv4 Unicast] 10.1.45.4 Inbound route-map
   R4-IN, action permit
21:04:56.175146 bgp:  (default) UPD: Received UPDATE message from 10.1.45.4
21:04:56.175160 bgp:  (default) UPD: 10.1.45.4 parsed UPDATE message from peer,
   len 61 , withdraw len 0, attr len 38, nlri len 0
21:04:56.175173 bgp:  (default) UPD: Attr code 1, length 1, Origin: Incomplete
21:04:56.175186 bgp:  (default) UPD: Peer 10.1.45.4 nexthop length in MP reach: 4
21:04:56.175202 bgp:  (default) UPD: Recvd NEXTHOP 10.1.45.4
21:04:56.175228 bgp:  (default) UPD: Attr code 14, length 13, Mp-reach
21:04:56.175242 bgp:  (default) UPD: 10.1.45.4 Received attr code 2, length 14,
   AS-Path: <200 100 600 >
21:04:56.175261 bgp:  (default) UPD: [IPv4 Unicast] 10.1.45.4 Inbound route-map
   R4-IN, action permit
21:04:56.175299 bgp:  (default) UPD: Received UPDATE message from 10.1.45.4
```

```
21:04:56.175313 bgp:   (default) UPD: 10.1.45.4 parsed UPDATE message from peer, len
   62 , withdraw len 0, attr len 39, nlri len 0
21:04:56.175325 bgp:   (default) UPD: Attr code 1, length 1, Origin: Incomplete
21:04:56.175337 bgp:   (default) UPD: Peer 10.1.45.4 nexthop length in MP reach: 4
21:04:56.175355 bgp:   (default) UPD: Recvd NEXTHOP 10.1.45.4
21:04:56.175381 bgp:   (default) UPD: Attr code 14, length 14, Mp-reach
21:04:56.175395 bgp:   (default) UPD: 10.1.45.4 Received attr code 2, length 14,
   AS-Path: <200 100 700 >
21:04:56.175436 bgp:   (default) UPD: [IPv4 Unicast] Received prefix 172.20.1.1/32
   from peer 10.1.45.4, origin 2, next hop 10.1.45.4, localpref 0, med 0
21:04:56.175592 bgp:   (default) UPD: [IPv4 Unicast] 10.1.45.4 Inbound route-map
   R4-IN, action deny
21:04:56.175608 bgp:   (default) UPD: [IPv4 Unicast] Prefix 172.20.1.1/32 from peer
   10.1.45.4 rejected by inbound policy
21:04:56.175622 bgp:   (default) UPD: [IPv4 Unicast] Dropping prefix 172.20.1.1/32
   from peer 10.1.45.4, due to prefix policy rejected
```

Summary

BGP route advertisement can be difficult to troubleshoot initially. After a network engineer fully understands how routes are installed and advertised to other routers, the troubleshooting process becomes easier.

For route advertisement, it is important to remember the following:

- The router must have an exact match in the RIB for the network statement.

- BGP aggregates are installed only if a smaller route that is in the aggregate range is present.

- A validity check is performed before a network prefix is installed in the Adj-RIB-in table. The validity check verifies that a loop is not present by checking the AS-Path, Originator-ID, or Cluster-ID. If a router detects a value that is present on itself, the network prefix is considered invalid and is discarded.

- The next-hop IP Address must be reachable for a network to be advertised. This is an issue with routes that are received from an iBGP peer that did not advertise the eBGP peering link or use the next-hop-self feature.

- The BGP communities no-advertise, no-export, and local-as impact the advertisement of routes to other routers and have varying behaviors, depending on the neighbor connection and whether the router is a member of a confederation.

- Troubleshooting a BGP routing policy ultimately requires that you manually examine the route policy to verify which route policy sequence the network prefix conditionally matches. Then that route policy sequence's action must be verified to ensure that the proper action is configured. If the network prefix does not match any route policy sequence, the network prefix is being dropped by an implicit deny.

Examining the three BGP tables and neighbor session provides a wealth of information that can rule out the reasons for a route to be dropped. After using the various tools and techniques, troubleshooting BGP route advertisement becomes second nature.

Further Reading

Some of the topics involving validity checks and next-hop resolution are explained further in the following books:

Halabi, Sam. *Internet Routing Architectures*. Indianapolis: Cisco Press, 2000. Print.

Zhang, Randy, Bartell, Micah. *BGP Design and Implementation*. Indianapolis: Cisco Press, 2003. Print.

White, Russ, Retana, Alvaro, Slice, Don. *Optimal Routing Design*. Indianapolis: Cisco Press, 2005. Print.

Edgeworth, Brad, Foss, Aaron, Garza Rios, Ramiro. *IP Routing on Cisco IOS, IOS XE and IOS XR*. Indianapolis: Cisco Press, 2014. Print.

References in This Chapter

Edgeworth, Brad, Foss, Aaron, Garza Rios, Ramiro. *IP Routing on Cisco IOS, IOS XE and IOS XR*. Indianapolis: Cisco Press, 2014. Print.

Cisco. Cisco IOS Software Configuration Guides. http://www.cisco.com.

Cisco. Cisco IOS XR Software Configuration Guides. http://www.cisco.com

Cisco. Cisco NX-OS Software Configuration Guides: http://www.cisco.com

## Chapter 5

Troubleshooting BGP Convergence

The following topics are covered in this chapter:

- Understanding BGP route convergence
- Troubleshooting convergence Issues
- BGP slow peer
- Troubleshooting BGP route churns

Understanding BGP Route Convergence

Every network design needs to be planned and tested before it is deployed and ready for use. There are various tests that should be performed, such as load test, failure test, convergence test, and so on before the network is ready to carry production traffic. The main problem faced when testing any network design is during convergence testing. The purpose of the convergence testing is to identify how convergent the network is when it is brought into production and actual production traffic will be carried over it. It is challenging when it comes to defining how convergent the network is. *Routing convergence* can be broadly defined as how quickly a routing protocol can become stable after changes occur in the network—for example, a protocol or link flap. In terms of Border Gateway Protocol (BGP), it can be defined as converged when all BGP neighbor sessions have been established and neighbors have been updated, routes have been learned from all neighbors and installed into the routing table, and all routing tables across the network are consistent after a network event or any change in the network.

Faster convergence leads to higher availability and improved network stability. Thus it is important that before the network is deployed in production, convergence time is properly calculated with thorough testing. But what is convergence time? Consider the topology shown in Figure 5-1. There are multiple paths from the source router in order to reach the destination router, but for simplicity, consider the two paths—primary and secondary. The primary extends from R1 to R2 to R4 to R6, whereas the secondary path extends from R1 to R3 to R5 to R6. If a link on primary path fails, the best path is impacted and leads to a traffic loss. Because of the failure event, a next-best path is computed. The amount of time during which there was a traffic loss in the network while the alternate path was not available to forward the traffic to the point where traffic starts flowing again is called the *convergence time*.

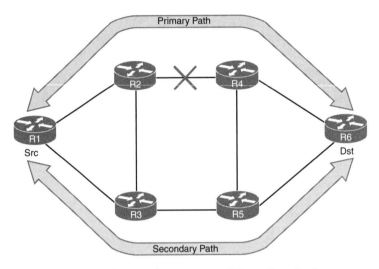

Figure 5-1   *Topology with Primary and Secondary Path*

Like any other dynamic routing protocol, BGP accepts routing updates from its neighbors. It then advertises those updates to its peers except to the one from which it received, only if the route is a best route. BGP uses an explicit withdrawal section in the update message to inform the peers on loss of the path so they can update their BGP table accordingly. Similarly, BGP uses implicit signaling to check if there is an update for the learned prefix and to update the existing path information in case newer information is available. Looking closely at the BGP update message as shown in Figure 5-2, it can be seen that new BGP update message is bounded with a set of BGP attributes. Thus, any update with different set of attributes needs to be formatted as a different update message to be replicated to its peers.

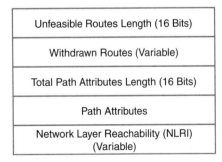

Figure 5-2   *BGP Update Message*

As the networks grow larger, this could eventually pose scalability challenges and convergence issues especially to the service provider and enterprise networks to maintain an ever-increasing number of Transmission Control Protocol (TCP) sessions and routes. If the scale of the network has increased, the BGP process will have to process all the routes present in the BGP table and update its peers. In addition, the router processing the updates in such a scaled environment demand more memory and CPU resources. Because BGP is a key protocol for the Internet, it is important to ensure that BGP is highly convergent even with increased scale.

BGP convergence depends on various factors. BGP convergence is all about the speed of the following:

- Establishing sessions with a number of peers

- Locally generate all the BGP paths (either via network statement, redistribution of static/connected/IGP routes), and/or from other component for other address-family for example, Multicast Virtual Private Network (MVPN) from multicast, Layer 2 Virtual Private Network (L2VPN) from l2vpn manager, and so on.)

- Send and receive multiple BGP tables; that is, different BGP address-families to/from each peer

- Upon receiving all the paths from peers, perform the best-path calculation to find the best path and/or multipath, additional-path, backup path

- Installing the best path into multiple routing tables, such as the default or Virtual Routing and Forwarding (VRF) routing table

- Import and export mechanism

- For another address-family, like l2vpn or multicast, pass the path calculation result to different lower layer components

BGP uses lot of CPU cycles when processing BGP updates and requires memory for maintaining BGP peers and routes in the BGP table. Based on the role of the BGP router in the network, appropriate hardware should be chosen. The more memory a router has, the more routes it can support, much like how a router with a faster CPU can support a larger number of peers.

BGP updates rely on TCP, optimization of router resources such as memory and TCP session parameters such as maximum segment size (MSS), path MTU discovery, interface input queues, TCP window size, and so on help improve convergence.

BGP Update Groups

An update group is a collection of peers with an identical outbound policy. The update groups are dynamically formed during the time of the configuration. Two peers will be part of same update group if one of the following conditions is met:

- Peers are in same peer group.

- Peers are having the same template.

■ If the peers are not part of any of the preceding two, they will be in same update group if they have the same outbound policy.

After an update group is formed, a peer within the update group is selected as a group leader. The BGP process walks the BGP table of the leader and then formats the messages that are then replicated to the other members of the update group. This is so because the router needs to format the update only once and replicate the formatted update to all the peers in the update group because they all need to have the same information. Because the messages are not required to be formatted for all the peers but only for the leader of the update group, this saves lot of resources and processing time on the router.

On IOS, an update group is verified using the command **show bgp ipv4 unicast update-group** [*group-index*]. This command displays the update group index, the address-family under which the update group is formed, messages formatted in the update group, the messages replicated to the peers in the update group, and all the peers in the update group. If a particular peer is in process of being replicated or not yet converged, an asterisk (*) is seen beside the peer, indicating that the peer is still being updated. The topology in Figure 5-3 is used for understanding the update groups and the update generation process. In this topology, R1, R10, and R20 are the three route reflectors (RR) whereas R2, R3, R4, and R5 are the RR clients.

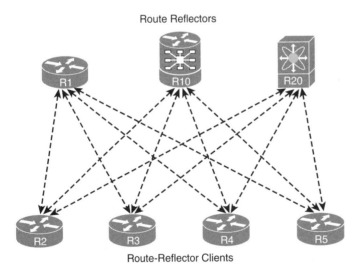

Figure 5-3 *Topology with Route Reflectors*

Example 5-1 displays the command output of **show bgp ipv4 unicast update-group** and previously discussed information. Also, this command shows the BGP update version, which generally matches the update version in the **show bgp ipv4 unicast summary** command. If the peers of the update group are configured as route-reflector clients, it is displayed in the command output. This command also displays any outbound policy attached to the update group.

Example 5-1 *BGP Update Group on IOS*

```
R1# show bgp ipv4 unicast update-group
BGP version 4 update-group 2, internal, Address Family: IPv4 Unicast
  BGP Update version : 7/0, messages 0, active RGs: 1
  Route-Reflector Client
  Route map for outgoing advertisements is dummy
  Topology: global, highest version: 7, tail marker: 7
  Format state: Current working (OK, last not in list)
               Refresh blocked (not in list, last not in list)
  Update messages formatted 4, replicated 16, current 0, refresh 0, limit 1000
  Number of NLRIs in the update sent: max 1, min 0
  Minimum time between advertisement runs is 0 seconds
  Has 4 members:
    10.1.12.2        10.1.13.2        10.1.14.2        10.1.15.2
R1# show bgp ipv4 unicast summary | in table
BGP table version is 7, local router ID is 192.168.1.1
```

Use the command **clear bgp ipv4 unicast update-group** *group-index* [**soft**] to clear or soft clear the neighbors in the update group. The debug command **debug bgp ipv4 unicast groups** is used to see the events happening in the update group. Example 5-2 demonstrates a neighbor being added to peer group and the debug output during the event.

Example 5-2 **debug bgp ipv4 unicast groups** *Command Output*

```
R1(config)# router bgp 65530
R1(config-router)# neighbor 10.1.15.2 peer-group group1

R1# debug bgp ipv4 unicast groups
! Output generated by debug command
11:19:24.459: BGP-DYN(0): 10.1.15.2 cannot join update-group 2
     due to an outbound route-map mismatch
11:19:24.459: BGP(0): Scheduling withdraws and update-group
     membership change for 10.1.15.2
11:19:24.459: BGP-DYN(0): 10.1.15.2 cannot join update-group 2
     due to an outbound route-map mismatch
11:19:24.459: BGP-DYN(0): Initializing the update-group 2 fields
     with 10.1.15.2
11:19:24.459: BGP-DYN(0): Merging update-group 2 into update-group 4
11:19:24.459: BGP-DYN(0): Removing 10.1.15.2 from update-group 2
11:19:24.459: BGP-DYN(0): Adding 10.1.15.2 to update-group 4
11:19:24.475: %BGP-5-ADJCHANGE: neighbor 10.1.15.2 Down Member added to peergroup
11:19:24.475: BGP-DYN(0): 10.1.15.2's policies match with update-group 4
```

Update groups on IOS XR are a bit different. In IOS XR, there is a concept of hierarchical update group. At the top of the hierarchy is a parent update group with multiple child subgroups beneath it. Each subgroup is a subset of neighbors within an update group that have the same version and are running at a same pace for sending updates. Figure 5-4 illustrates how BGP updates are replicated in IOS XR using update groups and subgroups. The update groups have multiple subgroups. Each subgroups points to multiple neighbors in that subgroup and also to the formatted update messages for that update group. Each neighbor then maintains the pointer toward the current message that is being processed and written on the socket.

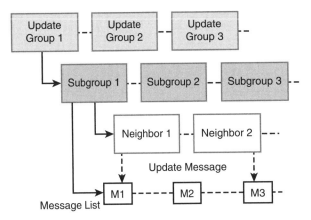

Figure 5-4   *BGP Update Message*

Barring desynchronization, an update group can contain multiple subgroups if neighbors having the same outbound behavior are configured at different times. Because the previous neighbors have already advanced to a table version, the neighbors being configured now are put in a new subgroup, and after they catch up to the other subgroup's update version number, the subgroups are merged. Example 5-3 displays the output of command **show bgp update-group** on IOS XR. A new neighbor that is configured later is put into a different subgroup, and once that neighbor has synchronized the update and reaches the same table version, its moved to the other subgroup where all the other peers are present.

Example 5-3   show bgp update-group *Command Output*

```
RP/0/0/CPU0:R10# show bgp update-group
Update group for IPv4 Unicast, index 0.2:
  Attributes:
    Neighbor sessions are IPv4
    Internal
    Common admin
    First neighbor AS: 65530
    Send communities
    Send extended communities
    Route Reflector Client
```

```
     4-byte AS capable
      Non-labeled address-family capable
      Send AIGP
      Send multicast attributes
      Minimum advertisement interval: 0 secs
    Update group desynchronized: 0
   Sub-groups merged: 0
   Number of refresh subgroups: 0
   Messages formatted: 6, replicated: 23
   All neighbors are assigned to sub-group(s)

! Sub-Group 0.2 is for a new neighbor that was configured later

     Neighbors in sub-group: 0.2, Filter-Groups num:1
       Neighbors in filter-group: 0.2(RT num: 0)
       10.1.105.2
       Neighbors in sub-group: 0.1, Filter-Groups num:1
       Neighbors in filter-group: 0.1(RT num: 0)
       10.1.102.2        10.1.103.2         10.1.104.2
```

```
! Output after the neighbor 10.1.105.2 has synchronized
RP/0/0/CPU0:R10# show bgp update-group
Update group for IPv4 Unicast, index 0.2:
  Attributes:
     Neighbor sessions are IPv4
     Internal
     Common admin
     First neighbor AS: 65530
     Send communities
     Send extended communities
     Route Reflector Client
     4-byte AS capable
     Non-labeled address-family capable
     Send AIGP
     Send multicast attributes
     Minimum advertisement interval: 0 secs
    Update group desynchronized: 0
   Sub-groups merged: 1
   Number of refresh subgroups: 0
   Messages formatted: 11, replicated: 28
   All neighbors are assigned to sub-group(s)
     Neighbors in sub-group: 0.2, Filter-Groups num:1
       Neighbors in filter-group: 0.2(RT num: 0)
       10.1.102.2        10.1.103.2        10.1.104.2        10.1.105.2
```

Two peers can be part of same update group within a particular address-family but can be in different update groups in a different address-family. Thus you need to ensure that a correct update group is being looked at while troubleshooting convergence issues.

Note   At the time of writing, the update group feature is not present in NX-OS.

BGP Update Generation

Update generation is the process of generating the update messages that need to be replicated to peer(s). The update generation process starts when one of the following events takes place:

- When a session is established with the peer
- When the import scanner is run with the importing prefixes
- When there is a change in the network
- Whenever there is an addition or removal of **neighbor** *ip-address* **soft-reconfiguration inbound** configuration
- Whenever the BGP table is repopulated or the **clear bgp ipv4 unicast * soft** command is used
- When a route refresh message is received from a neighbor

The BGP update generation process varies as to whether the peer is part of an update group or not. Without peer groups or update groups, BGP walks the table of each peer, filters the update based on the outbound policy, and generates the update that is then sent to that neighbor. In the case of update group, a peer group leader is elected for each peer group or update group. BGP walks the table for the leader only; the prefixes are then filtered through the outbound policies. Updates are then generated and sent to the peer group or update group leader and are then replicated for peer group or update group members that are synchronized with the leader.

Before the messages are replicated, the update messages are formatted and stored in an update group cache. The size of the cache depends on variables; thus it can change over time. The cache has a maximum upper limit to help the following:

- Control the maximum transient memory BGP would use to generate update messages
- Throttling the update group messages in case of the cache getting full

In earlier Cisco IOS software, the cache size was calculated based on the number of peers within the update group. The following criteria was used to calculate the cache size:

- For route refresh groups, always set the cache size to 1000
- For update group of RR clients with more than half the BGP peers on the router having max queue size configured, the cache size is the max queue size

Table 5-1 shows the queue depth (cache) calculation methodology:

Table 5-1 *Cache Size Calculation in Older IOS Releases*

Number of Peers	Queue Depth (Cache Size)
=1	100
>1 and <10	(Number of peers) * 100
>1 and <10 and number of peers in update group >= (total number of peers) / 8	1000
>= 10	1000
>= 1000	5000

The new behavior was introduced with an enhancement—CSCsz49626. For the newer IOS releases, the cache size is calculated based on the following:

- Number of peers in an update group

- Installed system memory

- Type of peers in an update group

- Type of address-family (for example, vpnv4 have a larger cache size)

Table 5-2 shows the calculation method for cache size in newer releases:

Table 5-2 *Cache Size Calculation in Newer IOS Releases*

Number of Peers	Queue Depth (Cache Size)
=1	100 * mem_multiply_factor
>1 and <10	(Number of peers) * 100 * mem_multiply_factor
>1 and <10 and number of peers in update group >= (total number of peers) / 8	1000 * mem_multiply_factor
>= 10	1000 * mem_multiply_factor
>= 1000	5000

The mem_multiply_factor or memory multiply factor variable in Table 5-2 is calculated based on the system memory. Table 5-3 shows the memory multiplier factor calculation based on system memory.

Table 5-3 *Memory Multiplier Factor*

Mem_multiply_factor	System Memory
1	≤1GB
2	1GB < and ≤5GB
5	>5GB

The cache size and number of messages within it can be seen with the help of the command **show bgp ipv4 unicast replication**. Example 5-4 shows the output of **show bgp ipv4 unicast replication**. From the output it can be noticed that the cache size (Csize) column is in a format of x/y, where x is the current number of messages in cache and y is the dynamically calculated cache size. It also displays the number of messages formatted and replicated for the update group.

Example 5-4 *BGP Replication* **show** *Command*

```
R1# show bgp ipv4 unicast replication

                                                     Current    Next
Index   Members          Leader      MsgFmt   MsgRepl   Csize   Version Version
   1        4        10.1.12.2          10        28    0/1000     10/0
! Output omitted due to brevity
```

In IOS XR, there is no cache size. In IOS XR, there is a *write limit*, which can be treated as a cap on the number of messages per update generation walk. The write limit has a maximum value of 5,000 messages. There is also a *total limit*, which refers to the maximum number of outstanding messages in the system across all subgroups or update groups. It has a max value of 25,000 messages. The update generation process is described in the following steps:

Step 1.   Whenever there is a table change, the Minimum Router Advertisement Interval (MRAI) is started.

Step 2.   When the timer expires, a subgroup within the update group is selected.

Step 3.   After a subgroup is selected, update messages are generated up to the value of *write limit* or until the total number of messages is less than the *total limit*. These messages are stored in the hash table in the system. The *io write* thread is then invoked to write the messages to each neighbor's socket.

Step 4.   Return to Step 2 to find another subgroup.

Step 5.   If there are a few subgroups for which the messages could not be generated, and the walk is completed, the update generation process is rescheduled for that update group, which is based on the MRAI value.

To verify the update generation process, use the debug command **debug bgp update**. Example 5-5 demonstrates the BGP update generation process in IOS XR with the help of debug output. It can be seen that when the prefix is received, the update message is then replicated to all the peers in the update group. One important thing to notice in the output is **[default-iowt]**. This indicates the *io write* thread as mentioned in Step 3 of the update generation process.

Example 5-5   *IOS XR Update Generation Process*

```
RP/0/0/CPU0:R10# debug bgp update level detail
! Truncating timestamp in the debug output
bgp[1052]: [default-rtr] (ip4u): Received UPDATE from 10.1.102.2 with attributes:
bgp[1052]: [default-rtr] (ip4u): nexthop 10.1.102.2/32, origin i, localpref 100,
    metric 0
bgp[1052]: [default-rtr] (ip4u): Received prefix 192.168.2.2/32 (path ID: none)
    from 10.1.102.2
! Output omitted for brevity
bgp[1052]: [default-upd] (ip4u): Created msg elem 0x10158ffc (pointing to message
  0x100475b8), for filtergroup 0.1
bgp[1052]: [default-upd] (ip4u): Generated 1 updates for update sub-group 0.1
    (average size = 70 bytes, maximum size = 70 bytes)
bgp[1052]: [default-upd] (ip4u): Updates replicated to neighbor 10.1.104.2
bgp[1052]: [default-upd] (ip4u): Updates replicated to neighbor 10.1.103.2
bgp[1052]: [default-upd] (ip4u): Updates replicated to neighbor 10.1.105.2
bgp[1052]: [default-upd] (ip4u): Updates replicated to neighbor 10.1.102.2
bgp[1052]: [default-iowt]: 10.1.104.2 send UPDATE length (incl. header) 70
bgp[1052]: [default-iowt]: 10.1.103.2 send UPDATE length (incl. header) 70
bgp[1052]: [default-iowt]: 10.1.105.2 send UPDATE length (incl. header) 70
bgp[1052]: [default-iowt]: 10.1.102.2 send UPDATE length (incl. header) 70
```

The update generation process on NX-OS is a bit different than on both IOS and IOS XR because there is no update group concept as of yet. BGP processes receive route update messages from its peers, runs the prefixes and attributes through any configured inbound policy, and installs the new paths in the BGP Routing Information Base (BRIB). BRIB is same as Loc-RIB, also known as BGP table. After the route has been updated in the BRIB, BGP then marks the route for further update generation. Before the prefixes are packaged, they are processed through any configured outbound policies. The BGP puts the marked routes into the update message and sends them to peers. Example 5-6 illustrates the BGP update generation on NX-OS. To understand the update generation process, enable debug commands **debug ip bgp update** and **debug ip bgp brib**. From the debug output shown, notice that the update received from peer 10.1.102.2 (withdraw message for prefix 192.168.2.2/32) is updated into the BRIB and then further updates are generated for the peers.

Example 5-6 *BGP Update Generation on NX-OS*

```
R20# debug logfile bgp
R20# debug ip bgp update
R20# debug ip bgp brib
R20# show debug logfile bgp
2015 Oct 11 14:26:33.613109 bgp: 65530 [7046] (default) UPD: Received UPDATE mes
sage from 10.1.202.2
2015 Oct 11 14:26:33.613332 bgp: 65530 [7046] (default) UPD: 10.1.202.2 parsed U
PDATE message from peer, len 28 , withdraw len 5, attr len 0, nlri len 0
2015 Oct 11 14:26:33.613381 bgp: 65530 [7046] (default) BRIB: [IPv4 Unicast] Mar
king path for dest 192.168.2.2/32 from peer 10.1.202.2 as deleted, pflags = 0x11
, reeval=0
! Output omitted for brevity
2015 Oct 11 14:26:33.616412 bgp: 65530 [7046] (default) UPD: [IPv4 Unicast] cons
ider sending 192.168.2.2/32 to peer 10.1.203.2, path-id 1, best-ext is off
2015 Oct 11 14:26:33.616437 bgp: 65530 [7046] (default) UPD: [IPv4 Unicast] 10.1
.203.2 192.168.2.2/32 path-id 1 withdrawn from peer due to: no bestpath
2015 Oct 11 14:26:33.616466 bgp: 65530 [7046] (default) UPD: [IPv4 Unicast] 10.1
.203.2 Created withdrawal (len 28) with prefix 192.168.2.2/32 path-id 1 for peer

2015 Oct 11 14:26:33.616495 bgp: 65530 [7046] (default) UPD: [IPv4 Unicast] (#66
) Finished update run for peer 10.1.203.2 (#66)
2015 Oct 11 14:26:33.616528 bgp: 65530 [7046] (default) UPD: [IPv4 Unicast] Star
ting update run for peer 10.1.204.2 (#65)
2015 Oct 11 14:26:33.616560 bgp: 65530 [7046] (default) UPD: [IPv4 Unicast] cons
ider sending 192.168.2.2/32 to peer 10.1.204.2, path-id 1, best-ext is off
2015 Oct 11 14:26:33.616585 bgp: 65530 [7046] (default) UPD: [IPv4 Unicast] 10.1
.204.2 192.168.2.2/32 path-id 1 withdrawn from peer due to: no bestpath
2015 Oct 11 14:26:33.616612 bgp: 65530 [7046] (default) UPD: [IPv4 Unicast] 10.1
.204.2 Created withdrawal (len 28) with prefix 192.168.2.2/32 path-id 1 for peer

! Output omitted for brevity
```

The BGP update generation process is helpful in understanding and troubleshooting convergence issues due to BGP.

Troubleshooting Convergence Issues

A BGP speaker faces convergence issues primarily because of a large BGP table size and an increase in the number of BGP peers. The different dimensional factors while investigating BGP convergence issues that need to be considered include the following:

- Number of peers

- Number of address-families

- Number of prefixes/paths per address-family

- Link speed of individual interface, individual peer

- Different update group settings and topology

- Complexity of attribute creation and parsing for each address-family

While troubleshooting convergence issues, the first and foremost thing to verify is the time when the problem started happening, and whether there have been any recent changes that happened in the network that led to slow convergence. The changes could be an addition of single or multiple new customers, hardware or software changes, recent increase in size of the routing table or BGP table, and so on. If there has been addition of new customers or a new BGP session, it is important to understand what the scale is of BGP sessions that a BGP speaker can handle on a router. Sometimes, a single peer might be added physically, but it might be forming a BGP neighbor relationship in multiple address-families. Remember that if the new peer is forming a neighbor relationship in multisession mode, then a session is established for each address-family respectively.

While performing the convergence testing, collect statistical data to serve as the baseline for future tests. Perform the baseline convergence test during deployment followed by periodic retesting. This process helps uncover various convergence and other problems in the network and identifies the root cause of any outage situation. Without a baseline, it is hard to know when a problem started, which increases the scope of investigation for finding the root cause.

Another variable that has the most impact on the convergence is how big the BGP table is and how many paths are available in the network. In the present day world, redundancy is the need of the hour. Thus, it is being noticed that lot of designs not only have one or two redundant paths, but multiple redundant paths, and these redundant paths have a cost attached to it. Where multipath is good for providing redundancy, there is an additional overhead added on CPU and memory for calculating and holding multiple redundant paths.

While designing a network, the network operators should also consider providing enough capacity for optimal operation, not just enough to meet requirements. It has been seen many times that a link is overstretched for the amount of traffic it can handle, or a lower speed link is used than what is required, just to save some cost. Such compromises can cost the organizations a lot more than they can anticipate. If the link is over utilized, it is very likely that it can impact convergence and can impact critical traffic. For example, if there is excess traffic on the link, it is likely to drop the excess traffic that it cannot handle. In such situations, if any BGP update gets dropped, those packets have to be retransmitted back to the peer, thus adding to the delay in processing an update by the peer. Overutilized links can also cause the BGP sessions to flap because the BGP peer might be looking for a BGP keepalive or BGP update packet, but it never receives it. To overcome such issues, quality-of-service (QoS) policies can be applied on the interface as a workaround to give more preference to important traffic, such as control-plane traffic or high IP precedence traffic.

Last but not least is the BGP attribute. If multiple set of attributes are being applied or being received for BGP prefixes, it causes multiple update packets to be generated, and if the BGP table is huge—for example, having one million prefixes that need to be updated with various attributes—this can cause delay in the update generation process along with consumption of a lot of CPU cycles. Also, if there is complex regex or filtering applied on the inbound policy for a peer, the updates can take a longer time to converge.

Faster Detection of Failures

One of the biggest factors leading to slower convergence is the mechanism to detect failures. The capability to detect failures quickly is an often overlooked aspect of fast convergence. Unless you are able to quickly detect a failure, you cannot achieve fast convergence. Most of the network operators try to figure out a solution for improvising on convergence but stay behind on detecting failures and thus are never able to achieve faster convergence. A stable and reliable network should have three primary features:

- Faster convergence
- Availability
- Scalability

When talking about failure detection, the failures should be detected not just at the control-plane level but also at the data plane level.

Bidirectional Fast Detection (BFD) is a detection protocol that is used for subsecond detection of data plane (forwarding path) failures. BFD is used in conjunction with BGP to help detect failures in the forwarding path that significantly increase BGPs reconvergence time. BFD is a single, common standardized mechanism that is independent of media and routing protocols. It can be used in place of fast-hellos for multiple protocols. A single BFD session provides fast detection for multiple client protocols, thus reducing the control-plane overhead. BFD does not replace the protocol hello packets; it just provides a method for failure detection.

Another feature that helps in faster detection of failures for BGP sessions is *fast peering session deactivation*. BGP fast peering session deactivation improves BGP convergence and response time to adjacency changes with BGP neighbors. This feature introduces an event-driven interrupt system that allows the BGP process to monitor the peering based on the adjacency. When there is an adjacency change detected, it triggers the termination of BGP sessions between the default or configured BGP scanning interval. Enable this feature on Cisco IOS using **neighbor** *ip-address* **fall-over** [**bfd**] command. Example 5-7 illustrates the configuration for implementing the fast peering session deactivation feature.

Example 5-7 *BGP Fast Peering Session Deactivation Feature Configuration*

```
R1(config)# router bgp 65530
R1(config-router)# neighbor 10.1.12.2 fall-over ?
  bfd        Use BFD to detect failure
  route-map  Route map for peer route
  <cr>
R1(config-router)# neighbor 10.1.12.2 fall-over bfd
R1(config-router)# end
```

With the fall-over option, BGP reacts immediately to any adjacency change detected locally. With the fall-over BFD option, not only faster convergence can be achieved but also a faster reaction. BFD can also help detect failures where the line protocol remains up, but peer reachability is lost.

Jumbo MTU for Faster Convergence

It is a well-known fact that the default MSS value without Path MTU discovery for BGP session is 536 bytes. In modern networks, an MSS of 536 results in an inefficient exchange of information because more packets are required to send the same amount of update data than if the MSS was 1460. This can be improved using Path maximum transmission unit (MTU) Discovery, which allows sending the update of size 1460 bytes with default MTU setting of 1500 across the path. So ~3 updates of 536 bytes can be packaged in the update and sent over to the peer. But the update can still be improved with Jumbo MTU of 9216 bytes. If the MTU is set to 9216 bytes and Path MTU discovery is enabled, as discussed in Chapter 3, "Troubleshooting Peering Issues," 9176 byte update messages can be sent to the neighbors instead of the default 536 byte update messages. This increases the efficiency because fewer update messages need to be sent to the peer. In case slow convergence is seen, it may be worth checking the TCP MSS negotiation and verify if Path MTU Discovery is enabled or not. If Path MTU Discovery is not enabled on one of the devices in the path, it will cause the TCP to negotiate with default MSS value of 536 bytes.

Slow Convergence due to Periodic BGP Scan

In case of convergence issues, IOS devices seem to show a symptom of high CPU or a high memory utilization condition on the routers. This is because the IOS platforms are not distributed and multithreaded platforms, like IOS XR and NX-OS. But the first distinct part that makes BGP convergence slow is the periodic validity check mechanism of next-hop reachability performed by the traditional BGP Scanner process in each BGP node. The default BGP scan time is 60 seconds. Thus, if the next-hop becomes unreachable, it is not updated until the BGP Scanner process is invoked to verify if the next-hop is valid.

Figure 5-5 demonstrates an ineffective BGP next-hop validity check with BGP Scanner. In this topology, R1 is the route reflector and R2, R3, and R4 are the route-reflector clients. The routers R3 and R4 are advertising the same prefix 192.168.5.5/32 toward the route reflector (RR) with the respective next-hop values. Because of the lower router-id, path via R3 is selected as the best path on the RR for prefix 192.168.5.5/32. When the next-hop advertised by R3 becomes unreachable, the update is still not advertised to the RR. This causes a black hole of traffic for that destination until the next-hop is updated. The RR must wait for the BGP scan time to pass before it detects that the next-hop learned via R3 is not valid anymore. This is explained with outputs in Example 5-8.

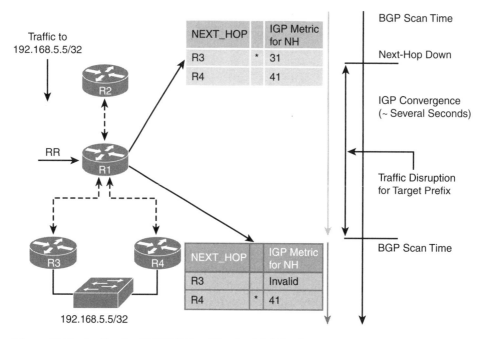

Figure 5-5   *Ineffective NH Validity Check with BGP Scanner*

Example 5-8   *Ineffective NH Validity Check with BGP Scanner*

```
! Output before 10.1.35.1 becomes unreachable
R2# show bgp ipv4 unicast
BGP table version is 60, local router ID is 192.168.2.2
Status codes: s suppressed, d damped, h history, * valid, > best, i - internal,
              r RIB-failure, S Stale, m multipath, b backup-path, f RT-Filter,
              x best-external, a additional-path, c RIB-compressed,
Origin codes: i - IGP, e - EGP, ? - incomplete
RPKI validation codes: V valid, I invalid, N Not found

     Network          Next Hop         Metric LocPrf Weight Path
 * i 192.168.5.5/32   10.1.45.1             0    100      0 ?
 *>i                  10.1.35.1             0    100      0 ?



!Output after 10.1.35.1 becomes unreachable
R2# show bgp ipv4 unicast 192.168.5.5
BGP routing table entry for 192.168.5.5/32, version 60
Paths: (2 available, best #2, table default)
  Advertised to update-groups:
    2
```

```
   Refresh Epoch 9
   Local, (Received from a RR-client), (received & used)
     10.1.45.1 (metric 41) from 192.168.4.4 (192.168.4.4)
       Origin incomplete, metric 0, localpref 100, valid, internal
       rx pathid: 0, tx pathid: 0
   Refresh Epoch 7
   Local, (Received from a RR-client), (received & used)
     10.1.35.1 (metric 31) from 192.168.3.3 (192.168.3.3)
       Origin incomplete, metric 0, localpref 100, valid, internal, best
       rx pathid: 0, tx pathid: 0x0
R2# show bgp ipv4 unicast
    Network          Next Hop          Metric LocPrf Weight Path
 * i 192.168.5.5/32  10.1.45.1              0    100      0 ?
 *>i                 10.1.35.1              0    100      0 ?
```

```
! Output after BGP Scan time expires
R2# show bgp ipv4 unicast
BGP table version is 61, local router ID is 192.168.2.2
Status codes: s suppressed, d damped, h history, * valid, > best, i - internal,
              r RIB-failure, S Stale, m multipath, b backup-path, f RT-Filter,
              x best-external, a additional-path, c RIB-compressed,
Origin codes: i - IGP, e - EGP, ? - incomplete
RPKI validation codes: V valid, I invalid, N Not found

    Network          Next Hop          Metric LocPrf Weight Path
 *>i 192.168.5.5/32  10.1.45.1              0    100      0 ?
 * i                 10.1.35.1              0    100      0 ?
R2# show bgp ipv4 unicast 192.168.5.5
BGP routing table entry for 192.168.5.5/32, version 61
Paths: (2 available, best #1, table default)
  Advertised to update-groups:
     2
  Refresh Epoch 9
  Local, (Received from a RR-client), (received & used)
     10.1.45.1 (metric 41) from 192.168.4.4 (192.168.4.4)
       Origin incomplete, metric 0, localpref 100, valid, internal, best
       rx pathid: 0, tx pathid: 0x0
  Refresh Epoch 7
  Local, (Received from a RR-client), (received & used)
     10.1.35.1 (Inaccessible) from 192.168.3.3 (192.168.3.3)
       Origin incomplete, metric 0, localpref 100, valid, internal
       rx pathid: 0, tx pathid: 0
```

To overcome this issue, the BGP scan time is reduced by using the command **bgp scan-time** *time-in-seconds*, where the timer can be set to any value between 5 seconds and 60 seconds. But this is not an effective solution, because it still does not resolve the essential characteristic of the BGP Scanner process. Also, this could cause an impact on the router if the router is having a large BGP table, and scanning through all the prefixes frequently to validate the next-hop can continuously degrade the router's performance. Thus it is always recommended to have BGP scan time set to its default value. A better way to overcome this issue is by using the BGP next-hop tracking (NHT) feature, which is discussed later in the chapter.

Slow Convergence due to Default Route in RIB

Default route makes the configuration simpler by allowing all traffic, but it is very important to understand where the default route needs to be advertised in the network and what impact it can potentially have. Although at times a default route is required, if configured inappropriately, it can lead to convergence issues and traffic black hole problems. Referring to the same topology as shown in Figure 5-5, R1 advertises a default route using default-originate command option toward the RR. Now taking Example 5-8, 192.168.5.5/32 has a best path through next-hop 10.1.35.1, but if that next-hop becomes unreachable, the BGP table still selects the best path for that path but with a lower metric because the RR now thinks that 10.1.35.1 is reachable via a default route which has a lower metric. Example 5-9 shows the output when this issue happens. Notice that the later output shows that the next-hop is still 10.1.35.1, but the next-hop has actually become unreachable. Thus, any traffic forwarded towards 192.168.5.5/32 will be black holed and dropped.

Example 5-9   *Traffic Black Hole due to Default Route in RIB*

```
! Output before 10.1.35.1 becomes unreachable
R2# show bgp ipv4 unicast
     Network          Next Hop          Metric LocPrf Weight Path
 *>i 0.0.0.0          192.168.1.1            0    100      0 i
 *  i 192.168.5.5/32  10.1.45.1              0    100      0 ?
 *>i                  10.1.35.1              0    100      0 ?
R2# show bgp ipv4 unicast 192.168.5.5
BGP routing table entry for 192.168.5.5/32, version 65
Paths: (2 available, best #2, table default)
  Advertised to update-groups:
     2
Refresh Epoch 9
  Local, (Received from a RR-client), (received & used)
    10.1.45.1 (metric 41) from 192.168.4.4 (192.168.4.4)
      Origin incomplete, metric 0, localpref 100, valid, internal
      rx pathid: 0, tx pathid: 0
```

```
Refresh Epoch 7
Local, (Received from a RR-client), (received & used)
   10.1.35.1 (metric 31) from 192.168.3.3 (192.168.3.3)
      Origin incomplete, metric 0, localpref 100, valid, internal, best
      rx pathid: 0, tx pathid: 0x0
```

```
! Output after 10.1.35.1 becomes unreachable
R2# show bgp ipv4 unicast 192.168.5.5
BGP routing table entry for 192.168.5.5/32, version 66
Paths: (2 available, best #2, table default)
  Advertised to update-groups:
     2
  Refresh Epoch 9
  Local, (Received from a RR-client), (received & used)
     10.1.45.1 (metric 41) from 192.168.4.4 (192.168.4.4)
        Origin incomplete, metric 0, localpref 100, valid, internal
        rx pathid: 0, tx pathid: 0
  Refresh Epoch 7
  Local, (Received from a RR-client), (received & used)
     10.1.35.1 (metric 2) from 192.168.3.3 (192.168.3.3)
        Origin incomplete, metric 0, localpref 100, valid, internal, best
        rx pathid: 0, tx pathid: 0x0
```

Similar issues can be seen when there is a summarized route in IP RIB. These kind of issues can be resolved using the BGP Selective Next-Hop Tracking feature, which is discussed later in the chapter.

BGP Next-Hop Tracking

The BGP NHT feature was designed to overcome some of the challenges of the BGP Scanner process and convergence issues that are seen with default or summarized routes in RIB. BGP NHT feature is designed on Address Tracking Filter (ATF) infrastructure, which enables event-driven NEXT_HOP reachability updates. ATF provides a scalable event-driven model for dealing with IP RIB changes. A standalone component, ATF allows for selective monitoring of IP RIB updates for registered prefixes. The following actions are taken after ATF tracks all prefixes that are registered:

■ Notify client about route changes.

■ Client, in this case BGP, is responsible for taking action based on ATF notifications.

For event-driven NEXT_HOP reachability, BGP registers its next-hops from all available paths with ATF during the best-path calculation. ATF maintains all the information regarding the next-hops and tracks any IP RIB events in a dependency database. When a route for BGP next-hop changes (add/modify/delete) in the RIB, ATF notifies BGP about the change of its next-hop. Upon notification, BGP triggers a table walk to compute the best path for each prefix. This table walk is known as a lightweight "BGP Scanner" run. Figure 5-6 illustrates the interaction between BGP, ATF, and the IP RIB.

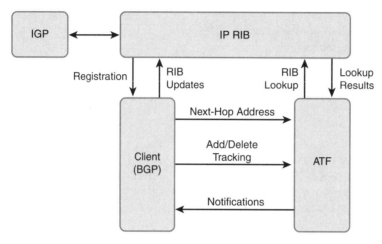

Figure 5-6   *Interaction Between BGP, ATF, and IP RIB*

Because BGP is capable of holding a large number of prefixes, and each prefix can have multiple paths, reacting to each notification from ATF could be costly for BGP. For this reason, the table walk is scheduled after a calculated time.

BGP NHT feature is enabled by default in almost all releases where the feature is supported, unless it is explicitly disabled on the router using the command **no bgp nexthop trigger enable** under the BGP address-family on Cisco IOS. BGP NHT cannot be disabled on IOS XR and NX-OS platforms. On Cisco IOS devices, a list of next-hops that are registered with ATF is viewed using the hidden command **show ip bgp attr nexthop**. Example 5-10 displays the output of all next-hops registered with ATF on the route-reflector router in Figure 5-5.

Example 5-10   *Next-Hops Registered with ATF*

```
R2# show ip bgp attr nexthop
 Next-Hop            Metric       Address-Family   Table-id  rib-filter
 10.1.13.3           0            ipv4 unicast     0         0x10B624C3
 10.1.45.5           3            ipv4 unicast     0         0x10B62400
 10.1.35.5           2            ipv4 unicast     0         0x10B62493
 10.1.14.4           0            ipv4 unicast     0         0x10B62433
```

After an ATF notification is received, BGP waits 5 seconds (by default) before triggering the next-hop scan. This timer is called the NHT trigger delay. The NHT trigger delay is changed for an address-family by using the command **bgp nexthop trigger delay** *seconds* on Cisco IOS. IOS XR and NX-OS platforms categorize the delay timers differently. The RIB notifications are classified based on the severity—critical and noncritical. The delay timers on IOS XR are configured by using the address-family command **nexthop trigger-delay** [**critical** | **non-critical**] *seconds*. NX-OS only provides command-line interface (CLI) to configure a trigger delay just for critical notifications using the address-family command **nexthop trigger-delay critical** *seconds*.

Note   The trigger delay is 5 seconds by default in almost all releases, except for 12.0(30)S or earlier (it is 1 second).

Selective Next-Hop Tracking

BGP NHT overcomes the problem faced because of periodic BGP scan by introducing the event-driven quick scan paradigm, but it still does not resolve the inconsistencies caused by default route or summarized route present in the RIB. To overcome these problems, a new enhancement was introduced in BGP NHT called the BGP Selective Next-Hop Tracking or BGP Selective Next-Hop Route Filtering.

A route map is used during best-path calculation and is applied on the routes in IP RIB that cover the next-hop of BGP prefixes. If the route to the next-hop fails the route-map evaluation during a BGP NHT scan triggered by a notification from ATF, the route to the next-hop is marked as unreachable. Selective Next-Hop Tracking is configured per address-family; this allows for different route maps to be applied for next-hop routes in different address-families.

Selective NHT is enabled using the command **bgp nexthop route-map** *route-map-name* on Cisco IOS software. Examine the Selective NHT feature configuration in Example 5-11.

Example 5-11   *Selective NHT Configuration*

```
router bgp 100
address-family ipv4 unicast
 bgp nexthop route-map Loop32
!
ip prefix-list le-31 seq 5 per 0.0.0.0/0 le 31
!
route-map Loop32 deny 10
 match ip address prefix-list le-31
!
route-map Loop32 permit 20
```

On Cisco IOS XR, use the command **nexthop route-policy** *route-policy-name* to implement the Selective Next-Hop Tracking feature.

> **Note**   The IOS XR implementation for BGP Next-Hop Tracking and Selective Next-Hop Tracking supports every address-family identifier (AFI)/subaddress-family identifier (SAFI), whereas IOS supports only IPv4/VPNv4 and VPNv6.

Slow Convergence due to Advertisement Interval

BGP neighbor advertisement interval or MRAI causes delays in update generation if set to a higher value configured manually. It is a good practice to have the same MRAI timer at both ends of the neighbor and also across different platforms. Cisco IOS has advertisement interval of 0 seconds for IBGP as well as EBGP session in a VRF and 30 seconds for EBGP session, whereas IOS XR and NX-OS has the advertisement interval of 0 seconds for both IBGP and EBGP sessions. Thus if there is an IOS router and an IOS XR router both having EBGP sessions, then IOS router advertises any update after the MRAI timer has passed, which is 30 seconds, whereas IOS XR advertises the update immediately. The higher advertisement interval can cause slow convergence because the updates are not replicated before the MRAI timer expires.

The advertisement interval or MRAI value is modified using the command **neighbor** *ip-address* **advertisement-interval** *time-in-seconds* on Cisco IOS and the command **advertisement-interval** *time-in-seconds* under the neighbor configuration mode on IOS XR. The MRAI value is not configurable on the NX-OS platform.

Computing and Installing New Path

By default, BGP always selects only one best path (assuming BGP multipath is not configured). In case of failure of the best path, BGP has to go through the path selection process again to compute the alternative best path. This takes time and thus impacts convergence time. Also, features such as BGP NHT help improve the convergence time by providing fast reaction to IGP events, but that is still not significant because it depends on the total number of prefixes to be processed for best-path selection. With the BGP multipath feature, equal cost paths can be used for both redundancy and faster failover.

The question is, what happens when there are unequal cost paths available in the network? Can the backup path be programmed in the forwarding engine (that is, Cisco Express Forwarding in case of Cisco devices) of the router? And how can multiple paths be received across a route reflector? There have been new enhancements in past few years in this area with which all these problems can be resolved. Features such as BGP Best External, BGP Add Path, and BGP Prefix Independent Convergence (PIC) are a few of the features that are answers to all these questions. These features highly enhance the convergence for BGP and provide high availability in the network. Backup paths are now precomputed and installed in the forwarding engine. Thus in case of any failure, the traffic switches to the installed backup path.

Note BGP PIC and other High Availability topics are covered in Chapter 14, "BGP High Availability."

Troubleshooting BGP Convergence on IOS XR

BGP convergence troubleshooting techniques that are specific to IOS XR are covered. When troubleshooting IOS XR BGP convergence issues, the first thing you need to do is to verify whether the issue is seen right after the router boots or if it's seen after a link or protocol flap, if fast convergence features are enabled, availability of an alternate path, and how fast the other supporting infrastructure functions (Label Switch Database (LSD), RIB, forwarding information base (FIB), and the like) are updated. It is also important to verify if any route policy is implemented or a route map on the peer router is attached to the BGP peer. Other possible scenarios that could lead to slow convergence on IOS XR could be a memory leak condition on the BGP process or by any critical application running in the system. This may cause the BGP to either converge slowly or hinder the BGP process from processing messages in a timely manner.

Verifying Convergence During Initial Bring Up

Verification needs to be performed when the router is rebooted, the BGP process has restarted or crashed, or BGP is configured for the first time. The following actions confirm convergence:

- **BGP process state:** Ensure that the BGP process is in Run state when it is started or restarted. If it is in a different state or is continuously restarting, then it needs further investigation and a Technical Assistance Center (TAC) case has to be opened.

- **bgp update-delay configuration:** Sometimes the BGP update-delay parameter is modified as part of the design requirements. BGP stays in Read-Only (RO) mode until the update-delay time elapses, unless it receives End of Row (EoR) from all peers.

- **Non-Stop Routing (NSR):** If NSR is configured, a Stateful Switchover (SSO) is achieved by using the **nsr process-failures switchover** configuration knob. Verify the state using the command **show redundancy** on the IOS XR platforms.

- **Verify BGP process performance statistics:** Check BGP performance statistics, such as when the first BGP peer was established, what time it moved out of RO mode, and so on. This is checked by using the command **show bgp process**. When a new session is established and when the router begins exchanging OPEN messages, the router enters into BGP RO mode.

- **performance-statistics detail:** This command is AFI/SAFI aware and should be checked for relevant AFI/SAFI.

Example 5-12 demonstrates the verification of the preceding points to troubleshoot any BGP convergence issue on the router.

Example 5-12   *Troubleshooting Convergence on IOS XR*

```
RP/0/0/CPU0:R10# show process bgp | include Process state
         Process state: Run


! Verifying bgp update-delay configuration
RP/0/0/CPU0:R10# show run router bgp | include update-delay
 bgp update-delay 360


! Verifying BGP in RO mode or Normal mode
RP/0/0/CPU0:R10# show bgp process detail | include State
State: Normal mode.


RP/0/0/CPU0:R10# show bgp process performance-statistics detail | begin First nei
First neighbor established:   Oct 13 23:40:05
Entered DO_BESTPATH mode:     Oct 13 23:46:09
Entered DO_IMPORT mode:       Oct 13 23:46:09
Entered DO_RIBUPD mode:       Oct 13 23:46:09
Entered Normal mode:          Oct 13 23:46:09
Latest UPDATE sent:           Oct 13 23:46:14
```

Note   The difference between the first established neighbor and update sent should be approximately the same as the update-delay time.

Verifying BGP Reconvergence in Steady State Network

To troubleshoot BGP reconvergence in steady state, always wait for the BGP application to be in RW (read/write) or Normal mode. After the BGP is in any of these states, check the router to see whether it exhibits any of the following symptoms:

■ Check whether the router is not exceeding maximum allowed BGP peers and prefixes.

■ Check for memory leaks by BGP application or any critical process.

■ Check for constant link/peer flaps and troubleshoot based on that.

■ Check whether the slow convergence is noticed for a particular peer or multiple peers. Compare the peers converging at a slower pace to the ones converging faster.

■ Check for any inefficiently configured route policy.

■ Ensure whether Path MTU Discovery is enabled.

■ Check for any issues with RIB/FIB/BCDL infrastructure that are adding to the convergence delay

Ensure there is no memory leak on the router by any process that could be impacting BGP convergence. Troubleshooting memory leaks is covered in Chapter 6, "Troubleshooting Platform Issues Due to BGP."

Check the logging buffer for any exception events, such as link flaps, peer flaps, BGP notifications, and core dumps for any process crashes. All these events can cause the BGP process to constantly calculate the best path for a given prefix that is learned from the flapping peer or across the flapping link. Consider configuring route dampening (applicable for prefixes learned from an external BGP peer) or interface dampening. In such situations, it might also be worth disabling **fast-external-fallover** knob under **router bgp** configuration, which is enabled by default.

Path maximum transmission unit (MTU) Discovery (PMTUD) was discussed in detail in Chapter 3. It is recommended to use PMTUD for improving convergence time in the network. While troubleshooting convergence issues, check the negotiated MSS value and current rx/tx queue size for the socket connection.

In Example 5-13, TCP stats show the details for this socket for the tx/rx toward application and toward netio/XIPC queue. TCP Non-Stop Routing (NSR) statistics are also listed for the protocol control block (PCB) associated with the BGP peer. Check the TCP PCB stats and NSR stats for the PCB on both the Active and Standby Route Processor (RP).

Example 5-13   *Verifying Any Drops on the TCP Session*

```
RP/0/8/CPU0:R10# show tcp brief | include 10.1.102.2
0x10146a20 0x60000000  0  0  10.1.102.1:62233    10.1.102.2:179     ESTAB


RP/0/8/CPU0:R10# show tcp statistics pcb 0x10146a20 location 0/8/CPU0
================================================================
 Statistics for PCB 0x10146a20, vrfid 0x60000000
Send:    0 bytes received from application
         0 segment instructions received from partner
         0 xipc pulses received from application
         0 packets sent to network (v4/v6 IO)
         722 packets sent to network (NetIO)
         0 packets failed getting queued to network (v4/v6 IO)
         0 packets failed getting queued to network (NetIO)
         0 write operations by application
         1 times armed, 0 times unarmed, 0 times auto-armed
         Last written at: Wed Oct 14 05:20:19 2015

Rcvd:    722 packets received from network
         380 packets queued to application
         0 packets failed queuing to application
         0 send-window shrink attempts by peer ignored
         0 read operations by application
         0 times armed, 0 times unarmed, 0 times auto-armed
         Last read at: Wed Oct 14 05:19:43 2015
```

```
AsyncDataWrite: Data Type Data
        380 successful write operations to XIPC
        0 failed write operations to XIPC
        7318 bytes data has been written
AsyncDataRead: Data Type Data
        343 successful read operations from XIPC
        0 failed read operations from XIPC
        6968 bytes data has been read
AsyncDataWrite: Data Type Terminate
        0 successful write operations to XIPC
        0 failed write operations to XIPC
        0 bytes data has been written
AsyncDataRead: Data Type Terminate
        0 successful read operations from XIPC
        0 failed read operations from XIPC
        0 bytes data has been read
! Output omitted for brevity
```

```
RP/0/8/CPU0:R10# show tcp nsr statistics pcb 0x10146a20 location 0/8/CPU0
--------------------------------------------------------------
                    Node: 0/8/CPU0
--------------------------------------------------------------
==============================================================
PCB 0x10146a20
Number of times NSR went up: 1
Number of times NSR went down: 0
Number of times NSR was disabled: 0
Number of times switch-over occured : 0
IACK RX Message Statistics:
        Number of iACKs dropped because SSO is not up          : 0
        Number of stale iACKs dropped                          : 0
        Number of iACKs not held because of an immediate match : 0
TX Messsage Statistics:
        Data transfer messages:
            Sent 118347, Dropped 0, Data (Total/Avg.) 2249329/19
                IOVAllocs       : 0
            Rcvd 0
                Success         : 0
                Dropped (Trim)  : 0
                Dropped (Buf. OOS): 0
        Segmentation instructions:
            Sent 6139724, Dropped 0, Units (Total/Avg.) 6139724/1
            Rcvd 0
```

```
          Success           : 0
              Dropped (Trim)    : 0
              Dropped (TCP)     : 0
        NACK messages:
            Sent 0, Dropped 0
            Rcvd 0
              Success           : 0
              Dropped (Data snd): 0
        Cleanup instructions    :
            Sent 118346, Dropped 0
            Rcvd 0
              Success           : 0
              Dropped (Trim)    : 0
Last clear at: Never Cleared
```

A complex route policy applied for a specific BGP peer can cause slowdown of BGP convergence. In Example 5-14, examine a complex route policy for a peer advertising 400K prefixes. The route policy performs multiple if-else statements, where each if statement tries to match either an as-path-set or prefix sets. If every prefix out of 400K prefixes goes through one of these if statements, it consumes a lot of CPU resources and slows BGP performance. This in turn can cause serious convergence issues. Complex route policies can be used for neighbors that are not advertising huge numbers of prefixes. The simpler the route policy, the faster the convergence for that BGP neighbor.

Example 5-14 *Complex BGP Route Policy*

```
as-path-set match-ases
  ios-regex '^(.*65531)$',
  ios-regex '^(.*65532)$',
  ios-regex '^(.*65533)$',
! Output omitted for brevity
!
prefix-set K1-routes
  10.170.53.0/24
end-set
!
prefix-set K2-routes
  10.147.4.0/24
end-set
!
prefix-set K3-routes
  198.168.44.0/23,
  198.168.46.0/24
end-set
!
```

```
route-policy Inbound-ROUTES
  if destination in K1-routes then
    pass
  elseif destination in K2-routes then
    pass
  elseif destination in K3-routes then
    pass
  elseif as-path in match-ases then
    drop
  else
    pass
  endif
end-policy
!
router bgp 65530
neighbor-group IGW
  remote-as 65530
  cluster-id 10.1.110.2
  address-family ipv4 unicast
   multipath
   route-policy Inbound-ROUTES in
```

If BGP has not converged after it has come out of RO mode, use the **show bgp all all convergence** command to identify in which AFI/SAFI the BGP is not converged, and troubleshooting can be performed accordingly. Example 5-15 shows the output of the **show bgp all all convergence** command. It displays how few address-families are in *not converged* state.

Example 5-15   show bgp all all convergence *Command*

```
RP/0/0/CPU0:R10# show bgp all all convergence
Address Family: IPv4 Labeled-unicast
=====================================
Not converged.
Received routes may not be entered in RIB.
One or more neighbors may need updating.


Address Family: IPv4 Unicast
=============================
Not converged.
```

```
Received routes may not be entered in RIB.
One or more neighbors may need updating.


Address Family: IPv6 Unicast
=============================
Converged.
All received routes in RIB, all neighbors updated.
All neighbors have empty write queues.
```

The convergence can also be verified for respective AFI/SAFI by using the CLI on the AFI/SAFI of interest. For instance, the command **show bgp vpnv4 unicast convergence** is used to verify the convergence state for the vpnv4 address-family. If a particular AFI/SAFI is flagged as *not converged*, further checks can be done to ascertain the reasons. One of the conditions that can lead to *not converged* state is that not all the configured peers in the address-family are in established state. If a peer is not expected to be in established state, the peer should be administratively shut down under the **router bgp** configuration. Another reason for a peer not being converged could be because either the local or remote peer router is busy and is not able to catch up with the processing of the incoming update message, or the transport is busy and not able to send the message out to the peer.

If a remote peer is not receiving an update in a timely manner, verify the update group performance statistics for the update group that the peer is member of. Example 5-16 shows the output of the command **show bgp ipv4 unicast update-group performance-statistics**. Use this command to verify how many messages have been formatted and how many replications have happened. Although it becomes a bit complex if the update group has a huge number of members, this command is really helpful for convergence issues seen for a set of peers.

Example 5-16 *Update Group Performance Statistics*

```
RP/0/0/CPU0:R10# show bgp ipv4 unicast update-group 0.2 performance-statistics
Update group for IPv4 Unicast, index 0.2:
  Attributes:
    Neighbor sessions are IPv4
    Internal
    Common admin
    First neighbor AS: 65530
    Send communities
    Send extended communities
    Route Reflector Client
    4-byte AS capable
    Non-labeled address-family capable
    Send AIGP
    Send multicast attributes
    Minimum advertisement interval: 0 secs
```

```
Update group desynchronized: 0
 Sub-groups merged: 0
 Number of refresh subgroups: 0
 Messages formatted: 0, replicated: 0
 All neighbors are assigned to sub-group(s)
   Neighbors in sub-group: 0.1, Filter-Groups num:1
     Neighbors in filter-group: 0.1(RT num: 0)
       10.1.102.2        10.1.103.2        10.1.104.2        10.1.105.2


 Updates generated for 0 prefixes in 10 calls(best-external:0)
           (time spent: 10.000 secs)
 Update timer last started: Oct 13 23:42:12.404
 Update timer last stopped: not set
 Update timer last processed: Oct 13 23:42:12.434
```

If the update group is showing 0 messages formatted, and 0 updates generated, there seems to be some problem. One possible reason could be the route policy configuration. It might have a deny statement blocking all the updates from being sent to the peer.

Troubleshooting BGP Convergence on NX-OS

Like IOS XR, NX-OS also provides CLI for verifying convergence. There is a process that should be followed to verify if the BGP has converged and the routes are installed in the BRIB.

If there is a traffic loss, after BGP has completed its convergence for a given address-family, the routing information in the Unicast RIB (URIB) and the forwarding information in the FIB should be verified. Example 5-17 demonstrates a BGP route getting refreshed. The command **show bgp** *afi safi ip-address* can be used to validate that the prefix is installed in the BRIB table, and the command **show ip route bgp** can be used to check that the route has been installed in the URIB. In the URIB, verify the timestamp of when the route was downloaded to the URIB. If the prefix was recently downloaded to the URIB, there might have been an event that caused the route to get refreshed.

In Example 5-17, notice that the prefix 192.168.2.2 was installed two days and eleven hours ago, but the other prefixes were installed more than five days ago.

Example 5-17   *Verifying BGP and Routing Table for Prefix*

```
R20# show bgp ipv4 unicast 192.168.2.2
BGP routing table information for VRF default, address family IPv4 Unicast
BGP routing table entry for 192.168.2.2/32, version 67
Paths: (1 available, best #1)
Flags: (0x08001a) on xmit-list, is in urib, is best urib route
```

```
 Advertised path-id 1
  Path type: internal, path is valid, is best path
  AS-Path: NONE, path sourced internal to AS
     10.1.202.2 (metric 0) from 10.1.202.2 (192.168.2.2)
        Origin IGP, MED 0, localpref 100, weight 0


  Path-id 1 advertised to peers:
     10.1.203.2          10.1.204.2          10.1.205.2
R20# show ip route bgp
IP Route Table for VRF "default"
'*' denotes best ucast next-hop
'**' denotes best mcast next-hop
'[x/y]' denotes [preference/metric]
'%<string>' in via output denotes VRF <string>


192.168.2.2/32, ubest/mbest: 1/0
    *via 10.1.202.2, [200/0], 2d11h, bgp-65530, internal, tag 65530,
192.168.3.3/32, ubest/mbest: 1/0
    *via 10.1.203.2, [200/0], 5d12h, bgp-65530, internal, tag 65530,
192.168.4.4/32, ubest/mbest: 1/0
    *via 10.1.204.2, [200/0], 5d12h, bgp-65530, internal, tag 65530,
192.168.5.5/32, ubest/mbest: 1/0
    *via 10.1.205.2, [200/0], 5d12h, bgp-65530, internal, tag 65530,
```

If the route is a vpnv4 prefix, that route has an associated label and a labeled next-hop. This is verified by using the command **show forwarding route** *prefix* **vrf** *vrf-name*. BGP convergence for the relevant address-family is checked by using the command **show bgp convergence detail vrf all**. Example 5-18 shows the output of the **show bgp convergence details vrf all** command. This command shows when the best-path selection process was started and the time to complete it.

Example 5-18   show bgp convergence detail vrf all *Command*

```
R20# show bgp convergence detail vrf all
Global settings:
BGP start time 5 day(s), 13:55:45 ago
Config processing completed 0.119865 after start
BGP out of wait mode 0.119888 after start
LDP convergence not required
Convergence to ULIB not required


Information for VRF default
Initial-bestpath timeout: 300 sec, configured 0 sec
BGP update-delay-always is not enabled
```

```
First peer up 00:09:18 after start
Bestpath timer not running

  IPv4 Unicast:
  First bestpath signalled 00:00:27 after start
  First bestpath completed 00:00:27 after start
  Convergence to URIB sent 00:00:27 after start
  Peer convergence after start:
    10.1.202.2          (EOR after bestpath)
    10.1.203.2          (EOR after bestpath)
    10.1.204.2          (EOR after bestpath)
    10.1.205.2          (EOR after bestpath)

! Output omitted for brevity
```

Note   If the BGP best-path has not run yet, the problem is likely not related to BGP on that node.

If the best-path runs before EOR is received, or if a peer fails to send the EOR marker, it can lead to traffic loss. In such situations, enable **debug for bgp updates** with relevant debug filters for VRF, address-family, and peer, as shown in Example 5-19.

Example 5-19   debug *Command with Filter*

```
debug bgp events updates rib brib import
debug logfile bgp
debug-filter bgp vrf vpn1
debug-filter bgp address-family ipv4 unicast
debug-filter bgp neighbor 10.1.202.2
debug-filter bgp prefix 192.168.2.2/32
```

From the debug output, check the event log to look at the timestamp when the most recent End of RIB (EOR) was sent to the peer. This also shows how many routes were advertised to the peer before the sending of the EOR. A premature EOR sent to the peer can also lead to traffic loss if the peer flushes stale routes early.

If the route in URIB has not been downloaded, it needs to be further investigated because it may not be a problem with BGP. The following commands can be run to check the activity in URIB that could explain the loss:

- **show routing internal event-history ufdm**

- **show routing internal event-history ufdm-summary**

- **show routing internal event-history recursive**

BGP Slow Peer

A *BGP slow peer* is a peer that cannot keep up with the rate at which the sender is generating update messages. The slow peer condition doesn't happen in one or two updates, but this condition occurs over a prolonged period of time (usually minutes). There are several reasons for a peer to exhibit this problem, including the following:

- The peer is not having enough CPU capacity to process the incoming updates.

- The CPU is running high on the peer router and cannot service the TCP connection at the required frequency.

- The throughput of the BGP TCP connection is very low as the result of excess traffic or traffic loss on the link.

For further understanding the problem of BGP slow peer, it is important to understand the TCP Flow Control mechanism. The receiving side of the TCP application has a receive buffer that stores the data it received for reading it and processing it. If the receiver's application doesn't read the data fast enough, the buffer may fill up. Figure 5-7 illustrates the correlation between the RcvBuffer and RcvWnd.

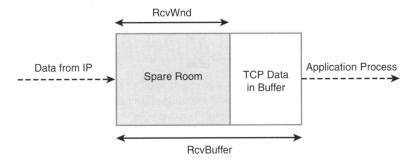

Figure 5-7 *TCP Flow Control Mechanism*

The TCP Flow Control mechanism prevents the sender from sending more data than the receiver can store. The receiver sends the information of spare room in the buffer using the *RcvWindow* field as part of each TCP segment.

$$RcvWindow = RcvBuffer - (LastByteReceived - LastByteRead)$$

How does this impact the BGP update processing in the update group? When an update group peer is slow in processing the TCP updates, the update group's number of updates pending transmission builds up and thus starts filling up the cache size (CSize). When that quota limit is reached, the BGP process does not format any new update messages for the update group leader. Because of this, even peers that are processing updates normally are not able to receive updates. Therefore, if there are any new updates to advertise new prefixes or any withdrawals, none of the peers in the update group receive the update. Thus, when one of the peers that is slow in consuming or processing the updates stops the formatting and replication of messages for all other peers in the update group, it is known as a slow peer condition.

> **Note**   At the time of writing, BGP slow peer condition is not applicable for IOS XR and NX-OS platforms. The reason is on IOS XR, because of the concept of subgroups within update groups, slow peer issues are overcome. The slow peer condition does not apply to NX-OS because there is no concept of update groups in NX-OS.

BGP Slow Peer Symptoms

There are two common symptoms when the BGP slow peer condition is seen:

- High CPU due to BGP Router process
- Prefixes not getting replicated and traffic black hole

High CPU due to BGP Router Process

Often a BGP slow peer condition is not identified because of the high CPU condition on the router. The problem is reported as a high CPU condition due to BGP Router process.

Traffic Black Hole and Missing Prefixes in BGP table

No BGP update messages are formatted until the cache is freed up, which causes the other neighbors that are processing updates normally to miss all the newer updates that might have been there. Thus if a prefix is withdrawn from one peer, it does not get replicated to rest of the other peers that are interested in that update. Therefore, all the other remaining peers still maintain that prefix in their BGP table and thus the routing table (RIB). This situation can lead to traffic black holing.

In Figure 5-8, R1 is acting as a RR, R2 is a slow peer, and R3 through R10 are other peers that are part of the same update group. Because of the slow peer condition, the CSize has filled up for the update group, and a lot of updates are pending to be replicated to router R2.

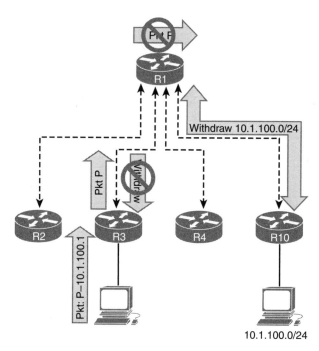

Figure 5-8   *Topology with Slow Peer*

R10 had a locally learned prefix (10.1.100.0/24) that becomes unreachable. R10 sends the withdraw message to R1 for this prefix. R1 updates that information in its BGP table, but it doesn't format the update for any of the RR clients because it is still waiting for the CSize to have room for new messages. This information is thus not replicated to R3. R3 has a host locally connected to it that is sending traffic for the hosts in subnet 10.1.100.1.0/24. The traffic is forwarded from R3 out, but it gets dropped because the upstream device doesn't have any information about the prefix 10.1.100.0/24 in its BGP table or routing table. This causes black holing of the traffic.

BGP Slow Peer Detection

BGP slow peer condition can be easily detected with the help of show commands. The following steps help identify a BGP slow peer:

Step 1.   Verify OutQ in **show bgp ipv4 unicast summary** output.

Step 2.   Verify SndWnd field in the **show bgp ipv4 unicast neighbor** *ip-address* command.

Step 3.   Verify CSize along with Current Version and Next Version fields in **show bgp ipv4 unicast replication** output.

Step 4.   Verify CPU utilization due to BGP Router process.

Verifying OutQ value

The **show bgp ipv4 unicast summary** or **show bgp vpnv4 unicast all summary** is a very useful command during troubleshooting BGP slow peer issues. The most important field to look in this output is the OutQ value, which should be high against a slow peer. Example 5-20 displays two neighbors with high OutQ value.

Example 5-20   *High OutQ for BGP Slow Peer*

```
R1# show bgp ipv4 unicast summary
Neighbor        V     AS MsgRcvd MsgSent    TblVer   InQ OutQ Up/Down  State/PfxRcd
10.1.12.2       4    109      42    87065        0     0 1000 00:10:00      3000
10.1.14.2       4    109      42    87391        0     0  674 00:10:00      2000
10.1.13.2       4    109      42    87391        0     0    0 00:10:00      1000
!Output omitted for brevity
```

The **show bgp ipv4 unicast summary** output is useful when the slow peer condition is seen in regular IPv4 BGP setup. But if there is a MPLS VPN setup, check the **show bgp vpnv4 unicast all summary** command as the peers are establishing neighbor relationship in the vpnv4 address-family. Also, it's important to note that the BGP slow peer condition is mostly seen in RR deployments unless it's a full-mesh BGP deployment. This is because the RR is peering with all its clients, most commonly using **peer-group** and with the same outbound policy, forming a single update group.

Verifying SndWnd

Now verify the **show bgp ipv4 unicast neighbor** *ip-address* command on both the sender and the receiver router. This command not only contains information related to BGP but also related to TCP. It shows the *SndWnd/RcvWnd* field based on the output on sending and the receiving routers, respectively. The sending side has the *SndWnd* value, which is very low or equal to 0. The *RcvWnd* field on the receiving router is very low or equal to 0. Example 5-21 demonstrates the low send window on the sending router and the low receive window in the receiving router. In this example, the sending router R1 is having the SndWnd as 0 and the receiving router R2 (the slow peer) is having the RcvWnd value as 0.

Example 5-21   show bgp ipv4 unicast neighbor *ip-address* Output

```
! Output from Sender side
R1# show bgp ipv4 unicast neighbor 10.1.12.2
! Output omitted for brevity
iss: 3662804973   snduna: 3668039487   sndnxt: 3668039487      sndwnd:       0
irs: 1935123434   rcvnxt: 1935222998   rcvwnd:       16003 delrcvwnd:     381

SRTT: 300 ms, RTTO: 303 ms, RTV: 3 ms, KRTT: 0 ms
minRTT: 0 ms, maxRTT: 512 ms, ACK hold: 200 ms
```

```
Status Flags: passive open, gen tcbs
Option Flags: nagle, path mtu capable


Datagrams (max data segment is 1436 bytes):
Rcvd: 3556 (out of order: 0), with data: 117, total data bytes: 99563
Sent: 5229 (retransmit: 17 fastretransmit: 0),with data: 5105, total data bytes:
  5234513
```

```
! Output from Receiver side
R2# show bgp ipv4 unicast neighbor 10.1.12.1
! Output omitted for brevity
iss: 1935123434   snduna: 1935223160   sndnxt: 1935223160      sndwnd:  15841
irs: 3662804973   rcvnxt: 3668039487   rcvwnd:            0  delrcvwnd:      0

SRTT: 304 ms, RTTO: 338 ms, RTV: 34 ms, KRTT: 0 ms
minRTT: 0 ms, maxRTT: 336 ms, ACK hold: 200 ms
Status Flags: none
Option Flags: higher precendence, nagle, path mtu capable
```

Verifying Cache Size and Pending Replication Messages

As stated, the cache size of the update group keeps increasing without returning to zero when the formatted update messages keep building up for transmission. This is verified by using the **show ip bgp replication** command. Example 5-22 displays the show ip bgp replication output. In this output, the update group 1 has 348 members and the cache size (CSize) of 1000, but the cache is almost full because there are 999 messages in the cache. Another important thing to note is that for the same update group, there is a huge difference between the Current Version and the Next Version values. If this difference is temporary, then this can be ignored, but if the difference in version remains for a long period of time along with high Csize utilization, then this indicates a slow peer. Ideally, both the Current Version and Next Version fields should be equal or 0.

Example 5-22   show ip bgp replication *Output*

```
R1# show bgp ipv4 unicast replication

                                                        Current Next
Index  Members    Leader       MsgFmt    MsgRepl   Csize   Version Version
  1      348     10.1.20.2    1726595727 1938155978 999/1000 1012333000/1012351142
  2       2     192.168.78.19   79434677   79398843  0/200  1012351503/1012351503
  3       1     10.37.187.24          0          0  0/100       0/0
  4       2     10.19.30.249    79219618   97412908  0/200  1012351504/1012351504
```

The neighbors having the high OutQ value are also part of the same update group that is having high CSize usage. Remember that if it is a MPLS VPN setup, use the command **show bgp vpvn4 unicast all replication** to verify the CSize for an update group.

Workaround

A simple workaround to mitigate the slow peer condition and prevent it from impacting the other peers is to move the slow peer into a separate update group. There are three manual ways to accomplish this:

■ Changing the outbound policy of that neighbor can move the neighbor to a separate update group.

■ Change the advertisement interval from the default value.

■ BGP Slow Peer feature.

Changing Outbound Policy

If the outbound policy of all the peers is the same, then creating a new outbound policy different from the one being used for the other peers moves the slow peer into a different update group.

Example 5-23 demonstrates moving a neighbor from one update group to another update group by changing the outbound policy using route-map.

Example 5-23   *Changing Outbound Route Policy*

```
R1# show bgp ipv4 unicast update-group
BGP version 4 update-group 5, internal, Address Family: IPv4 Unicast
  BGP Update version : 18/0, messages 0, active RGs: 1
  Topology: global, highest version: 18, tail marker: 18
  Format state: Current working (OK, last not in list)
              Refresh blocked (not in list, last not in list)
  Update messages formatted 9, replicated 11, current 0, refresh 0, limit 1000
  Number of NLRIs in the update sent: max 2, min 0
  Minimum time between advertisement runs is 0 seconds
  Has 4 members:
    10.1.12.2        10.1.13.2        10.1.14.2        10.1.15.2
```

```
R1(config)# route-map R5_Out permit 10
R1(config-route-map)# set community 65530:5
R1(config-route-map)# exit
R1(config)# router bgp 65530
R1(config-router)# address-family ipv4
R1(config-router-af)# neighbor 10.1.15.2 route-map R5_Out out
R1(config-router-af)# end
```

```
R1# show bgp ipv4 unicast update-group
BGP version 4 update-group 5, internal, Address Family: IPv4 Unicast
  BGP Update version : 19/0, messages 0, active RGs: 1
  Topology: global, highest version: 19, tail marker: 19
```

```
    Format state: Current working (OK, last not in list)
                  Refresh blocked (not in list, last not in list)
    Update messages formatted 9, replicated 11, current 0, refresh 0, limit 1000
    Number of NLRIs in the update sent: max 2, min 0
    Minimum time between advertisement runs is 0 seconds
    Has 3 members:
      10.1.12.2          10.1.13.2          10.1.14.2

BGP version 4 update-group 6, internal, Address Family: IPv4 Unicast
  BGP Update version : 19/0, messages 0, active RGs: 1
  Route map for outgoing advertisements is R5_Out
  Topology: global, highest version: 19, tail marker: 19
  Format state: Current working (OK, last not in list)
                Refresh blocked (not in list, last not in list)
  Update messages formatted 4, replicated 4, current 0, refresh 0, limit 1000
  Number of NLRIs in the update sent: max 3, min 0
  Minimum time between advertisement runs is 0 seconds
  Has 1 member:
    10.1.15.2
```

If the members are part of a peer group, then removing the slow peer from that peer group moves it to a separate update group. Alternatively, if the peer group or peers already have a route map, create a route map with the same functionality but with a different name and apply it to the slow peer. This moves the slow peer to a separate update group.

Advertisement Interval

The BGP advertisement interval or MRAI is a measure to limit the advertisement of routes. Rather than having flash updates, the router waits for the advertisement interval to expire and then it sends the update to its peers. The advertisement interval was 5 seconds for IBGP peers and 30 seconds for EBGP peers. But this was later updated to 0 seconds for IBGP peers and 30 seconds for EBGP peers on Cisco IOS software. Changing the MRAI value moves the peer to a separate update group because the update is not packaged at the same time as compared to the other neighbors. Example 5-24 demonstrates how changing the advertisement interval moves the peer to a separate update group. In the first output, it is seen that the advertisement interval is 0 seconds for all the members in the update group 5, but after changing the advertisement interval to 6 for neighbor 10.1.13.2, it was moved to a separate update group.

Example 5-24 *MRAI and Update Groups*

```
R1# show bgp ipv4 unicast update-group
BGP version 4 update-group 5, internal, Address Family: IPv4 Unicast
  BGP Update version : 24/0, messages 0, active RGs: 1
  Topology: global, highest version: 24, tail marker: 24
  Format state: Current working (OK, last not in list)
               Refresh blocked (not in list, last not in list)
  Update messages formatted 16, replicated 25, current 0, refresh 0, limit 1000
  Number of NLRIs in the update sent: max 2, min 0
  Minimum time between advertisement runs is 0 seconds
  Has 4 members:
   10.1.12.2        10.1.13.2        10.1.14.2        10.1.15.2
```

```
R1(config)# router bgp 65530
R1(config-router)# address-family ipv4
R1(config-router-af)# neighbor 10.1.13.2 advertisement-interval 6
R1(config-router-af)# end
```

```
R1# show bgp ipv4 unicast update-group
BGP version 4 update-group 8, internal, Address Family: IPv4 Unicast
  BGP Update version : 5/0, messages 0, active RGs: 1
  Topology: global, highest version: 5, tail marker: 5
  Format state: Current working (OK, last not in list)
               Refresh blocked (not in list, last not in list)
  Update messages formatted 0, replicated 0, current 0, refresh 0, limit 1000
  Number of NLRIs in the update sent: max 0, min 0
  Minimum time between advertisement runs is 0 seconds
  Has 3 members:
   10.1.12.2        10.1.14.2        10.1.15.2

BGP version 4 update-group 9, internal, Address Family: IPv4 Unicast
  BGP Update version : 5/0, messages 0, active RGs: 1
  Topology: global, highest version: 5, tail marker: 5
  Format state: Current working (OK, last minimum advertisement interval)
               Refresh blocked (not in list, last not in list)
  Update messages formatted 0, replicated 0, current 0, refresh 0, limit 1000
  Number of NLRIs in the update sent: max 0, min 0
  Minimum time between advertisement runs is 6 seconds
  Has 1 member:
   10.1.13.2
```

Both methods mentioned are manual methods of moving the slow peer to a separate update group.

BGP Slow Peer Feature

Starting with the 12.2(33)SRE release, Cisco IOS software introduced the slow peer detection feature that automatically detects and moves the slow peer into its own update group. The three mechanisms available are as follows:

- Static slow peer

- Dynamic slow peer detection

- Slow peer protection

Static Slow Peer

Static slow peer is a configuration option to move a peer into its own update group, similar to the manual methods mentioned previously. When enabled, this feature moves the statically configured peer to a separate update group. The command **neighbor** [*ip-address* | *peer-grp-name*] **slow-peer split-update-group static** allows statically setting a neighbor as a slow peer. The benefit of the static slow peer feature is that it takes less overhead on the system resources. If there are two or more neighbors marked as slow peer, all of them are part of the same update group and progress at the pace of the slowest peer of them all.

Dynamic Slow Peer Detection

The feature is enabled by default on the newer IOS releases that has support for slow peer detection. When this feature is enabled, the router monitors its peers to see if any exhibit the symptoms shared before. If a peer is found to be having those symptoms, it is marked as slow and dynamically moved to a separate update group. At this point, a syslog message is printed indicating the peer that is found to be slow. When the neighbor recovers from the slow peer condition, it is then moved back to the existing update group along with a syslog message indicating the recovery of the peer.

The **bgp slow-peer detection** [**threshold** *seconds*] command is used to enable the dynamic slow peer detection feature. The threshold value in this command defines the time to detect a peer as a slow peer. The default value is 300 seconds.

Example 5-25 displays a syslog message generated for a slow peer detection and recovery.

Example 5-25 *BGP Slow Peer Syslog Message*

```
Sept 24 22:54:32.982 IST: %BGP-5-SLOWPEER_DETECT: Neighbor IPv4 Unicast 10.1.12.2
   has been detected as a slow peer

! Output omitted for brevity

Sept 24 22:57:28.816 IST: %BGP-5-SLOWPEER_RECOVER: Slow peer IPv4 unicast 10.1.12.2
   has recovered.
```

> **Note**   The Dynamic Slow Peer feature is enabled per address-family.

Slow Peer Protection

This feature depends on the dynamic BGP slow peer detection. When this feature is enabled, the peer after recovering from slow peer state is not moved back automatically to the default update group. Rather, it is marked permanently to remain in the new update group. After the root cause of the slow peer condition is identified, the peer can then be moved to the default update group by using the **clear bgp** *ip-address* **slow** command. If there are multiple address families, the clear command has to be used within the affected address-family. The slow peer protection feature is enabled by using the **bgp slow-peer split-update-group dynamic [permanent]** configuration command. The **permanent** keyword is the one that enables slow peer protection.

Slow Peer Show Commands

The CLI for **show** commands for slow peer is no different from the regular BGP **show** commands, but the output can be filtered to slow peers using the **slow** keyword at the end of the command. The CLI is applicable when the IOS slow peer configuration is being used. To verify the update group created for the slow peer, use the **show bgp ipv4 unicast update-group slow** command. To verify the summary information of all slow peers, use the **show bgp ipv4 unicast summary slow** command. The slow keyword is available for both **show** and **clear** commands.

Troubleshooting BGP Route Flapping

In a huge enterprise or in service provider deployments, it's very common to see flapping routes. For example, a customer shuts down some servers at its end, and it causes the route to be updated on the service provider edge router and also on the remote customer router. These expected flaps are not cause for worry because they do not create a large table version update on the routers, but if there are 100K prefixes getting updated every few seconds, this can cause serious performance issues in the network and especially with BGP, because such route churns causes the CPU to spike up due to the BGP router process and slow down BGP convergence.

To investigate BGP route churn issues, the troubleshooting has to be performed on a hop-by-hop basis. Figure 5-9 shows the topology where the route reflector is seeing a huge amount of route churns. In this topology, R2, R3, and R4 are the route-reflector clients of router R1. R2 is peering with an ISP through which it is learning the Internet routing table.

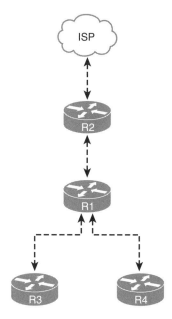

Figure 5-9 *Topology*

The initial problem is, in most cases, reported as high CPU due to BGP Router process. Example 5-26 shows the high CPU utilization on the router due to BGP Router process. If the BGP prefixes are supposed to get installed in the routing table (RIB), the IP RIB Update process may also consume the CPU utilization.

Example 5-26 *High CPU due to BGP Router Process*

```
R1# show process cpu sorted
CPU utilization for five seconds: 99%/4%; one minute: 98%; five minutes: 98%
  PID Runtime(ms)    Invoked     uSecs    5Sec    1Min   5Min TTY Process
    3    1892358    1306768      1448  50.65%  58.59%  63.87%   0 BGP Router
  198     101510        566    179346  34.61%  23.68%  21.04%   0 IP RIB Update
  100    1118683    1274370       877   6.81%   2.56%   1.03%   0 BGP I/O
  137    1752230    1275486      1373   1.86%   0.74%   0.67%   0 IP Input
   82     157775      41329      3817   0.40%   0.39%   0.39%   0 Per-Second Jobs
  339       8417        690     12198   0.32%   0.81%   0.20%   0 BGP Task
  104     110554     640268       172   0.16%   0.13%   0.12%   0 VRRS Main thread
```

To verify whether the route flapping is happening, the BGP table version and the routing table need to be checked. Because the routes learned over BGP are flapping, it causes the BGP table version to continuously increase by a huge number (a small increase is not much of a concern and is expected in a large network).

To verify the table version, use the **show ip bgp summary** command multiple times to see how frequently the table version is incrementing. It's better to capture this output along with the **show clock** command so as to understand the number of flaps that occurred since the last execution of the command. Example 5-27 demonstrates how to check the BGP table for flapping routes. The output shows that in 6 seconds the BGP table version has increased by 10,000. This output needs to be captured multiple times to understand how frequently the route churn is happening.

Example 5-27   *Verifying BGP Table Version*

```
R1# show clock
*14:54:24.240 UTC Sun Oct 25 2015
R1# show bgp ipv4 unicast summary
BGP router identifier 192.168.1.1, local AS number 65530
BGP table version is 277142, main routing table version 276802
39499 network entries using 5687856 bytes of memory
39499 path entries using 3159920 bytes of memory
3952/3952 BGP path/bestpath attribute entries using 600704 bytes of memory
! Output omitted for brevity


R1# show clock
*14:54:30.500 UTC Sun Oct 25 2015
R1# show bgp ipv4 unicast summary | include table
BGP table version is 289662, main routing table version 281302
```

If the routes are flapping in the global routing table, verify the routing table for flapping routes using the **show ip route | include 00:00:0** command. To verify the routes for the vpnv4 prefixes, use the **show ip route vrf * all | include 00:00:0 | Routing Table:** command. The command displays the routes that got installed in the routing table in last 10 seconds. Example 5-28 shows the routing table having flapped routes in last 10 seconds. From this output it is seen that the next-hop 10.1.12.2 is the node from where all the prefixes were received that are flapping.

Example 5-28   *Verifying Flapping Routes in RIB*

```
R1# show ip route | in 00:00:0
B        172.31.117.0 [200/2373] via 10.1.12.2, 00:00:09
B        172.31.118.0 [200/2373] via 10.1.12.2, 00:00:09
B        172.31.119.0 [200/2373] via 10.1.12.2, 00:00:09
B        172.31.120.0 [200/1324] via 10.1.12.2, 00:00:09
B        172.31.121.0 [200/1324] via 10.1.12.2, 00:00:09
B        172.31.122.0 [200/1324] via 10.1.12.2, 00:00:09
B        172.31.123.0 [200/1324] via 10.1.12.2, 00:00:09
B        172.31.124.0 [200/1324] via 10.1.12.2, 00:00:09
B        172.31.125.0 [200/1324] via 10.1.12.2, 00:00:09
B        172.31.126.0 [200/1324] via 10.1.12.2, 00:00:09
B        172.31.127.0 [200/1324] via 10.1.12.2, 00:00:09
```

```
B          172.31.128.0 [200/1324] via 10.1.12.2, 00:00:09
B          172.31.129.0 [200/1324] via 10.1.12.2, 00:00:09
B          172.31.130.0 [200/2964] via 10.1.12.2, 00:00:09
! Output omitted for brevity
```

Verify the next-hop for the flapping prefixes. In most cases, the flapping routes are coming from a common next-hop. Check the next-hop for a few of the flapping prefixes and track down that next-hop in the network. Go to that next-hop router and perform the preceding steps again by checking the table version, and then checking the routing table. If that router is receiving the prefixes from another eBGP peer, or those prefixes are learned via redistribution, then check the peer router to understand why those prefixes are flapping. One common reason could be a flapping link that is causing the BGP session or redistributing IGP to flap and create a route churn. Example 5-29 demonstrates how to track down the flapping prefixes. On the RR, a high amount of churn is noticed and further understood that the prefixes are learned via the next-hop 10.1.12.2. On the 10.1.12.2 router, those prefixes are being learned via another eBGP peer 10.1.26.2 from where those prefixes are being received. Further checking on the BGP peer shows that a BGP session has been flapping continuously, causing the BGP route churn.

Example 5-29   *Verifying the Prefixes on the Next-Hop Router*

```
R2# show ip route | in 00:00:0
B          172.47.117.0 [20/2370] via 10.1.26.2, 00:00:09
B          172.47.118.0 [20/2370] via 10.1.26.2, 00:00:09
B          172.47.119.0 [20/2370] via 10.1.26.2, 00:00:09
B          172.47.120.0 [20/2370] via 10.1.26.2, 00:00:09
B          172.47.121.0 [20/2370] via 10.1.26.2, 00:00:09
B          172.47.122.0 [20/2370] via 10.1.26.2, 00:00:09
B          172.47.123.0 [20/2370] via 10.1.26.2, 00:00:09
B          172.47.124.0 [20/2430] via 10.1.26.2, 00:00:09
B          172.47.125.0 [20/2430] via 10.1.26.2, 00:00:09
B          172.47.126.0 [20/2430] via 10.1.26.2, 00:00:09
B          172.47.127.0 [20/2430] via 10.1.26.2, 00:00:09
B          172.47.128.0 [20/2430] via 10.1.26.2, 00:00:09
B          172.47.129.0 [20/2430] via 10.1.26.2, 00:00:09
! Output omitted for brevity


R2# show logging
*Oct 25 06:03:45.585: %BGP-5-ADJCHANGE: neighbor 10.1.26.2 Up
*Oct 25 14:23:01.331: %BGP-5-NBR_RESET: Neighbor 10.1.26.2 reset (Peer closed the
  session)
*Oct 25 14:23:03.093: %BGP-5-ADJCHANGE: neighbor 10.1.26.2 Down Peer closed the
  session
*Oct 25 14:23:03.094: %BGP_SESSION-5-ADJCHANGE: neighbor 10.1.26.2 IPv4 Unicast
  topology base removed from session  Peer closed the session
*Oct 25 14:25:01.052: %BGP-5-ADJCHANGE: neighbor 10.1.26.2 Up
```

```
*Oct 25 14:28:01.122: %BGP-5-NBR_RESET: Neighbor 10.1.26.2 reset (Peer closed the
  session)
*Oct 25 14:28:05.354: %BGP-5-ADJCHANGE: neighbor 10.1.26.2 Down Peer closed the
  session
*Oct 25 14:28:05.354: %BGP_SESSION-5-ADJCHANGE: neighbor 10.1.26.2 IPv4 Unicast
  topology base removed from session  Peer closed the session
*Oct 25 14:28:15.183: %BGP-5-NBR_RESET: Neighbor 10.1.26.2 active reset (BGP
  Notification sent)
! Output omitted for brevity
```

There can be situations in which the router is receiving continuous route churns from the next-hop router, but the routing table of the next-hop router shows that those prefixes have been stable. This could be an indication that there is something more to the problem than just a flapping link. At this point, the update group and replication needs to be verified. Use the **debug bgp ipv4 unicast update** debug command to verify why the update is being generated.

Until the actual reason for the route churn is identified, apply a temporary patch on the devices running BGP using the dampening feature. With the use of BGP dampening, flapping routes can be avoided to be installed in the BGP table back and forth until those routes become stable. If the churn is happening due to a flapping link, in that case, the interface dampening feature can be applied along with BGP dampening. Another benefit of dampening is that it provides a nice view of which prefixes are flapping frequently by using the command **show bgp** *afi safi ip-address* or the command **show bgp** *afi safi* [**dampened-paths | flap-statistics**].

Summary

This chapter discussed various BGP convergence problems that could severely degrade network performance or can cause traffic black holes. The chapter explains in detail the BGP update groups and the BGP update generation process on various Cisco platforms. The chapter then describes various scenarios that lead to BGP convergence issues, such as the problems faced because of periodic BGP scan, slow convergence due to default route in the RIB, and so on. The chapter then discussed various steps to troubleshoot BGP convergence issues on IOS XR and NX-OS platforms. On Cisco IOS platforms, slow convergence issues due to a BGP slow peer problem are discussed along with the methods to resolve them. Finally, the chapter discussed techniques to troubleshoot flapping BGP routes issues.

Reference

RFC 7747, *Basic BGP Convergence Benchmarking Methodology for Data-Plane Convergence*, R. Papneja, B., Parise, S. Hares, D. Lee, I. Varlashkin, IETF, https:// tools.ietf.org/html/rfc7747, April 2016.

Chapter 6

Troubleshooting Platform Issues Due to BGP

The following topics are covered in this chapter:

- Troubleshooting High CPU due to BGP

- Troubleshooting Memory Issues due to BGP

- Troubleshooting BGP and Related Processes

There are situations in which a router might experience high CPU utilization or a memory leak which can severely impact the services on the router or even the whole network. In some instances, BGP protocol may just be a victim of such a situation. But there can also be situations where BGP protocol is not just the victim but also the cause of the problem. These situations cause instability in the functioning of any routing protocols, including BGP. This chapter primarily focuses on troubleshooting scenarios that impact the services on the router due to high CPU conditions, high memory utilization, or a memory leak condition on the router due to BGP. This chapter also covers BGP problems caused due to resource constraints, software problems, or platform limitations.

Troubleshooting High CPU Utilization due to BGP

A high CPU condition may be seen on the router due to two primary reasons:

- Interrupt (Traffic)

- Process

If the CPU utilization is high due to interrupts, it indicates that either there is traffic that is destined toward the router or the transit network traffic (traffic that is not destined to the router's IP addresses but is only transiting the router) is not switched in hardware and is instead handled by software processes on the router. When the CPU utilization is high because of a process, this scenario means that a process is consuming too many CPU cycles and is not releasing the CPU control for other processes.

The Cisco Internetwork Operating System (IOS), IOS XR, and NX-OS platforms have different architectures and manage the underlying processes differently. Troubleshooting high CPU utilization issues that are caused by BGP requires understanding how the different operating systems handle the BGP process.

Troubleshooting High CPU due to BGP on Cisco IOS

Cisco IOS is not a multithreaded platform and uses various processes relating to BGP to perform different tasks. All the BGP functionality is spread across multiple processes that are individually threaded (not multithreaded). Table 6-1 lists the various BGP processes on Cisco IOS devices.

Table 6-1   *BGP Processes on Cisco IOS*

BGP Open	Performs BGP peer establishment. It is usually not seen under the **show process cpu** command output unless there is a BGP session in Open State.
BGP Scanner	Runs every 60 seconds to verify the next-hop reachability of all prefixes in the BGP table.
BGP Router	Runs once per second. Its primary functions include establishing peering, sending and receiving routes, calculate any best path, processing route churns, and interacting with the RIB for route installation or deletion.
BGP I/O	Runs when BGP control packets are received. It handles queuing and processing of BGP packets.
BGP Scheduler	BGP Scheduler process takes care of monitoring and scheduling tasks for various BGP processes.
BGP BMP Server	BGP Monitoring Protocol (BMP) Server process is intended to be used for monitoring BGP sessions.
BGP Consistency	BGP consistency checker process checks against each network in the BGP table for label next-hop inconsistency and checks against each update-group's update policy.
BGP Task	BGP Task process performs task parceling (means breaking of a task into smaller portions, also called parcels, requiring less CPU time) for BGP.
BGP VA	VA stands for Virtual Aggregation. BGP VA process helps perform Forwarding Information Base (FIB) suppression by not loading the prefixes in FIB for which it is not responsible.

Note   Some older IOS versions have fewer processes than mentioned in Table 6-1.

Of all the processes listed in Table 6-1, BGP Scanner, BGP Router, and BGP I/O are the most CPU-intensive processes; they can cause severe impact on the services running on the router and performance degradation. It is essential to understand how these processes are coupled together to provide BGP functionality. Figure 6-1 shows the functioning model of BGP processes on Cisco IOS software.

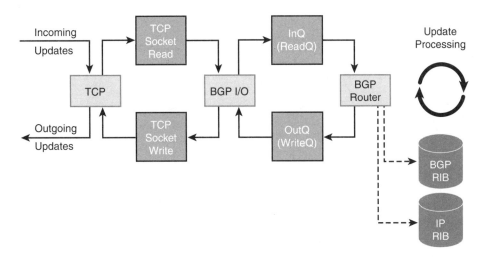

Figure 6-1 *BGP Processes on Cisco IOS Software*

High CPU due to BGP Scanner Process

The BGP Scanner process is a low-priority process that runs every 60 seconds by default. This process checks the entire BGP table to verify the next-hop reachability and updates the BGP table accordingly in case there is any change for a path. The BGP Scanner process runs through the Routing Information Base (RIB) for redistribution purposes.

The BGP Scanner process has to run the entire BGP RIB and global RIB and consumes a lot of CPU cycles if the BGP table and the routing table are holding a large number of prefixes. For example, for routers that consume the Internet routing table from their service provider, the router installs the route into the BGP table and the global RIB. The CPU will have a high utilization rate on routers with low performance CPUs due to the BGP Scanner process. Even on the high performance CPUs that are capable of performing much faster actions, the CPU may still spike up every 60 seconds.

Example 6-1 shows the CPU utilization on the router using the command **show process cpu sorted**. Notice that in the output below, the BGP Scanner process is consuming most of the CPU resources. Also notice that BGP is holding large number of prefixes from two different neighbors. When there are so many prefixes being held by BGP, the spike in the CPU utilization due to BGP Scanner process may not be an abnormal condition. The CLI shows % utilization over time, so if BGP scanner has run just prior to the CLI execution, the % CPU used by BGP scanner process will be high.

> **Note** The CPU utilization on the router is viewed using the command **show process cpu**. This command shows all the processes on the Cisco IOS router and their respective 5sec, 1Min, and 5Min average CPU utilization. The **sorted** keyword used with the command sorts the output based on the processes utilizing the most CPU resources.

Example 6-1 *High CPU due to BGP Scanner Process*

```
R1# show processes cpu sorted | exclude 0.00
CPU utilization for five seconds: 99%/0%; one minute: 30%; five minutes: 23%
 PID Runtime(ms)    Invoked    uSecs   5Sec   1Min   5Min TTY Process
 323   329026720   48369088     6802 93.83% 24.83% 17.73%   0 BGP Scanner
 162   166795336    1070414   155825  3.67%  0.51%  0.54%   0 IP Background
 321 1745832641952035493        89  0.71%  0.35%  0.38%   0 BGP Router
 281    84696032  687563142      123  0.23%  0.14%  0.12%   0 Port manager per
 163    65754676  168855372      389  0.15%  0.18%  0.14%   0 IP RIB Update
 322    48597036  799815299       60  0.15%  0.10%  0.08%   0 BGP I/O
 179    24667616   89018581      277  0.07%  0.03%  0.02%   0 CEF process


R1# show bgp ipv4 unicast summary
! Output omitted for brevity
Neighbor        V    AS MsgRcvd MsgSent   TblVer  InQ OutQ Up/Down   State/PfxRcd
10.1.12.2       4 65531 13490982  346982 44061045    0    0 4d01h         274061
10.1.13.2       4 65531   342135 11710057 44061063    0    0 4d01h              5
10.1.14.2       4 65531   341966 11627860 44061063    0    0 4d01h              1
10.1.15.2       4 65531   341970 11627869 44061063    0    0 4d01h              4
192.168.10.10   4 65531  3879885 11846203 44061063    0    0 4d01h         255020
```

When the BGP Scanner is running, even though it is a low priority process, it may affect other low priority processes that need to run. For example, Internet Message Control Protocol (ICMP) may have to wait a longer time to gain access to the CPU. This thus causes latency and delay in ping response.

The command **show processes** displays the various processes and their priority on the system. The column *QTy* in the command output is a combination of two variables. Variable *Q* basically has three values. The value *L* refers to low priority process, *H* refers to high priority process, and *M* refers to medium priority process. The variable *Ty* indicates various states based on the value. All the values of various states are described in Table 6-2.

Table 6-2 *Process States as Indicated by Ty*

Ty Value	Process State
*	Currently running
E	Waiting for an event
S	Ready to run, voluntarily relinquished processor

Ty Value	Process State
rd	Ready to run, wakeup conditions have occurred
we	Waiting for an event
sa	Sleeping until an absolute time
si	Sleeping for a time interval
sp	Sleeping for a time interval (alternate call)
st	Sleeping until a timer expires
hg	Hung; the process will never execute again
xx	Dead; the process has terminated, but has not yet been deleted

Example 6-2 illustrates the use of the **show processes** command that shows the BGP Scanner process is a low-priority process.

Example 6-2 *High CPU due to BGP Scanner Process*

```
R1# show processes
CPU utilization for five seconds: 0%/0%; one minute: 0%; five minutes: 0%
PID QTy      PC Runtime (ms)   Invoked   uSecs   Stacks TTY Process
323 Lsi   8892A3        9891      5107   193632416/36000   0 BGP Scanner
! Output omitted for brevity
```

When troubleshooting BGP Scanner issues, the platform scale should also be thoroughly checked, because in most cases it is due to an overloaded device that leads into such situations. Also, it should be ensured that there is proper ternary content addressable memory (TCAM) space available on the router.

Another important thing to verify is the routing table (RIB). Typically for IPv4 address-family, the prefixes are downloaded to RIB even on the route reflector, but for VPNv4 address-family, that is not the case. Use the **show ip route summary** command to verify how many routes are present in the RIB. The bigger the routing table, the longer the BGP Scanner process can take the CPU cycles.

Note In an MPLS VPN environment, BGP Scanner performs the route import and export into a particular VPN routing and forwarding (VRF) table. The BGP scanner process also checks for conditional advertisements and ensures whether a BGP prefix should be advertised. It also performs BGP route dampening.

High CPU due to BGP Router Process

This process is invoked when BGP is first configured on the router using the **router bgp** *autonomous-system-number* command. The BGP Router process runs once per second to safeguard faster convergence. To ensure faster convergence, it can consume all the free

CPU cycles. Example 6-3 shows the high CPU condition on the router due to BGP Router process.

Example 6-3 *High CPU due to BGP Router Process*

```
R2# show process cpu sorted
CPU utilization for five seconds: 98%/0%; one minute: 68%; five minutes: 68%
PID Runtime(ms)    Invoked     uSecs   5Sec   1Min   5Min TTY Process
185   281442004 683481796       411 98.24% 66.32% 65.09%    0 BGP Router
```

One scenario that can lead to high CPU utilization due to BGP Router process is huge route churn. Troubleshooting BGP route churn issues is discussed in detail in Chapter 5, "Troubleshooting Convergence Issues." BGP will have slow convergence if the CPU is busy with other tasks of equal or higher priority. The CPU itself could be busy with BGP churn; in that case, BGP is causing the CPU utilization problems, but the convergence may not be slower. In other words, if the CPU has a certain speed, and if BGP is using all of it, this may not really affect the convergence.

High CPU Utilization due to BGP I/O Process

The BGP I/O process runs when BGP control packets are received and manages the queuing and processing of BGP packets. High CPU utilization due to BGP I/O process is less common as compared to BGP Scanner or BGP Router processes. If there are excessive packets being received in the BGP queue for a longer period, or if there is a problem with TCP, the router shows symptoms of high CPU due to BGP I/O process. Example 6-4 illustrates a high CPU condition on the router due to BGP I/O process. Note the unread input bytes by TCP.

Example 6-4 *High CPU due to BGP I/O Process*

```
R1# show process cpu sorted
CPU utilization for five seconds: 81%/4%; one minute: 82%; five minutes:82%
 PID Runtime(ms)    Invoked     uSecs   5Sec   1Min   5Min TTY Process
 322  2087098100-1504383242        0 75.33% 73.65% 74.02%    0 BGP I/O
  78    66735804 235709575       283  0.49%  0.53%  0.51%    0 IP Input
! Output omitted for brevity
R1# show ip bgp vpn all neighbors | i BGP neighbor|Connnection state
BGP neighbor is 10.1.12.2,  remote AS 65530, internal link
Connection state is ESTAB, I/O status: 1, unread input bytes: 0
BGP neighbor is 10.1.13.2,  remote AS 65530, internal link
Connection state is ESTAB, I/O status: 1, unread input bytes: 108
BGP neighbor is 10.1.14.2,  remote AS 65530, internal link
Connection state is ESTAB, I/O status: 1, unread input bytes: 0
```

```
BGP neighbor is 10.1.15.2,   remote AS 65530, internal link
Connection state is ESTAB, I/O status: 1, unread input bytes: 0
```

```
! The TCB value 686B83C8 is achieved from the command show tcp brief
R2# show tcp tcb 686B83C8
Load for five secs: 79%/0%; one minute: 79%; five minutes: 81%
Connection state is ESTAB, I/O status: 1, unread input bytes: 108
Connection is ECN Disabled, Mininum incoming TTL 0, Outgoing TTL 255
Local host: 10.1.13.1, Local port: 179
Foreign host: 10.1.13.2, Foreign port: 62796
Connection tableid (VRF): 0
! Output omitted for brevity
```

Note   The TCP control block (tcb) value can be attained using **show tcp brief** command.

If the unread bytes keep incrementing, clearing the TCP session using command **clear tcp tcb** *value* resolves the issue with the TCP connection. This normalizes the CPU utilization as well. If the problem keeps happening again and again, running TCP debugs or performing packet captures may be useful.

The following steps summarize the process of troubleshooting a high CPU condition on the router due to one of the preceding BGP processes.

Step 1.   Verify the BGP process causing high CPU utilization. The process consuming high CPU utilization is verified by using the **show process cpu sorted** command.

Step 2.   Check the BGP Scanner. If the CPU has high utilization due to the BGP Scanner process, check the BGP and the routing table to verify how many routes are being learned by BGP. Elevated CPU utilization due to BGP scanner process may be normal every few seconds and should not be a problem as long as it is not causing impact to other functions of the router.

Step 3.   BGP Router. If the CPU is high due to the BGP Router process, verify the BGP table version to see if there is high BGP route churns being observed. Use the command **show bgp** *afi safi* **summary** to view the table version information for respective address-families. The RIB can also be checked for flapping routes using the **show ip route [vrf** *vrf-name*] | **include 00:00:0** command.

Step 4.   Verify that the path MTU discovery is enabled. Check that the **ip tcp path-mtu-discovery** command is enabled on the router global configuration mode. Also ensure there is no ICMP being blocked in the path. Use the **show bgp address-family unicast neighbor** *ip-address* command to verify the MSS value for the BGP neighbor. Also, perform the ping with DF-bit set to the remote destination. IOS XR and recent IOS software have path MTU discovery enabled by default. The TCP session can be verified for path MTU discovery by verifying the TCP tcb using the command **show tcp** *tcb*.

Step 5. If the route churn is noticed—that is, if the BGP table and/or the routing table are unstable—find the source of the route churn and troubleshoot the cause of it.

Step 6. Check for unread input bytes by using TCP. Use the **show tcp tcb value** command to check whether there are unread input bytes by the TCP session.

Step 7. Ensure that the system has sufficient resources. Confirm that there are enough system resources (DRAM, TCAM) to accommodate the Internet routing table. Also ensure that the latest hardware is being used. New hardware allows for a better and more powerful CPU that helps in faster processing of BGP requests and updates. It is important to verify that the production routers are capable of handling the scale and platform documentation and data sheets have been consulted to ensure the same.

Troubleshooting High CPU due to BGP on IOS XR

On IOS XR, there are multiple threads running under the BGP process performing various tasks. So if the CPU is high due to BGP, it might mean that a particular thread under the BGP process is consuming the CPU cycle. Example 6-5 illustrates the use of the command **show processes cpu** to check the CPU utilization statistics for last 1Min, 5Min, and 15Min. Notice in the command output that the BGP process is consuming the maximum CPU resources.

Example 6-5 show processes cpu *Command on IOS XR*

```
RP/0/RSP0/CPU0:R20# show processes cpu
CPU utilization for one minute: 98%; five minutes: 98%; fifteen minutes: 98%
PID     1Min    5Min    15Min  Process
1         0%      0%       0%  kernel
8195      0%      0%       0%  dllmgr
12290     0%      0%       0%  wd-critical-mon
12295     0%      0%       0%  p40x0mc
12296     0%      0%       0%  pkgfs
663922   87%     88%      88%  bgp
12297     0%      0%       0%  serdrvr
16394     0%      0%       0%  devc-pty
```

But this output does not yield much information on what really is happening within BGP that is causing high CPU utilization. Use the **show processes bgp [detail]** command to view all the threads under the *bgp* process and their respective CPU utilization. Example 6-6 illustrates the use of **show process bgp** command to view the threads consuming the most CPU cycle. From the output it is clear that thread 7 and thread 18 are consuming the most CPU resources.

Example 6-6 show processes bgp *Command Output*

```
RP/0/RSP0/CPU0:R20# show processes bgp
                  Job Id: 1054
                     PID: 663922
         Executable path: /disk0/iosxr-routing-5.1.3.sp5-1.0.0/0x100000/bin/bgp
             Instance #: 1
              Version ID: 00.00.0000
                 Respawn: ON
           Respawn count: 1
  Max. spawns per minute: 12
            Last started: Tue Oct 20 10:49:44 2015
           Process state: Run
           Package state: Normal
       Started on config: default
            Feature name: ON
                     Tag : default
           Process group: v4-routing
                    core: MAINMEM
               Max. core: 0
               Placement: Placeable
            startup_path: /pkg/startup/bgp.startup
                   Ready: 1.873s
               Available: 85.675s
        Process cpu time: 46.547 user, 1.837 kernel, 48.384 total
JID   TID CPU Stack pri state       TimeInState     HR:MM:SS:MSEC   NAME
1054   1   1  444K  10 Receive       0:00:08:0487    0:00:02:0224 bgp
1054   2   2  444K  10 Receive     305:21:48:0391    0:00:00:0000 bgp
1054   3   1  444K  10 Receive       0:00:01:0170    0:00:00:0381 bgp
1054   4   3  444K  10 Receive     305:21:44:0587    0:00:00:0000 bgp
1054   5   2  444K  10 Receive      58:10:54:0330    0:00:00:0022 bgp
1054   6   0  444K  10 Sigwaitinfo 305:21:45:0272    0:00:00:0000 bgp
1054   7  42  444K  10 Receive      29:14:41:0198    0:00:00:0028 bgp
1054   8   1  444K  10 Receive      49:05:21:0265    0:00:00:0221 bgp
!Output omitted for brevity
1054  16   1  444K  10 Receive       0:00:04:0515    0:00:04:0461 bgp
1054  17   3  444K  10 Receive      29:14:41:0199    0:00:00:0012 bgp
1054  18  37  444K  10 Receive      29:14:41:0198    0:00:00:0014 bgp
1054  19   3  444K  10 Receive      29:14:41:0184    0:00:00:0028 bgp
1054  20   1  444K  10 Receive      58:10:41:0906    0:00:00:0002 bgp
1054  21   3  444K  10 Receive       0:00:26:0826    0:00:00:0071 bgp
1054  22   3  444K  10 Receive       0:00:50:0343    0:00:36:0920 bgp
1054  23   3  444K  10 Receive     305:20:48:0097    0:00:00:0000 bgp
1054  24   2  444K  10 Receive       0:00:19:0698    0:00:00:0082 bgp
1054  25   0  444K  10 Receive     305:20:48:0097    0:00:00:0000 bgp
```

Although the thread consuming the most CPU resource is identified, it still does not reveal what a particular thread is doing. Each thread has a relevant threadname attached to it that can be viewed using the command **show process threadname** *jid*, where *jid* stands for Job Id.

Example 6-7 shows the output of **show processes threadname** *jid* output for the *bgp* process. Using this command, all the threads and their respective names under the *bgp* process are seen. The two threads in this case consuming the most CPU cycles are *bgp-label* thread and *bgp-import* thread.

Example 6-7   show processes threadname jid *Command Output*

```
RP/0/RSP0/CPU0:R20# show processes threadname 1054
JID    TID   ThreadName    pri state      TimeInState       NAME
1054   1     bgp-io-control 10 Receive       0:00:02:0694 bgp
1054   2                   10 Receive     305:23:23:0495 bgp
1054   3     bgp-rpki      10 Receive       0:00:01:0255 bgp
1054   4                   10 Receive     305:23:19:0691 bgp
1054   5     async         10 Receive      58:12:29:0433 bgp
1054   6                   10 Sigwaitinfo 305:23:20:0375 bgp
1054   7     bgp-label     10 Receive      29:16:16:0301 bgp
1054   8     bgp-mgmt      10 Receive      49:06:56:0368 bgp
1054   9     cdm_monitor_rs 10 Receive    305:23:19:0739 bgp
1054   10    bgp-rib-upd-0 10 Receive      29:16:16:0301 bgp
1054   11    lspv_lib BGPv4 10 Reply      305:23:20:0166 bgp
1054   12    bgp-rib-upd-1 10 Receive      29:16:16:0303 bgp
1054   13    cdm_monitor_rs 10 Receive    305:23:09:0530 bgp
1054   14    cdm_monitor_rs 10 Receive    305:22:59:0029 bgp
1054   15    bgp-io-read   10 Receive       0:00:08:0291 bgp
1054   16    bgp-io-write  10 Receive       0:00:08:0291 bgp
1054   17    bgp-router    10 Receive      29:16:16:0304 bgp
1054   18    bgp-import    10 Receive      29:16:16:0303 bgp
1054   19    bgp-upd-gen   10 Receive      29:16:16:0288 bgp
1054   20    bgp-sync-active 10 Receive    58:12:17:0010 bgp
1054   21    bgp-crit-event 10 Receive      0:00:01:0928 bgp
1054   22    bgp-event     10 Receive       0:00:25:0441 bgp
1054   23    bgp-mib-trap  10 Receive     305:22:23:0202 bgp
1054   24    bgp-io-ka     10 Receive       0:00:13:0184 bgp
1054   25    bgp-l2vpn-thr 10 Receive     305:22:23:0202 bgp
```

Although the names give a hint on what each thread does, it does not complete the picture. Table 6-3 elaborates the task of each thread under the *bgp* process.

Table 6-3 *BGP Process Threads*

Thread Name	Thread Function
bgp-io-control	Performs all functions related to listen socket creation (based on neighbor configuration), maintain per neighbor session timers, manage active and passive connections, install Local Packet Transport Service (LPTS) static policies, and manage connection collision.
bgp-io-read	Read the BGP messages from the neighbor socket buffer and queue it to the neighbor read queue (to be processed by bgp-router thread).
bgp-io-write	Write the BGP update messages from the neighbor OutQ to the associated socket buffer, and it also adjusts the next-hops of the update messages.
bgp-router	One of the most important threads, it reads the bgp update message. Validates the prefixes/networks and attributes, next-hop after unpacking the BGP updates.
	Update the per AFI/SAFI (Address-Family Identifier/Subsequent Address Family Identifier) network/prefix table and attribute table.
	Perform best-path calculation.
	Remove the prefix/path for prefixes withdrawn.
	Triggers BGP notification messages.
bgp-rib-update	Update global RIB with the final best path for the received prefixes/path for unipath and multipath.
	It also downloads to RIB as *opaque data* if attribute download is configured.
	Receives redistributed routes from global RIB into BGP RIB/table.
bgp-label	For VPNv4 prefix, prefixes that needs labels, *bgp-label* thread requests global label switch database (LSD) with label info.
	When LSD allocates labels, bgp receives them and uses it with route advertisements (with labels) as applicable.
bgp-import	Performs Virtual Private Network (VPN) prefix import/export.
bgp-crit-events	Critical-event thread in the speaker process handles only next-hop, Bidirectional Forwarding Detection (BFD), and fast-external-failover (FEF) notifications.
	When the prefix Next-Hop (NH) property changes (such as metric change or NH changes), RIB notifies *bgp-crit-event* thread. The *bgp-crit-event* thread then runs the best path calculation for all prefixes that use this NH (for all AFI/SAFI).

Thread Name	Thread Function
bgp-mgmt	Responsible for processing configuration, show, and clear command requests.
bgp-events	Performs housekeeping, Outbound Route Filtering (ORF), Route refresh, soft-reconfiguration.
bgp-sync-active	Syncing various databases between BGP on the active and the standby node.
bgp-update-gen	Generates the update message per filter-group.
bgp-io-ka	Generates the keepalives for all neighbors.
bgp-mib-trap	Generates BGP Management Information Base (MIB) traps that can be used for Simple Network Management Protocol (SNMP).
bgp-rpki	Performs prefix validation with a trusted source to overcome prefix hijacking.
lspv_lib BGPv4	Performs label switch path (LSP) verification.
bgp-l2vpn-thr	Responsible for BGP Autodiscovery mechanism.

Coming back to the problem shown in Example 6-7, the following factors can be checked on the router when the high CPU is due to the two highlighted threads:

- Flapping VPN prefixes

- Table version updates for the virtual routing and forwarding (*VRF*) instances

- Any routing loop condition due to mutual redistribution between Route Distinguishers (RD) in the network

If the problem is happening due to an expected configuration as highlighted in the last point, label and import processing can be delayed by using **bgp label-delay** *delay-in-seconds delay in milliseconds* and **bgp import-delay** *delay-in-seconds delay in milliseconds* configuration commands under the **address-family vpnv4 unicast** section. This eases the load on the CPU as it delays the batch processing of labels and imports for VPN prefixes in VRF tables. Similarly, if the high CPU utilization condition is noticed because of other threads, troubleshooting can be done according to the task(s) performed by that thread and appropriate actions can be taken.

Troubleshooting High CPU due to BGP on NX-OS

Because NX-OS is also a multithreaded architecture like IOS XR, there are multiple threads working under the *bgp* process to accomplish various tasks of BGP. Though the method to troubleshoot high CPU due to BGP remains the same, it is easier to look at the thread and know what task that particular thread is supposed to do. Based on that, further investigation can be done. On Nexus platforms, to verify high CPU utilization conditions due to a particular process such as bgp, use the **show processes cpu sort** command.

Example 6-8 shows the high CPU utilization on the Nexus device due to the *bgp* process. The important information to note in the output is the Process ID (PID) field, because that value is used to further look at the thread-level information for a particular process.

Example 6-8 *High CPU on Nexus Device*

```
R20# show processes cpu sort
PID     Runtime(ms)   Invoked    uSecs   1Sec    Process
-----   -----------   --------   -----   ------  -----------
7387            135         70    1935   47.5%   bgp
  34         390169   36175963      10    0.9%   kirqd
3572        2406238    6249848     385    0.9%   pltfm_config
5406            138         32    4336    0.9%   adjmgr
5488            353         87    4058    0.9%   netstack
5546       67783184  264737324     256    0.9%   snmpd
! Output omitted for brevity
```

Note   Some newer versions of NX-OS may show the CPU utilization output for 5 seconds, 1 minute, and 5 minutes. Also, the output may vary a bit based on the Nexus platform.

The **show system internal processes cpu** command is another command equivalent to **top** command in Linux. This command provides an ongoing look at processor activity in real time. Example 6-9 shows the output of the **show system internal processes cpu** command. The command output shows that the CPU has been high due to the *bgp* process.

Example 6-9 *Real-Time Processor Activity on Nexus*

```
R20# show system internal processes cpu
top - 14:55:39 up 108 days, 57 min,  2 users,  load average: 1.82, 1.53, 1.48
Tasks: 348 total,   1 running, 347 sleeping,   0 stopped,   0 zombie
Cpu(s): 30.4%us, 14.4%sy,  0.0%ni, 54.4%id,  0.0%wa,  0.1%hi,  0.6%si,  0.0%st
Mem:   8260784k total,  3139388k used,  5121396k free,    82360k buffers
Swap:        0k total,        0k used,        0k free,  1452676k cached
  PID USER      PR  NI  VIRT  RES  SHR S %CPU %MEM    TIME+  COMMAND
 7387 cisco     20   0  820m  24m  10m S 98.0  0.3 114481:15 bgp
 9998 cisco     20   0  3600 1592 1140 R  3.8  0.0   0:00.03 top
 2357 root      15  -5  114m 9860 4656 S  1.9  0.1  89:51.07 sysmgr
 3210 cisco     20   0  137m  13m 6464 S  1.9  0.2  92:10.98 urib
 5488 root      20   0  625m  50m  12m S  1.9  0.6  1965:49 netstack
    1 root      20   0  1988  604  524 S  0.0  0.0   1:08.34 init
    2 root      15  -5     0    0    0 S  0.0  0.0   0:00.00 kthreadd
    3 root      RT  -5     0    0    0 S  0.0  0.0   0:00.98 migration/0
!Output omitted due to brevity
```

The CPU stats can also be checked at the thread level using the **show process cpu details** *pid* command. Example 6-10 shows the CPU utilization on a per-thread level for the *bgp* process.

Example 6-10   show process cpu details *pid Output*

```
R20# show process cpu detailed 7387
CPU utilization for five seconds: 1%/0%; one minute: 1%; five minutes: 1%
PID     Runtime(ms)   Invoked   uSecs   5Sec    1Min    5Min    TTY   Process
-----   -----------   -------   -----   ------  ------  ------  ---   -----------
7387          150        61        2    0.00%   0.00%   0.00%    -    bgp
7388          210     10082        0    0.00%   0.00%   0.00%    -    bgp:active-time
7389           20        59        0    0.00%   0.00%   0.00%    -    bgp:bgp-cli-thr
7390           20        52        0    0.00%   0.00%   0.00%    -    bgp:bgp-mts
7391            0         2        0    0.00%   0.00%   0.00%    -    bgp:bgp-cmi
7392           20       597        0    0.00%   0.00%   0.00%    -    bgp:txthread-ha
7393            0         2        0    0.00%   0.00%   0.00%    -    bgp:bgp-soft-re
7394            0         2        0    0.00%   0.00%   0.00%    -    bgp:bgp-import
7395           70      1265        0    0.00%   0.00%   0.00%    -    bgp:bgp-peer-se
7396         1430       550        2    0.00%   0.02%   0.02%    -    bgp:bgp-cleanup
7397          290     10304        0    0.19%   0.01%   0.00%    -    bgp:bgp-session
7398          350      6531        0    0.00%   0.00%   0.00%    -    bgp:bgp-incomin
7399           10        16        0    0.00%   0.00%   0.00%    -    bgp:bgp-bestpat
7400            0         3        0    0.00%   0.00%   0.00%    -    bgp:bgp-vrf-bes
7401           10       160        0    0.00%   0.00%   0.00%    -    bgp:bgp-update-
7402           20       626        0    0.00%   0.00%   0.00%    -    bgp:bgp-send-up
7403            0       126        0    0.00%   0.00%   0.00%    -    bgp:sosend-0
7404            0       125        0    0.00%   0.00%   0.00%    -    bgp:sosend-1
7405           10       125        0    0.00%   0.00%   0.00%    -    bgp:sosend-2
7406           10       121        0    0.00%   0.00%   0.00%    -    bgp:sosend-3
7407            0       125        0    0.00%   0.00%   0.00%    -    bgp:sosend-4
7408            0       123        0    0.00%   0.00%   0.00%    -    bgp:sosend-5
7409           10       123        0    0.00%   0.00%   0.00%    -    bgp:sosend-6
7410            0       123        0    0.00%   0.00%   0.00%    -    bgp:sosend-7
7411           10       122        0    0.00%   0.00%   0.00%    -    bgp:sosend-8
7412            0       124        0    0.00%   0.00%   0.00%    -    bgp:sosend-9
7413           30      5140        0    0.00%   0.00%   0.00%    -    bgp:bgp-worker-
7414           50       180        0    0.00%   0.00%   0.00%    -    bgp:bgp-fd-clos
7415            0        12        0    0.00%   0.00%   0.00%    -    bgp:bgp-mts-con
7416            0         3        0    0.00%   0.00%   0.00%    -    bgp:ipv6-client
```

If the high CPU is due to BGP route churn, use the **show bgp vrf all all summary** command to verify the table version incrementing for all VRF contexts, and also use the command **show routing unicast event-history add-route** to view the prefixes that recently flapped.

Capturing CPU History

While troubleshooting a high CPU condition on the router (not necessarily due to BGP), it's important to know when the problem actually started and when the device is experiencing a high CPU utilization. In most cases, SNMP keeps polling the CPU statistics, which gives a historical data of the baseline CPU utilization. But if SNMP is not configured, the Cisco platforms have support for commands to verify the CPU utilization history for up to 72 hours. Use the **show processes cpu history** command to verify the history for last 60 seconds, 60 minutes, and 72 hours. This command is available only on IOS and NX-OS running devices. If using SNMP to collect statistics, use SNMP OID *1.3.6.1.4.1.9.9.109.1.1.1.1.3.1* to collect total CPU utilization of the route processor.

Troubleshooting Sporadic High CPU Condition

On most instances, the high CPU condition on the router may be sporadic and may happen for few seconds before any command is captured, and the CPU normalizes again.

To investigate such issues, a very powerful tool built in to Cisco Operating Systems can be used—Embedded Event Manager (EEM). EEM is an event-driven tool that takes various trigger inputs and allows the user to set what actions can be taken when the event gets triggered. With EEM, there is an option to capture the output when a particular problem is happening and also when an event has occurred.

For example, an action can be taken when high CPU utilization is being seen on the router, or logs can be procured when a BGP session has flapped. Example 6-11 shows the EEM configuration on all the platforms. The EEM has the trigger event set for a high CPU condition and the actions include BGP **show** commands that can be captured when the high CPU condition is noticed.

Example 6-11 *EEM Configuration for High CPU Utilization*

```
IOS
event manager applet High_CPU
event snmp oid 1.3.6.1.4.1.9.9.109.1.1.1.1.3.1 get-type exact entry-op ge
    entry-val 50 poll-interval 0.5
  action 0.0 syslog msg "High CPU DETECTED"
  action 0.1 cli command "enable"
  action 0.2 cli command "show clock | append disk0:high_cpu.txt"
  action 1.2 cli command "term length 0"
  action 1.3 cli command "show process cpu sorted | append     disk0:high_cpu.txt"
  action 1.4 cli command "show ip bgp summary | append disk0:high_cpu.txt"
  action 1.5 cli command "show clock | append disk0:high_cpu.txt"
  action 1.4 cli command "show ip bgp summary | append disk0:high_cpu.txt"
```

```
IOS XR
::cisco::eem::event_register_wdsysmon timewin 5 sub1 cpu_tot op ge val 70 maxrun_
  sec 600
```

```
#
# errorInfo gets set by namespace if any of the auto_path directories do not
# contain a valid tclIndex file.  It is not an error just left over stuff.
# So we set the errorInfo value to null so that we don't have left
# over errors in it.
#
set errorInfo ""


namespace import ::cisco::eem::*
namespace import ::cisco::lib::*

#
# errorInf gets set by namespace if any of the auto_path directories do not
# contain a valid tclIndex file.  It is not an error just left over stuff.
# So we set the errorInfo value to null so that we don't have left
# over errors in it.
#
set errorInfo ""

#Notify users that we're collecting
set output_msg "High CPU Collecting Commands"
action_syslog priority info msg $output_msg


# Set the list of commands to run
set cmd_list [list \
                "show proc blocked location all" \
                "show bgp ipv4 unicast summary" \
                "show bgp vrf all summary" \
                ]

# open a cli connection

if [catch {cli_open} result] {
    error $result $errorInfo
} else {
    array set cli1 $result
}

# Loop through the command list (cmd_list), executing each command
foreach command $cmd_list {
    append cmd_output "\nXXXXXXXXXXXXXXXXXXXXXXXXXXXXXXXXX "
    append cmd_output $command
```

```
    append cmd_output "\nXXXXXXXXXXXXXXXXXXXXXXXXXXXXXXXXX "

    if [catch {cli_exec $cli1(fd) $command} result] {
       error $result $errorInfo
    } else {
    append cmd_output $result
 }}
```

```
#close the cli connection
if [catch {cli_close $cli1(fd) $cli1(tty_id)} result] {
    error $result $errorInfo
}
```

```
set tdate [clock format [clock seconds] -format %Y%m%d%S]
set filename  [format "/harddisk:/cpu-log-%s.txt" $tdate]
set outfile [open $filename w]
puts $outfile "$cmd_output"
close $outfile
```

```
#Notify users that task is completed
set output_msg "Saved data to file $filename"
action_syslog priority info msg $output_msg
```

```
NX-OS
event manager applet HIGH-CPU
 event snmp oid 1.3.6.1.4.1.9.9.109.1.1.1.1.6.1 get-type exact entry-op ge
          entry-val 70 exit-val 30 poll-interval 1
 action 1.0 syslog msg High CPU hit $_event_pub_time
 action 2.0 cli enable
 action 3.0 cli show clock >> bootflash:high-cpu.txt
 action 4.0 cli show processes cpu sort >> bootflash:high-cpu.txt
 action 5.0 cli show bgp vrf all all summary >> bootflash:high-cpu.txt
 action 6.0 cli show clock >> bootflash:high-cpu.txt
 action 7.0 cli show bgp vrf all all summary >> bootflash:high-cpu.txt
```

Note   Refer to Cisco documentation at www.cisco.com for more details on configuring EEM on various Cisco Operating Systems.

Troubleshooting Memory Issues due to BGP

Every process and almost every piece of feature configuration consumes some amount of memory. If the feature or process starts consuming more memory than expected, then other features and processes may face a memory resource constraint. Every process on the router requires memory to execute and store its data; thus, it is crucial to have sufficient memory available for proper functioning of the router. Memory used by the BGP process depends on the following factors:

- Number of BGP peers

- Number of BGP prefixes

- BGP Attributes

- Number of paths

- Soft-reconfiguration inbound

- Neighbor Route-map, both Inbound and Outbound

- Filter-list

If there is not enough memory on the router, BGP sessions can fail to come up or existing sessions may go down. Also, the lack of free memory from one process may cause an impact to another process running on the system. For example CEF might get disabled when BGP has consumed too much memory on the router. Example 6-12 shows syslog messages of BGP sessions going down due to lack of memory on the router. The log shows that the BGP session starts going down just after the router faces a Memory Allocation Failure condition.

Example 6-12 *BGP Sessions Down due to No Memory*

```
Aug 30 01:56:36 89.200.128.90 306: 000292: Aug 30 01:56:34.909 BST:
%SYS-2-MALLOCFAIL: Memory allocation of 65536 bytes failed from 0x6063111C
Aug 30 01:56:36 89.200.128.90 310: -Process= "BGP Router", ipl= 0, pid=133
Aug 30 01:56:36 89.200.128.90 311: -Traceback= 605807A8 606357A0 60639EDC
60631124 609ED9D0 6099F7B4 609C5B6C 609C9A98 609CB0D0 609CBB7C 609B5FEC
Aug 30 01:56:39 89.200.128.90 312: 000293: Aug 30 01:56:38.986 BST:
%BGP-5-ADJCHANGE: neighbor 10.1.12.2 Down No memory
Aug 30 01:56:39 89.200.128.90 313: 000294: Aug 30 01:56:38.986 BST:
%BGP-5-ADJCHANGE: neighbor 10.1.13.2 Down No memory
Aug 30 01:56:39 89.200.128.90 314: 000295: Aug 30 01:56:38.986 BST:
%BGP-5-ADJCHANGE: neighbor 10.1.14.2 Down No memory
```

In Example 6-12, there is also a log message pointing toward the BGP Router process. This log message means that the BGP Router was requesting allocation of memory that failed because of insufficient memory on the router.

The insufficient memory on the router could be due to one of the following reasons:

- Insufficient memory installed on the router

- Memory leak condition on the router

Before investigating any memory issues on the router, the first insufficient memory issues are easy to deal with. The software version running on the router has a minimum memory requirement, which should always be verified. However, for certain features, which when enabled and based on their scale, memory beyond the minimum requirement may be required, such as large BGP tables. Upgrading the DRAM on the router resolves the problem. As a best practice when deploying a router, have the router installed with maximum memory supported to allow for future growth of the network. If the router continuously keeps on increasing the memory consumption without the addition of new feature or without multiple events on the router, that's the possible indication of memory leak on the router. Various platforms have their own set of CLI to troubleshoot memory issues.

TCAM Memory

Along with the physical memory, the other important space to verify is the TCAM memory. Routers use the TCAM space to store the forwarding information to make fast lookups and thus speed up the forwarding process. In addition, the ACL entries, QoS, and other information associated with upper-layer processing is also stored in the TCAM space. Most of the high-end routers have sufficient TCAM space, but their default configurations might require adjustments. While deploying a router, ensure that the platform not only has sufficient DRAM but also has good TCAM space.

One such example is from August 8, 2014; the Classless Inter-Domain Routing (CIDR) Report reported that the global Internet routing table had passed 512,000 routes. Multiple routers were hit, including some of the high-end routers like the Cisco 7600. On the 7600, most of the Supervisor cards, such as WS-SUP720-3BXL or RSP720-3CXL-GE, have the maximum IPv4 TCAM space for 1,000,000 routes, but the default configuration splits this space so that IPv4 has 512,000. The rest is divided among MPLS, IPv6, and multicast entries. This caused the platforms to run out of TCAM space, which caused the routers to run into a FIB Exception state that caused the overflowing route entries to be software switched.

The exception status is verified using the **show mls cef exception status** command. The **show mls cef maximum-routes** command is used to verify the current maximum routes system configuration on the 7600 series platform. Increasing the TCAM value to accommodate the increased routing table helped resolve the problem. It is also important to understand that the platform hardware limitation may differ from what the software BGP table can hold. Platform limitations should always be considered and properly understood before implementing any scaled featured in a production environment.

Troubleshooting Memory Issues on Cisco IOS Software

There are two types of memory spaces on IOS devices: Process memory and Input/Output (IO) memory. When a feature is enabled on IOS devices, such as BGP, protocol independent multicast (PIM), and so on, IOS allocates the memory from the process memory pool. When software switched traffic hits the CPU, the IO memory comes into use. The CPU allocates IO memory to temporarily store the frame. There are two primary reasons why a Cisco IOS device runs out of memory:

■ A process not freeing up memory after the memory is no longer in use. This behavior is generally known as *memory leak.*

■ A process does not limit the amount of memory it allocates, eventually using up all memory space on the router/switch.

The first problem can be identified using the **show memory debug leaks [chunks]** command. This command runs through the memory and tells which process is leaking memory. Because it has to run though the whole memory, this command is intrusive and might cause service disruptions due to high CPU utilization during the execution of the command (which does not last more than 2 to 3 minutes). So it is recommended to schedule a downtime (maintenance window) to offload the traffic to a backup device before running this command. But this command is helpful if the router is about to run out of memory and the only option is to reload the router to recover from the condition. There are also a set of show commands that can be used to identify a memory leak in a nonintrusive manner. These same commands can be used to identify if a process is not limiting the amount of memory it is allocating.

Note If a router has run out of memory due to a memory leak condition, a reload on the router helps recover from the leaked condition, but the memory will most likely leak again. Thus, identifying the process causing the memory leak is important to fix the problem.

The second problem cannot be identified so easily and requires a set of commands to investigate the problem. The first step is to ensure there is a continuous decrement in the free memory available on the router. If the memory leak is happening very frequently or the memory utilization is incrementing rapidly, perform the command collection every 10 to 15 minutes. If the leak is happening slowly (over a period of time), collect the statistics and monitor them at least every week. The command **show memory statistics** is used to verify the summary usage of both the process memory and IO memory, as shown in Example 6-13.

Example 6-13 show memory statistics *Command Output*

```
IOS# show memory statistics
            Head    Total(b)   Used(b)    Free(b)    Lowest(b)   Largest(b)
Processor   2196404  72886064   10511756   17438236   12365600    11045704
      I/O   2C00000  4194304    1669276    2525028    2489984     2523744
```

After it is clear from the output that the free memory is dropping, it needs to be understood which process is holding the most memory and if it's releasing the memory or not. The command **show processes memory sorted** shows the information of various memory pools along with per process memory consumption statistics like Allocated,

Freed, and Holding. These counters are useful to understand whether the consumption is continuously incrementing or the memory is getting freed up as well. Example 6-14 demonstrates the use of **show processes memory sorted** command to verify increasing consumption of memory by a process. The output shows that the free process memory went down from 20692936 bytes to 19001540 bytes.

Example 6-14 **show processes memory sorted** *Command Output*

```
IOS# show processes memory sorted
Processor Pool Total:    72886064 Used:   52193128 Free:   20692936
        I/O Pool Total:  12582912 Used:    8576324 Free:    4006588
Driver te Pool Total:     1048576 Used:         40 Free:    1048536


PID TTY  Allocated      Freed    Holding    Getbufs    Retbufs Process
  0   0  49649092   11944860   34657140          0          0 *Init*
100   0  74848892   55133364   18754060          0          0 Bgp Router
  0   0  51087472   50258644     846184   12086456    3864680 *Dead*
 67   0    599948      10784     532384          0          0 Stack Mgr Notifi

IOS# show processes memory sorted
Processor Pool Total:    72886064 Used:   53884524 Free:   19001540
        I/O Pool Total:  12582912 Used:    8576324 Free:    4006588
Driver te Pool Total:     1048576 Used:         40 Free:    1048536


PID TTY  Allocated      Freed    Holding    Getbufs    Retbufs Process
  0   0  49649092   11944860   34657140          0          0 *Init*
100   0  81711876   60216436   20448016          0          0 Bgp Router
  0   0  51139456   50313836     846184   12086456    3864680 *Dead*
```

After identifying the process that is increasingly consuming the memory on the router, use the command **show process memory** *pid* to get the program counter (PC) values that can then be used by Cisco Technical Assistance Center (TAC) for further investigation.

Note A memory leak is an indication of a software defect; thus it is recommended to engage Cisco TAC to prevent the issue from happening again. A software upgrade or a patch may be required to fix the bad code causing the memory leak on the device.

From the BGP perspective, use the command **show bgp** *afi safi* **summary** to identify the memory consumption under each address-family. The output shows the following:

■ Memory consumption by the network entries

■ Number of path entries

■ Path/best path attribute entries

- BGP community entries

- Route-map cache entries

- Filter-list cache entries

- Total memory consumed by a particular address-family

Example 6-15 illustrates how attaching a simple community increases the memory consumption. The first output shows there are two path/best path attribute entries consuming 304 bytes of memory and there is no BGP community entry. But as soon as a BGP community is attached, the path/best path attribute entry increases by 1, and now there is an entry for BGP community.

Example 6-15   *BGP Memory Consumption*

```
R1# show bgp ipv4 unicast summary
BGP router identifier 192.168.1.1, local AS number 65530
BGP table version is 3, main routing table version 3
2 network entries using 288 bytes of memory
2 path entries using 160 bytes of memory
2/2 BGP path/bestpath attribute entries using 304 bytes of memory
0 BGP route-map cache entries using 0 bytes of memory
0 BGP filter-list cache entries using 0 bytes of memory
BGP using 752 total bytes of memory
BGP activity 2/0 prefixes, 2/0 paths, scan interval 60 secs


Neighbor      V    AS MsgRcvd MsgSent   TblVer  InQ OutQ Up/Down  State/PfxRcd
10.1.12.2     4 65530   4502    4498        3    0    0 2d20h               1
```

```
R1(config)# route-map TEST permit 10
R1(config-route-map)# set community 100:2
R1(config-route-map)# exit
R1(config)# router bgp 65530
R1(config-router)# address-family ipv4 unicast
R1(config-router-af)# neighbor 10.1.12.2 route-map TEST in
R1(config-router-af)# end
```

```
R1# show bgp ipv4 unicast summary
BGP router identifier 192.168.1.1, local AS number 65530
BGP table version is 4, main routing table version 4
2 network entries using 288 bytes of memory
2 path entries using 160 bytes of memory
3/2 BGP path/bestpath attribute entries using 456 bytes of memory
1 BGP community entries using 24 bytes of memory
0 BGP route-map cache entries using 0 bytes of memory
0 BGP filter-list cache entries using 0 bytes of memory
```

```
BGP using 928 total bytes of memory
BGP activity 2/0 prefixes, 2/0 paths, scan interval 60 secs

Neighbor       V       AS MsgRcvd MsgSent   TblVer  InQ OutQ Up/Down  State/
  PfxRcd
10.1.12.2      4    65530    4508    4505        4    0    0 2d20h.         1
```

Monitor the overall memory usage of the BGP process using the commands in Example 6-15 to see if there are any changes that are causing the increase in memory or if the memory is continuously incrementing without any changes. One issue that was noticed in some old IOS software was memory utilization incrementing due to Idle neighbor sessions. As a best practice, it is recommended to shutdown the neighbors in the Idle state or remove the respective neighbor configuration if they have been down for a very long time and are supposed to stay down.

Another important factor that could lead to an increase in memory consumption is **neighbor** *ip-address* **soft-reconfiguration inbound** configuration, which was explained in Chapter 1, "BGP Fundamentals." Using this configuration, BGP keeps the received routes from each of its peers in the Adj-RIB-In table, even after ingress routing policy has been applied and the routes are installed into the Loc-RIB table. Because the Adj-RIB-In is not purged and stays in memory, the memory consumption increases.

If a peer is receiving an Internet routing table, it is not a good idea to have **soft-reconfiguration inbound** configured. This command is useful if there are fewer routes being received by the router. The memory consumption might also vary on different IOS versions because of the code enhancements made over the years. Also, **soft-reconfiguration inbound** configuration has been discouraged since the introduction of BGP Soft Reset enhancement. Example 6-16 demonstrates the increase in memory consumption due to soft-reconfiguration inbound configuration.

Example 6-16 *Increasing Memory Consumption due to* **soft-reconfiguration inbound**

```
R1# show bgp ipv4 unicast summary
BGP router identifier 192.168.1.1, local AS number 65530
BGP table version is 5, main routing table version 5
2 network entries using 288 bytes of memory
2 path entries using 160 bytes of memory
3/2 BGP path/bestpath attribute entries using 456 bytes of memory
1 BGP community entries using 24 bytes of memory
0 BGP route-map cache entries using 0 bytes of memory
0 BGP filter-list cache entries using 0 bytes of memory
BGP using 928 total bytes of memory
BGP activity 4/2 prefixes, 5/3 paths, scan interval 60 secs
```

```
Neighbor        V        AS MsgRcvd MsgSent    TblVer  InQ OutQ Up/Down  State/
  PfxRcd
10.1.12.2       4     65530   1066    1068       5    0    0 16:04:58         1
```

```
R1(config)# router bgp 65530
R1(config-router)# address-family ipv4 unicast
R1(config-router-af)# neighbor 10.1.12.2 soft-reconfiguration inbound
R1(config-router-af)# end
```

```
R1# show bgp ipv4 unicast summary
BGP router identifier 192.168.1.1, local AS number 65530
BGP table version is 5, main routing table version 5
2 network entries using 288 bytes of memory
3 path entries using 240 bytes of memory
3/2 BGP path/bestpath attribute entries using 456 bytes of memory
1 BGP community entries using 24 bytes of memory
0 BGP route-map cache entries using 0 bytes of memory
0 BGP filter-list cache entries using 0 bytes of memory
BGP using 1008 total bytes of memory
1 received paths for inbound soft reconfiguration
BGP activity 4/2 prefixes, 6/3 paths, scan interval 60 secs

Neighbor        V        AS MsgRcvd MsgSent    TblVer  InQ OutQ Up/Down  State/
  PfxRcd
10.1.12.2       4     65530   1718    1715       5    0    0 1d01h            1
```

Troubleshooting Memory Issues on IOS XR

Unlike IOS, there is a maximum limit that can be allocated by each process on IOS XR. By default, the limit is 300 Mb but the process can expand its limit. For example, *bgp* process sets its limit to 2 Gb. Example 6-17 shows the present memory allocated and the maximum limit for each process.

Example 6-17   *Memory Allocation by Processes on IOS XR*

```
RP/0/0/CPU0:R10# run show_processes -m -h -t
JID    Text    Data    Stack   Dynamic  Dyn-Limit  Shm-Tot  Phy-Tot  Process
-----  ------- ------  -------- -------- ---------  -------- -------  -------
1145   400K    624K    128K     20M      2048M      22M      21M      ipv6_rib
1144   400K    468K    156K     16M      2048M      22M      16M      ipv4_rib
1052   1000K   5M      384K     16M      2048M      21M      22M      bgp
1161   2M      1M      204K     13M      1024M      23M      15M      pim6
1160   2M      1M      216K     11M      1024M      22M      13M      pim
1158   472K    1M      232K     10M      512M       16M      12M      igmp
1159   416K    1M      120K     10M      512M       16M      12M      mld
1146   784K    920K    112K     6M       300M       20M      7M       mrib
! Output omitted for brevity
```

> **Note**   The IOS XR command **show processes memory** is an alternate command to **run show_processes -m -h -t** command. The **show_processes** command is run on the shell and not on the router prompt.

Processes can get notification that they reached their limit, but if the process keep leaking memory and crosses its limit, it receives a signal 31 from the kernel. In this scenario, the process crashes and respawns. Every time a process crashes and respawns, the respawn counter increments in the **show processes** *process-name* command output.

On IOS XR, Watchdog System Monitor (wdsysmon) monitors how much free memory is present on each node (Route Processor [RP], LC, and so on). A router might still reach a low memory condition even when no process has reached its maximum limit. This happens when multiple processes try to allocate memory at the same time. The wdsysmon maintains multiple thresholds defined based on the % free memory available. These thresholds are seen by using the **show watchdog threshold memory [default | configured]** command. Example 6-18 shows the various wdsysmon thresholds on the IOS XR router.

Example 6-18   *Memory Allocation by Processes on IOS XR*

```
RP/0/0/CPU0:R10# show watchdog threshold memory configured location 0/0/CPU0
Configured memory thresholds:
    Minor:      309      MB,
    Severe:     247      MB
    Critical:   154.780 MB
```

```
RP/0/0/CPU0:R10# show watchdog threshold memory defaults location 0/0/CPU0
Default memory thresholds:
  Minor:      309     MB
  Severe:     247     MB
  Critical:   154.780 MB
Memory information:
    Physical Memory: 3095     MB
    Free Memory:     1610.335 MB
    Memory State:        Normal
```

In the case of BGP, the *bgp* process takes different actions when different thresholds are reached and include the following:

- In minor memory state, *bgp* can stop bringing up new peers and reduce the write limits when not set to default.

- In severe state, *bgp* brings down some peers.

- In critical state, the *bgp* process shuts down. This is a severe error state and all routing protocol processes are shut down and it is required to manually bring them back up for recovery.

The different thresholds work well in situations where a memory problem is due to scale (too many neighbors, too many prefixes, and the like) but if there is a memory leak problem, the leaking process continues to leak more memory, and the only way to recover is to restart the process.

To troubleshoot memory issues on IOS XR, the first step is to verify the **show logging** output from the router to see if there is any process crash due to signal 31 or if wdsysmon reports that the memory threshold is crossed. Use the **show memory summary detail** command output to view how much memory is in use and free memory on the node. Example 6-19 shows the output of the **show memory summary detail** command. The node has about 208 MB free memory available.

Example 6-19   show memory summary *Output*

```
RP/0/0/CPU0:R10# show memory summary detail location 0/0/CPU0
node:      node0_0_CPU0
------------------------------------------------------------------
Physical Memory: 2.000G total
 Application Memory : 1.813G (208.652M available)
 Image: 62.794M (bootram: 62.794M)
 Reserved: 128.000M, IOMem: 1.980G, flashfsys: 0
 Shared window mfwdv6: 721.867K
 Shared window ether_ea_shm: 79.171K
 Shared window ether_ea_tcam: 203.378K
! Output omitted for brevity
```

Use the **show processes memory** command to identify the top users of the application memory. This commands needs to be collected from time to time as the leaking process keeps on consuming more and more memory shown under the Dynamic column of the output. If a particular process, such as *bgp* process, is holding the most memory, this does not mean that *bgp* is leaking memory on the router. The high memory utilization can be due to various reasons, like the number of neighbors or number of prefixes. The memory consumed should be periodically checked and compared to the total number of routes to be able to recognize a problem.

The commands previously mentioned can help in identifying memory issues, but they do not help in identifying if a particular process is causing a memory leak. To find a leaking process, IOS XR has an inbuilt tool that automatically computes which processes have allocated some memory between two snapshots. The **show memory compare** command provides this functionality in three easy steps:

Step 1.   Take Initial Snapshot.

Step 2.   Take the Delta Snapshot.

Step 3.   Generate report on Delta from Initial Snapshot.

The **show memory compare start** command takes the first snapshot and saves it in the */harddisk:/malloc_dump/memcmp_start.out* file. After the first snapshot is taken, wait for few minutes and then take the second snapshot using the **show memory compare end** command. This command saves the snapshot at the same location but with a different filename—*memcmp_end.out*. The final step is to compare both snapshots. The comparison is done using the **show memory compare report** command. After the comparison is made and the report is generated, the two files can be deleted from the disk. Example 6-20 demonstrates how memory leak can be identified using the **show memory compare** command.

Example 6-20 show memory compare *Command*

```
RP/0/0/CPU0:R10# show memory compare start
Sun Nov  8 07:21:01.040 UTC
Successfully stored memory snapshot /harddisk:/malloc_dump/memcmp_start.out

RP/0/0/CPU0:R10# show memory compare end
Sun Nov  8 07:24:36.545 UTC
Successfully stored memory snapshot /harddisk:/malloc_dump/memcmp_end.out

RP/0/0/CPU0:R10# show memory compare report
JID    name          mem before   mem after    difference malloc restart/exit/new
---    ----          ----------   ----------   ---------- ------- ----------------
1052   bgp           12715116     12743212     28096      68
283    licmgr        1210552      1226676      16124      29
389    tcp           1389648      1399904      10256      111
220    gsp           2837968      2847168      9200       2
315    nvgen_server  8515960      8522636      6676       258
1144   ipv4_rib      16709492     16715080     5588       48
373    sysdb_mc      2727856      2731288      3432       51
65712  exec          219660       220364       704        27
66     qnet          77472        77560        88         2
290    lpts_pa       465996       465924       -72        -1
309    netio         1165164      1164996      -168       -5
```

This process has to be performed multiple times to get to any conclusion. If the memory increases in the first iteration but reduces in the second or third iteration, this indicates that there might not be a memory leak. The trend needs to be monitored over a time period to determine if memory is actually leaking.

Note After the preceding information is collected along with core files that are generated during the process, the crash can be shared with Cisco TAC for further investigation and root cause analysis.

Troubleshooting Memory Issues on NX-OS

NX-OS has different memory architecture from IOS or IOS XR. Linux by default is not designed to keep track of memory held by processes. With NX-OS, an intelligent mechanism called MTRACK is used for allocating and tracking memory held by Process IDs (PID) within the system.

In NX-OS, the total system memory is 4 GB. This system memory is further split into three regions:

- High Region
- Low Region
- Preallocated

The preallocated region is a non-accessible memory space. The processes allocate their memory from the high region. The high region space is 3 GB in size. If the space in high region is exhausted (which is very unlikely), then the processes might use the space from low region. The low region memory space is responsible for kernel variable storage and Kernel Loadable Modules (KLM). The preallocated space and low region combine to hold 1 GB memory.

There are basically two types of memory issues that could occur on NX-OS platforms:

- Platform memory alerts
- Process memory issues

The kernel generates the platform memory alerts. The alert is first generated when a threshold called Minor threshold for total system usage or total kernel memory usage in the low region is reached. There are three thresholds defined within NX-OS: Minor, Severe, and Critical. Example 6-21 shows the alerts generated on the NX-OS platform. Use the **show system internal memory-alerts-log** command to view the platform memory alerts.

Example 6-21   *Platform Memory Alerts*

```
PLATFORM-2-MEMORY_ALERT:Memory Status Alert: MINOR. Usage 85% of available memory
PLATFORM-2-MEMORY_ALERT:Memory Status Alert: SEVERE. Usage 90% of available memory
PLATFORM-2-MEMORY_ALERT_RECOVERED: Memory Status Alert : SEVERE ALERT RECOVERED
PLATFORM-2-MEMORY_ALERT_RECOVERED: Memory Status Alert : MINOR ALERT RECOVERED
```

Use the **show system resources** command to investigate the cause of platform memory alerts.

The primary focus in this chapter is to investigate process memory issues. Process memory issues typically manifest themselves in the form of a crash. Each feature in NX-OS runs as a process on kernel. Any problem with an individual process does not impact other processes on the system. Though each process has its upper limit, there are no thresholds defined to notify the system that the memory is reaching its limit for a process. If the memory is exhausted, the process crashes, a core file is generated, and the process is then respawned.

Use the **show processes memory [sort]** command to view the processes consuming the most memory on a Nexus switch. Example 6-22 shows the sorted output of the **show processes memory** command. The *bgp* and the *netstack* processes are the two highest consumers as seen from the output.

Example 6-22   show processes memory sort *Command*

```
R20# show processes memory sort
PID    MemAlloc  MemLimit    MemUsed      StackBase/Ptr       Process
-----  --------  ----------  ----------   -----------------   ---------

6480   62111744  0           348655616    ff890870/ffffffff   bgp
3530   45162496  726328806   329355264    ffe7a040/ffffffff   netstack
3485   63488000  620038028   315682816    fffb27c0/ffffffff   arp
4652   20865024  733660403   259649536    ffa8c050/ffffffff   igmp
5323   13197312  603750566   250421248    ff832ef0/ffffffff   mrib
5337   8732672   440584345   237690880    fffe4cf0/ffffffff   mcastfwd
4646   12001280  583227392   233857024    fff8b4f0/ffffffff   l2rib
4615   8589312   497931763   230301696    ffae16b0/ffffffff   rpm
3489   5660672   490357440   228876288    ff9bdd10/ffffffff   icmpv6
4778   12382208  253751052   228454400    ffb74c70/ffffffff   ethpm
5326   7077888   487893286   225775616    ffdb5df0/ffffffff   m6rib
! Output omitted due to brevity
```

The two important fields in this output are MemLimit and MemUsed. There are few processes like *bgp* that do not have an upper limit (MemLimit) set. The **show processes memory** command is useful but does not give granular information of the memory usage behind a process. To view more granular information, use the **show system internal process-name mem-stats detail** command. Some feature processes like *bgp* are not available under this command.

To view more granular information for the *bgp* process, use the **show bgp internal mem-stats detail** command. Example 6-23 shows the output of this command. The output shows various slabs like BGP IPv4 destination, BGP path, and so on. In this command, all the various address-families supported are shown as slabs and show the memory consumed under them.

Example 6-23   show bgp internal mem-stats detail *Command*

```
R20# show bgp internal mem-stats detail
bgp-65530, Memory statistics
BGP Memory status: OK

BGP memory usage stats

Private memory
Total mallocs/frees/failed : 2962/2912/0
Memory requested/allocated : 6021624/0 bytes
HWM requested/allocated    : 6159416/0 bytes
Peer send buffer mallocs/reuses/frees/failed/hwm: 1709/3888/1708/0/2
Peer recv buffer mallocs/frees/failed/hwm: 4349/4349/0/1
Peer data buffer mallocs/frees/failed: 10/8/0
Peer data buffer allocated/hwm: 2/3

Shared memory
Total mallocs/frees/failed    : 10028/16/0
Memory requested/allocated    : 1199905/2919272 bytes
Memory requested by attr slab : 1200000
HWM requested/allocated       : 1199905/2919272 bytes

Statistics of SLABs used by BGP

SLAB: BGP path slab (100 x 3000)
Slab alloc count          : 100003
Slab max allocs           : 100003
Slab total allocs         : 100044
Slab total frees          : 41
Slab total block allocs   : 34
Slab block alloc failures : 0
Slab total block frees    : 0
Slab max blocks           : 34

SLAB: BGP IPv4 dest slab (68 x 3000)
Slab alloc count          : 2
Slab max allocs           : 4
Slab total allocs         : 13
Slab total frees          : 11
Slab total block allocs   : 1
Slab block alloc failures : 0
Slab total block frees    : 0
Slab max blocks           : 1
!Output omitted for brevity
```

There is no simple method to investigate memory leaks on the NX-OS platform. The best indication of a memory leak for a process in NX-OS is a process crash. After it is known that a process is leaking memory from time to time, the memory utilization can be monitored. Debug plug-ins can be used to further diagnose the problem if needed with the assistance from Cisco TAC.

Note   Troubleshooting memory leaks on NX-OS requires debug plug-ins and is outside the scope of this book.

Restarting Process

If a process is facing memory issues, it either crashes or needs to be manually restarted to restore the process to its normal functionality. On IOS, there is no option to restart a process. A process crash actually triggers a router reload. Because IOS XR and NX-OS are distributed environments, each process is an individual entity and can be restarted. Use the **process restart** [*job-id* | *process-name*] command to restart the process on IOS XR. Use **restart** *process-name instance-tag* to restart an instance of the process on NX-OS. For example, use **restart bgp** *autonomous-system-number* to restart the *bgp* instance on NX-OS. However, some processes, like SNMP, cannot be restarted using this method. Not all processes can be restarted using this method.

Note   If BGP process is required to be restarted, BGP should be gracefully shut down first using the **shutdown** command under the **router bgp** configuration.

Summary

This chapter explained the various BGP processes functions and how different processes interact with each other. This chapter explained under what circumstances certain BGP processes and threads could cause a high CPU condition on the router, therefore producing an impact. Later, the chapter illustrated how to use different command-line tools to investigate memory leak conditions due to BGP process on various platforms. A few recommendations that can help prevent any network outages or service impact due to platform issues were also provided in this chapter, such as the following:

- Ensure the device has proper memory and resources to run the intended features.

- Ensure the device is running latest software release.

- Periodically baseline memory and resource utilization on the device.

- Maintain redundancy in place in case of a process or router restart.

■ Examine the scale of the network.

■ Based on the process consuming the most CPU resources, troubleshoot the problem.

References

Cisco, Configuring and Managing Embedded Event Manager Policies, www.cisco.com.

Cisco, Cisco IOS EEM Command Reference, www.cisco.com.

Cisco, Troubleshooting Memory Problems, www.cisco.com.

Chapter 7

Scaling BGP

The following topics are covered in this chapter:

- Impact of growing Internet routing tables
- Scaling Internet table on various Cisco platforms
- Scaling Border Gateway Protocol (BGP) functions
- Scaling BGP with route reflectors and confederations

The Impact of Growing Internet Routing Tables

The Internet routing table has seen an inexorable growth since early 1990s, at a rate that has at the very least doubled in size each year. With such expansion, it has been a challenge for various vendors as well as ISPs to keep upgrading their platforms to meet the increasing needs. The requirements for maintaining the Internet routing table has long been an area of discussion and research, including the speed of transmission systems, the switching capacity of routers and switches, routing convergence, and more importantly, stability of the routing system.

The number of entries in the Internet routing table has steadily grown and reached the 256,000 routes milestone as per the Classless Inter-Domain Routing (CIDR) report. August 8, 2014, marked another milestone when the Internet routing table passed 512,000 routes. It was around that time, because of the Ternary Content-Addressable Memory (TCAM) size limitations, many router platforms required upgrading or recon-figuration to cope with the increased routing table size. As of November 2015, the CIDR report shows that the Internet routing table is nearing 581K routes. Figure 7-1 shows the graph of the growing IPv4 Internet routing table over the years. The graph plots the data from June 1988 to November 2015. Notice that the graph has been continuously showing a steep growth.

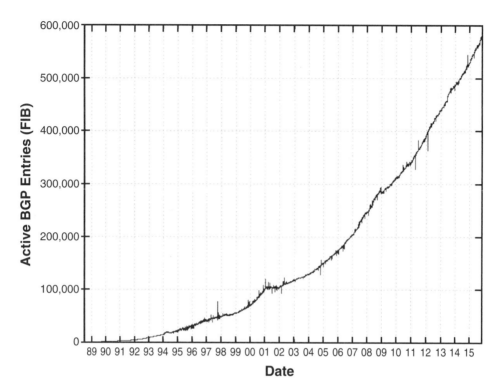

Figure 7-1 *IPv4 Internet Routing Table Growth from 1989–2015*

Note   Currently, the IPv4 Internet routing table is holding over 638K prefixes.

Because of this dramatic increase, there are no IPv4 addresses that can be allocated. In fact, the American Registry for Internet Numbers (ARIN)—the regional authority for North America that distributes IP addresses, officially announced on September 24, 2015, that its general IPv4 address pool was depleted. There are some Regional Internet Registries (RIRs) that still have their IPv4 address pool. Sooner or later, those will get depleted as well. Because of this limitation, the ISPs have started upgrading their networks to completely support IPv6 or function in dual-stack mode. Because the IPv6 addresses have 128 bits, it has a bigger address space. Many enterprises are now developing applications to support IPv6 addresses or dual-stack capabilities so that they don't have to migrate their applications or redesign them from scratch.

Because of the rapidly growing Internet table, there is a rapid increase in the IPv6 Internet routing table as well. The active IPv6 BGP entries have crossed the 27,000 prefixes mark. The increase in IPv6 addresses also poses a great challenge to resource requirements because the IPv6 prefixes need more memory and TCAM space because of the 128-bit address space. They require more CPU resources as compared to IPv4 prefixes for the same reason. Figure 7-2 shows the IPv6 Internet routing table growth over the past few years.

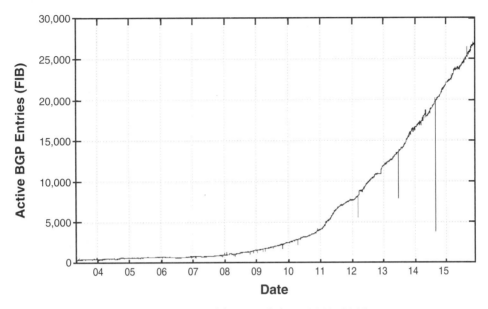

Figure 7-2   *Ipv6 Internet Routing Table Growth from 2003–2015*

There has also been a massive increase in the assigned autonomous system (AS) numbers. The total of assigned AS numbers, both 2-byte autonomous system number (ASN) and 4-byte ASN, has already crossed 82,000 at the time of writing. The Internet routing table sees an average of ~2.41 prefixes per BGP update and an average of 2.56 BGP update messages per second. The biggest challenge that the growing Internet poses today is the need for better CPU and higher memory.

Scaling Internet Table on Various Cisco Platforms

Not every Cisco platform (router/switch) is capable of handling the Internet routing table. Only a few routers can handle such a large number of prefixes. Even if certain routers exhaust their resources, they can still be tweaked to meet the present Internet routing table requirements.

Not many options can be controlled in a scaled network environment. The two choices are to either buy a router with more routing table capacity or design the network properly.

Buying a new router means upgrading a device which has more powerful CPU and memory to accommodate the present and near-future needs. But as the network grows, the demand for more memory and CPU resources will increase, and the device will again have to be replaced. The better option is to make proper use of the technology and redesign the network to make proper use of the available resources. Although a bigger router may still be required, it will sustain in the network for a longer period of time.

Often there is a discussion of how much memory is required to hold the Internet routing table, and which router should be used as a route reflector (RR). The answer is—it depends. Earlier, a Cisco 7200 series router with 512 MB Dynamic Random Access Memory (DRAM) was sufficient for holding the Internet routing table, but with the size of the routing table, not anymore. On top of that, many organizations now have peering with two ISPs to maintain redundancy. This doubles the memory requirement on the router.

The Cisco 6500 series or Cisco 7600 series hit the ternary content addressable memory (TCAM) limitation with the default configuration, but the TCAM can be tweaked to hold the Internet routes. Only the SUP720-3BXL or SUP720-3CXL Supervisor cards on Cisco 6500 or RSP720-3BXL or RSP720-3CXL supervisor cards on Cisco 7600 are capable of holding up to 1,000,000 IPv4 routes. The non-XL versions do not support more than 256,000 IPv4 routes and are not capable of holding full Internet routing tables. It is important to note that mixing XL and non-XL cards in the chassis results in the non-XL capacity.

ASR9000 series platforms that are configured with a Typhoon-based line card are capable of holding the Internet routing table. The Trident-based line cards are not recommended for Internet routing tables. When the Trident-based line card reaches its prefix limit, the error message '%ROUTING-FIB-4-RSRC_LOW' appears on the router, causing potential traffic loss on the line cards.

The Aggregation Services Router (ASR) 1000 series routers running 4 GB DRAM can scale up to 500,000 IPv4 routes, but to hold the Internet routing table, the router should be upgraded to 8 GB DRAM or a higher size DRAM to accommodate 1,000,000 routes.

On the Nexus side, Nexus7000 XL series line cards are capable of holding multiple copies of the Internet routes in the forwarding information base (FIB) along with VRF and Virtual Device Context (VDC) support. The XL series line cards are capable of holding up to 1,000,000 IPv4 routes or up to 350,000 IPv6 routes. The non-XL line cards can support only about 128,000 IPv4 or 64,000 IPv6 routes.

Cisco has a range of routers that are good choices for deploying as RRs, especially in the scenario where the provider is holding a large number of routes along with a substantial number of customers. Earlier, the Cisco 7200 series router was as good a choice as an RR. But with the increase in the Internet routing table and the faster expansion of the service provider networks, the Cisco 7200 series is out of the league. ASR1000 series or even CSR1000v (virtual router) series routers are now the preferred routers for deploying as an RR. However, based on the scale of the network and the feature requirements, the appropriate memory, route process (RP), and forwarding engine have to be chosen. Nexus devices are not really a good choice for deployment as RR for networks carrying Internet routing tables. ASR9000 series routers are recommended as Provider Edge (PE) or aggregation routers but can be used as RRs. RRs are often deployed so that they are not in the forwarding path, and thus large devices such as ASR9000 or Nexus switches do not make sense. Because of the form factor and resource capability, the ASR 1000 fits nicely as an RR.

BGP as a protocol is a victim of its own success. Being such a simple, robust, and scalable protocol, the networking community noticed a lot of opportunity to use BGP for new features from time to time. When the BGP was first developed in 1990, it was implemented only for interdomain routing, but over the years, the scalability increased with the increase in various address-families. Now BGP is not just used for IPv4 or IPv6, but also provides various features such as Multiprotocol Label Switching (MPLS) Virtual Private Network (VPN),

Multicast VPN, and the like. BGP has now been expanded in data-center environments to carry Virtual Extensible LAN (VXLAN) information using VXLAN-EVPN. Table 7-1 shows the control-plane evolution with BGP between 2000 and 2014.

Table 7-1 *Control-Plane Evolutions with BGP*

Service/Transport	200x	2014
IDR (Peering)	BGP	BGP (IPv6)
SP L3VPN	BGP	BGP + FRR + Scalability
SP Multicast VPN	Protocol Independent Multicast (PIM)	BGP Multicast VPN
DDOS Mitigation	Command-Line Interface (CLI)	BGP Flowspec
Network Monitoring	Simple Network Management Protocol (SNMP)	BGP Monitoring Protocol
Security	Filters	BGP Sec (RPKI), DDoS Mitigation
Proximity		BGP connected app API
SP-L3VPN-DC		BGP Inter-AS, VPN4DC
Business & CE L2VPN	Label Distribution Protocol (LDP)	BGP PW Signaling (VPLS)
DC Interconnect L2VPN		BGP MAC Signaling (EVPN)
MPLS Transport	LDP	BGP + Label (Unified MPLS)
Data Center	Open Shortest Path First (OSPF) / Intermediate System to Intermediate System (IS-IS)	BGP + Multipath
Massive Scale DMVPN	Next-Hop Resolution Protocol (NHRP) / Enhanced Interior Gateway Routing Protocol (EIGRP)	BGP + Path Diversity
Campus/Enterprise L3VPN	BGP	BGP
VXLAN		BGP VXLAN-EVPN

With so many address-families being supported, there are more challenges that BGP has to face, which include the following:

- More prefixes
- More BGP routers
- Multipath
- Attributes and policies
- More resilience

With so many challenges, it is possible to extend the life cycle or enhance the performance of a router by focusing on scalability. It is thus very important and crucial to know how to tune BGP rather than keep upgrading routers in the network.

Scaling BGP Functions

BGP is one of the most feature-rich protocols ever developed that provides ease of routing and control using policies. Although BGP has many built-in features that can allow it to scale very well, these enhancements are not always utilized properly. This poses various concerns when BGP is deployed in a scaled environment.

BGP is a heavy protocol because it uses the most CPU and memory resources on a router. And there are many factors that explain why it keeps utilizing more and more resources. The three major factors for BGP memory consumption are as follows:

- Prefixes

- Paths

- Attributes

BGP can hold many prefixes, and each prefix consumes some amount of memory. But when the same prefix is learned via multiple paths, that information is also maintained in the BGP table. Each path requires additional memory space. Because BGP was designed to give control to each AS to manage the flow of traffic through various attributes, each prefix can have several attributes per path. This is shown as a mathematical function:

- **Prefixes:** $(O(N))$

- **Paths:** $(O(M \times N))$

- **Attributes:** $(O(L \times M \times N))$

The topology in Figure 7-3 shows three paths to reach a prefix learned from router R5 on router R1.

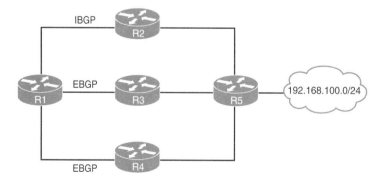

Figure 7-3 *Topology with BGP Multipath*

Example 7-1 demonstrates various BGP paths with various communities and attributes. Notice that each attribute or community learned from an individual neighbor for the prefix 192.168.100.0/24 is stored in the BGP table, thereby increasing memory consumption. Three paths are available for the prefix, out of which path number 3 is chosen as the best. The various paths within the address-family can be seen using the command **show bgp** *afi safi* **paths**.

Example 7-1 *BGP Multipath Prefix*

```
R1# show bgp ipv4 unicast 192.168.100.0
BGP routing table entry for 192.168.100.0/24, version 35
Paths: (3 available, best #3, table default, not advertised to EBGP peer)
  Advertised to update-groups:
    1
  Refresh Epoch 5
  400 500
    192.168.2.2 (metric 2) from 192.168.2.2 (192.168.2.2)
      Origin IGP, metric 0, localpref 100, valid, internal
      Community: internet 400:100 500:100
      rx pathid: 0, tx pathid: 0
  Refresh Epoch 4
  300 500
    10.1.13.3 from 10.1.13.3 (192.168.3.3)
      Origin IGP, localpref 100, valid, external
      Community: internet 300:100 500:100
      rx pathid: 0, tx pathid: 0
  Refresh Epoch 3
  400 500
    10.1.14.4 from 10.1.14.4 (192.168.4.4)
      Origin IGP, localpref 100, valid, external, best
      Community: 400:100 no-export
      rx pathid: 0, tx pathid: 0x0
R1# show bgp ipv4 unicast paths
Address     Hash Refcount Metric Path
0xCB130EC   2852        1     0 300 500 i
0xCB132E4   2889        1     0 400 500 i
0xCB1323C   2890        1     0 400 500 i
```

Example 7-1 showed how the memory consumption per BGP prefix depends on the number of paths, path attributes, and AS-Paths associated with it. When the prefix scale increases, the memory consumption on the router increases, and services could be impacted. It is therefore imperative to have the BGP memory tuned properly.

Tuning BGP Memory

To reduce or tune the BGP memory consumption, adjustments should be made to the three major factors leading to most BGP memory consumption as previously discussed. The various adjustments that can be made for each factor are discussed in the sections that follow.

Prefixes

BGP memory consumption becomes critical when BGP is holding a large number of prefixes or holding the Internet routing table. In most cases, not all the BGP prefixes are required to be maintained by all the routers running BGP in the network. To reduce the number of prefixes, the following actions can be taken:

- Aggregation
- Filtering
- Partial routing table instead of full routing table

With the use of aggregation, multiple specific routes can be aggregated into one route. But aggregation is challenging when performed on a fully deployed running network. After the network is up and running, the complete IP addressing scheme has to be examined to execute aggregation. Aggregation is a good option for green field deployments. The green field deployments give more control on the IP addressing scheme, which makes it easier to apply aggregation.

Filtering provides control over the number of prefixes that should be maintained in the BGP table or advertised to BGP peers. BGP provides filtering based on prefix, BGP attributes, and communities. One important point to remember is that complex route filtering or route filtering applied for a large number of prefixes helps reduce the memory required but also requires additional CPU resources to apply the policy on BGP updates.

Many deployments do not require all the BGP speakers to maintain a full BGP routing table. The BGP speakers can maintain even a partial routing table, containing the most relevant and required prefixes. Such designs greatly reduce the resources being used throughout the network and increase scalability.

Managing the Internet Routing Table

If an enterprise is peering with an ISP, the ISP can advertise the full Internet routing table using BGP or a default routing table using BGP or Interior Gateway Protocol (IGP). Generally, an enterprise doesn't need access to the complete Internet routing table. If the ISP is advertising a full Internet table, there are few ways of managing the Internet routing table:

- Ask the ISP to not send the whole Internet routing table by either filtering the needed routes or by advertising a default route. The enterprise should perform the route filtering as a fail-safe in case the ISP makes a mistake and sends the full Internet routing table.

- If the ISP cannot filter the routes, filtering can be performed at the enterprise edge router for the required prefixes. This option gives more control over the Internet routing table within the network.

- If resource conservation is the primary focus, ask the ISP to advertise a default route and regional ISP specific routes. This saves a lot of resources.

Figure 7-4 illustrates how using the preceding three points scales the network and consumes fewer resources. The topology has three routers: R1, Internet-GW, and ISP-RTR. The Internet-GW router is the enterprise edge router peering with the ISP router named ISP-RTR.

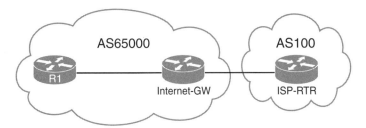

Figure 7-4 *Enterprise-ISP BGP Peering*

For the sake of understanding, only fewer routes, say 50,000 routes, are being advertised by the ISP-RTR router. Example 7-2 illustrates that the BGP memory consumption on Internet-GW router is high with the ISP router advertising the Internet routing table. But after filtering those routes and configuring a default route, the memory utilization is much better as compared to what was before.

Example 7-2 *Scaling Enterprise Edge Router with Default Route*

```
Internet-GW# show bgp ipv4 unicast summary
BGP router identifier 192.168.2.2, local AS number 65000
BGP table version is 50001, main routing table version 50001
50001 network entries using 7200144 bytes of memory
50001 path entries using 4000080 bytes of memory
5000/5000 BGP path/bestpath attribute entries using 760000 bytes of memory
5000 BGP AS-PATH entries using 225920 bytes of memory
0 BGP route-map cache entries using 0 bytes of memory
0 BGP filter-list cache entries using 0 bytes of memory
BGP using 12186296 total bytes of memory
BGP activity 170000/120000 prefixes, 200000/150000 paths, scan interval 60 secs


Neighbor        V    AS MsgRcvd MsgSent   TblVer  InQ OutQ Up/Down  State/PfxRcd
10.1.23.3       4   100    5010      14    50001    0    0 00:09:26     50000
192.168.1.1     4 65000      32    5105    50001    0    0 00:24:39        1
```

```
Internet-GW(config)# route-map DENY-ALL deny 10
Internet-GW(config-route-map)# match ip address prefix-list DENY-IP
Internet-GW(config-route-map)# exit
Internet-GW(config)# ip prefix-list DENY-IP seq 5 permit 0.0.0.0/0 le 32
Internet-GW(config)# router bgp 65000
Internet-GW(config-router)# address-family ipv4 unicast
Internet-GW(config-router-af)# neighbor 10.1.23.3 route-map DENY-ALL in
Internet-GW(config-router-af)# end
```

```
Internet-GW# show bgp ipv4 unicast summary
BGP router identifier 192.168.2.2, local AS number 65000
BGP table version is 100003, main routing table version 100003
1 network entries using 144 bytes of memory
1 path entries using 80 bytes of memory
1/1 BGP path/bestpath attribute entries using 152 bytes of memory
0 BGP route-map cache entries using 0 bytes of memory
0 BGP filter-list cache entries using 0 bytes of memory
BGP using 376 total bytes of memory
BGP activity 170001/170000 prefixes, 200001/200000 paths, scan interval 60 secs

Neighbor        V     AS MsgRcvd MsgSent   TblVer  InQ OutQ Up/Down  State/PfxRcd
10.1.23.3       4    100    5580     641   100002    0    0 09:37:57            0
192.168.1.1     4  65000     674    5797   100003    0    0 10:07:04            1
```

After the route filtering is performed and the static default route is configured toward the ISP, the command **neighbor** *ip-address* **default-originate** can be configured on the Internet-GW router toward the neighbor R1 to advertise the default route. This way, R1 has a path to reach the Internet.

Paths

Sometimes the BGP table carries fewer prefixes but still holds more memory because of multiple paths. A prefix can be learned via multiple paths, but only the best or multiple best paths can be installed in the routing table. To reduce the memory consumption by BGP due to multiple paths, the following solutions should be adopted:

- Reduce the number of peerings

- Use RRs instead of IBGP full mesh

Multiple BGP paths are caused by multiple BGP peers. Especially in an internal BGP (IBGP) full mesh environment, the number of BGP sessions increases exponentially, as does the number of paths. A lot of customers increase the number of IBGP neighbors to have more redundant paths, but two paths are sufficient to maintain redundancy.

Increasing the number of peerings can cause scaling issues both from the perspective of the number of sessions and from the perspective of BGP memory utilization.

It is a well-known fact that IBGP needs to be in full mesh. Figure 7-5 illustrates an IBGP full-mesh topology. In an IBGP full-mesh deployment of n nodes, there are a total of $n * (n-1) / 2$ IBGP sessions and $(n-1)$ sessions per BGP speaker.

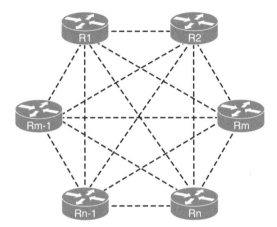

Figure 7-5 *IBGP Full Mesh*

This not only affects the scalability of an individual node or router, but it affects the whole network. To increase the scalability of IBGP network, two design approaches can be used:

- Confederations

- Route reflectors

Note BGP route reflectors are discussed later in this chapter.

Attributes

A BGP route is a "bag" of attributes. Every BGP prefix has certain default or mandatory attributes that are assigned automatically, such as next-hop or AS-PATH or attributes that are configured manually, such as Multi-Exit Discriminator (MED), assigned by custom-ers. Each attribute carried with the prefix contributes to the total amount of memory consumed. Along with attributes, communities—both standard and extended—add to increased memory consumption. To reduce the BGP memory consumption due to various attributes and communities, the following solutions can be adopted:

- Reduce the number of attributes

- Filter standard or extended communities

■ Limit local communities

■ Reduce the newer types of attributes (that is, AIGP, IBGP PE-CE)

There is no method to get rid of the default BGP attributes, but the use of other elements can be controlled. Using attributes that can make things more complex is not advantageous. For example, using MED and various MED-related CLI, such as the command **bgp always-compare-med** or **bgp deterministic-med**, may have an adverse impact on the network as described in RFC 3345 and lead to route instability or routing loop conditions. Thus the MED attribute and other related CLIs mentioned previously should be carefully configured in the network. User assigned attributes will consume more BGP memory, which can easily be avoided.

BGP community attributes make it easier to have more control over the BGP learned prefixes, both from Inter-AS and Intra-AS. Each destination can belong to multiple communities. Although there are no recommended ISP BGP communities apart from what is defined in RFC1998 or the four standard well-known communities, communities are very useful in an ISP network because it helps give control over the prefix to the customers. Communities are usually applied with route-maps. Extended communities such as Site of Origin (SOO) have specific requirements that are not always used and required, whereas standard communities provide policy-based routing.

Community attributes are numbers that represents specific meaning in the network. Based on the assigned value, certain actions are defined for the prefix in the network. As the network grows older and more mature, more communities are added over the period of time. Some of the older assigned community values lose their meaning or are not needed. But they are never touched, because network operators are afraid of breaking something in the network since they have no knowledge about those communities. Network administrators should try to reduce the number of BGP communities being used in the network. It not only makes the network much simpler to manage but also saves on network resources.

A router can receive a prefix with a community attribute attached and forward the community attached prefix to its peers, but the router controls the advertisement of the locally assigned community to another BGP peer using the command **neighbor** *ip-address* **send-community**. If the command is not specified, the locally assigned community is not advertised to BGP peers.

The newer features, such as IBGP PE-CE or Accumulated Interior Gateway Protocol (AIGP), introduce newer BGP attributes. When enabling IBGP between the Provider Edge (PE) and Customer Edge (CE) routers, a BGP attribute named ATTR_SET is added to the VPN prefix that allows all path attributes from the CE router to be carried across the service provider cloud. Using the AIGP metric attribute, BGP speakers receive knowledge about the end-to-end metric of all the paths. The AIGP metric attribute copies the IGP metric into BGP and helps to improve the path selection process.

Note   Both IBGP PE-CE and AIGP are covered extensively in Chapter 10, "MPLS Layer 3 VPN (L3VPN)."

Tuning BGP CPU

BGP is a heavy protocol and can consume a lot of CPU cycles. This has been detailed in Chapter 6, "Troubleshooting Platform Issues due to BGP." But using certain features and changing certain command lines helps save a lot of CPU resources. Use the following features to improve the CPU resources:

- Peer-groups and templates

- BGP soft reset

- IOS peer groups

- IOS peer templates

- NXOS peer templates

- IOS XR BGP templates

IOS Peer-Groups

Peer-groups are templates that can be used to assign common policies and attributes, such as an AS number or source-interface, and the like for multiple neighbors. This saves a lot of time and effort while configuring, when multiple neighbors have the same policy. But the peer-groups were not designed to save typing. By grouping neighbors with common policy together, routers save a lot of CPU resources by creating a one-time route object and then advertising that object to multiple peers. Example 7-3 illustrates the peer-group configuration on Cisco IOS software. Notice that after the peer-group is configured and the parameters are defined for the peer-group, the network administrator only needs to add neighbors to that peer-group. This saves a lot of time to bring up new neighbors.

Example 7-3 *BGP Peer-Group Configuration*

```
R1(config)# router bgp 65530
R1(config-router)# neighbor iBGP-RRC peer-group
R1(config-router)# neighbor iBGP-RRC remote-as 65530
R1(config-router)# neighbor iBGP-RRC update-source loopback0
R1(config-router)# neighbor 192.168.2.2 peer-group iBGP-RRC
R1(config-router)# neighbor 192.168.3.3 peer-group iBGP-RRC
R1(config-router)# address-family ipv4 unicast
R1(config-router-af)# neighbor iBGP-RRC route-reflector-client
R1(config-router-af)# neighbor 192.168.2.2 activate
R1(config-router-af)# neighbor 192.168.3.3 activate
```

IOS XR BGP Templates

There is no concept of peer-groups in IOS XR. IOS XR provides template support for neighbor configuration using the **af-group**, **session-group**, and **neighbor-group** commands. Table 7-2 states the use of these three BGP template configurations.

Table 7-2   *BGP Templates on IOS XR*

Template Command	Description
af-group	Configure address-family–dependent neighbor configuration, such as **route-reflector-client** or **next-hop-self**.
session-group	Configure address-family–independent neighbor configuration, such as **remote-as** or **update-source** configuration.
neighbor-group	Apply same configuration to one or more neighbors.

BGP neighbors may choose to override some of the inherited attributes from the templates. Example 7-4 illustrates the use of BGP templates on IOS XR.

Example 7-4   *BGP Templates on IOS XR*

```
RP/0/0/CPU0:R10(config)# router bgp 65530
! Configure af-group
RP/0/0/CPU0:R10(config-bgp)# af-group IPv4-AFI address-family ipv4 unicast
RP/0/0/CPU0:R10(config-bgp-afgrp)# route-reflector-client
RP/0/0/CPU0:R10(config-bgp-afgrp)# next-hop-self
RP/0/0/CPU0:R10(config-bgp-afgrp)# exit
! Configure session-group
RP/0/0/CPU0:R10(config-bgp)# session-group IPv4-SG
RP/0/0/CPU0:R10(config-bgp-sngrp)# remote-as 65530
RP/0/0/CPU0:R10(config-bgp-sngrp)# update-source loopback 0
RP/0/0/CPU0:R10(config-bgp-sngrp)# exit
! Configure neighbor-group
RP/0/0/CPU0:R10(config-bgp)# neighbor-group IBGP-GRP
RP/0/0/CPU0:R10(config-bgp-nbrgrp)# advertisement-interval 5
RP/0/0/CPU0:R10(config-bgp-nbrgrp)# exit
RP/0/0/CPU0:R10(config-bgp)# neighbor 192.168.2.2
RP/0/0/CPU0:R10(config-bgp-nbr)# use session-group IPv4-SG
RP/0/0/CPU0:R10(config-bgp-nbr)# use neighbor-group IBGP_GRP
RP/0/0/CPU0:R10(config-bgp-nbr)# address-family ipv4 unicast
RP/0/0/CPU0:R10(config-bgp-nbr-af)# use af-group IPv4-AFI
RP/0/0/CPU0:R10(config-bgp-nbr-af)# commit
```

NX-OS BGP Peer Templates

NX-OS uses peer templates to provide more concise peer configuration model. The NX-OS implementation of peer templates consists of three template types: **peer-policy**, **peer-session**, and **peer template**.

A **peer-policy** defines the address-family–dependent policy aspects for a peer, including inbound and outbound policy, filter-list and prefix-lists, soft-reconfiguration, and so on. A **peer-session** template defines "session" attributes such as transport details and session timers. Both the **peer-policy** and **peer-session** templates are inheritable; that is, a **peer-policy** or **peer-session** can inherit attributes from another **peer-policy** or **peer-session**, respectively. A peer template pulls the peer-session and peer-policy sections together to allow "cookie-cutter" neighbor definitions.

Example 7-5 illustrates peer template configurations on NX-OS.

Example 7-5   *BGP Peer Templates on NX-OS*

```
R20(config)# router bgp 65530
! Configure peer-policy template
R20(config-router)# template peer-policy PEERS-V4
R20(config-router-ptmp)# route-reflector-client
R20(config-router-ptmp)# next-hop-self
R20(config-router-ptmp)# exit
! Configure peer-session template
R20(config-router)# template peer-session PEER-DEFAULT
R20(config-router-stmp)# remote-as 65530
R20(config-router-stmp)# update-source loopback0
R20(config-router-stmp)# password cisco
R20(config-router-stmp)# exit
! Configure peer template
R20(config-router)# template peer IBGP-RRC
R20(config-router-neighbor)# inherit peer-session PEER-DEFAULT
R20(config-router-neighbor)# address-family ipv4 unicast
R20(config-router-neighbor-af)# inherit peer-policy PEERS-V4 10
R20(config-router)# neighbor 192.168.1.1
R20(config-router-neighbor)# inherit peer IBGP-RRC
R20(config-router-neighbor)# exit
```

BGP Peer Templates on Cisco IOS

In older versions of Cisco IOS, the peer-group configuration was used to group update messages for the peers using the BGP update groups feature. The update generation process on Cisco IOS is explained in great detail in Chapter 5, "Troubleshooting BGP Convergence." But there were a few challenges with the peer-group configuration on the Cisco IOS software, as follows:

■ All peer-group members had to share the same outbound policy.

■ All neighbors should be part of same peer-group and address-family. Neighbors configured in different address-families cannot belong to different peer-groups.

Such behaviors limited the scalability of neighbor configuration and reduced efficiency of the update message generation.

The separation of peer-group with the update-group generation process was introduced with BGP Dynamic Update Peer-Groups feature. The restriction of BGP neighbor configuration to outbound policy for an update-group is no longer applicable. But the **peer-group** configuration still retains the following limitations:

■ A BGP neighbor can belong to only one peer-group.

■ Neighbors belonging to different address-families cannot be part of same peer-group.

■ Only one outbound policy can be configured per peer-group.

Peer templates were introduced to overcome the limitations of peer-group configuration. Similar to NX-OS, the peer template configuration is inheritable and can form multiple hierarchies. There are two types of peer templates: peer-session and peer-policy.

The **peer-session** template allows configuring session-related parameters, whereas the **peer-policy** template allows for address-family–dependent configuration. Both the **peer-session** and **peer-policy** templates give more flexibility on configuring neighbors and provide faster convergence. Example 7-6 illustrates the configuration of peer-templates.

Example 7-6   *BGP Peer Templates on Cisco IOS*

```
R1(config)# router bgp 65530
! Configuring peer-session template
R1(config-router)# template peer-session IBGP-SESSION
R1(config-router-stmp)# remote-as 65530
R1(config-router-stmp)# update-source loopback0
R1(config-router-stmp)# exit
! Configuring peer-policy template
R1(config-router-stmp)# template peer-policy IBGP-NHS
R1(config-router-ptmp)# next-hop-self
R1(config-router-ptmp)# exit
R1(config-router)# template peer-policy IBGP-POLICY
R1(config-router-ptmp)# route-reflector-client
! Inheriting peer-policy NHS
R1(config-router-ptmp)# inherit peer-policy NHS 10
R1(config-router-ptmp)# exit
R1(config-router)# neighbor 192.168.2.2 inherit peer-session IBGP-SESSION
R1(config-router)# address-family ipv4 unicast
R1(config-router-af)# neighbor 192.168.2.2 activate
R1(config-router-af)# neighbor 192.168.2.2 inherit peer-policy IBGP-POLICY
```

Soft Reconfiguration Inbound Versus Route Refresh

BGP peers are requested for resending updates to peers when making adjustments to inbound BGP policies. BGP updates are incremental; that is, after the initial update is completed, only the changes are received. So BGP sessions are required to be reset, to request peers to send a BGP UPDATE message with all the NLRIs, so those updates can be rerun via the new filter. There are two methods to perform the session reset:

- **Hard Reset:** Dropping and reestablishing a BGP session. Can be performed by command **clear bgp** *afi safi* [* | *ip-address*].

- **Soft Reset:** A soft reset uses the unaltered prefixes, stored in the Adj-RIB-In table, to reconfigure and activate BGP routing tables without tearing down the BGP session.

A hard reset of a BGP session is disruptive to an operational network. If a BGP session is reset repeatedly over a short period of time because of multiple changes in BGP policy, it can result in other routers in the network dampening prefixes, causing destinations to be unreachable and traffic to be black holed.

A soft reconfiguration is a traditional way to allow route policy to be applied on the inbound BGP route update. BGP soft reconfiguration is enabled by using the **neighbor** *ip-address* **soft-reconfiguration inbound** configuration. When configured, the BGP stores an unmodified copy of all routes received from that peer at all times, even when the routing policies did not change frequently. One of the benefits of soft reconfiguration is that it helps test your filtering policies. Enabling soft reconfiguration means that the router also stores prefixes/attributes received prior to any policy application. This caused an extra overhead on memory and CPU on the router.

To manually perform a soft reset, use the command **clear bgp ipv4 unicast** [* | *ip-address*] **soft** [**in** | **out**]. The soft-reconfiguration feature is useful when an operator wants to know which prefixes have been sent to a router prior to the application of any inbound policy.

To overcome the challenges of **soft-reconfiguration inbound** configuration, BGP route refresh capability was introduced and is defined in RFC 2918. The BGP route refresh capability has a capability code of 2 and the length of 0. Using the route refresh capability, the router sends out a route refresh request to a peer to get the full table from the peer again. The advantage of route refresh capability is that no preconfiguration is needed to enable it. The ROUTE-REFRESH message is a new BGP message type, as shown in Figure 7-6.

Figure 7-6 *BGP ROUTE-REFRESH Message*

The AFI and SAFI in the ROUTE-REFRESH message point to the address-family where the configured peer is negotiating the route refresh capability. The Reserved bits are unused and are set to 0 by the sender and ignored by the receiver.

A BGP speaker can send a ROUTE-REFRESH message only if it has received a route refresh capability from its peer. This implies that all the participating routes should support the route refresh capability. The router sends a route refresh request (*REFRESH_REQ*) to the peer. After the speaker receives a route refresh request, the BGP speaker readvertises to the peer the Adj-RIB-Out of the Address-Family Identifier (AFI), and Subaddress-Family Identifier (SAFI) carried in the message, to its peer. The requesting peer receives the prefixes after any outbound policy applied on the peer is executed.

The **clear ip bgp** *ip-address* **in** or **clear bgp** *afi safi ip-address* **in** command tells the peer to resend a full BGP announcement by sending a route refresh request, whereas the **clear bgp** *afi safi ip-address* **out** command resends a full BGP announcement to the peer, and it does not initiate a route refresh request. The route refresh capability is verified by using the **show bgp** *afi safi* **neighbor** *ip-address* command. Example 7-7 displays the route refresh capability negotiated between the two BGP peers.

Example 7-7 *BGP Route-Refresh Capability*

```
R1# show bgp ipv4 unicast neighbor 10.1.12.2
BGP neighbor is 10.1.12.2,  remote AS 65530, internal link
  BGP version 4, remote router ID 192.168.2.2
  BGP state = Established, up for 2d03h
  Neighbor sessions:
    1 active, is not multisession capable (disabled)
  Neighbor capabilities:
    Route refresh: advertised and received(new)
    Four-octets ASN Capability: advertised and received
    Address family IPv4 Unicast: advertised and received
! Output omitted for brevity
```

Note When the soft-reconfiguration feature is configured, the BGP route refresh capability is not used, even though the capability is negotiated. The soft-reconfiguration configuration controls the processing or initiating route refresh.

To further understand the route refresh capability, examine the flow of messages during an update request using the route refresh capability between routers in Figure 7-7.

Figure 7-7 *BGP Route Refresh*

Example 7-8 illustrates how the BGP route refresh capability works with the help of
debug commands. An inbound policy is applied on the router R1 to set the community
value of 100:2 for the prefixes received from R2. To view the message exchange, enable
debug command **debug bgp ipv4 unicast in** and **debug bgp ipv4 unicast update**. After
the debug is enabled, issue the command **clear bgp ipv4 unicast** *ip-address* **in**, which
triggers the router to initiate a refresh request. Notice that the value highlighted in braces
is the message type. The message type 5 represents the ROUTE-REFRESH message.

Example 7-8 *BGP Update Using Route Refresh*

```
R1# debug bgp ipv4 unicast in
R1# debug bgp ipv4 unicast 192.168.2.2 updates


R1(config)# route-map SET_COMM permit 10
R1(config-route-map)# set community 100:2
R1(config-route-map)# exit
R1(config)# router bgp 100
R1(config-router)# address-family ipv4 unicast
R1(config-router-af)# neighbor 192.168.2.2 route-map SET_COMM in
R1(config-router-af)# end


! Initiating Route Refresh using clear command
R1# clear bgp ipv4 unicast 192.168.2.2 in


17:46:36: BGP: 192.168.2.2 sending REFRESH_REQ(5) for afi/safi: 1/1,
 refresh code is 0
17:46:36: BGP(0): 192.168.2.2 rcvd UPDATE w/ attr: nexthop 192.168.2.2,
 origin i, localpref 100, metric 0
R1# debug bgp ipv4 unicast out
R1# debug bgp ipv4 unicast 192.168.1.1 updates


17:46:36: BGP: 192.168.1.1 rcvd REFRESH_REQ for afi/safi: 1/1,
 refresh code is 0
17:46:36: BGP(0): (base) 192.168.1.1 send UPDATE (format) 192.168.2.2/32,
 next 192.168.2.2, metric 0, path Local
```

Notice the refresh code 0 in Example 7-8. The value 0 indicates that BGP route refresh is
being requested.

The BGP refresh request (REFRESH_REQ) is sent in one of the following cases:

- **clear bgp** *afi safi* [* | *ip-address*] **in** command is issued.

- **clear bgp** *afi safi* [* | *ip-address*] **soft in** command is issued.

- Adding or changing inbound filtering on the BGP neighbor via route-map.

- Configuring **allowas-in** for the BGP neighbor.

- Configuring **soft-reconfiguration inbound** for the BGP neighbor.

- Adding a **route-target import** to a VRF in MPLS VPN (for AFI/SAFI value 1/128 or 2/128).

Note   It is recommended to use **soft-reconfiguration inbound** only on EBGP peering whenever it is required to know what the EBGP peer previously advertised that has been filtered out. It is not recommended to configure **soft-reconfiguration inbound** command when there are large numbers of prefixes being learned, such as the Internet routing table over the EBGP connection.

Dynamic Refresh Update Group

To perform efficient formatting and replication, an update group mandates that the peers with the oldest table version in an update group must be processed first. This is done to allow such unprogressive peers to catch up with other peers in the update group. The behavior is achieved by processing the peers with the lowest BGP table version first until they reach the next-lowest peer's table version from where these peers would be processed together, and so on.

Replication based on the oldest table first approach has an obvious disadvantage of introducing serialization. This becomes far more apparent whenever peers are servicing route refresh requests for large table sizes in an update group.

When the route refresh request is received from a member of an update group (typically generated by PE as part of VRF provisioning), a BGP update group resets the neighbor table version to 0. This causes an update group to process peers servicing route refresh requests until they catch up with either the latest BGP table version or the version number of the second-lowest peer. The behavior of an update group imposes an update group peer delay to process any other transient network churn after all the peers have synced up to the latest version number.

To overcome this problem, *dynamic refresh update groups* were introduced. The dynamic refresh update groups implement a mechanism that decouples part of the peer members so that both the route refresh peers as well as other peer members in an update group are not serialized by the update group design.

Whenever a route refresh request is received, BGP schedules a route refresh timer of 60 seconds (default to an update group) if it is not already scheduled. The refresh process is initiated at the timer expiration. After the route refresh is processed, the "refresh state" is tracked under a separate dynamic refresh update group. The refresh state handles resetting of the peer table versions in the dynamically created update group; therefore, the current peer state is not affected.

If the refresh service is in progress for the corresponding update group, any other route refresh request is queued on the route refresh timer. This ensures that at any given time, only one set of refresh requests is serviced by an update group and its peers. In other words, several route refresh requests from one peer or several peers are processed together when the BGP refresh timer expires in the new dynamic refresh update group. It is important to remember that peers in the dynamic refresh update group receive the full RIB, whereas the peers in the regular update group receive the regular BGP updates.

Figures 7-8 through 7-10 explain the difference between regular update groups and dynamic refresh update groups with an example. Figure 7-8 displays the flow of a regular update group in which the peer with the lowest BGP table version is updated until it reaches the next lowest peer table version, and then both are replicated to the next table version until all the updates are replicated.

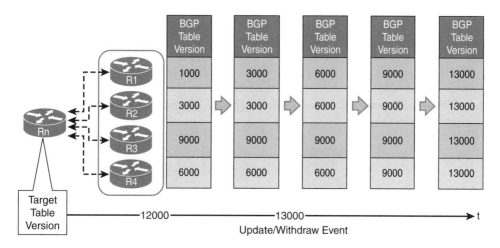

Figure 7-8 *Update Group Behavior*

If a route refresh request is received from a member—for example, when a new VRF is provisioned, a BGP update group resets the table version to 0, as shown in Figure 7-9. This causes an update group to process the peer servicing route refresh requests until they catch up either with the latest BGP table version or the version number of the second lowest peer in an update group.

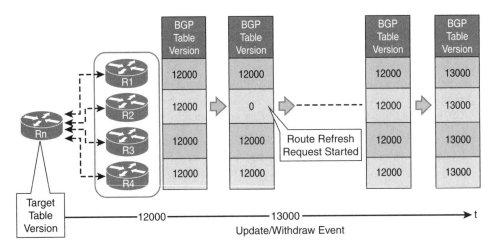

Figure 7-9   *Updates When Route Refresh Is Received*

Figure 7-10 shows that with dynamic route refresh update groups, the refresh state is tracked under a separate dynamic refresh update group. The refresh state handles the resetting of the peer table versions in a separate update group that does not affect the current peer states.

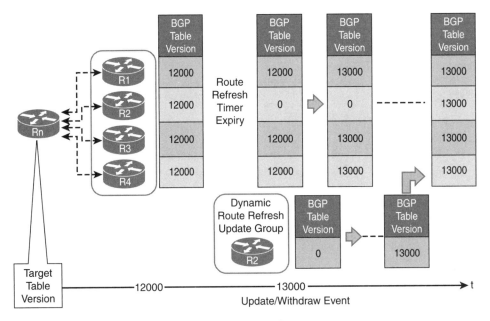

Figure 7-10   *Updates with Dynamic Refresh Update Groups*

The dynamic refresh update group feature is supported starting from Cisco IOS release 12.2(33)XNE or 12.2(31)SB13. There is no special configuration required to enable dynamic refresh update groups. IOS XR already implements more structured logic for handling update generation by using update groups and subgroups.

Note   IOS XR dynamically forms subgroups, which is a subset of neighbors within an update group based on the table version approximation. The subset of neighbors in a subgroup run at the same pace with regard to sending updates. If there are some neighbors that have a distinct table version, these are decoupled to different subgroups.

The dynamic refresh update group is created when any of the following events occur:

- Receiving route-refresh request
- Receiving Outbound Route Filtering (ORF) immediate request
- New peer establishment
- Any outbound policy change
- Reset of BGP sessions (hard reset or outbound soft reset)

The dynamic refresh update groups are recommended for RRs, typically L3VPN RRs, which have large numbers of IBGP peers within the same update group and may receive a route refresh request from any PE peers on VRF provisioning. The feature significantly reduces BGP convergence time of stable peers for update events during servicing of route refresh requests.

Note   In case of a large scaled number of VPN prefixes, generally seen in a tier-1 VPN provider, the convergence time could be reduced to under 10 to 20 seconds from 15 to 30 minutes.

Enhanced Route Refresh Capability

The toughest challenges to troubleshoot in BGP are route inconsistencies between peers. For example, withdraw or update not advertised to a peer can lead to a traffic black-hole problem. It takes a long time for customers to know and understand the problem and fix it. When the problem is identified, the most common solution is issuing the **clear ip bgp** *ip-address* **soft in** command. This workaround might not resolve the problem every time.

BGP enhanced route refresh capability is a new BGP capability with new enhancements to the route refresh capability that prevents any kind of inconsistency between the BGP peers. This capability is enabled in most of the recent Cisco IOS releases. During the BGP session establishment, a router sends Enhanced Refresh Capability via BGP capabilities advertisement (BGP-CAP). The capability is advertised with capability code 70 and length 0.

The message format for enhanced route refresh capability is same as the route refresh capability with a minute difference of the value in the reserved bits, a.k.a. Status bits. The three values of the status bits are as follows:

■ **0:** Normal Route Refresh Request

■ **1:** Start-of-RIB Route Refresh Message (*BoRR: Beginning of Route Refresh*)

■ **2:** End-of-RIB Route Refresh Message (*EoRR: Ending of Route Refresh*)

After the enhanced route refresh capability is negotiated, the BGP peer generates route refresh *Start-of-RIB* (SOR) before advertisement of *Adj-Rib-Out* and generates route refresh *End-of-RIB* (EOR) post advertisement of *Adj-RIB-Out*. A BGP speaker receiving an EOR message from its peer cleans up all the routes that were not readvertised as part of the route refresh response by the peer using the route refresh SOR. The route refresh EOR assists BGP to clear out any stale entries in the BGP table.

There might still be situations when continuous route churns occur in the network. During the same time, enhanced refresh EOR is not advertised by the peer, and the stale routes are cleaned up after expiration of the refresh EOR stale-path timer. The refresh stale-path timer is started when it receives SOR. Also, if the EOR is not advertised because of route churn, the EOR message is generated after the expiration of maximum refresh EOR timer. The following steps walk through the process of refresh processing with enhanced route refresh capability:

Step 1.   Initiate a refresh request by using the clear command **clear bgp** *afi safi* **soft in** or using the other triggers defined previously.

Step 2.   The peer sends a refresh SOR announcement and starts advertising the routes.

Step 3.   On the receiving peer, existing and new entries receive a new version (epoch) number, which indicates they have been refreshed.

Step 4.   After the peer finishes sending all paths, it advertises Refresh EOR.

Step 5.   After receiving Refresh EOR, if the received routes epoch is less than the number of routes from the neighbor previously present, it indicates the presence of a stale route. The stale route is then logged and purged. The stale route purging is performed by the BGP Scanner process (reducing the CPU overhead).

Step 6.   During the stale-path deletion process, a new SOR is received, and the stale-path deletion process is aborted.

The enhanced route refresh capability is enabled by default, but the EOR stale-path timer and maximum refresh EOR timer is disabled by default. The EOR stale-path timer is enabled by using the configuration command **bgp refresh stalepath-time** *seconds*. The maximum refresh EOR timer is enabled by using the configuration command **bgp refresh max-eor-time** *seconds*. Example 7-9 illustrates the configuration of the **bgp refresh** [stalepath-time | max-eor-time] *seconds* command. The minimum timer interval that can be set for both the commands is 600 seconds. If the value is set to 0, the timer is disabled.

Example 7-9 *BGP Enhanced Route Refresh Timer Configuration*

```
R1(config)# router bgp 100
R1(config-router)# bgp refresh stalepath-time ?
  <0-0>        Refresh stale-path timer disable
  <600-3600>  Timer interval (seconds)

R1(config-router)# bgp refresh stalepath-time 600
R1(config-router)# bgp refresh max-eor-time ?
  <0-0>        Refresh max-eor timer disable
  <600-3600>  Timer interval (seconds)

R1(config-router)# bgp refresh max-eor-time 600
R1(config-router)# end
```

With enhanced route refresh capability enabled, BGP generates syslog messages when a peer deletes stale routes after receiving an enhanced refresh EOR message (or when the stale-path timer expires). Example 7-10 examines the syslog messages generated when a BGP peer deletes stale routes after receiving an EOR message. The first part of the output displays the syslog notification when a stale entry is found after an EOR is received or when the stale-path timer expires. The second part of the output displays the number of stale paths that were from the neighbor.

Example 7-10 *BGP Stale Entry Removal Syslog Messages*

```
Net 200:200:192.168.193.0/0 from bgp neighbor IPv4 192.168.2.2 is stale after
 refresh EOR (rate-limited)
Net 200:200:192.168.193.0/0 from bgp neighbor IPv4 192.168.2.2 is stale after
 refresh stale-path timer expiry (rate-limited)
15 stale-paths deleted from bgp neighbor IPv4 192.168.2.2 after refresh EOR
15 stale-paths deleted from bgp neighbor IPv4 192.168.2.2 after refresh
 stale-path timer expiry
```

It is a best practice, though not mandatory, to configure enhanced route refresh timers. It is important to remember that network operators cannot configure the soft-reconfiguration inbound feature under vpnv4 address-family and should rely heavily on route refresh or enhanced route refresh capability.

To further examine the exchange of route refresh messages between the two routers as shown in Figure 7-6, use the debug commands **debug bgp** *afi safi* **update** and **debug bgp** *afi safi ip-address* [**in** | **out**]. Example 7-11 illustrates the exchange of SOR and EOR refresh messages between the two peers. Notice that when the SOR is received, the router R1 starts the stale-path timer, which is scheduled for 600 seconds. The time is stopped after the router receives the EOR message.

Example 7-11   *Enhanced Route Refresh Message Exchange*

```
R1# debug bgp ipv4 unicast updates
R1# debug bgp ipv4 unicast 192.168.2.2 in


19:23:19: BGP: 192.168.2.2 sending REFRESH_REQ(5) for afi/safi: 1/1,
 refresh code is 0
19:23:19: BGP: 192.168.2.2 rcv message type 5, length (excl. header) 4
19:23:19: BGP: 192.168.2.2 rcvd REFRESH_REQ for afi/safi: 1/1,
 refresh code is 1
19:23:19: BGP: nbr_topo global 192.168.2.2 IPv4 Unicast:base (0x10E5FD48:1)
 rcvd Refresh Start-of-RIB
19:23:19: BGP: nbr_topo global 192.168.2.2 IPv4 Unicast:base (0x10E5FD48:1)
 refresh_epoch is 43
19:23:19: BGP: nbr_topo global 192.168.2.2 IPv4 Unicast:base (0x10E5FD48:1)
 refresh stale-path timer scheduled for 600 seconds
19:23:19: BGP(0): 192.168.2.2 rcvd UPDATE w/ attr: nexthop 192.168.2.2,
 origin i, localpref 100, metric 0
19:23:19: BGP: 192.168.2.2 rcv message type 5, length (excl. header) 4
19:23:19: BGP: 192.168.2.2 rcvd REFRESH_REQ for afi/safi: 1/1,
 refresh code is 2
19:23:19: BGP: nbr_topo global 192.168.2.2 IPv4 Unicast:base (0x10E5FD48:1)
 rcvd Refresh End-of-RIB
19:23:19: BGP: nbr_topo global 192.168.2.2 IPv4 Unicast:base (0x10E5FD48:1)
 Enhanced refresh: Stopping stalepath timer
19:23:19: BGP: 192.168.1.1 rcv message type 5, length (excl. header) 4
19:23:19: BGP: 192.168.1.1 rcvd REFRESH_REQ for afi/safi: 1/1,
 refresh code is 0
19:23:19: BGP: 192.168.1.1 sending REFRESH_REQ(5) for afi/safi: 1/1,
 refresh code is 1
19:23:19: BGP(0): 192.168.1.1 NEXT_HOP is set to self for net 192.168.2.2/32,
19:23:19: BGP(0): (base) 192.168.1.1 send UPDATE (format) 192.168.2.2/32,
 next 192.168.2.2, metric 0, path Local
19:23:19: BGP: 192.168.1.1 sending REFRESH_REQ(5) for afi/safi: 1/1,
 refresh code is 2
```

Although it is good to have the enhanced route refresh capability enabled, the capability can be disabled using the hidden command **neighbor** *ip-address* **dont-capability-negotiate enhanced-refresh.**

Note   Both IOS XR and NX-OS do not support enhanced route refresh capability (RFC 7313) at the time of this writing.

Outbound Route Filtering (ORF)

The default route distribution model for BGP deployments is "send everything every-where," and then filter unwanted information at the receiving peer based on the local routing policy. Network operators desire the opposite—a mechanism to restrict routing information from reaching their node (router) to avoid such filtering. To overcome this challenge, Outbound Route Filtering (ORF) was introduced.

There are a number of ways that ORF can be partially achieved using features such as RR-Groups, extended community-list filters, route-maps, and so on. However, all these mechanisms require some form of manual provisioning by the operator to establish the initial filters, and then to maintain them as new customers are added to the infrastructure.

For ORF to function, ORF capability should be exchanged between the participating peers. The BGP ORF capability is announced with the capability code of 3 with variable capability length.

The BGP ORF capability provides two types of filtering mechanisms:

- Prefix-based ORF

- Extended community (route target)–based ORF

Prefix-Based ORF

BGP ORF provides a BGP-based mechanism that allows a BGP peer to send to the BGP speaker a set of route filters using a prefix list that the speaker may use to filter its out-bound routing updates toward the advertising peer. This feature is generally implemented between a PE and a CE router. An ISP usually advertises a full BGP table or a default route or a subset of the BGP table, but the ISPs do not generally implement any kind of complex outbound filtering toward their customers. Most of the times, the CE router has to do most of the filtering using inbound filters, which is again not a good method because the routes are already received by the CE router before they are filtered, and thus the resources have been consumed.

After ORF capability is exchanged, an operator on the CE router defines a set of prefix-list entries of required routes and advertises it toward PE. The PE then adds that prefix list in its outbound filter along with its existing outbound route filter (if any).

Extended Community–Based ORF

In MPLS VPN deployment, the control plane distributes VPN routing information everywhere within the local AS. Provider Edge Routers (PE-routers) filter unwanted routing information based on Automatic Route Filtering (ARF). ARF allows the PE-routers to filter based on the route target values carried within incoming routing updates.

There are a number of ways that filtering updates coming to PE can be partially achieved in Cisco IOS; rr-groups, extended community-list filters and route-maps are some exam-ples. However, all these mechanisms require some form of manual provisioning by the operator to establish the initial filters and then maintain them as new customers are added to the infrastructure.

Using route target–based ORF as defined in draft *Extended Community–Based ORF*, PE routers advertise ORF messages to RRs, but not vice versa. The content of the ORFs may be used to filter the routes advertised by RRs to PE routers. Each ORF entry consists of a single route target. A remote peer considers only those routes whose extended communities attribute has at least one route target in common with the list specified within the ORF update.

Note   In general, it is expected that PE routers have no requirement to restrict their routing updates toward the route reflectors, except in the case of multiple control-plane hierarchies.

BGP ORF Format

An ORF entry has the format <AFI/SAFI, ORF-type, Action, Match, ORF-value>. An ORF update may consist of one or more ORF entries that have a common AFI/SAFI and ORF-type. Table 7-3 elaborates the components of an ORF entry.

Table 7-3   *ORF Components*

Components	Description
AFI/SAFI	Provides a coarse granularity control by limiting the ORF to only the routes whose NLRI matches the "AFI/SAFI" component of the ORF.
ORF-Type	Determines the content of the ORF-value.
Action	Controls the handling of the ORF request by the remote peer. Action can be one of ADD, REMOVE, and REMOVE-ALL. ADD adds an ORF entry to the Outbound Route Filter on the remote peer; REMOVE deletes a previously installed ORF entry on the remote peer; REMOVE-ALL deletes the previously installed entries in the specified ORF on the remote peer.
Match	Used when support of matching granularity on a per ORF entry basis is needed, in which case the "Match" component can be one of PERMIT or DENY. The semantics of PERMIT is to ask the peer to pass updates for the set of routes that matches the ORF entry. The semantics of DENY is to ask the peer not to pass updates for the set of routes that matches the ORF entry.

ORF entries are carried within BGP ROUTE-REFRESH messages and can be distinguished between normal ROUTE-REFRESH messages, such as those not carrying ORF

entries, by using the message length field within the BGP message header. A single
ROUTE-REFRESH message can carry multiple ORF entries, although they will all share
the same AFI/SAFI and ORF-type.

As defined in RFC 5291, the encoding of each ORF entry consists of a common part
and a type-specific part. The common part consists of <AFI/SAFI, ORF-Type, Action,
Match>, and is encoded as follows:

- The AFI/SAFI component of an ORF entry is encoded in the AFI/SAFI field of the
  ROUTE-REFRESH message.

- Following the AFI/SAFI component is a one-octet "When-to-refresh" field. The
  value of this field can be one of IMMEDIATE (0x01) or DEFER (0x02).

- Following the "When-to-refresh" field is a collection of one or more ORFs, grouped
  by ORF-Type.

- The ORF-Type component is encoded as a one-octet field.

- The Length of ORFs component is a two-octets field that contains the length (in
  octets) of the ORF entries that follow, as shown in Figure 7-11.

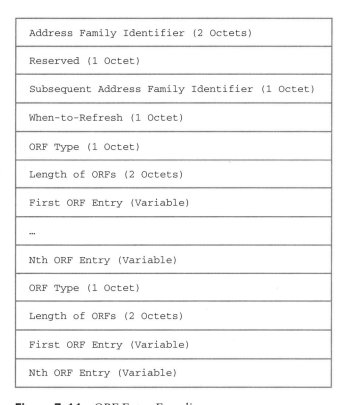

Figure 7-11 *ORF Entry Encoding*

The each ORF entry is a variable length field that consists of four primary fields: Action, Match, Reserved, and Type, as shown in Figure 7-12.

Action (2 Bits)
Match (1 Bit)
Reserved (5 Bits)
Type Specific Part (Variable)

Figure 7-12 *ORF Entry Field*

The reserved bit is set to 0 on transmit and ignored on receipt. The Extended Community ORF-type is defined with a value of 3, and the type-specific part of this entry consists of a single route target.

BGP ORF Configuration Example

As previously stated, before ORF messages are exchanged, the ORF capability should be negotiated. The ORF capability can be negotiated using the neighbor configuration command **capability orf** [**receive** | **send** | **both**]. The ORF capability is supported on Cisco IOS as well as on IOS XR software. Examine the topology shown in Figure 7-13. PE4 (IOS) and PE5(IOS XR) are connected to CE2. The PE routers are configured with a VRF named ABC and are importing routes advertised by remote CE router CE1.

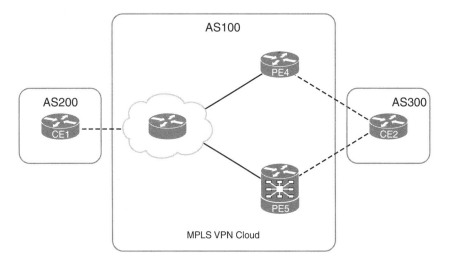

Figure 7-13 *MPLS VPN Topology with ORF Filtering on PE*

Example 7-12 illustrates the update processing on the CE2 router without ORF capability. Two prefix lists are configured on the CE2 router for neighbors on PE4 and PE5, allowing three prefixes from each side. When the prefix list is applied in the inbound direction and a soft clear of the BGP table using the **clear bgp ipv4 unicast * soft in** command is performed on the CE router, the CE2 router performs the filtering and denies all the other prefixes that do not match the prefix list.

Example 7-12 *BGP Route Filtering Without ORF*

```
ip prefix-list FROM-PE4 seq 5 permit 192.168.100.0/24
ip prefix-list FROM-PE4 seq 10 permit 192.168.102.0/24
ip prefix-list FROM-PE4 seq 15 permit 192.168.104.0/24
!
ip prefix-list FROM-PE5 seq 5 permit 192.168.101.0/24
ip prefix-list FROM-PE5 seq 10 permit 192.168.103.0/24
ip prefix-list FROM-PE5 seq 15 permit 192.168.105.0/24
!
router bgp 300
 neighbor 172.16.42.4 remote-as 100
 neighbor 172.16.52.5 remote-as 100
 address-family ipv4
  neighbor 172.16.42.4 activate
  neighbor 172.16.42.4 prefix-list FROM-PE4 in
  neighbor 172.16.52.5 activate
  neighbor 172.16.52.5 prefix-list FROM-PE5 in
```

```
CE2# debug bgp ipv4 unicast update
CE2# clear bgp ipv4 unicast * soft in
03:46:05.211: BGP: nbr_topo global 172.16.42.4 IPv4 Unicast:base
 (0xEDA8C38:1) rcvd Refresh Start-of-RIB
03:46:05.212: BGP: nbr_topo global 172.16.42.4 IPv4 Unicast:base
 (0xEDA8C38:1) refresh_epoch is 2
03:46:05.240: BGP(0): 172.16.42.4 rcvd UPDATE w/ attr: nexthop 172.16.42.4, origin e,
 merged path 100 200 8550 63704 {10584}, AS_PATH
03:46:05.241: BGP(0): 172.16.42.4 rcvd 192.168.14.0/24 -- DENIED due to: distribute/
 prefix-list;
03:46:05.246: BGP(0): 172.16.42.4 rcvd 192.168.15.0/24 -- DENIED due to: distribute/
 prefix-list;
03:46:05.248: BGP(0): 172.16.42.4 rcvd 192.168.16.0/24 -- DENIED due to: distribute/
 prefix-list;
:46:05.250: BGP(0): 172.16.42.4 rcvd 192.168.17.0/24 -- DENIED due to:
distribute/prefix-list;
03:46:05.252: BGP(0): 172.16.42.4 rcvd 192.168.18.0/24 -- DENIED due to: distribute/
 prefix-list;
03:46:05.253: BGP(0): 172.16.42.4 rcvd 192.168.19.0/24 -- DENIED due to: distribute/
 prefix-list;
03:46:05.254: BGP(0): 172.16.42.4 rcvd 192.168.20.0/24 -- DENIED due to: distribute/
 prefix-list;
! Output omitted for brevity
```

If a large number of prefixes are being advertised by PE, a lot of inbound filter processing happens on the CE router as those routes are already advertised by PE and received by CE. The inbound filtering only saves some resources when installing the prefixes in the BGP table and the routing information base (RIB).

Example 7-13 illustrates the configuration process of ORF capability. Notice that the PE routers PE4 and PE5 advertise the ORF capability with ORF type receive, whereas the CE2 advertises as send. The CE2 router configures the inbound prefix list to filter the prefixes being received from the PE routers PE4 and PE5.

Example 7-13 *BGP ORF Capability Configuration*

```
IOS
PE4(config)# router bgp 100
PE4(config-router)# address-family ipv4 vrf ABC
PE4(config-router-af)# neighbor 172.16.42.2 capability orf prefix-list receive
PE4(config-router-af)# end
```

```
IOS XR
RP/0/0/CPU0:PE5(config)# router bgp 100
RP/0/0/CPU0:PE5(config-bgp)# vrf ABC
RP/0/0/CPU0:PE5(config-bgp-vrf)# neighbor 172.16.52.2
RP/0/0/CPU0:PE5(config-bgp-vrf-nbr)# address-family ipv4 unicast
RP/0/0/CPU0:PE5(config-bgp-vrf-nbr-af)# capability orf prefix receive
RP/0/0/CPU0:PE5(config-bgp-vrf-nbr-af)# commit
```

```
IOS
CE2(config)# router bgp 300
CE2(config-router)# address-family ipv4 unicast
CE2(config-router-af)# neighbor 172.16.42.4 capability orf prefix-list send
CE2(config-router-af)# neighbor 172.16.52.5 capability orf prefix-list send
CE2(config-router-af)# end
```

After the ORF capability is negotiated, the CE router advertises the inbound prefix list to the respective PE routers. Use the command **show bgp vrf ABC all neighbors** *ip-address* **received prefix-filter** to view the received prefix-list filter on the PE router. This command is applicable for both IOS and IOS XR devices. Example 7-14 illustrates the use **show bgp vrf ABC all neighbors** *ip-address* **received prefix-filter** on both PE4 and PE5 routers to verify the prefix-list filter received from the CE2 router. Notice that the received prefix filter is the same prefix list that was configured on the CE2 router toward PE4 and PE5 routers.

Example 7-14 *BGP ORF Received Prefix-List Filter*

```
IOS
PE4# show bgp vrf ABC all neighbors 172.16.42.2 received prefix-filter
For address family: IPv4 Unicast
Address family: VPNv4 Unicast
ip prefix-list 172.16.42.2: 3 entries
   seq 5 permit 192.168.100.0/24
   seq 10 permit 192.168.102.0/24
   seq 15 permit 192.168.104.0/24

For address family: VPNv4 Unicast
Address family: VPNv4 Unicast
ip prefix-list 172.16.42.2: 3 entries
   seq 5 permit 192.168.100.0/24
   seq 10 permit 192.168.102.0/24
   seq 15 permit 192.168.104.0/24
```

```
IOS XR
RP/0/0/CPU0:PE5# show bgp vrf ABC neighbors 172.16.52.2 received prefix-filter
Number of entries: 3
ipv4 prefix ORF 172.16.52.2
  5 permit 192.168.101.0/24 ge 24 le 24
  10 permit 192.168.103.0/24 ge 24 le 24
  15 permit 192.168.105.0/24 ge 24 le 24
```

With ORF, the result remains the same for the prefixes in the BGP table (that was previously achieved using an inbound prefix list on the CE router) and the RIB. But in the background, there is a major difference in processing done by the CE and the PE routers. Example 7-15 illustrates the processing performed by the PE and the CE for filtering the prefixes. With the debug output, notice that only three prefixes are received and processed for the neighbor 172.16.42.4, which is as per the prefix filter on the PE4 router.

Example 7-15 *BGP ORF Capability Configuration*

```
CE2# debug bgp ipv4 unicast update

06:37:10.893: %BGP-5-ADJCHANGE: neighbor 172.16.42.4 Up
06:37:11.096: BGP(0): 172.16.42.4 rcvd UPDATE w/ attr: nexthop 172.16.42.4,
 origin e, merged path 100 200 33299 51178 47751 {27016}, AS_PATH
06:37:11.097: BGP(0): 172.16.42.4 rcvd 192.168.100.0/24
06:37:11.097: BGP(0): 172.16.42.4 rcvd 192.168.102.0/24
06:37:11.098: BGP(0): 172.16.42.4 rcvd 192.168.104.0/24
```

> **Note**   Cisco IOS and IOS XR do not support extended community–based ORF.

Maximum Prefixes

By default, a BGP peer holds all the routes advertised by the peering router. The number of routes can be filtered either on the inbound of the local router or on the outbound of the peering router. But there can still be instances where the number of routes are more than what a router anticipates or can handle. To prevent such situations, use the BGP maximum-prefix feature.

All three Cisco OSs support the BGP maximum-prefix feature that limits the number of prefixes on a per-neighbor basis. Typically, this feature is enabled for EBGP sessions but can also be used for IBGP sessions. This feature helps scale and prevent the network from an excess number of routes and thus should be carefully configured. The BGP maximum-prefix feature can be enabled in the following situations:

- Know how many BGP routes are anticipated from the peer.

- What actions should be taken if the number of routes exceeded the specified value. Should the BGP connection be reset or should a warning message be logged?

To limit the number of prefixes, use the command **neighbor** *ip-address* **maximum-prefix** *maximum* [*threshold*] [**restart** *restart-interval* | **warning-only**] for each neighbor. Table 7-4 describes each of the fields in the command.

Table 7-4   *BGP* **maximum-prefix** *Command Options*

Options	Description
maximum	Defines the maximum prefix limit.
threshold	Defines the threshold percentage at which a warning is generated.
restart *restart-interval*	Default behavior. Resets the BGP connection after the specified prefix limit is exceeded. The *restart-interval* is configured in minutes. BGP tries to reestablish the peering after the specified time interval is passed. When the restart option is set, a cease notification is sent to the neighbor and the BGP connection is terminated.
warning-only	Only gives a warning message when the specified limit is exceeded.
discard-extra-paths	Only supported on IOS XR. When configured, BGP drops all excess prefixes received from the neighbor after it reaches the maximum limit value.

An important point to remember is that when the **restart** option is configured with the **maximum-prefix** command, the only other way apart from waiting for the restart-interval timer to expire, to re-establish the BGP connection, is to perform a manual reset of the peer using the **clear bgp** *afi safi ip-address* command.

Example 7-16 illustrates the configuration of the **neighbor maximum-prefix** command on all three Cisco OSs. Notice that on IOS XR, the discard-extra-paths option is configured. The threshold value, if not specified, is set to 75% default.

Example 7-16   *BGP* maximum-prefix *Configuration*

```
! Configuration on Cisco IOS
CE2(config)# router bgp 300
CE2(config-router)# address-family ipv4 unicast
CE2(config-router-af)# neighbor 172.16.42.4 maximum-prefix 2 warning-only
CE2(config-router-af)# neighbor 172.16.52.5 maximum-prefix 2 restart 2


! Configuration on IOS XR
RP/0/0/CPU0:PE5(config)# router bgp 100
RP/0/0/CPU0:PE5(config-bgp)# vrf ABC
RP/0/0/CPU0:PE5(config-bgp-vrf)# neighbor 172.16.52.2
RP/0/0/CPU0:PE5(config-bgp-vrf-nbr)# address-family ipv4 unicast
RP/0/0/CPU0:PE5(config-bgp-vrf-nbr-af)# maximum-prefix 2 discard-extra-paths
RP/0/0/CPU0:PE5(config-bgp-vrf-nbr-af)# commit


! Configuration on NX-OS
PE6(config)# router bgp 100
PE6(config-router)# neighbor 172.16.62.2
PE6(config-router-neighbor)# address-family ipv4 unicast
PE6(config-router-neighbor-af)# maximum-prefix 4 warning-only
```

The maximum-prefix command takes immediate effect. Based on the action set, either the warning message is logged or the BGP session is reset. There is no control over which prefix is dropped or removed from the BGP table. Example 7-17 illustrates the syslog generated and the BGP connection reset due to maximum-prefix limit exceeded.

Example 7-17   *BGP* maximum-prefix *Configuration*

```
! Warning Message with warning-only option
00:09:04: %BGP-4-MAXPFX: Number of prefixes received from 172.16.42.4
 (afi 0) reaches 2, max 2
00:09:04: %BGP-3-MAXPFXEXCEED: Number of prefixes received from 172.16.42.4
 (afi 0): 3 exceeds limit 2
! Warning and BGP session reset with reset option
```

```
00:38:28: %BGP-4-MAXPFX: Number of prefixes received from 172.16.52.5
(afi 0) reaches 2, max 2
00:38:28: %BGP-3-MAXPFXEXCEED: Number of prefixes received from 172.16.52.5
(afi 0): 3 exceeds limit 2
00:38:28: %BGP-3-NOTIFICATION: sent to neighbor 172.16.52.5 6/1
(Maximum Number of Prefixes Reached) 7 bytes 00010100 000002
00:38:28: %BGP-5-NBR_RESET: Neighbor 172.16.52.5 reset (Peer over prefix limit)
00:38:28: %BGP-5-ADJCHANGE: neighbor 172.16.52.5 Down Peer over prefix limit
```

On IOS XR, a preset limit is placed on the number of prefixes that are accepted from a peer for each supported address-family. This default limit can be modified using the **maximum-prefix** command. Table 7-5 lists the limit of prefixes per each address-family on IOS XR.

Table 7-5 *Default Maximum Number of Prefixes per Address-Family*

Address-Family	Prefixes
IPv4 Unicast	1048576
IPv4 Labeled Unicast	131072
IPv4 Tunnel	1048576
IPv6 Unicast	524288
IPv6 Labeled Unicast	131072
IPv4 Multicast	131072
IPv6 Multicast	131072
VPNv4 Unicast	2097152
IPv4 MDT	131072
VPNv6 Unicast	1048576
L2VPN EVPN	2097152

BGP Max AS

There are various attributes that are, by default, assigned to every BGP prefix. The length of attributes that can be attached to a single prefix can grow up to size of 64K bytes, which can cause scaling as well as convergence issues for BGP.

Many times, the **as-path prepend** option is used to increase the AS-PATH list to make a path with lower AS-PATH list preferred. This operation does not have much of an impact. But from the perspective of Internet, a longer AS-PATH list can cause convergence issues and also cause security loopholes. The AS-PATH list actually signifies a router's position on the Internet.

IOS releases prior to 12.2 SRC or 12.4 T releases were not very efficient in handling AS-PATHs with over 255 AS numbers. They caused BGP session flaps. To limit the maximum number of AS-PATH lengths supported in the network, a **bgp maxas-limit** command was introduced. Using the **bgp maxas-limit** *1-254* command in IOS and the **maxas-limit** *1-512* command in NX-OS, any route with an AS-PATH length higher than the specified number is discarded.

IOS XR does not have a direct command to set the maxas-limit, but rather uses Route Policy Language (RPL) to achieve the same result. The **as-path length** feature of RPL helps achieve the same behavior as the **bgp maxas-limit** command.

Examine the topology in Figure 7-14. ISP1 and ISP2 routers are peering with IOS router R1, IOS XR router R2, and NX-OS router R3. The ISP router is advertising one prefix with an AS-PATH length of 4, whereas the ISP2 router is advertising two prefixes with an AS-PATH length of 1.

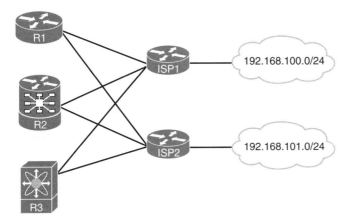

Figure 7-14   *Topology*

Example 7-18 displays the BGP table of routers R1, R2, and R3 before the maximum AS limit is configured. The prefix 192.168.100.0 is having four ASs in its AS-PATH list, whereas prefix 192.168.101.0 only has two ASs.

Example 7-18   *BGP Table Before Maximum AS Limit*

```
IOS
R1# show bgp ipv4 unicast
! Output omitted for brevity
Network            Next Hop      Metric LocPrf Weight Path
 *>   192.168.100.0   10.1.101.2    2219              0 200 134 115 149 i
 *>   192.168.101.0   10.1.201.2    2219              0 300 110 i
```

```
IOS XR
RP/0/0/CPU0:R2# show bgp ipv4 unicast
! Output omitted for brevity
   Network              Next Hop        Metric LocPrf Weight Path
*> 192.168.100.0/24     10.1.102.2       2219                0 200 134 115 149 i
*> 192.168.101.0/24     10.1.202.2       2219                0 300 110 i
```

```
NX-OS
R3# show bgp ipv4 unicast
! Output omitted for brevity
   Network              Next Hop        Metric  LocPrf Weight Path
*>e192.168.100.0/24     10.1.103.2      2219              0 200 134 115 149 i
*>e192.168.101.0/24     10.1.203.2      2219              0 300 110 i
```

Example 7-19 demonstrates the configuration on R1, R2, and R3 that will only accept prefixes with AS-PATH lengths of 3 or lower.

Example 7-19   *BGP Maximum AS Configuration*

```
R1
router bgp 100
 bgp maxas-limit 3
```

```
R2
router bgp 100
address-family ipv4 unicast
 !
 neighbor 10.1.102.2
  remote-as 100
  address-family ipv4 unicast
   route-policy MAXAS-LIMIT in
!
route-policy MAXAS-LIMIT
  if as-path length ge 3 then
    drop
  endif
   pass
end-policy
```

```
R3
router bgp 100
 maxas-limit 3
```

The command verifies the AS-PATH list during the update processing and does not have any impact on the BGP sessions. If there are any BGP prefixes with a higher AS-PATH length than specified in the BGP table before configuring the **bgp maxas-limit** command, those prefixes are not affected until the next update processing.

Example 7-20 provides the BGP table on R1, R2, and R3 after BGP maxas-limit is set.

Example 7-20 *BGP Table After Maximum AS Limit*

```
IOS
R1# show bgp ipv4 unicast
! Output omitted for brevity
Network            Next Hop        Metric LocPrf Weight Path
 *>  192.168.101.0    10.1.201.2      2219              0 300 110 i
```

```
IOS XR
RP/0/0/CPU0:R2# show bgp ipv4 unicast
! Output omitted for brevity
   Network         Next Hop        Metric LocPrf Weight Path
*> 192.168.101.0/24  10.1.202.2     2219              0 300 110 i
```

```
NX-OS
R3# show bgp ipv4 unicast
! Output omitted for brevity
   Network         Next Hop     Metric  LocPrf Weight Path
*>e192.168.101.0/24  10.1.203.2    2219            0 300 110 i
```

Along with discarding the route, all three routers also log a syslog message indicating that the prefix was discarded. Example 7-21 displays the logged syslog message on all three routers.

Example 7-21 *Syslog Message*

```
R1 - IOS
06:18:51.765: %BGP-6-ASPATH: Long AS path 200 134 115 149 received from
10.1.101.2: BGP(0) Prefixes: 192.168.100.0/24
```

```
R2 - IOS XR
bgp[1052]: %ROUTING-BGP-3-MALFORM_UPDATE : Malformed UPDATE message received from
  neighbor 10.1.102.2 (VRF: default) - message length 73 bytes, error flags
  0x00200000, action taken "DiscardAttr". Error details: "Error 0x00200000,
  Field "Attr-unexpected", Attribute 5 (Flags 0x40, Length 4), Data [400504]".
  NLRIs: [IPv4 Unicast] 192.168.100.0/24
```

```
R3 - NX-OS
R3# show bgp event-history logs
bgp-100 logs events
06:18:50.040318 bgp 100 [7373]: [7382]: [IPv4 Unicast] Path for 192.168.100.0/24
 from peer 10.1.103.2 found to exceed the maxas-limit
```

BGP Maximum Neighbors

Every platform has a limitation on the scale of BGP neighbors that it can support, but not all platforms provide a configuration to limit the number of BGP neighbors. IOS XR provides the BGP maximum neighbors feature that allows the users to limit the maximum number of BGP sessions that can be configured on the router. The default limit of maximum BGP neighbors that can be configured on the router is 4,000. IOS XR supports configuring of the maximum number of neighbors set between 1 to 15,000.

Use the command **bgp maximum neighbor** *1-15000* to set the maximum number of BGP neighbors that can be configured on the router. Example 7-22 illustrates the configuration of the **bgp maximum neighbor** command.

Example 7-22 bgp maximum neighbor *Command*

```
RP/0/0/CPU0:R2(config)# router bgp 100
RP/0/0/CPU0:R2(config-bgp)# bgp maximum neighbor ?
  <1-15000>  Maximum number of neighbors
RP/0/0/CPU0:R2(config-bgp)# bgp maximum neighbor 10
RP/0/0/CPU0:R2(config-bgp)# commit
```

An important point to remember is if there are 100 neighbors configured on the router, the value in the **bgp maximum neighbor** command cannot be set to below 100.

Scaling BGP with Route Reflectors

As explained earlier in this chapter and in Chapter 1, "BGP Fundamentals," route reflectors (RR) and confederations are the two options for scaling IBGP sessions. The RR design allows the IBGP peering to be configured like a hub-and-spoke instead of a full mesh. The RR clients are either regular IBGP peers—that is, they are not directly connected to each other—or the other design could have RR clients that are interconnected. Examine the two RR design scenarios as shown in Figure 7-15. Notice (a) has R1 acting as the RR, whereas R2, R3, and R4 are the RR clients, and (b) has a similar setup to that of (a) with a difference that the RR clients are fully meshed with each other.

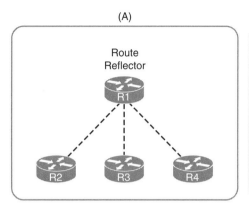 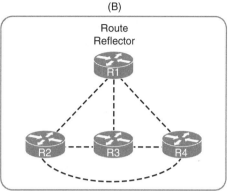

Figure 7-15 *Topology with RR and RR Clients and Topology with RR with Full-Mesh RR Clients*

The RR and the client peers form a cluster and are not required to be fully meshed. Because the topology in (b) has a RR along with fully meshed IBGP client peers, which actually defies the purpose of having RR, the BGP RR reflection behavior should be disabled. The BGP RR client-to-client reflection is disabled by using the command **no bgp client-to-client reflection**. This command is required only on the RR and not on the RR clients. Example 7-23 displays the configuration for disabling BGP client-to-client reflection.

Example 7-23 bgp maximum neighbor *Command*

```
IOS
R1(config)# router bgp 100
R1(config-router)# address-family ipv4 unicast
R1(config-router-af)# no bgp client-to-client reflection
```

```
IOS XR
RP/0/0/CPU0:R2(config)# router bgp 100
RP/0/0/CPU0:R2(config-bgp)# address-family ipv4 unicast
RP/0/0/CPU0:R2(config-bgp-af)# bgp client-to-client reflection disable
RP/0/0/CPU0:R2(config-bgp-af)# RP/0/0/CPU0:R2(config-bgp-af)#commit
```

```
NX-OS
R3(config)# router bgp 100
R3(config-router)# address-family ipv4 unicast
R3(config-router-af)# no client-to-client reflection
```

There are often questions about how many RRs should be added in the topology. The answer to this question depends on the design and network requirements. More RRs in the network means more redundancy. But having more RRs means more management work and more memory utilization on the RR routers. Generally, two RRs are sufficient in the network to provide redundancy. But each network runs its own set of services, such as IPv4, IPv6, VPNv4, and so on. An ideal design is to have two RRs per each service set; that is, two RRs for IPv4 address-family, two RRs for VPNv4 address-family, and so on. Although it is also important to remember that more RRs mean an increased number of paths on the RR clients. If the RRs are placed as autonomous system boundary routers (ASBRs), the RRs become the part of the forwarding path, which is typically not a best practice for a large service provider.

Note   When implementing RRs in a scaled environment, it is recommended to have the interface queue limit set to a higher value than the default value, especially on Cisco IOS platforms. The reason for that is when the RR router restarts or when there is a session flap, TCP packets will be coming toward the RR router from every part of the network, and the RR router must send an ACK to those received TCP packets. If the interface input queue size or buffer size is set to the default value (75 on IOS platforms and 375 on IOS XE platforms), those packets might get dropped if they exceed the number of packets the interface buffer can handle while the router is busy processing the updates. Therefore, increasing the interface buffer size to a value of 1500 to 2000 would help overcome any of these challenges. It is not necessary to increase the buffer size on the RR client routers, but it can be increased for consistency.

BGP Route Reflector Clusters

BGP RR uses two attributes as defined in RFC 2796—ORIGINATOR_ID and CLUSTER_ LIST, to provide loop prevention mechanism in RR design. A BGP cluster is a set of RR and its clients. When a single RR is deployed in a cluster, the cluster is identified by the router-id of the RR. But when there are two or more RRs in the cluster, the command **bgp cluster-id** [*number* | *ip-address*] in IOS and IOS XR or the command **cluster-id** [*number* | *ip-address*] in NX-OS can be used to set the cluster ID for the cluster. The *number* is a 32-bit numeric value that can be set as the cluster-id. Example 7-24 displays the **bgp cluster-id** configuration.

Example 7-24   bgp cluster-id *Configuration*

```
IOS
R1(config)# router bgp 65530
R1(config-router)# bgp cluster-id 0.0.0.1

IOS XR
RP/0/0/CPU0:R2(config)# router bgp 100
RP/0/0/CPU0:R2(config-bgp)# bgp cluster-id 0.0.0.1

NX-OS
R3(config)# router bgp 100
R3(config-router)# cluster-id 0.0.0.1
```

An RR router not only peers with the RR client router but also with the nonclient router. If there are nonclient routers in the topology, they have to be peered with the RR to allow proper route propagation within the network. An RR is also treated as a nonclient router to another RR. Therefore, all the RRs and the nonclient routers should form a full mesh.

Having the same cluster ID allows all RRs in the cluster to recognize updates from the RR clients in same cluster and reduce the number of updates to be stored in BGP table. When reflecting a route, RR appends the global cluster-id to the CLUSTER_LIST and when receiving a route, it discards the route if the global cluster-id is present in the CLUSTER_LIST of the route.

Figure 7-16 displays how a topology of BGP clusters with RR, RR clients, and nonclients R1, R2, and R3 are part of cluster 0.0.0.1. R4 is another RR with cluster-id of 0.0.0.2 and RR client R5. R6 is having an external BGP (EBGP) connection to R2 advertising loopback 192.168.6.6/32. R10 is a nonclient BGP router connected to both R1 and R4.

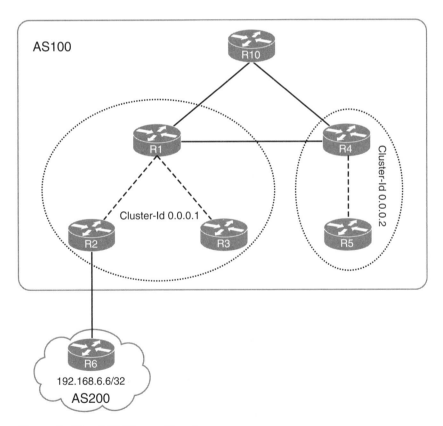

Figure 7-16 *BGP Cluster Topology*

R6 advertises the loopback address 192.168.6.6/32 toward R2. R2 then advertises the prefix to R1, which is the RR, but the BGP table of R3 does not show the prefix 192.168.6.6/32 because it is blocked due to the cluster list. The prefix advertised by RR router R1 has the cluster ID of 0.0.0.1, which is same as that of R3. R3 drops the prefix from getting installed in the BGP table. But 192.168.6.6/32 is successfully advertised to R4 and is seen in the BGP table as R6 having a different cluster ID i.e. 0.0.0.2. When R4 advertises the prefix to R5, it adds 0.0.0.2 in its prefix-list and R5 drops the update as it belongs to the same cluster 0.0.0.2.

Example 7-25 illustrates the loop prevention mechanism in the BGP cluster by displaying the BGP table of all the routers in AS100.

Example 7-25 *BGP Cluster Loop Prevention Mechanism*

```
R2# show bgp ipv4 unicast
     Network         Next Hop         Metric LocPrf Weight Path
r>i 192.168.1.1/32  192.168.1.1          0    100      0 i
*>  192.168.2.2/32  0.0.0.0              0         32768 i
*>  192.168.6.6/32  10.1.26.6                         0 200 i
```

```
R1# show bgp ipv4 unicast
     Network         Next Hop         Metric LocPrf Weight Path
*>  192.168.1.1/32  0.0.0.0              0         32768 i
r>i 192.168.2.2/32  192.168.2.2          0    100      0 i
r>i 192.168.3.3/32  192.168.3.3          0    100      0 i
r>i 192.168.4.4/32  192.168.4.4          0    100      0 i
r>i 192.168.5.5/32  192.168.5.5          0    100      0 i
*>i 192.168.6.6/32  192.168.2.2          0    100      0 200 i
```

```
R3# show bgp ipv4 unicast
     Network         Next Hop         Metric LocPrf Weight Path
r>i 192.168.1.1/32  192.168.1.1          0    100      0 i
*>  192.168.3.3/32  0.0.0.0              0         32768 i
```

```
R4# show bgp ipv4 unicast
     Network         Next Hop         Metric LocPrf Weight Path
r>i 192.168.1.1/32  192.168.1.1          0    100      0 i
r>i 192.168.2.2/32  192.168.2.2          0    100      0 i
r>i 192.168.3.3/32  192.168.3.3          0    100      0 i
*>  192.168.4.4/32  0.0.0.0              0         32768 i
r>i 192.168.5.5/32  192.168.5.5          0    100      0 i
*>i 192.168.6.6/32  192.168.2.2          0    100      0 200 i
```

```
R5# show bgp ipv4 unicast
     Network         Next Hop         Metric LocPrf Weight Path
r>i 192.168.4.4/32  192.168.4.4          0    100      0 i
*>  192.168.5.5/32  0.0.0.0              0         32768 i
```

If both RRs are in different clusters, the second RR holds the paths from the first RR and consumes more memory and CPU. The two methods of using the same cluster-id or different cluster-id have their own disadvantages, which should be understood when choosing an RR design. The disadvantages are as follows:

- Different cluster-id

    - Additional memory and CPU overhead on RR

- Same cluster-id

    - Less redundant paths

If the **bgp cluster-id** command is removed from router R5 as shown in Example 7-26, then both the prefix 192.168.6.6/32 can be viewed in R5 BGP table. The prefix is also seen with both the cluster IDs in the CLUSTER-LIST.

Example 7-26 *Removing the* bgp cluster-id *Command*

```
R5(config)# router bgp 100
R5(config-router)# no bgp cluster-id
R5# show bgp ipv4 unicast 192.168.6.6
BGP routing table entry for 192.168.6.6/32, version 12
Paths: (1 available, best #1, table default)
  Not advertised to any peer
  Refresh Epoch 1
  200
    192.168.2.2 (metric 4) from 192.168.4.4 (192.168.4.4)
      Origin IGP, metric 0, localpref 100, valid, internal, best
      Originator: 192.168.2.2, Cluster list: 0.0.0.2, 0.0.0.1
      rx pathid: 0, tx pathid: 0x0
```

Note It is not a recommended design to have the **bgp cluster-id** command configured on the RR client routers and should only be configured on the RR routers. The configuration here on the RR client is just used for demonstration purposes.

If the RR clients are fully meshed within the cluster, the **no bgp client-to-client reflection** command can be enabled on the RR.

Note As a best practice, full mesh between the RRs and the nonclients should be kept small.

Starting with the 15.2(1)S IOS release and 3.8 XR release, Cisco added the support for the Multi-Cluster ID (MCID) feature. The MCID functionality allows for a router-reflector to configure a cluster-id per neighbor. When a cluster-id is configured on a per-neighbor basis, functionality is changed in two ways:

■ CLUSTER_LIST–based loop detection mechanism

■ Disabling client to client route reflection based on cluster-id

When propagating a route with the MCID feature, the RR appends the cluster-id of the router from which the route was received to the CLUSTER_LIST. If the neighbor does not have an associated cluster-id, it uses the global cluster-id instead. For loop prevention with MCID, the receiving router discards the route if any of the global or per-neighbor cluster-id is found in the CLUSTER_LIST.

Example 7-27 illustrates how to configure per-neighbor cluster-id.

Example 7-27 *MCID Configuration*

```
IOS
R5(config)# router bgp 100
R5(config-router)# cluster-id 0.0.0.1
R5(config-router)# neighbor 192.168.4.4 cluster-id 0.0.0.1

IOS XR
RP/0/0/CPU0:R4(config)# router bgp 100
RP/0/0/CPU0:R4(config-bgp)# bgp cluster-id 0.0.0.2
RP/0/0/CPU0:R4(config-bgp)# neighbor 192.168.1.1
RP/0/0/CPU0:R4(config-bgp-nbr)# remote-as 100
RP/0/0/CPU0:R4(config-bgp-nbr)# cluster-id 0.0.0.1
RP/0/0/CPU0:R4(config-bgp-nbr)# update-source loopback0
RP/0/0/CPU0:R4(config-bgp-nbr)# address-family ipv4 unicast
```

Note   In Example 7-27, router R4 is replaced from IOS to IOS XR.

In Example 7-25, R4 learned the prefix from R1 because R4 was having a different cluster-id. But with the new MCID configuration, R4 no longer learns the prefixes from R1. This is because router R4 is now configured as the cluster-id 0.0.0.1 for neighbor 192.168.1.1. Example 7-28 displays the BGP table after the MCID implementation. In the output, notice that R4 does not contain the loopback routes from R2, R3, and R6.

Example 7-28 *MCID Configuration*

```
RP/0/0/CPU0:R4# show bgp ipv4 unicast
! Output omitted for brevity
Status codes: s suppressed, d damped, h history, * valid, > best
              i - internal, r RIB-failure, S stale, N Nexthop-discard
```

```
Origin codes: i - IGP, e - EGP, ? - incomplete
   Network             Next Hop            Metric LocPrf Weight Path
*>i192.168.1.1/32      192.168.1.1              0    100      0 i
*>  192.168.4.4/32     0.0.0.0                  0         32768 i
*>i192.168.5.5/32      192.168.5.5              0    100      0 i


Processed 3 prefixes, 3 paths
```

With the MCID feature, an RR client can peer not only with the RR in the same cluster but also with an RR in another cluster. Example 7-29 illustrates RR client R3 in cluster 0.0.0.1 peering with RR router R4 in cluster 0.0.0.2. The session is part of cluster 0.0.0.2. Notice that after the BGP peering, R4 has the prefix 192.168.3.3/32 in its BGP table. This prefix is not advertised to R5. Any prefix from R5 is advertised to R3.

Example 7-29 *Intercluster Peering*

```
IOS
R3(config)# router bgp 100
R3(config-router)# neighbor 192.168.4.4 remote-as 100
R3(config-router)# neighbor 192.168.4.4 update-source loopback0
R3(config-router)# neighbor 192.168.4.4 cluster-id 0.0.0.2
R3(config-router)# address-family ipv4 unicast
R3(config-router-af)# neighbor 192.168.4.4 activate
R3(config-router-af)# neighbor 192.168.4.4 next-hop-self


R3# show bgp ipv4 unicast
! Output omitted for brevity
     Network             Next Hop           Metric LocPrf Weight Path
r>i 192.168.1.1/32       192.168.1.1             0    100      0 i
*>  192.168.3.3/32       0.0.0.0                 0         32768 i
r>i 192.168.4.4/32       192.168.4.4             0    100      0 i
```

```
IOS XR
RP/0/0/CPU0:R4(config)# router bgp 100
RP/0/0/CPU0:R4(config-bgp)# neighbor 192.168.3.3
RP/0/0/CPU0:R4(config-bgp-nbr)# remote-as 100
RP/0/0/CPU0:R4(config-bgp-nbr)# update-source loopback0
RP/0/0/CPU0:R4(config-bgp-nbr)# address-family ipv4 unicast
RP/0/0/CPU0:R4(config-bgp-nbr-af)# route-reflector-client
RP/0/0/CPU0:R4(config-bgp-nbr-af)# commit
```

```
RP/0/0/CPU0:R4# show bgp ipv4 unicast
! Output omitted for brevity
   Network          Next Hop        Metric LocPrf Weight Path
*>i192.168.1.1/32   192.168.1.1          0    100      0 i
*>i192.168.3.3/32   192.168.3.3          0    100      0 i
*> 192.168.4.4/32   0.0.0.0              0         32768 i
*>i192.168.5.5/32   192.168.5.5          0    100      0 i

Processed 4 prefixes, 4 paths
```

With the introduction of the MCID feature, there have also been some enhancements with client-to-client reflection functionality. By default, in classical mode, the command **no bgp client-to-client reflection** helps disable the reflection of routes by the RR when the clients are fully meshed within the BGP cluster. But this command does not help when the clients have peering in different clusters; that is, intercluster peering.

The command to disable client-to-client route reflection for a particular cluster-id is **no bgp client-to-client reflection intra-cluster cluster-id** [**any** | *cluster-id1 cluster-id2 …*].

The *any* keyword is used to specify that client-to-client reflection is disabled for any cluster. The old command for disabling all client-to-client reflection is still used: **no bgp client-to-client reflection** [**all**]. The **all** keyword is optional and disables both inter-cluster and intra-cluster client-to-client reflection.

In summary, three levels of commands are used to disable client-to-client reflection:

■ **Level 1: no bgp client-to-client reflection** [**all**]. Disables intra-cluster and inter-cluster client-to-client reflection.

■ **Level 2: no bgp client-to-client reflection intra-cluster cluster-id any**. Disables intra-cluster client-to-client reflection for any cluster-id.

■ **Level 3: no bgp client-to-client reflection intra-cluster cluster-id** [*cluster-id1 cluster-id2 …*]. Disables intra-cluster client-to-client reflection for the specified cluster-ids.

Cisco IOS also provides the command **show bgp** *afi safi* **cluster-ids** [**internal**] to view the configured and used BGP client-to-client reflection method. The keyword **internal** is hidden and displays additional information.

Example 7-30 displays the output of the **show bgp ipv4 unicast cluster-ids internal** command, which shows the global cluster-id as 0.0.0.1 and configured per-neighbor cluster-id as 0.0.0.2. Notice that in the first part of the output, the C2C-rfl-CFG and C2C-rfl-USE fields show the value as ENABLED, which means that client-to-client reflection is happening. Later when the client-to-client reflection is disabled, the output shows the state of these fields as DISABLED. This is a quick method to verify the behavior when using cluster-ids.

Example 7-30 *Intercluster Peering*

```
R1# show bgp ipv4 unicast cluster-ids internal
Global cluster-id: 0.0.0.1 (configured: 0.0.0.1)
BGP client-to-client reflection:            Configured    Used
  all (inter-cluster and intra-cluster): ENABLED
  intra-cluster:                            ENABLED       ENABLED
Cluster-id head : 0x102AF5A8
Cluster-id chunk: 0xEFF5AE0

List of cluster-ids:
Cluster-id      #-neighbors C2C-rfl-CFG C2C-rfl-USE Refcount Address
0.0.0.2                   1 ENABLED     ENABLED            2 0x11BCE08C
```

```
R1(config)# router bgp 100
R1(config-router)# no bgp client-to-client reflection all
```

```
R1# show bgp ipv4 unicast cluster-ids internal
Global cluster-id: 0.0.0.1 (configured: 0.0.0.1)
BGP client-to-client reflection:            Configured    Used
  all (inter-cluster and intra-cluster): ENABLED
  intra-cluster:                            ENABLED       ENABLED
Cluster-id head : 0x102AF5A8
Cluster-id chunk: 0xEFF5AE0

List of cluster-ids:
Cluster-id      #-neighbors C2C-rfl-CFG C2C-rfl-USE Refcount Address
0.0.0.1                   0 DISABLED    DISABLED           2 0x11BCE034
0.0.0.2                   1 DISABLED    DISABLED           2 0x11BCE08C
```

Hierarchical Route Reflectors

It is so far clear that RRs help in scaling the full-mesh IBGP sessions. But in large-scale deployments, a single layer of RRs might not be enough to scale the whole network. With additional RR clients attached to an RR, more BGP updates and BGP keepalives are required to be processed by the RR router. This can consume a lot of CPU and memory resources.

Network designers can build route reflector clusters in hierarchies. With hierarchies, a router serving as an RR in one cluster can act as a client in another cluster. When a first level of BGP cluster is built, the remaining full mesh IBGP sessions are usually smaller. But if the remaining nonclient sessions are large, then additional levels of RRs can be configured. Figure 7-17 illustrates hierarchical RR topology design. In this topology, the first level of an RR cluster is built by creating cluster 10 and 20. This step reduced the original full mesh of 14 routers to a full mesh of eight routers. The second level of RR cluster is then built by creating cluster 100. This step further reduced the full mesh of eight routers to a full mesh consisting of only two routers. Only the two RRs in the cluster 100 are required to form peering with the RR routers in other clusters and also a full mesh peering with the nonclient routers.

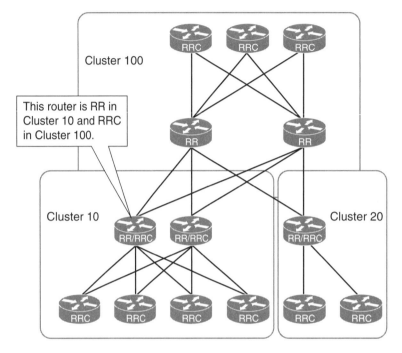

Figure 7-17   *Hierarchical Route Reflector*

When a client in the lowest level receives an EBGP update, it forwards it on to all configured RRs in the first level. The RR recognizes the update and forwards the update to the other clients within the same cluster and the other IBGP sessions (nonclients). The nonclient sessions are the second-level RRs. The second-level RRs receive the update and then replicate it to their clients and to the other peer in a full mesh.

Though hierarchical RR provides scalability in the number of full-mesh IBGP sessions, it does not provide scalability in terms of routes that it can handle. Hierarchical RRs add complexity with additional RRs and may possibly lead to performance degradations.

Note   It is recommended to have hierarchical RRs implemented using clusters, and a cluster-id should be configured on the RRs.

Partitioned Route Reflectors

Sometimes dedicated RRs in large-scale environments (especially service provider networks) do not scale to the demands of a large customer, who might be acting as a provider for their customers that are carrying a large number of VPNv4 prefixes. In such scenarios, partitioning of the RR roles between multiple RR routers help scale the requirements. RR partitioning is achieved by using two methods:

■ **Using BGP RR groups:** BGP RR groups is an inbound route target (RT) filtering method that is available only for VPNv4 and VPNv6 address-families. Configure inbound RT filtering using the command **bgp rr-groups** *extcommunity-list-name*. The configured extcommunity-list specifies the RT values to be permitted by the RR. The **bgp rr-groups** command applies to all neighbors configured under the address-family.

■ **Using Standard BGP communities:** Standard BGP communities can be used as inbound filters on RR and outbound filters on the PE router to filter the VPNv4 or VPNv6 prefixes. A community value is set for the CE prefixes and sent across toward the RR router. The RR routers filter those prefixes based on the community value assigned by the PE. This method allows for per-neighbor–based filtering but may increase CPU resource consumption on the RR routers and also adds an additional burden of maintenance for the configured filters.

Note   You can still use redundant route reflectors even when partitioning.

For further understanding, examine the topology shown in Figure 7-18. Four routers are part of the service provider network. PE1 and PE2 are the edge routers, RR1 and RR2 are the provider as well as RR routers. Each PE provides VPN services to two customers, VPN_A and VPN_B.

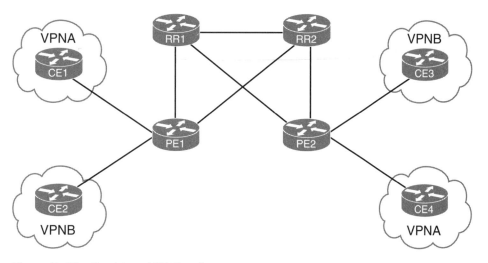

Figure 7-18 *Partitioned RR Topology*

RR1 and RR2 are both participating in the control plane and data plane forwarding. To demonstrate route partitioning, RR1 accepts routes only from VPN_A, and RR2 accepts routes only from VPN_B. Example 7-31 demonstrates the configuration of PE as well the RR routers; RR1 is filtering the RT value 100:1, which is for customer VPN_A, and RR2 is filtering RT value 100:2, which is for customer VPN_B.

Example 7-31 *Partitioned RR with Inbound RT Filters*

```
PE Config
ip vrf VPN_A
 rd 100:1
 route-target export 100:1
 route-target import 100:1
!
ip vrf VPN_B
 rd 100:2
 route-target export 100:2
 route-target import 100:2
!
router bgp 100
 neighbor 192.168.10.10 remote-as 100
 neighbor 192.168.10.10 update-source Loopback0
 neighbor 192.168.20.20 remote-as 100
 neighbor 192.168.20.20 update-source Loopback0
 !
 address-family vpnv4
  neighbor 192.168.10.10 activate
  neighbor 192.168.10.10 send-community both
  neighbor 192.168.10.10 next-hop-self
  neighbor 192.168.20.20 activate
  neighbor 192.168.20.20 send-community both
  neighbor 192.168.20.20 next-hop-self
 exit-address-family
 !
 address-family ipv4 vrf VPN_A
  . . .
 !
 address-family ipv4 vrf VPN_B
  . . .

RR1 Config
router bgp 100
 no bgp default ipv4-unicast
 neighbor 192.168.1.1 remote-as 100
 neighbor 192.168.1.1 update-source Loopback0
 neighbor 192.168.2.2 remote-as 100
```

```
 neighbor 192.168.2.2 update-source Loopback0
 neighbor 192.168.20.20 remote-as 100
 neighbor 192.168.20.20 update-source Loopback0
 !
address-family vpnv4
  neighbor 192.168.1.1 activate
  neighbor 192.168.1.1 send-community both
  neighbor 192.168.1.1 route-reflector-client
  neighbor 192.168.2.2 activate
  neighbor 192.168.2.2 send-community both
  neighbor 192.168.2.2 route-reflector-client
  neighbor 192.168.20.20 activate
  neighbor 192.168.20.20 send-community both
  bgp rr-group VPNA
 exit-address-family
 !
ip extcommunity-list standard VPNA permit rt 100:1
```

```
RR2 Config
router bgp 100
 neighbor 192.168.1.1 remote-as 100
 neighbor 192.168.1.1 update-source Loopback0
 neighbor 192.168.2.2 remote-as 100
 neighbor 192.168.2.2 update-source Loopback0
 neighbor 192.168.10.10 remote-as 100
 neighbor 192.168.10.10 update-source Loopback0
 !
 address-family vpnv4
  neighbor 192.168.1.1 activate
  neighbor 192.168.1.1 send-community both
  neighbor 192.168.1.1 route-reflector-client
  neighbor 192.168.2.2 activate
  neighbor 192.168.2.2 send-community both
  neighbor 192.168.2.2 route-reflector-client
  neighbor 192.168.10.10 activate
  neighbor 192.168.10.10 send-community both
  bgp rr-group VPNB
 exit-address-family
 !
ip extcommunity-list standard VPNB permit rt 100:2
```

If the RR partitioning is not performed, the PE2 learns the routes from PE1 for each customer VRF VPN_A and VPN_B via two paths: RR1 and RR2. One of them is chosen as the best path. But because RR partitioning is implemented, PE2 only sees one path for prefixes from VPN_A and VPN_B. Examine the output in Example 7-32. VPN_A prefixes are learned or reflected via RR1, whereas VPN_B prefixes are learned via RR2.

Example 7-32 *Partitioned RR with Inbound RT Filters*

```
PE2# show bgp vpnv4 unicast all 172.16.11.0
BGP routing table entry for 100:1:172.16.11.0/24, version 10
Paths: (1 available, best #1, table VPN_A)
  Not advertised to any peer
  Refresh Epoch 1
  Local
    192.168.1.1 (metric 3) (via default) from 192.168.10.10 (192.168.10.10)
      Origin incomplete, metric 0, localpref 100, valid, internal, best
      Extended Community: RT:100:1
      Originator: 192.168.1.1, Cluster list: 192.168.10.10
      mpls labels in/out nolabel/22
      rx pathid: 0, tx pathid: 0x0
PE2# show bgp vpnv4 unicast all 172.16.21.0
BGP routing table entry for 100:2:172.16.21.0/24, version 14
Paths: (1 available, best #1, table VPN_B)
  Not advertised to any peer
  Refresh Epoch 1
  Local
    192.168.1.1 (metric 3) (via default) from 192.168.20.20 (192.168.20.20)
      Origin incomplete, metric 0, localpref 100, valid, internal, best
      Extended Community: RT:100:2
      Originator: 192.168.1.1, Cluster list: 192.168.20.20
      mpls labels in/out nolabel/23
      rx pathid: 0, tx pathid: 0x0
```

Implementing partitioned RRs using inbound route target filters is very easy to implement because it uses the BGP rr-group feature. The other method to implement partitioned RRs is to use standard BGP communities. This method involves route-maps to set the community tags and match them on the RR to filter the updates. Example 7-33 shows the configuration of both the PE and RR routers for partitioning RR using standard BGP communities.

Example 7-33 *Partitioned RR with Standard BGP Communities*

```
PE1 Config
router bgp 100
 address-family vpnv4
  neighbor 192.168.10.10 activate
  neighbor 192.168.10.10 send-community both
  neighbor 192.168.10.10 route-map VPNA out
  neighbor 192.168.20.20 activate
  neighbor 192.168.20.20 send-community both
  neighbor 192.168.20.20 route-map VPNB out
 exit-address-family
 !
ip bgp-community new-format
!
access-list 10 permit 172.16.11.0 0.0.0.255
access-list 20 permit 172.16.21.0 0.0.0.255
!
route-map VPNA permit 10
 match ip address 10
 set community 100:1
!
route-map VPNB permit 10
 match ip address 20
 set community 100:2
```

```
PE2 Config
! Rest of the Config is same as PE1
access-list 10 permit 172.16.23.0 0.0.0.255
access-list 20 permit 172.16.24.0 0.0.0.255
!
route-map VPNA permit 10
 match ip address 10
 set community 100:1
!
route-map VPNB permit 10
 match ip address 20
 set community 100:2
```

```
RR1 Config
router bgp 100
 address-family vpnv4
```

```
  neighbor 192.168.1.1 activate
  neighbor 192.168.1.1 send-community both
  neighbor 192.168.1.1 route-reflector-client
  neighbor 192.168.1.1 route-map VPNA in
  neighbor 192.168.2.2 activate
  neighbor 192.168.2.2 send-community both
  neighbor 192.168.2.2 route-reflector-client
  neighbor 192.168.2.2 route-map VPNA in
  neighbor 192.168.20.20 activate
  neighbor 192.168.20.20 send-community both
  neighbor 192.168.20.20 route-map VPNA in
exit-address-family
!
ip bgp-community new-format
ip community-list 1 permit 100:1
!
route-map allow-VPNA permit 10
 match community 1
```

```
RR2 Config
router bgp 100
 address-family vpnv4
  neighbor 192.168.1.1 activate
  neighbor 192.168.1.1 send-community both
  neighbor 192.168.1.1 route-reflector-client
  neighbor 192.168.1.1 route-map VPNB in
  neighbor 192.168.2.2 activate
  neighbor 192.168.2.2 send-community both
  neighbor 192.168.2.2 route-reflector-client
  neighbor 192.168.2.2 route-map VPNB in
  neighbor 192.168.10.10 activate
  neighbor 192.168.10.10 send-community both
  neighbor 192.168.10.10 route-map VPNB in
exit-address-family
!
ip bgp-community new-format
ip community-list 1 permit 100:2
!
route-map allow-VPNB permit 10
 match community 1
```

Example 7-33 achieves the same results as shown in Example 7-32. The only difference is the method used. The later method is more complex and resource consuming because it has more customers. Additional community attributes have to be set and the route-map becomes larger.

BGP Selective Route Download

There are two ways RRs are deployed in the network from the perspective of forwarding path:

- When RRs are present in the forwarding path

- When RRs are separated from the forwarding path

When RRs are part of the forwarding path, the RR router not only has to perform RR activities but participate in the lookup and forwarding decisions of the packet. When RRs are separated from the forwarding path and are supposed to only perform RR activities, they are saved from the lookup and forwarding decision-making activities on the router, which saves a lot of CPU cycles. Such RRs are also called Out-of-Band Route Reflectors or Dedicated RRs, often also called off-path RRs or RR-on-a-stick.

The default behavior for any BGP router in the path, and even for RRs, requires the route to be downloaded to the RIB before the prefixes are replicated or advertised to the peers. In case of Out-of-Band RRs, there is no real need to have the routes downloaded into the RIB because such RRs are not in the forwarding path (data path).

To avoid the BGP routes from getting installed in the RIB, specifically on the RRs, use the BGP selective route download or selective RIB download feature. The BGP selective route download feature saves on both memory and CPU resources on the router. This feature is implemented using the **filter** keyword with the **table-map** command. Example 7-34 illustrates the implementation of the selective route download feature using the topology shown in Figure 7-19.

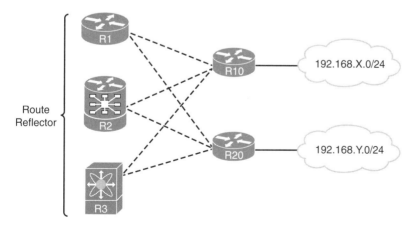

Figure 7-19 *Selective Route Download Topology*

In Example 7-34, an empty route-map BLOCK-INTO-FIB is configured with the deny option. This denies all the routes from getting downloaded into the RIB and the FIB.

Example 7-34 *BGP Selective Route Download Configuration*

```
IOS
R1(config)# route-map BLOCK-INTO-FIB deny 10
R1(config)# router bgp 100
R1(config-router)# address-family ipv4 unicast
R1(config-router-af)# table-map BLOCK-INTO-FIB filter
R1(config-router-af)# end
```

```
IOS XR
RP/0/0/CPU0:R2(config)# route-policy BLOCK-INTO-FIB
RP/0/0/CPU0:R2(config-rpl)# drop
RP/0/0/CPU0:R2(config-rpl)# exit
RP/0/0/CPU0:R2(config)# router bgp 100
RP/0/0/CPU0:R2(config-bgp)# address-family ipv4 unicast
RP/0/0/CPU0:R2(config-bgp-af)# table-policy BLOCK-INTO-FIB
RP/0/0/CPU0:R2(config-bgp-af)# commit
```

```
NX-OS
R3(config)# route-map BLOCK-INTO-FIB deny 10
R3(config)# router bgp 100
R3(config-router)# address-family ipv4 unicast
R3(config-router-af)# table-map BLOCK-INTO-FIB filter
R3(config-router-af)# end
```

With the configuration shown in Example 7-34, the command **show ip route bgp** will not display any routes in the output, whereas BGP table will hold all the routes in the BGP table. If only certain prefixes are required to be downloaded into the RIB and the FIB, the route-map or the route-policy statements can be modified accordingly. Example 7-35 illustrates the modification of routing policy for partial download of the routes in the RIB. It shows the BGP table and the routing table after the route-map is modified to deny two prefixes and allow the rest of the prefixes, unless the permit statement is configured as part of the route-map, even if the selected prefixes are denied in the sequence 10 statement. All the prefixes are blocked from being downloaded into the RIB.

Example 7-35 *BGP Selective Route Download Configuration*

```
IOS
R1(config)# route-map BLOCK-INTO-FIB deny 10
R1(config-route-map)# match ip address prefix-list BLOCK-IP
R1(config-route-map)# exit
R1(config)# route-map BLOCK-INTO-FIB permit 20
R1(config-route-map)# exit
R1(config)# ip prefix-list BLOCK-IP seq 5 permit 192.168.102.0/24
R1(config)# ip prefix-list BLOCK-IP seq 10 permit 192.168.103.0/24
R1(config)# end


! Verifying BGP Table
R1# show bgp ipv4 unicast
! Output omitted for brevity
     Network          Next Hop         Metric LocPrf Weight Path
 *>  192.168.100.0    10.1.101.2       2219             0 200 134 115 149 {117} e
 *>  192.168.101.0    10.1.101.2       2219             0 200 134 115 149 {117} e
 *>  192.168.102.0    10.1.101.2       2219             0 200 134 115 149 {117} e
 *>  192.168.103.0    10.1.101.2       2219             0 200 134 115 149 {117} e
 *>  192.168.104.0    10.1.101.2       2219             0 200 134 115 149 {117} e


! Verifying Routing Table
R1# show ip route bgp
! Output omitted for brevity
B       192.168.100.0/24 [20/2219] via 10.1.101.2, 10:29:04
B       192.168.101.0/24 [20/2219] via 10.1.101.2, 10:29:04
B       192.168.104.0/24 [20/2219] via 10.1.101.2, 10:29:04


IOS XR
! RPL Configuration
route-policy BLOCK-INTO-FIB
  if destination in (192.168.102.0/24) or destination in (192.168.103.0/24) then
    drop
  else
    pass
  endif
end-policy


! Verifying BGP Table
RP/0/0/CPU0:R2# show bgp ipv4 unicast
! Output omitted for brevity
```

```
Network               Next Hop        Metric LocPrf Weight Path
*> 192.168.100.0/24   10.1.102.2      2219                 0 200 134 115 149 {117} e
*> 192.168.101.0/24   10.1.102.2      2219                 0 200 134 115 149 {117} e
*> 192.168.102.0/24   10.1.102.2      2219                 0 200 134 115 149 {117} e
*> 192.168.103.0/24   10.1.102.2      2219                 0 200 134 115 149 {117} e
*> 192.168.104.0/24   10.1.102.2      2219                 0 200 134 115 149 {117} e

! Verifying Routing Table
RP/0/0/CPU0:R2# show route bgp
B     192.168.100.0/24 [20/2219] via 10.1.102.2, 00:00:00
B     192.168.101.0/24 [20/2219] via 10.1.102.2, 00:00:00
B     192.168.104.0/24 [20/2219] via 10.1.102.2, 00:00:00
```

A similar configuration of Cisco IOS can be used to modify the route-map on Nexus devices.

Note   It is important that the RRs should not be configured with **next-hop-self** when using this feature because this may cause the traffic to be black holed. This is because the command **next-hop-self** will make the RR participate in the forwarding path, but because it does not have the prefix in the RIB, traffic may get black holed. The **next-hop-self** should be configured on the ASBRs or Internet edge routers.

Virtual Route Reflectors

BGP Route Reflection as defined in RFC 4456 has been the de facto choice for scaling IBGP deployments for both service providers and enterprises worldwide. Traditionally, RRs were deployed using either core routers or dedicated physical hardware solely for control-plane route-reflection purposes. Although this has proven to be a viable solution that meets the demands of BGP with all the CPU and memory required, it lacks flexibility, elasticity, and agility to meet the constantly changing demands of the services.

Dedicated RRs, often also called off-path RRs or RR-on-a-stick, require a powerful CPU for intensive path computation and sufficient memory to store all the learned routes (even if it is required to store multiple copies of the Internet routing table). The two main functions or features required on dedicated RR are the following:

■ IGP

■ BGP

Throughput is not really a key factor because RRs in such deployments are not in forwarding path, although bandwidth is a key requirement for communication of BGP path updates.

Over the years, memory and CPU has become less expensive, and the industry has expanded its acceptance toward virtualization technologies. Virtualization technologies are a faster and more reliable method of deploying new services and reducing capital expenditure (CapEx) and operating expenses (OpEx).

The networking industry has revolutionized toward Network Function Virtualization (NFV). Deploying virtualized network function (VNF) in the form of virtual route reflector (vRR) is proving to be the solution to the problems faced with physical hardware to perform the same task. It is cheaper to add CPU and memory to a server that can perform the same tasks as a physical router and at the same time run multiple virtual instances from the same physical server, which saves on power consumption significantly.

There are many benefits of using vRR, which include the following:

■ Scalability (64bit OS)

■ Performance (Multicore)

■ Manageability

■ Same software version as deployed on edge (IOS XE / IOS XR)

■ vMotion (Hypervisor)

Figure 7-20 illustrates a sample topology with four virtual route reflectors (vRR).

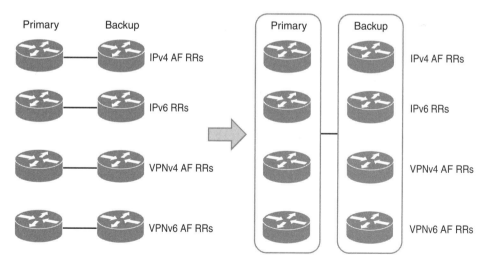

Figure 7-20 *vRR Routing Design*

Cisco provides a vRR solution using two main products:

■ Cloud Services Router (CSR) 1000v

■ IOS XRv

CSR 1000v can also be described as a virtualized IOS XE router. CSR 1000v is generalized to work on any x86-based processor with control plane and data plane mapped to virtual CPUs (vCPUs.) The CSR 1000v now comes in both 32-bit and 64-bit IOS XE OS. Because CSR 1000v leverages IOS XE code-base from ASR1000, RR features are part of the code-base. Figure 7-21 displays the architecture of the CSR1000v platform.

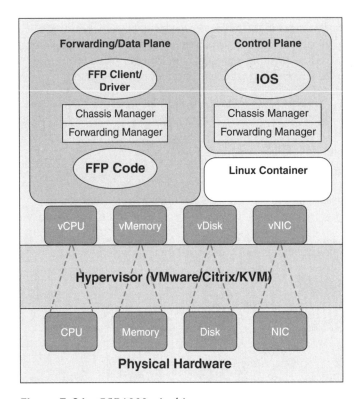

Figure 7-21   *CSR1000v Architecture*

The various components for packet path within CSR 1000v include the following:

- Ethernet Driver (ingress)

- Receive (Rx) thread

- PPE Thread (packet processing)

- HQF Thread (egress queueing)

- Ethernet Driver (egress)

Note   Explanation of all the components of packet processing within CSR 1000v is outside the scope of this book. Please refer to the "Reference" section for more information on CSR 1000v.

IOS XRv is a virtual router that uses the same carrier-class Cisco IOS XR operating system powering the ASR9000 and Carrier Routing System (CRS) series high-end routers. It provides the same key benefits as IOS XR while providing elasticity, agility, and flexibility that VNF brings.

IOS XRv is a virtual machine-based platform-independent representation of classic 32-bit x86 IOS XR with a QNX kernel. It is a single VM router, with the hardware model presented being a single VM containing the route processor (RP) functionality and line card interfaces with both the RP control-plane functionality, and the network interfaces and line card functionality running on the same virtual card.

Figure 7-22 displays the IOS XRv platform. There are four major components in the architecture:

- Full standard XR Platform Independent (PI) binaries

- Platform Layer

- Software Packet Path (SPP) Data Plane

- QNX (Kernel)

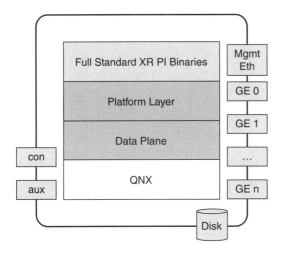

Figure 7-22   *IOS XRv Architecture*

Table 7-6 describes all the IOS XRv components.

Table 7-6 *Default Maximum Number of Prefixes per Address-Family*

Components	Description
IOS XR PI binaries	The standard platform independent XR packages, built in the same manner as for other XR platforms.
Platform Layer	A virtual platform layer providing the minimal functionality for the PI code to run, including platform services such as nodeid and chassis management, and various capability and utility libraries.
SPP Data Plane	The software data plane (NETIO/SPP) providing a software packet path for XR features, enabling forwarding and a host-stack to the router.
QNX	The standard XR QNX micro kernel.

Both CSR 1000v and IOS XRv are available as individual images for download as well as part of Cisco Modelling Labs (CML), previously known as VIRL.

Cisco recently launched the IOS XRv 9000 cloud-based router that is deployed as a VM instance on an x86 server running 64-bit IOS XR software. The IOS XRv 9000 provides traditional provider edge services along with vRR capabilities. The major difference between IOS XRv and IOS XRv 9000 is that the IOS XR 9000v router combines RP, line card, and virtualized forwarding capabilities into a single, centralized forwarding instance; that is, IOS XRv 9000 supports a high speed virtual x86 data plane.

BGP Diverse Path

BGP route reflectors have been the de facto feature in any network deployment for IBGP sessions and provides various capabilities as discussed in this chapter. But with benefits, there are certain limitations and problems that come along with this feature. The BGP-4 protocol specification requires the router to advertise only the best path for a destination. The BGP multipath feature helps provide load-balancing features over multiple paths along with resiliency and faster recovery from failures. The RR router only selects and advertises a single best path for each prefix, even if there are multiple paths available for the prefix on the RR. This breaks the BGP multipath functionality when RR is present in the path.

Note   BGP Multipath is discussed in detail in Chapter 8, "Troubleshooting BGP Edge Architectures."

To better understand the issues in detail, examine the topology in Figure 7-23. R4 and R41 are acting as the RR, whereas R2, R3, and R5 are the RR clients. R2 and R3 are having an EBGP session with R1. Now examine the topology with the single RR router R4. There are two paths from R4 to reach R1—via R4 - R2 - R1 and R4 - R3 - R1. But when the route is reflected to R5, it receives only one best path that is chosen by the RR. RR router R4 receives two paths but because of the best-path selection algorithm, RR only advertises the best path to R5. This makes R5 think it has only one path and cannot utilize the BGP multipath.

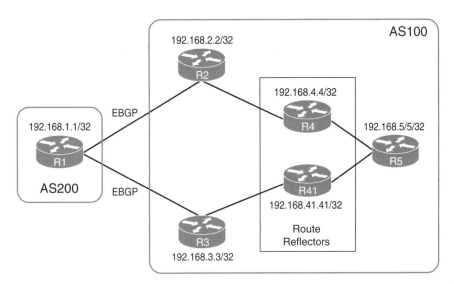

Figure 7-23 *RR Topology with Multiple IGP Paths*

Example 7-36 illustrates the RR problem explained in Figure 7-23. The EBGP peer R1 advertises prefix 192.168.1.1/32 toward R2 and R3. Routers R2 and R3 then advertises that prefix toward the RR router R4. R4 sees the prefix via two paths but selects the path via R2 as the best. R4 then reflects the best path toward R5. The router R5 can only see the best path with the next-hop as R2.

Example 7-36 *BGP RR Advertising Only Best Path*

```
R4# show bgp ipv4 unicast 192.168.1.1
BGP routing table entry for 192.168.1.1/32, version 3
Paths: (2 available, best #2, table default)
  Advertised to update-groups:
    1
```

```
Refresh Epoch 1
200, (Received from a RR-client)
   192.168.3.3 (metric 2) from 192.168.3.3 (192.168.3.3)
      Origin IGP, metric 0, localpref 100, valid, internal
      rx pathid: 0, tx pathid: 0
Refresh Epoch 1
200, (Received from a RR-client)
   192.168.2.2 (metric 2) from 192.168.2.2 (192.168.2.2)
      Origin IGP, metric 0, localpref 100, valid, internal, best
      rx pathid: 0, tx pathid: 0x0
```

```
R5# show bgp ipv4 unicast
! Output omitted for brevity
     Network          Next Hop          Metric LocPrf Weight Path
 *>i 192.168.1.1/32   192.168.2.2            0    100      0 200 i
```

Even if a second RR was added in the topology beside R4—for instance, R41—it would also advertise the best path; that is, via R2. Example 7-37 displays the output on R5 for prefix 192.168.1.1 after adding another RR. Notice that both the prefixes are being learned from the next-hop 192.168.2.2, which is the loopback IP of R2.

Example 7-37 *BGP RR Advertising Only Best Path*

```
R5# show bgp ipv4 unicast 192.168.1.1
BGP routing table entry for 192.168.1.1/32, version 3
Paths: (2 available, best #2, table default)
  Not advertised to any peer
  Refresh Epoch 1
  200
    192.168.2.2 (metric 3) from 192.168.41.41 (192.168.41.41)
      Origin IGP, metric 0, localpref 100, valid, internal
      Originator: 192.168.2.2, Cluster list: 192.168.41.41
      rx pathid: 0, tx pathid: 0
  Refresh Epoch 2
  200
    192.168.2.2 (metric 3) from 192.168.4.4 (192.168.4.4)
      Origin IGP, metric 0, localpref 100, valid, internal, best
      Originator: 192.168.2.2, Cluster list: 192.168.4.4
      rx pathid: 0, tx pathid: 0x0
```

When the exit point fails, traffic loss occurs until the control-plane converges. In such a scenario, the BGP Prefix Independent Convergence (PIC) feature doesn't get triggered as well. Not knowing about other exit points apart from the one advertised also means that the ingress routers cannot do load balancing. To overcome this problem, the BGP diverse path distribution feature can be used. The BGP diverse path was introduced in the Cisco IOS 15.4(2)M and IOS XE 3.1.0S release. There are four methods to use the BGP diverse path distribution mechanism:

- Using unique RD on each PE

- Using BGP best external feature

- Shadow route reflectors

- Shadow sessions

The first two options are discussed in Chapter 10, "MPLS Layer 3 VPN (L3VPN)," and Chapter 14, "BGP High Availability," because they are more relevant to MPLS VPN deployments. Chapter 14 also covers the BGP PIC feature. This chapter focuses on using shadow RRs and shadow sessions.

Shadow Route Reflectors

A shadow RR is another RR router that is added within the AS to provide diverse path functionality. The role of the shadow RR, a.k.a. Diverse-Path route reflector, is to advertise a diverse path to its clients. In other words, a shadow RR advertises the second-best path to its RR clients. It is recommended to have the same physical and control-plane connectivity for the shadow RR as that of the primary RR.

Note   Only one shadow RR per existing RR can be configured in the AS. Also, this feature is meant to provide path diversity within a cluster.

There is a caveat to consider before implementing shadow RR. In certain designs, it is required to disable the IGP metric check for the shadow RR to function properly. There are two possibilities of how primary and shadow RR are located in the topology:

- Both RRs are co-located.

- Both RRs are not co-located.

To understand both the design caveat, examine the two topologies shown in Figure 7-24. In topology A, both the RRs are co-located; that is, both RRs are either in a common subnet/VLAN connected via a switch or are deployed equidistant from both Internet Edge or PE routers. Because they are on the same VLAN with the same IGP metric toward the prefix, they do not require disabling the IGP metric check.

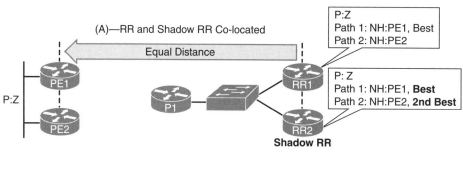

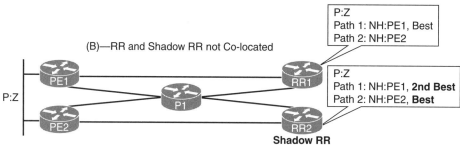

Figure 7-24   *Shadow Routers Design Scenarios*

In topology B, both RRs are not co-located; that is, with all equal cost links, both RR1 and RR2 do not have the same IGP metric/cost to reach one of the PE routers. There is an extra hop in the middle, router P1, which adds to the IGP metric. This causes RR1 to have the link connected to PE1 as the best path to reach the prefix, whereas RR2 learns the best path to reach the prefix via the link connected to PE2 and not via router PE1. On router RR2, the path learned via PE1 becomes the second-best path, thus causing both the RRs to advertise the same path as the primary as well as the diverse path. To avoid this situation, disable the IGP metric check on both the primary and the shadow RR. To disable the IGP metric check, use the command **bgp bestpath igp-metric ignore**. This command causes BGP to ignore the IGP metric during the BGP best-path calculation.

Table 7-7 shows the commands required to configure shadow RR.

Table 7-7   *Configuration Commands for Shadow Route Reflector*

Command	Description
bgp additional-paths select backup	Enables the router to calculate a second best path. Configured on shadow RR router.
neighbor *ip-address* advertise diverse-path backup	Enables the RR to advertise a diverse path to a RR client. Configured on shadow RR router.
bgp bestpath igp-metric ignore	Ignore IGP metric in BGP best-path calculation. Configured on both primary and shadow RR router.

Examine the same topology as shown in Figure 7-23. RR R41 is the shadow RR, and R4 is the primary RR. R2 advertises the prefix 192.168.1.1/32 to both R4 and R41 with the next-hop value set to R2. Likewise, R3 advertises the same prefix with the next-hop value set to R3. R4 then sends an update to R5 that R2 is the next-hop router in order to reach 192.168.1.1/32. R41, which is the shadow RR advertising the second-best path, and announces the update that the next-hop to reach 192.168.1.1/32 prefix is via R3. This is how R5 has two diverse paths received from both the RRs.

Example 7-38 displays the additional configuration on router R41 and the output on router R5 after making R41 a shadow RR. The prefix 192.168.1.1/32 is being learned via two next-hops: R2 and R3.

Example 7-38 *BGP Shadow RR Configuration and Output*

```
R41(config)# router bgp 100
R41(config-router)# address-family ipv4 unicast
R41(config-router-af)# neighbor 192.168.5.5 advertise diverse-path backup
R41(config-router-af)# end

R5# show bgp ipv4 unicast 192.168.1.1
BGP routing table entry for 192.168.1.1/32, version 2
Paths: (2 available, best #2, table default)
Multipath: eBGP
  Not advertised to any peer
  Refresh Epoch 4
  200
    192.168.3.3 (metric 3) from 192.168.41.41 (192.168.41.41)
      Origin IGP, metric 0, localpref 100, valid, internal
      Originator: 192.168.3.3, Cluster list: 192.168.41.41
      rx pathid: 0, tx pathid: 0
  Refresh Epoch 3
  200
    192.168.2.2 (metric 3) from 192.168.4.4 (192.168.4.4)
      Origin IGP, metric 0, localpref 100, valid, internal, best
      Originator: 192.168.2.2, Cluster list: 192.168.4.4
      rx pathid: 0, tx pathid: 0x0
```

Example 7-39 displays the output of **show bgp ipv4 unicast neighbor** *ip-address* **advertised-routes** command on R41, which shows that the route being advertised is a backup path.

Example 7-39 *BGP Shadow RR Configuration and Output*

```
R41# show bgp ipv4 unicast neighbors 192.168.5.5 advertised-routes
BGP table version is 5, local router ID is 192.168.41.41
Status codes: s suppressed, d damped, h history, * valid, > best, i - internal,
              r RIB-failure, S Stale, m multipath, b backup-path, f RT-Filter,
              x best-external, a additional-path, c RIB-compressed,
Origin codes: i - IGP, e - EGP, ? - incomplete
RPKI validation codes: V valid, I invalid, N Not found

     Network          Next Hop          Metric LocPrf Weight Path
 *bia192.168.1.1/32   192.168.3.3            0    100      0 200 i

Total number of prefixes 1
```

Now if the direct link from R2 to R41 and R3 to R4 is removed, and another router R6 is added in the middle for providing this cross connectivity as shown in Figure 7-25, then the IGP metric is different between R2 to R41 and R2 to R4. Similarly, the IGP metric is different from R3 to R4 and R3 to R41.

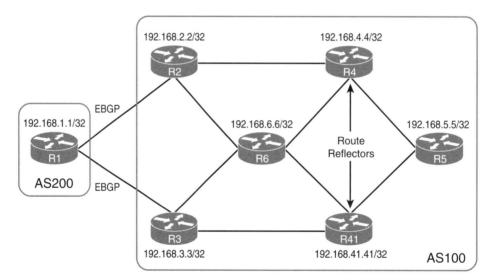

Figure 7-25 *RR Topology with Multiple IGP Paths of Different Metric*

This makes R4 choose R2 as the best path and R41 choose R3 as the best path to reach R1. This causes the shadow RR router R41 to advertise the second-best path, which is via R2 as well. It breaks the purpose of having shadow RR in the topology. Example 7-40 illustrates this behavior with the help of outputs on R4, R41, and R5. This is the same scenario as explained when both the RRs are not co-located.

Example 7-40 *Non Co-located RR Behavior*

```
R4# show bgp ipv4 unicast 192.168.1.1
BGP routing table entry for 192.168.1.1/32, version 13
Paths: (2 available, best #1, table default)
  Advertised to update-groups:
     1
  Refresh Epoch 1
  200, (Received from a RR-client)
    192.168.2.2 (metric 2) from 192.168.2.2 (192.168.2.2)
      Origin IGP, metric 0, localpref 100, valid, internal, best
      rx pathid: 0, tx pathid: 0x0
  Refresh Epoch 1
  200, (Received from a RR-client)
    192.168.3.3 (metric 3) from 192.168.3.3 (192.168.3.3)
      Origin IGP, metric 0, localpref 100, valid, internal
      rx pathid: 0, tx pathid: 0

R41# show bgp ipv4 unicast 192.168.1.1
BGP routing table entry for 192.168.1.1/32, version 12
Paths: (2 available, best #1, table default)
  Advertised to update-groups:
     2
  Refresh Epoch 2
  200, (Received from a RR-client)
    192.168.3.3 (metric 2) from 192.168.3.3 (192.168.3.3)
      Origin IGP, metric 0, localpref 100, valid, internal, best
      rx pathid: 0, tx pathid: 0x0
  Refresh Epoch 2
  200, (Received from a RR-client)
    192.168.2.2 (metric 3) from 192.168.2.2 (192.168.2.2)
      Origin IGP, metric 0, localpref 100, valid, internal, backup/repair
      rx pathid: 0, tx pathid: 0

R5# show bgp ipv4 unicast 192.168.1.1
BGP routing table entry for 192.168.1.1/32, version 2
Paths: (2 available, best #2, table default)
Multipath: eBGP
  Not advertised to any peer
  Refresh Epoch 5
  200, (received & used)
    192.168.2.2 (metric 3) from 192.168.41.41 (192.168.41.41)
      Origin IGP, metric 0, localpref 100, valid, internal
```

```
      Originator: 192.168.2.2, Cluster list: 192.168.41.41
      rx pathid: 0, tx pathid: 0
 Refresh Epoch 4
 200, (received & used)
   192.168.2.2 (metric 3) from 192.168.4.4 (192.168.4.4)
      Origin IGP, metric 0, localpref 100, valid, internal, best
      Originator: 192.168.2.2, Cluster list: 192.168.4.4
      rx pathid: 0, tx pathid: 0x0
```

This is where disabling the IGP metric check comes into play. By disabling the IGP metric check, both the primary and shadow RR do not advertise the same best path.

Example 7-41 demonstrates the behavior after the IGP metric check is disabled on both the RR routers.

Example 7-41 *Non Co-located RR Behavior*

```
R41# show bgp ipv4 unicast 192.168.1.1
BGP routing table entry for 192.168.1.1/32, version 8
BGP Bestpath: igpmetric-ignore
Paths: (2 available, best #1, table default)
  Advertised to update-groups:
     4
  Refresh Epoch 4
  200, (Received from a RR-client), (received & used)
    192.168.2.2 (metric 3) from 192.168.2.2 (192.168.2.2)
      Origin IGP, metric 0, localpref 100, valid, internal, best
      rx pathid: 0, tx pathid: 0x0
  Refresh Epoch 4
  200, (Received from a RR-client), (received & used)
    192.168.3.3 (metric 2) from 192.168.3.3 (192.168.3.3)
      Origin IGP, metric 0, localpref 100, valid, internal, backup/repair
      rx pathid: 0, tx pathid: 0

R5# show bgp ipv4 unicast 192.168.1.1
BGP routing table entry for 192.168.1.1/32, version 9
Paths: (2 available, best #2, table default)
Multipath: eBGP
  Not advertised to any peer
  Refresh Epoch 1
  200, (received & used)
```

```
   192.168.3.3 (metric 3) from 192.168.41.41 (192.168.41.41)
      Origin IGP, metric 0, localpref 100, valid, internal
      Originator: 192.168.3.3, Cluster list: 192.168.41.41
      rx pathid: 0, tx pathid: 0
 Refresh Epoch 1
 200, (received & used)
   192.168.2.2 (metric 3) from 192.168.4.4 (192.168.4.4)
      Origin IGP, metric 0, localpref 100, valid, internal, best
      Originator: 192.168.2.2, Cluster list: 192.168.4.4
      rx pathid: 0, tx pathid: 0x0
```

Shadow Sessions

Shadow RR is an effective solution for advertising diverse paths or backup paths, but it requires an additional physical router to be installed in the cluster. This is not a very cost-effective solution and not every organization can afford to purchase an extra router or bear the cost of extra links. To overcome cost challenges, a shadow sessions feature can be used.

With shadow sessions, the primary RR is used to advertise both the primary as well as the backup path. This requires an extra BGP peering between the peer from the RR, where the backup path needs to be advertised. Because it is not possible to have two BGP sessions in same address-family on the same peering IPs, an extra loopback interface can be created to form the peering. After the peering is formed on the new loopback address, the **neighbor** *ip-address* **advertise diverse-path backup** command can then be used to advertise the backup path.

Examine the topology shown in Figure 7-23 with a single RR router R4 and ignoring another RR router R41. Example 7-42 illustrates the configuration of a shadow session on router R4 and R5. In this configuration, an additional loopback is created apart from loopback0 interface, and an additional peering is formed between R4 and R5, where R4 is the RR and R5 is the RR client. Notice that the command **bgp additional-paths select backup** is now configured on the primary router itself. Because this router is acting as both the primary and the backup router, this command is required.

Example 7-42 *Shadow Session Configuration*

```
R4
R4(config)# router bgp 100
R4(config-router)# neighbor 192.168.55.55 remote-as 100
R4(config-router)# neighbor 192.168.55.55 update-source loopback1
R4(config-router)# address-family ipv4 unicast
R4(config-router-af)# neighbor 192.168.55.55 activate
R4(config-router-af)# neighbor 192.168.55.55 route-reflector-client
R4(config-router-af)# neighbor 192.168.55.55 advertise diverse-path backup
R4(config-router-af)# bgp additional-paths select backup
```

```
R5
R5(config)# router bgp 100
R5(config-router)# neighbor 192.168.44.44 remote-as 100
R5(config-router)# neighbor 192.168.44.44 update-source loopback1
R5(config-router)# address-family ipv4 unicast
R5(config-router-af)# neighbor 192.168.44.44 activate
```

After the shadow peering comes up between R4 and R5 over loopback1 interface, R5 receives the backup path via R3. Example 7-43 displays the output for the command **show bgp ipv4 unicast 192.168.1.1**, showing both the primary and backup path. Also notice that on R4, the advertised route for neighbor 192.168.55.55 shows the backup path being advertised.

Example 7-43 *Diverse-Path Verification*

```
R4
R4# show bgp ipv4 unicast neighbors 192.168.55.55 advertised-routes
BGP table version is 6, local router ID is 192.168.4.4
Status codes: s suppressed, d damped, h history, * valid, > best, i - internal,
              r RIB-failure, S Stale, m multipath, b backup-path, f RT-Filter,
              x best-external, a additional-path, c RIB-compressed,
Origin codes: i - IGP, e - EGP, ? - incomplete
RPKI validation codes: V valid, I invalid, N Not found

     Network          Next Hop          Metric LocPrf Weight Path
 *bia192.168.1.1/32   192.168.3.3            0    100      0 200 i

Total number of prefixes 1
```

```
R5
R5# show bgp ipv4 unicast 192.168.1.1
BGP routing table entry for 192.168.1.1/32, version 9
Paths: (2 available, best #2, table default)
Multipath: eBGP
  Not advertised to any peer
  Refresh Epoch 2
  200
```

```
   192.168.3.3 (metric 3) from 192.168.44.44 (192.168.4.4)
      Origin IGP, metric 0, localpref 100, valid, internal
      Originator: 192.168.3.3, Cluster list: 192.168.4.4
      rx pathid: 0, tx pathid: 0
 Refresh Epoch 1
 200, (received & used)
   192.168.2.2 (metric 3) from 192.168.4.4 (192.168.4.4)
      Origin IGP, metric 0, localpref 100, valid, internal, best
      Originator: 192.168.2.2, Cluster list: 192.168.4.4
      rx pathid: 0, tx pathid: 0x0
```

Route Servers

To understand what a route server is, it is first important to understand what an Internet Exchange (IX) is and how it works. An IX is a physical location that provides infrastructure for the service providers to exchange Internet traffic between their networks (autonomous systems). The infrastructure includes rack space, electricity, cooling resources, and a common switching infrastructure for service providers to directly connect their network.

There are two types of peerings that service providers form in order to share networks: private peering and public peering.

In private peering, two service providers, with a common agreement and contract, decide to provide one-to-one connectivity to each other. In such deployments, the infrastructure is agreed upon by the two service providers in the contract. Private peerings may be technically possible, but there are lot of operational difficulties involved with it. Also, it is almost impossible to negotiate business with all ISPs.

In public peering, a service provider connects to an IX, where the IX provides all the infrastructure resources and allows the service provider to connect to multiple peers at a single location. Although all the service providers are on the shared subnet, they have to maintain peering with other service providers individually. Public peering at an IX is a cost-saving option for smaller service providers who do not have resources to maintain multiple one-to-one connections.

Figure 7-26 displays the shared public peering at IX. Notice that, in the physical topology shown in (A), all the service providers are sharing a common subnet across the same switching infrastructure. The topology in (B) represents the logical topology, where all the service providers (in different ASs) are establishing a BGP peering with other service providers and thus form full mesh EBGP sessions to share the prefix advertisements.

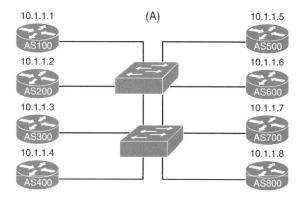

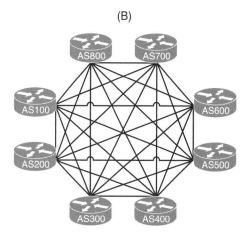

Figure 7-26 *Public Peering at IX*

The full-mesh peerings of a service provider presents scaling and administrative challenge. All the EBGP sessions are formed across a single link, and a flap on one link causes a BGP session to flap on multiple SP networks, which can lead to service impacts. Also, there is a huge operational overhead from the contracts that are negotiated between the service providers for each peering.

Route servers solve this problem by providing RR functionality for EBGP sessions. Route servers facilitate multilateral peering. Instead of maintaining multiple EBGP sessions, a provider only peers with the route server that takes care of reflecting the routes. A single BGP session to the route server allows a service provider to see the prefixes from all the other providers peering with the route server.

There are multiple route servers that are available for both IPv4 and IPv6 peerings and include the following:

- **IPv4 Route Servers:** http://www.bgp4.net/rs

- **IPv6 Route Servers:** http://www.bgp4.net/rs6

Route server solutions based on Linux OS and GNU software already exist. But those are not very stable solutions. A router-based solution provides better stability and faster performance.

Cisco introduced a route server feature beginning with the Cisco IOS 15.2(3)T release and IOS XE release 3.3S. The BGP route server feature is designed for IX operators to provide EBGP route reflection with a customizable policy for each service provider.

The BGP route server provides AS-path, MED, and next-hop transparency; that is, the peering is actually transparent outside the IX even though the service providers may be directly connected at the IX.

To understand the functioning of the route server and configuring the route server, examine the topology in Figure 7-27. There are four service providers with AS numbers ranging from AS100 to 400. The router server is present in AS500. All the service providers ranging from AS100 to 400, including the route server, are in the same subnet 10.1.0.1/24, as shown in the topology. AS100 is connected to private AS65000, and AS400 is connected to private AS65001.

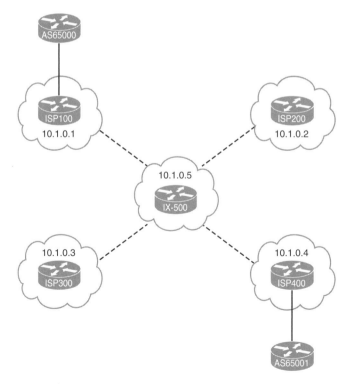

Figure 7-27 *Topology with EBGP Peers and Route Server*

To configure a basic route server functionality, use the command **neighbor** *ip-address* **route-server-client**. The command is applicable for both IPv4 as well as IPv6 peering.

Example 7-44 demonstrates the configuration of a route server and also a route server client.

Example 7-44   *BGP Route Server Configuration*

```
IX-500(config)# router bgp 500
IX-500(config-router)# neighbor 10.1.0.1 remote-as 100
IX-500(config-router)# neighbor 10.1.0.2 remote-as 200
IX-500(config-router)# neighbor 10.1.0.3 remote-as 300
IX-500(config-router)# neighbor 10.1.0.4 remote-as 400
IX-500(config-router)# address-family ipv4 unicast
IX-500(config-router-af)# neighbor 10.1.0.1 activate
IX-500(config-router-af)# neighbor 10.1.0.1 route-server-client
IX-500(config-router-af)# neighbor 10.1.0.2 activate
IX-500(config-router-af)# neighbor 10.1.0.2 route-server-client
IX-500(config-router-af)# neighbor 10.1.0.3 activate
IX-500(config-router-af)# neighbor 10.1.0.3 route-server-client
IX-500(config-router-af)# neighbor 10.1.0.4 activate
IX-500(config-router-af)# neighbor 10.1.0.4 route-server-client
```

```
ISP100(config)# router bgp 100
ISP100(config-router)# neighbor 10.1.0.5 remote-as 500
ISP100(config-router)# address-family ipv4 unicast
ISP100(config-router-af)# neighbor 10.1.0.5 activate
ISP100(config-router-af)# network 192.168.1.1 mask 255.255.255.255
```

```
ISP200(config)# router bgp 200
ISP200(config-router)# neighbor 10.1.0.5 remote-as 500
ISP200(config-router)# address-family ipv4 unicast
ISP200(config-router-af)# neighbor 10.1.0.5 activate
ISP200(config-router-af)# network 192.168.2.2 mask 255.255.255.255
```

This brings up the BGP neighbor relationship between the route server and all the route server clients. But as soon as the sessions come up and updates are received by one ISP and replicated to other ISPs, the ISP drops those messages, marking them as malformed. BGP does not install any update coming from the route server. Example 7-45 highlights the error message and the BGP summary output.

Example 7-45 *BGP Route Server Client Error Message and BGP Summary*

```
ISP100# show bgp ipv4 unicast summary
BGP router identifier 192.168.1.1, local AS number 100
BGP table version is 1, main routing table version 1
Neighbor    V    AS MsgRcvd MsgSent   TblVer  InQ OutQ Up/Down  State/PfxRcd
10.1.0.5    4   500       5       2        1    0    0 00:00:09            0


04:44:13.718: %BGP-6-MSGDUMP_LIMIT: unsupported or mal-formatted message
 received from 10.1.0.5:
FFFF FFFF FFFF FFFF FFFF FFFF FFFF FFFF 0037 0200 0000 1B40 0101 0040 0206 0201
0000 00C8 4003 040A 0100 0280 0404 0000 0000 20C0 A802 02
04:44:13.719: %BGP-6-MALFORMEDATTR: Malformed attribute in (BGP(0)
 Prefixes: 192.168.2.2/32 ) received from 10.1.0.5,
```

Because a route server provides AS-path transparency, this causes a route server to not to put its own AS in the AS_PATH list. BGP, by default, denies any updates received from an EBGP peer that does not list its own AS number at the beginning of the AS_PATH list. To receive updates from the route server, the route server clients should disable this behavior by using the command **no bgp enforce-first-as**. After enabling this command, a route server client—that is, an ISP edge router, starts receiving updates from the route server.

Example 7-46 demonstrates the use of the **no bgp enforce-first-as** command and the BGP table. Notice that in the BGP table, neither the next-hop value of the prefixes or the AS_PATH list is changed when the prefixes are reflected by the route server. The AS_PATH list does not contain AS500 (AS number of the route server). This shows the next-hop and AS-path transparency provided by route server.

Example 7-46 *Disabling First AS Check for EBGP Neighbors*

```
ISP100(config)# router bgp 100
ISP100(config-router-af)# no bgp enforce-first-as
ISP100# show bgp ipv4 unicast
! Output omitted for brevity
     Network          Next Hop          Metric LocPrf Weight Path
 *>  192.168.1.1/32   0.0.0.0                0         32768 i
 *>  192.168.2.2/32   10.1.0.2               0             0 200 i
 *>  192.168.3.3/32   10.1.0.3               0             0 300 i
 *>  192.168.4.4/32   10.1.0.4               0             0 400 i
! Output omitted for brevity
```

Route servers also allow a flexible routing policy to only selected routes to be advertised to a particular service provider. To enable flexible routing policy, contexts are created that maintain a virtual table of the filtered routes based on the policy. The selected routes are imported into the route server context using an import map. A route-map with at least one permit statement for the filter condition is configured and referenced in the import map. After the contexts are created, they are mapped to the neighbor using the context keyword after the **neighbor** *ip-address* **route-server-client** command.

The following steps explain how to configure a flexible routing policy on a route server.

Step 1.   Create a route-map with at least one permit statement. The matching criteria under a route-map could be an as-path or a next-hop value or any other attribute on the received prefix.

Step 2.   Create route server context using the command **route-server-context** *ctx-name* under the router bgp configuration. Under the route server context, import the route-map using the command **import-map** *route-map-name*.

Step 3.   Assign the context to the route server client using the address-family command **neighbor** *ip-address* **route-server-client context** *ctx-name*.

A BGP route server performs the filtering in three steps:

Step 1.   The incoming BGP updates from a route server client are stored in the global BGP table.

Step 2.   A virtual table is created based on the filtered routes using the **import-map** command. For the route server clients that are associated with a context, the route server overrides the global table routes with that of the filtered routes in the virtual table for that specific context before generating the updates.

Step 3.   Outbound policies can be applied to a route server client using the **neighbor** *ip-address* **route-map** *route-map-name* **out** command. The filter is applied on the global table routes of the route server and also to the virtual table routes that are already filtered.

Example 7-47 illustrates the configuration of a flexible routing policy for filtering incoming updates from a route server client. AS200; that is, peer 10.1.0.2, is advertising 100 prefixes with AS_PATH list containing prefixes ranging from AS65520 to AS65530. A route-map is configured to match all routes that have AS65530 in their AS_PATH list and advertise it to the peer 10.1.0.1.

Example 7-47 *Flexible Routing Policy Configuration*

```
IX-500(config)# route-map AS65530 per 10
IX-500(config-route-map)# match as-path 1
IX-500(config-route-map)# exit
IX-500(config)# ip as-path access-list 1 permit 65530
IX-500(config)# router bgp 500
IX-500(config-router)# route-server-context ASN-65530
IX-500(config-router-rsctx)# address-family ipv4 unicast
IX-500(config-router-rsctx-af)# import-map AS65530
IX-500(config-router-rsctx-af)# exit
IX-500(config-router-rsctx)# exit
IX-500(config-router)# address-family ipv4 unicast
IX-500(config-router-af)# neighbor 10.1.0.1 route-server-client context ASN-65530
```

```
ISP100# show bgp ipv4 unicast summary
! Output omitted for brevity


Neighbor      V      AS MsgRcvd MsgSent   TblVer  InQ OutQ Up/Down   State/PfxRcd
10.1.0.5      4     500      14       5      808    0    0 00:00:04           80


ISP100# show bgp ipv4 unicast
     Network         Next Hop       Metric LocPrf Weight Path
 *>  100.2.10.0/24   10.1.0.2         2563             0 200 65530 65526
 *>  100.2.11.0/24   10.1.0.2         2563             0 200 65530 65526
 *>  100.2.12.0/24   10.1.0.2         2563             0 200 65530 65526
 *>  100.2.13.0/24   10.1.0.2         2563             0 200 65530 65526
 *>  100.2.14.0/24   10.1.0.2         2563             0 200 65530 65526
! Output omitted for brevity
```

The virtual table for the context is seen by using the command **show bgp** *afi safi* **route-server context** *ctx-name*. Example 7-48 displays the virtual table based on the import-map on the route server. Notice that the routes that have been marked as suppressed are the ones that do not match the **import-map** statement; that is, having AS65530 in their AS_PATH list.

Example 7-48   *Virtual Table on Route Server*

```
IX-500# show bgp ipv4 unicast route-server context ASN-65530
Networks for route server context ASN-65530:
   Network          Next Hop       Metric LocPrf Weight Path
   100.2.0.0/24     (suppressed)
   100.2.1.0/24     (suppressed)
   100.2.2.0/24     (suppressed)
   100.2.3.0/24     (suppressed)
   100.2.4.0/24     (suppressed)
   100.2.5.0/24     (suppressed)
   100.2.6.0/24     (suppressed)
   100.2.7.0/24     (suppressed)
   100.2.8.0/24     (suppressed)
   100.2.9.0/24     (suppressed)
*>  100.2.10.0/24    10.1.0.2       2563            0 200 65530 65526
*>  100.2.11.0/24    10.1.0.2       2563            0 200 65530 65526
*>  100.2.12.0/24    10.1.0.2       2563            0 200 65530 65526
*>  100.2.13.0/24    10.1.0.2       2563            0 200 65530 65526
*>  100.2.14.0/24    10.1.0.2       2563            0 200 65530 65526
! Output omitted for brevity
```

Note   In case any issues occur with the route server, use the debug command **debug bgp** *afi safi* **route-server** [**client** | **context** | **event** | **import** | **policy**] [**detail**] to investigate the problem.

Summary

This chapter explained various techniques and features that can be deployed and implemented and that can be used to scale the BGP environment. It began by explaining the impact of the growing Internet table and how various methods are used to tweak the CPU and memory utilization for BGP. There was a brief comparison on using soft-reconfiguration inbound vs. route refresh and enhanced route refresh capability, and also how dynamic route refresh update groups help with scaling and convergence issues. Other features were discussed that help in scale routers running BGP protocol, such as ORF, maximum prefixes, max-as, maximum neighbors, and so on.

This chapter covers in great detail various methods on how BGP route reflectors can be deployed to scale the network. The primary benefit that the BGP route reflector provides is the reduction in the number of BGP connections that are required in a full-mesh IBGP topology. This also helps in reducing the number of paths for a prefix by reducing the number of BGP connections. The features that helps scale the BGP deployment are as follows:

- BGP clustering
- Hierarchical route reflectors
- Partitioned route reflectors
- Virtual route reflectors

All these functions are examined that help utilize the BGP route reflection functionality in an efficient and scalable manner. The chapter finally ends by discussing route servers that are highly required for service providers, especially those who are peering at Internet Exchanges.

References

RFC 2918, *Route Refresh Capability for BGP-4*, E. Chen, IETF, https://tools.ietf.org/html/rfc2918, September 2000.

RFC 7313, *Enhanced Route Refresh Capability for BGP-4*, K. Patel, E. Chen, B. Venkatachalapathy, IETF, https://tools.ietf.org/html/rfc7313, July 2014.

BRKSPG-2519, *Cisco Live*, Matthias Falkner, ORF Cisco.com—http://www.cisco.com/c/en/us/td/docs/ios/12_2s/feature/guide/fsbgporf.html.

## Chapter 8

Troubleshooting BGP Edge Architectures

The following topics are covered in this chapter:

- Border Gateway Protocol (BGP) Multihoming and BGP Multipath

- Understanding and Troubleshooting BGP Path Selection

- Common Issues with BGP Peering Between Multiple Service Providers

The Internet has become a vital component for businesses today. At a minimum, Internet connectivity is required for email and research. Other organizations host e-commerce servers, Voice over IP (VoIP) telephony, or for terminating VPN tunnels. An organization must incorporate redundancies in the network architecture to ensure that there are not any single points of failure (SPOF) with Internet connectivity.

A company can connect to the Internet with a simple default route via a single connection. However, if a company wants to use multiple service providers for redundancy or additional throughput, BGP is required. BGP is the routing protocol used on the Internet.

A company's use of BGP is not limited to Internet connectivity. If companies use a Multiprotocol Label Switched (MPLS) L3VPN from a SP, then they probably are using BGP to exchange the LAN networks with the service provider. Routes are typically redistributed between BGP and the LAN-based routing protocol.

In both of these scenarios, BGP is used at the edge of the network (Internet or WAN) and has redundant connections to ensure a reliable network. It provides advanced path selection and connectivity for an organization. This chapter focuses on troubleshooting BGP edge architectures.

BGP Multihoming and Multipath

The simplest method of providing redundancy is to provide a second circuit. Adding a second circuit and establishing a second BGP session across that peering link is known as *BGP multihoming* because there are multiple sessions to learn routes and establish connectivity. BGP's default behavior is to advertise only the best path to the routing information base (RIB), which means that only one path for a network prefix is used when forwarding network traffic to a destination.

BGP *multipath* allows for multiple paths to be presented to the RIB, so that both paths can forward traffic to a network prefix at the same time. BGP multipath is an enhanced form of BGP multihoming.

Note   It is vital to understand that the primary difference between BGP multihoming and BGP multipath is how load balancing works. BGP multipath attempts to distribute the load of the traffic dynamically. BGP multihoming is distributed somewhat by the nature of the BGP best path algorithm, but manipulation to the inbound/outbound routing policies is required to reach a more equally distributed load among the links.

There are three types of BGP multipath: External BGP (EBGP), Internal BGP (IBGP), and EIBGP multipath. EBGP multipath and IBGP multipath cannot be configured on the router at the same time.

In all three types of BGP multipath, the following BGP path attributes (PA) must match for multipath to be eligible:

- Weight

- Local Preference

- AS-Path length and content
  (confederations can contain a different AS_CONFED_SEQ path)

- Origin

- Multi-Exit Discriminator (MED)

- Advertisement method must match (IBGP or EBGP): If the prefix is learned via an IBGP advertisement, the Interior Gateway Protocol (IGP) routing protocol cost must match to be considered equal.

Figure 8-1 illustrates the differences between BGP multihoming and multipath from four common scenarios, as follows:

- **Scenario 1:** R1 connects to two different Internet SPs with two different circuits. R1 cannot use EBGP multipath because the AS-Paths are different for any prefix on the Internet. R1 is multihomed only.

- **Scenario 2:** R1 connects to the same Internet SP with two different circuits. R1 can use EBGP multipath for any Internet prefixes because the routes are learned via the same service provider (regardless whether R1 connects to the same router or different routers in service provider ABC). This assumes that all other BGP PAs are identical between R1's perspective.

- **Scenario 3:** R3 connects via IBGP to R1 and R2. R1 connects to SP ABC, whereas R2 connects to SP XYZ. R3 cannot use IBGP multipath because the AS-Paths are different for any Internet prefixes. R3 is multihomed only.

- **Scenario 4:** R3 connects via IBGP to R1 and R2. R1 and R2 connect to the same Internet SP. R3 uses IBGP multipath for any Internet prefixes because the AS-Path is the same (along with the other required BGP PAs.)

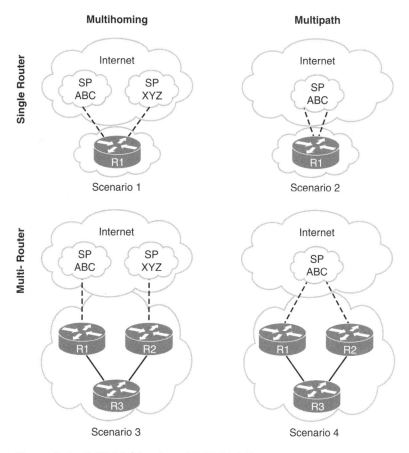

Figure 8-1 *BGP Multipath and BGP Multihome*

Note   Some engineers think that if a router establishes a single IBGP session using a loop-back address that can be reached via equal-cost multipath (ECMP) (because of the IGP) is BGP multipath. Although it receives the same benefits of BGP multipath, this is not BGP multipath. In this scenario, the forwarding decisions happen due to the recursive lookup of the next-hop in the IGP table, which is then balanced by the Cisco express forwarding (CEF) engine.

Resiliency in Service Providers

BGP multipath simplifies redundancy and the capability to load-balance traffic across the redundant link. However, organizations typically choose a different SP for each circuit, thereby hindering BGP multipath support. A second service provider could be selected for a variety of reasons but typically comes down to cost, circuit availability for remote locations, or separation of control plane.

By using a different SP, if one SP has problems in its network, network traffic can still flow across the other SP. Most of the examples in this chapter display different SPs for this reason. Along with this notion, companies will prefer one SP over a different SP so that traffic remains synchronous (that is, traffic takes the same path in both directions).

Note   An organization can have multiple circuits to multiple service providers, which allows for multipath and multihoming at the same time.

EBGP and IBGP Multipath Configuration

EBGP multipath is enabled on IOS and NX-OS devices with the BGP configuration command **maximum-paths** *number-paths*. The number of paths indicates the allowed number of EBGP paths to install in the RIB. The command **maximum-paths ibgp** *number-paths* sets the number of IBGP routes to install in the RIB. The commands are placed under the appropriate address-family.

IOS XR routers set the number of paths for installation into the RIB with the BGP configuration command **maximum-paths {ebgp | ibgp}** *number-paths* [**unequal-cost**]. The **unequal-cost** keyword allows for IBGP paths to install if the metrics to the next-hop do not match.

Example 8-1 demonstrates the IBGP multipath configuration for R3 from scenario 4 in Figure 8-1.

Example 8-1   *IBGP Multipath Configuration*

```
R3
router bgp 200
 neighbor 192.168.1.1 remote-as 200
 neighbor 192.168.1.1 update-source Loopback0
 neighbor 192.168.2.2 remote-as 200
 neighbor 192.168.2.2 update-source Loopback0
 !
 address-family ipv4
```

```
   neighbor 192.168.1.1 activate
   neighbor 192.168.2.2 activate
   maximum-paths ibgp 4
```

```
XR3
router bgp 200
 address-family ipv4 unicast
  maximum-paths ibgp 4
 !
 neighbor 192.168.1.1
  remote-as 200
  update-source Loopback0
  address-family ipv4 unicast
   !
 !
 neighbor 192.168.2.2
  remote-as 200
  update-source Loopback0
  address-family ipv4 unicast
```

```
NXOS3
router bgp 100
 address-family ipv4 unicast
   maximum-paths ibgp 4
 neighbor 192.168.1.1 remote-as 200
   update-source loopback0
   address-family ipv4 unicast
 neighbor 192.168.2.2 remote-as 200
   update-source loopback0
   address-family ipv4 unicast
```

Example 8-2 provides verification that R3 was able to identify the second path as multipath capable. Multipath eligibility begins only after the BGP best path algorithm executes. Alternate paths must match the exact BGP best path attributes listed earlier for BGP multipath consideration. In the output, the path from R1 (192.168.1.1) was identified as the best path, so the path from R2 (192.168.2.2) was eligible for multipath. Finally the RIB is verified, showing that both of the next-hop addresses are installed.

Example 8-2 *BGP Multipath Verification*

```
R3# show bgp ipv4 unicast
BGP table version is 23, local router ID is 192.168.3.3
Status codes: s suppressed, d damped, h history, * valid, > best, i - internal,
              r RIB-failure, S Stale, m multipath, b backup-path, f RT-Filter,
              x best-external, a additional-path, c RIB-compressed,
Origin codes: i - IGP, e - EGP, ? - incomplete
RPKI validation codes: V valid, I invalid, N Not found

     Network          Next Hop          Metric LocPrf Weight Path
 *mi 100.64.0.0/16    192.168.2.2            0    100      0 100 50 i
 *>i                  192.168.1.1            0    100      0 100 50 i
```

```
R3# show bgp ipv4 unicast 100.64.0.0
BGP routing table entry for 100.64.0.0/16, version 23
Paths: (2 available, best #2, table default)
Multipath: iBGP
  Not advertised to any peer
  Refresh Epoch 3
  100 50, (aggregated by 50 192.168.50.50)
    192.168.2.2 (metric 2) from 192.168.2.2 (192.168.2.2)
      Origin IGP, metric 0, localpref 100, valid, internal, atomic-aggregate,
        multipath(oldest)
      rx pathid: 0, tx pathid: 0
  Refresh Epoch 4
  100 50, (aggregated by 50 192.168.50.50)
    192.168.1.1 (metric 2) from 192.168.1.1 (192.168.1.1)
      Origin IGP, metric 0, localpref 100, valid, internal, atomic-aggregate,
        multipath, best
      rx pathid: 0, tx pathid: 0x0
```

```
R3# show ip route bgp | begin Gateway
Gateway of last resort is not set
      100.0.0.0/16 is subnetted, 1 subnets
B        100.64.0.0 [200/0] via 192.168.2.2, 00:03:10
                    [200/0] via 192.168.1.1, 00:03:10
```

EIBGP Multipath

The rules of IBGP or EBGP multipath prevents a router from installing an EBGP and IBGP route into the RIB at the same time. However, in some environments this can prevent an organization from using the full bandwidth available. EIBGP multipath allows for an EBGP and IBGP path with unequal next-hop metrics to be selected as the best path.

EIBGP multipath configuration on IOS and IOS XR routers uses the BGP address-family configuration command **maximum-paths eibgp** *number-paths*. At the time of this writing, NX-OS devices do not have support for this feature.

Figure 8-2 is used to explain how EIBGP works further and provides the following information:

- R1, R2, R3, R4, and R5 have established an IBGP full mesh for AS100.

- R1, R3, and R5 set the next-hop-self to IBGP peers.

- AS100 routers are using Open Shortest Path First (OSPF) as the IGP with the appropriate link costs in parentheses.

- EIBGP maximum paths have been set to 5 for all routers in AS100.

- The BGP table for all the routers is displayed after BGP best path calculation.

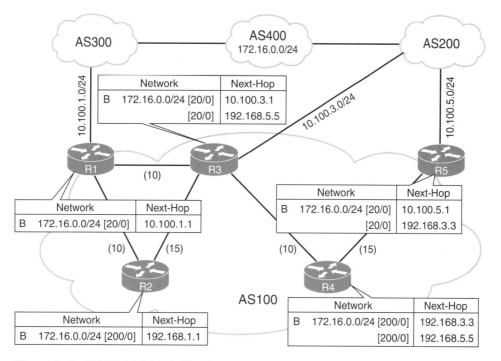

Figure 8-2 *EIBGP Multipath Topology*

In Figure 8-2, notice that R1 and R2 installed only one BGP path for 172.16.0.0/24 network, whereas R3, R4, and R5 utilized EIBGP multipath and installed multiple routes.

R1

R1 identifies the EBGP path via 10.100.1.1 as the best path because EBGP paths are preferred over IBGP paths. Notice that the other 172.16.0.0/24 paths are ineligible for multipath installation because the AS-Path does not match the AS-Path of the best path (300 400). Example 8-3 displays R1's BGP table for the 172.16.0.0/24 route.

Example 8-3   *R1's BGP Table*

```
R1# show bgp ipv4 unicast
! Output omitted for brevity
     Network          Next Hop         Metric LocPrf Weight Path
 * i 172.16.0.0/24    192.168.3.3                100      0 200 400 i
 * i                  192.168.5.5                100      0 200 400 i
 *>                   10.100.1.1                          0 300 400 i
```

R2

R2 identifies the IBGP path via R1 as the best path because the IGP metric to R1 is lower than the IGP metric to R3 and R5. Notice that the other 172.16.0.0/24 paths are ineligible for multipath because the AS-Path does not match the AS-Path of the best path (300 400). Example 8-4 displays R2's BGP table for the 172.16.0.0/24 route.

Example 8-4   *R2's BGP Table*

```
R2# show bgp ipv4 unicast
! Output omitted for brevity
     Network          Next Hop         Metric LocPrf Weight Path
 *>i 172.16.0.0/24    192.168.1.1          0    100      0 300 400 i
 * i                  192.168.3.3               100      0 200 400 i
 * i                  192.168.5.5               100      0 200 400 i
```

R3

R3 identifies the BGP best path via 10.100.3.1 as the best path because EBGP paths are preferred over IBGP paths. A second 172.16.0.0/24 path has an identical AS-Path to the BGP best path (300 400) and can be installed into the RIB even though it uses an IBGP path. Example 8-5 displays R3's BGP table for the 172.16.0.0/24 route.

Example 8-5   *R3's BGP Table*

```
R3# show bgp ipv4 unicast
! Output omitted for brevity
     Network          Next Hop         Metric LocPrf Weight Path
 *> 172.16.0.0/24     10.100.3.1                          0 200 400 i
 * i                  192.168.1.1          0    100      0 300 400 i
 *mi                  192.168.5.5               100      0 200 400 i

R3# show bgp ipv4 unicast 172.16.0.0/24
BGP routing table entry for 172.16.0.0/24, version 4
```

```
Paths: (3 available, best #3, table default)
Multipath: eiBGP
  Advertised to update-groups:
     1
  Refresh Epoch 2
  200 400
    192.168.5.5 (metric 3) from 192.168.5.5 (192.168.5.5)
      Origin IGP, metric 0, localpref 100, valid, internal, multipath(oldest)
      rx pathid: 0, tx pathid: 0
  Refresh Epoch 2
  300 400
    192.168.1.1 (metric 2) from 192.168.1.1 (192.168.1.1)
      Origin IGP, metric 0, localpref 100, valid, internal
      rx pathid: 0, tx pathid: 0
  Refresh Epoch 2
  200 400
    10.200.3.1 from 10.200.3.1 (192.168.0.9)
      Origin IGP, localpref 100, valid, external, multipath, best
      rx pathid: 0, tx pathid: 0x0
```

```
R3# show ip route bgp
      172.16.0.0/24 is subnetted, 1 subnets
B        172.16.0.0 [20/0] via 192.168.5.5, 00:02:21
                    [20/0] via 10.200.3.1, 00:02:21
```

Note If an IBGP route is used with a primary EBGP path, the administrative distance (AD) is changed to 20 so that both routes install into the RIB.

Note IOS XR routers do not display the *m* flag (status code) for EIBGP multipath routes in the BGP output.

R4

R4 identifies the BGP best path through R3 because the IGP cost is lower than the path through R5. A second 172.16.0.0/24 path has an identical AS-Path to the BGP best path (300 400) and can be installed into the RIB even though the IGP metric is different from the metric to R3. Example 8-6 displays R4's BGP table for the 172.16.0.0/24 route.

Example 8-6   *R4's BGP Table*

```
R4# show bgp ipv4 unicast
! Output omitted for brevity

   Network              Next Hop          Metric LocPrf Weight Path
 * i172.16.0.0/24       192.168.1.1            0    100      0 300 400 i
 *>i                    192.168.3.3                 100      0 200 400 i
 *mi                    192.168.5.5                 100      0 200 400 i


Processed 1 prefixes, 3 paths
```

R5

R5 identifies the BGP best path via 10.100.5.1 as the best path because the EBGP path is preferred over IBGP paths. R3's 172.16.0.0/24 path has an identical AS-Path to the BGP best path (300 400) and can be installed into the RIB even though it uses an IBGP path. Example 8-7 displays R5's BGP table for the 172.16.0.0/24 route.

Example 8-7   *R5's BGP Table*

```
RP/0/0/CPU0:XR5# show bgp ipv4 unicast
! Output omitted for brevity

   Network              Next Hop          Metric LocPrf Weight Path
 *> 172.16.0.0/24       10.100.5.1                          0 200 400 i
 * i                    192.168.1.1            0    100      0 300 400 i
 *mi                    192.168.3.3                 100      0 200 400 i


Processed 1 prefixes, 3 paths
```

Note   The use of EIBGP multipath can introduce a routing loop into a topology and should be used only after mapping out all the traffic flows. EIBGP multipath is typically used in the context of MPLS L3VPNs. Using this feature from the global table could result in routing loops if not designed properly.

Figure 8-3 displays a MPLS L3VPN topology to demonstrate an EIBGP multipath real-world use case. All the customer edge (CE) routers belong to the same Virtual Routing and Forwarding (VRF) instance that is hosted on the provider edge (PE) routers. Network traffic from CE3, CE4, and CE5 to 172.16.1.0/24 could saturate the network link between PE2 and CE1. PE2 selects this path because of the EBGP peering versus the paths by PE1 and PE3 that are IBGP paths. By enabling EIBGP multipath on PE2, traffic can be distributed across all three links. The customer prefers this because it does not have to increase bandwidth on the circuits between CE1 and PE2.

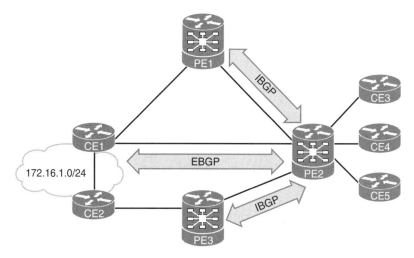

Figure 8-3 *EIBGP Multipath with MPLS L3VPN Topology*

AS-Path Relax

BGP multipath works well if an organization uses the same service provider for Internet connectivity. However, if an organization uses different service providers, the AS-Path is not identical and does not meet the requirements for BGP multipath. The AS-Path relax feature allows for BGP multipath to work when the AS-Path length is the same, but the AS-Paths are different.

The AS-Path relax feature is configured with the BGP configuration command **bgp bestpath as-path multipath-relax** on IOS, IOS XR, and NX-OS devices.

Understanding BGP Path Selection

The BGP best path selection algorithm influences how traffic enters or leaves an autonomous system (AS). Some router configurations modify the BGP attributes to influence inbound traffic, outbound traffic, or inbound and outbound traffic depending on the network design requirements. The BGP best path selection is not fully understood by a lot of network engineers and can often result in suboptimal routing.

This section explains the logic used by a router that uses BGP when forwarding routes.

Routing Path Selection Longest Match

Routers always select the path a packet should take by examining the prefix length of a network entry. The path selected for a packet is based on the prefix length, where the longest prefix length is always preferred. For example, /28 is preferred over /26, and /26 is preferred over /24.

This logic can be used to influence path selection in BGP. Assume that an organization owns the 100.64.0.0/16 network range, but needs to advertise only two subnets (100.64.1.0/24 and 100.64.2.0/24). It could advertise both prefixes (100.64.1.0/24 and 100.64.2.0/24) from all of its routers, but how could it distribute the load for each subnet if all traffic comes in on one router (that is, R1)?

It could modify various BGP PAs that are advertised externally, but a SP could have a BGP routing policy that ignores those path attributes, thereby resulting in random receipt of network traffic

A more elegant way that guarantees that paths are selected deterministically outside of your organization is to advertise a summary prefix (100.64.0.0/16) out of both routers. Then advertise a longer matching prefix out of the router that should receive network traffic for that prefix. Figure 8-4 displays the concept where R1 advertises the 100.64.1.0/24 prefix, R2 advertises the 100.64.2.0/24 prefix, and both routers advertise the 100.64.0.0/16 summary network prefix.

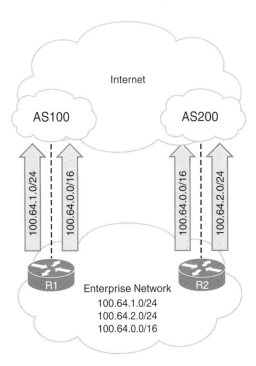

Figure 8-4   *BGP Path Selection Using Longest Match*

Regardless of an SP's routing policy, the more specific prefixes are advertised out of only one router. Redundancy is provided by advertising the summary address. If R1 crashes, devices will use R2's route advertisement of 100.64.0.016 to reach the 100.64.1.0/24 network.

Note Ensure that the network summaries that are being advertised from your organization are within only your network range. In addition, service providers typically will not accept IPv4 routes longer than /24 (that is, /25 or /26) or IPv6 routes longer than a /48. Routes are restricted to control the size of the Internet routing table.

BGP Best-Path Overview

BGP installs the first received path as the best path automatically. When additional paths are received for the same network prefix length, the newer paths are compared against the current best path. If there is a tie, processing continues onto the next step, until a best path winner is identified.

The following list provides the attributes that the BGP best path algorithm uses for the best route selection process. These attributes are processed in the following order:

1. Weight

2. Local Preference

3. Local originated (network statement, redistribution, aggregation)

4. Accumulated Interior Gateway Protocol (AIGP)

5. Shortest AS Path

6. Origin Type. IGP is preferred over EGP, and EGP is preferred over Incomplete.

7. Lowest MED

8. EBGP over IBGP

9. Lowest IGP next-hop metric

10. If both paths are external (EBGP), prefer the first (oldest).

11. Prefer the route that comes from the BGP peer with the lower RID.

12. Prefer the route with the minimum cluster list length.

13. Prefer the path that comes from the lowest neighbor address.

Note After Step 9, routes become eligible for BGP multipath, as explained earlier in this chapter.

The BGP routing policy can vary from organization to organization based on the manipulation of the BGP path attributes (PAs). Because some PAs are transitive and carry from one AS to another AS, those changes could impact downstream routing for other SPs, too. Other PAs are nontransitive and influence only the routing policy within the organization. Network prefixes are conditionally matched on a variety of factors, such as AS-Path length, specific autonomous system number (ASN), BGP communities, or other attributes.

The best path algorithm is explained in the following sections.

Weight

BGP weight is a Cisco defined attribute, and the first step for selecting the BGP best path. Weight is a 16-bit value (0-65,535) assigned locally on the router, and is not advertised to other routers. The path with the higher weight is preferred. Weight is not advertised to peers and influences only outbound traffic from a router or autonomous system. Because it is the first step in the best path algorithm, it should be used when other attributes should not influence the best path for a specific network.

The command **set weight** *weight* in a route-map or route policy sets the weight value for a prefix. The weight can also be set for all prefixes received by a neighbor using the command **neighbor** *ip-address* **weight** *weight* on IOS routers, and the command **weight** *weight* underneath the address-family on NX-OS and IOS XR routers.

Local Preference

Local preference (LOCAL_PREF) is a well-known discretionary path attribute and is included with path advertisements throughout an autonomous system. The local preference attribute is a 32-bit value (0–4,294,967,295) that indicates the preference for exiting the autonomous system to the destination network. A higher value is preferred over a lower value. The local preference is not advertised between EBGP peers and is typically used between IBGP peers to influence the next-hop address for outbound traffic (that is, leaving an autonomous system).

Setting the local preference for specific routes can be accomplished via a route-map or route policy with the action **set local-preference** *preference*. Local preference for all routes received by a neighbor can also be set with the BGP neighbor address-family configuration command **neighbor** *ip-address* **local-preference** *preference* on IOS routers, or the IOS XR equivalent command **local-preference** *preference*.

> **Note**   NX-OS devices can only set local preference by route-map.

If an edge BGP router does not define the local preference upon receipt of a prefix, the default local preference value of 100 is used during best path calculation and is included in advertisements to other IBGP peers.

Locally Originated via Network or Aggregate Advertisement

The third decision point in the best path algorithm is to determine if the route originated locally. Preference is given in the following order:

- Routes that were advertised locally
- Networks that have been aggregated locally
- Routes received by BGP peers (that is, not locally originated)

Accumulated Interior Gateway Protocol (AIGP)

AIGP is an optional nontransitive path attribute that is included with advertisements throughout an autonomous system. IGP protocols typically use the lowest path metric to identify the shortest path to a destination, but cannot provide the scalability of BGP. BGP uses an autonomous system (AS) to identify a single domain of control for a routing policy. BGP does not use path metric due to scalability issues combined with the notion that each AS may use a different routing policy to calculate metrics.

AIGP provides the capability for BGP to maintain and calculate a conceptual path metric in environments that use multiple ASs with unique IGP routing domains in each AS. The ability for BGP to make routing decisions based upon a path metric is a viable option because all of the ASs are under the control of a single domain with consistent routing policies for BGP and IGP protocols.

> **Note**   The IGP routing protocol should remain consistent between the routing domains. Every IGP routing protocol path metric has a different default value. For example, the EIGRP path metric is much higher than OSPF's.

In Figure 8-5, AS100, AS200, and AS300 are all under the control of the same service provider. AIGP has been enabled on the BGP sessions between all the routers, and the IGP protocols are redistributed into BGP. The AIGP metric is advertised between AS100, AS200, and AS300, allowing BGP to use the AIGP metric for best path calculations between the autonomous systems.

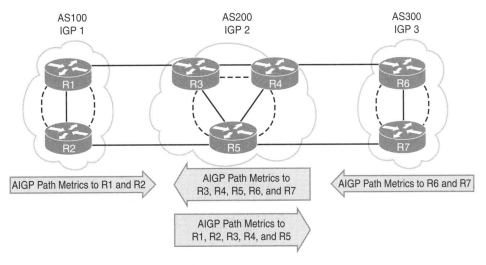

Figure 8-5 *AIGP Path Attribute Exchange Between Autonomous Systems*

Exchanging AIGP PAs must be agreed upon between the BGP peers, and is included only in prefix advertisements between AIGP enabled peers. IOS routers enable AIGP metrics for BGP neighbors with the address-family configuration command **neighbor** *ip-address* **aigp**.

IOS XR enables AIGP for all IBGP sessions automatically, but requires EBGP sessions to be configured with the BGP neighbor address-family configuration command **aigp**.

The AIGP metric is a 32-bit (0–4,294,967,295) value that can be set during redistribution or during receipt of a prefix with a route-map or route policy. Route-maps and route policies use the configuration command **set aigp-metric** {**igp-metric** | *metric*}. The **igp-metric** keyword sets the value to the IGP path metric on the redistributing router for the specific route. Static routes and network advertisements populate the AIGP metric with the path metric to the next-hop address of the route.

> **Note** Route-maps or route policies must be used to populate the AIGP metric during redistribution.

The following guidelines apply to AIGP metrics:

■ A path with an AIGP metric is preferred to a path without an AIGP metric

■ If the next-hop address requires a recursive lookup, the AIGP path needs to calculate a derived metric to include the distance to the next-hop address. This ensures that the cost to the BGP edge router is included.

  The formula is as follows:

  derived AIGP metric =(original AIGP metric + next-hop AIGRP metric)

  ■ If multiple AIGP paths exist and one next-hop address contains an AIGP metric and the other does not, the non-AIGP path is not used.

  ■ The next-hop AIGP metric is recursively added if multiple lookups are performed.

■ AIGP paths are compared based on the derived AIGP metric (with recursive next-hops) or the actual AIGP metric (nonrecursive next-hop). The path with the lower AIGP metric is preferred.

■ When a router R2 advertises an AIGP-enabled path that was learned from R1, if the next-hop address changes to an R2 address, *R2* increments the AIGP metric to reflect the distance (the IGP path metric) between R1 and R2.

> **Note** It is recommended that BGP best-external and additional-path features are used with AIGP metrics. These topics are covered in detail in Chapter 14, "BGP High Availability."

The AIGP metric is fairly new; it was added in IOS XR version 4.2.0, IOS 15.4(2)S, and IOS XE 3.12S. It is not supported on NX-OS at the time of this writing. Cisco allows for the conversion of the AIGP metric into MED for traffic selection when the neighboring router does not support AIGP metrics. MED comparison occurs later in the BGP best path algorithm but is a well-known mandatory attribute that all routers support.

To convert the AIGP metric to MED on IOS XR routers, use the BGP neighbor address-family configuration command **aigp send med [disable]**, and on IOS routers use the equivalent command **neighbor** *ip-address* **aigp send med**.

Shortest AS-Path

The next decision factor for the BGP best path algorithm is the AS-Path length. The path length typically correlates to the AS hop count. A shorter AS-Path is preferred over a longer AS-Path.

> **Note** When working with confederations, AS_CONFED_SEQUENCE (Confederation AS-Path) is not counted, and for aggregated addresses with multiple ASNs under the AS_SET portion of the AS-Path, the AS_SET counts for only one AS-Path entry.

Prepending ASNs to the AS-Path makes it longer, thereby making that path less desirable when compared with other paths. Typically, the AS-Path is prepended by the network owner, with the owner's ASN used for the prepending.

In general, paths that have had the AS-Path prepended are not selected as the BGP best path because the AS-Path is longer than the nonprepended path advertisement. Inbound traffic is influenced by prepending AS-Path length in advertisement to other ASs, and outbound traffic is influenced by prepending advertisements received from other ASs.

Each platform has its own method of prepending routes:

- IOS and NX-OS devices prepend a path with the command **set as-path prepend** {*as-number* | **last-as** *number*} on a route-map. The **last-as** option uses the last AS-Path value and allows a value of 1–10 prepends.

- IOS XR devices prepend a path with the command **prepend as-path** {*as-number* | **most-recent** *number*} in a route policy. The **most-recent** option uses the last AS-Path value and allows a value of 1–63.

> **Note** The shortest AS-Path criteria can be skipped by the best path algorithm on IOS and IOS XR routers with the BGP configuration command **bgp bestpath as-path ignore**. Some versions of IOS do not have a context-sensitive help for this command and require the complete command typed in correctly to function. Many network engineers consider this a hidden feature. This option is not available on NX-OS devices.

Origin Type

The next BGP best path decision factor is the well-known mandatory BGP attribute named *Origin*. By default, networks that are advertised via the network statement are set with the IGP or i Origin, and redistributed networks are assigned the Incomplete or ?

Origin attribute. The Exterior Gateway Protocol (EGP) or e Origin must be set explicitly by IOS XR and NX-OS devices. The Origin preference order is as follows:

1. IGP Origin (most preferred)

2. EGP Origin

3. Incomplete Origin (least preferred)

A prefix's Origin attribute can be modified with the command **set origin** {**igp** | **incomplete**} on a route-map, or with the command **set origin** {**egp** | **igp** | **incomplete**} on an IOS XR route policy.

Multi-Exit Discriminator (MED)

The next BGP best path decision factor is the nontransitive BGP attribute MED, which uses a 32-bit value (0–4,294,967,295) called a metric. BGP sets the MED automatically to the IGP path metric during network advertisement or redistribution. If the MED is received from an EBGP session, it can be advertised to other IBGP peers, but should not be sent outside of the AS that received it. MED's purpose is to influence traffic flows inbound from a different AS. A lower MED is preferred over a higher MED.

RFC 4451 guidelines state that a prefix without a MED value should be given priority and in essence should be compared with a value of 0. Some organizations require that a MED be set to a specific value for all the prefixes and declare that paths without the MED be treated as the least preferred. By default, if the MED is missing from a prefix learned from an EBGP peer, IOS, IOS XR, and NX-OS devices use a MED of 0 for the best path calculation. IOS routers advertise a MED of 0 to IBGP peers, and IOS XR advertises the path to IBGP peers without a MED.

Note   RFC 3345 and 4451 also provide scenarios that MED could introduce route oscillation. Evaluating these scenarios may impact the network design to use or not use MED as part of the best path selection.

IOS, IOS XR, and NX-OS routers by default do not compare MED between Member-ASs (Sub-ASs) in BGP confederations. The BGP configuration command **bgp bestpath med confed** changes the behavior so that MED is compared between Member-ASs on IOS and IOS XR routers, whereas the command **bestpath med confed** enables the behavior on NX-OS devices.

Missing MED Behavior

An organization may expect that its different SPs advertise a MED value for every prefix. If the MED is missing, that path is preferred over the other path. An organization can modify the default behavior so that prefixes without MED are always selected last.

IOS and IOS XR routers are configured with the command **bgp bestpath med missing-as-worst** under the BGP router process, which sets the MED to infinity (2^{32}-1) or (4,294,967,295) if the MED is missing from a path. NX-OS devices use the command **bestpath med missing-as-worst** under the BGP process.

An alternative solution is to use the BGP configuration command **default-metric** *metric*, which sets the metric to the value specified when a path is received without a MED. This allows the devices to calculate the BGP best path for prefixes without the MED attribute with a value different from 0 or infinity.

Always Compare Med

The default MED comparison mechanism requires the AS-Path to be identical because the policies used to set the MED could vary from AS to AS. This means that MED can influence traffic only when multiple links are from the same service provider. Typically, organizations use different service providers for redundancy. In these situations, the default BGP rules for MED comparison need to be relaxed to compare MED between different service providers.

The always compare MED feature allows for the comparison of MED regardless of the AS-Path. The always compare MED feature is enabled with the BGP configuration command **bgp always-compare-med** on IOS and NX-OS devices, and with the BGP configuration command **bgp bestpath med always** on IOS XR routers.

Note   Enable this feature on all BGP routers in the AS, or routing loops can occur.

BGP Deterministic MED

The best path algorithm compares a route update to the existing best path and processes the paths in the order they are stored in the Loc-RIB table. The paths are stored in the order that they are received in the BGP table. If always compare MED is not enabled, the path MED is compared only against the existing best path and not all the paths in the Loc-RIB table, which can cause variations in the MED best path comparison process.

Figure 8-6 demonstrates a topology where MED is not compared because of the order of the path advertisement. In this topology

- R4 advertises the 172.16.0.0/24 prefix with a MED of 200, and R5 selects R4's path as the best path because no other paths exist.

- R3 advertises the 172.16.0.0/24 prefix with a MED of 100. The AS-Path is from a different AS compared to R4's, so MED is not considered in the BGP best path calculation. R4's path remains the best path because it is the oldest EBGP learned route.

- R2 advertises the 172.16.0.0/24 prefix with a MED of 150. The AS-Paths are different from R4's, so MED is not considered in the BGP best path calculation. R4's path remains the best path because it is the oldest EBGP learned route.

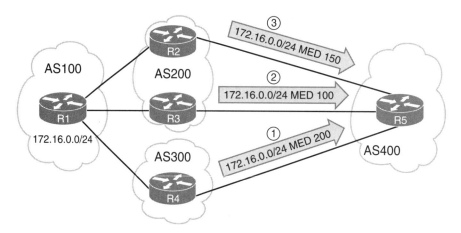

Figure 8-6 *Problems with MED Comparison*

BGP deterministic MED corrects the problem by grouping paths together with an identical AS-Path for identifying the best path. Each group is compared against each other.

With BGP deterministic MED enabled, the best path selection outcome is different. R2 and R3's paths are grouped together because they have an identical AS-Path (200 100). R4 is placed into a separate group, by itself because of its AS-Path (300 100). R3 is the best path for AS-Path group 200 100, and R4 is the best path for AS-Path group 300 100. The two AS-Path groups are then compared against each other, and because R3's MED is lower than R4's, R3's path is chosen as the best path.

In IOS, BGP deterministic MED is enabled with the BGP configuration command **bgp deterministic-med** and is recommended for all BGP deployments. In IOS XR, deterministic MED is enabled by default and cannot be disabled. NX-OS devices enable BGP deterministic med by default, but can disable this feature with the command **bestpath med non-deterministic** under the BGP process.

EBGP over IBGP

The next BGP best path decision factor is whether the route comes from an IBGP, EBGP, or Confederation Member-AS (Sub-AS) peering. The best path selection order is as follows:

1. EBGP peers (most desirable)

2. Confederation Member-AS peers

3. IBGP peers (least desirable)

Lowest IGP Metric

The next decision is to use the lowest IGP cost to the BGP next-hop address.

Figure 8-7 illustrates a topology where R2, R3, R4, and R5 are in AS 400. All of the AS 400 routers peer in a full mesh and establishes BGP sessions using Loopback 0 interfaces. R1 advertises the 172.16.0.0/24 network to R2 and R4.

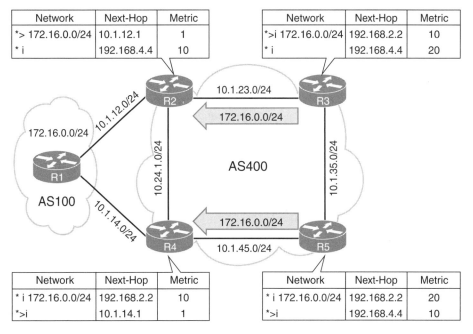

Network	Next-Hop	Metric
*> 172.16.0.0/24	10.1.12.1	1
* i	192.168.4.4	10

Network	Next-Hop	Metric
*>i 172.16.0.0/24	192.168.2.2	10
* i	192.168.4.4	20

Network	Next-Hop	Metric
* i 172.16.0.0/24	192.168.2.2	10
*>i	10.1.14.1	1

Network	Next-Hop	Metric
* i 172.16.0.0/24	192.168.2.2	20
*>i	192.168.4.4	10

Figure 8-7 *Lowest IGP Metric Topology*

R3 prefers the path from R2 compared to the IBGP path from R4 because the metric to reach the next-hop address is lower. R5 prefers the path from R4 compared to the IBGP path from R2 because the metric to reach the next-hop address is lower.

> **Note**   IOS and IOS XR routers can disable the lowest IGP metric step with the BGP address-family configuration command **bgp bestpath igp-metric ignore**. The feature cannot be disabled on NX-OS devices.

Prefer the Oldest EBGP Path

BGP can maintain large routing tables, and unstable sessions result in the BGP best path calculation to execute frequently. BGP maintains stability in a network by preferring the oldest (established) BGP session.

The downfall to this technique is that it does lead to a nondeterministic method of identifying the BGP best path from a design perspective. This step can be skipped on IOS, IOS XR, and NX-OS devices with the BGP configuration command **bgp bestpath compare-routerid**.

Router ID

The next step for the BGP best path algorithm is to select the best path using the lowest router-id of the advertising EBGP router. If the route was received by a route-reflector, the originator-id is substituted for the router-id.

Minimum Cluster List Length

The next step in the BGP best path algorithm is to select the best path using the lowest *cluster list* length. The cluster list is a nontransitive BGP attribute that is appended (not overwritten) by a route-reflector with its *cluster-id*. The cluster-id attribute is used by route reflectors as a loop prevention mechanism. The cluster-id is not advertised between ASs and is locally significant. In simplest terms, this step locates the path that has traveled the least amount of IBGP advertisement hops.

Figure 8-8 demonstrates the how the minimum cluster list length is used as part of the BGP best path calculation.

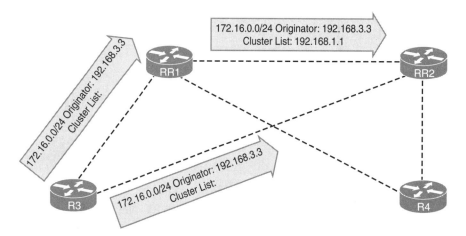

Figure 8-8   *Minimum Cluster List Length*

Figure 8-8 illustrates the following:

- R3 advertises the 172.16.0.0/24 network to RR1 and RR2 with only the Originator-ID.

- RR1 reflects the advertisement to RR2 after appending its RID to the cluster list.

- RR2 selects the path advertisement directly from R3. R3's cluster list length is 0, which is more desirable compared to RR1's cluster list length of 1.

Lowest Neighbor Address

The last step of the BGP best path algorithm selects the path that comes from the lowest BGP neighbor address. This step is limited to IBGP peerings because EBGP peerings used the oldest received path as the tie breaker.

Figure 8-9 demonstrates the concept of choosing the router with the lowest neighbor address. R1 is advertising the 172.16.0.0/24 network to R2. R1 and R2 have established two BGP sessions using the 10.12.1.0/24 and 10.12.2.0/24 network. R2 will select the path advertised from 10.12.1.1 because it is the lower IP address.

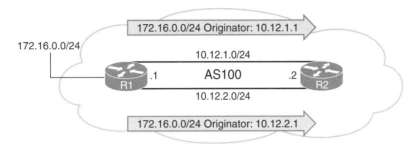

Figure 8-9 *Lowest IP Address*

> **Note** This design is inefficient in most scenarios because only one link is used. A better solution is to peer via a loopback interface and let the IGP load-balance across the link accordingly or use 802.3ad Link Aggregation (LAG) bundles.

Troubleshooting BGP Best Path

All the BGP prefix paths are shown in complete detail (including PAs) with the command **show bgp** *afi safi network prefix-length*. This allows for a manual comparison of the path attributes to identify why a router may have selected a different path than the one that was intended. The devices indicate which path was identified as the best path.

> **Note** The output also indicates if a path was multipath eligible. If a route is not multipath capable, be sure to verify that the weight, local preference, AS-Path, Origin, Med, and advertisement method all match.

IOS routers can display only the best path with the command **show bgp** *afi safi network prefix-length* **bestpath**. Example 8-8 displays the BGP best path for the 172.16.0.0/24 network.

Example 8-8 *IOS Best Path*

```
R6# show bgp ipv4 unicast 172.16.0.0/24 bestpath
BGP routing table entry for 172.16.0.0/24, version 5
Paths: (2 available, best #2, table default)
  Advertised to update-groups:
     2
  Refresh Epoch 2
  300 100
    10.36.1.3 from 10.36.1.3 (100.2.2.254)
      Origin IGP, localpref 100, weight 333, valid, external, best
```

IOS XR provides similar functionality with the command **show bgp** *afi safi network prefix-length* **bestpath-compare**. In addition, the output explains why a path was *not* selected as the best path. In Example 8-9, path 2 is not the best path because it has a lower weight than path 1.

Example 8-9   *IOS XR Best Path Compare*

```
RP/0/0/CPU0:R4# show bgp ipv4 unicast 172.24.0.0/24 bestpath-compare
BGP routing table entry for 172.24.0.0/24
Paths: (2 available, best #1)
  Path #1: Received by speaker 0
  200 100
    10.24.1.2 from 10.24.1.2 (100.1.1.254)
      Origin IGP, localpref 100, weight 444, valid, external, best, group-best
      Origin-AS validity: not-found
      best of AS 200, Overall best
  Path #2: Received by speaker 0
  300 100
    192.168.6.6 (metric 3) from 192.168.6.6 (192.168.6.6)
      Origin IGP, metric 0, localpref 100, valid, internal, group-best
      best of AS 300
      Lower weight than best path (path #1)
```

Visualizing the Topology

Examining the output for a specific network prefix may be enough to fully understand the path selection, whereas other times may help to visualize the process. In larger topologies, not all paths are present, even if all the routers within the AS are fully meshed. Drawing out the topology and identifying the ways a path is advertised within an AS is very helpful.

Figure 8-10 demonstrates the example. All the routers in AS400 (R4, R5, and R6) are fully meshed via IBGP. AS100 is advertising the 172.16.0.0/24 and 172.20.0.0/24 network prefixes. R6 is prepending AS-Path 300 (making the AS-Path longer) to only the 172.16.0.0/24 network prefix.

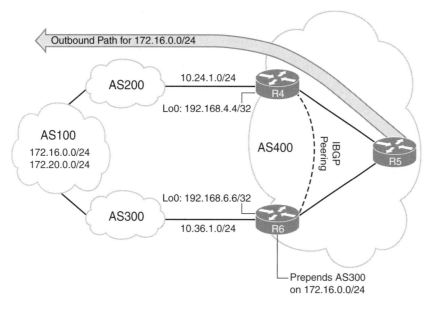

Figure 8-10 *Modifying BGP AS-Path*

Example 8-10 displays the BGP table for R5. A network engineer may think that R5 identified the path through AS200 as preferred and delete it from the BGP table.

Example 8-10 displays the BGP table for R4, R5, and R6.

Example 8-10 *R5 BGP Table After AS Prepending*

```
R5# show bgp ipv4 unicast
! Output omitted for brevity


  Network           Next Hop         Metric LocPrf Weight Path
*>i172.16.0.0/24    192.168.4.4                  100      0 200 100 i
*>i172.20.0.0/24    192.168.4.4                  100      0 200 100 i
*  i                192.168.6.6           0      100      0 300 100 i
```

This is not what happens. To fully understand what has happened, let's review the processing logic that occurs on each router during three phases (time cycles).

Phase I—Initial BGP Edge Route Processing

This is the phase where routes are initially processed by the BGP edge routers R4 and R6.

R4:

- R4 receives the 172.16.0.0/24 and 172.20.0.0/24 prefixes from AS200.

- No other paths for the prefix exist, so all paths are marked as best path.

- R4 advertises these paths to R5 and R6.

R6:

- R6 receives the prefix for 172.16.0.0/24 from AS300 and prepends 300 to the AS-Path a second time.

- R6 receives the 172.20.0.0/24 prefixes from AS300.

- No other paths for the prefix exist, so all paths are marked as best path.

- R6 advertises these paths to R4 and R5.

Example 8-11 displays what the BGP table on R4 and R6 are during this phase. Notice the AS-Path for the 172.16.0.0/24 network on R6, and that it has an additional 300 listed.

Example 8-11   *BGP Table After Phase I Processing*

```
R4# show bgp ipv4 unicast
! Output omitted for brevity
   Network          Next Hop          Metric LocPrf Weight Path
*> 172.16.0.0/24    10.24.1.2                         0 200 100 i
*> 172.20.0.0/24    10.24.1.2                         0 200 100 i
```

```
R6# show bgp ipv4 unicast
! Output omitted for brevity
   Network          Next Hop          Metric LocPrf Weight Path
*>i172.16.0.0/24    10.36.1.3                       0 300 300 100 i
*>172.20.0.0/24     10.36.1.3                       0 300 100 i
```

Phase II—BGP Edge Evaluation of Multiple Paths

This is the phase where R4 and R5 have received each other's routes and compare each path for a prefix. Ultimately, R6 advertises a route withdrawal for the 172.16.0.0/24. R5 receives routes from R4 and R6 at the same time, resulting in both paths being present in the BGP Adj-RIB table.

R4:

- R4 receives R6's paths for all the prefixes from AS300.

- R4 detects that the 172.16.0.0/24 path from R6 has a longer AS-Path than the path from AS200. R4 leaves the path from AS200 as the best path for the prefix.

- R4 detects that the 172.20.0.0/24 path from R6 has the same AS-Path length. Because of the tie, the best path is selected using steps after AS-Path length in the best path algorithm (EBGP over IBGP). AS200 is the best path.

R5:

- R5 receives paths for all network prefixes from R4 and R6.

- R5 detects that the 172.16.0.0/24 path from AS200 has a shorter AS-Path than the path from R6. R5 marks the path from R4 as the best path for the prefix.

- R5 detects that both the 172.20.0.0/24 paths have identical AS-Path length and proceeds to steps after AS-Path length in the best path algorithm (Lower RID for IBGP routes). The path from R4 is the best path.

R6:

- R6 receives R4's path advertisement for all the prefixes from AS200.

- R6 detects that the 172.16.0.0/24 path from R4 has a shorter AS-Path than the path from AS300. R6 marks that path from R4 as the best path for the prefix and sends route withdrawals for the path via AS300.

- R6 detects that the 172.20.0.0/24 path from AS300 has the same AS-Path length as the path from R4. Because of the tie, the best path is selected using steps after AS-Path length in the best path algorithm (EBGP over IBGP). AS300 is the best path.

Example 8-12 displays the BGP tables for R4, R5, and R6 after phase II processing.

Example 8-12 *BGP Tables After Phase II Processing*

```
R4# show bgp ipv4 unicast
! Output omitted for brevity
   Network          Next Hop         Metric LocPrf Weight Path
*> 172.16.0.0/24    10.24.1.2                         0 200 100 i
*> 172.20.0.0/24    10.24.1.2                         0 200 100 i
*  i                192.168.6.6          0    100     0 300 100 i


R5# show bgp ipv4 unicast
! Output omitted for brevity
   Network          Next Hop         Metric LocPrf Weight Path
*>i172.16.0.0/24    192.168.4.4              100     0 200 100 i
*  i                192.168.6.6              100     0 300 300 100 i
*>i172.20.0.0/24    192.168.4.4              100     0 200 100 i
*  i                192.168.6.6          0    100     0 300 100 i


R6# show bgp ipv4 unicast
! Output omitted for brevity
   Network          Next Hop         Metric LocPrf Weight Path
*>i172.16.0.0/24    192.168.4.4              100     0 200 100 i
*                   10.36.1.3                        0 300 300 100 i
*  i172.20.0.0/24   192.168.4.4              100     0 200 100 i
*>                  10.36.1.3                        0 300 100 i
```

Phase III—Final BGP Processing State

This is the last phase processing for topology. In this topology, R4 and R5 process R6's route withdrawal for the 172.16.0.0/24 prefix because the path from AS300 is not the best path in R6's BGP table.

- **R4:** R4 receives R6's withdraw for 172.16.0.0/24 and removes it from the BGP table.

- **R5:** R5 receives R6's withdraw for 172.16.0.0/24 and removes it from the BGP table.

Example 8-13 displays the BGP tables for R4, R5, and R6 after phase III processing.

Example 8-13 *BGP Processing After Phase III*

```
R4# show bgp ipv4 unicast
! Output omitted for brevity
   Network          Next Hop          Metric LocPrf Weight Path
*> 172.16.0.0/24    10.24.1.2                          0 200 100 i
*> 172.20.0.0/24    10.24.1.2                          0 200 100 i
*  i                192.168.6.6           0    100     0 300 100 i
```

```
R5# show bgp ipv4 unicast
! Output omitted for brevity
   Network          Next Hop          Metric LocPrf Weight Path
*>i172.16.0.0/24    192.168.4.4                100     0 200 100 i
*>i172.20.0.0/24    192.168.4.4                100     0 200 100 i
*  i                192.168.6.6           0    100     0 300 100 i
```

```
R6# show bgp ipv4 unicast
! Output omitted for brevity
   Network          Next Hop          Metric LocPrf Weight Path
*>i172.16.0.0/24    192.168.4.4                100     0 200 100 i
*                   10.36.1.3                           0 300 300 100 i
*  i172.20.0.0/24   192.168.4.4                100     0 200 100 i
*>                  10.36.1.3                           0 300 100 i
```

Path Selection for the Routing Table

As each routing protocol receives updates and other routing information, it chooses the best path to any given destination and attempts to install this path into the routing table. For example, after BGP calculates the best path toward 10.0.1.0/24, BGP first checks to see if an entry exists in the routing table. If it does not exist, the route is installed into the RIB. If the route already exists in the RIB, the router decides whether to install the route presented by BGP based upon the AD of the route in BGP and the AD of the existing route in the RIB. If this route has the *lowest administrative distance* to the destination (when compared to the other route in the table), it's installed in the routing table. If this route isn't the route with the best administrative distance, then the route is rejected. Not understanding the order of processing can lead to confusion for the installation of a route in to the global routing table.

For example, suppose that a prefix is available via OSPF (110 AD), EBGP (20 AD), and IBGP (200 AD). If the BGP best path algorithm selects the IBGP path over the EBGP path (because of AS-Path), the router installs the route learned via OSPF into the RIB because the AD of 120 is lower than 200. However, this conflicts with the logic from a pure AD perspective because the EBGP learned route has an AD of 20 versus OSPF's AD of 110. Remember that AD determines preference during installation into the RIB between competing routing protocols and not within a protocol.

Common Issues with BGP Multihoming

The following section discusses multiple common scenarios that happen with BGP when multihomed. The issues are caused by bad design and not accommodating all the scenarios from a control plane or from forwarding packets. Additional planning is required when connecting to multiple service providers.

Transit Routing

When you are running BGP with more than one service provider, you run the risk that your AS will become a transit AS. In Figure 8-11, AS500 is connecting to two service providers (SP3 and SP4) for resiliency.

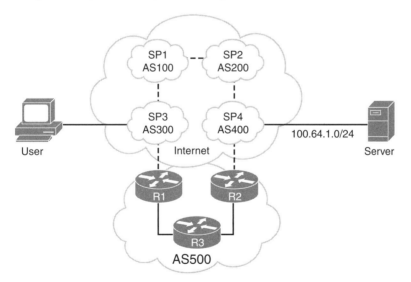

Figure 8-11 *Transit Routing*

Problems can arise if R1 and R2 use the default BGP routing policy. A user that connects to SP3 (AS300) routes through the enterprise network (AS500) to reach a server that attaches to SP4 (AS400). SP3 receives the 100.64.1.0/24 prefix from AS100 and AS500. SP3 selects the path through AS500 because the AS-Path is much shorter than going through SP1 and SP2's networks.

The AS500 network is providing transit routing to everyone on the Internet, which can saturate AS500's peering links. In addition to causing problems for the users in AS500, it impacts traffic from the users that are trying to transverse AS500.

Transit routing can be avoided by applying outbound route policies that allow only for locally advertised routes to be advertised from the router. The simplest method is to use the regex pattern ^$ as shown in Example 8-14. IOS XR can simplify the query by using the built-in filter of **is-local** too.

Example 8-14   *Methods of Preventing Transit Routing*

```
IOS
router bgp 500
 neighbor 100.64.1.1 remote-as 300
 !
 address-family ipv4
  neighbor 100.64.1.1 activate
  neighbor 100.64.1.1 route-map AS300-OUT out
 exit-address-family
!
route-map AS300-OUT permit 10
 match as-path 1
 !
ip as-path access-list 1 permit ^$
```

```
IOS XR
router bgp 500
 address-family ipv4 unicast
 !
 neighbor 100.64.1.1
  remote-as 300
  address-family ipv4 unicast
   route-policy PASS-ALL in
   route-policy AS300-OUT out
 !
route-policy AS300-OUT
  if as-path is-local then
    pass
  endif
end-policy
```

Note   It is considered a best practice to use a different route policy for inbound and outbound prefixes for each BGP neighbor.

Note Transit routing is not restricted to Internet connectivity. It is very common to have transit routing on MPLS L3VPNs when two service providers are used. Typically, one SP is preferred over another SP. Trying to fix WAN-related issues when transit routing is occurring is similar to playing *whack-a-mole* because the problem appears in various sites during the isolation phase of troubleshooting. Use the same steps that are shown in Example 8-14 for use in your WAN, too.

Problems with Race Conditions

Adding a second circuit for redundancy provides redundancy at the transport level. If both circuits connect to the same CE router, then the CE router becomes a SPOF. This is overcome by adding a second router (that is, one router per circuit/transport). A variety of problems can occur due to design or configuration, and other problems can occur due to timing. These problems occur because of race conditions that directly correlate to the timing of events or actions that occur on a router. A race condition problem occurs due to a certain order of events or actions that occur on a router.

Figure 8-12 displays a topology where R1 and R2 are branch routers that receive the 100.64.1.0/24 network from two service provider routers. R1 and R2 mutually redistribute BGP in the IGP routing protocol. There is not a BGP session between R1 and R2. This configuration provides R1 and R2 with routes from both paths (EBGP and IGP) and provides connectivity for any downstream branch routers (if present).

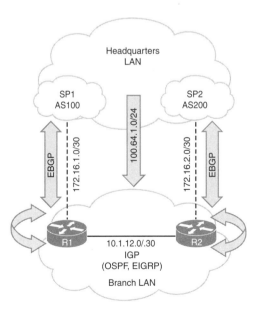

Figure 8-12 *Topology for BGP Race Condition*

Example 8-15 displays the BGP and EIGRP configuration for R1 and R2. Both routers mutually redistribute routes between BGP and EIGRP.

Example 8-15 *R1 and R3 Configuration for BGP and EIGRP*

```
R1
router eigrp LAN
 address-family ipv4 unicast autonomous-system 1
  topology base
   default-metric 100000 1 255 1 1500
   redistribute bgp 300
  exit-af-topology
  network 10.0.0.0
  network 192.168.0.0
 exit-address-family
!
router bgp 300
 neighbor 172.16.1.2 remote-as 100
 !
 address-family ipv4
  redistribute eigrp 1
  neighbor 172.16.1.2 activate
 exit-address-family
```

```
R2
router eigrp LAN
 address-family ipv4 unicast autonomous-system 1
  topology base
   default-metric 100000 1 255 1 1500
   redistribute bgp 300
  exit-af-topology
  network 10.0.0.0
  network 192.168.0.0
 exit-address-family
!
router bgp 300
 neighbor 172.16.2.2 remote-as 200
 !
 address-family ipv4
  redistribute eigrp 1
  neighbor 172.16.2.2 activate
exit-address-family
```

Example 8-16 displays the BGP table for R1 and R2 when working properly. Notice that both routers have only one path for the 100.64.1.0/24, with the next-hop referring to the appropriate service provider router. R1 has a next-hop IP address of 172.16.1.2 and R2 has a next-hop IP address of 172.16.2.2.

Example 8-16 *R1 and R2's BGP Table Working Properly*

```
R1# show bgp ipv4 unicast | begin Network
       Network          Next Hop          Metric LocPrf Weight Path
 *>  10.1.12.0/24      0.0.0.0                0            32768 ?
 *>  100.64.1.0/24     172.16.1.2             0                0 100 ?
 r>  172.16.1.0/30     172.16.1.2             0                0 100 ?


R2# show bgp ipv4 unicast | begin Network
       Network          Next Hop          Metric LocPrf Weight Path
 *>  10.1.12.0/24      0.0.0.0                0            32768 ?
 *>  100.64.1.0/24     172.16.2.2             0                0 200 ?
 r>  172.16.2.0/30     172.16.2.2             0                0 200 ?
```

Example 8-17 displays R1 and R2's routing table for the 100.64.1.0/24 network. Notice how both routers have installed the routes from the BGP table. Both routes have an administrative distance (AD) of 20 because they were learned from EBGP peers.

Example 8-17 *R1 and R2's Routing Table for the 100.64.1.0/24 Network*

```
R1# show ip route
! Output omitted for brevity
      100.0.0.0/24 is subnetted, 1 subnets
B        100.64.1.0 [20/0] via 172.16.1.2, 00:12:36


R2# show ip route
! Output omitted for brevity
      100.0.0.0/24 is subnetted, 1 subnets
B        100.64.1.0 [20/0] via 172.16.2.2, 00:01:29
```

Up to this point things are working properly because R1 established the BGP session with AS100 at the same time that R2 established the BGP session with AS200. The race condition is triggered in either of the following scenarios:

■ **R1 and R2 establish BGP sessions at different times.** For example, R1 establishes the BGP session with AS100 first, and then R2 establishes a BGP session with AS200 one minute later.

■ **BGP session failure occurs.** For example, the circuit between R2 and AS200 fails. This takes down the BGP session between R2 and AS200.

In a triggered state, R2 forwards packets to R1 when trying to reach the 100.64.1.0/24 network instead of sending them toward AS200.

Example 8-18 provides the BGP table for R1 and R2 while in a problem state, along with R2's routing table. Notice that R2 has two paths for the 100.64.1.0/24 network. The best path has a next-hop of 10.1.12.1 (R1) and a weight of 32,768 that was redistributed from EIGRP into BGP. The other path was learned via AS200. R2's routing table for 100.64.1.0/24 shows that the path was learned from EIGRP with an administrative distance of 170.

Example 8-18 *R1 and R2's BGP and Routing Table in Triggered State*

```
R1# show bgp ipv4 unicast | begin Network
     Network          Next Hop        Metric LocPrf Weight Path
 *>  10.1.12.0/24     0.0.0.0              0         32768 ?
 *>  100.64.1.0/24    172.16.1.2           0             0 100 ?
 r>  172.16.1.0/30    172.16.1.2           0             0 100 ?


R2# show bgp ipv4 unicast | begin Network
     Network          Next Hop        Metric LocPrf Weight Path
 *>  10.1.12.0/24     0.0.0.0              0         32768 ?
 *   100.64.1.0/24    172.16.2.2           0             0 200 ?
 *>                   10.1.12.1        61440         32768 ?
 r>  172.16.2.0/30    172.16.2.2           0             0 200 ?


R2# show ip route
Gateway of last resort is not set


      10.0.0.0/8 is variably subnetted, 2 subnets, 2 masks
C        10.1.12.0/24 is directly connected, GigabitEthernet0/2
      100.0.0.0/24 is subnetted, 1 subnets
D EX     100.64.1.0 [170/61440] via 10.1.12.1, 00:03:23, GigabitEthernet0/2
      172.16.0.0/16 is variably subnetted, 2 subnets, 2 masks
C        172.16.2.0/30 is directly connected, GigabitEthernet0/1
      192.168.2.0/32 is subnetted, 1 subnets
C        192.168.2.2 is directly connected, Loopback0
```

The problem occurs because the 100.64.1.0/24 network was learned first from R1. R1 then redistributed the route into EIGRP, which was then advertised to R2. R2 then redistributes the route into BGP with a weight of 32,768. After R2 establishes a BGP session with AS200, that path has a weight of zero (0). The redistributed path is always selected as the best path.

It is important to understand why the problem did not occur earlier in this section to understand the solution. Assume that R1 and R2 establish a BGP session with the service provider at the same time. R1 and R2 redistribute the 100.64.1.0/24 network into EIGRP at the same time. Both routers learn about the path from BGP and EIGRP.

The EBGP path has a lower AD of 20, whereas the EIGRP path has an AD of 170. The router installs the BGP path into the routing table because of the lower AD. EIGRP is unable to redistribute the 100.64.1.0/24 network into BGP because the EIGRP route is not installed in the routing table.

> **Note** The source routing protocol must be installed into the routing table when redistributing routes into a destination routing protocol. The rules of route redistribution can be complicated, but are explained thoroughly in the book *IP Routing on Cisco IOS, IOS XE, and IOS XR*, as listed at the end of this chapter.

After R2's BGP session fails, BGP removes the 100.64.1.0/24 network from the BGP table and the BGP entry for the routing table. The EIGRP entry is installed in the routing table and is then redistributed into BGP. After BGP reestablishes, the EBGP path is not selected as the best path because of the lower weight.

If BGP were able to select the EBGP path as the best path, the router would install the BGP path into the routing table and remove the EIGRP path. After this happens, the redistributed route is then removed from the BGP table.

One solution involves changing the weight for the EBGP peers on R1 and R2 to a value that is higher than 32,768 (the value set at redistribution). Another solution is to block routes that are redistributed into an IGP from being redistributed back into BGP (which is shown later in this chapter). This also prevents the site from becoming a transit site for those prefixes.

Example 8-19 demonstrates the configuration where R1 and R2 set the weight to 40,000 for all routes learned from AS100 and AS200, respectively.

Example 8-19 *BGP Configuration to Overcome Race Conditions*

```
R1
router bgp 300
 neighbor 172.16.1.2 remote-as 100
 !
 address-family ipv4
  redistribute eigrp 1
  neighbor 172.16.1.2 weight 40000
 exit-address-family
```

```
R2
router bgp 300
 neighbor 172.16.2.2 remote-as 200
 !
 address-family ipv4
  redistribute eigrp 1
  neighbor 172.16.2.2 activate
  neighbor 172.16.2.2 weight 40000
 exit-address-family
```

Example 8-20 verifies that BGP weight has been set properly on all routes learned from AS100 and AS200. This ensures that the race condition does not occur again for this scenario.

Example 8-20   *Verification of BGP Peer Weight*

```
R1# show bgp ipv4 unicast | begin Network
     Network          Next Hop          Metric LocPrf Weight Path
 *>  10.1.12.0/24     0.0.0.0                0         32768 ?
 *>  100.64.1.0/24    172.16.1.2             0         40000 100 ?
 r>  172.16.1.0/30    172.16.1.2             0         40000 100 ?


R2# show bgp ipv4 unicast | begin Network
     Network          Next Hop          Metric LocPrf Weight Path
 *>  10.1.12.0/24     0.0.0.0                0         32768 ?
 *>  100.64.1.0/24    172.16.2.2             0         40000 200 ?
 r>  172.16.2.0/30    172.16.2.2             0         40000 200 ?
```

Peering on Cross-Link

Establishing a BGP session between the BGP edge routers helps prevent race conditions and allows for all routers to identify the best path for every prefix. When peering between BGP edge routers, providing Internet connectivity to downstream devices (further in to the organization's network) can be achieved as follows:

- **Scenario 1:** Configure BGP on the downstream routers so that they can forward packets directly to the appropriate Internet edge router.

  Some of the devices may not be capable of running BGP or taking the full Internet routing table. In these scenarios, route summarization may be required, or use the technique in scenario 2.

- **Scenario 2:** Configure an IGP on the Internet edge routers and advertise a default route into the IGP protocol. When traffic reaches either Internet edge router, they can forward traffic out their direct connection or to the other Internet edge router for forwarding based on the BGP best path algorithm.

  In this technique, a link is required between the Internet edge routers to send traffic between each other. In a failure scenario, each edge router should forward traffic only out of its Internet circuit. Although this may create asynchronous routing (outbound traffic takes one path and inbound traffic takes a different path), this is the simplest method to implement.

Figure 8-13 demonstrates an Internet edge architecture where a dedicated link is installed between R1 and R2. If R1 identifies the path through AS200 as the best path, R1 should forward packets across the 10.1.12.0/24 network toward R2; and if R2 identifies the path through AS100 as the best path, R2 should forward traffic across the 10.1.12.0/24 network toward R1.

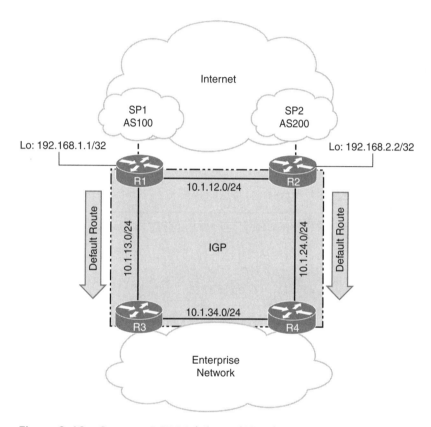

Figure 8-13 *Common BGP Multihomed Topology*

Expected Behavior

In the current design, R1 and R2 have enabled the IGP (OSPF) on all the internal LAN interfaces (including the 10.1.12.0/24 network and their loopback interfaces). The BGP session between them is established using their loopback addresses (192.168.1.1 for R1 and 192.168.2.2 for R2).

Example 8-21 displays the BGP table for R1 and R2. R1 and R2 prefer their own path for the 100.64.100.0/24 network. R1 and R2 also prefer the path through AS100 for the 8.8.0.0/16 network, which means that traffic received by R2 for this network must be forwarded across the 10.1.12.0/24 network to R1.

Example 8-21   *BGP Table from R1 and R2*

```
R1# show bgp ipv4 unicast | begin Network
     Network          Next Hop         Metric LocPrf Weight Path
 *>  8.8.0.0/16       100.64.101.254                      0 100 50 i
 *  i 100.64.100.0/24 192.168.2.2           0    100      0 200 50 i
 *>                   100.64.101.254                      0 100 50 i
 *  i 192.168.0.0/16  192.168.2.2           0    100      0 i
 *>                   0.0.0.0               0          32768 i


R2# show bgp ipv4 unicast | begin Network
     Network          Next Hop         Metric LocPrf Weight Path
 *>i 8.8.0.0/16       192.168.1.1           0    100      0 100 50 i
 *                    100.64.102.254                      0 200 50 2222 i
 *>  100.64.100.0/24  100.64.102.254                      0 200 50 i
 *  i                 192.168.1.1           0    100      0 100 50 i
 *  i 192.168.0.0/16  192.168.1.1           0    100      0 i
 *>                   0.0.0.0               0          32768 i
```

Note The 192.168.0.0/16 range is advertised by R1 and R2 for connectivity by devices on the Internet. This IP range is in RFC1918 space and should never be seen on the Internet; it is used only for demonstration purposes.

Internet connectivity is provided to the rest of the organization by a default route that R1 and R2 advertise into the IGP (OSPF). Example 8-22 displays the routing table for R3 and R4. Notice that none of the Internet routes (100.64.0.0/24 or 8.8.0.0/16) are present.

Example 8-22   *IGP Routing Table of R3 and R4*

```
R3# show ip route
! Output omitted for brevity
Gateway of last resort is 10.1.13.1 to network 0.0.0.0


O*E2  0.0.0.0/0 [110/1] via 10.1.13.1, 06:15:23, GigabitEthernet0/1
      10.0.0.0/8 is variably subnetted, 7 subnets, 3 masks
O        10.1.12.0/24 [110/2] via 10.1.13.1, 06:16:45, GigabitEthernet0/1
C        10.1.13.0/24 is directly connected, GigabitEthernet0/1
O        10.1.24.0/24 [110/2] via 10.1.34.4, 06:16:16, GigabitEthernet0/2
C        10.1.34.0/24 is directly connected, GigabitEthernet0/2
O        192.168.1.1 [110/2] via 10.1.13.1, 06:16:45, GigabitEthernet0/1
O        192.168.2.2 [110/3] via 10.1.34.4, 06:15:46, GigabitEthernet0/2
                    [110/3] via 10.1.13.1, 06:16:45, GigabitEthernet0/1
```

```
C        192.168.3.3 is directly connected, Loopback0
O        192.168.4.4 [110/2] via 10.1.34.4, 06:16:16, GigabitEthernet0/2
```

```
R4# show ip route
! Output omitted for brevity
Gateway of last resort is 10.1.24.2 to network 0.0.0.0

O*E2  0.0.0.0/0 [110/1] via 10.1.24.2, 06:13:50, GigabitEthernet0/1
         10.0.0.0/8 is variably subnetted, 7 subnets, 3 masks
O        10.1.12.0/24 [110/2] via 10.1.24.2, 06:14:22, GigabitEthernet0/1
O        10.1.13.0/24 [110/2] via 10.1.34.3, 06:14:52, GigabitEthernet0/2
C        10.1.24.0/24 is directly connected, GigabitEthernet0/1
C        10.1.34.0/24 is directly connected, GigabitEthernet0/2
O        192.168.1.1 [110/3] via 10.1.34.3, 06:14:52, GigabitEthernet0/2
                     [110/3] via 10.1.24.2, 06:14:22, GigabitEthernet0/1
O        192.168.2.2 [110/2] via 10.1.24.2, 06:14:22, GigabitEthernet0/1
O        192.168.3.3 [110/2] via 10.1.34.3, 06:14:52, GigabitEthernet0/2
C        192.168.4.4 is directly connected, Loopback0
```

Example 8-23 provides verification that connectivity works properly between the hosts to the 8.8.8.8 host, and that R2 is forwarding traffic received by R4 across the 10.1.12.0/30 link to R1.

Example 8-23 *Connectivity Test*

```
R3# ping 8.8.8.8 source loopback 0
Sending 5, 100-byte ICMP Echos to 8.8.8.8, timeout is 2 seconds:
Packet sent with a source address of 192.168.3.3
!!!!!
Success rate is 100 percent (5/5), round-trip min/avg/max = 3/5/7 ms
```

```
R3# traceroute 8.8.8.8 source Loopback 0
Tracing the route to 8.8.8.8
  1 10.1.13.1 3 msec 3 msec 3 msec
  2 100.64.101.254 4 msec 4 msec 4 msec
  3 100.64.1.1 5 msec *  13 msec
```

```
R4# ping 8.8.8.8 source loopback 0
Sending 5, 100-byte ICMP Echos to 8.8.8.8, timeout is 2 seconds:
```

```
Packet sent with a source address of 192.168.4.4
!!!!!
Success rate is 100 percent (5/5), round-trip min/avg/max = 3/5/7 ms
```

```
R4# traceroute 8.8.8.8 source Loopback 0
Tracing the route to 8.8.8.8
  1 10.1.24.2 5 msec 4 msec 3 msec
  2 10.1.12.1 5 msec 6 msec 9 msec
  3 100.64.101.254 7 msec 4 msec 3 msec
  4 100.64.1.1 7 msec *   9 msec
```

Unexpected Behavior

In this design, there are two possible causes for an unexpected behavior:

- Circuit failure between the 10.1.12.0/30 circuit/network link.

- LAN interfaces have a higher speed/bandwidth than the peer link between the Internet edge routers.

Assume that the LAN interfaces on the 10.1.13.0/24, 10.1.34.0/24, and 10.1.24.0/24 network have all been upgraded from 1 Gb interfaces to 10 Gb interfaces. Users attached to R4 have reported sporadic loss of network connectivity to the Internet, whereas users attached to R3 are operating properly. Example 8-24 demonstrates the connectivity tests performed by R3 and R4 and demonstrates the following:

- R3 and R4 can connect to the 100.64.100.0/24 without issues.

- R3 can connect to the 8.8.0.0/16 without issues.

- R4 cannot connect to the 8.8.0.0/16.

Example 8-24 *Verification of Connectivity After Link Failure*

```
R3# ping 100.64.100.100 source Loopback 0
Sending 5, 100-byte ICMP Echos to 100.64.100.100, timeout is 2 seconds:
Packet sent with a source address of 192.168.3.3
!!!!!
Success rate is 100 percent (5/5), round-trip min/avg/max = 6/7/9 ms

R3# ping 8.8.8.8 source loopback 0
Sending 5, 100-byte ICMP Echos to 8.8.8.8, timeout is 2 seconds:
Packet sent with a source address of 192.168.3.3
!!!!!
Success rate is 100 percent (5/5), round-trip min/avg/max = 3/5/7 ms
```

```
R4# ping 100.64.100.100 source Loopback 0
Sending 5, 100-byte ICMP Echos to 100.64.100.100, timeout is 2 seconds:
```

```
Packet sent with a source address of 192.168.4.4
!!!!!
Success rate is 100 percent (5/5), round-trip min/avg/max = 6/8/12 ms


R4# ping 8.8.8.8 source Loopback 0
Sending 5, 100-byte ICMP Echos to 8.8.8.8, timeout is 2 seconds:
Packet sent with a source address of 192.168.4.4
.....
Success rate is 0 percent (0/5)
```

The next step is to examine the BGP tables on R1 and R2, which look the same as in
Example 8-21. If possible, a traceroute is performed by R4 to the failing host (8.8.8.8) to
see where the packet is being dropped. Example 8-25 displays the traceroute from R4 to
the 8.8.8.8 host.

Notice that the packet is forwarded by R2 toward R4, which sends the packet back to R2.
The link failure has caused a routing loop between R2 and R4 for networks that should
be sent to the Internet by R1. Packets never reach their final destination when in a routing
loop. They are forwarded hop by hop while the packet TTL decrements until it is zero
and is discarded.

Example 8-25 *Identification of Where Packet Is Dropped in Network*

```
R3# traceroute 8.8.8.8 source Loopback 0
Tracing the route to 8.8.8.8
VRF info: (vrf in name/id, vrf out name/id)
  1 10.1.13.1 5 msec 3 msec 3 msec
  2 100.64.101.254 5 msec 5 msec 7 msec
  3 100.64.1.1 7 msec *  6 msec
```

```
R4# traceroute 8.8.8.8 source Loopback 0
Tracing the route to 8.8.8.8
VRF info: (vrf in name/id, vrf out name/id)
  1 10.1.24.2 3 msec 3 msec 3 msec
  2 10.1.24.4 1 msec 2 msec 1 msec
  3 10.1.24.2 4 msec 5 msec 4 msec
  4 10.1.24.4 3 msec 3 msec 6 msec
  5 10.1.24.2 4 msec 4 msec 5 msec
  6 10.1.24.4 4 msec 4 msec 3 msec
  7 10.1.24.2 5 msec 5 msec 6 msec
  8 10.1.24.4 5 msec 6 msec 4 msec
```

```
 9 10.1.24.2 8 msec 10 msec 7 msec
10 10.1.24.4 5 msec 6 msec 7 msec
11 10.1.24.2 8 msec 8 msec 7 msec
12 10.1.24.4 6 msec 6 msec 7 msec
13 10.1.24.2 7 msec 12 msec 9 msec
14 10.1.24.4 7 msec 8 msec 10 msec
15 10.1.24.2 11 msec 8 msec 9 msec
16 10.1.24.4 8 msec 8 msec 10 msec
17 10.1.24.2 11 msec 11 msec 12 msec
18 10.1.24.4 10 msec 11 msec 11 msec
19 10.1.24.2 13 msec 12 msec 11 msec
20 10.1.24.4 13 msec 9 msec 9 msec
21 10.1.24.2 13 msec 13 msec 13 msec
22 10.1.24.4 13 msec 19 msec 13 msec
23 10.1.24.2 13 msec 14 msec 12 msec
24 10.1.24.4 14 msec 12 msec 12 msec
25 10.1.24.2 12 msec 16 msec 12 msec
26 10.1.24.4 13 msec 13 msec 13 msec
27 10.1.24.2 14 msec 14 msec 15 msec
28 10.1.24.4 15 msec 17 msec 17 msec
29 10.1.24.2 18 msec 19 msec 19 msec
30 10.1.24.4 16 msec 13 msec 10 msec
```

The next step is to examine the 8.8.0.0/16 network prefix on R2 to identify what might be causing the problem. Example 8-26 displays the explicit BGP path where R2 shows the path via R1 as the best path with a next-hop IP address of 192.168.1.1.

Example 8-26   *Examination of the 8.8.0.0/16 Prefix on R2*

```
R2# show bgp ipv4 unicast 8.8.0.0
BGP routing table entry for 8.8.0.0/16, version 17
Paths: (2 available, best #1, table default)
  Advertised to update-groups:
     1
  Refresh Epoch 2
  100 50
    192.168.1.1 (metric 4) from 192.168.1.1 (192.168.1.1)
      Origin IGP, metric 0, localpref 100, valid, internal, best
      rx pathid: 0, tx pathid: 0x0
  Refresh Epoch 2
  200 50 2222
    100.64.102.254 from 100.64.102.254 (100.64.102.254)
      Origin IGP, localpref 100, valid, external
      rx pathid: 0, tx pathid: 0
```

The next-hop for BGP has been confirmed as R1's loopback interface. Because loopback interfaces are virtual and always up, the outbound interface must be identified for R1 (192.168.1.1). Example 8-27 displays R2's RIB for the next-hop IP address 192.168.1.1. Notice that the outbound interface is Te0/3 with a next-hop of R4 (10.1.24.4) instead of R1 (10.1.12.1).

Example 8-27 *Examination of Next-Hop Resolution for R1*

```
R2# show ip route 192.168.1.1
Routing entry for 192.168.1.1/32
  Known via "ospf 1", distance 110, metric 4, type intra area
  Last update from 10.1.24.4 on TenGigabitEthernet0/3, 00:06:23 ago
  Routing Descriptor Blocks:
  * 10.1.24.4, from 192.168.1.1, 00:06:23 ago, via TenGigabitEthernet0/3
      Route metric is 4, traffic share count is 1
```

The problem is that the path via the 10 Gb interfaces (toward R4) has more hops but is a lower cost of 4, whereas the path via the 10.1.12.0/24 link (1 Gb interface) has only one hop but has a forwarding cost of 10.

Any packet that R2 needs to forward to R1 is sent on the 10.1.24.0/24 link back to R4. R4 does not have visibility to the Internet routing table and forwards the packet back to R2. The packet stays in a loop until the TTL is decremented to zero and the packet is dropped.

Secondary Verification Methods of a Routing Loop

At times, the destination network may not be known, and the end user cannot report it to the network team. A routing loop can be deducted by adding an internal access control list (ACL) that matches TTL. Placing the ACL on a network interface that faces toward the organization's LAN displays counts of TTL.

It is important to remember that the TTL of a traceroute starts at 1 and increments to 30 after a response is received on a hop-by-hop basis by devices in the path. Most normal IP traffic starts with a TTL of 255. To see the loop, the ACL should start with a value of 255 and decrement one by one or in ranges to zero.

An access control entry (ACE) entry in the ACL can include the **log** keyword so that the destination network can be identified and then checked in the BGP table to see whether traffic is trying to cross to the other Internet edge router. Be sure to account for normal traffic flow, so logging may start at a TTL value of 240 or lower. Be aware that packets that match the ACE entry with the **log** keyword are punted to the CPU for processing.

Example 8-28 demonstrates the configuration of the ACL and placement on R2's interface facing toward R4.

Example 8-28 *ACL to Check TTL of Packets*

```
R2# configuration t
Enter configuration commands, one per line. End with CNTL/Z.
R2(config)# ip access-list extended TTL
R2(config-ext-nacl)# permit ip any any ttl eq 255
R2(config-ext-nacl)# permit ip any any ttl eq 254
! Keep continue the number of TTL without the log keyword until after the
! expected number of TTL hops should not be
! reached by normal traffic.
R2(config-ext-nacl)# permit ip any any ttl eq 240 log
! Continued on the number until the TTL reaches 0
R2(config-ext-nacl)# permit ip any any ttl eq 4 log
R2(config-ext-nacl)# permit ip any any ttl eq 3 log
R2(config-ext-nacl)# permit ip any any ttl eq 2 log
R2(config-ext-nacl)# permit ip any any ttl eq 1 log
R2(config-ext-nacl)# permit ip any any ttl eq 0 log
R2(config-ext-nacl)# int Te0/3
R2(config-if)# ip access-group TTL out
```

Normally this next step is not required, because the traffic flow triggers the ACL counters on the router. However, traffic is going to be simulated on R4 toward a network in Example 8-29. Notice that even though one packet was transmitted, there are multiple matches in increments of two. When the packet reaches the ACE entry for a TTL of 240, the log action triggers the packet with a destination of 8.8.8.8. This information can then be used to research the BGP table for that network.

Example 8-29 *Secondary Verification Method*

```
R4# ping 8.8.8.8 source Loopback 0 repeat 1
Type escape sequence to abort.
Sending 5, 100-byte ICMP Echos to 8.8.8.8, timeout is 2 seconds:
Packet sent with a source address of 192.168.4.4
.....
Success rate is 0 percent (0/5)
18:25:53.767: %SEC-6-IPACCESSLOGDP: list TTL permitted icmp 192.168.4.4 -> 8.8.8.8
(0/0), 1 packets


R2(config)# do show ip access-list TTL
! Output omitted for brevity
Extended IP access list TTL
    10 permit ip any any ttl eq 255 log
    20 permit ip any any ttl eq 254 (1 match)
```

```
30 permit ip any any ttl eq 253
40 permit ip any any ttl eq 252 (matches)
50 permit ip any any ttl eq 251
60 permit ip any any ttl eq 250 (1 match)
.....
160 permit ip any any ttl eq 240 log (1 match)
170 permit ip any any ttl eq 239 log
180 permit ip any any ttl eq 238 log (1 match)
190 permit ip any any ttl eq 237 log
200 permit ip any any ttl eq 236 log (1 match)
210 permit ip any any ttl eq 235 log
220 permit ip any any ttl eq 234 log (1 match)
```

Note The ACL should probably include an early ACE entry for routing protocols or network management so that only normal traffic is captured in the counters.

Design Enhancements

Now that the problem has been identified, let's explore some of the better design solutions to prevent this from happening.

- Do not peer Internet edge BGP sessions via Loopback interfaces. If this is a requirement, do not advertise the loopback interface for peering into the IGP protocol. Use a fully specified static route (include outbound interface and IP address of the next-hop). This prevents issues with recursive lookups.

- Peer the Internet edge routers with the IP address of the peering link. Do not advertise this network into the IGP.

- Create a generic routing encapsulation (GRE) tunnel between the two Internet edge routers. It could use the loopback 0 interface as the encapsulating/decapsulating interface. A new unique network (172.16.12.0/24) is added to the GRE tunnel that is not added to the IGP.

  The BGP peering is established between the devices using the new GRE network (172.16.12.0/24). Internet traffic that must be forwarded from the other Internet edge router can traverse across non-BGP devices because the packets are encapsulated by the GRE tunnel. The outermost destination IP in the header of the GRE packet exists in the IGP. Be aware of the additional overhead of the GRE packets that cross the LAN network.

Full Mesh with IBGP

Figure 8-14 displays four routers and their routing table in AS200. All four routers connect only with the router directly attached to it, and use the **next-hop-self** feature to
modify the next-hop IP address of routes that are exchanged between routers. R1 and R2
are the Internet edge BGP routers, whereas R3 and R4 are interior routers.

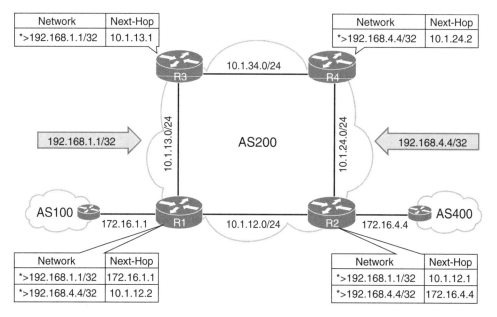

Figure 8-14 *Common BGP Multihomed Topology*

The following BGP peering exists in this topology:

- R1 peers with AS100, R3, and R2. R1 uses the **next-hop-self** feature with R2 and R3.

- R2 peers with AS400, R1, and R4. R2 uses the **next-hop-self** feature with R1 and R4.

- R3 peers with R1 and R4.

- R4 peers with R2 and R3.

The users attached to R3 claim that they can reach AS100 but cannot reach anything connected to AS400. The users attached to R4 claim that they can reach AS400 but cannot
reach AS100.

A junior network engineer verifies that all the BGP sessions are established, and that
some routes are being exchanged, but cannot identify why R3 and R4 do not have complete BGP tables, like R1 and R2 have.

The reason is that a router does not advertise IBGP routes to a different IBGP peer as part
of a loop prevention mechanism. The solution to this scenario is to make R3 and R4 route
reflectors, or to establish an IBGP full mesh in this topology.

Problems with Redistributing BGP into an IGP

Redistributing BGP into the IGP—EIGRP, OSPF, intermediate-system to intermediate-system (IS-IS)—is not recommended on routers that contain the full Internet routing table, because IGPs are not designed to carry that many network prefixes. Depending on the platform, they start to max out around 20,000 routes or fewer. However, BGP is used to exchange routes between the SP's routers for MPLS VPNs, which contain a much smaller number of routes.

Figure 8-15 displays two common scenarios for how routes are exchanged between the corporate network and the SP's MPLS L3VPN network. R1 and R2 are acting CE devices and mutually redistribute BGP between OSPF.

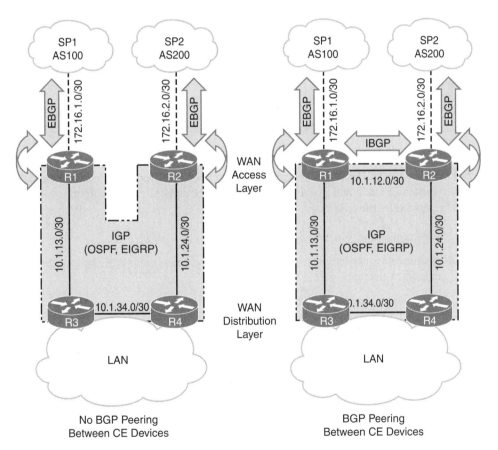

Figure 8-15 *Options for Exchanging Routes Between LAN and WAN*

Redistributing between different routing protocols causes a loss of path information, preventing a complete topology of the routers between the source and destination networks. This can cause *route feedback*, which is a redistributed route that is redistributed back into the original routing domain at a different point in the network topology.

Figure 8-16 illustrates that two routing domains exist (domain A and domain B), and R2 and R4 are mutually redistributing between the two domains. The 10.1.1.0/24 route from domain A is redistributed into domain B by R2 and eventually reaches R4. R4 then redistributes the 10.1.1.0/24 network back into domain A as route feedback. Incomplete routing topologies and route feedback introduce the possibility for suboptimal routing or routing loops in a topology.

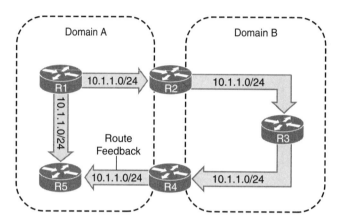

Figure 8-16 *Route Feedback*

In both scenarios of Figure 8-15, there is a chance of a routing loops between the mutual redistribution of OSPF and BGP because of the loss of path information. Routing loops can be avoided by the following:

■ Blocking the route feedback by using distribute-lists.

■ Conditional redistribution to prevent route feedback based on route tags or explicit prefix identification.

■ Modification of administrative distance (AD).

■ Summarizing routes in the destination routing domain.

The most common method is to use route tags because of the dynamic nature of it. The logic consists of the following:

■ OSPF routes that are redistributed to BGP and have a specific BGP community set to indicate the route was redistributed (i.e. 1:1). BGP checks routes for the redistribution community (1:1) during redistribution and prevent these routes from being advertised back in to OSPF.

■ BGP sets a tag in OSPF for all routes that are redistributed to indicate that route was redistributed (1). OSPF checks routes for the redistribution tag (1) during redistribution and prevents these routes from being inserted into BGP.

This logic is commonly referred to as the *Tag and Block Redistribution.*

Example 8-30 displays the mutual redistribution configuration for R1 and R2 of Figure 8-15. The redistribution of OSPF into BGP uses the optional commands to match external OSPF networks, as explained earlier in Chapter 4, "Troubleshooting Route Advertisement and BGP Policies." Notice how routes injected into BGP have the BGP community set, and routes injected into OSPF have a route tag set. Additional logic could be added to set different metrics during redistribution to prefer one CE over another depending on the overall network design.

Example 8-30 *Tag and Block Configuration Between OSPF and BGP*

```
R1 and R2
router ospf 1
 redistribute bgp 300 subnets route-map REDIST-BGP-TO-OSPF
!
router bgp 300
 address-family ipv4
  redistribute ospf 1 match internal external 1 external 2 route-map REDIST-OSPF-TO-
  BGP
!
route-map REDIST-OSPF-TO-BGP deny 10
 description Deny routes originally redistributed earlier from BGP
 match tag 1
route-map REDIST-OSPF-TO-BGP permit 20
 description Set BGP community to tag routes sourced from OSPF
 set community 1:1
!
route-map REDIST-BGP-TO-OSPF deny 10
 description Deny routes originally redistributed earlier from OSPF
 match community 1
route-map REDIST-BGP-TO-OSPF permit 20
 description Set OSPF Tag for routes sourced from BGP
 set tag 1
 set metric-type type-1
!
ip community-list 1 permit 1:1
```

R3's loopback has been redistributed from OSPF into BGP on R1. Examining the 192.168.3.3 network prefix on R1's BGP table verifies that the BGP community was set properly to 1:1 as shown in Example 8-31.

Example 8-31   *Verification of BGP Community Being Set*

```
R1# show bgp ipv4 unicast 192.168.3.3
BGP routing table entry for 192.168.3.3/32, version 53
Paths: (1 available, best #1, table default)
  Advertised to update-groups:
     2
  Refresh Epoch 1
  Local
    10.1.13.3 from 0.0.0.0 (192.168.1.1)
      Origin incomplete, metric 2, localpref 100, weight 32768, valid, sourced, best
      Community: 1:1
      rx pathid: 0, tx pathid: 0x0
```

The next step is to verify that a BGP network was redistributed into OSPF. The 172.31.2.0/24 network was specifically selected on R1 because the route was learned via R2's BGP session and then redistributed into OSPF. The route tag should not be present in R1's BGP table because it should have been blocked because of its tag. In addition, R1 and R2 do not have an IBGP session, so the route could not have been exchanged via BGP.

Example 8-32 verifies that the route tag is properly set in OSPF and that the prefix is not in R1's BGP table.

Example 8-32   *Verification of Route Tag Being Set and Blocked During Redistribution*

```
R1# show ip route 172.31.2.0
Routing entry for 172.31.2.0/24
  Known via "ospf 1", distance 110, metric 4
  Tag 1, type extern 1
  Redistributing via bgp 300
  Advertised by bgp 300 match internal external 1 & 2 route-map REDIST-OSPF-TO-BGP
  Last update from 10.1.13.3 on GigabitEthernet0/3, 00:06:50 ago
  Routing Descriptor Blocks:
  * 10.1.13.3, from 100.64.102.1, 00:06:50 ago, via GigabitEthernet0/3
      Route metric is 4, traffic share count is 1
      Route tag 1

R1# show bgp ipv4 unicast 172.31.2.0/24
% Network not in table
```

Note   Some network engineers like to set the tag and community to a specific value to quickly locate the router that performed the redistribution. These techniques can work quite well, but add to the configuration and could lead to problems later because of the complexity involved with keeping track of multiple route tags/BGP communities.

Summary

This chapter focused on the routing and troubleshooting process when redundancy is added through BGP multihoming. BGP multipath functionality enhances the capability of load balancing of network traffic between routers. However, identifying the BGP best path has more steps than the traditional IGP protocol. Because BGP is a vector-based routing protocol, the best path can influence the paths contained in other BGP routers in the organization.

Troubleshooting suboptimal routes and routing loops requires a solid understanding of how a router selects the outbound interface for a packet. A router uses the following logic:

■ Longest matching prefix.

■ Best path algorithm for the routing protocol.

■ Administrative distance is checked when a route is already installed in the RIB by another routing protocol. The protocol with the lower AD is deemed more trustworthy and will install into the RIB.

Network engineers can uses this logic to influence traffic into and out of their organization, as shown in Table 8-1.

Table 8-1 *Common Techniques to Influence BGP Path Selection*

Logical Order	Description	Technique	Single or Multiple Routers	Influences Which Traffic
1st	Longest Match	Advertise summary routes out of both BGP edge routers, single explicit route out of only one BGP Edge router.	Multiple	Inbound
2nd	Weight	Set a higher path weight of the preferred egress Edge router.	Single	Outbound
3rd	Local Preference	Set a higher local preference of the preferred egress Edge router.	Multiple	Outbound
4th	AIGP	Set costing of path prefixes to match IGP cost link.	Multiple	Outbound
5th	AS-Path	Prepending additional AS-Path to prefix makes that router less preferred.	Multiple	Inbound
6th	MED	Set a lower MED value on preferred routers.	Multiple	Inbound

In addition to path selection, failure to accommodate different scenarios in multihomed BGP topologies can result in suboptimal routing, saturated links, or packet loss. Transit routing should be eliminated on Internet-based connections and restricted to specific sites (that is, headquarters) for the WAN. The design will change between edge BGP routers depending on the capabilities of the surrounding routers. If surrounding routers support BGP, the peerings can be dynamic and use loopback interfaces. If they cannot, the BGP peering should be based off of the peering link (which should not be advertised into the IGP).

References

RFC 4451, *BGP MULTI_EXIST_DISC (MED) Considerations*, D. McPherson, V. Gill, http://www.ietf.org/rfc/rfc4451.txt, March 2006.

Informational RFC, *The Accumulated IGP Metric Attribute for BGP*, P. Mohapatra et al., http://tools.ietf.org/html/draft-ietf-idr-aigp-18, April 2014.

Informational RFC, *Advertisement of Multiple Paths in BGP*, D. Walton et al., http://tools.ietf.org/html/draft-ietf-idr-add-paths-09, October 2013.

Edgeworth, Brad, Foss, Aaron, Garza Rios, Ramiro. *IP Routing on Cisco IOS, IOS XE and IOS XR*. Indianapolis: Cisco Press, 2014. Print.

Cisco. Cisco IOS Software Configuration Guides. http://www.cisco.com.

Cisco. Cisco IOS XR Software Configuration Guides. http://www.cisco.com.

## Chapter 9

Securing BGP

The following topics are covered in this chapter:

- Need for securing Border Gateway Protocol (BGP)
- Securing BGP Sessions
- Securing Inter-Domain Routing
- BGP Remote Triggered Black Hole (RTBH)
- BGP Flowspec

The Need for Securing BGP

BGP is one protocol that literally makes the Internet work. Because of its criticality and importance in the Internet, BGP has been the target protocol for most hackers and attackers around the world. The main focus of any attacker is to find a vulnerability in a system, in this case BGP, and then exploit it. The attackers know very well that if they are able to find a loophole in BGP, they can cause a major instability in the Internet. This is the primary reason why it is important to secure BGP.

Before thinking of securing BGP, there are few primary areas where the focus should be concentrated:

- **Authentication:** It is important to authenticate the identity of BGP neighbors in the same or two different ASs. Only the authenticated BGP neighbors should be allowed to establish a BGP session and share routing information with each other.

- **Integrity:** It should be ensured that the BGP messages were not illegally modified en route.

- **Availability:** It should be ensured that the BGP speaker is protected from any kind of Denial-of-Service (DoS) or Distributed Denial-of-Service (DDoS) attacks.

- **Prefix origination validation:** A mechanism should be implemented to validate between invalid and legitimate routes for a BGP destination.

- **AS path verification:** Ensure that an AS_PATH is not falsified (modified with a wrong AS number or deleted) by an illegal entity. This can result in traffic black holes for the destination prefix as AS_PATH is used by the route selection process.

Unless all the preceding areas are covered, BGP cannot be said to be securely implemented. RFC 4272, *BGP Security Vulnerabilities Analysis*, presents various weak areas in BGP that every enterprise or service provider should consider when implementing BGP. Security was not made an integral part of BGP protocol when it was initially developed. Though various security enhancements were made over the years, BGP is affected with the same vulnerabilities that Transmission Control Protocol (TCP) is.

BGP provides no confidentiality, and it provides only limited integrity and authentication services. Furthermore, BGP messages can be replayed; that is, if an attacker intercepts a BGP UPDATE message that adds a route, the hacker can resend that message after the route has been withdrawn and cause an inconsistent and invalid route to be present in the routing information base (RIB).

A security loophole in BGP can either be due to a misconfiguration or a faulty or malicious source. Some of the vulnerabilities include the following:

- BGP session hijacking

- Man-in-the-Middle (MITM) attacks

- DoS and DDoS attacks

- Disabling an autonomous system (AS)

- Bogus routing information

- Domain Name Service (DNS) attacks

This chapter focuses on various techniques that can be implemented to overcome some of the vulnerabilities that BGP possesses.

Securing BGP Sessions

The first step in implementing security for BGP is by securing a BGP session itself. BGP is a stateful transport layer protocol and thus provides some level of security, as TCP does, but this property is also BGP's weakness. Some methods can be used to implement secured BGP sessions.

Note   Some of the features are specific to external BGP (EBGP) sessions, but BGP sessions should be secured both for internal BGP (IBGP) as well as EBGP sessions.

Explicitly Configured Peers

A BGP session requires both BGP speakers to be explicitly configured for forming a BGP session. The BGP session is not established if only one router is configured for BGP, whereas the other side is not. But even a TCP session can be opened and established with single-sided configuration especially when peering is formed between physical links. Example 9-1 illustrates the opening of TCP port 179 via a Telnet command. In this example, router R1 is configured with BGP configuration to form a peering on the physical interface, whereas the other side, router Rn, does not have BGP configuration. Performing a Telnet command to the peer from any host (connected router in this case) can still open the TCP port 179 although the BGP connection is not established.

Example 9-1   *Establishing a TCP Connection on Port 179*

```
Rn# telnet 10.1.110.1 179
Trying 10.1.110.1, 179 ... Open
ˇˇˇˇ9d¥¿®ÃFAdˇˇˇˇ
[Connection to 10.1.110.1 closed by foreign host]


R1# show tcp brief
TCB        Local Address            Foreign Address          (state)
0F21BA98   10.1.110.1.179           10.1.110.10.44106        ESTAB
```

An attacker can try to compromise the network with this open TCP port 179. To overcome this security loophole, a best practice is to form a neighbor relationship over a loopback interface. When forming a neighborship with a loopback address, either use a static route or an IGP to share the loopback information with the peer. It is more difficult to figure out a peering loopback IP address than a physical interface IP address, because the physical interface IP can still be discovered using an IP scanner software or even traceroute by the attacker.

Coming back to the open TCP port, threats against a long-lived TCP session are prone to session hijacking. This is done by predicting the TCP sequence number. To overcome this problem, strong sequence number randomization should be implemented in BGP. Cisco Adaptive Security Appliance (ASA) and Private Internet Exchange (PIX) firewalls support strong sequence number randomization and can be placed between the EBGP peers. But the sequence number randomization can cause the BGP session not to come up when using MD5 authentication, which is discussed in the next section.

IPv6 BGP Peering Using Link-Local Address

IPv6 BGP peers are configured the same way as IPv4 peers. With IPv6, there are two kinds of IPv6 addresses on an interface: global IPv6 address and link-local address. The global IPv6 addresses are globally unique addresses that are manually assigned to an interface. Link-local addresses, on the other hand, are automatically configured IPv6 addresses with the prefix FE80::/10 (binary—1111 1110 10) and the interface identifier in the modified EUI-64 format. Manually configure link-local IPv6 addresses by using the **ipv6 address** *v6-address* **link-local** command on Cisco IOS and IOS XR or the command **ipv6 link-local** *v6-address* on NX-OS.

> **Note**   To identify an IPv6 link-local address of an interface, use the command **show ipv6 interface** *interface-name*.

Generally, IPv6 BGP peering is configured on global IPv6 unicast addresses, but it can also be configured on IPv6 link-local addresses. The benefit of using link-local addresses for BGP peering is that an attacker could neither form a BGP peering on the link-local addresses nor communicate with either peer. Example 9-2 illustrates the IPv6 BGP peering configuration using a link-local address between the two routers. When using a link-local address for peering on Cisco IOS, the command to configure the BGP neighbor is **neighbor** *link-local-address%Interface-name* **remote-as** *asn*. Also, it is very important to configure the **update-source** command for link-local–based IPv6 BGP peering because it is possible that multiple interfaces may share the same link-local address. If the link local addresses are manually configured and are unique, it is not required to use the **update-source** command option.

Example 9-2   *Establishing BGP Peering on Link-Local Address*

```
IOS
interface GigabitEthernet0/1
 ip address 10.1.110.1 255.255.255.0
 ipv6 address 2001:10:1:110::1/64
 ipv6 address FE80::1 link-local
!
router bgp 100
 bgp router-id 192.168.1.1
 neighbor FE80::2%GigabitEthernet0/1 remote-as 200
!
 address-family ipv6
  neighbor FE80::2%GigabitEthernet0/1 activate
  neighbor FE80::2%GigabitEthernet0/1 route-map SET_NH out
!
route-map SET_NH permit 10
 set ipv6 next-hop 2001:10:1:110::1
```

```
IOS XR
interface GigabitEthernet0/0/0/1
 ipv4 address 10.1.110.1 255.255.255.0
 ipv6 address 2001:10:1:110::1/64
 ipv6 address FE80::1 link-local
!
router bgp 100
 bgp router-id 192.168.1.1
 address-family ipv6 unicast
!
```

```
neighbor fe80::2
 remote-as 200
 update-source gigabitethernet0/0/0/1
address-family ipv6 unicast
 route-policy PASS-ALL in
 route-policy PASS-ALL out
!
route-policy PASS-ALL
 pass
end-policy
```

```
NX-OS
interface Ethernet2/1
 ip address 10.1.110.1 255.255.255.0
 ipv6 address 2001:10:1:110::1/64
 ipv6 link-local FE80::1
!
router bgp 100
 router-id 192.168.1.1
 neighbor FE80::2
 remote-as 200
  address-family ipv6
   route-map SET_NH out
!
route-map SET_NH permit 10
 set ipv6 next-hop 2001:10:1:110::1
```

Notice that in Example 9-2, an outbound route-map is configured to set the next-hop value to the global IPv6 unicast address. The reason for doing this is that the BGP next-hop attribute, MP_REACH_NLRI, might not always contain a global IPv6 unicast address and a link-local address, especially when the peering addresses are not on a common subnet. The link-local addresses are local to a subnet and thus can be used across multiple interfaces. Thus there needs to be a global IPv6 address that can be used for the BGP next-hop verification process.

Using the link-local peering method also has its disadvantages. First, if a hardware problem is noticed and requires replacement, the new hardware has a different MAC address. This in turn changes the link-local address on the interface because the address is partially based on the MAC address of the interface. This can easily be fixed by manually assigning the link-local address as shown in Example 9-2. Second, using a link-local address is a complex method. There are plenty of global IPv6 unicast addresses that can be used, and by implementing various methods, such as Message Digest 5 (MD5) authentication and time-to-live (TTL) security, the same level of security can be achieved for global addresses as compared to link-local addresses. The benefit of using global

IPv6 addresses over link-local addresses is that you do not have to worry about the next-hop attribute. The other big challenge faced with link-local addresses is typo errors when configuring the BGP neighbors, which is very common because of the complex addressing scheme of the link-local addresses.

BGP Session Authentication

Like any other routing protocol, BGP can be configured for authentication. It is recommended to have authentication configured, at least for the EBGP peers. Because BGP forms point-to-point TCP connections to exchange information, although secure, it is still possible to hijack an existing TCP connection or can cause TCP resets between two BGP peers and may inject bad routes.

With BGP authentication, this type of attack is considerably more difficult. The reason is that an attacker not only must get the TCP sequence numbers right but must also insert the correct encrypted authentication key.

BGP supports the Message Digest 5 (MD5) hash-based authentication mechanism defined in RFC 2385. The RFC defines TCP option 19, which is an extension to enhance security for BGP using MD5 authentication. Using MD5, TCP creates an MD5 digest hash for each packet that is sent as part of a BGP session.

The TCP payload that includes the BGP route advertisements and the shared secret key is used to generate the MD5 hash by the sending router. The created MD5 hash is then stored in TCP option 19. The receiving BGP speaker neighbor uses the same algorithm and shared secret key to regenerate and compute its own version of the MD5 hash. The receiving BGP speaker neighbor compares its own version with the one it received; if the received and computed MD5 hash values are not identical, the packet is discarded. Otherwise, the packet is accepted and processed by BGP.

Example 9-3 illustrates enabling of MD5 authentication on all three Cisco operating systems. In this example, the peers are configured with an unencrypted password.

Example 9-3 *Configuring MD5 Authentication*

```
IOS
R1(config)# router bgp 100
R1(config-router)# neighbor 10.1.110.10 password cisco


IOS XR
RP/0/0/CPU0:R2(config)# router bgp 100
RP/0/0/CPU0:R2(config-bgp)# neighbor 10.1.102.10
RP/0/0/CPU0:R2(config-bgp-nbr)# password cisco
RP/0/0/CPU0:R2(config-bgp-nbr)# commit


NX-OS
R3(config)# router bgp 100
R3(config-router)# neighbor 10.1.103.10
R3(config-router-neighbor)# password cisco
```

> **Note**   There are two common options when specifying passwords in all three operating systems. The value 0 indicates an unencrypted clear text password, and value 7 indicates Cisco proprietary type 7 encrypted passwords.

Clear text or unencrypted passwords are encrypted in the configuration on Cisco IOS using the command **service password-encryption**. This command automatically encrypts the password in the configuration. IOS XR does the encryption of the passwords by default. NX-OS also encrypts the password to type 3 by default.

Although Cisco type 7 passwords are easy to break, all three operating systems now support strong Advanced Encryption Standard (AES) to encrypt the passwords in the configuration. Refer to the Cisco configuration guide for respective operating systems for enabling AES password encryption.

> **Note**   Regardless of how the password is stored on the router, what BGP sends on the wire for BGP authentication remains the same.

BGP uses TCP authentication, which enables the authentication option and sends the message authentication code based on a cryptographic algorithm configured as part of the key chain configuration. The key chain configuration is permitted only for BGP on IOS XR platforms. Although multiple cryptographic algorithms can be configured under the key chain, only HMAC-MD5 and HMAC-SHA1-12 are the two algorithms supported for BGP. Example 9-4 demonstrates the configuration for key chain–based authentication codes for BGP.

Example 9-4   *Configuring* key chain *for BGP*

```
RP/0/0/CPU0:R2(config)# key chain BGP_PWD
RP/0/0/CPU0:R2(config-BGP_PWD)# key 1
RP/0/0/CPU0:R2(config-BGP_PWD-1)# cryptographic-algorithm ?
  HMAC-MD5      Configure HMAC-MD5 as cryptographic algorithm
  HMAC-SHA1-12  Configure HMAC-SHA1-12 as cryptographic algorithm
  HMAC-SHA1-20  Configure HMAC-SHA1-20 as cryptographic algorithm
  MD5           Configure MD5 as cryptographic algorithm
  SHA-1         Configure SHA-1-20 as cryptographic algorithm

RP/0/0/CPU0:R2(config-BGP_PWD-1)# cryptographic-algorithm HMAC-SHA1-12
RP/0/0/CPU0:R2(config-BGP_PWD-1)# exit
RP/0/0/CPU0:R2(config-BGP_PWD)# exit
RP/0/0/CPU0:R2(config)# router bgp 100
RP/0/0/CPU0:R2(config-bgp)# neighbor 10.1.102.10
RP/0/0/CPU0:R2(config-bgp-nbr)# keychain BGP_PWD
RP/0/0/CPU0:R2(config-bgp-nbr)# commit
```

An important thing to remember while enabling the key chain–based authentication mechanism is that both MD5-based password authentication and key chain–based authentication cannot be configured together. Second, the peering router should also support the same cryptographic algorithm as configured on the IOS XR router.

BGP Pass Through

As stated before, the Cisco ASA firewall, by default, offsets the TCP sequence number with a random number for every TCP session passing through it. This may cause MD5 authentication to fail. Also, the ASA firewall strips off TCP option 19 by default, which is used for BGP MD5 authentication. These two behaviors of the ASA firewall cause problems for a BGP session passing through it. This problem is resolved by the following the four simple steps:

Step 1.   Create an ACL to permit BGP traffic. The ACL entry should be made on two places: on the ACL that is applied on the outside interface for permitting BGP traffic and on the ACL to be used under class-map.

Step 2.   Create a TCP map to allow TCP option 19. TCP map is created using the **tcp-map** command. Use the subcommand **tcp-option** under the **tcp-map** to specify option 19.

Step 3.   Create a class-map to match BGP traffic.

Step 4.   Disable sequence number randomization and enable TCP option 19 in global policy. Under the **policy-map global_policy**, call the class-map created in step 3. Under the class-map, disable TCP sequence number randomization and enable TCP Option 19.

If the hash number is different because of the random sequence number generated by ASA, the TCP session drops and an MD5 failed message is logged as follows:

```
%TCP-6-BADAUTH: Invalid MD5 digest from 10.1.110.2:64323 to 10.1.110.10:179
```

Example 9-5 illustrates the configuration on the Cisco ASA firewall to disable TCP sequence number randomization and enable TCP Option 19 using the steps previously laid out.

Example 9-5   *ASA Configuration for BGP Traffic*

```
access-list OUT extended permit tcp host 10.1.110.2 host 10.1.110.10 eq bgp
access-list OUT extended permit tcp host 10.1.110.2 eq bgp host 10.1.110.10
!
access-list BGP-TRAFFIC extended permit tcp host 10.1.110.2 host 10.1.110.10 eq bgp
access-list BGP-TRAFFIC extended permit tcp host 10.1.110.2 eq bgp host 10.1.110.10
!
tcp-map TCP-OPTION-19
  tcp-options range 19 19 allow
!
access-group OUT in interface Outside
!
```

```
class-map BGP_TRAFFIC
 match access-list BGP-TRAFFIC
!
policy-map global_policy
 class inspection_default
  ! Output omitted for brevity
 class BGP_TRAFFIC
  set connection random-sequence-number disable
  set connection advanced-options TCP-OPTION-19
```

This configuration is applicable for the ASA firewall running in either Routed mode or Transparent mode. This configuration is required on ASA version 7.x and higher.

Note For ASA running below 7.x, use the **norandomseq** keyword at the end of the command **static (inside,outside)**. For more details on the configuration, refer to the documentation link in the "References" section of this chapter.

EBGP-Multihop

EBGP connections are usually configured on directly connected links. BGP uses the IP TTL value of 1 within the IP header of the BGP packets to protect eBGP sessions from attacks. BGP by default, assumes that the EBGP peer is one hop away or directly connected. But if the neighbors are multiple hops away—that is, more than one hop away—the command **neighbor** *ip-address* **ebgp-multihop** *hop-count* is required to form the BGP neighborship, where hop-count is the number of hops the peering device is. The middle hop can be a routed firewall or another routing entity.

When the **ebgp-multihop** command is configured without the hop count value, the default hop count value is set to 255. In most cases, when EBGP connections are established, it is already known how many hops away the device is located. But when the hop count value is set to 255, this leaves an opportunity open for attackers to spoof packets multiple hops away to try to establish an EBGP session.

To avoid spoofing attacks by ensuring BGP traffic cannot reach devices further than the specified number of hops, configure the exact number of hops of the peering router using the **ebgp-multihop** command.

In case of directly connected neighbors peering over the loopback address, a hop count of 2 is required to form a BGP session. Use the command **neighbor** *ip-address* **disable-connected-check** to avoid this. This prevents both the routers from specifying command **ebgp-multihop 2** while configuring neighborship. When the **neighbor disable-connected-check** command is configured, the TTL value of the BGP packet is still set to 1.

BGP TTL Security

As stated earlier, when an EBGP session is configured, all the neighbor session packets are sent with a TTL value of 1. This concept proved useful for EBGP peers that were a single hop away; however, this concept does not take into account attackers who could be 255 hops away and could send spoofed packets. An attacker could send large amounts of TCP SYN (synchronize) packets, from a single host or distributed hosts, toward the BGP peer to overwhelm the BGP process. Because BGP is a high priority process, it consumes a lot of CPU resources and thus causes a service outage in the network. Figure 9-1 depicts how an attacker sends spoofed BGP messages to attack an ISP BGP router. If routers R1 and R2 are running MD5 authentication, R1 uses MD5 to filter out the bogus messages. But the problem with this method is that the MD5 authentication is done on the RP. The MD5 packets are forwarded to the CPU and thus overwhelm the CPU, causing a service impact.

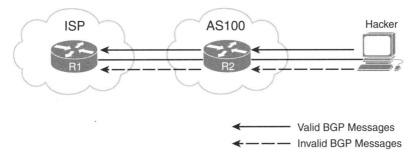

Figure 9-1   *BGP Spoofing Attack*

The BGP TTL security mechanism is applicable to eBGP peering sessions between routers that are either directly connected interfaces or multiple hops away. The TTL security sets the TTL value to 255. When the receiver obtains the packet, it checks for a TTL value of 254 (for a directly connected neighbor). Based on the number of hop counts, a lower acceptable TTL value is decided for multi-hop neighbors.

> **Note**   This concept was originally defined in *The BGP TTL Security Hack (BTSH)* and later extended beyond BGP in *The Generalized TTL Security Mechanism (GTSM)* in RFC 3682.

The **neighbor** *ip-address* **ttl-security hops** *hop-count* is used in place of the **neighbor** *ip-address* **ebgp-multihop** *hop-count* command. For TTL security to work, both the peering devices must be configured with the **ttl-security** command, or the BGP session will not come up. Example 9-6 demonstrates how to configure TTL security for a one-hop router with loopback peering. Notice that in IOS XR, the peering is being performed with the physical link address rather than using a loopback interface. The reason is that IOS XR does not presently support multi-hop TTL security.

Example 9-6 *TTL Security Configuration*

```
IOS
IOS(config)# router bgp 100
IOS(config-router)# neighbor 192.168.10.10 remote-as 200
IOS(config-router)# neighbor 192.168.10.10 update-source Loopback0
IOS(config-router)# neighbor 192.168.10.10 ttl-security hops 2
IOS(config-router)# address-family ipv4 unicast
IOS(config-router-af)# neighbor 192.168.10.10 activate
```

```
IOS XR
RP/0/0/CPU0:IOS-XR(config)# router bgp 100
RP/0/0/CPU0:IOS-XR(config-bgp)# neighbor 10.1.102.10
RP/0/0/CPU0:IOS-XR(config-bgp-nbr)# remote-as 200
RP/0/0/CPU0:IOS-XR(config-bgp-nbr)# ttl-security
RP/0/0/CPU0IOS-XR(config-bgp-nbr)# update-source loopback0
RP/0/0/CPU0:IOS-XR(config-bgp-nbr)# address-family ipv4 unicast
RP/0/0/CPU0:IOS-XR(config-bgp-nbr-af)# commit
```

If the hop count is set to 2, BGP only accepts packets with a TTL value that is equal to or greater than 253 (253 or 254). If a packet is received with any other TTL value in the packet header (252 or lower), the packet is silently discarded.

Note BGP TTL Security is not supported on NX-OS at the time of this writing.

The main benefit of using TTL security is that if the attacker sends a spoofed packet, it has a lower TTL value than the receiving router is anticipating. The receiving router compares the incoming packet TTL value, and if it doesn't match` the expected value, it discards the packet. Thus, the only cost on the receiving router for the spoofed packets is comparing the TTL value, which is much cheaper than comparing MD5. Secondly, the TTL check is performed in hardware itself in most of the platforms, rather than sending the packet to RP. This saves CPU resources if the device is under attack.

MD5 authentication should still be used to authenticate any message that makes it past BTSH. There are always possibilities that an attacker can breach the BGP TTL security. In such cases, MD5 authentication ensures that the network is still protected from spoofed attacks with a minimal CPU cost.

Filtering

Filtering is not usually required within an AS, but it is a good practice to have it implemented on the Internet edge routers that are having EBGP connections with service providers. By default, all the packets are permitted on a given interface. This makes the router vulnerable to unwanted traffic from the Internet. To protect the router from unwanted traffic from Internet, use the following filtering methods for deployment:

- Filtering using ACL

- Filtering using the firewall

With regard to filtering using ACL, an ACL (both IPv4 and IPv6) can be configured on the interface permitting traffic from certain source and destinations. In the case of BGP, TCP port 179 should be permitting between the source and the destination IPs, and all other TCP traffic on port 179 should be denied. This helps securing the BGP peer from forged BGP traffic by the attackers. Example 9-7 illustrates the configuration for permitting specific BGP neighbor traffic on the physical port.

Example 9-7 *ACL Permitting BGP Traffic*

```
IOS
R1(config)# ip access-list extended ALLOW_BGP
R1(config-ext-nacl)# permit tcp host 10.1.110.10 host 10.1.110.1 eq bgp
R1(config-ext-nacl)# permit tcp host 10.1.110.10 eq bgp host 10.1.110.1
R1(config-ext-nacl)# permit ip host 10.1.110.10 host 10.1.110.1
R1(config-ext-nacl)# deny tcp any any eq bgp
R1(config-ext-nacl)# deny tcp any eq bgp any
R1(config-ext-nacl)# permit ip any any
R1(config-ext-nacl)# exit
R1(config)# interface gigabitEthernet 0/1
R1(config-if)# ip access-group ALLOW_BGP in
```

```
IOS XR
RP/0/0/CPU0:R2(config)# ipv4 access-list ALLOW_BGP
RP/0/0/CPU0:R2(config-ipv4-acl)# permit tcp host 10.1.102.10 host 10.1.102.2 eq bgp
RP/0/0/CPU0:R2(config-ipv4-acl)# permit tcp host 10.1.102.10 eq bgp host 10.1.102.2
! Output omitted for brevity
RP/0/0/CPU0:R2(config)# interface gigabitEthernet 0/0/0/0
RP/0/0/CPU0:R2(config-if)# ipv4 access-group ALLOW_BGP ingress
RP/0/0/CPU0:R2(config-if)# commit
```

Note Configuration on Cisco IOS and NX-OS is same, except that on NX-OS an access-list is configured using the command **ip access-list** *acl-name*.

With regard to filtering using the firewall, as mentioned in Chapter 3, "Troubleshooting Peering Issues," recall that firewalls run in two modes: Routed mode and Transparent mode. In either of the modes, the method of configuring an ACL remains the same. The benefit of using a firewall is that the firewall is capable of handling more ACL entries than a regular router can.

It is not a good practice to have large ACLs configured on the interface on a router, because the ACL entries consume a lot of ternary content addressable memory (TCAM) space on the router. Also, when the ACL is configured with a log option, it requires CPU processing of those packets that hit that entry. The main function of the router is routing and forwarding traffic, and performing other tasks similar to that of a firewall is always going to be an overhead. A firewall, on the other hand, is designed and optimized to perform filtering and thus is capable of handling a huge number of ACL entries.

Protecting BGP Traffic Using IPsec

There are various mechanisms of protecting data over the network. Internet Protocol Security (IPsec) is one secure method of protecting critical data from DoS or MITM attacks. With the IPsec tunneling mechanism, the keys are refreshed from time to time, which makes it a more secure method than using MD5 authentication.

It is a common design practice for enterprises and banking organizations, where protecting data is primary goal, to set up IPsec tunnels between hub and spoke or between different sites. After the tunnel is set up, either IGP is run across the tunnel interface or BGP. The benefit of running IGP or BGP across IPsec tunnel is not only having reachability, but even the routing protocol messages are encrypted. This security mechanism can be used to protect BGP sessions from integrity violations, replay, and DoS attacks through its authentication header. Using encapsulated security payload (ESP), a higher level of confidentiality can be achieved.

Although much more effective than the previous other solutions, IPsec is not widely used by the ISPs, and it does not cover other attacks previously mentioned. Although running IPsec tunnels in the network comes with an additional cost of system resources like CPU and memory that is used for encrypting and decrypting the packets, it is the most secure that provides data integrity. Some platforms have specific ASICs and line cards that take care of performing the encryption and decryption for the IPsec tunnels.

Securing Interdomain Routing

A typical Internet deployment scenario is one in which multiple customer sites are interconnected through an SP network. Figure 9-2 shows three customer sites interconnected to each other through an SP. In steady state, the customer edge (CE) routers advertise their prefixes to the provider edge (PE) routers via BGP update messages; each PE, on receiving the updates, processes the updates, applies local incoming policies, and installs the prefixes in its BGP table. BGP then runs the best-path calculation algorithm and selects the best path for each prefix and advertises the best path for each prefix to its IBGP peers.

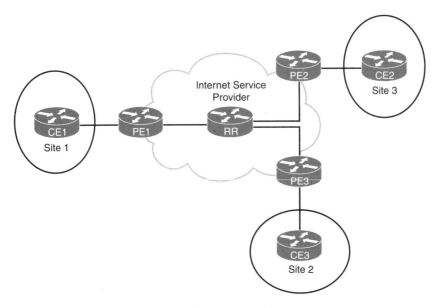

Figure 9-2 *Typical Internet Deployment Topology*

The BGP protocol provides rich information, such as path attributes carried with each prefix for an AS to select paths based on each ASs policies. The BGP protocol does not currently have any intrinsic way to validate the payload of a BGP update message that is used for path selection.

Service providers establish their policies by creating filters that are applied on the received paths. However, these filters are created based on non-signed information that cannot always be trusted; for example, through Internet Routing Registries, the WHOIS database, or through customer provided information. Creating a filter to apply a policy using these non-signed information implies that there is a high chance that a customer announcing any IP prefix to its transit provider can cause an IP hijacking event.

BGP Prefix Hijacking

In a normal BGP operation, any AS can inject any prefixes into the BGP network; this can be due to either an unintentional or a malicious activity. The effect leads to prefix hijacking by the AS, if it does not have a path to the prefix and black holes all traffic for that prefix. This prefix hijacking occurs when an AS is announcing someone else's prefix or when an AS is announcing a more specific range of someone else's prefix.

There are two variations to prefix hijacking:

- The same prefix advertised with a smaller AS path

- Advertisement of a more specific prefix

To understand a prefix advertised with a smaller AS path scenario, examine the topology in Figure 9-3. The client host resides in AS 100, whereas the destination web server resides in AS 500 and the packet traverses the path from AS 100 to AS 500 via AS 200 and AS 300.

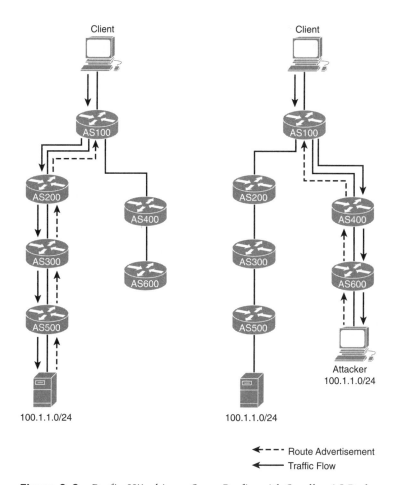

Figure 9-3 *Prefix Hijacking—Same Prefix with Smaller AS Path*

The following sequence of events occur when the prefix hijacking occurs:

1. AS 500 advertises its origin route 100.1.1.0/24 to the connected PEs.

2. The PEs in different ASs elect the best path for that prefix and advertise to its connected PEs.

3. When the client sends the traffic for that prefix, the traffic flows via connected AS and reaches AS 500.

4. The host in AS 600 advertises the same prefix 100.1.1.0/24 to its connected PEs, either by mistake or as a malicious attack on the prefix.

5. On AS 100, there are now two paths available for the same prefix; AS 100 prefers the option with the shorter path through AS 600 and elects that as its best path. Traffic for that prefix is forwarded toward AS 600.

This leads to traffic black holing for the prefix originated by AS 500 as the traffic is diverted to AS 600. Example 9-8 demonstrates the traffic black holing in the previously described scenario.

Example 9-8 *Traffic Black Holing Due to Prefix with Smaller AS Path*

```
AS100
AS100# show bgp ipv4 unicast
! Output omitted for brevity

     Network          Next Hop        Metric LocPrf Weight Path
r>   10.1.12.0/24     10.1.12.2          0            0 200 ?
*>   10.1.23.0/24     10.1.12.2          0            0 200 ?
*>   10.1.35.0/24     10.1.12.2                       0 200 300 ?
*>   100.1.1.0/24     10.1.12.2                       0 200 300 500 i

! Ping from the Client host
```

```
CLIENT
cisco@client-1:~$ ping 100.1.1.2
PING 100.1.1.2 (100.1.1.2) 56(84) bytes of data.
64 bytes from 100.1.1.2: icmp_seq=1 ttl=60 time=4.69 ms
64 bytes from 100.1.1.2: icmp_seq=2 ttl=60 time=5.76 ms
64 bytes from 100.1.1.2: icmp_seq=3 ttl=60 time=3.47 ms
```

```
AS100
! Output after 100.1.1.0/24 advertised by AS 600
AS100# show bgp ipv4 unicast

     Network          Next Hop        Metric LocPrf Weight Path
r>   10.1.12.0/24     10.1.12.2          0            0 200 ?
*>   10.1.23.0/24     10.1.12.2          0            0 200 ?
*>   10.1.35.0/24     10.1.12.2                       0 200 300 ?
*>   100.1.1.0/24     10.1.14.4                       0 400 600 ?
*                     10.1.12.2                       0 200 300 500 i
```

```
CLIENT
! Ping from the Client host

cisco@client-1:~$ ping 100.1.1.2
PING 100.1.1.2 (100.1.1.2) 56(84) bytes of data.
From 10.1.46.6 icmp_seq=1 Destination Host Unreachable
From 10.1.46.6 icmp_seq=2 Destination Host Unreachable
From 10.1.46.6 icmp_seq=3 Destination Host Unreachable
```

In the second scenario, an AS advertises a more specific prefix for a given address space for which it is not the actual originator and does not own that address space. Because the more specific prefix is not present in any routing table, this prefix forms a route with an invalid origin AS, shadows the prefix corresponding to the valid AS, and affects all networks receiving this advertisement.

Examine the topology in Figure 9-4. The web server is connected to AS 400, and the client system is connected on AS 100. The packet flows from AS 100 to AS 400 via AS 200 and AS 300. AS 300 is also peering AS 500.

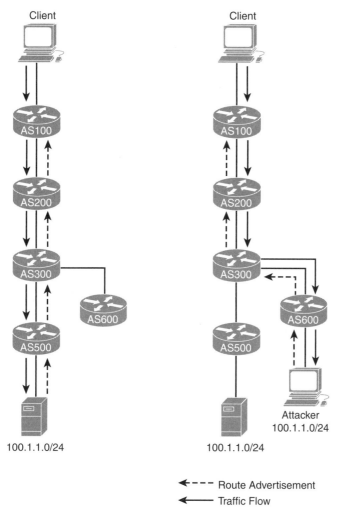

Figure 9-4 *Prefix Hijacking—More Specific Prefix*

The forwarding decision on the router is based on the longest prefix match to the destination. If a more specific prefix is present in the network, the forwarding happens to the prefix in that subnet.

The series of events that occur when a more specific prefix is advertised in the network is shown in Figure 9-4.

1. AS 400 advertises its origin route 100.1.1.0/24 to the connected PEs in different ASs.

2. Every PEs in each of the different ASs elects the best path for that prefix and advertises to its connected PEs.

3. When the client sends the traffic for that prefix, the traffic flows via connected AS and reaches AS 400.

4. AS 500 originates the same prefix 100.1.1.0/25 with a more specific mask to its connected PEs, either by mistake or as a malicious attack on the prefix.

5. On AS 300, when traffic is received for the more specific prefix, this traffic will be forwarded toward AS 500.

This leads to traffic black holing for the prefix originated by AS 400 as the traffic is diverted to AS 500.

Example 9-9 demonstrates the traffic black-hole situation with a more specific prefix advertised by another AS.

Example 9-9 *Traffic Black Holing Due to More Specific Prefix Advertisement*

```
AS100

AS100# show bgp ipv4 unicast

! Output omitted for brevity


      Network          Next Hop       Metric LocPrf Weight Path
 r>   10.1.12.0/24     10.1.12.2          0              0 200 ?
 *>   10.1.23.0/24     10.1.12.2          0              0 200 ?
 *>   100.1.1.0/24     10.1.12.2                         0 200 300 400 i


CLIENT

! Ping from the Client host


cisco@client-1:~$ ping 100.1.1.2

PING 100.1.1.2 (100.1.1.2) 56(84) bytes of data.

64 bytes from 100.1.1.2: icmp_seq=1 ttl=60 time=4.69 ms

64 bytes from 100.1.1.2: icmp_seq=2 ttl=60 time=5.76 ms

64 bytes from 100.1.1.2: icmp_seq=3 ttl=60 time=3.47 ms
```

```
AS100
! Output after more specific prefix is advertised


AS100# show bgp ipv4 unicast
! Output omitted for brevity
     Network          Next Hop      Metric LocPrf Weight Path
r>   10.1.12.0/24     10.1.12.2          0          0 200 ?
*>   10.1.23.0/24     10.1.12.2          0          0 200 ?
*>   100.1.1.0/25     10.1.12.2                     0 200 300 500 i
*>   100.1.1.0/24     10.1.12.2                     0 200 300 400 i
```

```
CLIENT
! Ping from the Client host


cisco@client-1:~$ ping 100.1.1.2
PING 100.1.1.2 (100.1.1.2) 56(84) bytes of data.
From 10.1.35.5 icmp_seq=1 Destination Host Unreachable
From 10.1.35.5 icmp_seq=2 Destination Host Unreachable
From 10.1.35.5 icmp_seq=3 Destination Host Unreachable
```

Thus, the manifestation of prefix hijacking is as follows:

- An AS announcing someone else's prefix

- An AS announcing a more specific prefix of someone else's prefix

Prefix hijacking issues are not just in theory but have actually caused some major outages in the past. One example goes back to February 2008, when Pakistan Telecom (AS 17557) made an unauthorized advertisement of the prefix 208.65.153.0/24 hijacking the YouTube subnet 208.65.152.0/22. One of Pakistan Telecom's upstream providers—PCCW Global (AS 3491)—forwarded this announcement to the rest of the Internet, which resulted in the hijacking of YouTube traffic on a global scale and caused a major outage for the website. Figure 9-5 illustrates the traffic diversion after the prefix hijacking for the YouTube website.

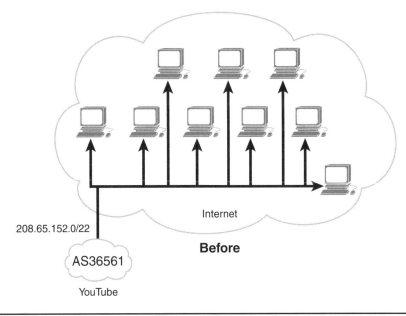

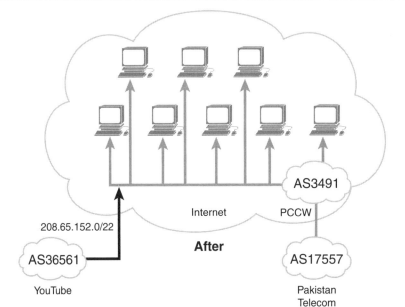

Figure 9-5   *YouTube Prefix Hijacking*

Such scenarios have caused some major outages to various websites in the past. To protect inter-domain routing, consider the following parameters before devising the solution:

■ The solution should be scalable.

■ The solution should not increase the memory consumption of BGP by multiple folds.

- BGP routers should be capable of validating all ASs in the path.

- The subscribers and ISPs should not rely on mutual trust between them.

To overcome the prefix hijacking issues, different vendors and universities came up with solutions to secure BGP. This chapter discusses the two most popular solutions:

- Secure BGP (S-BGP)

- Secure Origin BGP (soBGP)

S-BGP

S-BGP was developed by Stephen Kent, Charles Lynn, and Karen Seo from BBN Technologies. S-BGP was developed after assessing BGP vulnerabilities, and the solution was published in April 2000. S-BGP architecture consists of three main components:

- **IPsec:** Provides authenticity and integrity of peer-to-peer communication.

- **Public Key Infrastructure (PKI):** Provides secure identification of BGP speakers, ASs, and IP address blocks. It also supports AS number ownership and BGP router authorization to represent an AS.

- **Attestations:** Encapsulates authorization to advertise the specified prefix/address block into UPDATE messages.

IPsec

S-BGP uses IPsec to protect all BGP traffic between two peer routers. The IPsec features provide cryptographically enforced data authentication, data integrity and anti-replay features that help in providing a secure communication. IPsec is capable of refreshing the keys, providing automatic key management, which MD5 is not capable of. IPsec provides standards-based cryptographic protection. The main purpose of using IPsec is to secure BGP control traffic.

Public Key Infrastructure

Many types of certificates are used in S-BGP. To understand the requirements of various certificates, it is important to understand the IP address and AS allocation hierarchy.

Figure 9-6 shows the hierarchy of address allocation. Internet Assigned Numbers Authority (IANA) is the root of all addresses in the hierarchy. IANA assigns the address blocks to Regional Internet Registries (RIR), which then performs block allocation to ISPs and National Registries. The subscribers then nominally receive the address blocks from the ISPs.

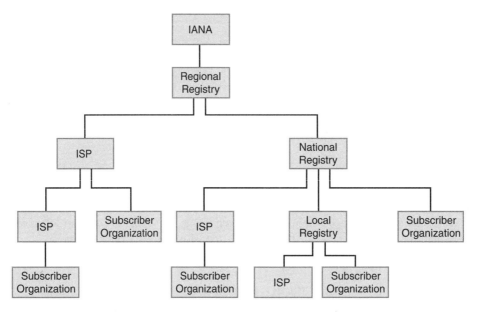

Figure 9-6   *Address Allocation Hierarchy*

Note   Hierarchy is not always followed in address allocation.

Figure 9-7 shows the hierarchy of AS number allocations. IANA is the root of all ASs in the hierarchy, which then delegates the AS numbers to regional registries. The regional registries then allocate the AS numbers to the ISPs or the subscriber organizations.

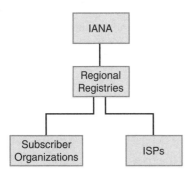

Figure 9-7   *AS Allocation Hierarchy*

An organization receives an IP address space and AS number directly from the RIR. Public Key (X.509) certificates are issued to ISPs and subscribers to identify the AS owners and prefix holders, as described in RFC 3779. Every AS is associated with a pair of public/private keys. The digital certificates provide the cryptographic mechanism to ensure integrity of the data.

When a BGP speaker sends a BGP message, it signs the message with its private key. The BGP peer, on receiving the message, verifies the message using the sender's public key. This helps provide secure identification of BGP speakers, ASs, and IP address blocks.

Attestations

Attestations are the crucial component of S-BGP architecture because they are used to encapsulate authorization information within the UPDATE message. There are two types of attestations in S-BGP:

- Address Attestation (AA)

- Route Attestation (RA)

AA is issued by the owner of the address block. Because the RIR allocates the address to either an ISP or a subscriber, the AA is issued by them. It is used to identify the origin AS authorized to advertise the address block. AA is used to protect BGP from erroneous updates—updates from authenticated but misbehaving or misconfigured BGP speakers.

RAs are issued by ASs and are used to provide authentication. The S-BGP speaker authorizes neighbor ASs to use the route in the UPDATE containing the RA. The RA is used to protect BGP from erroneous updates.

Each UPDATE message may include one or more address attestations and a set of route attestations, which are carried in a new, optional, transitive path attribute. The attestations are used by BGP speakers to validate the destination address blocks and end-to-end AS_PATH information in the update. Figure 9-8 shows the encoding of attestations.

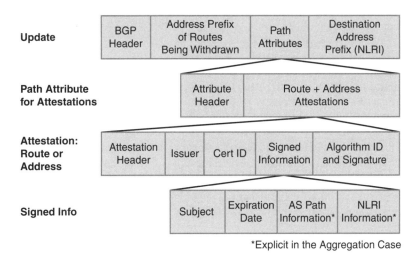

Figure 9-8 *Encoding of Attestations*

The S-BGP router generates an attestation when generating an UPDATE message for another S-BGP router. A new RA is generated that encompasses the path and prefixes along with the AS number of the neighbor AS. The S-BGP router validates attestations (AA) associated with each UPDATE message received from another S-BGP router to verify that the origin AS was authorized to advertise the prefix. The S-BGP router verifies that its AS number is in the first RA. It also validates the signature of each RA in the received UPDATE message.

soBGP

BGP as a routing protocol is prone to various threats, and solutions exist that have been deployed to counteract individual threats. Features like inbound filters, route limits, martian checks, and other feature enhancements within BGP are independent of each other and counter various vulnerabilities.

The soBGP draft was initially proposed by Russ White in April 2004. soBGP targets the need to verify the validity of an advertised prefix, if the originator is authorized to advertise the route. soBGP is based on few mechanisms, mainly certificates, to secure interdomain routing. It verifies that the originator of a route is authorized to advertise the route and that the AS_PATH represents a valid path to the originator.

soBGP follows the web-of-trust model to validate certificates. This means that there is no specific root, but it relies on distributed responsibility. soBGP uses certificates to advertise and correlate AS identity, prefix ownership, and route policy. It relies primarily on three types of certificates:

- Entity Certificate
- Authorization Certificate
- Policy Certificate

Entity Certificate

The first and most important point to start securing BGP is to have a strong authentication mechanism between peers. soBGP overcomes this issue by using Entity Certificates, or EntityCert, which are used for AS authentication between peers. An EntityCert binds an AS number to at least one public key. For a root-level trust, a small number of public key certificates are distributed and configured manually. An AS with a trusted AS public key certificate may further sign a public key certificate for another validated AS. This naturally forms a web-of-trust model.

Note   The root-level public key certificates are allocated to some tier-1 ISPs and some well-known authentication service providers, such as Verisign.

Authorization Certificate

Authorization Certificates, or AuthCert, are used to assign and delegate IP address space. Trusted ASs (using EntityCert) are authorized to advertise certain IP blocks of addresses. AuthCerts are used to bind an AS to the IP address space they are allowed to advertise.

Policy Certificate

Policy Certificates, or PolicyCerts, are used to define per-AS or per-prefix policies. AuthCerts are not advertised independently but are encapsulated into certificates that include a set of policies the originator enforces on the advertised prefixes. A PolicyCert encloses the following:

- An AuthCert

- Policies applied to the prefix

- Signature: signed by an authorized AS

BGP SECURITY Message

Certificates between the BGP peers or ASs are not transmitted using regular update messages. A new BGP SECURITY message was proposed to ensure transportation of certificates from one soBGP peer to another soBGP peer. To ensure that two peers are soBGP capable, the capability exchange occurs during the initial session formation process.

There is no sequence on whether the certificates are exchanged first or the BGP prefixes. The BGP sessions can also be used for exchanging just the certificates.

Note Unfortunately, both S-BGP and soBGP features are not supported on Cisco platforms. Cisco platforms support the BGP Origin AS Validation feature, which is discussed later in this chapter.

BGP Origin AS Validation

Looking at the S-BGP and soBGP solutions, it is clear that a mechanism is required that could differentiate between invalid and legit (valid) routes for a BGP destination. IETF SIDR workgroup has defined a framework based on Resource Public Key Infrastructure (RPKI) under RFC 6481, that describes the RPKI repository structure that enables a BGP operator to find all the repositories in a systematic way.

To adequately address the prefix hijacking issues discussed before, each AS must selectively choose the prefixes it wants to accept. For this to be effective, an AS needs authoritative information about the Origin AS for every prefix it wants to accept. A central authority to provide this information, in and of itself, is not likely to be sufficient.

The Route Information Registries (RIR) publish this information on a regular basis. However, this is not sufficient for a number of reasons:

- The RIR can only publish allocations made in the provider-independent space. The provider-dependent space is allocated by subdelegations from the various service providers.

- There is also the issue of how one can trust the published information in a reliable manner.

- Finally, there is the need to digest all this information in an automated process and be able to configure the BGP routers in the network.

Given the requirements, each mapping (Origin AS—prefix mapping) must be cryptographically signed by the entity that is delegating that prefix to a particular AS. This cryptographically signed delegation of a prefix to an AS is called a Route Origin Authorization (ROA). In this scheme the IANA, as the owner of the entire prefix space, provides ROAs for delegations of the prefix space to the RIRs. Each RIR can in turn generate ROA delegations for all the provider-independent and provider-dependent allocations that it makes. In turn, service providers who provide subdelegations in the provider-dependent space can generate similar ROAs for their actions. The hierarchical delegations of ROAs, with their cryptographic properties, provide the Origin AS to prefix mappings in a trusted manner. These mappings are published in well-known (or discoverable) RPKI repositories. The IANA, each of the RIRs, and the service providers all operate their own RPKI repositories. An operator who is configuring a BGP router needs to have a mechanism to find these repositories and retrieve the mappings from them.

Each RPKI repository maintains, in addition to ROAs, a manifest list that identifies all the sub-RPKI repositories that it is aware of or using. It can use this list to identify all the RPKI repositories and sync up the ROAs published by that repository. The repositories use rsync among themselves to sync their published objects.

Each AS operates at least one cache validator in its network. The cache validator has the role of pulling the ROAs in using rsync. The cache validator, as its name implies, caches the ROAs and validates their signature. Periodically, it probes all the RPKI servers to detect any changes to the ROA databases. Using a special RPKI-RTR protocol, the cache validator downloads validated Origin AS—Prefix mappings to the BGP router, that then enables the router to filter out bad routes—those routers with prefixes whose origin ASs do not match the published information from the RPKI repositories.

The router can communicate the result of its computation to its IBGP peers using an extended community that they can then use to optimize their validation of this route.

Figure 9-9 shows the complete BGP Origin AS validation system.

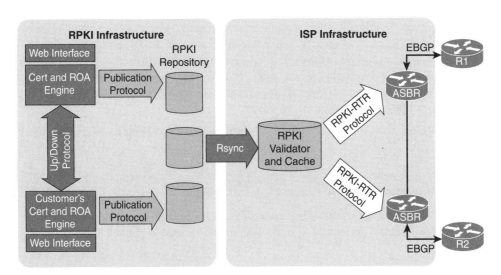

Figure 9-9 *BGP Origin AS Validation System*

Route Origination Authorization (ROA)

ROA is a digitally signed object distributed through the RPKI infrastructure. It indicates the address prefix holder's explicit authorization that an AS can rightfully originate a prefix. Figure 9-10 displays the ROA format for a particular prefix-AS mapping. The prefix-block covers BGP prefixes 172.25.0.0 with minimum mask-length of 16 and a maximum mask-length of 24. For example, this ROA entry covers the prefix 172.25.0.0/24 but not 172.25.50.5/32. Also, the AS number 12343 is authorized to announce the prefix covered by the ROA prefix-block.

ROA
172.25.0.0/16–24
12343
Signature

Figure 9-10 *ROA Format*

The ROA is verified with the public key of the organization creating the ROA, and the public key is available from the certificate of the AS.

Note Initial deployment of RPKI is expected to have far fewer ROAs covering BGP prefixes than there are BGP prefixes in the Internet tables of routers. Hence, most of the path validation done by routers initially results in an *unknown* validity state. As the RPKI is updated gradually to cover more Internet prefixes, the number of *unknown* state paths decrease.

RPKI Prefix Validation Process

The RPKI-Cache-to-Router connectivity can be many-to-many: one RPKI cache can provide origin-AS validation data to multiple routers, and one router can be connected to multiple RPKI caches. A router connects to RPKI servers/caches/peers to download information in order to build a special RPKI database that can be used by BGP to validate the origin-ASs for the Internet routing table. Typically, this validation is done at the edge routers in an AS for paths received from an outside AS (EBGP paths). Internal routers (RRs) do not take part in origin-AS validation.

The RPKI validation for the BGP prefixes is performed with an event-based approach at two places:

- When the router receives EBGP prefixes in the UPDATE message, those prefixes are verified against the RPKI database before they are inserted into the BGP table.

- When there is an insertion or deletion of ROA in the RPKI database, a back walk to the BGP table is performed to verify relevant prefixes that are affected by the ROA updates.

Figure 9-11 illustrates the prefix validation mechanism using RPKI with the preceding two scenarios. (A) illustrates the lookup being performed when the BGP update is received, whereas (B) illustrates the back walk being performed when the ROA is updated.

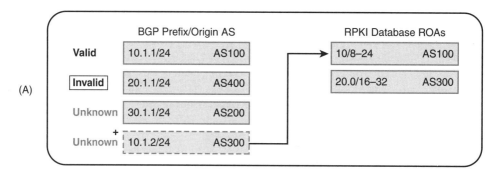

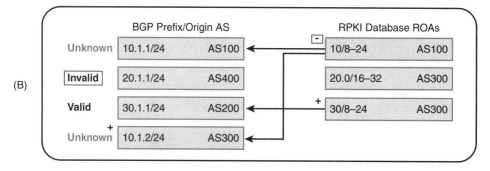

Figure 9-11 *RPKI Prefix Lookup*

A particular route in a BGP router is in one of many validation states, which include the following:

- **Valid:** Valid BGP Origin AS—The router applies its local policies on this route and uses it consistent with those local policies. When it announces this route to other BGP routers in its AS, it tags this route with the appropriate extended community, defined in RFC 6811, that then tells other IBGP peers in the AS that origin validation was successful for this route advertisement. These other peers can rely on this to avoid revalidating the origin AS for these routes.

- **Unknown:** No BGP origin AS—Prefix mapping was found for this prefix in the RPKI repositories that this cache validator connected with. The router applies its local policies on this route and uses it consistent with those local policies. When it announces this route to other BGP routers in its AS, it tags the route with appropriate extended community; that then tells other IBGP peers in the AS that origin validation was not done for this route advertisement. These other peers are then required to validate these routes before using them.

- **Invalid:** The origin AS on this route is invalid for the specific prefix for this route. The BGP router has different ways of handling these routes, which include

  - Lower preference relative to routes whose validation state is Valid or Unknown.

  - Disallow the route from being used in the best-path calculations.

The preferred action on the invalid routes is to drop them, but if the router is configured not to drop such routes, the prefix is attached with the appropriate extended community and updates the IBGP peers stating that the origin validation failed for the advertised routes.

Note   The routers do not drop or take any action on the invalid routes. It is left up to the operators to choose what actions to perform for the invalid routes.

The RPKI caches send validation data to the routers at their own pace (initial database dump, followed by incremental updates). The RPKI database is designed for fast and efficient lookup for verification of BGP paths. Given an IPv4 or IPv6 prefix/mask-length and its corresponding origin-AS, the RPKI database lookup quickly finds any covering prefix-blocks in the RPKI database.

The RPKI looks up the following algorithm for validating the prefixes:

- If the BGP prefix/mask-length has no covering ROAs in the BGP router local storage, the validity of the path is *Not Found*.

- If the BGP prefix is covered by one or more ROAs in the BGP router local storage, then

- If the route-prefix length is less than or equal to the ROA max prefix length and route origin AS matches the ROA origin AS, the validation state of the BGP route is *Valid*.

- If the route-prefix length is less than or equal to the ROA max prefix length but route origin AS does not match the ROA origin AS, the validation state of the BGP route is *Invalid*.

Figure 9-12 illustrates the outcomes of the lookup performed on the RPKI cache entries. Examine the prefix lookups (A) that illustrate two ROA entries covering the BGP prefix. The first ROA entry does not match the prefix. The second ROA covers the BGP prefix but has a different origin AS. The third entry matches the origin, making the RPKI lookup result *valid*. In (B), the two ROA entries cover the prefix but none of the entries match the origin AS number. This makes the RPKI lookup result *invalid*.

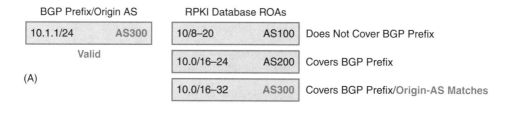

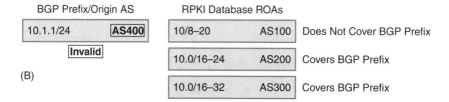

Figure 9-12   *Valid Prefix Based on ROA Entries*

Finally, in Figure 9-13, none of the ROA entries match the prefix that is being looked up. This makes the RPKI lookup result *unknown*.

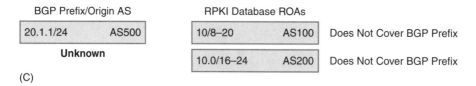

Figure 9-13   *Unknown Prefix Based on ROA Entries*

Configuring and Verifying RPKI

The origin AS validation feature can be configured on the edge or core routers in an AS as the validation of the incoming BGP prefixes runs for both EBGP and IBGP paths. To understand RPKI functionality, examine the topology shown in Figure 9-14. Routers R1, R2, R3, and R4 are part of the ISP network. Router R1 is running Cisco IOS, whereas R4 is running IOS XR. Both R1 and R4 are connected to the RPKI cache server located on host 172.16.1.100. The RPKI server is listening on port 8282.

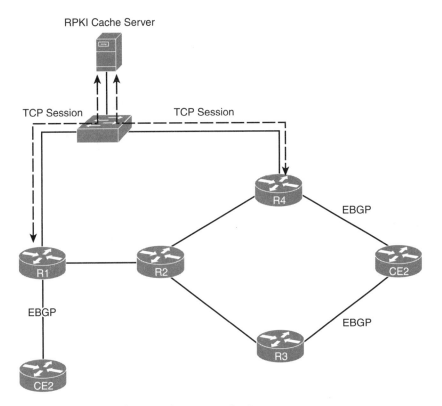

Figure 9-14 *Topology with RPKI Cache Server*

To enable the feature, use the command **bgp rpki server tcp** *ip-address* **port** *port-number* **refresh** *time-in-seconds* on Cisco IOS and the command **rpki server** *ip-address* **transport tcp port** *port-number* on IOS XR software. Example 9-10 demonstrates the configuration of RPKI on both Cisco IOS and IOS XR software. Use the command **refresh-time** *time-in-seconds* to specify the time BGP waits before sending periodic queries to the RPKI server.

Example 9-10 *BGP RPKI Configuration*

```
IOS
R1(config)# router bgp 100
R1(config-router)# bgp rpki server tcp 172.16.1.100 port 8282 refresh 600

IOS XR
RP/0/0/CPU0:R4(config)# router bgp 100
RP/0/0/CPU0:R4(config-bgp)# rpki server 172.16.1.100
RP/0/0/CPU0:R4(config-bgp-rpki-server)# transport tcp port 8282
RP/0/0/CPU0:R4(config-bgp-rpki-server)# refresh-time 600
RP/0/0/CPU0:R4(config-bgp-rpki-server)# commit
```

Note Usually, RPKI cache or RPKI Root Certificate Authority (CA) runs on TCP port 323. But when using RIPE NCC RPKI Validator, the connection is established on TCP port 8282. For testing purposes, RIPE NCC RPKI Validator is an easy option.

After the RPKI server has been configured, verify the connection. Initially, very few prefixes are received from the RPKI server, but over the period of time, those prefixes increase. The RPKI connection status is verified using the command **show bgp** *afi safi* **rpki servers** on Cisco IOS and the command **show bgp rpki server** [*ip-address* | **summary**] on IOS XR. Example 9-11 displays the output of the verification commands. Notice that the command on Cisco IOS software shows all the session-related information such as source port, destination port, refresh time, and so on, and also the command shows how many prefixes have been received. If there are connection failures due to reachability or firewall issues, the connection failure count increments, and the number of prefixes remains at 0. The **show** command on IOS XR displays more brief information on the connection details and ROA exchanged. The **show bgp rpki summary** command displays a summarized output with the server IP, port number, and the IPv4 and IPv6 ROAs received.

Example 9-11 *BGP RPKI Connection Verification*

```
IOS
R1# show bgp ipv4 unicast rpki servers
BGP SOVC neighbor is 172.16.1.100/8282 connected to port 8282
Flags 64, Refresh time is 600, Serial number is 460, Session ID is 13464
InQ has 0 messages, OutQ has 0 messages, formatted msg 121
Session IO flags 3, Session flags 4008
 Neighbor Statistics:
  Prefixes 19677
  Connection attempts: 1
  Connection failures: 0
  Errors sent: 0
```

```
  Errors received: 0



Connection state is ESTAB, I/O status: 1, unread input bytes: 0

Connection is ECN Disabled, Mininum incoming TTL 0, Outgoing TTL 255

Local host: 172.16.1.138, Local port: 54334

Foreign host: 172.16.1.100, Foreign port: 8282

Connection tableid (VRF): 0

Maximum output segment queue size: 50


Enqueued packets for retransmit: 0, input: 0   mis-ordered: 0 (0 bytes)


Event Timers (current time is 0x271B445):

Timer          Starts     Wakeups         Next

Retrans           122          0          0x0

TimeWait            0          0          0x0

AckHold         10962        518          0x0

SendWnd             0          0          0x0

KeepAlive       22985          0          0x271D66F

GiveUp              0          0          0x0

PmtuAger        31789      31788          0x271B648

DeadWait            0          0          0x0

Linger              0          0          0x0

ProcessQ            0          0          0x0


iss: 2699285131   snduna: 2699286340   sndnxt: 2699286340

irs: 2620767940   rcvnxt: 2646216517


sndwnd:  29200  scale:      0  maxrcvwnd:  16384

rcvwnd:  15732  scale:      0  delrcvwnd:    652


SRTT: 1000 ms, RTTO: 1003 ms, RTV: 3 ms, KRTT: 0 ms

minRTT: 1 ms, maxRTT: 1000 ms, ACK hold: 200 ms

uptime: 36114044 ms, Sent idletime: 6883 ms, Receive idletime: 6771 ms

Status Flags: active open

Option Flags: keepalive running, nagle, path mtu capable

IP Precedence value : 6

Datagrams (max data segment is 1460 bytes):

Rcvd: 20813 (out of order: 0), with data: 18518, total data bytes: 25448576

Sent: 27241 (retransmit: 0, fastretransmit: 0, partialack: 0, Second Congestion: 0),
with data: 121, total data bytes: 1208


 Packets received in fast path: 0, fast processed: 0, slow path: 0
```

```
  fast lock acquisition failures: 0, slow path: 0
TCP Semaphore      0x7F58C49882B8   FREE
```

```
IOS XR
RP/0/0/CPU0:R4# show bgp rpki server 172.16.1.100
RPKI Cache-Server 172.16.1.100
  Transport: TCP port 8282
  Connect state: NONE
  Conn attempts: 0
  Total byte RX: 0
  Total byte TX: 0
  Last reset
    Timest: Jan 16 08:40:53 (00:00:01 ago)
    Reason: protocol error
RPKI-RTR protocol information
  Serial number: 0
  Cache nonce: 0x3498
  Protocol state: NONE
  Refresh  time: 600 seconds
  Response time: 30 seconds
  Purge time: 60 seconds
  Protocol exchange
    ROAs announced:  14088 IPv4    2122 IPv6
    ROAs withdrawn:      0 IPv4       0 IPv6
    Error Reports :      0 sent       0 rcvd
  Last protocol error
    Reason: response timeout
    Detail: response timeout while in DATA_START state


RP/0/0/CPU0:R4# show bgp rpki server summary
Hostname/Address    Transport    State      Time          ROAs (IPv4/IPv6)
172.16.1.100        TCP:8282     ESTAB      00:00:25       11502/1762
```

Because the router receives ROA entries from the RPKI cache server, those entries/ prefixes are viewed using the command **show bgp** *afi safi* **rpki table** on Cisco IOS and the **show bgp rpki table** [**ipv4** | **ipv6** | *ip-address/length* | *ipv6-address/length*] command. Example 9-12 displays the output of the RPKI table.

Example 9-12 *BGP RPKI ROA Entries*

```
IOS
R1# show bgp ipv4 unicast rpki table
16479 BGP sovc network entries using 2636640 bytes of memory
17141 BGP sovc record entries using 548512 bytes of memory

Network          Maxlen   Origin-AS   Source   Neighbor
1.9.0.0/16       24       4788        0        172.16.1.100/8282
1.9.21.0/24      24       4788        0        172.16.1.100/8282
1.9.52.0/24      24       4788        0        172.16.1.100/8282
1.9.53.0/24      24       4788        0        172.16.1.100/8282
1.9.54.0/24      24       4788        0        172.16.1.100/8282
1.9.55.0/24      24       4788        0        172.16.1.100/8282
1.9.112.0/24     24       4788        0        172.16.1.100/8282
1.9.113.0/24     24       4788        0        172.16.1.100/8282
1.9.114.0/24     24       4788        0        172.16.1.100/8282
1.9.115.0/24     24       4788        0        172.16.1.100/8282
! Output omitted for brevity


R1# show bgp ipv6 unicast rpki table
2441 BGP sovc network entries using 449144 bytes of memory
2536 BGP sovc record entries using 81152 bytes of memory

Network            Maxlen   Origin-AS   Source   Neighbor
2001:608::/32      32       5539        0        172.16.1.100/8282
2001:610::/32      48       1103        0        172.16.1.100/8282
2001:610:240::/42  42       3333        0        172.16.1.100/8282
2001:620::/32      32       559         0        172.16.1.100/8282
2001:620::/29      29       559         0        172.16.1.100/8282
2001:630::/32      48       786         0        172.16.1.100/8282
2001:638::/32      32       680         0        172.16.1.100/8282
2001:638:30D::/48  48       8519        0        172.16.1.100/8282
! Output omitted for brevity


IOS XR
RP/0/0/CPU0:R4# show bgp rpki table ipv4
    Network        Maxlen      Origin-AS       Server
    1.9.21.0/24    24          4788            172.16.1.100
    1.9.52.0/24    24          4788            172.16.1.100
    1.9.53.0/24    24          4788            172.16.1.100
    1.9.55.0/24    24          4788            172.16.1.100
    1.9.112.0/24   24          4788            172.16.1.100
```

```
 1.9.113.0/24            24              4788            172.16.1.100
 1.9.114.0/24            24              4788            172.16.1.100
 1.9.115.0/24            24              4788            172.16.1.100
! Output omitted for brevity


RP/0/0/CPU0:R4# show bgp rpki table ipv6
 Network                Maxlen          Origin-AS       Server
 2001:648:2800::/48      48              5470            172.16.1.100
 2001:660:3203::/48      48              2094            172.16.1.100
 2001:678:3::/48         48              42              172.16.1.100
 2001:67c:224::/48       48              51164           172.16.1.100
 2001:67c:2e8::/48       48              3333            172.16.1.100
 2001:67c:348::/48       48              47426           172.16.1.100
 2001:67c:192c::/48      48              24940           172.16.1.100
 2001:67c:1b43::/48      48              60564           172.16.1.100
 2001:67c:2074::/48      48              57763           172.16.1.100
! Output omitted for brevity
```

After the ROA entries are populated in the RPKI table, the EBGP paths are then validated for Origin AS against those ROA entries. Based on the verification with the ROA entries, the prefixes are assigned validation codes, which can be valid, invalid, or not found.

Use the command **show bgp** *afi safi* on Cisco IOS to verify the RPKI validated prefixes. The command to verify the origin AS is a bit different on IOS XR. Use the command **show bgp origin-as validity [valid | invalid | not-found]** on IOS XR to verify the prefixes.

Example 9-13 demonstrates the origin AS prefix validation using the **show bgp ipv4 unicast** command. On Cisco IOS, the prefixes are marked with the RPKI validation codes in the show command output itself, where *V* implies valid, *I* implies invalid, and *N* implies Not found. The prefix 1.9.0.0/24 is marked *Invalid* because the ROA entry shows the prefix is being originated from AS 4788, whereas the prefix here is being originated from AS 4790. The prefix 1.9.50.0/24 is marked *Valid* because the prefix in the BGP table and ROA entry both show the Origin AS as AS 4788. Finally, the prefix 34.1.4.0/24 is marked *Not found* because the prefix is not found in any of the ROA entries.

Example 9-13 *BGP Origin-AS Prefix Validation on Cisco IOS*

```
IOS
R1# show bgp ipv4 unicast
BGP table version is 1892, local router ID is 192.168.1.1
Status codes: s suppressed, d damped, h history, * valid, > best, i - internal,
              r RIB-failure, S Stale, m multipath, b backup-path, f RT-Filter,
              x best-external, a additional-path, c RIB-compressed,
Origin codes: i - IGP, e - EGP, ? - incomplete
RPKI validation codes: V valid, I invalid, N Not found
     Network          Next Hop        Metric LocPrf Weight Path
I*>  1.9.0.0/24       10.1.15.5        1800            0 200 4789 4790 e
I*>  1.9.1.0/24       10.1.15.5        1800            0 200 4789 4790 e
I*>  1.9.2.0/24       10.1.15.5        1800            0 200 4789 4790 e
I*>  1.9.3.0/24       10.1.15.5        1800            0 200 4789 4790 e
I*>  1.9.4.0/24       10.1.15.5        1800            0 200 4789 4790 e
V*>  1.9.50.0/24      10.1.15.5        1193            0 200 4790 4788 e
V*>  1.9.51.0/24      10.1.15.5        1193            0 200 4790 4788 e
V*>  1.9.52.0/24      10.1.15.5        1193            0 200 4790 4788 e
V*>  1.9.53.0/24      10.1.15.5        1193            0 200 4790 4788 e
N*>  34.1.4.0/24      10.1.15.5        1657            0 200 4789 4790 4791 e
N*>  34.1.5.0/24      10.1.15.5        1657            0 200 4789 4790 4791 e
N*>  34.1.6.0/24      10.1.15.5        1657            0 200 4789 4790 4791 e
N*>  34.1.7.0/24      10.1.15.5        1657            0 200 4789 4790 4791 e
N*>  34.1.8.0/24      10.1.15.5        1657            0 200 4789 4790 4791 e
! Output omitted for brevity
```

Example 9-14 demonstrates the origin AS prefix validation on IOS XR software.
The command **show bgp origin-as validity valid** command displays the valid prefixes
that match the prefix and the origin AS with the ROA entries. The command **show
bgp origin-as validity invalid** command displays the invalid prefixes. Notice that
the output shows the origin AS as AS 300, whereas the prefix is supposed to be
originated from AS 3215, thus marking the prefixes as invalid. The command **show
bgp origin-as validity not-found** displays the prefixes that were not found during
the ROA lookup.

Example 9-14 *BGP Origin-AS Prefix Validation*

```
IOS XR
RP/0/0/CPU0:R4# show bgp origin-as validity valid
BGP router identifier 192.168.4.4, local AS number 100
BGP generic scan interval 60 secs
Non-stop routing is enabled
BGP table state: Active
```

```
Table ID: 0xe0000000   RD version: 25305
BGP main routing table version 25305
BGP NSR Initial initsync version 2 (Reached)
BGP NSR/ISSU Sync-Group versions 0/0
BGP scan interval 60 secs


Status codes: s suppressed, d damped, h history, * valid, > best
              i - internal, r RIB-failure, S stale, N Nexthop-discard
Origin codes: i - IGP, e - EGP, ? - incomplete
   Network            Next Hop           Metric LocPrf Weight Path
*> 2.1.0.0/16         10.1.46.6           2309          0 300 3215 e
*> 2.2.0.0/16         10.1.46.6           2309          0 300 3215 e
*> 2.3.0.0/16         10.1.46.6           2309          0 300 3215 e
*> 2.4.0.0/16         10.1.46.6           2309          0 300 3215 e
*> 2.5.0.0/16         10.1.46.6           2309          0 300 3215 e
*> 2.6.0.0/16         10.1.46.6           2309          0 300 3215 e
*> 2.7.0.0/16         10.1.46.6           2309          0 300 3215 e
*> 2.8.0.0/16         10.1.46.6           2309          0 300 3215 e
*> 2.9.0.0/16         10.1.46.6           2309          0 300 3215 e
*> 2.10.0.0/16        10.1.46.6           2309          0 300 3215 e


Processed 10 prefixes, 10 paths
RP/0/0/CPU0:R4# show bgp origin-as validity invalid
! Output omitted for brevity
   Network            Next Hop           Metric LocPrf Weight Path
*> 2.12.0.0/16        10.1.46.6           2747          0 300 e
*> 2.14.0.0/16        10.1.46.6           2747          0 300 e


Processed 2 prefixes, 2 paths
RP/0/0/CPU0:R4# show bgp origin-as validity not-found
! Output omitted for brevity
   Network            Next Hop           Metric LocPrf Weight Path
*> 2.16.0.0/16        10.1.46.6           2747          0 300 e
*> 2.17.0.0/16        10.1.46.6           2747          0 300 e


Processed 2 prefixes, 2 paths
```

Note   Similar to Cisco IOS, use the command **show bgp** *afi safi* **origin-as validity** [**valid** | **invalid** | **not-found**] to display the routes in the BGP table with their validity state. On IOS XR, a fourth validity state is seen in the command output *D*, which stands for *disabled*.

Use the command **show bgp** *afi safi* [*prefix*] to verify the validity state of the prefix received from each neighbor. Example 9-15 displays the prefix validation state using this command.

Example 9-15 *Verifying Prefix Validation State*

```
IOS
R1# show bgp ipv4 unicast 1.9.0.0/24
BGP routing table entry for 1.9.0.0/24, version 4466
Paths: (1 available, no best path)
  Not advertised to any peer
  Refresh Epoch 1
  200 4789 4790
    10.1.15.5 from 10.1.15.5 (10.1.15.5)
      Origin EGP, metric 1800, localpref 100, valid, external
      path 7F58A93D2C08 RPKI State invalid
      rx pathid: 0, tx pathid: 0

R1# show bgp ipv4 unicast 1.9.53.0/24
BGP routing table entry for 1.9.53.0/24, version 1746
Paths: (1 available, best #1, table default)
  Advertised to update-groups:
     12
  Refresh Epoch 1
  200 4790 4788
    10.1.15.5 from 10.1.15.5 (10.1.15.5)
      Origin EGP, metric 1193, localpref 100, valid, external, best
      path 7F58A93D0608 RPKI State valid
      rx pathid: 0, tx pathid: 0x0
```

```
IOS XR
RP/0/0/CPU0:R4# show bgp ipv4 unicast 2.1.0.0/16
! Output omitted for brevity
  300 3215
    10.1.46.6 from 10.1.46.6 (10.1.46.6)
      Origin EGP, metric 2309, localpref 100, valid, external, best, group-best
      Received Path ID 0, Local Path ID 1, version 33619
      Origin-AS validity: valid

RP/0/0/CPU0:R4# show bgp ipv4 unicast 2.11.0.0/16
! Output omitted for brevity
  300
    10.1.46.6 from 10.1.46.6 (10.1.46.6)
      Origin EGP, metric 2747, localpref 100, valid, external, best, group-best
      Received Path ID 0, Local Path ID 1, version 33630
      Origin-AS validity: invalid
RP/0/0/CPU0:R4#
```

With RPKI, the default behavior of BGP is that a router does not advertise the RPKI states of EBGP learned paths to IBGP peers. This is the reason that the outputs in both Examples 9-13 and 9-14 display the validated prefixes learned from local EBGP peers and not learned via remote IBGP peers. To allow the sharing of RPKI state information between the IBGP peers, use the command **neighbor** *ip-address* **announce rpki state** on Cisco IOS and the command **bgp origin-as validation signal ibgp** on IOS XR. Example 9-16 demonstrates the configuration for announcing RPKI states to IBGP peers.

Example 9-16   *Announcing RPKI States to IBGP Peers*

```
IOS
R1(config)# router bgp 100
R1(config-router)# address-family ipv4 unicast
R1(config-router-af)# neighbor 192.168.2.2 announce rpki state
R1(config-router-af)# neighbor 192.168.2.2 send-community

IOS XR
RP/0/0/CPU0:R4(config)# router bgp 100
RP/0/0/CPU0:R4(config-bgp)# address-family ipv4 unicast
RP/0/0/CPU0:R4(config-bgp-af)# bgp origin-as validation signal ibgp
RP/0/0/CPU0:R4(config-bgp-af)# send=community
RP/0/0/CPU0:R4(config-bgp-af)# commit
```

Note   For the **neighbor announce rpki state** command to function properly, configure the IBGP peer with the **neighbor send-community** [extended | both] command.

Upon receiving the validity state information via extended community, IBGP peers can derive their validity state without having to perform a lookup in the RPKI database. After configuring the commands to announce RPKI states to IBGP peers in Example 9-16, both R1 and R4 routers are able to see the prefixes validated by each other. Example 9-17 displays the output of validated prefixes from the IBGP peers on both R1 and R4, respectively. Notice the next-hop of the validated prefix. Router R1 shows the prefixes validated by router R4, whereas R4 displays the prefixes validated by router R1.

Example 9-17   *Validated Prefixes from IBGP Peer*

```
IOS
R1# show bgp ipv4 unicast

     Network          Next Hop         Metric LocPrf Weight Path
V*>i 2.1.0.0/16       192.168.4.4        2309    100      0 300 3215 e
V*>i 2.2.0.0/16       192.168.4.4        2309    100      0 300 3215 e
V*>i 2.3.0.0/16       192.168.4.4        2309    100      0 300 3215 e
! Output omitted for brevity
```

```
IOS XR
RP/0/0/CPU0:R4# show bgp origin-as validity valid
  Network           Next Hop            Metric LocPrf Weight Path
*>i1.9.50.0/24      192.168.1.1           1193    100      0 200 4790 4788 e
*>i1.9.51.0/24      192.168.1.1           1193    100      0 200 4790 4788 e
*>i1.9.52.0/24      192.168.1.1           1193    100      0 200 4790 4788 e
! Output omitted for brevity
```

When a BGP route enters an AS, the received path is checked for origin-AS validity because these routes are not under the local AS's control and can be potentially unsafe. To avoid repeating the Origin AS validation process at each router in the AS, the edge router that computes an EBGP route's validity signals the validity state of the route that it has calculated through a nontransitive BGP extended community. All its internal IBGP peers in the AS can, if they so choose, derive the validity of the route from this extended community setting.

To disable the RPKI validation process, use the command **bgp bestpath prefix-validate disable** on Cisco IOS and the command **bgp origin-as validation disable** on IOS XR. Using this command, prefix validation for all EBGP paths is disabled and all EBGP paths are marked as valid by default. It is important to remember that disabling the prefix validation does not disconnect the connection with the RPKI server. The server connection remains up, and the RPKI information downloads but is not used in any manner. Example 9-18 shows how to disable RPKI validation on the router. Notice that on IOS XR, the origin AS validation (RPKI validation) can be performed at four levels:

- **Global level:** Disables origin AS validation for all neighbors in all address-families.

- **Global address-family level:** Disables origin AS validation for all neighbors in a specified address-family.

- **Neighbor level:** Disables origin AS validation for all address-families for a neighbor. The neighbor should be an EBGP neighbor.

- **Neighbor address-family level:** Disables origin AS validation only for a particular address-family for a neighbor.

Example 9-18   *Disable RPKI Validation*

```
IOS
R1(config)# router bgp 100
R1(config-router)# address-family ipv4 unicast
R1(config-router-af)# bgp bestpath prefix-validate disable
```

```
IOS XR
RP/0/0/CPU0:R4(config)# router bgp 100
```

```
RP/0/0/CPU0:R4(config-bgp)# bgp origin-as validation disable
RP/0/0/CPU0:R4(config-bgp)# address-family ipv4 unicast
RP/0/0/CPU0:R4(config-bgp-af)# bgp origin-as validation disable
RP/0/0/CPU0:R4(config-bgp-af)# exit
RP/0/0/CPU0:R4(config-bgp)# neighbor 10.1.46.6
RP/0/0/CPU0:R4(config-bgp-nbr)# origin-as validation disable
RP/0/0/CPU0:R4(config-bgp-nbr)# address-family ipv4 unicast
RP/0/0/CPU0:R4(config-bgp-nbr-af)# origin-as validation disable
RP/0/0/CPU0:R4(config-bgp-nbr-af)# commit
```

Note On IOS XR, the command **bgp origin-as validation time** [off | *5-60*] can be used instead of the disable option. Use the **time** command option to either set off the automatic prefix validation after the RPKI update or set the time to wait between an RPKI update and a BGP table walk. This command option is only available globally and not under any neighbor or address-family.

RPKI Best-Path Calculation

The validation state of the prefixes can be used in the network to perform the best-path calculations. By default, BGP best-path algorithm allows prefixes that are marked valid and not-found. The prefixes marked invalid are disallowed for the best-path calculation process by default. However, this behavior can be overridden via configuration.

Before understanding how the best-path calculation can be influenced for origin AS validated prefixes, it is important to verify what functionality is enabled by default or from configuration. Although looking at the configuration is easy, it can also be verified using the show command **show bgp rpki summary** on IOS XR. Such a command is not available for Cisco IOS. Examine the output as shown in Example 9-19. In the command output, notice that three options can be seen, and this is with the default settings when RPKI is enabled. This command also displays a summarized view of the RPKI database.

Example 9-19 *BGP RPKI Summary*

```
IOS XR
RP/0/0/CPU0:R4# show bgp rpki summary
RPKI cache-servers configured: 1
RPKI global knobs
  Origin-AS validation is ENABLED globally
  Origin-AS validity WILL NOT affect bestpath selection globally
  Origin-AS validity signaling towards iBGP is DISABLED globally
RPKI database
  Total IPv4 net/path: 12278/12664
  Total IPv6 net/path: 1866/1927
```

On Cisco IOS, the RPKI best-path calculation is enabled by default, and the only way to disable it is by disabling the prefix validation. On IOS XR, the best-path calculation can be influenced based on the prefix validation using the knob **bgp bestpath origin-as use validity**. This command can either be enabled globally or under a particular address-family. Example 9-20 demonstrates the configuration for enabling RPKI for BGP best-path calculation. After the **bgp bestpath origin-as use validity** command is configured, the **show bgp rpki summary** command output displays the configured options.

Example 9-20 *Enabling RPKI for Best-Path Calculation*

```
IOS XR
RP/0/0/CPU0:R4(config)# router bgp 100
RP/0/0/CPU0:R4(config-bgp)# bgp bestpath origin-as use validity
RP/0/0/CPU0:R4(config-bgp)# address-family ipv4 unicast
RP/0/0/CPU0:R4(config-bgp-af)# bgp bestpath origin-as use validity
RP/0/0/CPU0:R4(config-bgp-af)# commit

RP/0/0/CPU0:R4# show bgp rpki summary
RPKI cache-servers configured: 1
RPKI global knobs
  Origin-AS validation is ENABLED globally
  Origin-AS validity WILL affect bestpath selection globally
    Origin-AS 'invalid' routes CANNOT be bestpaths
  Origin-AS validity signaling towards iBGP is DISABLED globally
RPKI database
  Total IPv4 net/path: 6800/6931
  Total IPv6 net/path: 1032/1054
```

To enable invalid marked routes to be used during the best-path calculation process, use the command **bgp bestpath prefix-validate allow-invalid** on Cisco IOS and the command **bgp bestpath origin-as allow invalid** on IOS XR. The command on IOS XR can be configured at multiple levels and takes effect only when the command **bgp bestpath origin-as use origin-as validity** is enabled. Example 9-21 demonstrates the configuration for allowing invalid prefixes to be accounted during best-path calculation.

Example 9-21 *Enabling Invalid Prefixes for Best-Path Calculation*

```
IOS
R1(config)# router bgp 100
R1(config-router)# address-family ipv4 unicast
R1(config-router-af)# bgp bestpath prefix-validate allow-invalid
```

```
IOS XR
RP/0/0/CPU0:R4(config)# router bgp 100
RP/0/0/CPU0:R4(config-bgp)# bgp bestpath origin-as allow invalid
```

```
RP/0/0/CPU0:R4(config-bgp)# address-family ipv4 unicast
RP/0/0/CPU0:R4(config-bgp-af)# bgp bestpath origin-as allow invalid
RP/0/0/CPU0:R4(config-bgp-af)# exit
RP/0/0/CPU0:R4(config-bgp)# neighbor 10.1.46.6
RP/0/0/CPU0:R4(config-bgp-nbr)# bestpath origin-as allow invalid
RP/0/0/CPU0:R4(config-bgp-nbr)# address-family ipv4 unicast
RP/0/0/CPU0:R4(config-bgp-nbr-af)# bestpath origin-as allow invalid
RP/0/0/CPU0:R4(config-bgp-nbr-af)# commit
```

Note   When the **bestpath origin-as allow invalid** command is configured at a neighbor or neighbor address-family level, ensure the command is enabled for EBGP neighbors.

Various controls on origin AS validity state are configured using route-maps on Cisco IOS and Route Policy Language (RPL) on IOS XR. Policies matching on validity state can be configured only at the neighbor inbound attach point for any BGP neighbor. Example 9-22 illustrates how routing policy can be used to influence the path selection process based on the prefix validity state. On Cisco IOS, a route-map is created to set the local-preference to 200 for prefixes that are marked valid, set local-preference to 50 if the prefixes are marked invalid, and the not-found marked prefixes are set with default local-preference value. On IOS XR, the similar action is taken, except for the invalid routes, which are dropped and thus not installed in the BGP table.

Example 9-22   *Influencing Path Selection Using Route Policies*

```
IOS
R1(config)# route-map Match_RPKI permit 10
R1(config-route-map)# match rpki valid
R1(config-route-map)# set local-preference 200
R1(config-route-map)# exit
R1(config)# route-map Match_RPKI permit 20
R1(config-route-map)# match rpki invalid
R1(config-route-map)# set local-preference 50
R1(config-route-map)# exit
R1(config)# route-map Match_RPKI permit 30
! Below match statement is not really required but here for
! demonstration purpose
R1(config-route-map)# match rpki not-found
R1(config-route-map)# set local-preference 100
R1(config-route-map)# exit
```

```
R1(config)# router bgp 100
R1(config-router)# address-family ipv4 unicast
R1(config-router-af)# neighbor 10.1.15.5 route-map Match_RPKI in
```

```
IOS XR
RP/0/0/CPU0:R4(config)# route-policy Match_RPKI
RP/0/0/CPU0:R4(config-rpl)# if validation-state is valid then
RP/0/0/CPU0:R4(config-rpl-if)# set local-preference 200
RP/0/0/CPU0:R4(config-rpl-if)# pass
RP/0/0/CPU0:R4(config-rpl-if)# exit
RP/0/0/CPU0:R4(config-rpl)# if validation-state is invalid then
RP/0/0/CPU0:R4(config-rpl-if)# drop
RP/0/0/CPU0:R4(config-rpl-if)# else
RP/0/0/CPU0:R4(config-rpl-else)# set local-preference 100
RP/0/0/CPU0:R4(config-rpl-else)# pass
RP/0/0/CPU0:R4(config-rpl-else)# exit
RP/0/0/CPU0:R4(config-rpl)# exit
RP/0/0/CPU0:R4(config)# router bgp 100
RP/0/0/CPU0:R4(config-bgp)# neighbor 10.1.46.6
RP/0/0/CPU0:R4(config-bgp-nbr)# address-family ipv4 unicast
RP/0/0/CPU0:R4(config-bgp-nbr-af)# route-policy Match_RPKI in
RP/0/0/CPU0:R4(config-bgp-nbr-af)# commit
```

Note   If the prefix validation is already performed, it is good to perform a clear on the BGP connection or clear the RPKI validation; this will instantiate the validation process and the route policy will be processed.

BGP Remote Triggered Black-Hole Filtering

DDOS attacks target network infrastructure or computer services by sending an overwhelming number of service requests to the server from many sources. Server and network resources are used up in serving the fake requests, resulting in denial or degradation of legitimate service requests to be served. A network under DDOS attack can face a major service and financial impact and requires immediate mitigation.

BGP RTBH filtering is a security technique used to mitigate or overcome DDOS attacks. When a network is under DDOS attack, many resources, such as bandwidth, CPU, and memory, can be used up along with the target server's service degradation. It is important to understand that RTBH is more of a reactive measure after a DDoS attack is reported. It does not prevent a DDoS attack from happening; rather, it is a way of dealing with the problem. The DDoS traffic is dropped at the edge of the network closest to the source.

Because the packets are dropped in CEF or fast path, there is little impact to the router doing the filtering. The RTBH mechanism should be considered from two perspectives:

- Destination based
- Source based

Source based is when you want to filter traffic from a specific or unwanted source address, and destination based is when you want to filter based on a specific destination.

Examine the topology in Figure 9-15 to further understand how BGP RTBH works. The internal network is composed of R1, R2, R3, and R4. R1 is connected toward the Internet. The target server is connected behind R4. A DDOS attack is coming from the Internet toward the target server. In this topology, the router R3 is the trigger router.

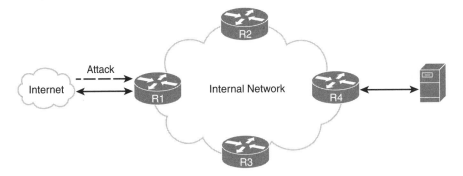

Figure 9-15 *DDOS Attack Mitigation with RTBH*

To mitigate the DDOS attack using destination-based RTBH, follow these steps:

Step 1. Create a Static Route Destined to Null0. The static route can be defined on Test-Net range IP addresses described in RFC 3330; that is, 192.0.2.0/24 subnet. This route forces any traffic destined to the IP in this subnet to be immediately dropped by the router. This command is configured on the trigger router and also on all the edge devices.

Step 2. Create a route-map or RPL policy with next-hop as the IP used in Step 1, set the community of the route to no-export, set origin to igp.

Step 3. Redistribute the static route defined in Step 1 in BGP using the route-map or RPL defined in Step 2.

Step 4. Create a Static Route for the Destination Server.

Note Steps 1 to 3 should be executed before the DDOS attack. After the DDOS attack is found, follow Step 4.

Notice that in Step 1, the static route points to Null0 interface. The Null0 interface is a pseudo-interface, which can neither receive nor forward traffic. Thus it makes sense to point the undesirable traffic toward that interface and drop it. In Step 2, the route is set with a community value of no-export. This is required to prevent the route from being accidently exported outside the local AS. Although not required, additional communities can also be attached to the route to assign a policy specific to the AS.

Example 9-23 illustrates the configuration of destination-based RTBH.

Example 9-23 *Destination-Based RTBH Configuration on Triggering Router and Edge Router*

```
Trigger Router Configuration
IOS
R3(config)# route-map RTBH permit 10
R3(config-route-map)# match tag 100
R3(config-route-map)# set ip next-hop 192.0.2.1
R3(config-route-map)# set origin igp
R3(config-route-map)# set community no-export
R3(config-route-map)# set local-preference 200
R3(config-route-map)# exit
R3(config)# router bgp 100
R3(config-router)# address-family ipv4 unicast
R3(config-router-af)# redistribute static route-map RTBH

! Configure the Static Route for the Server IP After the DDOS Attack is found
R3(config)# ip route 192.168.100.100 255.255.255.255 null0 tag 100
```

```
IOS XR
RP/0/0/CPU0:R3(config)# route-policy RTBH
RP/0/0/CPU0:R3(config-rpl)# if tag eq 100 then
RP/0/0/CPU0:R3(config-rpl-if)# set next-hop 192.0.2.1
RP/0/0/CPU0:R3(config-rpl-if)# set community (no-export)
RP/0/0/CPU0:R3(config-rpl-if)# set origin igp
RP/0/0/CPU0:R3(config-rpl-if)# set local-preference 200
RP/0/0/CPU0:R3(config-rpl-if)# exit
RP/0/0/CPU0:R3(config-rpl)# exit
RP/0/0/CPU0:R3(config)# router bgp 100
RP/0/0/CPU0:R3(config-bgp)# address-family ipv4 unicast
RP/0/0/CPU0:R3(config-bgp-af)# redistribute static route-policy RTBH
RP/0/0/CPU0:R3(config-bgp-af)# commit

! Configure the Static Route for the Server IP After the DDOS Attack is found
RP/0/0/CPU0:R3(config)# router static
```

```
RP/0/0/CPU0:R3(config-static)# address-family ipv4 unicast
RP/0/0/CPU0:R3(config-static-afi)# 192.168.100.100/32 null0 tag 100
RP/0/0/CPU0:R4(config-static-afi)# commit
```

```
Edge Router Configuration
R1(config)# ip route 192.0.2.1 255.255.255.255 null0
```

After the destination-based RTBH is configured, the edge router (even in case RTBH is not configured on the edge router), gets the best path for the server 192.168.100.100/32 from router R3. Because the next-hop for the prefix is set to 192.0.2.1, and a static route is configured on the edge router for this IP pointing toward null0 interface, the traffic is dropped at the edge itself.

Destination-based RTBH works on destination IP addresses and only prevents return traffic to an infected host. It is effective for connection-oriented protocols, but it does not prevent traffic flooding or DoS traffic from an infected host. Unicast Reverse Path Forwarding (uRPF) is a similar technique that works on source IP addresses to drop the traffic by sender at the edge of the network. This allows other legitimate sources to send their traffic toward the destination server.

uRPF is usually implemented in loose mode. In loose mode, uRPF performs a Forwarding Information Base (FIB) lookup for the source IP on the router. If the FIB has the information for the source IP, the packet is forwarded toward the destination. If the FIB does not have the information of the source IP, or if the FIB points toward Null0 interface, the reverse path forwarding (RPF) check fails, and the router drops the packet.

uRPF is configured on the edge devices in the network. Use the command **ip verify unicast source reachable-via**. Example 9-24 demonstrates the configuration of uRPF on the edge devices in the topology.

Example 9-24 *Source-Based RTBH Configuration*

```
IOS
R1(config)# interface gigabitethernet 0/1
R1(config-if)# ip verify unicast source reachable-via any
```

```
IOS XR
RP/0/0/CPU0:R3(config)# interface gigabitethernet 0/0/0/0
RP/0/0/CPU0:R3(config-if)# ipv4 verify unicast source reachable-via any
RP/0/0/CPU0:R3(config-if)# commit
```

BGP Flowspec

BGP Flow Specification (Flowspec) defined in RFC 5575, *Dissemination of Flow Specification Rules*, provides for a mechanism to encode flow specification rules for aggregated traffic flows so that they can be distributed as a BGP network layer reachability information (NLRI). Per the RFC: "*A flow specification is an n-tuple consisting of several matching criteria that can be applied to IP traffic. A given IP packet is said to match the defined flow if it matches all the specified criteria*". A flowspec is said to be n-tuple because there are multiple match criterias that can be defined, and all the match criteria should be matched. Traffic does not match the flowspec entry if all the tuples are not matched.

BGP flowspec has many possible applications, but the primary one for many network operators is the distribution of traffic filtering actions for DDoS attack mitigation.

To address the DDOS attacks, the focus should be first on its detection, such as invalid or malicious incoming requests, and then mitigation. Mitigation of DDOS attacks is performed in two steps:

Step 1.   **Diversion:** Send traffic to a specialized device that removes the invalid or malicious packets from the traffic stream while retaining the legitimate packets.

Step 2.   **Return:** Send back the clean and legitimate traffic to the server.

Examine the DDOS attack mitigation scenario in Figure 9-16. When an attack traffic enters into the edge of the network along with legitimate traffic, the DDOS attack is detected using Netflow data. By analyzing the Netflow data, suspected flows are exported to the security server, where the data is further analyzed to ensure if it is a DDOS attack or not. As soon as the DDOS attack is confirmed, the security server updates the edge routers using BGP flowspec to drop, rate-limit, or redirect traffic toward the DDOS scrubber where the DDOS traffic is further analyzed and cleaned.

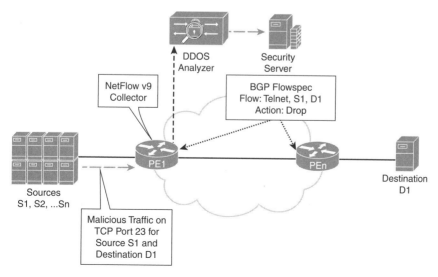

Figure 9-16   *DDOS Mitigation Scenario*

A few other applications of BGP flowspec include the following:

- "…automate inter-domain coordination of traffic filtering, such as what is required in order to mitigate (distributed) denial-of-service attacks" (RFC5575)

- "…traffic filtering in the context of a BGP/MPLS VPN service" (RFC5575)

- Bogon Feed: *http://www.cymru.com/jtk/misc/community-fs.html*

- SIDR feed: Propagation of rules related to the validity of the origin of prefix advertisements

- Kill switch: Ability for a central authority to apply filters at the edge of a wide range of service providers

Although BGP RTBH is one of the solutions to DDOS attacks, BGP flowspec provides a more granular approach to this problem by effectively constructing instructions to match a particular flow with source and destination, Layer 4 parameters, and packet specifics, such as length, fragment, and so on, and allow for a dynamic installation of an action at the border routers. To resolve these attacks, perform one of the following:

- Drop the traffic.

- Inject it in a different VRF for further inspection and analysis.

- Allow the traffic, but policing / rate limiting the traffic at a defined rate.

BGP flowspec defines a new NLRI with an AFI value of 1 and a SAFI value of 133 for unicast traffic filtering and a SAFI value of 134 for VPN traffic filtering. The NLRI is treated as an opaque string by BGP. This NLRI information is encoded using the MP_REACH_NLRI and MP_UNREACH_NLRI attributes. Every flowspec route can be understood as a rule consisting of two parts—match and action. The matching part is encoded in the NLRI field, and the action part is encoded as a BGP extended community.

BGP flowspec allows for the following parameters to be defined by using the various flowspec NLRI types that can be used for the match criteria, as shown in Table 9-1.

Table 9-1 *Flowspec NLRI Type for Match Criteria*

BGP Flowspec NLRI Type	QoS Match Fields
Type 1	Destination IP / IPv6 address
Type 2	Source IP / IPv6 address
Type 3	IP / IPv6 Protocol
Type 4	Source or destination port
Type 5	Destination port
Type 6	Source port
Type 7	ICMP Type

BGP Flowspec NLRI Type	QoS Match Fields
Type 8	ICMP Code
Type 9	TCP flags
Type 10	Packet length
Type 11	DSCP
Type 12	Fragmentation bits

The default action for a traffic filtering flow specification is to accept the traffic that matches a particular rule. Various actions can be defined based on the extended community values as described in Table 9-2.

Table 9-2   *Extended Community Value–Based Actions*

Type	Description	PBR Action
0x8006	traffic-rate	Drop	Police
0x8007	traffic-action	Terminal Action + Sampling
0x8008	redirect-vrf	Redirect VRF
0x8009	traffic-marking	Set DSCP
0x0800	Redirect IP NH	Redirect IPv4 or IPv6 Next-Hop

Configuring BGP Flowspec

BGP flowspec supports client/server architecture. The router acting as a server, a.k.a. controller, injects the flowspec NLRI entries, and the router acting as a client (BGP Speaker) receives the NLRI from the controller and programs the hardware according to the instructions defined in the flowspec NLRI entry.

Note   Devices running Cisco IOS can only be configured as flowspec client or route reflector. As of the time of writing, only the IOS XR device is capable of running as a flowspec controller. Virtual XR (XRv) devices cannot be configured as client devices because they are not hardware-forwarding capable. Thus they can only be configured as controller.

Because the controller is responsible for injecting flowspec entries, the controller should be configured with a policy-map and should be associated to enhanced Policy-Based Routing (ePBR). The controller configuration is done in the **flowspec** configuration mode. After the flowspec configuration is done, a new address-family is enabled on BGP for advertisement and connection establishment purposes between the server and the client. This configuration is similar on both the controller and the client. On the client side, the only thing to ensure is that the flowspec peering is functional between the controller (route reflector) and the client.

For illustrating the configuration and functioning of BGP flowspec, examine the topology in Figure 9-17. Router R3 is acting as a controller, and routers R2 and R4 are the BGP flowspec clients.

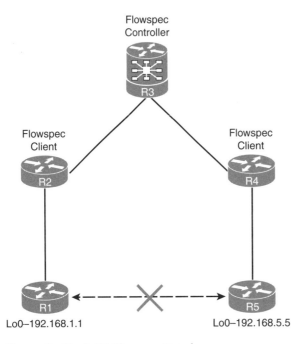

Figure 9-17 *BGP Flowspec Topology*

Example 9-25 illustrates the configuration of BGP flowspec peering between the server and the client router. This configuration helps bring up the BGP peering between the two peers for the ipv4 flowspec address-family.

Example 9-25 *BGP Flowspec Peering*

```
IOS XR
RP/0/0/CPU0:RR_R3(config)# router bgp 100
RP/0/0/CPU0:RR_R3(config-bgp)# bgp router-id 192.168.3.3
RP/0/0/CPU0:RR_R3(config-bgp)# address-family ipv4 flowspec
RP/0/0/CPU0:RR_R3(config-bgp-af)# exit
RP/0/0/CPU0:RR_R3(config-bgp)# neighbor 192.168.2.2
RP/0/0/CPU0:RR_R3(config-bgp-nbr)# remote-as 100
RP/0/0/CPU0:RR_R3(config-bgp-nbr)# update-source loopback0
RP/0/0/CPU0:RR_R3(config-bgp-nbr)# address-family ipv4 flowspec
RP/0/0/CPU0:RR_R3(config-bgp-nbr-af)# route-reflector-client
RP/0/0/CPU0:RR_R3(config-bgp-nbr-af)# commit

IOS
R2(config-if)# router bgp 100
```

```
R2(config-router)# bgp router-id 192.168.2.2
R2(config-router)# neighbor 192.168.3.3 remote-as 100
R2(config-router)# neighbor 192.168.3.3 update-source loopback0
R2(config-router)# address-family ipv4 flowspec
R2(config-router-af)# neighbor 192.168.3.3 activate
R2(config-router-af)# neighbor 192.168.3.3 next-hop-self
R2(config-router-af)# end
```

Example 9-26 displays the output of the **show bgp ipv4 flowspec summary** command on both IOS and IOS XR routers. Use the **show bgp** *afi* **flowspec summary** command to verify the neighborship in other address-families.

Example 9-26   *BGP Flowspec Neighborship Verification*

```
IOS XR
RP/0/0/CPU0:RR_R3# show bgp ipv4 flowspec summary
! Output omitted for brevity

Neighbor         Spk    AS MsgRcvd MsgSent   TblVer   InQ OutQ  Up/Down   St/PfxRcd
192.168.2.2        0   100      12      12        1     0    0 00:08:59           0


IOS
R2# show bgp ipv4 flowspec summary
BGP router identifier 192.168.2.2, local AS number 100
BGP table version is 1, main routing table version 1

Neighbor         V     AS MsgRcvd MsgSent   TblVer   InQ OutQ Up/Down   State/PfxRcd
192.168.3.3      4    100      14      15        1     0    0 00:11:54             0
```

Notice that in the command outputs, there are 0 prefixes received. Even if the IPv4 unicast address-family holds multiple prefixes, the number of prefixes for flowspec remains at 0 until a flowspec entry is advertised by the controller. The controller can be configured in few simple steps:

Step 1.   In the class definition, create a class-map and configure the required tuple definition. The tuple definitions are the various match statements that can be configured.

Step 2.   Define action. Create a policy-map and specify the required action for each class-map.

Step 3.   Configure flowspec using the **flowspec** command, and enable flowspec on all the interfaces using the subcommand **local-install interface-all**. Then define the address-families for which the flowspec will be injected.

Step 4.   Associate the flowspec with PBR using the command **service-policy type pbr** *policy-map-name* under the respective address-family. The flowspec can also be defined for address-families under VRF.

Example 9-27 demonstrates the configuration for defining the flowspec on the controller. The configuration illustrates blocking traffic sourced from the R1 loopback interface, 192.168.1.1/32, toward the R5 loopback address,192.168.5.5/32.

Example 9-27   *BGP Flowspec Controller Configuration*

```
IOS XR
RP/0/0/CPU0:RR_R3(config)# class-map type traffic match-all FS_RULE
RP/0/0/CPU0:RR_R3(config-cmap)# match source-address ipv4 192.168.1.1/32
RP/0/0/CPU0:RR_R3(config-cmap)# match destination-address ipv4 192.168.5.5/32
RP/0/0/CPU0:RR_R3(config-cmap)# exit
RP/0/0/CPU0:RR_R3(config)# policy-map type pbr FS_POLICY_MAP
RP/0/0/CPU0:RR_R3(config-pmap)# class FS_RULE
RP/0/0/CPU0:RR_R3(config-pmap-c)# drop
RP/0/0/CPU0:RR_R3(config-pmap-c)# exit
RP/0/0/CPU0:RR_R3(config-pmap)# class class-default
RP/0/0/CPU0:RR_R3(config-pmap-c)# exit
RP/0/0/CPU0:RR_R3(config-pmap)# exit
RP/0/0/CPU0:RR_R3(config)# flowspec
RP/0/0/CPU0:RR_R3(config-flowspec)# address-family ipv4
RP/0/0/CPU0:RR_R3(config-flowspec-af)# service-policy type pbr FS_POLICY_MAP
RP/0/0/CPU0:RR_R3(config-flowspec-af)# exit
RP/0/0/CPU0:RR_R3(config-flowspec)# exit
RP/0/0/CPU0:RR_R3(config)# commit
```

```
IOS
! Configuration required on Client side
R2(config)# flowspec
R2(config-flowspec)# local-install interface-all
R2(config-flowspec)# address-family ipv4
```

As stated in the previous steps, the command **local-install interface-all** is required to enable flowspec on all the interfaces and allow them to install the policies pushed by the controller. The command is only required on the controller if you want to install the entries on the controller as well. If the controller is being configured on XRv router, **local-install interface-all** command is not required. The reason is that this command will try to install the policies in the hardware, but the XRv instance is not hardware dependent; thus it will throw an error. Configuring the command **local-install interface-all** on the client router installs flowspec policies on all interfaces.

Note Flowspec can be disabled on specific interfaces using the interface subcommand [ip | ipv6] **flowspec disable**. On IOS XR, use [**ipv4** | **ipv6**] flowspec disable.

After configuring the controller with the necessary flowspec, BGP flowspec NLRI is sent to the BGP flowspec peer. At this point, the **show bgp** *afi* **flowspec summary** command shows 1 prefix (entry) received and advertised. When looking at the BGP table for the received flowspec entry, the same flowspec entry that was configured on the controller is seen on the client router.

Example 9-28 displays the BGP flowspec entry on the controller as well as on the client router. Before looking at the BGP flowspec table, notice the command **show bgp ipv4 flowspec summary** output on the client router. The number of prefixes received is increased to 1. This confirms that the flowspec entry was received from the controller.

Example 9-28 *BGP Flowspec Definition*

```
IOS XR
RP/0/0/CPU0:RR_R3# show bgp ipv4 flowspec
   Network          Next Hop          Metric LocPrf Weight Path
*> Dest:192.168.5.5/32,Source:192.168.1.1/32/96
                    0.0.0.0                                 0 i


Processed 1 prefixes, 1 paths
```

```
IOS
R2# show bgp ipv4 flowspec summary
! Output omitted for brevity

Neighbor      V    AS MsgRcvd MsgSent  TblVer  InQ OutQ Up/Down  State/PfxRcd
192.168.3.3   4   100    114    123       2    0    0 01:50:29          1

R2# show bgp ipv4 flowspec

   Network          Next Hop          Metric LocPrf Weight Path
*>i Dest:192.168.5.5/32,Source:192.168.1.1/32
                    0.0.0.0                         100      0 i
```

Both Cisco IOS / IOS XE and IOS XR platforms provide various flowspec verification commands that can be used during troubleshooting. To verify the BGP flowspec NLRI information, use the command **show flowspec [ipv4 | ipv6] nlri [internal | detail]**. This command shows the same information about the configured policy on the controller. Example 9-29 displays the output of command **show flowspec nlri** to view the NLRI information. The command with **detail** and **internal** options displays the Matched and Dropped counters, which tell about the number of packets matched and dropped.

Example 9-29 *Flowspec NLRI Information*

```
IOS XR
RP/0/0/CPU0:RR_R3# show flowspec ipv4 nlri detail
AFI: IPv4
  NLRI (hex)      :0x0120c0a805050220c0a80101
    Actions       :Traffic-rate: 0 bps  (policy.1.FS_POLICY_MAP.FS_RULE)


RP/0/0/CPU0:RR_R3# show flowspec ipv4 nlri internal
AFI: IPv4
  NLRI (hex)      :0x0120c0a805050220c0a80101
    Actions       :Traffic-rate: 0 bps  (policy.1.FS_POLICY_MAP.FS_RULE)
      Client Version: 0
      Unsupported:   FALSE
      RT:
        VRF Name Cfg:   0x00
        RT Cfg:         0x00
        RT Registered:  0x00
        RT Resolved:    0x00
      Class handles:
      Class Handle Version:     0
      Sequence:               1024
      Match Unsupported:      None
      Synced:                 FALSE
      Ref Count:              1
      Last Error:             0:No error
      Last Batch:             0
      Time Init:              Jan 19 06:29:06
      Time iClass Update:
```

```
IOS
R2# show flowspec ipv4 nlri detail
AFI: IPv4
  NLRI (hex)      :0x0120C0A805050220C0A80101
    Actions       :Traffic-rate: 0 bps  (bgp.1)
    Statistics                       (packets/bytes)
      Matched           :              0/0
      Dropped           :              0/0


R2# show flowspec ipv4 nlri internal
AFI: IPv4
  NLRI (hex)      :0x0120C0A805050220C0A80101
    Actions       :Traffic-rate: 0 bps  (bgp.1)
      Client Version: 0
      Unsupported:   FALSE
      RT:
```

```
      VRF Name Cfg:     0x00
      RT Cfg:           0x00
      RT Registered:    0x00
      RT Resolved:      0x00
   Class handles:
     Handle [0]:        4c9da1
   Class Handle Version:    1
   Sequence:               1024
   Synced:                 FALSE
   Match Unsupported:      None
   Ref Count:              1
   Last Error:             0x0:Unknown error 0
   Last Batch:             1
   Statistics                         (packets/bytes)
     Matched           :              0/0
     Dropped           :              0/0
```

Use the command **show flowspec client [internal]** to view the client-specific stats. The internal option provides more detailed counters and also shows the success and error counters for the connection and the client policy. This is useful when troubleshooting flowspec sending and receiving issues between the controller and client devices.

Example 9-30 displays the command output of the **show flowspec client [internal]** command. Because RR_R3 router is the controller, two clients are seen in the output. One is via BGP and the other is the flowspec policy. The client router R2 only is receiving the flow via BGP and thus shows just one client and one flow received. Ensure that the client state shows connected.

Example 9-30   show flowspec client *Command*

```
IOS XR
RP/0/0/CPU0:RR_R3# show flowspec client
Client: bgp.1
  State: Connected
  Flows: 0
Client: policy.1
  State: Connected
  Flows: 1

RP/0/0/CPU0:RR_R3# show flowspec client internal
Client: bgp.1
  State: Connected
    Time Create:            Jan 19 06:29:06
    Time Dormant:
     Remaining:             0
```

```
  Time Connected:          Jan 19 06:29:06
  Time Replay:
  Time Unconfigured:
Flows: 0
Version: 0
Node: 0/0/CPU0
PID: 704784
Manager IPC Handle: 0x20003008
Manager IPC Tx Would Block: FALSE
Manager IPC Tx MSG Q Size: 0
Manager Stats:               Success     Error
  Connect                        1          0          1          0
  Table Prod Reg                 1          0          1          0
  Table Prod Unreg               0          0          0          0
  Table Redist Reg               1          0          1          0
  Table Redist Unreg             0          0          0          0
  Table Replay End               2          0          2          0
  Table All Replay End           0          0          0          0
  Table GR EOR                   0          0          0          0
  Table NLRI Update              0          0          0          0
  Table NLRI Withdraw            0          0          0          0
  Notify Table NLRI Update       1          0          1          0
  Notify Table NLRI Withdraw     0          0          0          0
  Notify Table Replay End        1          0          1          0
  RT Update                      0          0          0          0
  RT Remove                      0          0          0          0
  RT Replay End                  1          0          1          0
  Notify RT Reg                  0          0          0          0
  Notify RT Unreg                0          0          0          0
  Notify RT Replay End           1          0          1          0
Client State: UP
Client PID: 704784
Client IPC Handle: 0x20003008
Client IPC Tx Would Block: FALSE
Client IPC Tx MSG Q Size: 0
Client Stats:                Success     Error
  Connect                        1          0          1          0
  Table Prod Reg                 1          0          1          0
  Table Prod Unreg               0          0          0          0
  Table Redist Reg               1          0          1          0
  Table Redist Unreg             0          0          0          0
  Table Replay End               2          0          2          0
  Table All Replay End           0          0          0          0
```

```
   Table GR EOR                         0          0          0          0
   Table NLRI Update                    0          0          0          0
   Table NLRI Withdraw                  0          0          0          0
   Notify Table NLRI Update             1          0          1          0
   Notify Table NLRI Withdraw           0          0          0          0
   Notify Table Replay End              1          0          1          0
   RT Update                            0          0          0          0
   RT Remove                            0          0          0          0
   RT Replay End                        1          0          1          0
   Notify RT Reg                        0          0          0          0
   Notify RT Unreg                      0          0          0          0
   Notify RT Replay End                 1          0          1          0
!Output omitted for brevity
```

```
IOS
R2# show flowspec client
Client: bgp.1
  State: Connected
  Flows: 1

R2#show flowspec client internal
Client: bgp.1
  State: Connected
    Time Create:              07:15:00
    Time Dormant:
      Remaining:          0
    Time Connected:           07:15:00
    Time Replay:
    Time Unconfigured:
  Flows: 1
  Version: 0
  Node: <n/a>
  PID: 568
  Manager IPC Handle: 0xdd7d3250
  Manager IPC Q size: 0
  Manager IPC Tx Would Block: FALSE
  Manager IPC Tx MSG Q Size: 0
Manager Stats:                  Success      Error
    Connect                           1          0          1          0
    Table Prod Reg                    1          0          1          0
    Table Prod Unreg                  0          0          0          0
    Table Redist Reg                  0          0          0          0
    Table Redist Unreg                0          0          0          0
    Table Replay End                  0          0          0          0
```

Table All Replay End	0	0	0	0
Table GR EOR	0	0	0	0
Table NLRI Update	1	0	1	0
Table NLRI Withdraw	0	0	0	0
Notify Table NLRI Update	0	0	0	0
Notify Table NLRI Withdraw	0	0	0	0
Notify Table Replay End	0	0	0	0
RT Update	0	0	0	0
RT Remove	0	0	0	0
RT Replay End	0	0	0	0
Notify RT Reg	0	0	0	0
Notify RT Unreg	0	0	0	0
Notify RT Replay End	0	0	0	0

```
Client State: UP
Client PID: 568
Client IPC Handle: 0xdd7d33f0
Client IPC Q Size: 0
! Output omitted for brevity
```

The **show flowspec client internal** command output has two sections. One is the manager stats and other is the client stats. Success and Error statistics are maintained for various fields under each of the stats sections. While troubleshooting, ensure that there is no error counter seen incrementing for any of those fields.

After the flowspec entries are installed on the client, and if a ping test is performed from router R1 loopback0 interface toward R5 loopback interface, the packet does not pass, and the drop counters for these packets are seen in the show flowspec ipv4 detail output. Example 9-31 demonstrates the ping test performed from 192.168.1.1/32 toward 192.168.5.5/32 and the drops counters incrementing on the client router R2.

Example 9-31 *Verifying Flowspec Functioning*

```
R1# show ip route 192.168.5.5
Routing entry for 192.168.5.5/32
  Known via "ospf 100", distance 110, metric 5, type intra area
  Last update from 10.1.12.2 on GigabitEthernet0/2, 00:04:46 ago
  Routing Descriptor Blocks:
  * 10.1.12.2, from 192.168.5.5, 00:04:46 ago, via GigabitEthernet0/2
      Route metric is 5, traffic share count is 1

! Ping to Blocked IP Address
R1# ping 192.168.5.5 source 192.168.1.1
Sending 5, 100-byte ICMP Echos to 192.168.5.5, timeout is 2 seconds:
```

```
Packet sent with a source address of 192.168.1.1

.....

Success rate is 0 percent (0/5)
```

```
! Ping Test to another Destination IP
R1# ping 192.168.4.4 source 192.168.1.1
Sending 5, 100-byte ICMP Echos to 192.168.4.4, timeout is 2 seconds:
Packet sent with a source address of 192.168.1.1
!!!!!
Success rate is 100 percent (5/5), round-trip min/avg/max = 6/9/11 ms
```

```
IOS - Flowspec Client
R2# show flowspec ipv4 detail
AFI: IPv4
  Flow            :Dest:192.168.5.5/32,Source:192.168.1.1/32
    Actions       :Traffic-rate: 0 bps  (bgp.1)
    Statistics                      (packets/bytes)
      Matched           :               8/912
      Dropped           :               8/912
```

Summary

This chapter explained various security threats that BGP is prone to and various solutions that can be applied to help mitigate those security loop holes. It began with exploring various features securing BGP peering using various methods such as MD5 authentication, using link-local addresses for IPv6 BGP peering, TTL security, and IPsec tunnels. Prefix hijacking issues and various methods available to secure interdomain routing in BGP were discussed. Solutions such as S-BGP and soBGP are explored, and RPKI is explained in great detail. With RPKI, the prefixes are validated into three states:

- Valid

- Invalid

- Unknown

Based on these states the best-path calculation in the network can be influenced, and the states can also be advertised to the IBGP peers upon enabling it from configuration.

Further DDOS attacks in BGP are discussed along with solutions such as RTBH and BGP Flowspec. It is important to remember that the BGP RTBH and BGP Flowspec are ways of using BGP as part of a domain security policy because they do not increase security for BGP itself

It is crucial to implement security at various points in a BGP deployment to keep the Internet as secure as possible.

References

RFC 3779, *X.509 Extensions for IP Addresses and AS Identifiers*, C. Lynn, S. Kent, K. Seo, IETF, https://tools.ietf.org/html/rfc3779, June 2004.

RFC 6811, *BGP Prefix Origin Validation*, P. Mohapatra, J. Scudder, D. Ward, R. Bush, R. Austein, IETF, https://tools.ietf.org/html/rfc6811, January 2013.

RFC 5575, *Dissemination of Flow Specification Rules*, P. Marques, N. Sheth, R. Raszuk, B. Greene, J. Mauch, D. McPherson, IETF, https://tools.ietf.org/html/rfc5575, August 2009.

DRAFT, *Secure BGP (S-BGP)*, C. Lynn, J. Mikkelson, K. Seo, IETF, https://tools.ietf.org/html/draft-clynn-s-bgp-protocol-01, June 2003.

DRAFT, *Architecture and Deployment Considerations for Secure Origin BGP*, R. White, IETF, https://tools.ietf.org/html/draft-white-sobgp-architecture-02, July 2006.

RFC 5635, *Remote Triggered Black Hole Filtering with Unicast Reverse Path Forwarding (uRPF)*, W. Kumari, D. McPherson, IETF, https://tools.ietf.org/html/rfc5635, August 2009.

YouTube Hijacking: A RIPE NCC RIS Case Study, https://www.ripe.net/publications/news/industry-developments/youtube-hijacking-a-ripe-ncc-ris-case-study.

BGP—Origin AS Validation, Cisco Documentation, www.cisco.com.

## Chapter 10

MPLS Layer 3 VPN (L3VPN)

The following topics are covered in this chapter:

- MPLS Layer 3 VPN (L3VPN) Overview

- MPLS Layer 3 VPN Configuration

- Virtual Routing and Forwarding (VRF) Instances

- Route Targets (RTs) and Route Distinguishers (RDs)

- Troubleshooting MPLS L3VPN

A *virtual private network (VPN)* provides connectivity to private networks over a public network. VPNs operate by tunneling, encrypting the payload, or both. With VPN tunneling, packets destined between private networks are encapsulated and assigned new packet headers that allow the packet to traverse the public network. Tunnels are a form of *overlay routing* because they exist on top of an existing network, known as the *underlay network* or a *transport network*.

The new packet headers provide a method of forwarding the packet across the public network without exposing the private network's original packet headers. This allows the packet to be forwarded between the two endpoints without requiring any routers from extracting information from the payload (original packet headers and data). After the packet reaches the remote endpoint, the VPN tunnel headers are decapsulated (that is, removed). The endpoint checks the original headers and then forwards the packet out the appropriate interface to the private network.

MPLS VPNs

ISPs use Multiprotocol Label Switching (MPLS) to provide a scalable peer-to-peer architecture that provides a dynamic method of tunneling for packets to transit from provider edge (PE) router to PE router without looking into the original packet's contents.

With traditional routing, a router receives a packet and checks the header for the destination IP address. It then locates the longest matching route in the forwarding table, performs a recursive lookup to find the outbound interface, and then forwards the packet out of that interface. This process continues for every hop (router) along the path to the packet's destination.

MPLS forwarding reduces the lookup process by all the routers in the path of a packet. A router assigns a locally significant label (numerical value) for the directly connected prefixes that are connected to it and then advertises this label to prefix binding to neighboring routers. The neighboring router receives that label and creates a corresponding locally significant label. The process continues where a label exists for all the routes for all the routers in the routing domain.

When a packet is received, the longest match lookup is performed in the forwarding table, and then the associated label is identified. All further forwarding occurs based on the MPLS label. The local router contains a table that correlates its local label with the downstream router's label, and outbound interface. Forwarding lookups are more explicit and do not require subsequent analysis by routers in the middle of the packet's path.

> **Note**   MPLS forwarding is more efficient than traditional route lookups and provides a method of tunneling packets that otherwise could not be forwarded in the underlay network. New technologies continue to be developed upon MPLS forwarding, which reinforces the brilliance of the technology.

MPLS networks forward traffic based on the outermost MPLS label of a packet. The MPLS labels are inserted after the Layer 2 information and before the IP headers (source IP and destination IP) in a packet, so none of the transit routers require the examination of the packet's inner header or payload. As packets cross the core of the network, the source and destination IP addresses are never checked as long as a label exists in the packet. Only the PE routers need to know how to send the packets toward the customer edge (CE) router. MPLS VPNs are considered an overlay network because they are forwarded on the SP's underlay network by using MPLS labels.

MPLS VPNs are categorized by two technologies on the PE router:

- **Layer 2 VPN (L2VPN):** PE routers provide connectivity to CE routers by creating a virtual circuit between the nodes. An interface on the PE router is associated directly to the virtual circuit. Packets received on the interface are then associated with the virtual circuit, labeled with the circuit-id, then labeled for the remote PE's IP address, and then forwarded toward the PE attaching to the other end of the circuit.

  The PE routers do not participate in the routing of the devices in the private networks.

- **Layer 3 VPN (L3VPN):** PE routers provide connectivity to CE routers by exchanging network prefixes with them. PE routers then exchange those network prefixes with remote PE routers that then advertise the prefixes to the remote CE routers.

  PE routers forward network traffic based on IP addresses and not based off circuit-ids.

> **Note**   MPLS VPNs provide a method of segmenting network traffic, but do not encrypt network traffic. Encryption of network traffic is required to ensure data confidentiality or data integrity.

MPLS Layer 3 VPN (L3VPN) Overview

MPLS L3VPNs participate in the routing tables of the CE and PE routers. The technology is based on the following components:

- Exchange of network prefixes between CE and PE routers.

- Exchange of network prefixes between local PE and remote PE routers. This can be a direct BGP session or through a route-reflector (RR).

- Exchange of MPLS labels that are used for forwarding packets between the local PE and remote PE routers.

- Forwarding of packets based on outermost MPLS labels.

PE routers use a virtual context known as a Virtual Routing and Forwarding (VRF) context for each customer. Every VRF context provides a method for routers to maintain a separate routing and forwarding table for each customer on a router.

The PE routers should have an abundant amount of CPU and RAM to hold all the routes for every VRF configured on them. The PE routers must contain all the routes for a particular customer (VRF), whereas the CE routers maintain only the routes for the customer that it belongs to. The route table on the PE routers can be programmed via a static route at the local PE router or is learned dynamically from routes that are advertised from the CE router.

PE routers exchange the VRF's routes with other PE routers using Multi-Protocol BGP (MP-BGP) using a special address family just for MPLS L3VPN networks. VPN labels are associated to each of the VRF's routes to identify which VRF the routes belong to.

Virtual Routing and Forwarding

Virtual Routing and Forwarding (VRF) is a technology that creates separate virtual routers on a physical router. Router interfaces, routing tables, and forwarding tables are completely isolated between VRFs, preventing traffic from one VRF to forward into another VRF. VRFs are an essential component of the L3VPN architecture and provide increased router functionality through segmentation in lieu of using multiple devices. All router interfaces belong to the global VRF (also known as default VRF) until they are specifically assigned to a different VRF. The global VRF is identical to the regular routing table of non-VRF routers.

Figure 10-1 demonstrates three VRFs in one physical router—the default global VRF and two user-defined VRFs: VPN01 and VPN02.

Figure 10-1 *VRFs on a Physical Router*

Every VRF configured on a router maintains a separate routing table that allows for over-lapping IP address ranges between different customers. Configuring VRFs on a router ensures that the paths are isolated, network security is increased, and encrypting traffic on the network is not needed to maintain privacy between VRFs.

Figure 10-2 displays a simple peer-to-peer topology where a service provider needs to deliver connectivity to two different customers while ensuring that routes are not mixed between customers.

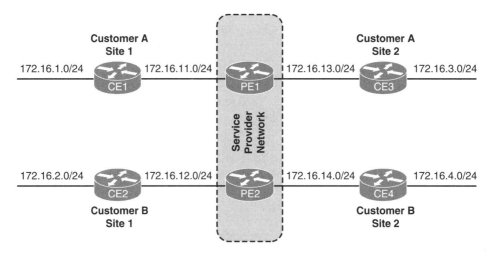

Figure 10-2 *Separate Routing Domains*

By using VRFs, the service provider can use one router instead of two. Figure 10-3 displays the same topology except that PE1 is using VRFs to separate the customer's network on PE1. CE1 and CE3 belong to VRF VPN01 for Customer A, and CE2 and CE4 belong to VRF VPN02 for Customer B. Configuration changes are needed only on PE1, and all the CE routers are configured normally (that is, no VRF configuration).

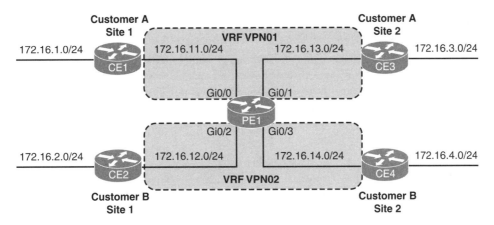

Figure 10-3 *Separate Routing Domains Through VRFs*

CE1 maintains connectivity with CE3, but neither router can see any VRF VPN02 networks (172.16.2.0/24, 172.16.4.0/24, 172.16.12.0/24, 172.16.14.0/24). CE2 maintains connectivity with CE4, but neither router can see any VRF VPN01 network (172.16.1.0/24, 172.16.3.0/24, 172.16.11.0/24, 172.16.13.0/24).

Route Distinguisher

A route distinguisher (RD) is a method of providing uniqueness to a network prefix regardless of which VRF context the route belongs to. Routes are exchanged between other service provider routers as a VPNv4 prefix that includes the following:

- 8-byte (64 bit) RD identifier.
- 4-bytes (32 bit) for the actual IPv4 network. IPv6 networks will use 16 bytes.

The RD identifier is commonly expressed by two 4-byte identifiers separated by a colon. The first 4 bytes of the RD generally refers to the autonomous system number (ASN) of the service provider, and the last 4 bytes of the RD is an incremental number. An example RD would be 100:1 within AS100's network. Only one RD can be configured on a PE router per VRF. A VPN prefix is the RD combined with the actual IPv4 or IPv6 network.

> **Note**   The RD is not used to link a network prefix to a specific VRF. It is used strictly to guarantee the uniqueness of a network prefix. The RD can be the same or a different value for the same VRF on two different PE routers based on design.

Route Target

BGP route targets (RTs) are extended BGP communities that identify the VPNv4 or VPNv6 routes that should be associated with a VRF. Route targets are an 8-byte value (64 bits) that are expressed by two 4-byte identifiers separated by a colon. The first set generally refers to the ASN of the service provider, and the second set is an incremental value. An example RT is 100:1 within AS100's network.

In the router's VRF definition, the RT is defined globally or for a specific address-family with one or more RTs for routes that are advertised. As the router advertises a VPN prefix to another PE router, the export RTs are added as a BGP path attribute to the VPN prefix. Upon receipt of a VPN prefix, the RTs are matched to the import RTs for the local router's VRF. If the VPN prefix's RTs match the local VRFs import RTs, the route is imported to that specific VRF.

Note   A router discards the VPN prefixes if the RT in the VPN prefix does not match any of the import RTs for the VRFs on the router. This is done to conserve router memory. Cisco refers to this as a *route-target filter*, and it is enabled by default.

A router can have multiple import RTs and multiple export RTs per VRF. The RTs do not have to match, but the export RTs of one router must match the import RTs of another router for the route to be associated to the VRF. Typically, a service provider keeps the RTs the same for import and export on all VRFs spread across all PE routers to simplify troubleshooting.

Note   The capability of having multiple RT path attributes increases scalability and functionality in the routing design. This concept is explained later in this chapter.

Multi-Protocol BGP (MP-BGP)

A BGP address-family identifier (AFI) correlates to a specific network protocol, such as IPv4, IPv6, and the like, and additional granularity through subsequent address-family identifier (SAFI), such as unicast and multicast. These attributes are carried inside BGP update messages and are used to carry network reachability information for different address families.

The additional length of a VPN prefix (RD + Network) requires a different address-family in BGP to exchange routes with other PE routers. MPLS L3VPN uses the AFI 1, SAFI 128 for IPv4 VPN prefixes and is referred to as the VPNv4 address-family. IPv6 network prefixes use the AFI 2, SAFI 128 and is referred to as VPNv6 address-family. For the remainder of this chapter, VPNv4 address families will be the implied address-family, but the same functionality exists with VPNv6 address-family too.

PE routers need to establish a VPNv4 BGP session with other PE routers. Like traditional IPv4 prefixes, a router does not advertise network prefixes learned from an IBGP peer to another IBGP peer. This means that a full mesh of VPNv4 BGP sessions must be formed between PE routers, or a route-reflector can be used.

Network Advertisement Between PE and CE Routers

All the LAN networks attached to the CE routers need to be advertised to the PE router so that it can advertise those routes to other PE routers. Network prefixes can be statically advertised with the network command, but dynamic redistribution from the connected interface database or from a routing protocol is considered more scalable.

The BGP VPNv4 address-family is how network prefixes are exchanged between PE routers. Traditionally the VPNv4 address-family is an IBGP session between other route reflectors (RR) and PE routers. The most intuitive solution is to use BGP as the PE-CE routing protocol because routes learned in the VRF context in BGP do not have to be redistributed into or out of BGP. The PE-CE BGP session is normally an EBGP session. Using other protocols like static routes, connected networks, Enhanced Interior Gateway Routing Protocol (EIGRP), Open Shortest Path First (OSPF), Intermediate-System to Intermediate System (IS-IS), and so on require redistribution (generally mutually with a tag-and-block technique to prevent routing loops) with the VRF context in BGP.

This book focuses only on BGP as the PE-CE routing protocol.

MPLS Layer 3 VPN Configuration

Now that an overview of the technologies and concepts has been provided, this chapter offers a brief overview of the components. Figure 10-4 displays a topology containing three PE routers: PE1 (IOS), PE2 (IOS-XR), and PE3 (NX-OS), and a VPNv4 route reflector (RR). This topology will be the primary topology to demonstrate how to troubleshoot BGP in a MPLS L3VPN network.

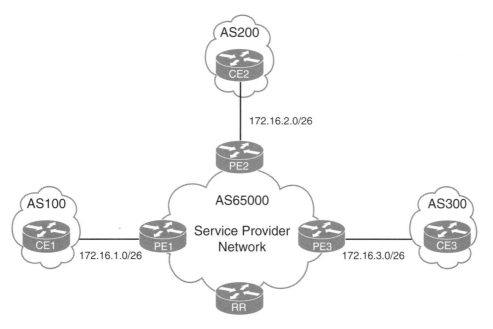

Figure 10-4 *MPLS L3VPN Sample Topology*

Table 10-1 displays a list of relevant networks, IP addresses, and BGP information for our topology. All three PE routers peer with the VPNv4 route-reflector at 192.168.100.100. The PE routers all use the same RD (1:1) and RT (1:1).

Table 10-1   *IP Addresses and Networks for the Sample MPLS L3VPN Topology*

Site	ASN	Peering Link	PE Global Loopback	PE VRF Loopback	CE Loopback
1	100	172.16.1.0/26	192.168.1.1/32	172.16.1.200/32	172.16.1.100/32
2	200	172.16.2.0/26	192.168.2.2/32	172.16.2.200/32	172.16.2.100/32
3	300	172.16.3.0/26	192.168.3.3/32	172.16.3.200/32	172.16.3.100/32

VRF Creation and Association

This section explains the VRF creation process and how a VRF is associated to an interface.

IOS VRF Creation

In IOS, the following steps are required to create a VRF and assign it to an interface:

Step 1.   Define the VRF. The VRF is defined with the command **vrf definition** *vrf-name*. The VRF name is locally relevant and does not impact connectivity with other routers.

Step 2.   Define the route distinguisher (RD). An RD ensures uniqueness of a route between multiple VRFs across multiple PE routers. The RD is configured with the command **rd** {*as-number:nn* | *ip-address:nn*}.

Step 3.   Initialize the address-family. Initialize the appropriate address-family with the command **address-family** {**ipv4** | **ipv6**}. The address-family can be IPv4, IPv6, or both. Failing to initialize the address-family prohibits the appropriate IPv4 or IPv6 addresses from being configured on a VRF-enabled interface.

Step 4.   Identify BGP route targets. BGP route targets (RT) are extended BGP communities that identify the VPNv4 or VPNv6 routes that should be associated with a VRF. The command **route-target** [**import** | **export** | **both**] *as-number:nn* identifies the RTs used upon the **import** or **export** of the routes to other VPNv4 or VPNv6 BGP neighbors. If the **import** or **export** keyword is not included, then **both** is implied. Multiple route targets can be associated to a VRF.

Step 5.   Associate the VRF to the interfaces. In interface configuration submode, specify the interface to be associated with the VRF with the interface parameter command **vrf forwarding** *vrf-name*. The VRF must be associated to the interface first before configuring an IP address. If an IP address is already configured on the interface, and the VRF is associated to the interface, IOS removes the IP address.

Step 6.   **Configure an IP address on the interface or subinterface.** The IP address needs to be associated to the interface with the command **ip address** *ip-address subnet-mask* [**secondary**].

> **Note**   Older IOS versions supported only IPv4 based VRFs and used the commands **ip vrf** *vrf-name* for the VRF definition and **ip vrf forwarding** *vrf-name* for associating the VRF to an interface. Eventually these commands will be deprecated.
>
> The command **vrf upgrade-cli multi-af-mode** {**common-policies** | **non-common-policies**} [**vrf** *vrf-name*] only upgrades IPv4-based VRF to a multiprotocol VRF. Cisco recommends using the multiprotocol VRF **vrf definition** and **vrf forwarding** commands.

Example 10-1 demonstrates the VRF creation and assignment to interfaces on the IOS router PE1. Notice how the previous IP address was automatically removed from the interface when the VRF was assigned.

Example 10-1   *VRF Creation and Interface Assignment for IOS*

```
PE1-IOS# configuration t
Enter configuration commands, one per line. End with CNTL/Z.
PE1-IOS(config)# vrf definition VPN01
PE1-IOS(config-vrf)# rd 1:1
PE1-IOS(config-vrf)# address-family ipv4 unicast
PE1-IOS(config-vrf-af)# route-target 1:1
PE1-IOS(config-vrf-af)# interface gi0/2
PE1-IOS(config-if)# vrf forwarding VPN01
% Interface GigabitEthernet0/2 IPv4 disabled and address(es) removed due to enabling
  VRF VPN01
PE1-IOS(config-if)# ip address 172.16.1.1 255.255.255.192
PE1-IOS(config-if)# interface loopback100
PE1-IOS(config-if)# vrf forwarding VPN01
PE1-IOS(config-if)# ip address 172.16.1.200 255.255.255.255
```

IOS XR VRF Creation

The following steps are required to create a multiprotocol VRF and assign it to an interface on an IOS XR node:

Step 1.   **Define the VRF.** The VRF is defined with the command **vrf** *vrf-name*. The VRF name is locally relevant and does not impact connectivity with other routers.

Step 2.   **Initialize the address-family.** Initialize the appropriate address-family with the command **address-family** {**ipv4** | **ipv6**} **unicast**. The address-family can be IPv4, IPv6, or both. Failing to initialize the address-family prohibits the appropriate IPv4 or IPv6 address from being configured on a VRF-enabled interface.

Step 3.   **Identify BGP route targets.** BGP route targets are extended BGP communities that identify the VPNv4 or VPNv6 routes that should be associated with a VRF. The import RT is configured with the command **import route-target** *as-number:nn* and identifies the RTs that should be imported to the VRF from VPNv4 prefixes. The command **export route-target** *as-number:nn* sets the RT on VPNv4 prefixes that are advertised to other PE routers. Multiple route targets can be associated to a VRF.

Step 4.   **Associate the VRF to the interfaces.** In interface configuration submode, specify the interface to be associated with the interface parameter configuration command **vrf** *vrf-name*. The VRF needs to be associated to the interface first before configuring an IP address. Unlike IOS and NX-OS, the IP address is not automatically removed and prohibits the change from being committed. If an IP address is already configured, remove the IP address and commit the change first.

Step 5.   **Configure an IP address on the interface or subinterface.** The IP address is configured by entering the commands **ipv4 address** *ipv4-address subnet-mask*.

Example 10-2 demonstrates the VRF creation and assignment to interfaces on the IOS XR router PE2. An IP address was not present on the Gi0/0/0/1 interface before the configuration because this can cause the commit to fail.

Example 10-2   *VRF Creation and Interface Assignment for IOS-XR*

```
RP/0/0/CPU0:PE2-XR# configuration t
RP/0/0/CPU0:PE2-XR(config)# vrf VPN01
RP/0/0/CPU0:PE2-XR(config-vrf)# address-family ipv4 unicast
RP/0/0/CPU0:PE2-XR(config-vrf-af)# import route-target 1:1
RP/0/0/CPU0:PE2-XR(config-vrf-af)# export route-target 1:1
RP/0/0/CPU0:PE2-XR(config-vrf-af)# interface gi0/0/0/1
RP/0/0/CPU0:PE2-XR(config-if)# vrf VPN01
RP/0/0/CPU0:PE2-XR(config-if)# ipv4 address 172.16.2.1 255.255.255.192
RP/0/0/CPU0:PE2-XR(config-if)# interface loopback 100
RP/0/0/CPU0:PE2-XR(config-if)# vrf VPN01
RP/0/0/CPU0:PE2-XR(config-if)# ipv4 address 172.16.2.200 255.255.255.255
RP/0/0/CPU0:PE2-XR(config-if)# commit
```

NX-OS VRF Creation

In NX-OS, the following steps are required to create a VRF and assign it to an interface:

Step 1.   **Define the VRF.** The VRF is defined with the command **vrf context** *vrf-name*. The VRF name is locally relevant and does not impact connectivity with other routers.

Step 2.   **Define the route distinguisher.** An RD ensures uniqueness of a route between multiple VRFs across multiple PE routers. The RD is configured with the command **rd** {*as-number:nn* | *ip-address:nn*}.

Step 3.   **Initialize the address-family.** Initialize the appropriate address family with the command **address-family** {**ipv4** | **ipv6**}. The address-family can be IPv4, IPv6, or both. Failing to initialize the address-family prohibits the appropriate IPv4 or IPv6 addresses from being configured on a VRF-enabled interface.

Step 4.   **Identify BGP route targets.** BGP RTs are extended BGP communities that identify the VPNv4 or VPNv6 routes that should be associated with a VRF. The command **route-target** {**import** | **export** | **both**} *as-number:nn* identifies the route targets used on the **import** or **export** of the routes to other VPNv4 or VPNv6 BGP neighbors. Multiple route targets can be associated to a VRF.

Step 5.   **Associate the VRF to the interfaces.** In interface configuration submode, specify the interface to be associated with the VRF with the interface parameter command **vrf member** *vrf-name*. The VRF needs to be associated to the interface first before configuring an IP address. If an IP address is already configured on the interface, and the VRF is associated to the interface, NX-OS removes the IP address.

Step 6.   **Configure an IP address on the interface or subinterface.** The IP address needs to be associated to the interface with the command **ip address** *ip-address /prefix-length* [**secondary**].

Example 10-3 demonstrates the VRF creation and assignment to interfaces on the NX-OS device PE3. Notice how the previous IP address was automatically removed from the interface when the VRF was assigned.

Example 10-3   *VRF Creation and Interface Assignment for NX-OS*

```
PE3-NXOS# configuration t
PE3-NXOS(config)# vrf context VPN01
PE3-NXOS(config-vrf)# rd 1:1
PE3-NXOS(config-vrf)# address-family ipv4 unicast
PE3-NXOS(config-vrf-af-ipv4)# route-target both 1:1
PE3-NXOS(config-vrf-af-ipv4)# interface e2/2
PE3-NXOS(config-if)# vrf member VPN01
04:26:57 PE3-NXOS %CLIS-6-CLIS_SYSLOG_CMD_REMOVED: Command deleted from the NVDB: ip
  address 172.16.3.1/26
Warning: Deleted all L3 config on interface Ethernet2/2
PE3-NXOS(config-if)# ip address 172.16.3.1/26
PE3-NXOS(config-if)# interface loopback100
PE3-NXOS(config-if)# vrf member VPN01
PE3-NXOS(config-if)# ip address 172.16.3.200/32
```

Verification of VRF Settings and Connectivity

After creating VRFs and assigning them to an interface, it is recommended to verify the changes. This section also explains some of the commands to view the routing table and provide connectivity tests with in the VRF context.

Viewing VRF Settings and Interface IP Addresses

IOS routers display a quick summary of the VRF(s) that include the VRF name, RD, IP protocols, and interfaces, with the command **show vrf** [*vrf-name*] [**detail**]. The *vrf-name* is optional, and the optional **detail** keyword provides additional information, such as route targets, and import/export route-maps.

IOS XR routers display the VRF name, RD, RT(s), and IP protocols with the command **show vrf** [*vrf-name* | **all**]. IOS XR includes the RD, import/export route targets and the address-families that have been initialized for that VRF.

NX-OS devices display the VRF information with the command **show vrf** [*vrf-name* | **all**] [**interface** | **detail**]. Only the internal VRF-ID and state is shown if the optional keywords are not used. The interface keyword displays the interfaces that are associated to the VRF.

Example 10-4 provides sample output of the commands. This is the first step of trouble-shooting PE-CE connectivity in verifying that the CE is in the correct VRF on the PE.

Example 10-4 *Display of VRF Interface Information*

```
PE1-IOS# show vrf
  Name                            Default RD          Protocols    Interfaces
  VPN01                           1:1                 ipv4         Gi0/2
                                                                   Lo100


RP/0/0/CPU0:PE2-XR# show vrf all
VRF                 RD                  RT                        AFI    SAFI
VPN01               not set
                                        import   1:1              IPV4   Unicast
                                        export   1:1              IPV4   Unicast


PE3-NXOS# show vrf VPN01 interface
Interface                VRF-Name                      VRF-ID  Site-of-Origin
loopback100              VPN01                              3  --
Ethernet2/2              VPN01                              3  --
```

IOS routers display IP addresses in all VRFs (default, and custom defined) with the command **show ip interface** [**brief**]. The interface status can be narrowed to all VRFs or a specific VRF with the command **show vrf** {**ipv4** | **ipv6**} **interface** [*vrf-name*] on IOS routers. Example 10-5 demonstrates the output.

Example 10-5 *Viewing VRF IP Interfaces on IOS Routers*

```
PE1-IOS# show ip interface brief
Interface              IP-Address       OK? Method Status              Protocol
GigabitEthernet0/0     10.255.1.89      YES NVRAM  administratively down down
GigabitEthernet0/1     10.1.11.1        YES manual up                  up
GigabitEthernet0/2     172.16.1.1       YES manual up                  up
Loopback0              192.168.1.1      YES NVRAM  up                  up
Loopback100            172.16.1.200     YES manual up                  up


PE1-IOS# show vrf ipv4 interface VPN01
Interface              VRF                         Protocol   Address
GigabitEthernet0/2     VPN01                       up         172.16.1.1
Loopback100            VPN01                       up         172.16.1.200
```

IOS XR and NX-OS devices only show the IP addresses in the default routing table with the command **show ip interface brief**. To see the IP addresses in the global routing table and all VRFs, use the command **show ipv4 vrf all interface brief** on IOS XR routers, and the command **show ip interface brief vrf all** on NX-OS devices. Example 10-6 provides sample output of these commands.

Example 10-6 *Viewing VRF IP Interfaces on IOS XR and NX-OS Devices*

```
RP/0/0/CPU0:PE2-XR# show ip vrf all interface brief
Interface              IP-Address       Status          Protocol Vrf-Name
Loopback0              192.168.2.2      Up              Up       default
Loopback100            172.16.2.200     Up              Up       VPN01
GigabitEthernet0/0/0/0 10.1.22.2        Up              Up       default
GigabitEthernet0/0/0/1 172.16.2.1       Up              Up       VPN01


PE3-NXOS# show ip interface brief vrf all
IP Interface Status for VRF "default"(1)
Interface       IP Address       Interface Status
Lo0             192.168.3.3      protocol-up/link-up/admin-up
Eth2/1          10.1.33.3        protocol-up/link-up/admin-up


IP Interface Status for VRF "VPN01"(2)
Interface       IP Address       Interface Status
Lo100           172.16.3.200     protocol-up/link-up/admin-up
Eth2/2          172.16.3.1       protocol-up/link-up/admin-up
```

Viewing the VRF Routing Table

Examining the routing table from the VRF context is a vital component of troubleshooting. The commands for displaying the routing table on all three operating systems are as follows:

- IOS routers allow only the viewing of the routing table of one VRF with the command **show ip route vrf** *vrf-name*.

- IOS XR routers use the command **show route vrf** {*vrf-name* | **all**}.

- NX-OS devices use the command **show ip route vrf** {*vrf-name* | **all**}.

IOS XR and NX-OS devices allow for the viewing of multiple VRF routing tables by using the **all** keyword in lieu of specifying a VRF name. With all three command sets, additional information can be seen by appending other keywords like *network /prefix-length* after the initial command. Example 10-7 displays sample content for all three types of routers.

Example 10-7 *Viewing the VRF Routing Table*

```
PE1-IOS# show ip route vrf VPN01
! Output omitted for brevity
Routing Table: VPN01
Gateway of last resort is not set
      172.16.0.0/16 is variably subnetted, 10 subnets, 2 masks
C        172.16.1.0/26 is directly connected, GigabitEthernet0/2
L        172.16.1.1/32 is directly connected, GigabitEthernet0/2
B        172.16.1.100/32 [20/0] via 172.16.1.11, 1w3d
C        172.16.1.200/32 is directly connected, Loopback100


RP/0/0/CPU0:PE2-XR# show route vrf VPN01
! Output omitted for brevity
Gateway of last resort is not set
C    172.16.2.0/26 is directly connected, 1d11h, GigabitEthernet0/0/0/1
L    172.16.2.1/32 is directly connected, 1d11h, GigabitEthernet0/0/0/1
L    172.16.2.200/32 is directly connected, 1d11h, Loopback100


PE3-NXOS# show ip route vrf VPN01
! Output omitted for brevity
IP Route Table for VRF "VPN01"
172.16.3.0/26, ubest/mbest: 1/0, attached
    *via 172.16.3.1, Eth2/2, [0/0], 1d10h, direct
172.16.3.1/32, ubest/mbest: 1/0, attached
    *via 172.16.3.1, Eth2/2, [0/0], 1d10h, local
172.16.3.200/32, ubest/mbest: 2/0, attached
    *via 172.16.3.200, Lo100, [0/0], 1d10h, local
    *via 172.16.3.200, Lo100, [0/0], 1d10h, direct
```

VRF Connectivity Testing Tools

The **ping** and **traceroute** utilities are vital tools for troubleshooting path failure issues. When working with VRF contexts, the vrf must be specified.

For IOS and IOS XR routers, the command is **ping vrf** *vrf-name destination-ip-address* [**source** {*interface-id* | *ip-address*}] or the command **traceoute vrf** *vrf-name destination-ip-address* [**source** {*interface-id* | *ip-address*}]. NX-OS devices use the command **ping** *destination-ip-address* **vrf** *vrf-name* [**source** *ip-address*] or the command **traceroute** *destination-ip-address* **vrf** *vrf-name* [**source** *ip-address*].

Example 10-8 displays the use of the **ping** command on the PE routers with their local peer CE device.

Example 10-8   *VRF Connectivity Test Tools*

```
PE1-IOS# ping vrf VPN01 172.16.1.11
Sending 5, 100-byte ICMP Echos to 172.16.1.11, timeout is 2 seconds:
!!!!!
Success rate is 100 percent (5/5), round-trip min/avg/max = 2/3/7 ms

RP/0/0/CPU0:PE2-XR# ping vrf VPN01 172.16.2.22
Sending 5, 100-byte ICMP Echos to 172.16.2.22, timeout is 2 seconds:
!!!!!
Success rate is 100 percent (5/5), round-trip min/avg/max = 1/4/9 ms

PE3-NXOS# ping 172.16.3.33 vrf VPN01
PING 172.16.3.33 (172.16.3.33): 56 data bytes
64 bytes from 172.16.3.33: icmp_seq=0 ttl=254 time=2.333 ms
64 bytes from 172.16.3.33: icmp_seq=1 ttl=254 time=2.237 ms
64 bytes from 172.16.3.33: icmp_seq=2 ttl=254 time=2.413 ms
64 bytes from 172.16.3.33: icmp_seq=3 ttl=254 time=2.856 ms
64 bytes from 172.16.3.33: icmp_seq=4 ttl=254 time=4.028 ms

--- 172.16.3.33 ping statistics ---
5 packets transmitted, 5 packets received, 0.00% packet loss
round-trip min/avg/max = 2.237/2.773/4.028 ms
```

MPLS Forwarding

MPLS forwarding needs to be enabled in the service provider network. There are multiple ways that MPLS labels can be exchanged between routers. MPLS Label Distribution Protocol (LDP) is common and is enabled fairly quickly.

On IOS routers the **mpls ip** command is placed under each of the interfaces in the service provider network that may forward labeled packets. On older IOS versions of code, MPLS may need to be enabled globally with the command **mpls ip**.

IOS XR routers require the usage of an MPLS package that must be installed before configuration. IOS XR routers initialize the LDP process with the command **mpls ldp**. All the interfaces listed under the LDP process will be LDP enabled. MPLS operations, administration, and maintenance (OAM) must be enabled with the command **mpls oam** so that the path can be verified with **ping** and **traceroute** commands.

NX-OS devices must enable MPLS-based services with the following commands in the order provided: **install feature-set mpls**, **feature-set mpls**, **feature mpls l3vpn**, and **feature mpls ldp**. After all the MPLS features have been enabled, LDP is enabled globally with the command **mpls ip** and then again under any MPLS interfaces.

Example 10-9 displays the basic configuration for enabling MPLS on the PE routers. All three PE routers have only one internal interface connecting to the service provider network. Only that interface needs MPLS enabled on it.

Example 10-9   *Sample MPLS LDP Configuration*

```
PE1-IOS
mpls ip
!
interface GigabitEthernet0/1
 description to P2
 ip address 10.1.11.1 255.255.255.0
 mpls ip
```

```
PE2-XR
mpls oam
!
mpls ldp
 router-id 192.168.2.2
 interface GigabitEthernet0/0/0/0
```

```
PE3-NXOS
mpls ip
!
interface Ethernet2/1
  description to P3
  no switchport
  mpls ip
  ip address 10.1.33.3/24
  ip router ospf 1 area 0.0.0.0
  no shutdown
```

BGP Configuration for VPNv4 and PE-CE Prefixes

The BGP configuration consists of the following components:

- Advertisement of VPNv4 prefixes to other PE routers or route reflector (RR).

- Establishment of the BGP session between the PE and CE routers. The BGP configuration resides under the VRF context.

- Route advertisement in the VRF context. Any routes that exist in the BGP VRF context are advertised as a VPNv4 prefix to other PE routers. This is where networks are specifically defined or redistributed.

The configuration for all three platforms varies slightly and is explained next:

IOS BGP Configuration for MPLS L3VPN

The following steps show how to configure BGP routing for MPLS L3VPN on an IOS router. The RD must be configured in the VRF definition before configuring BGP.

Step 1.   **Create the BGP routing process.** Initialize the BGP process with the global command **router bgp** *as-number*.

Step 2.   **Disable the Default IPv4 address-family.** IOS enables the IPv4 address-family by default. Disabling this behavior ensures that only the intended address-family is initialized. The IPv4 address-family is disabled with the command **no bgp default ipv4-unicast**.

Step 3.   **Define the VPNv4 neighbor session configuration.** The other PE routers (or route reflectors) need to have the session parameters defined. The remote ASs must be defined with the command **neighbor** *ip-address* **remote-as** *as-number* and the BGP session needs to be sourced by a loopback address with a /32 netmask with the command **neighbor** *ip-address* **update-source** *interface-id*. Additional session configuration options such as authentication can be added as well.

Step 4.   **Initialize the VPNv4 address-family.** The VPNv4 address-family needs to be initialized with the command **address-family vpnv4 unicast**.

Step 5.   **Activate the BGP VPNv4 address-family for the PE or RR session.** Now that the BGP session has been defined and the VPNv4 address-family is initialized, the BGP neighbor needs to be activated under the VPNv4 address-family with the command **neighbor** *ip-address* **activate**.

Step 6.   **Enable BGP extended communities.** MPLS L3VPN is dependent on the usage of extended BGP communities for the advertisement of route targets and other BGP path attributes. The command **neighbor** *ip-address* **send-community {extended | both}** is required.

> **Note**   Other BGP address-family commands, such as defining the route-reflector client or configuring route-maps, are defined here. This concludes the configuration of the VPNv4 configuration.

Step 7.   **Initialize the address-family for a specific VRF.** Initialize the address-family with the BGP router configuration command **address-family** *afi* [*safi*] **vrf** *vrf-name*.

Step 8.   **Configure the neighbor's CE configuration settings.** Identify the BGP neighbor's IP address and autonomous system number with the BGP router configuration command **neighbor** *ip-address* **remote-as** *as-number*. Additional neighbor configuration occurs under the BGP address-family VRF context for route-maps, BGP sessions, and the like. The BGP session options and address-family options are all listed under this section.

Step 9.   **Advertise or redistribute routes in the VRF.** Route advertisement or redistribution occurs under the BGP address-family VRF context. Typically, most service providers redistribute the connected routes into the VRF because it includes the peering link at a minimum.

Example 10-10 displays the BGP configuration for the VPNv4 address-family to the route reflector (192.168.100.100) and the CE1 router (172.16.1.11) in remote AS100.

Example 10-10   *IOS BGP VPNv4 and PE-CE Configuration*

```
PE1-IOS# show run | s router bgp
router bgp 65000
 bgp log-neighbor-changes
 no bgp default ipv4-unicast
 neighbor 192.168.100.100 remote-as 65000
 neighbor 192.168.100.100 description VPNv4 Route-Reflector
 neighbor 192.168.100.100 update-source Loopback0
 !
 address-family ipv4
 exit-address-family
 !
 address-family vpnv4
  neighbor 192.168.100.100 activate
  neighbor 192.168.100.100 send-community extended
 exit-address-family
 !
 address-family ipv4 vrf VPN01
  redistribute connected
  neighbor 172.16.1.11 remote-as 100
  neighbor 172.16.1.11 activate
 exit-address-family
```

IOS XR BGP Configuration for MPLS L3VPN

The following steps show how to configure BGP routing for MPLS L3VPN on an IOS XR router. The RD is defined as part of the BGP process:

Step 1. **Create the BGP routing process.** Initialize the BGP process with the global configuration command **router bgp** *as-number*.

Step 2. **Initialize the VPNv4 address-family.** The VPNv4 address-family needs to be initialized with the command **address-family vpnv4 unicast**.

Step 3. **Define the VPNv4 neighbors.** Configure the BGP VPNv4 neighbor's IP address with the BGP router configuration command **neighbor** *ip-address*.

Step 4. **Define the VPNv4 BGP neighbor's session information.** The remote AS must be defined with the command **remote-as** *as-number*. The BGP session needs to be sourced by a loopback address with a /32 netmask with the command **neighbor** *ip-address* **update-source** *interface-id*. Any other additional session information, such as passwords, can be defined here as well.

Step 5. **Activate the BGP VPNv4 address-family for the PE or RR session.** Activate the address-family for the BGP neighbor with the BGP neighbor configuration command **address-family** *afi safi*.

> **Note** Additional BGP address-family specific commands, such as defining a route-reflector client or route policies, are configured here. There is no need to enable extended communities because those are automatically advertised to IBGP peers by IOS XR routers. This concludes the VPNv4 configuration.

Step 6. **Define the VRF in BGP.** The VRF for the BGP instance is defined with the command **vrf** *vrf-name*.

Step 7. **Define the VRF's route distinguisher.** The RD is configured with the command **rd** {*as-number:nn* | *ip-address:nn*}.

Step 8. **Initialize the VRF's address-family.** Initialize the address-family for that VRF with the BGP router configuration command **address-family** *afi safi* so it can be associated to a BGP neighbor in that VRF. Any route advertisement or redistribution on the PE occurs under the VRF address-family.

Step 9. **Define the VRF's Neighbor's CE IP Address.** Configure the BGP neighbor's IP address with the BGP router configuration command **neighbor** *ip-address*.

Step 10. **Define the neighbor's BGP autonomous system number.** Configure the BGP neighbor's autonomous system number with the BGP neighbor configuration command **remote-as** *as-number*. Any additional BGP session information is configured here.

Step 11.   **Activate the address-family for the BGP neighbor.** Activate the address-family for the BGP neighbor with the BGP neighbor configuration command **address-family** *afi safi*. EBGP peers require the user of a route policy to allow the inbound/outbound exchange of BGP prefixes, as explained earlier in Chapter 4, "Troubleshooting Route Advertisement and BGP Policies."

Example 10-11 displays the BGP configuration for the VPNv4 address-family to the route-reflector (192.168.100.100) and the CE2 router (172.16.2.22) in remote AS200.

Example 10-11   *IOS XR BGP VPNv4 and PE-CE Configuration*

```
RP/0/0/CPU0:PE2-XR# show run router bgp
router bgp 65000
 address-family vpnv4 unicast
 !
 neighbor 192.168.100.100
  remote-as 65000
  update-source Loopback0
  address-family vpnv4 unicast
  !
 !
 vrf VPN01
  rd 1:1
  address-family ipv4 unicast
   redistribute connected
  !
  neighbor 172.16.2.22
   remote-as 200
   address-family ipv4 unicast
    route-policy PASS-ALL in
    route-policy PASS-ALL out
```

Note   IOS XR nodes do not establish a BGP session if the router identifier (RID) is set to zero because dynamic RID allocation did not find any *up* loopback interfaces. The RID needs to be set manually with the BGP router configuration command **bgp router-id** *router-id*.

NX-OS BGP Configuration for MPLS L3VPN

The following steps show how to configure BGP routing for MPLS L3VPN on an NX-OS router.

Step 1.   Create the BGP routing process. Initialize the BGP process with the global configuration command **router bgp** *as-number*.

Step 2.   Initialize the VPNv4 address-family. The VPNv4 address-family needs to be initialized with the command **address-family vpnv4 unicast**.

Step 3.   Define the VPNv4 neighbors. Configure the BGP VPNv4 neighbor's IP address with the BGP router configuration command **neighbor** *ip-address*.

Step 4.   Define the VPNv4 BGP neighbor's session information. The VPNv4 neighbor's session information needs to be defined. The remote-as must be defined with the command **remote-as** *as-number*. The BGP session needs to be sourced by a loopback address with a /32 netmask with the command **update-source** *interface-id*. Any other additional session information, such as passwords, can be defined here as well.

Step 5.   Activate the BGP VPNv4 address-family for the BGP PE or RR session. Activate the address-family for the BGP neighbor with the BGP neighbor configuration command **address-family** *afi safi*.

Step 6.   Enable BGP extended communities. MPLS L3VPN is dependent on the usage of extended BGP communities for the advertisement of route targets and other BGP path attributes. The command **send-community** {extended | both} is required. Additional BGP address-family specific commands, such as defining a route-reflector client or route policies, are configured here.

Step 7.   Define the VRF in BGP. The VRF for the BGP instance is defined with the command **vrf** *vrf-name*.

Step 8.   Initialize the VRF's address-family. Initialize the address-family for that VRF with the BGP router configuration command **address-family** *afi safi* so it can be associated to a BGP neighbor in that VRF. Any route advertisement or redistribution on the PE occurs under the VRF address-family.

Step 9.   Define the VRF's neighbor's CE IP address. Configure the BGP neighbor's IP address with the BGP router configuration command **neighbor** *ip-address*.

Step 10.   Define the neighbor's BGP autonomous system number. Configure the BGP neighbor's autonomous system number with the BGP neighbor configuration command **remote-as** *as-number*. Any additional BGP session information is configured here.

Step 11.   Activate the address-family for the BGP neighbor. Activate the address-family for the BGP neighbor with the BGP neighbor configuration command **address-family** *afi safi*. Any additional address-family configuration settings such as route-maps can be defined here.

Example 10-12 displays the BGP configuration for the VPNv4 address-family to the route-reflector (192.168.100.100) and the CE3 router (172.16.3.33) in remote AS300.

Example 10-12   *NX-OS BGP VPNv4 and PE-CE Configuration*

```
PE3-NXOS# show run bgp
feature bgp

router bgp 65000
  address-family vpnv4 unicast
  neighbor 192.168.100.100
    remote-as 65000
    update-source loopback0
    address-family vpnv4 unicast
      send-community extended
  vrf VPN01
    address-family ipv4 unicast
      redistribute direct route-map ALL
    neighbor 172.16.3.33
      remote-as 300
      address-family ipv4 unicast
! The following section is part of the show run bgp output, but is actually part
! of the VRF creation.
vrf context VPN01
  rd 1:1
  address-family ipv4 unicast
    route-target import 1:1
    route-target export 1:1
```

Verification of BGP Sessions and Routes

Now that the BGP session has been configured for the VPNv4 address-family and between the PE and CE routers, it is recommended that the sessions are validated.

The relevant BGP information for a specific VRF is seen with the command **show bgp** {**vpnv4** | **vpnv6**} **unicast** {**all** | **rd** *route-distinguisher* | **vrf** *vrf-name*} [**labels** | **summary** | **neighbors** [**ip-address** [**advertised-routes** | **received**]]] on IOS routers. The **labels** keyword displays the MPLS label that is first tagged with the packet. This is the label assigned from the router that learns the route from a CE router. If the **vrf** *vrf-name* option is used, the VPNv4 sessions are not included in the output.

> **Note**   The VRF BGP table should be a smaller subset of routes that are contained in the VPNv4 address-family for a router. On smaller topologies, it may be hard to differentiate between the two commands.

Example 10-13 displays the output of iterations of the preceding commands to verify that the BGP session is established and that routes have been received.

Example 10-13 *Display VPNv4 and PE-CE BGP Sessions on IOS*

```
PE1-IOS# show bgp vpnv4 unicast vrf VPN01 summary
! Output omitted for brevity


Neighbor        V    AS MsgRcvd MsgSent   TblVer  InQ OutQ Up/Down  State/PfxRcd
172.16.1.11     4    100      21      26       21    0    0 00:15:49          2
```

```
PE1-IOS# show bgp vpnv4 unicast summary
! Output omitted for brevity
Neighbor        V    AS MsgRcvd MsgSent   TblVer  InQ OutQ Up/Down  State/PfxRcd
172.16.1.11     4    100      21      26       21    0    0 00:16:16          2
192.168.100.100 4  65000      23      20       21    0    0 00:12:26          6
```

```
PE1-IOS# show bgp vpnv4 unicast all
! Output omitted for brevity
      Network          Next Hop        Metric LocPrf Weight Path
Route Distinguisher: 1:1 (default for vrf VPN01)
 *    172.16.1.0/26    172.16.1.11          0            0 100 ?
 *>                    0.0.0.0              0        32768 ?
 *>   172.16.1.100/32  172.16.1.11          0            0 100 ?
 *>   172.16.1.200/32  0.0.0.0              0        32768 ?
 *>i  172.16.2.0/26    192.168.2.2          0    100     0 ?
 *>i  172.16.2.100/32  192.168.2.2          0    100     0 200 ?
 *>i  172.16.2.200/32  192.168.2.2          0    100     0 ?
 *>i  172.16.3.0/26    192.168.3.3          0    100     0 ?
 *>i  172.16.3.100/32  192.168.3.3          0    100     0 300 ?
 *>i  172.16.3.200/32  192.168.3.3          0    100     0 ?
```

```
PE1-IOS# show bgp vpnv4 unicast vrf VPN01
! Output omitted for brevity
      Network          Next Hop        Metric LocPrf Weight Path
Route Distinguisher: 1:1 (default for vrf VPN01)
 *    172.16.1.0/26    172.16.1.11          0            0 100 ?
 *>                    0.0.0.0              0        32768 ?
 *>   172.16.1.100/32  172.16.1.11          0            0 100 ?
 *>   172.16.1.200/32  0.0.0.0              0        32768 ?
 *>i  172.16.2.0/26    192.168.2.2          0    100     0 ?
 *>i  172.16.2.100/32  192.168.2.2          0    100     0 200 ?
 *>i  172.16.2.200/32  192.168.2.2          0    100     0 ?
 *>i  172.16.3.0/26    192.168.3.3          0    100     0 ?
```

```
*>i 172.16.3.100/32  192.168.3.3                 0    100    0 300 ?
*>i 172.16.3.200/32  192.168.3.3                 0    100    0 ?
```

```
PE1-IOS# show bgp vpnv4 unicast vrf VPN01 labels
   Network          Next Hop        In label/Out label
Route Distinguisher: 1:1 (VPN01)
   172.16.1.0/26    172.16.1.11     25/nolabel
                    0.0.0.0         25/nolabel(VPN01)
   172.16.1.100/32  172.16.1.11     26/nolabel
   172.16.1.200/32  0.0.0.0         27/nolabel(VPN01)
   172.16.2.0/26    192.168.2.2     nolabel/24012
   172.16.2.100/32  192.168.2.2     nolabel/24013
   172.16.2.200/32  192.168.2.2     nolabel/24012
   172.16.3.0/26    192.168.3.3     nolabel/492287
   172.16.3.100/32  192.168.3.3     nolabel/22
   172.16.3.200/32  192.168.3.3     nolabel/492287
```

The command **show bgp {vpnv4 | vpnv6} unicast [summary]** displays the VPNv4 session with the PE or RRs on IOS XR and NX-OS devices. The command **show bgp vrf** {*vrf-name* | **all**}] [**labels** | **summary** | **neighbors** [**ip-address** [**advertised-routes** | **received**]]] provides additional information about the routes from the VRF context. The significant difference in the two commands is that IOS XR/NX-OS does not require the identification of a VRF, RD, or use the **all** keyword.

Example 10-14 displays the output of iterations of the commands that were just provided to verify that the BGP session is established and that routes have been received on the IOS XR router. Notice that the IP address for the BGP peer changes depending upon the command.

Example 10-14   *Display VPNv4 and PE-CE BGP Sessions on IOS XR*

```
RP/0/0/CPU0:PE2-XR# show bgp vpnv4 unicast summary
! Output omitted for brevity
Process        RcvTblVer    bRIB/RIB    LabelVer   ImportVer   SendTblVer  StandbyVer
Speaker               22          22          22          22           22           0


Neighbor         Spk    AS MsgRcvd MsgSent    TblVer  InQ OutQ  Up/Down   St/PfxRcd
192.168.100.100    0 65000      43      36        22    0    0 00:30:55           6
```

```
RP/0/0/CPU0:PE2-XR# show bgp vrf VPN01 ipv4 unicast summary
! Output omitted for brevity
Neighbor        Spk    AS MsgRcvd MsgSent   TblVer  InQ OutQ  Up/Down  St/PfxRcd
172.16.2.22       0   200     40      40       22    0    0 00:33:33          2
```

```
RP/0/0/CPU0:PE2-XR# show bgp vrf VPN01 ipv4 unicast
! Output omitted for brevity
   Network             Next Hop          Metric LocPrf Weight Path
Route Distinguisher: 1:1 (default for vrf VPN01)
*>i172.16.1.0/26      192.168.1.1            0    100      0 ?
*>i172.16.1.100/32    192.168.1.1            0    100      0 100 ?
*>i172.16.1.200/32    192.168.1.1            0    100      0 ?
*> 172.16.2.0/26      0.0.0.0                0         32768 ?
*                     172.16.2.22            0             0 200 ?
*> 172.16.2.100/32    172.16.2.22            0             0 200 ?
*> 172.16.2.200/32    0.0.0.0                0         32768 ?
*>i172.16.3.0/26      192.168.3.3            0    100      0 ?
*>i172.16.3.100/32    192.168.3.3            0    100      0 300 ?
*>i172.16.3.200/32    192.168.3.3            0    100      0 ?

Processed 9 prefixes, 10 paths
```

```
RP/0/0/CPU0:PE2-XR# show bgp vrf VPN01 ipv4 unicast labels
! Output omitted for brevity
Route Distinguisher: 1:1 (default for vrf VPN01)
*>i172.16.1.0/26      192.168.1.1       25           nolabel
*>i172.16.1.100/32    192.168.1.1       26           nolabel
*>i172.16.1.200/32    192.168.1.1       27           nolabel
*> 172.16.2.0/26      0.0.0.0           nolabel      24012
*                     172.16.2.22       nolabel      24012
*> 172.16.2.100/32    172.16.2.22       nolabel      24013
*> 172.16.2.200/32    0.0.0.0           nolabel      24012
*>i172.16.3.0/26      192.168.3.3       492287       nolabel
*>i172.16.3.100/32    192.168.3.3       22           nolabel
*>i172.16.3.200/32    192.168.3.3       492287       nolabel

Processed 9 prefixes, 10 paths
```

Example 10-15 displays the output of the previous commands to verify that the BGP session is established and that routes have been received on the NX-OS device.

Example 10-15   *Display VPNv4 and PE-CE BGP Sessions on NX-OS Devices*

```
PE3-NXOS# show bgp vpnv4 unicast summary
! Output omitted for brevity
Neighbor        V    AS MsgRcvd MsgSent    TblVer   InQ OutQ Up/Down  State/PfxRcd
192.168.100.100 4 65000     51      44       14     0    0 00:38:19 6
PE3-NXOS# show bgp vrf VPN01 ipv4 unicast summary
! Output omitted for brevity
Neighbor        V    AS MsgRcvd MsgSent    TblVer   InQ OutQ Up/Down  State/PfxRcd
172.16.3.33     4   300     39      41       13     0    0 00:32:21 2
```

```
PE3-NXOS# show bgp vrf VPN01 ipv4 unicast
! Output omitted for brevity
   Network          Next Hop          Metric     LocPrf     Weight Path
*>i172.16.1.0/26    192.168.1.1           0        100          0 ?
*>i172.16.1.100/32  192.168.1.1           0        100          0 100 ?
*>i172.16.1.200/32  192.168.1.1           0        100          0 ?
*>i172.16.2.0/26    192.168.2.2           0        100          0 ?
*>i172.16.2.100/32  192.168.2.2           0        100          0 200 ?
*>i172.16.2.200/32  192.168.2.2           0        100          0 ?
*>r172.16.3.0/26    0.0.0.0               0        100      32768 ?
* e                 172.16.3.33           0                     0 300 ?
*>e172.16.3.100/32  172.16.3.33           0                     0 300 ?
*>r172.16.3.200/32  0.0.0.0               0        100      32768 ?
```

```
PE3-NXOS# show bgp vrf VPN01 ipv4 unicast labels
! Output omitted for brevity
   Network          Next Hop          In label/Out label
*>i172.16.1.0/26    192.168.1.1       nolabel/25
*>i172.16.1.100/32  192.168.1.1       nolabel/26
*>i172.16.1.200/32  192.168.1.1       nolabel/27
*>i172.16.2.0/26    192.168.2.2       nolabel/24012
*>i172.16.2.100/32  192.168.2.2       nolabel/24013
*>i172.16.2.200/32  192.168.2.2       nolabel/24012
*>r172.16.3.0/26    0.0.0.0           492287/nolabel (VPN01)
* e                 172.16.3.33       492287/nolabel (VPN01)
*>e172.16.3.100/32  172.16.3.33       22/nolabel (VPN01)
*>r172.16.3.200/32  0.0.0.0           492287/nolabel (VPN01)
```

Troubleshooting MPLS L3VPN

The previous sections explained the concepts and technologies used in a MPLS L3VPN.
This section continues on the theory and explains the process for troubleshooting an
MPLS L3VPN network.

The first step of troubleshooting is to verify that the control plane is working properly. This includes verification that the CE routers contain routes for the source and destination network in their routing table. Sometimes access to the CE routers is not possible, so viewing the routing table is restricted to the VRF tables on the PE routers. If the packet's source or destination network is missing on either CE router, start tracing the missing route along the path from the source of the route's origination toward the CE missing the network.

Figure 10-5 displays a smaller version of the topology that displays only two sites and the BGP tables for all the CE and PE routers. The CE routers are advertising their networks to the PE routers. The PE routers are advertising their local routes and routes learned from their attached CE to the remote PE. The remote PE then advertises the networks to the remote CE. Both CEs contain routes for the source and destination network in the topology.

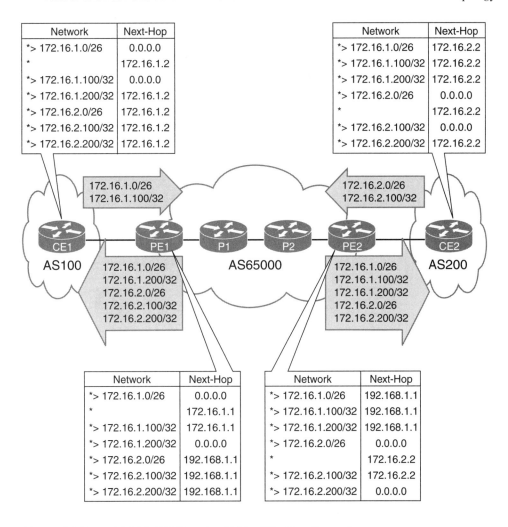

Figure 10-5 *MPLS L3VPN Routing Tables Working Properly*

> **Note**   The Loopback 100 interface was added to all the PE routers as a way to check route advertisement between CE and PE or between PE routers. This technique accelerates the ability to verify route advertisement between PE and CE routers.
>
> Production networks typically do not have a loopback interface in the VRF for this purpose, but they can be added as part of the troubleshooting step.

Default Route Advertisement Between PE-CE Routers

The CE routers need only a default route to forward packets toward the PE router. The PE router can have more routing entries for the VRF so that packets can be forwarded to the appropriate PE router. However, the PE routers need to know about the routes that are attached to the CE routers because BGP still needs to advertise the routes toward the PE routers.

Figure 10-6 demonstrates the concept where PE1 and PE2 advertise only a default route to the CE routers. The CE routers still advertise their local networks to the PEs. Notice that the routing table for the PE routers is the same as in Figure 10-5 when the CE routers receive the full routing table. In either scenario, the CE routers contain routes for the source and destination of the network traffic.

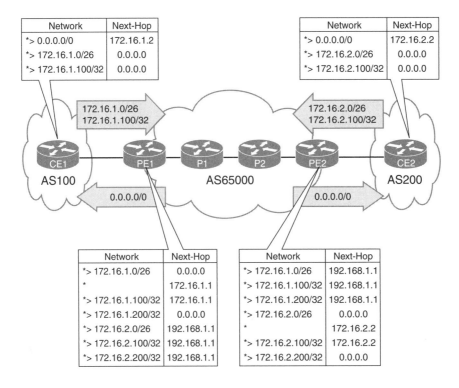

Figure 10-6   *CE Routers Receiving Only a Default Route*

Problems with AS-PATH

Most customers use the same ASN on their CE routers, or keep the number of ASNs fairly low. Keeping the ASN count to a low number simplifies their operations and deployment of CE routers by network management systems because the configurations can be placed in standardized templates. This also allows the company to keep the routing policies standardized. Regardless of the design reasons, if two locations use the same ASN, there could be routing problems between these sites while using MPLS L3VPN to connect them.

The problem is demonstrated by revisiting the sample topology depicted in Figure 10-4, which has all the CE routers using a different ASN. CE1 uses AS100, CE2 uses AS200, and CE3 uses AS300.

After changing all the CE routers (and corresponding changes on the PE routers) to use the same ASN (AS100), connectivity between all CE devices is broken. But any PE router can ping any CE router or its associated networks. To simplify troubleshooting for this scenario, focus will be directed toward CE1 connecting to CE2.

Example 10-16 displays the BGP tables for CE1 and CE2 as the first step of troubleshooting. In the output, CE1 and CE2 receive all the routes from the PE routers, but they do not have any routes from the remote CE routers. Notice that the CE routers are missing the loopback networks from the remote CE routers.

Example 10-16 *Viewing the BGP Table on CE1 and CE2*

```
CE1# show bgp ipv4 unicast
! Output omitted for brevity
      Network          Next Hop        Metric LocPrf Weight Path
 *    172.16.1.0/26    172.16.1.1           0             0 65000 ?
 *>                    0.0.0.0              0         32768 ?
 *>   172.16.1.100/32  0.0.0.0              0         32768 ?
 *>   172.16.1.200/32  172.16.1.1           0             0 65000 ?
 *>   172.16.2.0/26    172.16.1.1                         0 65000 ?
 *>   172.16.2.200/32  172.16.1.1                         0 65000 ?
 *>   172.16.3.0/26    172.16.1.1                         0 65000 ?
 *>   172.16.3.200/32  172.16.1.1                         0 65000 ?


CE2# show bgp ipv4 unicast
! Output omitted for brevity
      Network          Next Hop        Metric LocPrf Weight Path
 *>   172.16.1.0/26    172.16.2.1                         0 65000 ?
 *>   172.16.1.200/32  172.16.2.1                         0 65000 ?
 *    172.16.2.0/26    172.16.2.1           0             0 65000 ?
 *>                    0.0.0.0              0         32768 ?
 *>   172.16.2.100/32  0.0.0.0              0         32768 ?
 *>   172.16.2.200/32  172.16.2.1           0             0 65000 ?
 *>   172.16.3.0/26    172.16.2.1                         0 65000 ?
 *>   172.16.3.200/32  172.16.2.1                         0 65000 ?
```

Because the CE routers are missing some of the networks, it is time to check the PE routers to see if they have the CE's loopback networks in the BGP table. The PE router's VPNv4 BGP table is displayed in Example 10-17. All the CE loopback interfaces (172.16.1.100/32, 172.16.2.100/32, and 172.16.3.100/32) are present on PE1 and PE2.

Example 10-17   *Looking for the Remote CE Loopbacks on the PE Routers*

```
PE1-IOS# show bgp vpnv4 unicast vrf VPN01
! Output omitted for brevity
      Network            Next Hop         Metric LocPrf Weight Path
Route Distinguisher: 1:1 (default for vrf VPN01)
 *    172.16.1.0/26      172.16.1.11           0              0 100 ?
 *>                      0.0.0.0               0          32768 ?
 *>   172.16.1.100/32    172.16.1.11           0              0 100 ?
 *>   172.16.1.200/32    0.0.0.0               0          32768 ?
 *>i 172.16.2.0/26       192.168.2.2           0    100      0 ?
 *>i 172.16.2.100/32     192.168.2.2           0    100      0 100 ?
 *>i 172.16.2.200/32     192.168.2.2           0    100      0 ?
 *>i 172.16.3.0/26       192.168.3.3           0    100      0 ?
 *>i 172.16.3.100/32     192.168.3.3           0    100      0 100 ?
 *>i 172.16.3.200/32     192.168.3.3           0    100      0 ?


RP/0/0/CPU0:PE2-XR# show bgp vrf VPN01 ipv4 unicast
! Output omitted for brevity
      Network            Next Hop         Metric LocPrf Weight Path
Route Distinguisher: 1:1 (default for vrf VPN01)
 *>i172.16.1.0/26        192.168.1.1           0    100      0 ?
 *>i172.16.1.100/32      192.168.1.1           0    100      0 100 ?
 *>i172.16.1.200/32      192.168.1.1           0    100      0 ?
 *>  172.16.2.0/26       0.0.0.0               0          32768 ?
 *                       172.16.2.22           0              0 100 ?
 *>  172.16.2.100/32     172.16.2.22           0              0 100 ?
 *>  172.16.2.200/32     0.0.0.0               0          32768 ?
 *>i172.16.3.0/26        192.168.3.3           0    100      0 ?
 *>i172.16.3.100/32      192.168.3.3           0    100      0 100 ?
 *>i172.16.3.200/32      192.168.3.3           0    100      0 ?

Processed 9 prefixes, 10 paths
```

Next, check for any outbound filtering of prefixes toward the CE routers. But there are no route maps or filtering techniques applied to the PE routers during configuration. Upon further examination, the CE prefixes all contain the same AS-Path. The CE devices are dropping the prefixes as part of BGP's loop prevention mechanisms. Verify this by using the techniques shown in Chapter 4. Example 10-18 displays the BGP neighbor status on CE1 that shows that prefixes were dropped due to the AS-Path loop.

Example 10-18   *Checking for AS-Path Loops on CE1*

```
CE1# show bgp ipv4 unicast neighbors 172.16.1.1
! Output omitted for brevity
For address family: IPv4 Unicast


                                       Outbound      Inbound
  Local Policy Denied Prefixes:        --------      -------
    AS_PATH loop:                          n/a             2
    Bestpath from this peer:                 7           n/a
    Total:                                   7             2
```

Figure 10-7 displays a smaller subsection of the topology where CE1 and CE2 both use
AS100. In this topology, CE1 and CE2 advertise their prefixes to their local PE routers.
These PE routers exchange routes with each other, and thereby have complete BGP
tables. The PE routers then advertise the routes to the local CE router. Only the remote
CE routes are discarded because of the AS-Path loop check. The local PE loopback
networks are accepted by the CE routers.

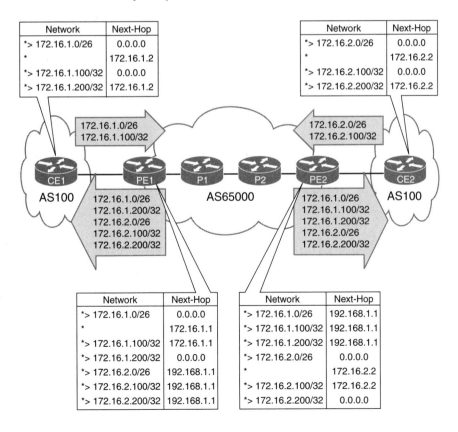

Figure 10-7   *Problems with CE Route Tables if CEs Use the Same ASN*

This scenario occurs frequently with MPLS L3VPNs and can be overcome with the AS-overide feature. The AS-override feature operates under the address-family and checks the AS-Path for network prefixes. When an AS-Path matches the ASN of the peering router, the local PE's ASN is used instead. AS-override is enabled on IOS PE devices with the command **neighbor** *ip-address* **as-override** within the VRF's BGP configuration. IOS XR and NX-OS PE devices enable AS-override with the command **as-override** within the address-family configuration for the CE router.

Example 10-19 displays the relevant configuration on the PE routers to use the **as-override** feature.

Example 10-19   *Configuration to Use* **as-override** *Feature*

```
PE1-IOS
router bgp 65000
 address-family ipv4 vrf VPN01
  redistribute connected
  neighbor 172.16.1.11 remote-as 100
  neighbor 172.16.1.11 activate
  neighbor 172.16.1.11 as-override
 exit-address-family


PE2-XR
router bgp 65000
 vrf VPN01
  neighbor 172.16.2.22
   address-family ipv4 unicast
    as-override


PE3-NXOS
router bgp 65000
  vrf VPN01
    neighbor 172.16.3.33
      address-family ipv4 unicast
        as-override
```

Example 10-20 displays the BGP table on CE1 and CE2 after the **as-override** feature has been configured on all the PE routers. Notice that the loopback addresses from the remote CE devices have an AS-Path length of two and that the second ASN is the same as the PE router. This verifies that the feature is working as intended.

Example 10-20 *Verification of Route Advertisements After* **as-override** *Configuration*

```
CE1# show bgp ipv4 unicast
! Output omitted for brevity
       Network          Next Hop          Metric LocPrf Weight Path
  *    172.16.1.0/26    172.16.1.1             0            0 65000 ?
  *>                    0.0.0.0                0        32768 ?
  *>   172.16.1.100/32  0.0.0.0                0        32768 ?
  *>   172.16.1.200/32  172.16.1.1             0            0 65000 ?
  *>   172.16.2.0/26    172.16.1.1                          0 65000 ?
  *>   172.16.2.100/32  172.16.1.1                          0 65000 65000 ?
  *>   172.16.2.200/32  172.16.1.1                          0 65000 ?
  *>   172.16.3.0/26    172.16.1.1                          0 65000 ?
  *>   172.16.3.100/32  172.16.1.1                          0 65000 65000 ?
  *>   172.16.3.200/32  172.16.1.1                          0 65000 ?


CE2# show bgp ipv4 unicast
! Output omitted for brevity
       Network          Next Hop          Metric LocPrf Weight Path
  *>   172.16.1.0/26    172.16.2.1                          0 65000 ?
  *>   172.16.1.100/32  172.16.2.1                          0 65000 65000 ?
  *>   172.16.1.200/32  172.16.2.1                          0 65000 ?
  *>   172.16.2.0/26    0.0.0.0                0        32768 ?
  *                     172.16.2.1             0            0 65000 ?
  *>   172.16.2.100/32  0.0.0.0                0        32768 ?
  *>   172.16.2.200/32  172.16.2.1             0            0 65000 ?
  *>   172.16.3.0/26    172.16.2.1                          0 65000 ?
  *>   172.16.3.100/32  172.16.2.1                          0 65000 65000 ?
  *>   172.16.3.200/32  172.16.2.1                          0 65000 ?
```

There are two alternatives to using the **as-override** feature:

- The use of the **allowas-in** feature on the CE routers, which disables the AS-Path loop check only for that neighbor.

- The PE routers advertise a default route to the CE routers. As explained earlier, the CEs forward the packets toward the PE router. The PE router then has the full routing table (no conflicts in AS-Path) so the PE can forward to the appropriate remote PE router.

This shrinks the size of the routing table on the CE but could cause traffic loss in certain scenarios. For example, imagine that every remote site is connected to two different SPs. The CE's routing table would have only two default routes that point to the different SPs. If a remote link failed, the CE would not know about it because the PE is not advertising more specific routes for the path that does work properly.

Suboptimal Routing with VPNv4 Route Reflectors

Large SP networks use RRs to overcome the scalability issue with using an IBGP full mesh. However, because BGP advertises the best path only to other BGP peers, the RR placement can potentially cause suboptimal routing. RRs do not pass all the paths to a client by default. It only advertises the BGP best path, which is calculated based on the RR's location in the network and not the route reflector client's location.

Figure 10-8 demonstrates an environment where suboptimal routing occurs because of the loss of path information at the route reflectors. Notice the following elements in Figure 10-8:

- CE1 and CE2 are advertising the 172.16.10.0/24 network to PE1 and PE2 accordingly.

- PE1 and PE2 advertise the VPNv4 prefix of 172.16.10.0/24 with the RD 1:1 to RR.

- The RR receives the prefix and stores them in the same topology database because they share the same RD.

- The RR compares both paths and picks the path via PE2 as the best path because of the IGP metric.

- The RR only advertises PE2's path to PE3.

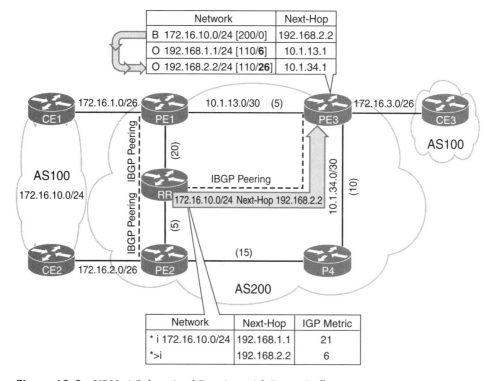

Figure 10-8 *VPNv4 Suboptimal Routing with Route Reflectors*

Looking at PE3's routing table to PE1 (192.168.1.1) and PE2 (192.168.2.2), the optimal path from CE3 to the 172.16.10.0/24 network should be sent directly to PE1 across the 10.1.13.0/30 network. Unfortunately, the RR only advertised the path that uses PE2, so PE3 forwards traffic out of the suboptimal path to reach the 172.16.10.0/24 network. Notice that the BGP route on PE3 does a recursive lookup to the PE2's next-hop address.

Example 10-21 verifies that the RR is advertising only one of the paths (from PE2) for the 172.16.10.0/24 prefix to PE3 router. This forces PE3 to forward traffic to PE2 even though PE1 is a better path.

Example 10-21   *172.16.10.0/24 Network Prefixes on the Route Reflector*

```
RR# show bgp vpnv4 unicast all
! Output omitted for brevity
     Network          Next Hop        Metric LocPrf Weight Path
Route Distinguisher: 1:1
 *>i 172.16.1.0/26    192.168.1.1          0    100      0 ?
 *>i 172.16.1.100/32  192.168.1.1          0    100      0 100 ?
 *>i 172.16.1.200/32  192.168.1.1          0    100      0 ?
 *>i 172.16.2.0/26    192.168.2.2          0    100      0 ?
 *>i 172.16.2.100/32  192.168.2.2          0    100      0 100 ?
 *>i 172.16.2.200/32  192.168.2.2          0    100      0 ?
 *>i 172.16.3.0/26    192.168.3.3          0    100      0 ?
 *>i 172.16.3.100/32  192.168.3.3          0    100      0 100 ?
 *>i 172.16.3.200/32  192.168.3.3          0    100      0 ?
 *>i 172.16.10.0/24   192.168.2.2          0    100      0 100 ?
 *  i                 192.168.1.1          0    100      0 100 ?
```

```
RR# show bgp vpnv4 unicast all neighbors 192.168.3.3 advertised-routes
! Output omitted for brevity

     Network          Next Hop        Metric LocPrf Weight Path
Route Distinguisher: 1:1
 *>i 172.16.1.0/26    192.168.1.1          0    100      0 ?
 *>i 172.16.1.100/32  192.168.1.1          0    100      0 100 ?
 *>i 172.16.1.200/32  192.168.1.1          0    100      0 ?
 *>i 172.16.2.0/26    192.168.2.2          0    100      0 ?
 *>i 172.16.2.100/32  192.168.2.2          0    100      0 100 ?
 *>i 172.16.2.200/32  192.168.2.2          0    100      0 ?
 *>i 172.16.3.0/26    192.168.3.3          0    100      0 ?
 *>i 172.16.3.100/32  192.168.3.3          0    100      0 100 ?
 *>i 172.16.3.200/32  192.168.3.3          0    100      0 ?
 *>i 172.16.10.0/24   192.168.2.2          0    100      0 100 ?

Total number of prefixes 10
```

Example 10-22 displays that PE3 has only one path from the RR to calculate the BGP best path. This is the suboptimal path to the 172.16.10.0/24 network.

Example 10-22   *Only One Path to 172.16.10.0/24 on PE3*

```
PE3-NXOS# show bgp vpnv4 unicast
! Output omitted for brevity
   Network            Next Hop         Metric     LocPrf     Weight Path
Route Distinguisher: 1:1    (VRF VPN01)
*>i172.16.1.0/26      192.168.1.1            0        100         0 ?
*>i172.16.1.100/32    192.168.1.1            0        100         0 100 ?
*>i172.16.1.200/32    192.168.1.1            0        100         0 ?
*>i172.16.2.0/26      192.168.2.2            0        100         0 ?
*>i172.16.2.100/32    192.168.2.2            0        100         0 100 ?
*>i172.16.2.200/32    192.168.2.2            0        100         0 ?
*>r172.16.3.0/26      0.0.0.0                0        100     32768 ?
* e                   172.16.3.33            0                    0 100 ?
*>e172.16.3.100/32    172.16.3.33            0                    0 100 ?
*>r172.16.3.200/32    0.0.0.0                0        100     32768 ?
*>i172.16.10.0/24     192.168.2.2            0        100         0 100 ?
```

If PE3 had received both paths (that is, a path from PE1 and PE2) from the RR, then PE3 could calculate the best path based on its IGP metric to reach each PE1 or PE2. By associating a unique RD to every VRF, the RR sees only one path for each RD and advertises all the unique VPN prefixes to PE3. Although there may be unique VPN prefixes, they have the same RT associated to them and are imported into the VRF table on the destination PE.

Note   Recall that the VPN prefix is the combination of the RD and a network prefix, and the function of the RD is to ensure that the VPN prefix is unique. The RD does not associate a VPNv4 prefix to a specific VRF; that is the role of the RT.

To explain the solution, imagine that the RD has been changed on PE2 to 1:2 and PE3 has changed its RD to 1:3 for the VPN01 VRF. Example 10-23 displays the VPNv4 addresses on the route reflector. Notice that all the routes advertised from a PE are contained in a different RD grouping. This is because the paths are considered unique.

Upon viewing the VPNv4 routes that are advertised to PE3, there are two paths to 172.16.10.0/24 (one from PE1 with RD 1:1 and another from PE2 with RD 1:2.

Example 10-23 *Viewing of VPNv4 Prefixes on the Route Reflector*

```
RR# show bgp vpnv4 unicast all
! Output omitted for brevity
     Network            Next Hop          Metric LocPrf Weight Path
Route Distinguisher: 1:1
 *>i 172.16.1.0/26      192.168.1.1            0    100      0 ?
 *>i 172.16.1.100/32    192.168.1.1            0    100      0 100 ?
 *>i 172.16.1.200/32    192.168.1.1            0    100      0 ?
 *>i 172.16.10.0/24     192.168.1.1            0    100      0 100 ?
Route Distinguisher: 1:2
 *>i 172.16.2.0/26      192.168.2.2            0    100      0 ?
 *>i 172.16.2.100/32    192.168.2.2            0    100      0 100 ?
 *>i 172.16.2.200/32    192.168.2.2            0    100      0 ?
 *>i 172.16.10.0/24     192.168.2.2            0    100      0 100 ?
Route Distinguisher: 1:3
 *>i 172.16.3.0/26      192.168.3.3            0    100      0 ?
 *>i 172.16.3.100/32    192.168.3.3            0    100      0 100 ?
 *>i 172.16.3.200/32    192.168.3.3            0    100      0 ?
```

```
RR# show bgp vpnv4 unicast all neighbors 192.168.3.3 advertised-routes
! Output omitted for brevity
     Network            Next Hop          Metric LocPrf Weight Path
Route Distinguisher: 1:1
 *>i 172.16.1.0/26      192.168.1.1            0    100      0 ?
 *>i 172.16.1.100/32    192.168.1.1            0    100      0 100 ?
 *>i 172.16.1.200/32    192.168.1.1            0    100      0 ?
 *>i 172.16.10.0/24     192.168.1.1            0    100      0 100 ?
Route Distinguisher: 1:2
 *>i 172.16.2.0/26      192.168.2.2            0    100      0 ?
 *>i 172.16.2.100/32    192.168.2.2            0    100      0 100 ?
 *>i 172.16.2.200/32    192.168.2.2            0    100      0 ?
 *>i 172.16.10.0/24     192.168.2.2            0    100      0 100 ?
Route Distinguisher: 1:3
 *>i 172.16.3.0/26      192.168.3.3            0    100      0 ?
 *>i 172.16.3.100/32    192.168.3.3            0    100      0 100 ?
 *>i 172.16.3.200/32    192.168.3.3            0    100      0 ?

Total number of prefixes 11
```

Note Notice that the number of advertised prefixes is different between Example 10-21 and Example 10-23. This is to accommodate the extra path from the different RD for the 172.16.10.0/24 network.

Example 10-24 displays the BGP table on PE3. The first two groups of VPN prefixes are specific to RD 1:1 and 1:2 where they each have a path to the 172.16.10.0/24 network prefix. The last group (RD 1:3) contains all the routes from any RD (1:1 or 1:2) because the VPN01 VRF import RT matches the RTs in both paths. PE3 installs all the paths for the 172.16.10.0/24 regardless of the RDs and can now calculate the best path (from PE1 or PE2) for that specific VRF.

Note   In essence, the last grouping shows the output from the command **show bgp ipv4 unicast vrf** *vrf-name*.

Example 10-24   *Verification of VPN Prefixes on PE3*

```
PE3-NXOS# show bgp vpnv4 unicast
! Output omitted for brevity
    Network             Next Hop          Metric      LocPrf      Weight Path
Route Distinguisher: 1:1
*>i172.16.1.0/26       192.168.1.1              0         100           0 ?
*>i172.16.1.100/32     192.168.1.1              0         100           0 100 ?
*>i172.16.1.200/32     192.168.1.1              0         100           0 ?
*>i172.16.10.0/24      192.168.1.1              0         100           0 100 ?

Route Distinguisher: 1:2
*>i172.16.2.0/26       192.168.2.2              0         100           0 ?
*>i172.16.2.100/32     192.168.2.2              0         100           0 100 ?
*>i172.16.2.200/32     192.168.2.2              0         100           0 ?
*>i172.16.10.0/24      192.168.2.2              0         100           0 100 ?

Route Distinguisher: 1:3      (VRF VPN01)
*>i172.16.1.0/26       192.168.1.1              0         100           0 ?
*>i172.16.1.100/32     192.168.1.1              0         100           0 100 ?
*>i172.16.1.200/32     192.168.1.1              0         100           0 ?
*>i172.16.2.0/26       192.168.2.2              0         100           0 ?
*>i172.16.2.100/32     192.168.2.2              0         100           0 100 ?
*>i172.16.2.200/32     192.168.2.2              0         100           0 ?
*>r172.16.3.0/26       0.0.0.0                  0         100       32768 ?
* e                    172.16.3.33             0                       0 100 ?
*>e172.16.3.100/32     172.16.3.33             0                       0 100 ?
*>r172.16.3.200/32     0.0.0.0                  0         100       32768 ?
*  i172.16.10.0/24     192.168.2.2             0         100           0 100 ?
*>i                    192.168.1.1             0         100           0 100 ?
```

Although this technique provides additional paths for every PE to calculate the BGP best path, it consumes additional router memory. The size of the BGP table and amount of memory on the router should be evaluated with this design.

All three of the platforms support the capability to view routes based on a specific RD with the command **show bgp vpnv4 unicast rd** *route-distinguisher*. Example 10-25 shows the use of the command.

Example 10-25   *Viewing All the Routes Based on the RD*

```
PE1-IOS# show bgp vpnv4 unicast rd 1:1
! Output omitted for brevity
      Network          Next Hop         Metric LocPrf Weight Path
Route Distinguisher: 1:1 (default for vrf VPN01)
   *    172.16.1.0/26    172.16.1.11            0            0 100 ?
   *>                    0.0.0.0                0        32768 ?
   *>   172.16.1.100/32  172.16.1.11            0            0 100 ?
   *>   172.16.1.200/32  0.0.0.0                0        32768 ?
```

```
RP/0/0/CPU0:PE2-XR# show bgp vpnv4 unicast rd 1:2
! Output omitted for brevity
      Network          Next Hop         Metric LocPrf Weight Path
Route Distinguisher: 2:1 (default for vrf VPN01)
*> 172.16.2.0/26        0.0.0.0                0        32768 ?
*                       172.16.2.22            0            0 100 ?
*> 172.16.2.100/32      172.16.2.22            0            0 100 ?
*> 172.16.2.200/32      0.0.0.0                0        32768 ?
```

```
PE3-NXOS# show bgp vpnv4 unicast rd 1:3
! Output omitted for brevity
      Network          Next Hop         Metric    LocPrf    Weight Path
Route Distinguisher: 3:1    (VRF VPN01)
*>r172.16.3.0/26        0.0.0.0                0      100     32768 ?
* e                     172.16.3.33            0                  0 100 ?
*>e172.16.3.100/32      172.16.3.33            0                  0 100 ?
*>r172.16.3.200/32      0.0.0.0                0      100     32768 ?
*>r172.16.3.200/32      0.0.0.0                0      100     32768 ?
```

Note   Running the **show bgp vpnv4 unicast rd** *route-distinguisher* command on a PE router also includes routes with a matching RT and RD. This command is used best on a RR to include only the routes on a RR. In large SP environments, it can be difficult to trace a network prefix on a route reflector because the RDs are different for every location and VRF. A troubleshooting trick involves the temporary creation of a VRF on the RR that includes all the RTs so that all the VRF's routes are visible. This allows for the use of **show bgp** commands from the VRF perspective versus the VPNv4 address-family.

Note   Newer versions of software support BGP Add-Path which allows for the advertisement of multiple paths to a peer. BGP Add-Path is covered in detail in Chapter 14, "BGP High Availability."

Troubleshooting Problems with Route Targets

The last aspect for troubleshooting MPLS L3VPN is to understand the import and export of *route targets (RT)*. As network prefixes are received from a CE router by a PE router, the export RTs are added to the prefix as part of the BGP path attributes in the VPN prefix. When a router receives a VPN prefix from another PE router (or RR), the network prefix is only installed into the VRF when the VPN prefix's RT matches the VRF's import RT. Any route that does not match the VRF's import RT with the prefix RT is discarded by default to save router resources.

Note   BGP route reflectors (RR)s generally do not have a VRF configured, which would mean that it drops all the VPN prefixes. Making a BGP router a RR disables the filtering of routes that do not import into a VRF. This allows for all routes to remain present in the RR's BGP database.

Figure 10-9 is a small subsection of the reference topology where PE1 is using an import/export RT of 1:1, and PE2 is using an import/export RT of 1:2 for the same VRF.

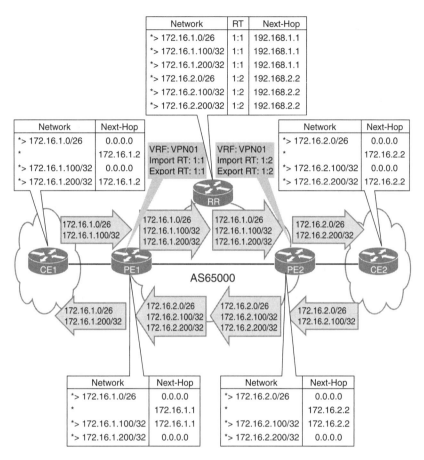

Figure 10-9 *Different Import and Export Route Targets*

Connectivity between the CE devices is failing, and after reviewing the BGP table of the CE routers, network engineering realizes that the CE routers are not learning any of the other CE prefixes from the PE routers. Examining the remote PE's routing table in Example 10-26 indicates that only the local routes and routes from the local CE are in the BGP table.

Example 10-26 *PE Router's BGP Table with Different Route Targets*

```
PE1# show bgp vpnv4 unicast all
! Output omitted for brevity


      Network          Next Hop          Metric LocPrf Weight Path
Route Distinguisher: 1:1 (default for vrf VPN01)
 *   172.16.1.0/26    172.16.11.1           0            0 100 ?
 *>                   0.0.0.0               0        32768 ?
```

```
*>  172.16.1.100/32  172.16.11.1                0               0 100 ?
*>  172.16.1.200/32  0.0.0.0                    0           32768 ?
```

```
PE2# show bgp vpnv4 unicast all
! Output omitted for brevity


     Network          Next Hop          Metric LocPrf Weight Path
Route Distinguisher: 1:2 (default for vrf VPN01)
 *   172.16.2.0/26    172.16.22.1                0               0 100 ?
 *>                   0.0.0.0                    0           32768 ?
 *>  172.16.2.100/32  172.16.22.1                0               0 100 ?
 *>  172.16.2.200/32  0.0.0.0                    0           32768 ?
```

The next step of troubleshooting is to check the VPN prefixes are on the RR. The local PE configuration should be checked after verifying that all the VPN prefixes are on the RR, and the RR displays that the routes are being advertised to the remote PE router. After examining the VRF configuration on both PE routers, the problem is found with the import RTs not matching the other PE router's export RT.

Enabling BGP debugs provides another method of verification that the import RT does not match the RT of the VPN prefix. Example 10-27 displays how using BGP debugs provides verification of an invalid RT import statement.

Example 10-27   *Verification of RT Import Failure with BGP Debug*

```
PE1# debug bgp vpnv4 unicast updates in
BGP updates debugging is on (inbound) for address family: VPNv4 Unicast
! A soft reset is done with the RR to resent all of the VPNv4 prefixes again
PE1# clear bgp vpnv4 unicast * soft
! Output omitted for brevity
02:06:06: BGP(4): (base) 192.168.2.2 send UPDATE (format) 2:1:172.16.2.0/24, next
  192.168.1.1, label 21, metric 0, path 200
02:06:07: BGP(4): 192.168.2.2 rcvd UPDATE w/ attr: nexthop 192.168.2.2, origin ?,
  localpref 100, metric 0, merged path 200, AS_PATH , extended community RT:1:2
02:06:07: BGP(4): 192.168.2.2 rcvd 2:3:172.16.2.0/26, label 21 -- DENIED due to:
  extended community not supported;
```

A quick solution is to add the other PE router's export RTs to the local PE router's import RTs. The new VRF configuration for PE1 and PE2 is displayed in Example 10-28.

Example 10-28 *VRF Configuration with Multiple Import Route Targets*

```
PE1-IOS
vrf definition VPN01
 rd 1:1
 !
 address-family ipv4
  route-target export 1:1
  route-target import 1:1
  route-target import 1:2
```

```
PE2-XR
vrf VPN01
 address-family ipv4 unicast
  import route-target
   1:1
   1:2
   !
  export route-target
   1:2
```

Example 10-29 provides verification that the PE routers accept multiple RTs. It contains the output of PE1's VRF definition and the BGP table for the prefixes learned from Site 2 (172.16.2.0/26) that have a RT of 1:2.

Example 10-29 *Verification of Multiple Import RTs*

```
PE1-IOS# show vrf detail VPN01
! Output omitted for brevity
VRF VPN01 (VRF Id = 1); default RD 1:1; default VPNID <not set>
  Interfaces:
    Lo100                 Gi0/2
Address family ipv4 unicast (Table ID = 0x2):
  Export VPN route-target communities
    RT:1:1
  Import VPN route-target communities
    RT:1:1                    RT:1:2
```

```
PE1-IOS# show bgp vpnv4 unicast all 172.16.2.0/26
BGP routing table entry for 1:1:172.16.2.0/26, version 41
```

```
Paths: (1 available, best #1, table VPN01)
  Advertised to update-groups:
     1
  Refresh Epoch 2
  Local
    192.168.2.2 (metric 4) (via default) from 192.168.100.100 (192.168.100.100)
       Origin incomplete, metric 0, localpref 100, valid, internal, best
       Extended Community: RT:1:2
       Originator: 192.168.2.2, Cluster list: 192.168.100.100
       mpls labels in/out nolabel/24012
```

MPLS L3VPN Services

A benefit to MPLS L3VPN is that routes can be exchanged between two different VRFs on the same service provider. The service provider can advertise all the network prefixes from a VRF into another customer's topology or be selective with the route advertisement. The process of advertisement networks between customers is referred to as *VRF route leaking* or just *route leaking*.

> **Note**   It is important to note that routes must be leaked in both directions to establish connectivity. One direction is for the forwarding of the initial packet, and the other direction is for the return of the packets.

Route leaking is used during company mergers and acquisitions when they use the same SP. Assuming that there is no overlapping IP addresses, all the routes could be mutually leaked to every VRF so that both companies are fully interconnected.

Another use case is for cloud-based providers that provide application services to multiple customers, like email hosting. Instead of providing connectivity across a public network such as the Internet, they could provide connectivity through a common MPLS L3VPN provider. The cloud provider could use Network Address Translation (NAT) and firewalls in its infrastructure to maintain separation of customer network space.

Figure 10-10 provides a sample topology where two companies (A & B) are subscribing to company C's email hosting service out of Site 2. The network design must accommodate the following:

- All the sites in Company A must be able to reach the email servers attached to CE3 that is located in Site 2.

- All the sites in Company B must be able to reach the hosted email servers attached to CE3 that is located in Site 2.

- All of Company C's email servers attached to CE3 must be able to reach all the networks in Company A's and Company B's sites.

■ Company A (CE1 and CE4) should not be able to reach any of the sites in Company B (CE2 and CE5).

■ Company B (CE2 and CE5) should not be able to reach any of the sites in Company A (CE1 and CE4).

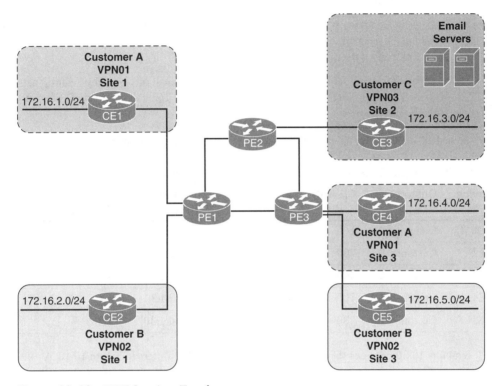

Figure 10-10 *VRF Services Topology*

This may seem like a challenging task that will require the use of many ACLs on routers for all three companies on a traditional network. If an additional network was added later—Company C's network that hosts email services—how many devices would require a configuration change? Fortunately, this is a very common scenario that provides flexibility and scalability by using different RTs in a VRF.

A VRF can have multiple import and export RTs. The first step is to define the logic for the export RT, which follows:

■ An export RT (that is, 1:10) is selected for all the sites in Company A.

■ An export RT (that is, 1:20) is selected for all the sites in Company B.

■ An export RT (that is, 1:30) is selected for Company C's site that is hosting email services. If there are normal sites for Company C's day-to-day operations (such as corporate LAN or human resource systems), those are assigned a different RT (i.e. 31) to prevent external companies from receiving those routes.

The second step is to define all the import RTs for every site, which uses the following logic:

- All sites in Company A import RT 1:10 (Company A sites) and 1:30 (Company C email hosted network on CE3). This allows users to send traffic to the email servers from Company A networks.

- All sites in Company B import RT 1:20 (Company B sites) and 1:30 (Company C email hosted network on CE3). This allows user to send traffic to the email servers from Company B networks.

- Company C's email servers require routes to connect to all of Company A and B networks. PE2 imports RT 1:10 (all Company A sites) and 1:20 (all Company B sites) in to VRF VPN03.

Table 10-2 displays the RT import/export logic for the VRF assigned to each CE device.

Table 10-2   *Route Target Import and Export Logic for Hosted Services*

Device	Customer	CE ASN	VRF Name	Import Route Targets	Export Route Targets
CE1	Company A	100	VPN01	1:10 and 1:30	1:10
CE2	Customer B	200	VPN02	1:20 and 1:30	1:20
CE3	Customer C	300	VPN03	1:10 and 1:20	1:30
CE4	Customer A	100	VPN01	1:10 and 1:30	1:10
CE5	Customer B	200	VPN02	1:20 and 1:30	1:20

Example 10-30 provides the BGP configuration for the PE routers in Figure 10-10. A unique RD has been assigned to every VRF where the first octet correlates to the VPN number and the second octet correlates to the site. Notice that the import/export RTs match those from Table 10-2.

Example 10-30   *Configuration for BGP Services*

```
PE1
vrf definition VPN01
 rd 1:1
!
 address-family ipv4
  route-target export 1:10
  route-target import 1:10
  route-target import 1:30
 exit-address-family
!
```

```
vrf definition VPN02
 rd 2:1
 !
 address-family ipv4
  route-target export 1:20
  route-target import 1:20
  route-target import 1:30
 exit-address-family
!
router bgp 65000
 no bgp default ipv4-unicast
 neighbor 192.168.2.2 remote-as 65000
 neighbor 192.168.2.2 update-source Loopback0
 neighbor 192.168.3.3 remote-as 65000
 neighbor 192.168.3.3 update-source Loopback0
 !
 address-family vpnv4
  neighbor 192.168.2.2 activate
  neighbor 192.168.2.2 send-community extended
  neighbor 192.168.3.3 activate
  neighbor 192.168.3.3 send-community extended
 exit-address-family
 !
 address-family ipv4 vrf VPN01
  redistribute connected
  neighbor 172.16.11.1 remote-as 100
  neighbor 172.16.11.1 activate
  neighbor 172.16.11.1 as-override
 exit-address-family
 !
 address-family ipv4 vrf VPN02
  redistribute connected
  neighbor 172.16.22.1 remote-as 200
  neighbor 172.16.22.1 activate
  neighbor 172.16.22.1 as-override
 exit-address-family
```

PE2
```
vrf definition VPN03
 rd 3:2
 !
 address-family ipv4
  route-target export 1:30
  route-target import 1:10
```

```
   route-target import 1:20
  exit-address-family
 !
router bgp 65000
 no bgp default ipv4-unicast
 neighbor 192.168.1.1 remote-as 65000
 neighbor 192.168.1.1 update-source Loopback0
 neighbor 192.168.3.3 remote-as 65000
 neighbor 192.168.3.3 update-source Loopback0
 !
 address-family vpnv4
  neighbor 192.168.1.1 activate
  neighbor 192.168.1.1 send-community extended
  neighbor 192.168.3.3 activate
  neighbor 192.168.3.3 send-community extended
 exit-address-family
 !
 address-family ipv4 vrf VPN01
  redistribute connected
  neighbor 172.16.33.1 remote-as 300
  neighbor 172.16.33.1 activate
  neighbor 172.16.33.1 as-override
 exit-address-family
```

```
PE3
vrf definition VPN01
 rd 1:3
 !
 address-family ipv4
  route-target export 1:10
  route-target import 1:10
  route-target import 1:30
 exit-address-family
 !
vrf definition VPN02
 rd 2:3
 !
 address-family ipv4
  route-target export 1:20
  route-target import 1:20
  route-target import 1:30
 exit-address-family
 !
router bgp 65000
```

```
no bgp default ipv4-unicast
 neighbor 192.168.1.1 remote-as 65000
 neighbor 192.168.1.1 update-source Loopback0
 neighbor 192.168.2.2 remote-as 65000
 neighbor 192.168.2.2 update-source Loopback0
 !
address-family vpnv4
  neighbor 192.168.1.1 activate
  neighbor 192.168.1.1 send-community extended
  neighbor 192.168.2.2 activate
  neighbor 192.168.2.2 send-community extended
 exit-address-family
 !
address-family ipv4 vrf VPN01
 redistribute connected
 neighbor 172.16.44.1 remote-as 100
 neighbor 172.16.44.1 activate
 neighbor 172.16.44.1 as-override
exit-address-family
 !
address-family ipv4 vrf VPN02
 redistribute connected
 neighbor 172.16.55.1 remote-as 200
 neighbor 172.16.55.1 activate
 neighbor 172.16.55.1 as-override
exit-address-family
```

Example 10-31 displays the import and export RTs for the VRFs on PE1, PE2, and PE3. The RDs are different for all the VRFs for every PE router, and the import/export RTs all match Table 10-2.

Example 10-31   *Verification of VRF Route Target Import and Export*

```
PE1# show vrf detail
! Output omitted for brevity
VRF VPN01 (VRF Id = 1); default RD 1:1; default VPNID <not set>
  Interfaces:
    Gi0/1
Address family ipv4 unicast (Table ID = 0x2):
  Export VPN route-target communities
    RT:1:10
  Import VPN route-target communities
    RT:1:10               RT:1:30
VRF VPN02 (VRF Id = 2); default RD 2:1; default VPNID <not set>
```

```
  Interfaces:
    Gi0/2
Address family ipv4 unicast (Table ID = 0x3):
  Flags: 0x0
  Export VPN route-target communities
    RT:1:20
  Import VPN route-target communities
    RT:1:20                RT:1:30
```

```
PE2# show vrf detail
! Output omitted for brevity
VRF VPN01 (VRF Id = 1); default RD 3:2; default VPNID <not set>
  Interfaces:
    Gi0/1
Address family ipv4 unicast (Table ID = 0x2):
  Export VPN route-target communities
    RT:1:30
  Import VPN route-target communities
    RT:1:10                RT:1:20
```

```
PE3# show vrf detail
! Output omitted for brevity
VRF VPN01 (VRF Id = 1); default RD 1:3; default VPNID <not set>
  Interfaces:
    Gi0/1
Address family ipv4 unicast (Table ID = 0x2):
  Export VPN route-target communities
    RT:1:10
  Import VPN route-target communities
    RT:1:10                RT:1:30

VRF VPN02 (VRF Id = 2); default RD 2:3; default VPNID <not set>
  Interfaces:
    Gi0/2
Address family ipv4 unicast (Table ID = 0x3):
  Export VPN route-target communities
    RT:1:20
  Import VPN route-target communities
    RT:1:20                RT:1:30
```

Example 10-32 demonstrates the routing tables of CE1 (VRF: VPN01), CE2 (VRF: VPN02), and CE3 (VRF:VPN03). CE1 and CE2 have the route to the email servers installed in their routing table even though it resides in a different VRF. The significance is that CE3 provides connectivity to the email servers and requires connectivity to all Company A and Company B networks so it has imported routes from VPN01 and VPN02 VRFs.

Example 10-32 *Verification of Routing Tables for MPLS Services*

```
CE1# show bgp ipv4 unicast
! Output omitted for brevity
      Network          Next Hop         Metric LocPrf Weight Path
 *>   172.16.1.0/24    0.0.0.0               0        32768 ?
 *>   172.16.3.0/24    172.16.11.2                        0 65000 300 ?
 *>   172.16.4.0/24    172.16.11.2                        0 65000 65000 ?
 *    172.16.11.0/24   172.16.11.2           0            0 65000 ?
 *>                    0.0.0.0               0        32768 ?
 *>   172.16.33.0/24   172.16.11.2                        0 65000 ?
 *>   172.16.44.0/24   172.16.11.2                        0 65000 ?


CE2# show bgp ipv4 unicast
! Output omitted for brevity
      Network          Next Hop         Metric LocPrf Weight Path
 *>   172.16.2.0/24    0.0.0.0               0        32768 ?
 *>   172.16.3.0/24    172.16.22.2                        0 65000 300 ?
 *>   172.16.5.0/24    172.16.22.2                        0 65000 65000 ?
 *    172.16.22.0/24   172.16.22.2           0            0 65000 ?
 *>                    0.0.0.0               0        32768 ?
 *>   172.16.33.0/24   172.16.22.2                        0 65000 ?
 *>   172.16.55.0/24   172.16.22.2                        0 65000 ?


CE3# show bgp ipv4 unicast
! Output omitted for brevity
      Network          Next Hop         Metric LocPrf Weight Path
 *>   172.16.1.0/24    172.16.33.2                        0 65000 100 ?
 *>   172.16.2.0/24    172.16.33.2                        0 65000 200 ?
 *>   172.16.3.0/24    0.0.0.0               0        32768 ?
 *>   172.16.4.0/24    172.16.33.2                        0 65000 100 ?
 *>   172.16.5.0/24    172.16.33.2                        0 65000 200 ?
 *>   172.16.11.0/24   172.16.33.2                        0 65000 ?
 *>   172.16.22.0/24   172.16.33.2                        0 65000 ?
 *    172.16.33.0/24   172.16.33.2           0            0 65000 ?
 *>                    0.0.0.0               0        32768 ?
 *>   172.16.44.0/24   172.16.33.2                        0 65000 ?
 *>   172.16.55.0/24   172.16.33.2                        0 65000 ?
```

Example 10-33 displays the VPNv4 prefixes on PE1. The prefixes in the RD 1:1 VPN01 VRF grouping include the routes with a RD of 1:1 (local), RD of 1:2 (Site 3), and RD of 3:2 (Site 3).

Example 10-33   *PE1's BGP Table with VPN Services*

```
PE1-IOS# show bgp vpnv4 unicast all
! Output omitted for brevity


      Network          Next Hop          Metric LocPrf Weight Path
Route Distinguisher: 1:1 (default for vrf VPN01)
 *>   172.16.1.0/24    172.16.11.1            0              0 100 ?
 *>i 172.16.3.0/24     192.168.2.2            0      100     0 300 ?
 *>i 172.16.4.0/24     192.168.3.3            0      100     0 100 ?
 *    172.16.11.0/24   172.16.11.1            0              0 100 ?
 *>                    0.0.0.0                0          32768 ?
 *>i 172.16.33.0/24    192.168.2.2            0      100     0 ?
 *>i 172.16.44.0/24    192.168.3.3            0      100     0 ?
Route Distinguisher: 1:3
 *>i 172.16.4.0/24     192.168.3.3            0      100     0 100 ?
 *>i 172.16.44.0/24    192.168.3.3            0      100     0 ?
Route Distinguisher: 2:1 (default for vrf VPN02)
      Network          Next Hop          Metric LocPrf Weight Path
 *>   172.16.2.0/24    172.16.22.1            0              0 200 ?
 *>i 172.16.3.0/24     192.168.2.2            0      100     0 300 ?
 *>i 172.16.5.0/24     192.168.3.3            0      100     0 200 ?
 *    172.16.22.0/24   172.16.22.1            0              0 200 ?
 *>                    0.0.0.0                0          32768 ?
 *>i 172.16.33.0/24    192.168.2.2            0      100     0 ?
 *>i 172.16.55.0/24    192.168.3.3            0      100     0 ?
Route Distinguisher: 2:3
 *>i 172.16.5.0/24     192.168.3.3            0      100     0 200 ?
 *>i 172.16.55.0/24    192.168.3.3            0      100     0 ?
Route Distinguisher: 3:2
      Network          Next Hop          Metric LocPrf Weight Path
 *>i 172.16.3.0/24     192.168.2.2            0      100     0 300 ?
 *>i 172.16.33.0/24    192.168.2.2            0      100     0 ?
```

> **Note**   In Example 10-32, CE3's BGP table contains the peering networks for the other company networks (172.16.11.0/24, 172.16.22.0/24, 172.16.44.0/24, and 172.16.55.0/24). Those network prefixes could be assigned a different RT on the PE routers (for example, RT 1:11 for Company A and RT 1:21 for Company B) as they are advertised to other PEs. The networks that should be imported into the other VRF should maintain the original RT for that VRF.
>
> The VRF definitions would then include three RTs: the two for each VRF marking and one for the cloud provider (Company C's). It is important to note that a route is exported only once. In other words, if VRF VPN01 imports a route from VRF VPN02, VRF VPN01 cannot export VRF VPN02's routes as its own. VRF VPN03 must import from VRF VPN01 directly. This is a similar concept to how IBGP learned routes are not reflected to other IBGP peers.

A VRF can use multiple different RTs at a time. Trying to find routes that match a specific RT may seem like a daunting task on a route-reflector. However the solution involves the creation of an extended community list on IOS and NX-OS devices or a route policy on IOS XR routers. The extended community list or route policy is then applied against the VPNv4 address family, as shown in Example 10-34.

Example 10-34   *Viewing Prefixes Based on RT*

```
IOS-RR# config t
IOS-RR(config)# ip extcommunity-list 1 permit rt 1:10
IOS-RR(config)# exit
IOS-RR# show bgp vpnv4 unicast all extcommunity-list 1
! Output omitted for brevity
BGP table version is 21, local router ID is 192.168.100.1
Status codes: s suppressed, d damped, h history, * valid, > best, i - internal,
              r RIB-failure, S Stale, m multipath, b backup-path, f RT-Filter,
              x best-external, a additional-path, c RIB-compressed,
Origin codes: i - IGP, e - EGP, ? - incomplete
RPKI validation codes: V valid, I invalid, N Not found


     Network          Next Hop            Metric LocPrf Weight Path
Route Distinguisher: 1:1
 *>i 172.16.1.0/24    192.168.1.1              0    100      0 100 ?
 *>i 172.16.11.0/24   192.168.1.1              0    100      0 ?
Route Distinguisher: 1:3
 *>i 172.16.4.0/24    192.168.3.3              0    100      0 100 ?
 *>i 172.16.44.0/24   192.168.3.3              0    100      0 ?

RP/0/0/CPU0:XR-RR# conf t
RP/0/0/CPU0:XR-RR(config)# route-policy RT
```

```
RP/0/0/CPU0:XR-RR(config-rpl)# if extcommunity rt matches-any ( 1:10) then
RP/0/0/CPU0:XR-RR(config-rpl)# pass endif
RP/0/0/CPU0:XR-RR(config-rpl)# end-policy
RP/0/0/CPU0:XR-RR(config)# commit
RP/0/0/CPU0:XR-RR(config)# end
RP/0/0/CPU0:XR-RR# show bgp vpnv4 unicast route-policy RT
! output ommitted for brevity
   Network            Next Hop          Metric LocPrf Weight Path
Route Distinguisher: 1:1
*>i172.16.1.0/24      192.168.1.1            0    100    0 100 ?
*>i172.16.11.0/24     192.168.1.1            0    100    0 ?
Route Distinguisher: 1:3
*>i172.16.4.0/24      192.168.3.3            0    100    0 100 ?
*>i172.16.44.0/24     192.168.3.3            0    100    0 ?
*
```

```
NXOS-RR# config t
NXOS-RR(config)# ip extcommunity-list standard RT permit rt 1:10
NXOS-RR(config)# exit
NXOS-RR# show bgp vpnv4 unicast extcommunity-list RT
! output ommitted for brevity
   Network            Next Hop         Metric     LocPrf    Weight Path
Route Distinguisher: 1:1
*>i172.16.1.0/24      192.168.1.1           0        100       0 100 ?
*>i172.16.11.0/24     192.168.1.1           0        100       0 ?
Route Distinguisher: 1:3
*>i172.16.4.0/24      192.168.3.3           0        100       0 100 ?
*>i172.16.44.0/24     192.168.3.3           0        100       0 ?
*>i172.16.44.0/24     192.168.3.3           0        100       0 ?
```

RT Constraints

As stated earlier, the PE router discards any VPN prefixes that contain an RT that does not match any of the import RTs for any of the VRFs. The filtering occurs on the PE router after it has received the prefixes. This is not much of an issue for environments that have a low number of VRFs or when the VRFs are consistently deployed across all VRFs.

However, most service providers have hundreds of PE routers that each hold thousands of VRFs on them. Only a small portion of the VRFs are located on a single router, which results in the PE router receiving a lot of routes that it does not need from the VPNv4 RR. This behavior causes a lot of wasted resources (CPU, memory, and network) between the PE and RR routers.

Figure 10-11 demonstrates the behavior where PE1 has two VRFs configured (VPN01 and VPN02) and PE2 has two VRFS configured (VPN02 and VPN03). Both PEs advertise their VPN prefixes to the RR. The RR advertises all VPN prefixes toward the PE routers. The VPN prefixes for the VPN03 VRF are not needed on PE1, and the VPN prefixes for VPN01 are not needed on PE2, but both unwanted prefixes are advertised.

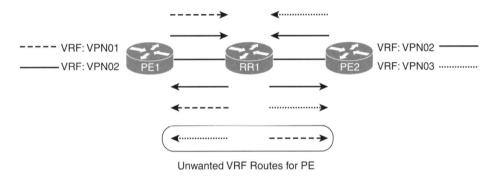

Unwanted VRF Routes for PE

Figure 10-11 *Unnecessary VPN Prefixes Advertised to PE Routers*

The same concept applies to VPN prefixes that are exchanged between RRs. Not only are there unwanted updates from RR to PE, there are unwanted updates between RRs. Figure 10-12 demonstrates the following:

- RR1 receives VPN prefixes from PE1 and PE2 (VPN01, VPN02, and VPN03).

- RR1 advertises these VPN prefixes to RR2, which then advertises the VPN prefixes to PE3 and PE4.

- RR2 receives VPN prefixes from PE3 and PE4 (VPN01, VPN03, and VPN04).

- RR2 advertises these VPN prefixes to RR1, which then advertises the VPN prefixes to PE1 and PE2.

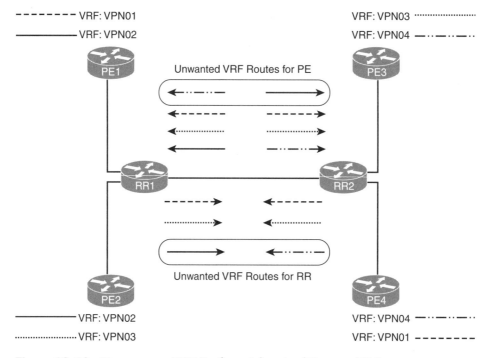

Figure 10-12 *Unnecessary VPN Prefixes Advertised Between RR Routers*

It should be apparent that the VPN03 VPN prefix is not needed on the RR2, PE3, or PE4 routers, and that the VPN04 VPN prefix is not needed on the RR1, PE1, or PE1 routers.

RT Constraint (RTC) is a mechanism to prevent the propagation of the VPN prefixes to a PE (or RR) that is not interested in the VPN prefix. RTC is defined in RFC 4684, and operates in a similar fashion to Outbound Route Filtering (ORF) of IPv4 prefixes.

RTC is based on the concept that every BGP peer advertises its list of RTs to a BGP peer. The BGP peer then applies a filter to the list of VPN prefixes it has and advertises only VPN prefixes that match the RTs that match the peer. In essence, the PE router tells the RR which VRFs it has and wants to receive.

On PE routers with low VPN membership, this functionality helps reduce the scaling requirements of the PE. The PE router does not have to spend resources on filtering out unwanted updates, and thus the memory and CPU requirements on the PE are reduced.

On the other hand, the resource requirements on the RR increase to accommodate holding a list of RTs because they are required to filter the VPN prefixes that it advertises. At the same time, the RR needs to process only the VPN routes used by its RR clients, and the resources that would be spend on the actual transmission of unwanted updates are saved.

RTC works through the usage of an additional address-family that contains all the RT membership information. This is known as the *RT-Filter address-family*. Routers that want to participate in RTC establish a VPNv4 (or VPNv6) session and a RT-Filter session.

> **Note**   A RR can advertise VPN prefixes to RTC and non-RTC clients at the same time. RT filtering occurs only for routers that establish a RT-Filter BGP session with it.

At the time of this writing, RTC is supported only on IOS and IOS XR routers. IOS initialize the RT-Filter address family with the command **address-family rtfilter unicast**. The BGP session is then activated, and route-reflector clients can be defined as well. An IOS XR router initializes the RT-Filter address family with the command **address-family ipv4 rt-filter**, and then the address-family is associated underneath each BGP peer as well.

Example 10-35 provides the sample configuration for PE1 (IOS) and PE2 (IOS XR).

Example 10-35   *RTC Configuration for IOS and IOS XR*

```
PE1-IOS
router bgp 65000
 neighbor 192.168.100.100 remote-as 65000
neighbor 192.168.100.100 update-source Loopback0
 !
address-family vpnv4
  neighbor 192.168.100.100 activate
  neighbor 192.168.100.100 send-community extended
 exit-address-family
 !
 address-family rtfilter unicast
  neighbor 192.168.100.100 activate
  neighbor 192.168.100.100 send-community extended
 exit-address-family
```

```
PE2-XR
router bgp 65000
 address-family vpnv4 unicast
 address-family ipv4 rt-filter
 !
 neighbor 192.168.100.100
  remote-as 65000
  update-source Loopback0
  address-family vpnv4 unicast
  address-family ipv4 rt-filter
```

> **Note**   The RR uses the same configuration as Example 10-35, but also configures the PE routers as route-reflector clients.

The RT-Filter address-family always sets the next-hop IP address to the router that advertised the RT-Membership prefix. This allows for RT-Membership to cascade or follow
the advertisement path across multiple RRs. The RT-Membership prefix is structured as
follows:

- The first 4 bytes are for the ASN of the advertising router.

- The second octet reflects the BGP extended community type.

- The third and fourth octets reflect the actual RT itself.

The contents of the RT-Filter table is displayed on IOS routers with the command **show
bgp rtfilter unicast {all | default | rt *rt*}**. IOS XR routers use the command **show bgp ipv4
rt-filter**.

Example 10-36 displays RT-Membership prefixes on the RR in Figure 10-4. Notice that
PE1 and PE2 have all advertised 65000:2:1:1, which signifies that both PE routers have
RT 1:1 configured on them. PE1 has the additional RTs of 1:10, 1:11, and 1:12 configured
as well.

Example 10-36   *RT-Membership Prefixes on the Route Reflector*

```
RR# show bgp rtfilter unicast all
! Output omitted for brevity
     Network          Next Hop           Metric LocPrf Weight Path
     0:0:0:0          0.0.0.0                              0 i
 * i 65000:2:1:1      192.168.2.2               100   32768 i
 *>i                  192.168.1.1          0    100   32768 i
 *>i 65000:2:1:10     192.168.1.1          0    100   32768 i
 *>i 65000:2:1:11     192.168.1.1          0    100   32768 i
 *>i 65000:2:1:12     192.168.1.1          0    100   32768 i
```

Notice the 0:0:0:0 RT-Membership prefix that is advertised on the RR. This prefix is
advertised to all the RT-Filter route-reflector clients to tell them that they should advertise all VPN prefixes to it. Failing to configure the route-reflector clients on the RR
prohibits the advertisement of RT-Membership prefixes to the RR.

Note   PE devices that want to receive all VPN prefixes but do not want the BGP session
to reset, which occurs when disabling the RT-Filter address-family, can advertise the
default route to the RR with the **neighbor default-originate** command.

MPLS VPN Label Exchange

After the CE routers have routes for source and destination networks, the focus shifts
toward the MPLS forwarding of the network traffic. As stated earlier, packets are forwarded by MPLS labels between PE routers to PE routers.

But how does a PE router differentiate one VRF's network traffic from another VRF when there are thousands of VRFs on the same router? After talking about import and export RTs, some network engineers might think that the export RTs are included as part of the packet header. The RT is 8 bytes in length, and multiple RTs on a packet would make the packet headers too big.

Instead, VRF identification works by adding a second MPLS label. When a packet is encapsulated at the source PE, the MPLS VPN label (inner) first, and then a second for-warding MPLS label (outer) is added to the packet. Forwarding between the PEs uses the outer label, and the inner label is used by the destination PE to identify which VRF it belongs to. Figure 10-13 displays the packet capture of a MPLS L3VPN packet, which should help with the visualization of the MPLS labels.

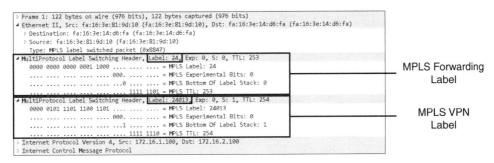

Figure 10-13 *Packet Capture of MPLS L3VPN Packet*

The destination PE router assigns a unique local MPLS VPN label for every network pre-fix that is attached to a VRF. The MPLS VPN PE label is advertised as part of the BGP path attribute. Upon receipt of a packet, the destination PE router looks up the MPLS VPN label and can identify which VRF it is associated with and the outbound interface that the packet should be sent out on. Regardless of the source PE router, the MPLS VPN label will be the same for that VPN prefix.

Note It is possible for the same MPLS VPN label to be used for two different VPN prefixes as long as the VPN prefixes are associated to different destination PEs. This is because the first differentiator is the packet's next-hop, which correlates to a different PE router.

Example 10-37 displays the BGP tables for the sample topology in Figure 10-4. PE2 is advertising the 172.16.2.100/32 VPN prefix with the MPLS VPN label of 24013 to the other PE routers. Notice that the PE1 and PE3 routers have the same *Out label* for the 172.16.2.100/32 network.

If the MPLS VPN labels are not the same, the packet does not forward out the correct port. Additional troubleshooting is needed to identify why the MPLS VPN label changed between the PE routers.

Example 10-37   *MPLS VPN Labels*

```
PE1-IOS# show bgp vpnv4 unicast vrf VPN01 labels
   Network           Next Hop        In label/Out label
Route Distinguisher: 1:1 (VPN01)
   172.16.1.0/26     172.16.1.11     25/nolabel
                     0.0.0.0         25/nolabel(VPN01)
   172.16.1.100/32   172.16.1.11     26/nolabel
   172.16.1.200/32   0.0.0.0         27/nolabel(VPN01)
   172.16.2.0/26     192.168.2.2     nolabel/24012
   172.16.2.100/32   192.168.2.2     nolabel/24013
   172.16.2.200/32   192.168.2.2     nolabel/24012
   172.16.3.0/26     192.168.3.3     nolabel/492287
   172.16.3.100/32   192.168.3.3     nolabel/22
   172.16.3.200/32   192.168.3.3     nolabel/492287


RP/0/0/CPU0:PE2-XR# show bgp vrf VPN01 ipv4 unicast labels
! Output omitted for brevity
Network            Next Hop        Rcvd Label      Local Label
Route Distinguisher: 1:1 (default for vrf VPN01)
*>i172.16.1.0/26      192.168.1.1      25              nolabel
*>i172.16.1.100/32    192.168.1.1      26              nolabel
*>i172.16.1.200/32    192.168.1.1      27              nolabel
*>  172.16.2.0/26     0.0.0.0          nolabel         24012
*                     172.16.2.22      nolabel         24012
*>  172.16.2.100/32   172.16.2.22      nolabel         24013
*>  172.16.2.200/32   0.0.0.0          nolabel         24012
*>i172.16.3.0/26      192.168.3.3      492287          nolabel
*>i172.16.3.100/32    192.168.3.3      22              nolabel
*>i172.16.3.200/32    192.168.3.3      492287          nolabel

Processed 9 prefixes, 10 paths


PE3-NXOS# show bgp vrf VPN01 ipv4 unicast labels
! Output omitted for brevity
   Network           Next Hop        In label/Out label
*>i172.16.1.0/26      192.168.1.1      nolabel/25
*>i172.16.1.100/32    192.168.1.1      nolabel/26
*>i172.16.1.200/32    192.168.1.1      nolabel/27
*>i172.16.2.0/26      192.168.2.2      nolabel/24012
*>i172.16.2.100/32    192.168.2.2      nolabel/24013
*>i172.16.2.200/32    192.168.2.2      nolabel/24012
*>r172.16.3.0/26      0.0.0.0          492287/nolabel (VPN01)
* e                   172.16.3.33      492287/nolabel (VPN01)
*>e172.16.3.100/32    172.16.3.33      22/nolabel (VPN01)
*>r172.16.3.200/32    0.0.0.0          492287/nolabel (VPN01)
```

MPLS Forwarding

The first portion of this section focused on the control plane aspect of troubleshooting MPLS L3VPNs. The other component is to verify that MPLS forwarding is working properly. Enabling MPLS operations, administration, and maintenance (OAM) is required on IOS XR for this troubleshooting technique. After it is enabled, a router can **ping** or **traceroute** using MPLS labels to verify PE-to-PE MPLS connectivity. The destination address should match the IP address associated with the next-hop IP address shown in BGP (that is, a loopback interface with a /32 IP address).

The command structure is **ping mpls ipv4** *destination-network /prefix-length*. If connectivity is successful in one direction, it needs to be checked in the other direction for return traffic. MPLS forwarding should be troubleshot as a unidirectional technology.

Example 10-38 displays the MPLS ping being performed on PE1, PE2, and PE3.

Example 10-38 *MPLS Ping*

```
PE1-IOS# ping mpls ipv4 192.168.2.2/32
Sending 5, 100-byte MPLS Echos to 192.168.2.2/32,
     timeout is 2 seconds, send interval is 0 msec:

Codes: '!' - success, 'Q' - request not sent, '.' - timeout,
  'L' - labeled output interface, 'B' - unlabeled output interface,
  'D' - DS Map mismatch, 'F' - no FEC mapping, 'f' - FEC mismatch,
  'M' - malformed request, 'm' - unsupported tlvs, 'N' - no label entry,
  'P' - no rx intf label prot, 'p' - premature termination of LSP,
  'R' - transit router, 'I' - unknown upstream index,
  'X' - unknown return code, 'x' - return code 0

Type escape sequence to abort.
!!!!!
Success rate is 100 percent (5/5), round-trip min/avg/max = 5/5/7 ms

RP/0/0/CPU0:PE2-XR# ping mpls ipv4 192.168.3.3/32
! Output omitted for brevity
Type escape sequence to abort.
!!!!!
Success rate is 100 percent (5/5), round-trip min/avg/max = 1/8/10 ms

PE3-NXOS# ping mpls ipv4 192.168.1.1/32
! Output omitted for brevity
Type Ctrl-C to abort.
!!!!!
Success rate is 100 percent (5/5), round-trip min/avg/max = 8/9/10 ms
 Total Time Elapsed 57 ms
```

In the event that the MPLS ping fails, a MPLS traceroute can be executed with the same command structure of **traceroute mpls ipv4** *destination-network /prefix-length*, which could help with isolating where the problem may exist.

> **Note**   The troubleshooting of MPLS forwarding is outside of the scope of this book and can be found in other Cisco Press books, such as MPLS Fundamentals by Luc de Ghein.

Summary

This chapter provided a general overview of MPLS VPNs. MPLS L3VPNs provide privacy of customer networks through the usage of VRFs and MPLS forwarding between PE routers.

Troubleshooting MPLS L3VPN consists of troubleshooting the control plane (VPN prefix exchange via BGP) and MPLS forwarding. Most of the complexity comes from troubleshooting the control plane component of MPLS L3VPN. Common issues to look for when troubleshooting are the following:

- AS-Path loops on the CE routers. This is overcome by the use of **as-override** on the PE router.

- Verify that the import RTs match the export RTs for the specific VRF. Making these the same where possible simplifies troubleshooting.

- Verify that MPLS VPN labels are the same on both PE routers.

- If RTC is enabled, make sure that the RR is advertising a default route in the RT-Filter address-family toward the route-reflector clients. Verify that the RTs are being advertised toward the RR.

When a route is missing on the CE or PE router, start to check the path of route advertisements toward the PE advertising the route.

References

RFC 4360, *BGP Extended Communities Attribute*, Srihari Sangli, Dan Tappan, Yakov Rekhter, IETF, http://www.ietf.org/rfc/rfc4360.txt, February 2006.

RFC 4364, *BGP/MPLS IP Virtual Private Networks (VPNs)*, Eric Rosen, Yakov Rekhter. IETF, https://tools.ietf.org/html/rfc4364, February 2006.

RFC 4684, *Constrained Route Distribution for Border Gateway Protocol/ Multiprotocol Label Switching (BGP/MPLS) Internet Protocol (IP) Virtual Private Networks (VPNs)*, Marques, R. Bonica, L. Fange, et al., IETF, https://tools.ietf.org/html/rfc4684, November 2006.

Cisco. Cisco IOS Software Configuration Guides. http://www.cisco.com.

Cisco. Cisco IOS XR Software Configuration Guides. http://www.cisco.com.

Cisco. Cisco NX-OS Software Configuration Guides. http://www.cisco.com.

Chapter 11

BGP for MPLS L2VPN Services

The following topics are covered in this chapter:

- L2VPN Services
- Virtual Private Wire Service
- Virtual Private LAN Service

L2VPN Services

The networking industry has seen development of various access services over the years. This includes IP, ATM, Frame-Relay (FR), Ethernet, and so on. As new innovations happen in the industry, more and more technologies are deployed, and some customers move to those newer technologies. Service providers (SP) still need to serve the old customers but also have to meet the requirements of customers who want to move to newer technologies. For example, customer ABC with 100 sites, using ATM or Frame-Relay connections from the service providers, wants to move Ethernet-based infrastructure. The service provider servicing customer ABC now has to upgrade its infrastructure to support customer ABC, but at the same time maintain the infrastructure to support other customers still using ATM, Frame-Relay, or broadband services.

Multiple access services require multiple core technologies. This adds heavily to the cost of production networks and also adds complexity to manage such network infrastructure. If there was a common infrastructure in the service provider core that could serve almost all access services, that would reduce the cost for the service providers to a great extent.

Over the years, Multiprotocol Label Switching (MPLS) and IP capabilities have evolved not just to provide Layer 3 VPN services but also provide Layer 2 Virtual Private Network (L2VPN) services. L2VPN enables SPs to carry multiple network services over a single converged network using IP/MPLS. In L2VPN, service providers extend a Layer 2 circuit to customers with literally any Layer 2 medium, and the customers can connect their network with the remote sites using the same or a different Layer 2 medium. For example, company ABC, having three sites, might be running Frame-Relay on site 1 but may run ATM on site 2 and Ethernet on site 3 and still maintain connectivity between each of them. The three sites are still getting a Layer 2 termination point from the service provider, but now company ABC does not have to maintain the same infrastructure at all sites to maintain connectivity. This gives more flexibility to the customers but at the same time reduces the cost of the service providers because they maintain a common infrastructure in their core network.

The main benefits of L2VPNs are as follows:

- Single infrastructure for both IP and legacy services.

- Seemless migration of legacy ATM / Frame-Relay services to IP/MPLS-based core without affecting any existing services.

- Incremental provisioning of new services.

- Cost saving due to reduced capital or operations expenses achieved through IP/MPLS infrastructure.

- Service providers do not participate in routing with customer's network and save resources on the provider routers.

The L2VPN services can be run across two cores:

- MPLS Core

- IP Core

The L2VPN services using IP/MPLS cores can be divided into two categories:

- **VPWS:** Wire Service

- **VPLS:** Local-Area Network (LAN) Service

Virtual Private Wire Service (VPWS) provides point-to-point services between two customer sites over the provider core. Virtual Private LAN Service (VPLS) provides multipoint-to-multipoint services between multiple customer sites using a mesh of point-to-point pseudowires over the provider core and a virtual switch to emulate a LAN. VPWS makes use of Any Transport over MPLS (AToM) pseudowires when the provider core is MPLS. VPLS service also uses the MPLS in the service provider core. Layer 2 Tunneling Protocol version 3 (L2TPv3) provides similar capabilities (only point-to-point services) but over an IP Core.

Figure 11-1 shows the various L2VPN models and their Layer 2 infrastructure support hierarchies. The MPLS-based L2VPNs provides point-to-point, point-to-multipoint, and multipoint-to-multipoint connections, whereas L2TPv3 provides only point-to-point connections.

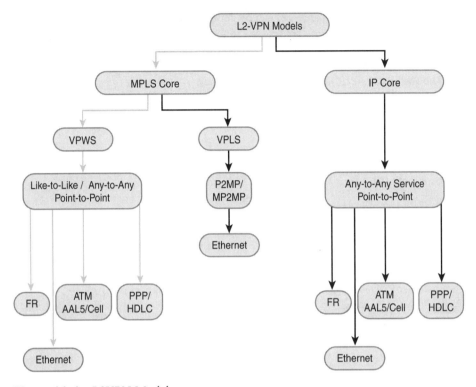

Figure 11-1 *L2VPN Models*

> **Note** Because there is no involvement for Border Gateway Protocol (BGP)-based services for L2TPv3 pseudowires, this chapter does not cover L2TPv3 concepts. It covers only MPLS-based L2VPN services; that is, VPWS and VPLS.

Terminologies

Let's take a look at a few terminologies frequently used in context of L2VPNs.

- **Attachment Circuit (AC):** A physical or a virtual circuit connecting the customer edge (CE) to a provider edge (PE). An attachment circuit (AC) may be an ATM virtual circuit identifier (VCI) / virtual path identifier (VPI) or FR data link connection identifier (DLCI), Virtual LAN (VLAN), an Ethernet port, or even an MPLS label switch path (LSP).

- **Terminating PE (T-PE):** A terminating PE is a PE where the endpoint of a pseudowire (PW) is terminated.

- **Switching PE (S-PE):** A switching PE is a one where one pseudowire segment is switched to another pseudowire segment. This is seen usually in case of multisegment pseudowires.

■ **Pseudowires (PW):** Pseudowires can be defined as a virtual tunnel between two provider edge routers that connect two attachment circuits and carry customer packet data units (PDUs) over the service provider core. A PW may connect the pseudowire end-services (PWESs), a.k.a. ACs, of the same or a different type. The PWES can be of any of the following types:

  ■ Ethernet

  ■ Ethernet Virtual Circuits (EVC)

  ■ ATM VCI/VPI

  ■ 802.1Q (VLAN)

  ■ High-level Data Link Control (HDLC)

  ■ Point-to-Point Protocol (PPP)

  ■ Frame-Relay VC

The customer PDU is encapsulated inside the header and is seen as a MPLS or IP packet inside the service provider core. This helps the service providers migrate from a traditional Layer 2 infrastructure, such as ATM or FR, to an IP/MPLS-based core. Figure 11-2 illustrates how the PWs connect different customer sites.

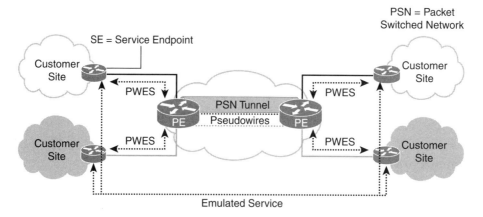

Figure 11-2   *Pseudowires over Packet Switched Network*

Table 11-1 lists the various PW types as defined by Request for Comments (RFC) 4446. There are some more PW types that are defined by IETF but not listed in Table 11-1.

Table 11-1 *Pseudowire Types*

VC Type (Pseudowire Type)	Attachment Circuit Type / PWES Type
0x0001	Frame Relay DLCI
0x0002	ATM AAL5 SDU VCC transport
0x0003	ATM transparent cell transport
0x0004	Ethernet Tagged Mode
0x0005	Ethernet
0x0006	HDLC
0x0007	PPP
0x0008	SONET/SDH Circuit Emulation Service Over MPLS (CEM)
0x000C	ATM one-to-one VCC Cell Mode
0x000E	ATM AAL5 PDU VCC transport
0x000F	Frame-Relay Port mode
0x0019	Frame Relay DLCI

- **VC Label:** A VC label is used to identify an AToM virtual circuit (VC).

- **Control Word:** The control word is an optional 4-byte field that takes care of address packet sequentiality, small packet size, control bits, and the like. It is used to maintain information provided in the header of various L2 PDUs. The control word has two formats:

  - **Generic:** Where first nibble is 0000

  - **Inband Virtual Circuit Connectivity Verification (VCCV):** Where first nibble is 0001

The following are the functions of generic control word:

- **Padding:** Pad small size packets

- **Sequence Number:** To detect out of order packets

- Carry control bits of the Layer 2 header of the transported protocol

- Facilitating fragmentation and reassembly

- Aids in load-balancing AToM frames in MPLS core

The inband VCCV is used as payload identifier. The control word is optional for some protocols but mandatory for others.

Virtual Private Wire Service

VPWS provides point-to-point services between two CE devices over the provider MPLS core network. The traffic from the CE devices is sent over the PW A VC label, or the PW label is used to process packets at each PE. Hence, each PE must reserve a PW label (local label) and advertise it to the peer. A tunnel label is then used to forward the PDU from one PE to another PE. Because the peer can be multiple hops away, a targeted Label Distribution Protocol (LDP) session is used for label distribution. The VC label bindings exchanged over this LDP session use the Forward Equivalence Class (FEC) element type 128 via the LDP—*downstream unsolicited mode*. Only one targeted session is created for multiple VCs between the PEs. If there is already a targeted session between the PEs by another application, that session is used. LDP uses the FEC type 128 to determine that the message is for AToM application. This is described in RFC 4447.

To understand the control plane of VPWS, examine the topology in Figure 11-3. A native service is provided by the PE router toward the CE using an AC. In the core, the P and the PE routers are running IGP and LDP between them for exchanging routing and label information. The two PEs can be discovered by manual configuration or by using the BGP autodiscovery mechanism. A targeted LDP session is used between the PE routers to exchange VC label information and control information.

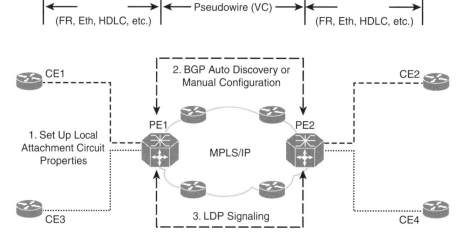

Figure 11-3 *VPWS Control Plane*

The following steps give a run down on the sequence of events between the two PE routers for exchanging VC label and control information:

Step 1.   Attachment circuit is configured with Peer Address and Virtual Circuit Identifier (VCID).

Step 2.   PE1 starts targeted LDP session with PE2 if one does not already exist.

Step 3.   PE1 allocates VC label for new circuit and binds to configured VC ID.

Step 4.   PE1 sends LDP label Mapping Message containing VC FEC TLV and VC label Type Length Value (TLV).

Step 5.   PE2 receives VC FEC TLV and VC label TLV that matches local VCID.

Step 6.   PE2 repeats Steps 1 through 5 so that bidirectional label/VCID mappings are established.

Note   The FEC element type used for LDP signaling is 128, whereas FEC element type used with BGP autodiscovery is 129.

Figure 11-4 illustrates the data plane for a VPWS circuit. Notice that customer PDU is followed by an optional field C that represents control word, VC label, and the Tunnel label. At each hop within the service provider core, packets are forwarded using the underlying label switching mechanism.

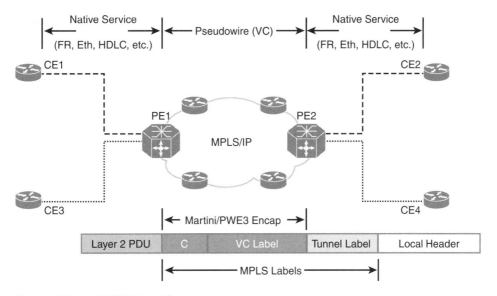

Figure 11-4   *VPWS Data Plane*

Interworking

VPWS service allows for establishment of PW across heterogeneous ACs. Each circuit type behaves and functions differently based on the underlying Layer 2 medium. Thus, it becomes difficult to forward traffic across PWs when either side is having a different type of AC. To overcome this problem, the Interworking feature is used. There are two types of interworking mainly supported in L2VPN:

■ **Ethernet Interworking:** This mode is also known as *bridged* mode. In this mode of operation, Ethernet frames are extracted from the AC and sent over the PW. AC on the other end of the PW performs the adaptation of the Ethernet frame to the Layer 2 technology used. In this mode, CE routers can natively bridge Ethernet or can use a bridged encapsulation model such as Bridge Virtual Interface (BVI). This mode provides LAN services and connectivity services.

■ **IP Interworking:** This mode is also known as the *routed* mode. In this mode of operation, the Layer 3 payload is extracted from the Layer 2 payload and sent over the PW. This method is used for providing IP connectivity between sites, regardless of their Layer 2 infrastructures.

Apart from the preceding two interworking methods, IOS XR and NX-OS also supports the VLAN Interworking mode. In this mode of operation, the VLAN ID is included in the payload along with the Layer 2 payload. Without this interworking, the packets on the main interface do not send the VLAN tag over the PW.

Note   Refer to Cisco.com documentation links in the reference section on how interworking functions between different types of ACs on both sides.

Configuration and Verification

The default method for configuring VPWS circuits is manual configuration. In other words, the PWs have to be manually configured between the PE routers. The configuration can be laid out in few simple steps, as follows:

Step 1.   Configure IGP. Configure IGP between the P and the PE routers in the service provider network. Open Shortest Path First (OSPF) and Intermediate System to Intermediate System (IS-IS) are recommended, and PE should advertise the LDP-ID as a /32 route.

Step 2.   Configure LDP. Configure LDP on the core interfaces using the command **mpls ip** on both Cisco IOS and NX-OS platforms or enabling the interfaces under **mpls ldp** configuration mode on IOS XR platform to allocate labels for Interior Gateway Protocol (IGP) learned prefixes. This ensures LSP is formed between the source and the terminating PE router.

Step 3.   Configure Attachment Circuit. Configure the AC on both PE routers. When configuring the AC, ensure the same maximum transmission unit (MTU) settings are defined on both sides.

Step 4.   Configure Interworking. Enable the relevant interworking mode between both the PE for the PW. This is configured by defining a **pseudowire-class**. Note that interworking is not required when using like-to-like PWs.

Step 5. Configure xconnect. Configure the xconnect between the PE routers using a unique VCID—that is, the VCID value should have been used on either of the PE routers. The VCID value should be same on both PE routers.

Step 6. Enable Attachment Circuit. After the xconnect is configured, enable the AC by bringing up the customer facing interfaces.

Examine the topology as shown in Figure 11-5. PE1, PE2, and PE3 are forming a VPWS circuit over Ethernet—that is, Ethernet over MPLS (EoMPLS). A PW is formed between PE1 and PE2 and between PE1 and PE3. For simplicity, the AC is the same on both sides—like-to-like.

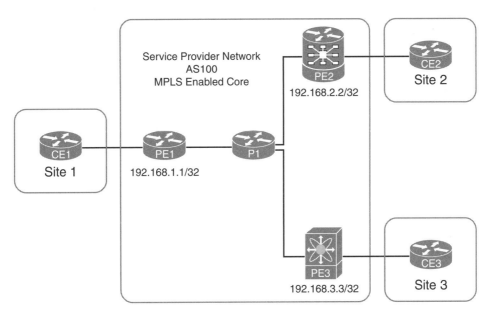

Figure 11-5 *Topology*

Note EoMPLS is a VPWS service for Ethernet attachment circuits. An Ethernet PW is used to carry Ethernet/802.3 PDUs over an MPLS network. This allows the service providers to offer emulated Ethernet services over existing MPLS networks. EoMPLS is a point-to-point service. EoMPLS encapsulation is defined in RFC 4448. The VC setup is performed as described in RFC 3985. Two type of modes are supported in EoMPLS: the raw (VC type 4) and the tagged (VC type 5) mode. The encapsulation performed depends on whether the VLAN tag is service-delimiting or non-service-delimiting. If non-service-delimiting, the tags are passed transparently over the PW as payload. If it's service-delimiting and tagged mode, the tags can be rewritten, stripped, or left unchanged in tagged mode. If it's service-delimiting and raw mode, no rewrite or removal of tags is required.

Example 11-1 illustrates the configuration for a EoMPLS circuit (VPWS) between PE1, PE2, and PE3, which are running Cisco IOS, IOS XR, and NX-OS software, respectively. The core facing interfaces on the PE routers and P router P1 are running IGP and LDP.

Example 11-1 *VPWS Configuration*

```
PE1 - Cisco IOS
pseudowire-class EOMPLS
 encapsulation mpls
 interworking ethernet


!
interface Loopback0
 ip address 192.168.1.1 255.255.255.255
!
interface GigabitEthernet1/1/2
 no ip address
 no keepalive
 service instance 100 ethernet
  encapsulation dot1q 100
  rewrite ingress tag pop 1 symmetric
  xconnect 192.168.2.2 100 encapsulation mpls pw-class EOMPLS
!
  service instance 101 ethernet
  encapsulation dot1q 101
  rewrite ingress tag pop 1 symmetric
  xconnect 192.168.3.3 101 encapsulation mpls pw-class EOMPLS
```

```
PE2 - IOS XR
interface Loopback0
 ipv4 address 192.168.2.2 255.255.255.255
!
interface GigabitEthernet0/0/0/1
!
interface GigabitEthernet0/0/0/1.2 l2transport
 encapsulation dot1q 100
!
l2vpn
 pw-class EOMPLS
  !
 xconnect group test
```

```
  p2p VPWS
    interface GigabitEthernet0/3/0/2.100
    neighbor 192.168.1.1 pw-id 100
    !
    interworking Ethernet
```

```
PE3 - NX-OS
feature-set mpls
feature mpls ldp
feature mpls l2vpn
feature evc
!
l2vpn xconnect context EOMPLS
  interworking ethernet
  member Ethernet3/3 service-instance 101
  member pseudowire101
!
interface pseudowire101
  neighbor 192.168.1.1 101
  encapsulation mpls
!
interface Ethernet3/3
  no shutdown
  service instance 101 ethernet
    encapsulation dot1q 101
    no shutdown
```

Note   In the preceding example, EVC is used on Cisco IOS and NX-OS devices. The Metro Ethernet forum describes EVC as a port-based point-to-point or multipoint-to-multipoint Layer 2 circuit. An EVC is configured using the interface level command **service instance** *instance-id* **ethernet**.

After the configuration is done, all the PE routers establish a targeted LDP session between them. To verify the targeted LDP session, use the command **show mpls ldp neighbor**. This command displays all the LDP sessions to the adjacent neighbors as well as targeted LDP neighbor sessions to the remote neighbors. Example 11-2 displays the targeted LDP session on all the PE routers.

Example 11-2   *Verifying Targeted LDP Session*

```
IOS

PE1# show mpls ldp neighbor
    Peer LDP Ident: 192.168.2.2:0; Local LDP Ident 192.168.1.1:0
        TCP connection: 192.168.2.2.35456 - 192.168.1.1.646
        State: Oper; Msgs sent/rcvd: 99/96; Downstream
        Up time: 01:03:14
        LDP discovery sources:
          Targeted Hello 192.168.1.1 -> 192.168.2.2, active, passive
        Addresses bound to peer LDP Ident:
          10.122.167.207   192.168.2.2     10.1.24.2
    Peer LDP Ident: 192.168.3.3:0; Local LDP Ident 192.168.1.1:0
        TCP connection: 192.168.3.3.44119 - 192.168.1.1.646
        State: Oper; Msgs sent/rcvd: 42/33; Downstream
        Up time: 00:17:18
        LDP discovery sources:
          Targeted Hello 192.168.1.1 -> 192.168.3.3, active, passive
        Addresses bound to peer LDP Ident:
          192.168.3.3     10.1.34.3
```

```
IOS XR

RP/0/1/CPU0:PE2# show mpls ldp neighbor
Peer LDP Identifier: 192.168.1.1:0
  TCP connection: 192.168.1.1:646 - 192.168.2.2:35456
  Graceful Restart: No
  Session Holdtime: 180 sec
  State: Oper; Msgs sent/rcvd: 99/101; Downstream-Unsolicited
  Up time: 01:05:11
  LDP Discovery Sources:
    Targeted Hello (192.168.2.2 -> 192.168.1.1, active)
  Addresses bound to this peer:
    1.1.1.1          10.1.14.1        13.13.13.1        192.168.1.1
```

```
NX-OS

PE3# show mpls ldp neighbor
Peer LDP Ident: 192.168.1.1:0; Local LDP Ident 192.168.3.3:0
        TCP connection: 192.168.1.1.646 - 192.168.3.3.44119
        State: Oper; Msgs sent/rcvd: 37/47; Downstream
        Up time: 00:21:34
        LDP discovery sources:
          Targeted Hello 192.168.3.3 -> 192.168.1.1, active, passive
        Addresses bound to peer LDP Ident:
          1.1.1.1          13.13.13.1        192.168.1.1       10.1.14.1
```

To view the details of the pseudowire connection, use the command **show mpls l2transport vc** *vcid* [**detail**] on Cisco IOS, **show l2vpn xconnect detail** on IOS XR, and **show l2vpn atom vc detail** on NX-OS. These commands display the VC status, local and remote VC label information, MTU settings, AC status, packets received and sent, and most importantly, the signaling mechanism being used. Example 11-3 displays the VC information using these commands.

Example 11-3 *Verifying VC Information*

```
PE1# show mpls l2transport vc 100 detail
Local interface: Gi1/1/2 up, line protocol up, Eth VLAN 100 up
  Interworking type is Ethernet
  Destination address: 192.168.2.2, VC ID: 100, VC status: up
    Output interface: Gi1/1/0, imposed label stack {23 16000}
    Preferred path: not configured
    Default path: active
    Next hop: 12.12.12.2
  Create time: 00:00:43, last status change time: 00:00:34
    Last label FSM state change time: 00:00:34
    Last peer autosense occurred at: 00:00:34
  Signaling protocol: LDP, peer 192.168.2.2:0 up
    Targeted Hello: 192.168.1.1(LDP Id) -> 192.168.2.2, LDP is UP
    Graceful restart: not configured and not enabled
    Non stop routing: not configured and not enabled
    Status TLV support (local/remote)   : enabled/supported
      LDP route watch                   : enabled
      Label/status state machine        : established, LruRru
      Last local dataplane   status rcvd: No fault
      Last BFD dataplane     status rcvd: Not sent
      Last BFD peer monitor  status rcvd: No fault
      Last local AC  circuit status rcvd: No fault
      Last local AC  circuit status sent: No fault
      Last local PW i/f circ status rcvd: No fault
      Last local LDP TLV     status sent: No fault
      Last remote LDP TLV    status rcvd: No fault
      Last remote LDP ADJ    status rcvd: No fault
    MPLS VC labels: local 40, remote 16000
    Group ID: local 0, remote 67110912
    MTU: local 1500, remote 1500
    Remote interface description: GigabitEthernet0_3_0_2.100
  Sequencing: receive disabled, send disabled
  Control Word: Off (configured: autosense)
  SSO Descriptor: 192.168.2.2/100, local label: 40
  Dataplane:
    SSM segment/switch IDs: 24588/12293 (used), PWID: 2
```

```
  VC statistics:
    transit packet totals: receive 0, send 0
    transit byte totals:   receive 0, send 0
! Output omitted for brevity
```

```
RP/0/1/CPU0:PE2# show l2vpn xconnect detail
Group test, XC VPWS, state is up; Interworking Ethernet
  AC: GigabitEthernet0/3/0/2.100, state is up
    Type VLAN; Num Ranges: 1
    VLAN ranges: [100, 100]
    MTU 1500; XC ID 0x4000001; interworking Ethernet
    Statistics:
      packets: received 0, sent 0
      bytes: received 0, sent 0
      drops: illegal VLAN 0, illegal length 0
  PW: neighbor 192.168.1.1, PW ID 100, state is up ( established )
    PW class not set, XC ID 0xff000001
    Encapsulation MPLS, protocol LDP
    Source address 192.168.2.2
    PW type Ethernet, control word disabled, interworking Ethernet
    PW backup disable delay 0 sec
    Sequencing not set

    PW Status TLV in use
      MPLS          Local                        Remote
      ------------  ---------------------------  -----------------------------
      Label         16000                        40
      Group ID      0x4000800                    0x0
      Interface     GigabitEthernet0/3/0/2.100   unknown
      MTU           1500                         1500
      Control word  disabled                     disabled
      PW type       Ethernet                     Ethernet
      VCCV CV type  0x2                          0x2
                    (LSP ping verification)      (LSP ping verification)
      VCCV CC type  0x6                          0x6
                    (router alert label)         (router alert label)
                    (TTL expiry)                 (TTL expiry)
      ------------  ---------------------------  -----------------------------
    Incoming Status (PW Status TLV):
      Status code: 0x0 (Up) in Notification message
    Outgoing Status (PW Status TLV):
      Status code: 0x0 (Up) in Notification message
    MIB cpwVcIndex: 4278190081
    Create time: 16/03/2016 23:01:25 (00:44:45 ago)
    Last time status changed: 16/03/2016 23:37:58 (00:08:11 ago)
```

```
   Statistics:
     packets: received 0, sent 0
     bytes: received 0, sent 0
```

```
PE3# show l2vpn atom vc detail
pseudowire101 is up, VC status is up PW type: Ethernet
  Create time: 00:43:15, last status change time: 00:03:11
    Last label FSM state change time: 00:03:11
  Destination address: 192.168.1.1 VC ID: 101
    Output interface: Ethernet3/2, imposed label stack {39 16}
    Preferred path: not configured
    Default path: active
    Next hop: 10.1.34.4
  Member of xconnect service EOMPLS
    Associated member EFP-Eth3/3.101 is up, status is up
    Interworking type is Like2Like
  Signaling protocol: LDP, peer 192.168.1.1:0 up
    Targeted Hello: 192.168.3.3(LDP Id) -> 192.168.1.1, LDP is UP
    Graceful restart: configured and not enabled
    Non stop routing: not configured and not enabled
    PWid FEC (128), VC ID: 101
    Status TLV support (local/remote)          : enabled/supported
      LDP route watch                          : enabled
      Label/status state machine               : established, LruRru
      Local dataplane status received          : No fault
      BFD dataplane status received            : Not sent
      BFD peer monitor status received         : No fault
      Status received from access circuit      : No fault
      Status sent to access circuit            : No fault
      Status received from pseudowire i/f      : No fault
      Status sent to network peer              : No fault
      Status received from network peer        : No fault
      Adjacency status of remote peer          : No fault
  Sequencing: receive disabled, send disabled
  Bindings
    Parameter    Local                          Remote
    -----------  -----------------------------  -----------------------------
    Label        16                             39
    Group ID     0                              0
    Interface
    MTU          1500                           1500
    Control word on (configured: autosense)    on
    PW type      Ethernet                       Ethernet
    VCCV CV type 0x02                           0x02
                 LSPV [2]                       LSPV [2]
```

```
   VCCV CC type 0x06                        0x07
                RA [2], TTL [3]             CW [1], RA [2], TTL [3]
   Status TLV   enabled                     supported
 Rx Counters
   0 input transit packets, 0 bytes
   0 drops, 0 seq err
 Tx Counters
   0 output transit packets, 0 bytes
   0 drops
```

Note Illustration on all the various VPWS circuit types is outside the scope of this book. Refer to the Cisco documentation as mentioned in reference section for more details. Also, refer to the Cisco Press book *Layer 2 VPN Architectures*.

VPWS BGP Signaling

VPWS services can also be set up using BGP signaling. RFC 6624 describes the autodiscovery and signaling mechanism for L2VPNs using BGP. Although the BGP autodiscovery mechanism for VPWS services is limited to IOS XR platforms, BGP provides signaling capability for VPWS circuits. BGP uses an NLRI update message with address-family identifier (AFI) 25 and sub-address-family identifier (SAFI) 65 for both VPWS and VPLS.

Examine the BGP network layer reachability information (NLRI) for VPWS, as shown in Figure 11-6. This new NLRI carries the individual VPWS information. The route distinguisher (RD), CE_ID, and CE Block Offset (Label Block Offset) are used to uniquely determine a VPWS NLRI. The CE_ID is nothing but the Site Id.

| Length (2 Octets) |
| CE ID (2 Octets) |
| RD (8 Octets) |
| CE Block Offset (2 Octets) |
| CE Block Size (2 Octets) |
| Label Block (3 Octets) |
| subTLV (Variable) |

Figure 11-6 *VPWS NLRI*

A new sub-TLV is carried on the NLRI and represents the state of the circuit, as shown in Figure 11-7. The bits correspond to each piece of CE information that is carried in the NLRI. Circuit status is represented by checking both the attachment circuit state and LSP state.

subTLV Type (1 Octet)
Length (2 Octets)
Bit Vector 1 = Down, 0 = Up

Figure 11-7 *Sub-TLV for VPWS*

A L2VPN extended community parameter is sent along with the NLRI with L2VPN information. The Encap Type is used to specify the type of attachment circuit (ATM, FR, Ethernet, and so on). Details of different assignments are described in *draft-kompella-ppvpn-l2vpn-03*. In addition to CE ID and label block information, BGP also signals *control flags*, as shown in Figure 11-8. The control flags indicate whether the control word is included in the encapsulation and if the sequence number is present for the packets being sent.

Extended Community Type (2) 0x800A
Encap Type (1 Octet)
Control Flags (1 Octet)
L2 MTU (2 Octets)
Reserved (2 Octets)

Figure 11-8 *Control Flags*

Note   If a control word mismatch occurs, the PW remains in down state.

VPWS service involves configuration where each PE defines the association between the local and remote CE ID via configuration. Along with this, the CE range, route target (RT), and RD information need to be specified in the configuration. This triggers the NLRI exchanged between the BGP peers, and L2VPN is informed about the remote circuit status and label binding information. This is used by L2VPN to set up the circuits.

Note   At the time of this writing, both IOS and NX-OS do not have support for BGP-based signaling and autodiscovery for VPWS circuits. Only IOS XR has support for BGP signaling and autodiscovery.

Configuration

When a VPWS xconnect is configured with BGP signaling and autodiscovery enabled, BGP distributes the NLRI with the appropriate BGP next-hop and CE_ID. Under the l2vpn configuration mode, an xconnect group is configured using the command **xconnect group** *group-name*. Under the xconnect group, both the autodiscovery mechanism and the signaling protocol are defined. It is important to remember that the signaling protocol can be either LDP or BGP. The RD can be set to auto mode but can also be manually assigned. The other important configuration under the xconnect group required is the **vpn-id** and the **ce-id**.

For both VPWS and VPLS, there is a new L2VPN address-family configuration introduced that is used for BGP signaling and autodiscovery purposes on IOS XR, named **address-family l2vpn vpls-vpws**. Example 11-4 displays the configuration for setting up the VPWS circuit on IOS XR with BGP signaling and autodiscovery.

Example 11-4   *BGP Signaling and Autodiscovery on IOS XR for VPWS*

```
! Configuring L2VPN Section
RP/0/1/CPU0:PE2(config)# l2vpn
RP/0/1/CPU0:PE2(config-l2vpn)# xconnect group VPWS
RP/0/1/CPU0:PE2(config-l2vpn-xc)# mp2mp EOMPLS
RP/0/1/CPU0:PE2(config-l2vpn-xc-mp2mp)# vpn-id 100
RP/0/1/CPU0:PE2(config-l2vpn-xc-mp2mp)# l2-encapsulation vlan
RP/0/1/CPU0:PE2(config-l2vpn-xc-mp2mp)# autodiscovery bgp
RP/0/1/CPU0:PE2(config-l2vpn-xc-mp2mp-ad)# rd auto
RP/0/1/CPU0:PE2(config-l2vpn-xc-mp2mp-ad)# route-target 192.168.2.2:100
RP/0/1/CPU0:PE2(config-l2vpn-xc-mp2mp-ad)# signaling-protocol bgp
RP/0/1/CPU0:PE2(config-l2vpn-xc-mp2mp-ad-sig)# ce-id 100
RP/0/1/CPU0:PE2(config-l2vpn-xc-mp2mp-ad-sig-ce)# int g0/3/0/2.100 remote-ce-id 1
RP/0/1/CPU0:PE2(config-l2vpn-xc-mp2mp-ad-sig-ce)# commit
! Configuring BGP Section
RP/0/0/CPU0:PE2(config)# router bgp 100
RP/0/0/CPU0:PE2(config-bgp)# address-family l2vpn vpls-vpws
RP/0/0/CPU0:PE2(config-bgp-af)# exit
RP/0/0/CPU0:PE2(config-bgp)# neighbor 192.168.3.3
RP/0/0/CPU0:PE2(config-bgp-nbr)# remote-as 100
RP/0/0/CPU0:PE2(config-bgp-nbr)# update-source loopback0
RP/0/0/CPU0:PE2(config-bgp-nbr)# address-family l2vpn vpls-vpws
RP/0/0/CPU0:PE2(config-bgp-nbr-af)# commit
```

Note   Verification and troubleshooting steps for VPWS and VPLS are same and are covered later in the chapter under the VPLS section.

Virtual Private LAN Service

VPWS is used for connecting two remote locations of the same or different attachment circuit type. For example, EoMPLS provides point-to-point Ethernet services by connecting two LAN environments. But when an organization's Layer 2 domains are expanded across multiple sites and geographical boundaries, creating multiple point-to-point VPWS connections can increase complexity for the network and requires more resources on the PE routers.

A multipoint service is required to maintain the communication between the distributed LAN infrastructure. VPLS provides multipoint services for LAN. The primary motivation behind VPLS is to provide connectivity between geographically dispersed sites across metropolitan-area networks (MAN) and wide-area networks (WAN) to a shared LAN segment, which is virtualized over a service provider core versus point-to-point circuits in VPWS. Figure 11-9 displays a VPLS deployment. Notice that in this topology there are three PE routers, each of which is connected to the different sites of the same customer. The service provider core network runs IP and MPLS services providing label switching paths between PE routers.

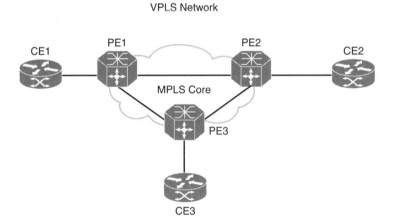

Figure 11-9 *Virtual Private LAN Services*

In VPLS, the sites belong to the same broadcast domain, are connected across a service provider MPLS network, and can transmit unicast, broadcast, and multicast traffic to the desired customer locations. Because of this capability, VPLS circuits require media access control (MAC) address learning/aging on a per pseudowire basis. Also, it requires packet replication for multicast/broadcast traffic and for flooding of unknown unicast frames. This is done at the platform (hardware) level on most of the Cisco platforms where hardware forwarding is supported to allow greater scalability (more customer circuits) on the PE router.

The customer packet forwarding decision is made by looking at the Layer 2 Virtual Forwarding Instance (VFI) of a particular VPLS domain. An Ethernet or Layer 2 frame received from the customer network can be forwarded to one or more local interfaces and/or emulated VCs in the VPLS domain. On receiving the frame, the source MAC address is learned just like in traditional switching. Based on the populated MAC entries, the PE router switches those frames to the appropriate LSP to be transmitted to remote PE routers. If the destination MAC address is not found in the MAC table, the frame is then replicated to all the remote PE routers by the originating PE router.

Note   To prevent forwarding loops in a full-mesh VPLS topology, enable Layer 2 split-horizon. It is a loop prevention mechanism that prevents packets received on one PW from being forwarded to another PW.

Configuration

Configuring VPLS is similar to configuring VPWS with a difference that in VPLS, the circuits are point-to-multipoint. Thus each router should be configured with the neighboring PE router in that VPLS domain. VPLS can be set up using various methods:

- Manual configuration with LDP signaling
- BGP Autodiscovery with LDP signaling
- BGP Autodiscovery with BGP signaling

The following steps can be used to configure VPLS using the first method.

Step 1.   On the PE router, configure Layer 2 interfaces that connect to the CE. These interfaces can be configured either as access ports, trunk ports, Q-in-Q, or using EVCs.

Step 2.   Based on platform requirements, configure VLANs or bridge domains on the PE router.

Step 3.   Configure MPLS in Service Provider Core. Enable MPLS LDP on core interfaces on both the PE and the P routers. This allows you to build an LSP between the PE routers.

Step 4.   Configure VFI. Configure L2VPN VFI context for VPLS domains. Under the VFI contexts, configure the vpn-id and other PE neighbor information within the same VPLS domain.

Step 5.   Associate AC with the VFI.

Step 6.   Enable AC. After the xconnect is configured, enable the AC by bringing up the customer facing interfaces.

For illustrating VPLS configuration, examine the same topology as shown in Figure 11-5. PE routers PE1, PE2, and PE3 are all part of same VPLS domain connecting three sites for the same customer. Example 11-5 illustrates the configuration for VPLS using manual configuration and LDP signaling. Notice that on all three PE routers, the other two PE routers are configured as the peer routers. This is required in case of a manual configuration method.

Example 11-5 *VPLS Configuration*

```
Configuration PE1 - Cisco IOS
l2 vfi VPLS-VFI manual
 vpn id 100
 bridge-domain 100
 neighbor 192.168.3.3 encapsulation mpls
 neighbor 192.168.2.2 encapsulation mpls
 !
interface GigabitEthernet1/1/2
 no ip address
 negotiation auto
 service instance 100 ethernet
  encapsulation dot1q 100
  rewrite ingress tag pop 1 symmetric
  bridge-domain 100
```

```
Configuration PE2 - IOS XR
l2vpn
 bridge group BD-GRP
  bridge-domain 100
    interface GigabitEthernet0/3/0/2.100
    !
    vfi VPLS-VFI
     neighbor 192.168.1.1 pw-id 100
     !
     neighbor 192.168.3.3 pw-id 100
 !
interface GigabitEthernet0/3/0/2.100 l2transport
 dot1q vlan 100
```

```
Configuration PE3 - NX-OS
l2vpn vfi context VPLS-VFI
  vpn id 100
  member pseudowire1
  member pseudowire2
bridge-domain 100
  member vfi VPLS-VFI
  member Ethernet3/3 service instance 100
 !
```

```
interface pseudowire1
  neighbor 192.168.1.1 100
  encapsulation mpls
!
interface pseudowire2
  neighbor 192.168.2.2 100
  encapsulation mpls
!
interface Ethernet3/3
  no shutdown
  service instance 100 ethernet
    encapsulation dot1q 100
    no shutdown
```

Verification

The very first step in verification and troubleshooting process for VPLS is to verify three primary things:

- PE to PE LSP is complete.

- AC is up.

- VFI status is up.

The PE to PE LSP is verified using the command **ping mpls ipv4** *ip-address subnet-mask*. Ensure that Layer 2 interfaces facing the customer equipment or CE router are up. The VFI status is verified using the command **show l2vpn vfi name** *vfi-name* on Cisco IOS and NX-OS and command **show l2vpn bridge-domain summary** on IOS XR. Example 11-6 displays the output of the command **show l2vpn vfi name** and **show l2vpn bridge-domain summary**. The **show l2vpn vfi name** *vfi-name* command displays the VFI status, Signaling protocol, VPN ID, and the PW status.

Example 11-6 *Verifying VFI Status*

```
IOS
PE1# show l2vpn vfi name VPLS-VFI
Legend: RT=Route-target, S=Split-horizon, Y=Yes, N=No

VFI name: VPLS-VFI, state: up, type: multipoint, signaling: LDP
  VPN ID: 100
  Bridge-Domain 100 attachment circuits:
  Pseudo-port interface: pseudowire100001
  Interface         Peer Address    VC ID     S
  pseudowire100003  192.168.2.2     100       Y
  pseudowire100002  192.168.3.3     100       Y
```

```
RP/0/1/CPU0:PE2# show l2vpn bridge-domain summary
Number of groups: 1, bridge-domains: 1, Up: 1, Shutdown: 0, Partially-
programmed: 0
Default: 1, pbb-edge: 0, pbb-core: 0
Number of ACs: 1 Up: 1, Down: 0, Partially-programmed: 0
Number of PWs: 2 Up: 2, Down: 0, Standby: 0, Partially-programmed: 0
```

```
NX-OS
PE3# show l2vpn vfi name VPLS-VFI
Legend: RT=Route-target, S=Split-horizon, Y=Yes, N=No

VFI name: VPLS-VFI, state: up, type: multipoint, signaling: LDP
  VPN ID: 100
  Bridge-Domain 100 attachment circuits:
  Pseudo-port interface: vfi100001
  Interface        Peer Address    VC ID       S
  pseudowire2      192.168.2.2     100         Y
  pseudowire1      192.168.1.1     100         Y
```

On IOS devices, the command **show xconnect all** also displays the status of the PWs and the VFI. Example 11-7 displays the output of the command show xconnect all on PE1.

Example 11-7 show xconnect all *Command Output*

```
PE1# show xconnect all
Legend:      XC ST=Xconnect State  S1=Segment1 State  S2=Segment2 State
  UP=Up        DN=Down             AD=Admin Down      IA=Inactive
  SB=Standby HS=Hot Standby        RV=Recovering      NH=No Hardware


XC ST   Segment 1                   S1 Segment 2                      S2
------+----------------------------+--+-------------------------------+--
UP pri  vfi VPLS-VFI                UP mpls 192.168.2.2:100           UP
UP pri  vfi VPLSA                   UP mpls 192.168.3.3:100           UP
UP pri  bd 100                      UP  vfi VPLSA                     UP
```

Similar to VPWS, for VPLS, multiple PWs are formed with multiple PEs with same VPN ID. Thus, the VPLS connection with each PE is verified using the command **show mpls l2transport vc** [**destination** *ip-address*] **vcid** *vc-id* [**detail**] on Cisco IOS, the command **show l2vpn bridge-domain** [**neighbor** *ip-address*] [**pw-id** *vc-id*] [**detail**] on IOS XR, and the command **show l2vpn atom vc** [**destination** *ip-address*] [**vcid** *vc-id*] [**detail**] on NX-OS. Example 11-8 displays the output of the commands to verify the VPLS PWs.

Example 11-8   *Verfying VPLS PWs*

```
IOS
PE1# show mpls l2transport vc destination 192.168.2.2 vcid 100 detail
Local interface: VFI VPLS-VFI vfi up
  Interworking type is Ethernet
  Destination address: 192.168.2.2, VC ID: 100, VC status: up
    Output interface: Gi1/1/0, imposed label stack {23 16000}
    Preferred path: not configured
    Default path: active
    Next hop: 12.12.12.2
  Create time: 01:23:36, last status change time: 01:12:09
    Last label FSM state change time: 01:12:11
    Last peer autosense occurred at: 01:12:11
  Signaling protocol: LDP, peer 192.168.2.2:0 up
    Targeted Hello: 192.168.1.1(LDP Id) -> 192.168.2.2, LDP is UP
    Graceful restart: not configured and not enabled
    Non stop routing: not configured and not enabled
    Status TLV support (local/remote)    : enabled/supported
      LDP route watch                    : enabled
      Label/status state machine         : established, LruRru
      Last local dataplane   status rcvd: No fault
      Last BFD dataplane     status rcvd: Not sent
      Last BFD peer monitor  status rcvd: No fault
      Last local AC  circuit status rcvd: No fault
      Last local AC  circuit status sent: No fault
      Last local PW i/f circ status rcvd: No fault
      Last local LDP TLV     status sent: No fault
      Last remote LDP TLV    status rcvd: No fault
      Last remote LDP ADJ    status rcvd: No fault
    MPLS VC labels: local 35, remote 16000
    Group ID: local 0, remote 0
    MTU: local 1500, remote 1500
    Remote interface description: VPLS-VFI
  Sequencing: receive disabled, send disabled
  Control Word: Off (configured: autosense)
  SSO Descriptor: 192.168.2.2/100, local label: 35
  Dataplane:
    SSM segment/switch IDs: 16391/8194 (used), PWID: 2
  VC statistics:
    transit packet totals: receive 7, send 213
    transit byte totals:   receive 664, send 17736
    transit packet drops:  receive 4, seq error 0, send 0

IOS XR
RP/0/1/CPU0:PE2# show l2vpn bridge-domain neighbor 192.168.1.1 pw-id 100 detail
```

```
Legend: pp = Partially Programmed.
Bridge group: BD-GRP, bridge-domain: 100, id: 0, state: up, ShgId: 0, MSTi: 0
! Output omitted for brevity
  Create time: 26/03/2016 21:51:28 (01:38:02 ago)
  No status change since creation
  ACs: 1 (1 up), VFIs: 1, PWs: 1 (1 up), PBBs: 0 (0 up)
  List of Access PWs:
  List of VFIs:
    VFI VPLS-VFI (up)
      PW: neighbor 192.168.1.1, PW ID 100, state is up ( established )
        PW class not set, XC ID 0xff000001
        Encapsulation MPLS, protocol LDP
        Source address 192.168.2.2
        PW type Ethernet, control word disabled, interworking none
        PW backup disable delay 0 sec
        Sequencing not set

        PW Status TLV in use
          MPLS          Local                          Remote
          ------------  -----------------------------  -----------------------
          Label         16000                          35
          Group ID      0x0                            0x0
          Interface     VPLS-VFI                       unknown
          MTU           1500                           1500
          Control word  disabled                       disabled
          PW type       Ethernet                       Ethernet
          VCCV CV type  0x2                            0x2
                        (LSP ping verification)        (LSP ping verification)
          VCCV CC type  0x6                            0x6
                        (router alert label)           (router alert label)
                        (TTL expiry)                   (TTL expiry)
          ------------  -----------------------------  -----------------------
        Incoming Status (PW Status TLV):
          Status code: 0x0 (Up) in Notification message
        MIB cpwVcIndex: 4278190081
        Create time: 26/03/2016 21:51:28 (01:38:02 ago)
        Last time status changed: 26/03/2016 21:57:17 (01:32:13 ago)
        MAC withdraw message: send 0 receive 0
        Static MAC addresses:
        Statistics:
          packets: received 328, sent 850
          bytes: received 21262, sent 73198
    DHCPv4 snooping: disabled
    IGMP Snooping profile: none
```

```
      VFI Statistics:
         drops: illegal VLAN 0, illegal length 0
```

```
NX-OS
PE3# show l2vpn atom vc destination 192.168.1.1 vcid 100 detail
pseudowire1 is up, VC status is up PW type: Ethernet
  Create time: 01:46:28, last status change time: 01:41:40
    Last label FSM state change time: 01:42:41
  Destination address: 192.168.1.1 VC ID: 100
    Output interface: Ethernet3/2, imposed label stack {16 16}
    Preferred path: not configured
    Default path: active
    Next hop: 10.1.34.4
  Member of vfi service VPLS-VFI
    Bridge-Domain id: 100
  Signaling protocol: LDP, peer 192.168.1.1:0 up
    Targeted Hello: 192.168.3.3(LDP Id) -> 192.168.1.1, LDP is UP
    Graceful restart: configured and not enabled
    Non stop routing: not configured and not enabled
    PWid FEC (128), VC ID: 100
    Status TLV support (local/remote)        : enabled/supported
      LDP route watch                        : enabled
      Label/status state machine             : established, LruRru
      Local dataplane status received        : No fault
      BFD dataplane status received          : Not sent
      BFD peer monitor status received       : No fault
      Status received from access circuit    : No fault
      Status sent to access circuit          : No fault
      Status received from pseudowire i/f    : No fault
      Status sent to network peer            : No fault
      Status received from network peer      : No fault
      Adjacency status of remote peer        : No fault
  Sequencing: receive disabled, send disabled
  Bindings
    Parameter    Local                           Remote
    -----------  ------------------------------  -----------------------------
    Label        16                              16
    Group ID     0                               0
    Interface
    MTU          1500                            1500
    Control word on (configured: autosense)     on
    PW type      Ethernet                        Ethernet
    VCCV CV type 0x02                            0x02
                 LSPV [2]                        LSPV [2]
```

```
  VCCV CC type 0x06                          0x06
                RA [2], TTL [3]              RA [2], TTL [3]
  Status TLV    enabled                     supported
Rx Counters
  322 input transit packets, 20608 bytes
  0 drops, 0 seq err
Tx Counters
  304 output transit packets, 28576 bytes
  0 drops
```

VPLS Autodiscovery Using BGP

Conventional VPLS implementation requires manual configuration of each neighbor remote PE router in the VPLS domain. When a new PE is added or removed from the VPLS domain, manual configuration changes are required on each PE router, which is part of the same VPLS domain. In a large service provider network, where there could be hundreds or thousands of customers availing VPLS services, manual configuration adds to a lot of operational cost and also increases the chance of misconfigurations.

Defined in RFC 4761, VPLS autodiscovery provides a mechanism to automatically discover neighbors in a VPLS domain, eliminating the need to manually provision a VPLS neighbor. This helps in automatically updating the VPLS domain whenever a neighbor is added or removed. To perform autodiscovery of VPLS neighbors in a domain, BGP sends the NLRI as an update, as shown in Figure 11-10.

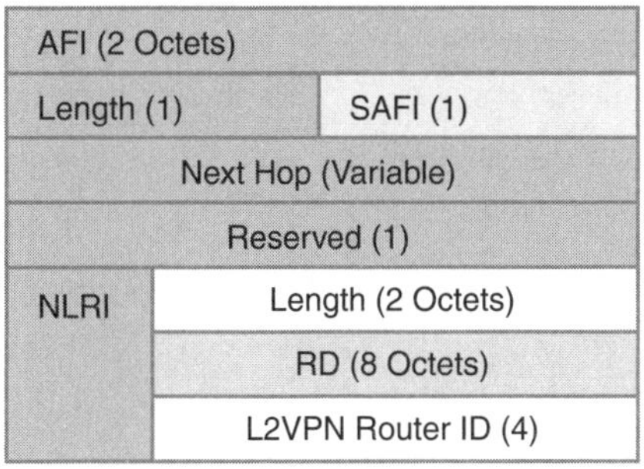

AFI (2 Octets)		
Length (1)	SAFI (1)	
Next Hop (Variable)		
Reserved (1)		
NLRI	Length (2 Octets)	
	RD (8 Octets)	
	L2VPN Router ID (4)	

Figure 11-10 *VPLS Autodiscovery NLRI*

After a PE is configured as part of a particular VPLS domain, the information needed to set up connection with remote PEs in the same VPLS domain is distributed through the discovery process. After the discovery process is complete, each PE forms a full mesh with other neighbors in the VPLS domain. The signaling for VPLS, by default, is taken care of by LDP. RFC 4762 defines the LDP-based signaling mechanism for VPLS.

Note   VPLS autodiscovery can also be achieved using RADIUS. In this method, each PE device is connected to one or more RADIUS servers. The RADIUS server keeps track of all PE requests per VPN. The RADIUS server then sends the list of PEs to the PE requesting authentication. The PE then sets the pseudowires using the information.

One major difference between VPLS autodiscovery and manual configuration is that in this method, FEC 129 is used. FEC 129 is also known as *Generalized FEC*. FEC 128 is used when using VPLS with manual configuration. Under FEC 128, both endpoints use a 32-bit identifier (PW ID) and should be same in order for PW to establish. But with FEC 129, each endpoint has its own distinct identifier. In other words, the generalized FEC 129 signaling may not be compatible with those endpoint identifiers provisioned with 32-bit PW ID values. Unlike FEC 128, the values of the PW ID with FEC 129 do not have to match on both the local and remote nodes. Figure 11-11 displays the FEC 129 element structure.

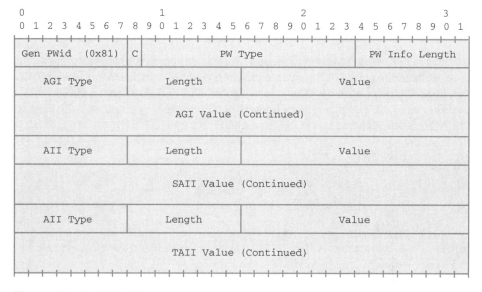

Figure 11-11   *FEC 129*

Under the FEC 129 structure, the three main elements are the following:

- **Attachment Group Identifier (AGI):** The identifier of the VPLS domain—VPLS-ID.

- **Source Attachment Individual Identifier (SAII):** The identifier of the local endpoint. The L2VPN Router ID of the local PE.

- **Target Attachment Individual Identifier (TAII):** The identifier of the remote endpoint. The L2VPN Router ID of the remote PE.

Other important feature that is essential for the BGP autodiscovery mechanism is *Flexible Target Address*. Targeted LDP session address is based on the next-hop received from BGP. This may be different from the LDP router-id on the remote end. Flexible Target Address functionality allows the LDP targeted hello accept-list to be modified by peer when the BGP NLRI is received.

To configure BGP VPLS autodiscovery, the BGP L2VPN address-family is used. Example 11-9 illustrates the configuration of BGP VPLS autodiscovery with LDP signaling. For enabling BGP autodiscovery, the **autodiscovery bgp** command is used in all the platforms, which is defined under the l2vpn context. In Example 11-9, on both IOS and IOS XR, additional configuration is also done, such as vpls-id, rd, route-target. These configurations are optional and are not required to be configured when establishing VPLS PWs using BGP autodiscovery and LDP signaling mechanism.

Example 11-9 *VPLS BGP Autodiscovery Configuration*

```
PE1 Configuration - Cisco IOS
l2vpn
 router-id 192.168.1.1
l2vpn vfi context VPLS-VFI
 vpn id 100
 autodiscovery bgp signaling ldp
  vpls-id 100:100
  rd 100:100
  route-target export 100:100
  route-target import 100:100
 !
router bgp 100
bgp router-id 192.168.1.1
neighbor 192.168.2.2 remote-as 100
 neighbor 192.168.2.2 update-source Loopback0
 neighbor 192.168.3.3 remote-as 100
 neighbor 192.168.3.3 update-source Loopback0
address-family l2vpn vpls
  neighbor 192.168.2.2 activate
  neighbor 192.168.2.2 send-community extended
  neighbor 192.168.2.2 prefix-length-size 2
  neighbor 192.168.3.3 activate
  neighbor 192.168.3.3 send-community extended
  neighbor 192.168.3.3 prefix-length-size 2

PE2 Configuration - IOS XR
l2vpn
 router-id 192.168.2.2
 bridge group BD-GRP
```

```
   bridge-domain 100
     interface GigabitEthernet0/3/0/2.100
     !
     vfi VPLS-VFI
      vpn-id 100
      autodiscovery bgp
       rd auto
       route-target 100:100
       signaling-protocol ldp
 !
router bgp 100
 bgp router-id 192.168.2.2
 address-family l2vpn vpls-vpws
 !
neighbor 192.168.1.1
  remote-as 100
  update-source Loopback0
  address-family l2vpn vpls-vpws
   Signalling bgp disable
   !
  !
 neighbor 192.168.3.3
  remote-as 100
  update-source Loopback0
  address-family l2vpn vpls-vpws
   Signalling bgp disable
```

```
PE3 Configuration - NX-OS
feature mpls l2vpn
l2vpn
  router-id 192.168.3.3
!
l2vpn vfi context VPLS-VFI
  vpn id 100
  autodiscovery bgp signaling ldp
!
bridge-domain 100
  member vfi VPLS-VFI
!
router bgp 100
  router-id 192.168.3.3
  address-family l2vpn vpls
  neighbor 192.168.1.1
    remote-as 100
```

```
   update-source loopback0
   address-family l2vpn vpls
     send-community both
 neighbor 192.168.2.2
   remote-as 100
   update-source loopback0
   address-family l2vpn vpls
     send-community both
```

Note   IOS XR supports configuration to support for automatic assignment of RD using the command **rd auto**. This command option is not available in other platforms, but RD is automatically assigned by default on all the other platforms.

One important thing to notice in Example 11-9 is that under the Cisco IOS configuration on router PE1, there is an additional neighbor configuration command **neighbor** *neighbor-ip* **prefix-length-size** [1-2]. This command is required for interoperability between Cisco IOS and IOS XR or Cisco IOS and NX-OS. The reason is that the IOS software encodes the NLRI length in the first byte in bits format in the BGP Update message. However, the Cisco IOS XR Software interprets the NLRI length in 2 bytes. Therefore, when the BGP neighbor with VPLS address-family is configured between the IOS and the IOS XR or NX-OS, NLRI mismatch can happen, leading to flapping between neighbors. To avoid this conflict, IOS supports the **prefix-length-size 2** command that needs to be enabled for IOS to work with IOS XR. Example 11-10 displays the output of the BGP notification message received when the IOS router tries forming a neighbor relationship with the IOS XR or NX-OS device under l2vpn vpls address-family. Notice that the Cisco IOS router (PE1) receives a notification from the peer 192.168.2.2 that it received an illegal network, which is of 1 byte.

Example 11-10   *Cisco IOS Interoperability Error Message*

```
09:41:01.872: %BGP-5-ADJCHANGE: neighbor 192.168.2.2 Up
09:41:01.880: %BGP-3-NOTIFICATION: received from neighbor 192.168.2.2 3/10
 (illegal network) 1 bytes 60
09:41:01.880: %BGP-5-NBR_RESET: Neighbor 192.168.2.2 reset
 (BGP Notification received)
09:41:01.880: %BGP-5-ADJCHANGE: neighbor 192.168.2.2 Down
BGP Notification received
09:41:01.880: %BGP_SESSION-5-ADJCHANGE: neighbor 192.168.2.2 L2VPN Vpls
 topology base removed from session  BGP Notification received
```

The BGP neighbors established under the L2VPN VPLS address-family is viewed using the command **show bgp l2vpn vpls summary**. Example 11-11 displays the established BGP neighbors and the prefixes received from those neighbors.

Example 11-11 *Autodiscovered VPLS Neighbors and Prefixes*

```
IOS
PE1# show bgp l2vpn vpls all summary
! Output omitted for brevity
Neighbor        V     AS MsgRcvd MsgSent   TblVer  InQ OutQ Up/Down  State/PfxRcd
192.168.2.2     4    100      70      78       17    0    0 01:06:57            1
192.168.3.3     4    100     101     109       17    0    0 01:33:30            1


PE1# show bgp l2vpn vpls all
! Output omitted for brevity


     Network              Next Hop        Metric LocPrf Weight Path
Route Distinguisher: 100:100
  *>   100:100:192.168.1.1/96
                         0.0.0.0                         32768 ?
  *>i 100:100:192.168.3.3/96
                         192.168.3.3             100        0 i
Route Distinguisher: 192.168.2.2:32768
  *>i 192.168.2.2:32768:192.168.2.2/96
                         192.168.2.2             100        0 i
```

```
IOS XR
RP/0/1/CPU0:PE2# show bgp l2vpn vpls summary
! Output omitted for brevity



Neighbor        Spk     AS MsgRcvd MsgSent   TblVer  InQ OutQ  Up/Down  St/PfxRcd
192.168.1.1       0    100     753     626       14    0    0 01:14:19          1
192.168.3.3       0    100     362     341       14    0    0 01:40:52          1


RP/0/1/CPU0:PE2# show bgp l2vpn vpls
! Output omitted for brevity

Network              Next Hop        Rcvd Label        Local Label
Route Distinguisher: 100:100
*>i192.168.1.1/32      192.168.1.1     nolabel           nolabel
*>i192.168.3.3/32      192.168.3.3     nolabel           nolabel
Route Distinguisher: 192.168.2.2:32768 (default for vrf BD-GRP:100)
*>i192.168.1.1/32      192.168.1.1     nolabel           nolabel
*> 192.168.2.2/32      0.0.0.0         nolabel           nolabel
```

```
*>i192.168.3.3/32       192.168.3.3     nolabel         nolabel

Processed 5 prefixes, 5 paths
```

```
NX-OS
PE3# show bgp l2vpn vpls summary
! Output omitted for brevity

Neighbor        V    AS MsgRcvd MsgSent   TblVer  InQ OutQ Up/Down  State/PfxRcd
192.168.1.1     4   100     122     112       14    0    0 01:45:06 1
192.168.2.2     4   100     109     112       14    0    0 01:45:07 1


PE3# show bgp l2vpn vpls
! Output omitted for brevity

   Network            Next Hop          Metric    LocPrf    Weight Path
Route Distinguisher: 100:100 BGP-AD     (VFI VPLS-VFI)
*>i192.168.1.1/32       192.168.1.1          0        100         0 ?
*>i192.168.2.2/32       192.168.2.2                   100         0 i
*>l192.168.3.3/32       0.0.0.0                       100     32768 i


Route Distinguisher: 192.168.2.2:32768 BGP-AD
*>i192.168.2.2/32       192.168.2.2                   100         0 i
```

After the BGP peering is established under the L2VPN VPLS address-family, the VPLS peers are discovered and verified on each PE router under the respective VFI using the command **show l2vpn vfi name** *vfi-name* on Cisco IOS and NX-OS and the command **show l2vpn discovery bridge-domain** on IOS XR. Example 11-12 examines the output of these commands. Notice the output in Example 11-12, that on IOS and NX-OS, dynamic PW interfaces are created for each VPLS peer in that domain. This is done automatically by the L2VPN process.

Example 11-12 *Autodiscovered VPLS Peers*

```
IOS
PE1# show l2vpn vfi name VPLS-VFI
Legend: RT=Route-target, S=Split-horizon, Y=Yes, N=No


VFI name: VPLS-VFI, state: up, type: multipoint, signaling: LDP
  VPN ID: 100, VPLS-ID: 100:100
  RD: 100:100, RT: 100:100, 100:100
  Bridge-Domain 100 attachment circuits:
  Pseudo-port interface: pseudowire100007
  Interface        Peer Address    VC ID        Discovered Router ID    S
```

```
pseudowire100011    192.168.2.2       100         192.168.2.2            Y
pseudowire100009    192.168.3.3       100         192.168.3.3            Y
```

```
IOS XR
RP/0/1/CPU0:PE2# show l2vpn discovery bridge-domain
Service Type: VPLS,  Connected
  List of VPNs (1 VPNs):
  Bridge group: BD-GRP, bridge-domain: 100, id: 0, signaling protocol: LDP
    VPLS-ID: (auto) 100:100
    Local L2 router id: 192.168.2.2
    List of Remote NLRI (2 NLRIs):
    Local Addr       Remote Addr       Remote L2 RID    Time Created
    --------------   --------------    ---------------  -------------------
    192.168.2.2      192.168.1.1       192.168.1.1      03/30/2016 08:42:58
    192.168.2.2      192.168.3.3       192.168.3.3      03/30/2016 08:22:51
```

```
NX-OS
PE3# show l2vpn vfi name VPLS-VFI
Legend: RT=Route-target, S=Split-horizon, Y=Yes, N=No
VFI name: VPLS-VFI, state: up, type: multipoint, signaling: LDP
  VPN ID: 100, VPLS-ID: 100:100
  RD: 100:100, RT: 100:100
  Bridge-Domain 100 attachment circuits:
  Pseudo-port interface: vfi100003
  Interface        Peer Address      VC ID       Discovered Router ID    S
  pseudowire100016 192.168.2.2       100         192.168.2.2             Y
  pseudowire100015 192.168.1.1       100         192.168.1.1             Y
```

After the VPLS peers are discovered in the VPLS domain, the allocated VC labels and the PW status is viewed using the command **show l2vpn service vfi name** *vfi-name* [detail] on both Cisco IOS and NX-OS and the commands **show l2vpn bridge-domain autodis-covery bgp** [detail] and **show l2vpn bridge-domain bd-name** *name* [detail] on IOS XR. Example 11-13 displays the output of the command **show l2vpn service vfi name** and also the command **show l2vpn bridge-domain autodiscovery bgp**. Notice that the command **show l2vpn service vfi name** *vfi-name* not only displays the label information but also the status of the PW interface and the xconnect status.

Example 11-13   *VC Information*

```
IOS
PE1# show l2vpn service vfi name VPLS-VFI detail
Legend: St=State      XC St=State in the L2VPN Service        Prio=Priority
        UP=Up         DN=Down           AD=Admin Down         IA=Inactive
        SB=Standby    HS=Hot Standby    RV=Recovering         NH=No Hardware
        m=manually selected
```

```
   Interface          Group      Encapsulation                    Prio  St  XC St
   ---------          -----      -------------                    ----  --  -----
VPLS name: VPLS-VFI, State: UP
   pw100004                      VPLS-VFI(VFI)                      0    UP  UP
   pw100006           core_pw    192.168.2.2:100(MPLS)             0    UP  UP
                                 Local VC label 29
                                 Remote VC label 16013

   pw100005           core_pw    192.168.3.3:100(MPLS)             0    UP  UP
                                 Local VC label 28
                                 Remote VC label 22
```

```
IOS XR
RP/0/1/CPU0:PE2# show l2vpn bridge-domain autodiscovery bgp detail
Legend: pp = Partially Programmed.
Bridge group: BD-GRP, bridge-domain: 100, id: 0, state: up, ShgId: 0, MSTi: 0
  Coupled state: disabled
  MAC learning: enabled
  MAC withdraw: enabled
    MAC withdraw for Access PW: enabled
    MAC withdraw sent on bridge port down: disabled
  Flooding:
    Broadcast & Multicast: enabled
    Unknown unicast: enabled
  MAC aging time: 300 s, Type: inactivity
  MAC limit: 4000, Action: none, Notification: syslog
  MAC limit reached: no
  MAC port down flush: enabled
  MAC Secure: disabled, Logging: disabled
  Split Horizon Group: none
  Dynamic ARP Inspection: disabled, Logging: disabled
  IP Source Guard: disabled, Logging: disabled
  DHCPv4 snooping: disabled
  IGMP Snooping profile: none
  Bridge MTU: 1500
  MIB cvplsConfigIndex: 1
  Filter MAC addresses:
  Create time: 30/03/2016 17:27:47 (11:40:36 ago)
  No status change since creation
  ACs: 1 (1 up), VFIs: 1, PWs: 2 (2 up), PBBs: 0 (0 up)
  List of VFIs:
    VFI VPLS-VFI (up)
      VPN-ID: 100, Auto Discovery: BGP, state is Provisioned (Service Connected)
      Route Distinguisher:  (auto) 192.168.2.2:32768
```

```
Import Route Targets:
  100:100
Export Route Targets:
  100:100
Signaling protocol: LDP
AS Number: 100
VPLS-ID: (auto) 100:100
L2VPN Router ID: 192.168.2.2
PW: neighbor 192.168.1.1, PW ID 100:100, state is up ( established )
  PW class not set, XC ID 0xff000001
  Encapsulation MPLS, Auto-discovered (BGP), protocol LDP
  Source address 192.168.2.2
  PW type Ethernet, control word disabled, interworking none
  PW backup disable delay 0 sec
  Sequencing not set

  PW Status TLV in use
    MPLS         Local                          Remote
    ------------ ------------------------------ -------------------------
    Label        16013                          29
    BGP Peer ID  192.168.2.2                    192.168.1.1
    LDP ID       192.168.2.2                    192.168.1.1
    AII          192.168.2.2                    192.168.1.1
    AGI          100:100                        100:100
    Group ID     0x0                            0x0
    Interface    VPLS-VFI                       unknown
    MTU          1500                           1500
    Control word disabled                       disabled
    PW type      Ethernet                       Ethernet
    VCCV CV type 0x2                            0x2
                 (LSP ping verification)        (LSP ping verification)
    VCCV CC type 0x6                            0x6
                 (router alert label)           (router alert label)
                 (TTL expiry)                   (TTL expiry)
    ------------ ------------------------------ -------------------------
  Incoming Status (PW Status TLV):
    Status code: 0x0 (Up) in Notification message
  MIB cpwVcIndex: 4278190081
  Create time: 30/03/2016 17:34:10 (11:34:13 ago)
  Last time status changed: 30/03/2016 23:34:22 (05:34:01 ago)
  MAC withdraw message: send 0 receive 0
  Static MAC addresses:
  Statistics:
```

```
          packets: received 0, sent 9996
            bytes: received 0, sent 859656
      DHCPv4 snooping: disabled
      IGMP Snooping profile: none
```

```
NX-OS
! Output omitted for brevity
PE3# show l2vpn service vfi name VPLS-VFI detail

Legend: St=State     XC St=State in the L2VPN Service     Prio=Priority
        UP=Up        DN=Down            AD=Admin Down      IA=Inactive
        SB=Standby   HS=Hot Standby     RV=Recovering      NH=No Hardware
        m=manually selected


  Interface        Group       Encapsulation                 Prio  St  XC St
  ---------        -----       -------------                 ----  --  -----
VPLS name: VPLS-VFI, State: UP
  vfi100001                    VPLS-VFI(VFI)                   0    UP  UP
  pw100002         core_pw     192.168.2.2:100(MPLS)           0    UP  UP
                               Local VC label 24
                               Remote VC label 16014
                               port-profile:
  pw100001         core_pw     192.168.1.1:100(MPLS)           0    UP  UP
                               Local VC label 22
                               Remote VC label 28
                               port-profile:
```

The following steps should be used when troubleshooting BGP VPLS autodiscovery issues:

Step 1. **BGP autodiscovery.** Ensure that BGP autodiscovery is enabled on all the PEs in the VPLS domain.

Step 2. **VPN ID.** Verify that the VPN ID (also referred to as VPLS-ID) is matching on both the local and remote PE routers. BGP protocol exchanges the VPLS-ID information as an extended community with other PEs. If VPLS-ID is not matching on one of the PEs, then VPLS autodiscovery won't happen for that PE.

Step 3. **Route target.** The BGP advertises and imports the associated VPLS instance information using BGP route-target ext community. If the PE is not configured with the correct import or export communities, then BGP autodiscovery may not work.

Step 4. **IOS and other OSs interoperability.** Ensure that the prefix-length-size is set to 2 when the remote PE router is a non-IOS router.

VPLS BGP Signaling

There are two primary tasks of the BGP control plane for VPLS:

- Autodiscovery
- Signaling

Signaling by default is handled by LDP, when using either manual configuration method or the BGP VPLS autodiscovery method. But BGP can also be used for signaling purposes, which involves setting up and tearing down of PWs. The BGP signaling mechanism for VPLS is defined in RFC 4761. When using BGP for signaling, BGP sends the NLRI as an update to the remote peer for updating the label information, as shown in Figure 11-12.

Length (2 Octets)
Route Target (8 Octets)
VE ID (2 Octets)
VE Block Offset (VBO) (2)
VE Block Size (VBS) (2)
VE Label Base (LB) (2)

Figure 11-12 *BGP NLRI for Updating Label Information*

- **VE ID:** Uniquely identify the VPLS Edge device (VE). This is typically configured by the network administrator.

- **Label Block (LB):** A label block is a set of de-multiplexor labels used to reach a given VE ID. The label block for a given VE ID is given next. There is one-to-one correspondence between the remote system and local system; that is, (VBO+n) corresponds to (LB + n).

  Label block for local system: LB = LB + VBS − 1

  Label block for remote system: VBO = VBO + VBS − 1

Along with this information, L2VPN information is carried in the L2VPN Extended Community attribute, as shown in Figure 11-13. Included in the extended community are control word and sequencing information, which is carried over in the control flag field.

| Extended Community Type (2)
0x800A |
| Encapsulation Type (1)
   VPLS = 19 |
| Control Flags (1) |
| L2 MTU (2) |
| Reserved (2) |

Figure 11-13   *L2VPN Extended Community Attribute*

BGP signaling carries label blocks for a set of VPLS edge devices. The logic employed by the edge device is shown in Example 11-14. Assume that the VE_ID 100 and 101 are used for the two edge devices PE1 and PE2 and that VE block size (VBS) of 10 is used. When the NLRI [100,100,10,5000] is sent to the PE2 device, it checks its own VE_ID (101) in the VE range received. Because 101 is in the range, it accepts the NLRI and calculates the remote label for the PE1 device from the LB = 5000. It is 5000 + 101 − 100 = 5001. It then checks whether it has sent any NLRI for VE_ID (100). If it has not, it constructs a NLRI [101, 100, 10, 6000] and sends it to the PE1 device. Now, because it has allocated both the local and remote label and associated bridge ID, it informs L2VPN to set up the PW to the PE1. PE1 sets up the PW to the PE2 after receiving the NLRI.

When the NLRI is received with a range that does not match with the VE_ID of the PE router, it creates a new block and sends it to the peers. This causes discovery of the new device and also triggers actions as illustrated in the preceding paragraph to perform label allocation.

Note   BGP signaling provides a mechanism to address the dual homed devices (DHD). DHD devices have same VE_ID and also are associated with a site-id. The DHD devices can set preferences for path selection via BGP. Therefore, DHD device selection is purely a BGP path selection decision and it is mostly used for active-standby type of forwarding from the DHD devices.

LDP signaling is a better choice than BGP signaling for VPLS for the following reasons:

- Route Reflector increases the signaling delays because the signaling updates have to go through the RR router to reach the remote PE.

- Route Reflector does not reduce the information to be sent as part of the update, hence it does not help in a scaled environment. In other words, RR helps in peer scaling but not in reducing the updates exchanged between PE routers.

- Preallocation of label is done in blocks. Hence, it increases the chances of label space exhaustion at the edge device because if a large block of label space is not available, the smaller blocks of labels are reserved, causing possible fragmentation of label space.

- Existing Route-Reflector software upgrades might be required to support the BGP signaling for VPLS.

To configure BGP signaling for VPLS, use the **autodiscovery bgp signaling bgp** command under l2vpn context. Along with setting the signaling to BGP, VE ID should also be assigned in the l2vpn configuration section. Example 11-14 illustrates the configuration for VPLS with BGP autodiscovery and BGP signaling. Notice the neighbor command **suppress-signaling-protocol ldp** on Cisco IOS and NX-OS or the command **signaling [ldp|bgp] disable** on IOS XR. These commands are used to disable LDP signaling when the signaling protocol is configured as BGP. This is required because the LDP signaling is enabled by default.

Example 11-14   *VPLS BGP Autodiscovery and Signaling*

```
PE1 Configuration - Cisco IOS
l2vpn
 router-id 192.168.1.1
l2vpn vfi context VPLS-VFI
 vpn id 100
 autodiscovery bgp signaling bgp
  ve id 1
  rd 100:100
  route-target export 100:100
  route-target import 100:100
!
router bgp 100
bgp router-id 192.168.1.1
neighbor 192.168.2.2 remote-as 100
 neighbor 192.168.2.2 update-source Loopback0
 neighbor 192.168.3.3 remote-as 100
 neighbor 192.168.3.3 update-source Loopback0
address-family l2vpn vpls
  neighbor 192.168.2.2 activate
  neighbor 192.168.2.2 send-community extended
  neighbor 192.168.2.2 suppress-signaling-protocol ldp
  neighbor 192.168.3.3 activate
  neighbor 192.168.3.3 send-community extended
  neighbor 192.168.3.3 suppress-signaling-protocol ldp
```

```
PE2 Configuration - IOS XR
l2vpn
```

```
  router-id 192.168.2.2
  bridge group BD-GRP
   bridge-domain 100
     interface GigabitEthernet0/3/0/2.100
     !
     vfi VPLS-VFI
      vpn-id 100
      autodiscovery bgp
       rd 100:100
       route-target 100:100
       signaling-protocol bgp
        ve-id 2
 !
 router bgp 100
  bgp router-id 192.168.2.2
  address-family l2vpn vpls-vpws
  !
  neighbor 192.168.1.1
   remote-as 100
   update-source Loopback0
   address-family l2vpn vpls-vpws
    Signalling ldp disable
    !
   !
  neighbor 192.168.3.3
   remote-as 100
   update-source Loopback0
   address-family l2vpn vpls-vpws
    Signalling ldp disable
```

```
PE3 Configuration - NX-OS
l2vpn vfi context VPLS-VFI
  vpn id 100
  autodiscovery bgp signaling bgp
    rd 100:100
    ve id 3
 !
bridge-domain 100
  member vfi VPLS-VFI
 !
router bgp 100
  router-id 192.168.3.3
  address-family l2vpn vpls
```

```
  neighbor 192.168.1.1
    remote-as 100
    update-source loopback0
    address-family l2vpn vpls
      send-community both
      suppress-signaling-protocol ldp
  neighbor 192.168.2.2
    remote-as 100
    update-source loopback0
    address-family l2vpn vpls
      send-community both
      suppress-signaling-protocol ldp
```

For VPLS BGP signaling, the Cisco IOS and NX-OS devices maintain the RIB information for all the signaling data. To view the information, use the command **show l2vpn signaling rib [detail]**. The command displays both the NLRI as well as routing information base (RIB) information for the signaling. Example 11-15 displays the output of the command **show l2vpn signaling rib detail** on both PE1 and PE3 running Cisco IOS and NX-OS, respectively.

Example 11-15   *L2VPN Signaling RIB*

```
IOS
PE1# show l2vpn signaling rib detail
Route 100:100:2 (epoch:1) from iBGP peer 192.168.2.2
Provisioned (Y) Stale (N)
  Route-Target: 100:100
NLRI [6A000002]
    VE-ID:2 VBO:1 VBS:10 LB:16000
    MTU: 1500 Control Word: off
RIB Filter [97000003]
    RD: 100:100
    VE-ID: 1, VBO: 1, VBS: 10 LB: 38
Forwarder [1A000002] VFI VPLS-VFI

Route 100:100:3 (epoch:1) from iBGP peer 192.168.3.3
Provisioned (Y) Stale (N)
  Route-Target: 100:100
NLRI [F0000001]
    VE-ID:3 VBO:1 VBS:10 LB:24
    MTU: 1500 Control Word: off
```

```
RIB Filter [97000003]
    RD: 100:100
    VE-ID: 1, VBO: 1, VBS: 10 LB: 38
Forwarder [1A000002] VFI VPLS-VFI
```

```
NX-OS
PE3# show l2vpn signaling rib detail
Route 100:100:1 (epoch:0) from iBGP peer 192.168.1.1
Provisioned (Y) Stale (N)
Route-Targets:
    [0] 100:100
NLRI [0x16000006]
    VE-ID:1 VBO:1 VBS:10 LB:38
    MTU: 1500 Control Word: off
RIB Filter [0x45000003]
    RD: 100:100
    VE-ID: 3, VBO: 1, VBS: 10 LB: 24
Forwarder [0xb0000003] VFI VPLS-VFI

Route 100:100:2 (epoch:0) from iBGP peer 192.168.2.2
Provisioned (Y) Stale (N)
Route-Targets:
    [0] 100:100
NLRI [0xa3000005]
    VE-ID:2 VBO:1 VBS:10 LB:16000
    MTU: 1500 Control Word: off
RIB Filter [0x45000003]
    RD: 100:100
    VE-ID: 3, VBO: 1, VBS: 10 LB: 24
Forwarder [0xb0000003] VFI VPLS-VFI
```

Note The BGP VPLS autodiscovery commands remain the same when using BGP VPLS autodiscovery and BGP signaling.

On IOS XR platforms, the command **show bgp l2vpn vpls** displays the local labels as well as remote labels for the prefixes. These labels are nothing but the LB and is viewed only when BGP signaling is enabled. Example 11-16 displays the output of the command **show bgp l2vpn vpls**. The local label can be viewed only for the locally originated PW.

Example 11-16   *VC Labels in BGP L2VPN VPLS Table*

```
IOS XR
RP/0/1/CPU0:PE2# show bgp l2vpn vpls
Fri Apr  1 03:29:54.805 UTC
BGP router identifier 192.168.2.2, local AS number 100
BGP generic scan interval 60 secs
BGP table state: Active
Table ID: 0x0   RD version: 2903485008
BGP main routing table version 17
BGP scan interval 60 secs


Status codes: s suppressed, d damped, h history, * valid, > best
              i - internal, r RIB-failure, S stale
Origin codes: i - IGP, e - EGP, ? - incomplete
   Network            Next Hop        Rcvd Label      Local Label
Route Distinguisher: 100:100 (default for vrf BD-GRP:100)
*>i1:1/32             192.168.1.1     38              nolabel
*> 2:1/32             0.0.0.0         nolabel         16000
*>i3:1/32             192.168.3.3     24              nolabel


Processed 3 prefixes, 3 paths
```

Troubleshooting

Cisco platforms also have support for internal event-traces or event-history, which maintains historical data related to events, errors, and finite state machines (FSM). These trace logs are useful for debugging l2vpn issues, especially in live production environments where running a debug could potentially be service impacting. To capture event-traces for l2vpn, use the command **show l2vpn internal event-trace [event | error | major]** on Cisco IOS software. Table 11-2 lists the options used in the **show l2vpn internal event-trace** command.

Table 11-2   *Cisco IOS L2VPN Event-Trace Options*

event	Displays any event-related traces
error	Displays only error-related information
major	Displays only major events

On IOS XR, use the command **show l2vpn trace**. This command displays all the trace logs related to the l2vpn component. The command **show l2vpn internal event-history [cli | errors | events | msgs]** displays the event-history information related to l2vpn on NX-OS. The command on NX-OS has two more options under the event-history command listed in Table 11-3.

Table 11-3 *Cisco IOS L2VPN Event-Trace Options*

cli	Displays the traces of action of each cli command entered
msgs	Displays the msgs received by L2VPN from other components

Example 11-17 displays the output of the event traces related to L2VPN errors.

Example 11-17 *L2VPN Error Event Traces*

```
PE1# show l2vpn internal event-trace error
! Output omitted for brevity


! The below error event occurs when one kind of signaling method is configured
! and other signaling mechanism is being tried to configure on top of the
! existing signaling method.

*Mar 31 10:04:53.754: error: XC ERROR: VFI auto-discovery signaling protocol
                              changes are not allowed. Delete the VFI and
                              reconfigure.
*Mar 31 10:04:53.754: error: XC ERROR: PRC_GEN_FAILURE:PRC_FAILURE_PERMANENT
*Mar 31 10:06:53.997: error: SSM ERROR SM[SSS:AToM:16399]: Unprovision failed
*Mar 31 10:06:53.997: error: SSM ERROR CM[SSS:AToM:16399]: unable to deallocate
                              segment 1
```

```
RP/0/1/CPU0:PE2# show l2vpn trace
! Output omitted for brevity


! The below trace logs displays the NLRI update received and the respective
! values received in the NLRI

11:29:41.527 l2vpn/ad 0/1/CPU0 t15 AUTO-DISCO:500: REQ_NLRI_REFRESH SVC=0
 VPNID=0 FLAGS=0x1
11:29:41.528 l2vpn/ad 0/1/CPU0 t15 AUTO-DISCO:604: VPN ADD PART1: SVC=1
 VPNID=0 NAME=BD-GRP:100 RD[0-3]=0x1c0a8 RD[4-7]=0x2028000 sig =1
11:29:41.528 l2vpn/ad 0/1/CPU0 t15 AUTO-DISCO:608: VPN ADD PART2: shutdown=0
 mtu = 1500 cfbv=0x0 encap=19, VPLS-ID[0-3] = 0 VPLS-ID[4-7] = 0
11:29:41.530 l2vpn/ad 0/1/CPU0 t1  AUTO-DISCO:218: AD_RCV_RESYNC_DONE SVC=0
```

```
PE3# show l2vpn internal event-histor errors
L2VPN Process Event History Error:
!Output omittied for brevity


23:19:18.73302: XC ERROR i/f: [pw100003]PW interface does not exist
in config PSS, can't delete it
23:19:18.21888: XC ERROR UFDM: [4] ack peer-id count is 0
```

```
23:14:55.70402: XC ERROR i/f: [pw100001]Failed to remove PW interfac
e from PSS
23:14:55.70401: XC ERROR i/f: [pw100001]PW interface does not exist
in config PSS, can't delete it
23:14:55.18887: XC ERROR UFDM: [4] ack peer-id count is 0


! The below error log indicates that there was a mis-match in the cbit field
! between the local PE and the remote PE router, causing the pseudowire not
! to come up.

10:33:11.24402: AToM ERROR[192.168.2.2, 100]: .. Remote is invalid
10:33:11.24390: AToM ERROR[192.168.2.2, 100]: .. Mismatch cbit, loca
l 1, remote 0
```

Note For a detailed set of trace logs and other event-history logs, **show tech-support l2vpn** and **show tech-support bgp** can be captured on NX-OS. On IOS XR platform, **show tech-support routing bgp** and **show tech-support l2vpn** and the command **show tech-platform l2vpn platform** can be captured during problematic conditions.

Summary

There are various methods used for L2VPN services over MPLS. The default signaling method is a manual method using LDP signaling. The L2VPN services such as VPWS and VPLS can also be enabled using BGP extensions to L2VPN. BGP provides autodiscovery and signaling services for both VPWS and VPLS. The VPWS provides point-to-point services, whereas VPLS provides multipoint services. It has to be carefully defined where to use VPWS versus VPLS solutions. Although BGP extension is available for both VPWS and VPLS, it is not a good method to use BGP for VPWS. BGP for VPLS provides the service providers with following benefits:

- Scalability
- Peer autodiscovery
- Less configuration load
- Advertise VC labels

This chapter explained how both the manual as well as the autodiscovery mechanism can be useful for VPLS services and how to troubleshoot them. The chapter then detailed the BGP signaling mechanism for VPLS and platform troubleshooting commands that can be used during troubleshooting. Because the BGP troubleshooting for L2VPN address family is similar to any other AFI/SAFI, it makes it easier for service providers to implement BGP for providing L2VPN services to customers while availing other benefits.

References

RFC 3985, *Pseudo Wire Emulation Edge-to-Edge (PWE3) Architecture*, S. Bryant, P. Pate, IETF, http://tools.ietf.org/html/rfc3985, March 2005.

RFC 4446, *IANA Allocations for Pseudowire Edge to Edge Emulation (PWE3)*, L. Martini, IETF, http://tools.ietf.org/html/rfc4446, April 2006.

RFC 4447, *Pseudowire Setup and Maintenance Using the Label Distribution Protocol (LDP)*, L. Martini, Ed., E. Rosen, N. El-Aawar, T. Smith, G. Heron, IETF, http://tools.ietf.org/html/rfc4447, April 2006.

RFC 4448, *Encapsulation Methods for Transport of Ethernet over MPLS Networks*, L. Martini, Ed., E. Rosen, N. El-Aawar, G. Heron, IETF, http://tools.ietf.org/html/rfc4448, April 2006.

RFC 6624, *Layer 2 Virtual Private Networking using BGP for Auto-Discovery and Signaling*, K. Kompella, B. Kothari, R. Cherukuri. IETF, https://tools.ietf.org/html/rfc6624, May 2012.

RFC 4761, *VPLS Using BGP for Auto-Discovery and Signaling*, K. Kompella, Y. Rekhter. IETF, https://tools.ietf.org/html/rfc4761, Jan 2007.

RFC 4762, *VPLS Using LDP for Signaling*, M. Lasserre, K. Kompella. IETF, https://tools.ietf.org/html/rfc4762, Jan 2007.

Cisco Press, *Layer 2 VPN Architectures*, Wei Luo, Carlos Pignataro, Anthony Chan, Dmitry Bokotey.

Cisco. L2VPN Interworking, http://www.cisco.com/c/en/us/td/docs/ios/ios_xe/mpls/configuration/guide/convert/mp_l2_vpns_book_xe/mp_l2vpn_intrntwkg_xe.html.

## Chapter 12

IPv6 BGP for Service Providers

The following topics are covered in this chapter:

- IPv6 BGP Features and Concepts
- IOS XR BGP Policy Accounting
- 6PE
- 6VPE

IPv6 BGP Features and Concepts

Routing protocols and features have expanded for IPv6 over the years. A great number of improvements and features have been added for BGP's support of IPv6 as well. Although most of BGP's features and behavior is the same between IPv4 and IPv6 peering, some features work differently on IPv6 than on IPv4. This section discusses all the various features and services for IPv6 using BGP that need clarification from the IPv4 behavior.

IPv6 BGP Next-Hop

Multiprotocol BGP Extensions for IPv6 is defined in RFC 2545 and RFC 2858, which also state how the IPv6 BGP Next-Hop information is shared with both internal BGP (IBGP) as well as external BGP (EBGP) connections. BGP connections can be formed over a global IPv6 address or link-local addresses, and unicast addresses can reside on physical interfaces or virtual loopback interfaces. When forming an IPv6 IBGP peering, the next-hop is the only global IPv6 address, regardless of the connection type. An EBGP peering in IPv6 address-family or VPNv6 address-family has different next-hop behavior based on the peering interfaces, as follows:

- **Peering between directly connected IPv6 addresses:** In this case, the MP_REACH_NLRI attribute contains two next-hop values:

  - The link-local IPv6 address

  - The global IPv6 address

- **Peering between loopback addresses:** In this case, only one next-hop information is shared in the MP_REACH_NLRI attribute, which is the global IPv6 address.

> **Note**   The Next-Hop Network Address field in the MP_REACH_NLRI attribute has the length of 16 bytes when just the global IPv6 address is present and 32 bytes when the link-local address is also present along with the global IPv6 address.

In Figure 12-1, CE1 has an eBGP session with PE1, and PE1 has an IBGP session with RR-P. The BGP sessions are established over the physical interfaces on both sides of PE1 router. All three routers advertise their IPv6 loopback addresses.

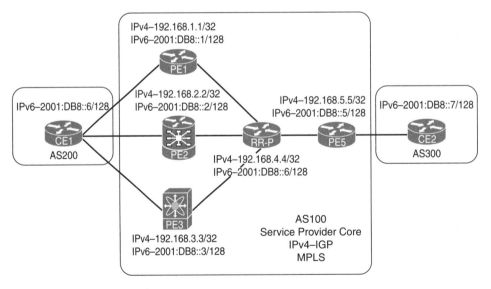

Figure 12-1   *IPv6 Topology*

Example 12-1 displays the configuration on all three routers. For the ease of understanding and verification, the link-local addresses are statically defined.

Example 12-1 *IPv6 Neighbor Configuration*

```
! PE1 Configuration
interface Loopback0
 ip address 192.168.1.1 255.255.255.255
 ipv6 address 2001:DB8::1/128
!
interface GigabitEthernet0/1
 ipv6 address FE80::1 link-local
 ipv6 address 2001:DB8:0:16::1/64
!
interface GigabitEthernet0/2
 ipv6 address FE80::1 link-local
 ipv6 address 2001:DB8:0:14::1/64
!
router bgp 100
 bgp router-id 192.168.1.1
 bgp log-neighbor-changes
 no bgp default ipv4-unicast
 neighbor 2001:DB8:0:14::4 remote-as 100
 neighbor 2001:DB8:0:16::6 remote-as 200
 !
 address-family ipv6
  network 2001:DB8::1/128
  neighbor 2001:DB8:0:14::4 activate
  neighbor 2001:DB8:0:14::4 next-hop-self
  neighbor 2001:DB8:0:16::6 activate
 exit-address-family
```

```
! RR-P Configuration
interface Loopback0
 ip address 192.168.4.4 255.255.255.255
 ipv6 address 2001:DB8::4/128
!
interface GigabitEthernet0/1
 ipv6 address FE80::4 link-local
 ipv6 address 2001:DB8:0:14::4/64
!
router bgp 100
 bgp router-id 192.168.4.4
 bgp log-neighbor-changes
 no bgp default ipv4-unicast
 neighbor 2001:DB8:0:14::1 remote-as 100
```

```
!
address-family ipv6
  network 2001:DB8::4/128
  neighbor 2001:DB8:0:14::1 activate
 exit-address-family
```

```
! CE1 Configuration
interface Loopback0
 ip address 192.168.6.6 255.255.255.255
 ipv6 address 2001:DB8::6/128
!
interface GigabitEthernet0/1
 ipv6 address FE80::6 link-local
 ipv6 address 2001:DB8:0:16::6/64
!
router bgp 200
 bgp router-id 192.168.6.6
 bgp log-neighbor-changes
 no bgp default ipv4-unicast
 neighbor 2001:DB8:0:16::1 remote-as 100
 !
 address-family ipv6
  network 2001:DB8::6/128
  neighbor 2001:DB8:0:16::1 activate
 exit-address-family
```

With this configuration, router CE1 advertises its loopback to router PE1, which further advertises its IPv6 BGP table to router RR-P router. Example 12-2 displays the output of the command **show bgp ipv6 unicast** *ipv6-address* on router PE1 for the loopback0 of router CE1. In this output, the next-hop shows two entries. The main next-hop shows the global IPv6 address of CE1's GigabitEthernet0/1 interface (2001:DB8:0:16::6), and it also shows the link-local address of CE1 (FE80::6). But when verifying the same output for the IBGP learned prefix, that is, loopback0 of RR-P router, notice that there is only single next-hop value.

Example 12-2 *IPv6 BGP Next-Hop Verification*

```
! Verification of prefixes learned via EBGP sessions
PE1# show bgp ipv6 unicast 2001:db8::6/128
BGP routing table entry for 2001:DB8::6/128, version 12
Paths: (1 available, best #1, table default)
  Advertised to update-groups:
     5
  Refresh Epoch 1
  200
```

```
   2001:DB8:0:16::6 (FE80::6) from 2001:DB8:0:16::6 (192.168.6.6)
      Origin IGP, metric 0, localpref 100, valid, external, best
      rx pathid: 0, tx pathid: 0x0
```

```
! Verification of prefixes learned via IBGP session
PE1# show bgp ipv6 unicast 2001:db8::4/128
BGP routing table entry for 2001:DB8::4/128, version 10
Paths: (1 available, best #1, table default)
  Advertised to update-groups:
     3
  Refresh Epoch 1
  Local
    2001:DB8:0:14::4 from 2001:DB8:0:14::4 (192.168.4.4)
      Origin IGP, metric 0, localpref 100, valid, internal, best
      rx pathid: 0, tx pathid: 0x0
```

When a wireshark capture is performed between PE1 and CE1, the BGP UPDATE message shows that it contains two next-hops in the Next-Hop Network Address field of the MP_REACH_NLRI attribute. In Figure 12-2, notice that the Next-Hop Network Address field is 32 bytes and lists both of the next-hop values—the IPv6 global address and the link-local address.

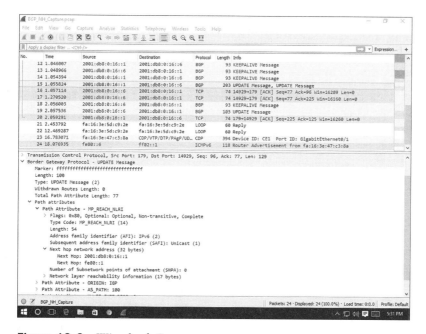

Figure 12-2 *Wireshark Capture*

If the same peering between PE1 and CE1 is performed over the loopback interface, the BGP next-hop has only one next-hop in the Network Layer Reachability Information (NLRI). Examine the output of the **show bgp ipv6 unicast** *ipv6-address* command on router CE1 for the PE1 loopback in Example 12-3. Notice that in this example, the BGP next-hop for the PE1 loopback shows the PE1 loopback. This is because the peering is from loopback to loopback between the two routers.

Example 12-3   *IPv6 EBGP BGP Next-Hop with Loopback Peering*

```
CE1# show bgp ipv6 unicast 2001:db8::1/128
! Output omitted for brevity
    2001:DB8::1 from 2001:DB8::1 (192.168.1.1)
      Origin IGP, metric 0, localpref 100, valid, external, best
      rx pathid: 0, tx pathid: 0x0

CE1# show bgp ipv6 unicast 2001:db8::4/128
! Output omitted for brevity
    2001:DB8::1 from 2001:DB8::1 (192.168.1.1)
      Origin IGP, localpref 100, valid, external, best
      rx pathid: 0, tx pathid: 0x0
```

IPv6 Reachability over IPv4 Transport

BGP supports the exchange of IPv6 prefixes via an IPv6 peering (peering established with IPv6 connectivity) or via an IPv4 peering (peering established with IPv4 connectivity). The BGP IPv6 NLRI over IPv4 established peering is an example of multiprotocol BGP (MP-BGP). This section focuses on exchanging IPv6 routes over an IPv4 peering. Often this is done to conserve resources by not running a second session for IPv6.

In Example 12-4, the neighbor is enabled for not just IPv4 address-family but also for IPv6 address-family. Examining the same topology in Figure 12-1, routers PE1, PE2, and PE3 form an EBGP neighborship with CE1 and form an IBGP neighbor relationship with RR-P over IPv4 addresses.

Example 12-4   *IPv6 AF BGP Neighbor over IPv4 Address*

```
IOS - PE1
router bgp 100
 bgp router-id 192.168.1.1
 bgp log-neighbor-changes
 no bgp default ipv4-unicast
 neighbor 10.1.14.4 remote-as 100
 neighbor 10.1.16.6 remote-as 200
 !
 address-family ipv6
  network 2001:DB8::1/128
```

```
  neighbor 10.1.14.4 activate
  neighbor 10.1.14.4 next-hop-self
  neighbor 10.1.16.6 activate
```

```
IOS XR - PE2
router bgp 100
 bgp router-id 192.168.2.2
 address-family ipv4 unicast
 !
 address-family ipv6 unicast
  network 2001:db8::2/128
 !
 neighbor 10.1.24.4
  remote-as 100
  address-family ipv6 unicast
   next-hop-self
  !
 !
 neighbor 10.1.26.6
  remote-as 200
  address-family ipv4 unicast
   route-policy pass in
   route-policy pass out
  !
  address-family ipv6 unicast
   route-policy pass in
   route-policy pass out
!
route-policy pass
  pass
end-policy
```

```
NX-OS - PE3
router bgp 100
  router-id 192.168.3.3
  address-family ipv4 unicast
  address-family ipv6 unicast
    network 2001:db8::3/128
  neighbor 10.1.34.4
    remote-as 100
    address-family ipv6 unicast
      next-hop-self
  neighbor 10.1.36.6
    remote-as 200
    address-family ipv6 unicast
```

When the BGP peering is established between the IBGP or EBGP peers, the routes are exchanged, but with a different behavior on the next-hop value.

■ On IOS devices, the next-hop field remains inaccessible because the next-hop value is in the format ::FFFF:[ip-address]—also known as the IPv4 mapped IPv6 address, where ip-address is the next-hop IPv4 address. The reason for this address being inaccessible is that the IOS devices do not assign a valid IPv6 address as the next-hop, but create an IPv6 next-hop address based on the IPv4 address, which may not exist.

■ The IOS XR devices exhibit the correct behavior by advertising both the global IPv6 address and the link-local address as the next-hop for the EBGP neighbor and the global IPv6 address for the IBGP neighbor.

■ NX-OS on the other hand, advertises the global IPV6 address as the next-hop for both the EBGP and IBGP neighbors.

Example 12-5 illustrates the different next-hop behaviors from all the three platforms (IOS, IOS XR, and NX-OS) for both the IBGP and EBGP connections. Notice that the prefix 2001:DB8::1/128 is having an inaccessible next-hop for both the EBGP as well as the IBGP peering. This causes reachability issues, and the prefix never gets installed in the IPv6 routing information base (RIB). This issue is not seen for the prefixes advertised by IOS XR and NX-OS devices.

Example 12-5   *IPv6 BGP Next-Hop with IPv4 Peering*

```
Outputs for EBGP Peerings
! Prefix from PE1 running IOS
CE1# show bgp ipv6 unicast 2001:db8::1/128
BGP routing table entry for 2001:DB8::1/128, version 0
Paths: (1 available, no best path)
Flag: 0x820
  Not advertised to any peer
  Refresh Epoch 1
  100
    ::FFFF:10.1.16.1 (inaccessible) from 10.1.16.1 (192.168.1.1)
      Origin IGP, metric 0, localpref 100, valid, external
      rx pathid: 0, tx pathid:


! Prefix from PE2 running IOS XR
CE1# show bgp ipv6 unicast 2001:db8::2/128
BGP routing table entry for 2001:DB8::2/128, version 14
Paths: (1 available, best #1, table default)
  Advertised to update-groups:
     1
  Refresh Epoch 1
100
```

```
    2001:DB8:0:26::2 (FE80::2) from 10.1.26.2 (192.168.2.2)
      Origin IGP, metric 0, localpref 100, valid, external, best
      rx pathid: 0, tx pathid: 0x0
```

```
! Prefix from PE3 running NX-OS
CE1# show bgp ipv6 unicast 2001:db8::3/128
BGP routing table entry for 2001:DB8::3/128, version 3
Paths: (1 available, best #1, table default)
  Advertised to update-groups:
      1
  Refresh Epoch 1
  100
    2001:DB8:0:36::3 from 10.1.36.3 (192.168.3.3)
      Origin IGP, localpref 100, valid, external, best
      rx pathid: 0, tx pathid: 0x0
```

```
! Output from IBGP Peering on all Prefix from PE1 running IOS
RR-P# show bgp ipv6 unicast 2001:db8::1/128
BGP routing table entry for 2001:DB8::1/128, version 27
Paths: (1 available, no best path)
  Not advertised to any peer
  Refresh Epoch 1
  Local
    ::FFFF:10.1.14.1 (inaccessible) from 10.1.14.1 (192.168.1.1)
      Origin IGP, metric 0, localpref 100, valid, internal
      rx pathid: 0, tx pathid: 0
```

```
! Prefix from PE2 running IOS XR
RR-P# show bgp ipv6 unicast 2001:db8::2/128
BGP routing table entry for 2001:DB8::2/128, version 2
Paths: (1 available, best #1, table default)
  Not advertised to any peer
  Refresh Epoch 1
  Local
    2001:DB8:0:24::2 from 10.1.24.2 (192.168.2.2)
      Origin IGP, metric 0, localpref 100, valid, internal, best
      rx pathid: 0, tx pathid: 0x0
```

```
! Prefix from PE3 running NX-OS
RR-P# show bgp ipv6 unicast 2001:db8::3/128
BGP routing table entry for 2001:DB8::3/128, version 3
Paths: (1 available, best #1, table default)
  Not advertised to any peer
```

```
Refresh Epoch 1
Local
  2001:DB8:0:34::3 from 10.1.34.3 (192.168.3.3)
    Origin IGP, localpref 100, valid, internal, best
    rx pathid: 0, tx pathid: 0x0
```

To overcome this problem, a route-map is configured on all the IOS devices to manually assign the IPv6 next-hop address. The next-hop value is assigned using a route-map. After the IPv6 next-hop is assigned, the prefixes learned from IOS devices get installed in the IPv6 RIB.

Example 12-6 demonstrates the configuration of assigning an IPv6 next-hop on IOS devices and the prefix information on the advertised neighboring devices. Notice that after the IPv6 next-hop value is assigned, the PE1 router automatically advertises two next-hop values—the global IPv6 address, which was assigned using route-map, and the link-local address. As soon as both the IBGP and EBGP peers receive valid next-hops for PE1 loopback, they are able to ping that loopback address.

Example 12-6 *Configuring and Verifying IPv6 Next-Hop on IOS Routers*

```
PE1(config)# route-map toCE1 permit 10
PE1(config-route-map)# set ipv6 next-hop 2001:DB8:0:16::1
PE1(config-route-map)# route-map toRR-P permit 10
PE1(config-route-map)# set ipv6 next-hop 2001:DB8:0:14::1
PE1(config-route-map)# exit
PE1(config)# router bgp 100
PE1(config-router)# address-family ipv6 unicast
PE1(config-router-af)# neighbor 10.1.14.4 route-map toRR-P out
PE1(config-router-af)# neighbor 10.1.16.6 route-map toCE1 out

! Verifying Prefix from PE1 on CE1 - EBGP Peering
CE1# show bgp ipv6 unicast 2001:db8::1/128
BGP routing table entry for 2001:DB8::1/128, version 97
Paths: (1 available, best #1, table default)
  Advertised to update-groups:
     4          7
  Refresh Epoch 1
  100
    2001:DB8:0:16::1 (FE80::1) from 10.1.16.1 (192.168.1.1)
      Origin IGP, metric 0, localpref 100, valid, external, best
      rx pathid: 0, tx pathid: 0x0
```

```
CE1# ping 2001:db8::1
Type escape sequence to abort.
Sending 5, 100-byte ICMP Echos to 2001:DB8::1, timeout is 2 seconds:
!!!!!
Success rate is 100 percent (5/5), round-trip min/avg/max = 1/2/3 ms
```

```
! Verifying Prefix from PE1 on RR-P - IBGP Peering
RR-P# show bgp ipv6 unicast 2001:db8::1/128
BGP routing table entry for 2001:DB8::1/128, version 32
Paths: (1 available, best #1, table default)
  Not advertised to any peer
  Refresh Epoch 1
  Local
    2001:DB8:0:14::1 from 10.1.14.1 (192.168.1.1)
      Origin IGP, metric 0, localpref 100, valid, internal, best
      rx pathid: 0, tx pathid: 0x0

RR-P# ping 2001:db8::1
Type escape sequence to abort.
Sending 5, 100-byte ICMP Echos to 2001:DB8::1, timeout is 2 seconds:
!!!!!
Success rate is 100 percent (5/5), round-trip min/avg/max = 1/2/3 ms
```

Note   The IPv6 next-hop is not required to be manually assigned on IOS XR or NX-OS devices. When NX-OS router receives a prefix from IOS router, it receives the default inaccessible next-hop address. When IOS XR router receives a prefix from the IOS device, the next-hop value is seen as the IPv4 address rather than as the inaccessible IPv6 address. In either case, the IOS device is required to manually configure an IPv6 next-hop address for the advertised prefixes.

IPv4 Routes over IPv6 Next-Hop

Imagine a large data center with a Spine-Leaf (clos) architecture that is based on IPv6 addressing. Because of the number of links and other reasons, the data center cannot run in a dual-stack environment while providing IPv4 connectivity between leaf devices.

Examine the Spine-Leaf topology of a data center deployment in Figure 12-3. A typical spine-leaf topology consists of less than 10 spine nodes, a few hundreds of leaf nodes, and couple of border leaves.

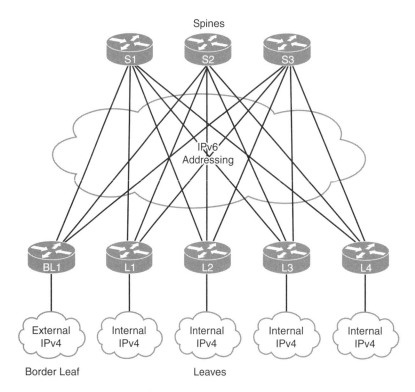

Figure 12-3 *Spine-Leaf Topology*

Internal IPv4 destinations are learned through the leaves while external IPv4 destinations are learned through the border leaves. The spine, leaf, and border leaf may have IPv4 loopback configured for management purpose. Other than that, only IPv6 addressing is used on them. Because global IPv6 addresses are assigned to the router's interfaces, this provides the ability to identify and manage individual interfaces. Bidirectional Forwarding Detection (BFD) could also be used to monitor the wellness of the next-hop address.

With such a design, the challenge is how to exchange IPv4 routes over IPv6 infrastructure. RFC 5549 describes the mechanism for allowing BGP to exchange IPv4 routes over IPv6 next-hop. The problem with this feature is the next-hop value. The BGP next-hop for the IPv4 prefix is an IPv6 address that has been converted to an IPv4 address which is an invalid address. The initial 32 bits of an IPv6 address are converted into an IPv4 address format and advertised to the BGP peer.

Example 12-7 demonstrates the configuration of the IPv6 BGP peering for IPv4 address-family.

Example 12-7 *IPv6 BGP Peering for IPv4 Address-Family*

```
IOS
PE1(config)# router bgp 100
PE1(config-router)# neighbor 2001:DB8:0:14::4 remote-as 100
PE1(config-router)# neighbor 2001:DB8:0:16::6 remote-as 200
PE1(config-router)# address-family ipv4 unicast
PE1(config-router-af)# neighbor 2001:DB8:0:14::4 activate
PE1(config-router-af)# neighbor 2001:DB8:0:14::4 next-hop-self
PE1(config-router-af)# neighbor 2001:DB8:0:16::6 activate
PE1(config-router-af)# network 192.168.1.1 mask 255.255.255.255
NX-OS
PE3(config)# router bgp 100
PE3(config-router)# address-family ipv4 unicast
PE3(config-router-af)# network 192.168.3.3/32
PE3(config-router-af)# exit
PE3(config-router)# neighbor 2001:db8:0:36::6
PE3(config-router-neighbor)# remote-as 200
PE3(config-router-neighbor)# address-family ipv4 unicast
PE3(config-router-neighbor-af)# exit
PE3(config-router-neighbor)# exit
PE3(config-router)# neighbor 2001:db8:0:34::4
PE3(config-router-neighbor)# remote-as 100
PE3(config-router-neighbor)# address-family ipv4 unicast
```

Note IPv6 BGP peering under IPv4 address-family is not supported on IOS XR at the time of this writing.

After the neighborship is established, the prefixes are advertised with an inaccessible IPv4 next-hop. In this scenario, the first 32 bits of the IPv6 address are 2001:DB8. When converted into an IPv4 address, it becomes 32.1.13.184, which is not an IP address assigned anywhere in this topology and thus is inaccessible. Example 12-8 displays the output of the advertised prefix by the PE toward CE1.

Example 12-8 *IPv4 Prefix Learned over IPv6 BGP Peer*

```
CE1# show bgp ipv4 unicast 192.168.1.1
BGP routing table entry for 192.168.1.1/32, version 0
Paths: (1 available, no best path)
  Not advertised to any peer
  Refresh Epoch 3
 100
```

```
32.1.13.184 (inaccessible) from 2001:DB8:0:16::1 (192.168.1.1)
  Origin IGP, metric 0, localpref 100, valid, external
  rx pathid: 0, tx pathid: 0
```

To overcome this problem, a route-map is required with the next-hop value set to the router's own address that is a valid next-hop address for the receiving router.

Note   Although the features are available to exchange IPv4 routes over IPv6 peering, or vice versa, it is recommended to exchange the routes over the same addressing peering (that is, the exchange of IPv4 routes over IPv4 peering and IPv6 routes over IPv6 peering). This simplifies the exchange of routes and reduces the operational complexity.

IPv6 BGP Policy Accounting

The BGP Policy Accounting (BGP-PA) feature provides per-interface accounting for network traffic that is matched against the autonomous system (AS) number, community-list, AS-Path, and so on. The prefixes are classified and are then installed into the RIB according to the routing policies. Based on the routing policy, BGP-PA assigns each prefix a bucket associated with an interface.

BGP-PA is a very useful tool for service providers because based on the accounted traffic, they can charge their customers for the traffic for the BGP routes that traverse through the links. It is important to remember that this feature is available both for IPv4 and IPv6 prefixes and only provides accounting for BGP learned prefixes. Other Interior Gateway Protocol (IGP) learned prefixes are not accounted.

To configure BGP-PA, a set of route policies are defined to match routing prefixes and classify the routing prefixes, and then assign each prefix a unique traffic index using the **route-map** or **route-policy** subcommand **set traffic-index** *bucket-number*. Example 12-9 demonstrates the configuration of the policy using route-map and RPL. When matching on community values, it can be used for both IPv4 as well as IPv6 accounting. When matching based on IP/IPv6 addresses, the separate accounting policies (route-map in case of IOS and route policy in case of IOS XR) are configured.

Example 12-9   *Configuring BGP Community and BGP-PA Buckets*

```
! Example shows Cisco IOS configuration for matching Community Values for
! assigning traffic buckets
PE1(config)# ip community-list 10 permit 10:10
PE1(config)# ip community-list 20 permit 20:20
PE1(config)# ip community-list 30 permit 30:30
PE1(config)# route-map SET_TRAFFIC_INDX permit 10
```

```
PE1(config-route-map)# match community 10
PE1(config-route-map)# set traffic-index 1
PE1(config-route-map)# route-map SET_TRAFFIC_INDX permit 20
PE1(config-route-map)# match community 20
PE1(config-route-map)# set traffic-index 2
PE1(config-route-map)# route-map SET_TRAFFIC_INDX permit 30
PE1(config-route-map)# match community 30
PE1(config-route-map)# set traffic-index 3
PE1(config-route-map)# exit
```

```
! Example shows IOS XR configuration for matching based on IP Addresses
RP/0/0/CPU0:PE2(config)# route-policy BGP-POL-ACCT
RP/0/0/CPU0:PE2(config-rpl)# if destination in (192.168.6.6/32) then
RP/0/0/CPU0:PE2(config-rpl-if)# set traffic-index 1
RP/0/0/CPU0:PE2(config-rpl-if)# else
RP/0/0/CPU0:PE2(config-rpl-else)# set traffic-index 2
RP/0/0/CPU0:PE2(config-rpl-else)# exit
RP/0/0/CPU0:PE2(config-rpl)# exit
RP/0/0/CPU0:PE2(config)# route-policy V6-BGP-PA
RP/0/0/CPU0:PE2(config-rpl)# if destination in (2001:db8::6/128) then
RP/0/0/CPU0:PE2(config-rpl-if)# set traffic-index 1
RP/0/0/CPU0:PE2(config-rpl-if)# else
RP/0/0/CPU0:PE2(config-rpl-else)# set traffic-index 2
RP/0/0/CPU0:PE2(config-rpl-else)# exit
RP/0/0/CPU0:PE2(config-rpl)# exit
RP/0/0/CPU0:PE2(config)# commit
```

After defining the match criteria, use the command **table-map** *route-map-name* on Cisco
IOS or **table-policy** *route-policy-name* on IOS XR under the address-family to classify
the traffic before enabling BGP-PA. Then assign a bucket for the traffic based on the
match criteria. The next step is to enable interfaces to perform the accounting for the
classified packets. The BGP-PA provides the following accounting for both input and output direction:

- Source accounting

- Destination accounting

- Source and destination accounting

The BGP-PA does not get initialized unless the interface is enabled for accounting.

To enable the BGP-PA, use the command **bgp-policy accounting [input | output] [source]**
on Cisco IOS and use the command **[ipv4 | ipv6] bgp policy accounting [input | output]**

[source-accounting | destination-accounting] on IOS XR. Example 12-10 demonstrates the configuration of BGP-PA on both IOS and IOS XR devices.

Example 12-10   *Initializing BGP-PA*

```
IOS
PE1(config)# router bgp 100
PE1(config-router)# address-family ipv6 unicast
PE1(config-router-af)# table-map SET_TRAFFIC_INDX
PE1(config-router-af)# exit
PE1(config)# interface gigabitEthernet0/1
PE1(config-if)# bgp-policy accounting input
PE1(config-if)# bgp-policy accounting output
```

```
IOS XR
RP/0/0/CPU0:PE2(config)# router bgp 100
RP/0/0/CPU0:PE2(config-bgp)# address-family ipv6 unicast
RP/0/0/CPU0:PE2(config-bgp-af)# table-policy V6-BGP-PA
RP/0/0/CPU0:PE2(config-bgp-af)# exit
RP/0/0/CPU0:PE2(config-bgp)# exit
RP/0/0/CPU0:PE2(config)# interface gigabitEthernet 0/0/0/0
RP/0/0/CPU0:PE2(config-if)# ipv6 bgp policy accounting in destination-accounting
RP/0/0/CPU0:PE2(config-if)# ipv6 bgp policy accounting out destination-accounting
RP/0/0/CPU0:PE2(config-if)# commit
```

Use the command **show [ip | ipv6] interface** *interface-name* to verify whether the BGP-PA has been enabled, and if enabled, then in which direction it is enabled. After the BGP-PA is enabled, and there is active traffic hitting the route-map or the route policy, the interface starts collecting the statistics for each bucket. The traffic statistics for each bucket is viewed by using the command **show cef interface** *interface-name* **policy-statistics [input | output]** on Cisco IOS and the command **show cef [ipv4 | ipv6] interface** *interface-name* **bgp-policy-statistics** on IOS XR.

Example 12-11 examines the BGP-PA interface statistics for the accounted packets. Notice that on IOS XR, there are two buckets. One is the default bucket and the other is the bucket number 1 which is for the traffic that has the destination of IPv6 address 2001:db8::6/128.

Example 12-11   *Verifying BGP-PA Statistics*

```
IOS
PE1# show cef interface gigabitEthernet0/1 policy-statistics
GigabitEthernet0/1 is up (if_number 3)
  Corresponding hwidb fast_if_number 3
  Corresponding hwidb firstsw->if_number 3
```

```
 BGP based Policy accounting on input is enabled
 Index           Packets              Bytes
    1              612               41244
    2                0                   0
    3                0                   0
    4                0                   0
    5                0                   0
! Output omitted for brevity
```

```
IOS XR
RP/0/0/CPU0:PE2# show cef ipv6 interface Gig0/0/0/0 bgp-policy-statistics
GigabitEthernet0/0/0/0 is UP
Input BGP policy accounting on dst IP address enabled
  buckets      packets       bytes
  default       10557      1055700
Output BGP policy accounting on dst IP address enabled
  buckets      packets       bytes
  default         818        57676
    1           10357      1035700
```

Note   The BGP-PA statistics can be cleared using the command **clear cef interface** *interface-name* **policy-statistics** on Cisco IOS and the command **clear cef [ipv4 | ipv6] interface** *interface-name* **bgp-policy-statistics** on IOS XR.

IPv6 Provider Edge Routers (6PE) over MPLS

After the ratification of IPv6 addressing standards, service providers needed to find a way to provide IPv6 connectivity to their customers. Service providers (SPs) typically standardized on a small set of devices that are deployed in massive quantities. Although networking vendors came out with newer routers that natively supported IPv6, upgrading the infrastructure to provide both IPv4 and IPv6 connectivity to their customers was too expensive. SPs had already deployed Multiprotocol Label Switching (MPLS) in their network and provided Layer 2 and Layer 3 MPLS VPN services to their customers. Three alternative MPLS tunneling solutions were created to deliver end-to-end IPv6 services to their customers:

- Tunneling over IPv4 signaled label switched paths (LSP) (MPLS-TE)

- IPv6 VPN Provider Edge (6VPE)

- IPv6 Provider Edge (6PE)

6PE is the most scalable and least disruptive mechanism for providing IPv6 services to end users over MPLS enabled IPv4 infrastructure. With 6PE, only the PE router is required to be upgraded to support IPv4 and IPv6 services. The other transit routers (P—provider) do not require any software or hardware upgrades. Benefits of using a 6PE solution include the following:

- **Minimal operational cost and risk:** There is no impact on the existing MPLS-enabled IPv4 core.

- **No impact to IPv4 customers:** The PE can still provide IPv4 services to existing customers and at the same time provide IPv6 services.

- **Nondisruptive:** 6PE routers can be added anytime in the network without any service disruptions and provide IPv6 services.

- **Easy connectivity between PE and CE:** PE and CE can run any IPv6-enabled IGP, static route, or EBGP peering to exchange IPv6 routing information.

Defined in RFC 4798, 6PE relies on BGP extensions to exchange IPv6 NLRI over an IPv4 peering session along with an MPLS label for each IPv6 prefix being advertised. The IPv6 packets are label switched across the MPLS backbone to form the reachability between two 6PE routers. In the core, the IPv6 traffic is forwarded from 6PE to 6PE based on MPLS labels, similar to the way VPN traffic is transported across the core in MPLS VPN.

When implementing 6PE architecture, there is no concept of VRFs. The CE facing interfaces are part of the global routing context. Two labels are carried for the IPv6 traffic:

- **MP-BGP Label:** This is used to identify the outgoing interface on the Egress PE router. The PE router allocates one label per IPv6 prefix.

- **IGP Label:** This is used to forward the traffic in the MPLS IPv4 core network. The IGP label identifies the LSP toward the next-hop address, which is the remote 6PE router.

Note   The reason for having two labels is that when the penultimate-hop popping (PHP) mechanism takes place, the packet on the penultimate-hop will perform an IPv6 lookup, but the router is not IPv6 enabled; thus, the packet will drop.

Figure 12-4 illustrates the architecture of 6PE. Notice that there is a full mesh of MP-IBGP sessions between the PE routers. The PE routers exchange IPv6 and label information to forward the IPv6 traffic across the MPLS cloud by switching the labeled packets.

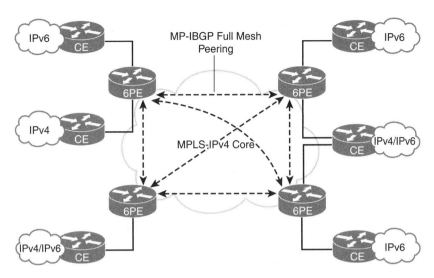

Figure 12-4 *6PE Architecture*

For understanding and troubleshooting 6PE, it is very important to understand the control plane and the data plane flow. The 6PE control plane and data plane is very similar to that of IPv4 MPLS VPN. For traffic flowing from left to right direction, the control-plane flow is in the opposite direction; that is, right to left.

Figure 12-5 gives a brief overview of the 6PE routing and label distribution (control plane) across the MPLS cloud. In this topology, the egress PE router PE5 allocates a BGP label 23 for the destination CE2 prefix 2001:DB8::7/128 and advertises it to its IPv6 peer PE1 with the next-hop value of PE5 loopback address. Because the core is MPLS enabled, the PE router then advertises an implicit-null label toward the P/RR router RR-P, which is the penultimate-hop for PE5. The RR-P router allocates a label value of 19 and advertises toward the PE1 router. Both the PE1 and PE5 routers are having EBGP peering with the CE routers, respectively. The PE1 routers advertise the CE2 loopback address as an EBGP prefix toward the CE1 router.

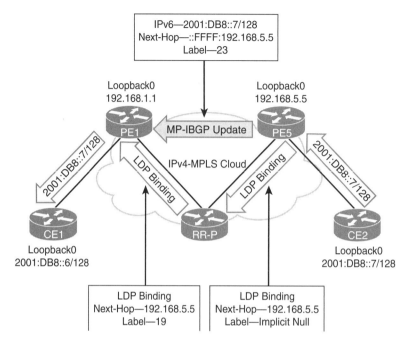

Figure 12-5 *6PE Control-Plane Flow*

After the control-plane information is exchanged, the traffic can start from CE1 toward CE2. When an IPv6 packet sent from router CE1 toward CE2 reaches PE1, the PE1 performs a lookup in its IPv6 routing table and finds the prefix with the outgoing label of 23 and the next-hop of PE5 loopback. Then the PE1 router performs a label forwarding information base (LFIB) lookup for the PE5 loopback and finds a label of 19 learned from the RR-P router. The PE1 router adds the BGP label 23 on top of the IPv6 packet received from CE1 and then adds the IGP label 19 on top of the BGP label and forwards the packet toward the RR-P router. This makes the IPv6 packet transparent inside the service provider core network. The RR-P router then receives the MPLS packet with a label value of 19, performs a LFIB lookup, and finds that it is the penultimate-hop for PE5. It then strips off the IGP label and forwards the packet with just the BGP label 23. When the packet is received by PE5, it performs a lookup in its BGP table and finds the next-hop to reach 2001:DB8::7/128 is 2001:DB8:0:57::7. PE5 then performs the forwarding information base (FIB) lookup and forwards the traffic of the outgoing interface toward CE2.

Figure 12-6 depicts the data forwarding in the 6PE deployment.

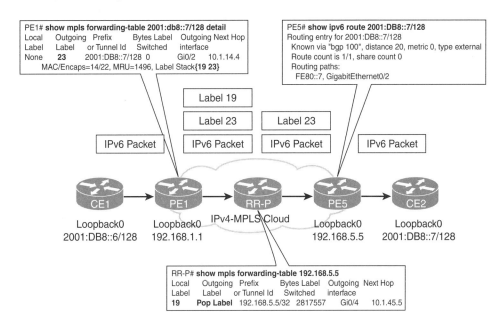

Figure 12-6 *6PE Data Plane Flow*

6PE Configuration

6PE is configured by following these simple steps:

Step 1. Configure IGP. IS-IS or OSPF is enabled in the service provider core to provide PE to PE reachability. The PE loopbacks should be advertised with the IGP as a /32 prefix.

Step 2. Configure MPLS. Enable MPLS on all the core network interfaces. After enabling MPLS, there should be an LSP between all the PE routers in the network.

Step 3. Configure MP-IBGP peering between PEs. Establish IPv6 peering between the PE routers. 6PE uses the MP-IBGP session to distribute IPv6 routes over the MPLS IPv4 network. When establishing an MP-IBGP session between the PE routers, ensure that the session is IPv6 MPLS label capable.

Step 4. Configure IPv6 routing between PE and CE. Use IPv6 static, IPv6 enabled dynamic routing, or IPv6 EBGP peering between the PE and the CE routers. Note that there is no VRF configured in case of 6PE. The PE-CE interfaces are part of the global IPv6 unicast routing table.

For configuration and verification of 6PE deployment, examine the same topology as shown in Figure 12-1. Example 12-12 displays the configuration of PE1, PE2, and PE3. PE1 is running IOS, PE2 is running IOS XR, and PE3 is running NX-OS. Notice that on IOS XR and NX-OS, the peering is established under **address-family ipv6 labeled-unicast**. This is because IOS XR and NX-OS do not support the send-label command, and it is using the peering under the labeled-unicast address-family BGP advertises labels to its peers. The address-family ipv6 labeled-unicast takes care of advertising the label to the peers. A 6PE router running IOS XR or NX-OS allocates a label for a prefix based on the **allocate-label** [**all** | *policy*] and sends an IPv6 labeled-unicast update to another 6PE router. The policy on IOS XR is defined using route policy and on NX-OS using route-maps.

Example 12-12   *6PE Configuration*

```
PE1 - IOS
ipv6 unicast-routing
ipv6 cef
!
interface Loopback0
 ip address 192.168.1.1 255.255.255.255
 ip ospf 100 area 0
!
interface GigabitEthernet0/1
 description Connected to CE1
 no ip address
 ipv6 address FE80::1 link-local
 ipv6 address 2001:DB8:0:16::1/64
!
interface GigabitEthernet0/2
 description Connected to RR-P
 ip address 10.1.14.1 255.255.255.0
 ip ospf 100 area 0
 mpls ip
!
router ospf 100
 router-id 192.168.1.1
!
router bgp 100
 bgp router-id 192.168.1.1
 bgp log-neighbor-changes
 no bgp default ipv4-unicast
 neighbor 2001:DB8:0:16::6 remote-as 200
 neighbor 192.168.5.5 remote-as 100
 neighbor 192.168.5.5 update-source Loopback0
```

```
!
address-family ipv6
  neighbor 2001:DB8:0:16::6 activate
  neighbor 192.168.5.5 activate
  neighbor 192.168.5.5 send-community both
  neighbor 192.168.5.5 send-label
 exit-address-family
!
mpls ldp router-id Loopback0 force
```

```
PE2 - IOS XR
interface Loopback0
 ipv4 address 192.168.2.2 255.255.255.255
 ipv6 address 2001:db8::2/128
!
interface GigabitEthernet0/0/0/0
 ipv6 address fe80::2 link-local
 ipv6 address 2001:db8:0:26::2/64
!
interface GigabitEthernet0/0/0/1
 ipv4 address 10.1.24.2 255.255.255.0
!
router ospf 100
 router-id 192.168.2.2
 area 0
  interface Loopback0
  !
  interface GigabitEthernet0/0/0/1
  !
 !
!
router bgp 100
 bgp router-id 192.168.2.2
 address-family ipv6 unicast
  allocate-label all
 !
 neighbor 192.168.5.5
  remote-as 100
  update-source Loopback0
  address-family ipv6 labeled-unicast
  !
 !
 neighbor 2001:db8:0:26::6
  remote-as 200
```

```
  address-family ipv6 unicast
   route-policy pass in
   route-policy pass out
  !
 !
!
route-policy pass
  pass
end-policy
!
mpls ldp
 router-id 192.168.2.2
 interface GigabitEthernet0/0/0/1
```

```
PE3 - NX-OS
install feature-set mpls
feature-set mpls
feature mpls l3vpn
feature-set bgp
!
interface loopback0
  ip address 192.168.3.3/32
!
interface Ethernet2/1
  no switchport
  ipv6 address 2001:db8:0:36::3/64
  no shutdown
!
interface Ethernet2/2
  no switchport
  ip address 10.1.34.3/24
  ip router ospf 100 area 0.0.0.0
  mpls ip
  no shutdown
!
mpls ldp configuration
  router-id Lo0
!
router ospf 100
  router-id 192.168.3.3
!
router bgp 100
  router-id 192.168.3.3
  address-family ipv6 unicast
```

```
   allocate-label all
neighbor 2001:db8:0:36::6
  remote-as 200
  address-family ipv6 unicast
neighbor 192.168.5.5
  remote-as 100
  update-source loopback0
  address-family ipv6 labeled-unicast
```

Note   If using a static route or dynamic IPv6 routing protocol, perform mutual redistribution between the IPv6 IGP and BGP IPv6 address-family.

6PE Verification and Troubleshooting

The first step to verify after configuring 6PE is to ensure that the 6PE have full mesh MP-IBGP peering, and they are exchanging the capability to advertise labels for IPv6 unicast. The established BGP sessions are verified using the command **show bgp ipv6 unicast summary** on Cisco IOS and the command **show bgp ipv6 [unicast | labeled-unicast] summary** on IOS XR and NX-OS.

Use the command **show bgp ipv6 unicast neighbors** *neighbor-ip* on Cisco IOS and the command **show bgp ipv6 labeled-unicast neighbors** *neighbor-ip* on IOS XR and NX-OS. Example 12-13 verifies that the 6PE routers are exchanging labeled-unicast capability to advertise labels to the peers. Notice that even though PE5 is an IOS router, on PE2 and PE3 labeled-unicast capability is being advertised and received.

Example 12-13   *6PE MPLS Labels Advertising Capability*

```
PE1 - IOS
PE1# show bgp ipv6 unicast neighbors 192.168.5.5
BGP neighbor is 192.168.5.5,  remote AS 100, internal link
  BGP version 4, remote router ID 0.0.0.0
  BGP state = Idle
  Neighbor sessions:
    0 active, is not multisession capable (disabled)
    Stateful switchover support enabled: NO
  Do log neighbor state changes (via global configuration)
  Default minimum time between advertisement runs is 0 seconds

 For address family: IPv6 Unicast
  BGP table version 19, neighbor version 1/19
  Output queue size : 0
```

```
     Index 0, Advertise bit 0
     Community attribute sent to this neighbor
     Sending Prefix & Label
     Slow-peer detection is disabled
! Output omitted for brevity
```

```
PE2 - IOS XR
RP/0/0/CPU0:PE2# show bgp ipv6 labeled-unicast neighbors 192.168.5.5
BGP neighbor is 192.168.5.5
 Remote AS 100, local AS 100, internal link
 Remote router ID 192.168.5.5
  BGP state = Established, up for 02:26:28
! Output omitted for brevity
  Non-stop routing is enabled
  Multi-protocol capability received
  Neighbor capabilities:
    Route refresh: advertised (old + new) and received (old + new)
    Graceful Restart (GR Awareness): advertised
    4-byte AS: advertised and received
    Address family IPv6 Labeled-unicast: advertised and received
  Received 170 messages, 0 notifications, 0 in queue
  Sent 150 messages, 0 notifications, 0 in queue
  Minimum time between advertisement runs is 0 secs
. . .
```

```
PE3 - NX-OS
PE3# show bgp ipv6 labeled-unicast neighbors 192.168.5.5
BGP neighbor is 192.168.5.5,  remote AS 100, ibgp link,  Peer index 1
  BGP version 4, remote router ID 192.168.5.5
! Output omitted for brevity
  Neighbor capabilities:
  Dynamic capability: advertised (mp, refresh, gr)
  Dynamic capability (old): advertised
  Route refresh capability (new): advertised received
  Route refresh capability (old): advertised received
  4-Byte AS capability: advertised received
  Address family IPv6 Unicast: received
  Address family IPv6 Label Unicast: advertised received
  Graceful Restart capability: advertised
. . .
```

After the capability has been confirmed, verify that the IPv6 BGP labels are being received on each of the 6PE routers. Example 12-14 illustrates the verification of the local BGP label allocation and received BGP labels information using the command **show bgp ipv6 unicast labels**. The In Label signifies the local allocated label and the Out Label signifies the label received from the remote peer. PE5 allocates label 23 for the prefix 2001:DB8::7/128, and this is verified on all the remote 6PE routers, and vice versa.

Example 12-14 *Verifying IPv6 BGP Labels*

```
IOS
PE1# show bgp ipv6 unicast labels
   Network          Next Hop       In label/Out label
   2001:DB8::6/128  2001:DB8:0:16::6
                                  23/nolabel
   2001:DB8::7/128  ::FFFF:192.168.5.5
                                  nolabel/23
```

```
IOS XR
RP/0/0/CPU0:PE2# show bgp ipv6 unicast labels
! Output omitted for brevity
   Network          Next Hop       Rcvd Label     Local Label
*> 2001:db8::6/128  2001:db8:0:26::6
                                  nolabel         24007
*>i2001:db8::7/128  192.168.5.5    23             nolabel
```

```
NX-OS
PE3# show bgp ipv6 unicast labels
! Output omitted for brevity
   Network          Next Hop       In label/Out label
*>e2001:db8::6/128  2001:db8:0:36::6
                                  27/nolabel (default)
*>i2001:db8::7/128  ::ffff:192.168.5.5
                                  nolabel/23
```

```
IOS
PE5# show bgp ipv6 unicast labels
   Network          Next Hop       In label/Out label
   2001:DB8::6/128  ::FFFF:192.168.3.3
                                  nolabel/27
                    ::FFFF:192.168.1.1
                                  nolabel/23
                    ::FFFF:192.168.2.2
                                  nolabel/24007
   2001:DB8::7/128  2001:DB8:0:57::7
                                  23/nolabel
```

Notice the next-hop for the remote prefixes on each 6PE router. Except on the IOS XR router, all the routers show the next-hop as the IPv4 mapped IPv6 address. But because the labels are exchanged between the 6PE routers, the reachability is present without even modifying the next-hop to a valid IPv4 address.

Even though the prefixes in the BGP table may show IPv4 mapped IPv6 address, the IPv6 RIB shows the next-hop as the peering loopback IP of the remote 6PE router. Based on the IPv4 next-hop, the packets are label switched in the core. This is verified based on the CEF table output. The command **show ipv6 cef** *ipv6-address* [**detail**] displays the IPv6 CEF entry, which shows the outgoing interface as well as the MPLS labels, which are used for forwarding the packets. Example 12-15 examines the output of the IPv6 routing table and the CEF table thereof. Notice that all three 6PE routers show the MPLS label value of 23, which they learned from the remote 6PE router PE5. The IGP label is the same on all three nodes because they all connect to the RR-P router, which allocated an IGP label of 19 for the 192.168.5.5/32 address.

Example 12-15 *IPv6 Routing Table and CEF Entry on 6PE*

```
IOS
PE1# show ipv6 route 2001:db8::7/128
Routing entry for 2001:DB8::7/128
  Known via "bgp 100", distance 200, metric 0, type internal
  Route count is 1/1, share count 0
  Routing paths:
    192.168.5.5%default indirectly connected
      MPLS label: 23
      Last updated 1d07h ago

PE1# show ipv6 cef 2001:db8::7/128 detail
2001:DB8::7/128, epoch 0, flags [rib defined all labels]
  recursive via 192.168.5.5 label 23
    nexthop 10.1.14.4 GigabitEthernet0/2 label 19
```

```
IOS XR
RP/0/0/CPU0:PE2# show route ipv6 2001:db8::7/128
Routing entry for 2001:db8::7/128
  Known via "bgp 100", distance 200, metric 0
  Tag 300, type internal
  Installed Jan 31 04:50:36.358 for 1d10h
  Routing Descriptor Blocks
    ::ffff:192.168.5.5, from ::ffff:192.168.5.5
      Nexthop in Vrf: "default", Table: "default", IPv4 Unicast, Table Id:
        0xe0000000
      Route metric is 0
  No advertising protos.
```

```
RP/0/0/CPU0:PE2# show cef ipv6 2001:db8::7/128 detail
! Output omitted for brevity
  via ::ffff:192.168.5.5, 3 dependencies, recursive [flags 0x6000]
    path-idx 0 NHID 0x0 [0xa1759050 0x0]
    recursion-via-/128
    next hop VRF - 'default', table - 0xe0000000
    next hop ::ffff:192.168.5.5 via ::ffff:192.168.5.5:0
      next hop 10.1.24.4/32 Gi0/0/0/1    labels imposed {19 23}


    Load distribution: 0 (refcount 1)


    Hash  OK  Interface              Address
    0     Y   Unknown                ::ffff:192.168.5.5:0
```

```
NX-OS
PE3# show ipv6 route 2001:db8::7/128 detail
2001:db8::7/128, ubest/mbest: 1/0
      cand ubest/mbest: 1/0, ufdm in/update: 1/0
  *via ::ffff:192.168.5.5%default:IPv4, [200/0], 1d07h, bgp-100, internal, tag
 300  (mpls)
        client-specific data: 1
        recursive next hop: ::ffff:192.168.5.5/128
        extended route information: BGP origin AS 300 BGP peer AS 300
        MPLS[0]: Label=23 E=0 TTL=0 S=0
```

Use the command **show mpls forwarding** to view the IGP label and the IPv6 prefix label. Example 12-16 demonstrates the verification of the BGP label and the IGP label. The command also shows the information of the outgoing interface, which is the core facing interface.

Example 12-16 *MPLS Forwarding Table Output*

```
PE1# show mpls forwarding-table 2001:db8::7/128 detail
Local     Outgoing    Prefix          Bytes Label   Outgoing     Next Hop
Label     Label       or Tunnel Id    Switched      interface
None      23          2001:DB8::7/128 0             Gi0/2        10.1.14.4
        MAC/Encaps=14/22, MRU=1496, Label Stack{19 23}
        FA163E8A3E23FA163EB62BA28847 0001300000017000
        No output feature configured


PE1# show mpls forwarding-table 192.168.5.5
Local     Outgoing    Prefix          Bytes Label   Outgoing     Next Hop
Label     Label       or Tunnel Id    Switched      interface
21        19          192.168.5.5/32  0             Gi0/2        10.1.14.4
```

The IPv6 addresses are only enabled on the service provider edge routers; the **traceroute** tool is used to verify the path for the IPv6 packet. The IPv4-only nodes in the path display the IPv4 mapped IPv6 address. Note that these addresses are used to represent the address of IPv4-only nodes as an IPv6 address.

Example 12-17 demonstrates the use of traceroute to trace the path for the IPv6 packet from CE2 to CE1. The first hop in the output is the PE router with IPv6 address. The next-hop is the RR-P router, which is an IPv4-only node and thus displays the IPv4 mapped IPv6 address.

Example 12-17   *IPv6 Traceroute*

```
CE2# traceroute
Protocol [ip]: ipv6
Target IPv6 address: 2001:db8::6
Source address: 2001:db8::7
Insert source routing header? [no]:
Numeric display? [no]:
Timeout in seconds [3]:
Probe count [3]:
Minimum Time to Live [1]:
Maximum Time to Live [30]:
Priority [0]:
Port Number [0]:
Type escape sequence to abort.
Tracing the route to 2001:DB8::6

  1 2001:DB8:0:57::5 13 msec 3 msec 3 msec
  2 ::FFFF:10.1.45.4 17 msec 18 msec
  3 2001:DB8:0:16::1 [MPLS: Label 23 Exp 0] 5 msec 6 msec 7 msec
  4 2001:DB8:0:16::6 13 msec 17 msec 13 msec
```

Note   If an IPv4-only node does not have IPv6 software at all, it cannot understand the IPv6 packet and hence cannot generate the ICMPv6 message. In that case, the P router drops the packet. This results in an output of "* * *" in the traceroute for that P router.

IPv6 VPN Provider Edge (6VPE)

With the introduction of RFC 4659, MPLS VPNs are extended to IPv6 VPN. IPv6 VPN Provider Edge (6VPE) routers provide the capability of providing IPv6 VPN services to customers over an IPv4 MPLS infrastructure.

Each IPv6 VPN has its own separate address space and is maintained in a separate routing table using virtual routing and forwarding (VRF). The VPN routes are exchanged across different sites via a new VPN-IPv6 or VPNV6 address-family. The VPNv6 address-family peering has the capability code 1 (multiprotocol BGP), AFI=2 (for IPv6), and SAFI=128 (MPLS labeled VPN-IPv6).

Like IPv4 MPLS Layer 3 VPNs, a VPNv6 route is made unique by attaching a route-distinguisher (RD) value before the prefix. The labeled VPN-IPv6 MP_REACH_NLRI itself is encoded as specified in [MPLS-BGP]—RFC 3107, which defines how label information is carried in BGP. The prefix belongs to the VPN-IPv6 address-family, or a VPNv6 route is a 24-byte address consisting of 8 bytes for RD followed by an IPv6 address, which is 16 bytes.

Figure 12-7 shows the 6VPE deployment architecture. In this topology, the PE routers (6VPE) provide both IPv4 and IPv6 VPN services to the customers. The service provider core network still runs on IPv4-MPLS, which means the service providers do not need to upgrade their core infrastructure but only make changes to the edge routers.

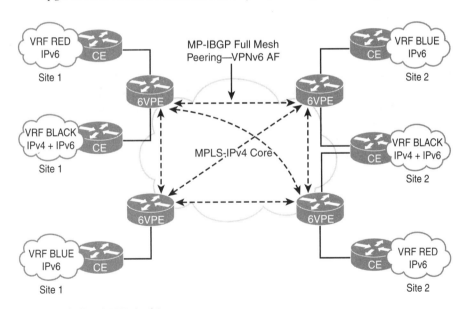

Figure 12-7 *6VPE Architecture*

6VPE routers perform the following functions:

- Participate in IPv4 IGP to establish internal reachability inside the MPLS cloud.

- Form LDP peering within the IPv4 core network for binding labels.

- Run MP-BGP4 to advertise IPv6 reachability and distribute VPN-IPv6 labels among them. The labels can be distributed as follows:

    - **Per-Prefix label:** The 6VPE node distributes labels for each IPv6 prefix learned via the VRF interfaces.

    - **Per-CE label:** The 6VPE node aggregates all the routes learned from one particular CE and advertises one label for them.

    - **Per-VRF label:** The 6VPE node advertises one label for all the IPv6 prefixes learned via the VRF interfaces.

> **Note**   The MP-IBGP peering between the 6VPE devices can be either full meshed or all the 6VPEs can exchange the relevant information via peering with RR over the VPNv6 address-family.

IPv6-Aware VRF

A service provider can provide both IPv4 as well as IPv6 VPN services to a customer in a single VRF. The older method of configuring VRF on Cisco IOS using the command **ip vrf** *vrf-name* only allows for IPv4-only VPNs. To allow a VRF to support both IPv4 as well as IPv6 VPN, use the command **vrf definition** *vrf-name*. Both IOS XR and NX-OS support both IPv4, as well as IPv6 address families under the VRFs. Example 12-18 illustrates the configuration of IPv6-capable VRF on all three platforms.

Example 12-18   *IPv6-Aware VRF Configuration*

```
PE1 - IOS
vrf definition red
 rd 100:1
 !
 address-family ipv4
  route-target export 100:1
  route-target import 100:1
 exit-address-family
 !
 address-family ipv6
  route-target export 100:1
  route-target import 100:1
 exit-address-family

PE2 - IOS XR
vrf red
 address-family ipv4 unicast
  import route-target
   100:1
  !
```

```
    export route-target
     100:1
    !
address-family ipv6 unicast
    import route-target
     100:1
    !
    export route-target
     100:1
```

```
PE3 - NX-OS
vrf context red
    rd 100:1
    address-family ipv4 unicast
        route-target import 100:1
        route-target export 100:1
    address-family ipv6 unicast
        route-target import 100:1
        route-target export 100:1
```

Note   Cisco IOS provides a migration command for conversion of VPNv4 to multiprotocol VRF using the command **vrf upgrade-cli multi-af-mode vrf** *vrf-name*. This command forces migration from old CLI for IPv4-only capable VRF to new Multi-AF capable VRF CLI.

6VPE Next-Hop

The next important concept to understand is the BGP next-hop with IPv6-VPN. MP-BGP currently has the constraint that the BGP Next-Hop field in the MP_REACH_NLRI attribute needs to be of the same address-family as the NLRI encoded in the MP_REACH_NLRI attribute. In case of VPN-IPv6 NLRI advertisement, this means that the BGP Next-Hop field must belong to the VPN-IPv6 address-family.

Because 6VPE feature supports IPv6 VPN service over an IPv4 backbone, the BGP Next-Hop field may be encoded (when peering over IPv4-MPLS) with a VPN-IPv6 prefix; that is, a VPNv6 prefix.

- RD is set to zero.

- The 16-byte IPv6 address is encoded as an IPv4-mapped IPv6 address, with the IPv4 address being the address of the advertising PE.

Note   IPv6 is also capable of peering over the IPv6 backbone. In such a case, the BGP next-hop is an RD followed with a plain IPv6 address.

The notation RD:IPv4-prefix, used for VPNv4 prefixes, could not be used for VPNv6 prefixes because it conflicts with the IPv6 prefix notation. For instance, 100:1:2001::/64 could be interpreted as an IPv6 prefix or as an VPNv6 prefix with a RD of 100:1. For that reason, VPNv6 prefixes use the notation [*RD*]*ipv6-address*. In this case, it would be [100:1]2001::/64.

Route Target

Each VRF is associated with Route Target (RT) import and export rules. Like IPv4 VPNs, 6VPE will also use the RT import and export rules in the following manner:

- Associated with each VRF is an export RT list. When a VPN route is exported into BGP and advertised to other PEs in MP-IBGP, all the RTs in the export RT list of the corresponding VRF are included in the BGP advertisement.

- Associated with each VRF is an import RT list. This list defines the values that should be matched against to decide whether a route is eligible to be imported into that VRF. The import rule is that all routes tagged with at least one RT associated with a given VRF will be imported into that VRF. Ingress PE performs such filtering during route import.

Unless it is a PE also acting as an RR, a PE router discards any VPNv6 route whose RT does not match any of the import RTs on any of the configured VRFs on the router. This behavior acts as an automatic inbound route filtering for both IPv4 as well as IPv6 VPNs.

When the policy of a PE router changes, such as a new VRF is added or a new import RT is added to an existing VRF, the PE router must acquire the routes it may previously have discarded. This is done using a BGP's Route Refresh capability described in RFC 2918. Note that ROUTE-REFRESH messages defined in RFC 2918 have an AFI value of 2 and a SAFI value of 128 for requesting refresh for VPNv6 routes. The 6VPE automatically triggers a ROUTE-REFRESH request on relevant PE changes.

Note   A PE providing both IPv4 as well as IPv6 VPN services as part of same VRF allows for sharing the same as well as a distinct RT between IPv4 and an IPv6 address-family under VRF.

6VPE Control Plane

Examine the 6VPE Control-Plane flow as shown in Figure 12-8. CE1 is running IPv6 services. The PE routers PE1 and PE5 may provide both IPv4 as well as IPv6 VPN services. The core facing interfaces are IPv4 and MPLS enabled. IPv6 is not enabled in the

MPLS core network. The 6VPE routers have a common peering with the RR router RR-P. The customer routers (CE1 and CE2) are part of IPv6 VRF routing table on the 6VPE and not the global IPv6 routing table as in the case of 6PE deployment.

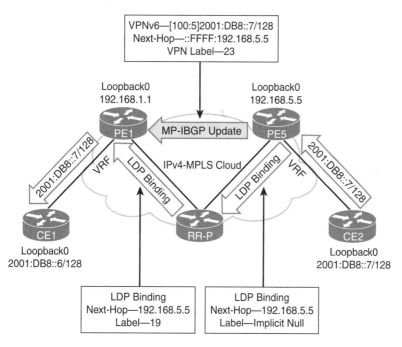

Figure 12-8   *6VPE Control Plane*

Figure 12-8 shows the process for signaling the control plane as listed in the following steps:

Step 1.   The 6VPE router learned a prefix 2001:DB8::7/128 from the CE2 router in the VRF. The 6VPE router PE5 then assigns a VPNv6 label for the prefix and advertises it toward the RR-P router, which is then replicated to the relevant 6VPE routers with valid import RT statements under the VRF.

Step 2.   The egress 6VPE router PE5 assigns the next-hop value for the VPNv6 prefix. The Next-Hop field for the VPNv6 prefix is set to the egress PE IPv4 address, which is typically the VPNv6 peering loopback IP.

Step 3.   In the IPv4-MPLS core, PE5 advertises an implicit-null or POP label (label value 3) toward the RR-P router. The RR-P router updates its LFIB table with this information and accordingly updates the FIB. The implicit-null label is added on top of the VPNv6 label for the prefix 2001:DB8::7/128.

Step 4.   The RR-P router then allocates a label value of 19, which is then swapped with the POP label and propagated toward the Ingress PE router. If RR router does not lie in the data or forwarding path of the MPLS VPN traffic, then RR just reflects the information received from a PE router to other PE routers.

Step 5.   On receiving an update from the RR router, the 6VPE router verifies which VRF has imported the advertised RT value of the egress 6VPE router. Based on the lookup, the VPNv6 prefix is then installed in the respective IPv6 VRF routing table and then downloaded to the FIB. Before installing the IPv6 prefix into the Cisco Express Forwarding (CEF) table, the 6VPE router resolves the next-hop label information for the next-hop value, which is in the ::ffff.[ip-address] format.

Step 6.   After the next-hop is resolved, CEF will install a label stack for the learned prefix where the outer label will be LDP label (**19**) learned via RR-P router and the inner VPN label is the one learned from BGP (**23**). It is important to note that the CEF table being referenced here is the VRF CEF table and not the global CEF table.

6VPE Data Plane

Based on the signaled 6VPE control-plane information, the data plane functions and forwards the traffic across the MPLS core. Figure 12-9 explains the IPv6 packet forwarding from the CE1 to the CE2 router across the MPLS IPv4 core network.

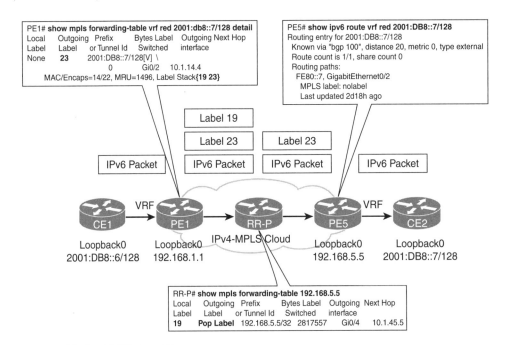

Figure 12-9   *6VPE Data Plane*

The 6VPE data plane operations shown in Figure 12-8 are also explained in the following steps:

Step 1.   Router PE1 receives an IPv6 packet from CE1 for the destination 2001:DB8::7/128.

Step 2.   On receiving the packet, PE1 performs a lookup in the VRF CEF table, which results in label stack (two labels) imposition: the BGP label 23 and the IGP label 19. After the labels are imposed on the packet, the packet is forwarded to the upstream router RR-P.

Step 3.   The RR-P router receives the labeled packet and performs an LFIB lookup on the top label, which is the IGP label. Because the next-hop is the PE router, it POPs the top label and forwards a single label packet (VPN label) to PE5.

Step 4.   On PE5, the label lookup in ingress VRF CEF yields egress interface toward CE2. The VPN label is disposed of and just the IPv6 packet is forwarded to the CE2 router.

6VPE Configuration

To understand the 6VPE deployment, examine the same topology as shown in Figure 12-1. The PE routers are now acting as 6VPE routers and are running all the services that are run on a 6VPE node. Example 12-19 illustrates the 6VPE configuration on all three 6VPE routers running different OSs. The MPLS and IPv4 core configuration remains the same as Example 12-12. Notice that the VRF on Cisco IOS is being attached to an interface using the **vrf forwarding** *vrf-name* command rather than **ip vrf forwarding** *vrf-name* command. This new command is used when the **vrf definition** command is being used to configure Multi-AF VRF.

Example 12-19   *6VPE Configuration*

```
PE1 - IOS
interface GigabitEthernet0/1
 vrf forwarding red
 ipv6 address FE80::1 link-local
 ipv6 address 2001:DB8:0:16::1/64
!
router bgp 100
 bgp router-id 192.168.1.1
 bgp log-neighbor-changes
 no bgp default ipv4-unicast
 neighbor 192.168.4.4 remote-as 100
 neighbor 192.168.4.4 update-source Loopback0
```

```
!
address-family vpnv6
  neighbor 192.168.4.4 activate
  neighbor 192.168.4.4 send-community extended
  neighbor 192.168.4.4 next-hop-self
 exit-address-family
 !
address-family ipv6 vrf red
  neighbor 2001:DB8:0:16::6 remote-as 200
  neighbor 2001:DB8:0:16::6 activate
 exit-address-family
```

```
PE2 - IOS XR
interface GigabitEthernet0/0/0/0
 vrf red
 ipv6 address fe80::2 link-local
 ipv6 address 2001:db8:0:26::2/64
!
router bgp 100
 bgp router-id 192.168.2.2
 address-family vpnv6 unicast
 !
 neighbor 192.168.4.4
  remote-as 100
  update-source Loopback0
  address-family vpnv6 unicast
   next-hop-self
  !
 !
vrf red
  rd 100:1
  address-family ipv6 unicast
  !
  neighbor 2001:db8:0:26::6
   remote-as 200
   address-family ipv6 unicast
    route-policy pass in
    route-policy pass out
```

```
PE3 - NX-OS
interface Ethernet2/1
  no switchport
  mac-address 0000.0101.002f
  vrf member red
```

```
  ipv6 address 2001:db8:0:36::3/64
!
router bgp 100
  router-id 192.168.3.3
  address-family ipv4 unicast
  address-family vpnv6 unicast
  neighbor 192.168.4.4
    remote-as 100
    update-source loopback0
    address-family vpnv6 unicast
      next-hop-self
  vrf red
    address-family ipv6 unicast
    neighbor 2001:db8:0:36::6
      remote-as 200
      address-family ipv6 unicast
```

The route reflector router RR-P only reflects the VPN prefixes to the other PE routers.

6VPE Control-Plane Verification

The first step of control-plane verification in 6VPE begins on the egress 6VPE router, which locally learns the destination IPv6 prefix in a VRF. Use the command **show ipv6 route vrf** *vrf-name ipv6-address* to verify whether the route is present in the VRF routing table. Example 12-20 demonstrates the verification of the IPv6 route present in the VRF routing table. Note that both the source and the destination CE route are present in the VRF routing table. 2001:DB8::6/128 is learned from CE1, whereas the 2001:DB8::7/128 is locally learned from the CE2 router. There may be multiple paths from which the prefix might be learned, but by default, only the best routes get installed in the RIB.

Example 12-20 *Verifying IPv6 Route in VRF Routing Table*

```
PE5# show ipv6 route vrf red
! Output omitted for brevity
B   2001:DB8::6/128 [200/0]
     via 192.168.1.1%default, indirectly connected
B   2001:DB8::7/128 [20/0]
     via FE80::7, GigabitEthernet0/2
```

After the route is verified to be present in the VRF V6-RIB, verify the prefix in the BGP VPNv6 table as well. When verifying the prefix present in the VPN table, also verify the VPN-IPv6 label allocated by the 6VPE router. On Cisco IOS and NX-OS, use the command **show bgp vpnv6 unicast vrf** *vrf-name ipv6-address* or use **show bgp vrf** *vrf-name* **vpnv6 unicast** *ipv6-address* to verify the prefix and the label allocated by the 6VPE router. Both of these commands are not supported on IOS XR. Use the same command **show bgp vpnv6 unicast vrf** *vrf-name ipv6-address* to verify the prefix and the label information on IOS XR.

Examine the output as displayed in Example 12-21. In this example, the prefix
2001:DB8::7/128 is a locally learned VPN-IPv6 prefix. Notice the format of the prefix
in the VPN-IPv6 table. Its in the format [RD]IPv6-Address. This is because the prefix is
learned from an IPv6-enabled peer. The 6VPE router PE5 allocates a label value of 23 for
the locally learned prefix.

Example 12-21   *Verifying the CE Prefix in VPNv6 Table*

```
PE5# show bgp vpnv6 unicast vrf red 2001:db8::7/128
BGP routing table entry for [100:5]2001:DB8::7/128, version 38
Paths: (1 available, best #1, table red)
  Advertised to update-groups:
     2
  Refresh Epoch 1
  300
    2001:DB8:0:57::7 (FE80::7) (via vrf red) from 2001:DB8:0:57::7 (192.168.7.7)
      Origin IGP, metric 0, localpref 100, valid, external, best
      Extended Community: RT:100:1
      mpls labels in/out 23/nolabel
      rx pathid: 0, tx pathid: 0x0
```

The next step is to verify that there is VPNv6 neighborship from the 6VPE router toward
the RR or the remote 6VPE router. If there is no RR in the network, a full mesh neighbor
relationship between all the 6VPE routers is required. Use the command **show bgp vpnv6
unicast all summary** on Cisco IOS or use **show bgp vpnv6 unicast summary** on IOS
XR and NX-OS platforms to verify the VPNv6 neighbor relationship.

After the peering is established, the 6VPE routers exchange the VPN prefixes and
labels between each other. Example 12-22 displays the output of the same command as
shown in Example 12-21 to verify the prefixes present in the remote 6VPE router. Notice
that all three 6VPE routers have the same label 23 as the received label or out label.
Because the RD on the advertising 6VPE router is 100:5, and on the receiving side it is
100:1, the prefix is viewed under two RDs on the receiving 6VPE routers.

Example 12-22   *Verifying VPNv6 Prefix on Ingress 6VPE*

```
PE1 - IOS
PE1# show bgp vpnv6 unicast vrf red 2001:db8::7/128
BGP routing table entry for [100:1]2001:DB8::7/128, version 7
Paths: (1 available, best #1, table red)
  Advertised to update-groups:
     1
  Refresh Epoch 1
  300, imported path from [100:5]2001:DB8::7/128 (global)
    ::FFFF:192.168.5.5 (metric 3) (via default) from 192.168.4.4 (192.168.4.4)
```

```
        Origin IGP, metric 0, localpref 100, valid, internal, best
        Extended Community: RT:100:1
        Originator: 192.168.5.5, Cluster list: 192.168.4.4
        mpls labels in/out nolabel/23
        rx pathid: 0, tx pathid: 0x0
```

```
PE2 - IOS XR
RP/0/0/CPU0:PE2# show bgp vpnv6 unicast vrf red 2001:db8::7/128
BGP routing table entry for 2001:db8::7/128, Route Distinguisher: 100:1
Versions:
  Process            bRIB/RIB   SendTblVer
  Speaker                 5            5
Last Modified: Feb  4 22:46:29.408 for 1d05h
Paths: (1 available, best #1)
  Not advertised to any peer
  Path #1: Received by speaker 0
  Not advertised to any peer
  300
    192.168.5.5 (metric 3) from 192.168.4.4 (192.168.5.5)
      Received Label 23
      Origin IGP, metric 0, localpref 100, valid, internal, best, group-best,
import-candidate, imported
      Received Path ID 0, Local Path ID 1, version 5
      Extended community: RT:100:1
      Originator: 192.168.5.5, Cluster list: 192.168.4.4
      Source VRF: default, Source Route Distinguisher: 100:5
```

```
PE3 - NX-OS
PE3# show bgp vrf red vpnv6 unicast 2001:db8::7/128
BGP routing table information for VRF default, address family VPNv6 Unicast
Route Distinguisher: 100:1      (VRF red)
BGP routing table entry for 2001:db8::7/128, version 6
Paths: (1 available, best #1)
Flags: (0x08001a) on xmit-list, is in u6rib, is best u6rib route
  vpn: version 8, (0x100002) on xmit-list

  Advertised path-id 1, VPN AF advertised path-id 1
  Path type: internal, path is valid, is best path
          Imported from 100:5:2001:db8::7/128
  AS-Path: 300 , path sourced external to AS
    ::ffff:192.168.5.5 (metric 42) from 192.168.4.4 (192.168.4.4)
      Origin IGP, MED 0, localpref 100, weight 0
      Received label 23
```

```
    Extcommunity:
          RT:100:1
      Originator: 192.168.5.5 Cluster list: 192.168.4.4


  VRF advertise information:
  Path-id 1 advertised to peers:
    2001:db8:0:36::6


  VPN AF advertise information:
  Path-id 1 not advertised to any peer
```

In most of the deployments, the role of RRs is not extended to PE and therefore does not have any VRFs configured. The VPNv6 prefixes can be verified on the RR using the RD values using the command **show bgp vpnv6 unicast rd** *asn:nn ipv6-address*.

The VPN labels are verified by using the command **show bgp vpnv6 unicast vrf** *vrf-name* **labels** or by using the command **show mpls forwarding vrf** *vrf-name ipv6-address*. The **show mpls forwarding** command is not available for verifying a specific prefix on IOS XR; thus the command **show bgp vpnv6 unicast vrf** *vrf-name* **labels** can be used. Example 12-23 displays both the locally allocated and remotely learned VPN labels.

Example 12-23 *Verifying VPN Labels*

```
IOS
PE1# show mpls forwarding-table vrf red 2001:db8::7/128
Local      Outgoing   Prefix          Bytes Label   Outgoing   Next Hop
Label      Label      or Tunnel Id    Switched      interface
None       23         2001:DB8::7/128[V]    \
                                      0             Gi0/2      10.1.14.4


PE1# show bgp vpnv6 unicast vrf red labels
   Network         Next Hop      In label/Out label
Route Distinguisher: 100:1 (red)
   2001:DB8::6/128 2001:DB8:0:16::6
                                  23/nolabel
   2001:DB8::7/128 ::FFFF:192.168.5.5
                                  nolabel/23


IOS XR
RP/0/0/CPU0:PE2# show bgp vpnv6 unicast vrf red labels
! Output omitted for brevity
Status codes: s suppressed, d damped, h history, * valid, > best
              i - internal, r RIB-failure, S stale, N Nexthop-discard
```

```
Origin codes: i - IGP, e - EGP, ? - incomplete
   Network              Next Hop        Rcvd Label      Local Label
Route Distinguisher: 100:1 (default for vrf red)
*  i2001:db8::6/128    192.168.1.1     23              24008
*>                     2001:db8:0:26::6
                                       nolabel         24008
*>i2001:db8::7/128     192.168.5.5     23              nolabel
```

```
NX-OS
PE3# show bgp vpnv6 unicast labels
! Output omitted for brevity
   Network              Next Hop          In label/Out label
Route Distinguisher: 100:1    (VRF red)
*>e2001:db8::6/128     2001:db8:0:36::6
                                          28/nolabel (red)
*>i2001:db8::7/128     ::ffff:192.168.5.5
                                          nolabel/23

Route Distinguisher: 100:5
*>i2001:db8::7/128     ::ffff:192.168.5.5
                                          nolabel/23
```

Note The control-plane verification of the MPLS core network is same as shown in the 6PE section.

6VPE Data Plane Verification

From the SP's perspective, the 6VPE control-plane verification begins from the ingress 6VPE routers. In the topology shown in Figure 12-1, the ingress 6VPE routers are PE1, PE2, and PE3. After the routes are received from the remote 6VPE router PE5, the best route is installed in the RIB, which then gets installed in the FIB—that is, the CEF table or on platforms that support non-CEF–based hardware-based forwarding such as Nexus. The CEF table is downloaded into the hardware, which then programs the ASICs to perform the packet forwarding.

When a packet comes from the CE1 router destined toward 2001:DB8::7/128, the 6PE router looks at the CEF table for the information. The CEF table contains the information on the outgoing interface and the label stack information. Examine the CEF table on the 6VPE routers as shown in Example 12-24. Notice that in this output, 23 is the VPNv6 label received from PE5, and label 19 is the IGP label received from router RR-P. Recall that the router RR-P allocated a local label of 19 for the destination 192.168.5.5/32.

Example 12-24 *6VPE CEF Table*

```
PE1# show ipv6 cef vrf red 2001:db8::7/128 detail
2001:DB8::7/128, epoch 0, flags [rib defined all labels]
  recursive via 192.168.5.5 label 23
    nexthop 10.1.14.4 GigabitEthernet0/2 label 19
```

Because the IOS XR platform maintains the CEF table on the ingress as well as the egress line cards, the CEF table is verified both on the RP as well as the ingress and egress line cards on the router. Use the command **show cef vrf** *vrf-name* **ipv6** *ipv6-address* **hardware** [**ingress** | **egress**] [**detail**] [**location** *location-id*], where the ingress or egress option is specified when the hardware entry is looked up on the ingress or the egress line card. The location option is useful when the command needs to be verified on a particular line card. If not specified, the command is executed on the active route processor on the router. Example 12-25 demonstrates the verification of hardware forwarding and CEF information on the IOS XR 6VPE router. Notice that in the hardware CEF entry output, the next-hop VRF is seen as the default. The table id *0xe0000000* represents the global (default) routing table.

Example 12-25 *6VPE Forwarding Information on IOS XR*

```
RP/0/0/CPU0:PE2# show cef vrf red ipv6 2001:db8::7/128
2001:db8::7/128, version 7, internal 0x5000001 0x0 (ptr 0xa140c5f4) [1],
 0x0 (0x0), 0x208 (0xa14db230)
 Updated Feb  4 22:46:29.731
 Prefix Len 128, traffic index 0, precedence n/a, priority 3
   via ::ffff:192.168.5.5, 3 dependencies, recursive [flags 0x6000]
     path-idx 0 NHID 0x0 [0xa176b0bc 0x0]
     recursion-via-/128
     next hop VRF - 'default', table - 0xe0000000
     next hop ::ffff:192.168.5.5 via ::ffff:192.168.5.5:0
      next hop 10.1.24.4/32 Gi0/0/0/1    labels imposed {19 23}


! Verify the Ingress Hardware Programming
RP/0/0/CPU0:PE2# show cef vrf red ipv6 2001:db8::7/128 hard ing det loc 0/0/CPU0
Sat Feb  6 14:32:56.241 UTC
2001:db8::7/128, version 7, internal 0x5000001 0x0 (ptr 0xa140c5f4) [1],
 0x0 (0x0), 0x208 (0xa14db230)
 Updated Feb  4 22:46:29.730
 Prefix Len 128, traffic index 0, precedence n/a, priority 3
  gateway array (0xa12a05a0) reference count 1, flags 0x4038, source rib (7),
 0 backups
              [1 type 1 flags 0x48089 (0xa14f5398) ext 0x0 (0x0)]
```

```
 LW-LDI[type=0, refc=0, ptr=0x0, sh-ldi=0x0]
 gateway array update type-time 1 Feb  4 22:46:29.730
LDI Update time Feb  4 22:46:29.730
  via ::ffff:192.168.5.5, 3 dependencies, recursive [flags 0x6000]
   path-idx 0 NHID 0x0 [0xa176b0bc 0x0]
   recursion-via-/128
   next hop VRF - 'default', table - 0xe0000000
   next hop ::ffff:192.168.5.5 via ::ffff:192.168.5.5:0
    next hop 10.1.24.4/32 Gi0/0/0/1    labels imposed {19 23}
Ingress platform showdata is not available.



   Load distribution: 0 (refcount 1)


   Hash  OK  Interface               Address
   0     Y   Unknown                 ::ffff:192.168.5.5:0

! Verify the Egress Hardware Programming
RP/0/0/CPU0:PE2# show cef vrf red ipv6 2001:db8::7/128 hard egr det loc 0/0/CPU0
2001:db8::7/128, version 7, internal 0x5000001 0x0 (ptr 0xa140c5f4) [1],
 0x0 (0x0), 0x208 (0xa14db230)
 Updated Feb  4 22:46:29.730
 Prefix Len 128, traffic index 0, precedence n/a, priority 3
  gateway array (0xa12a05a0) reference count 1, flags 0x4038, source rib (7),
 0 backups
                [1 type 1 flags 0x48089 (0xa14f5398) ext 0x0 (0x0)]
  LW-LDI[type=0, refc=0, ptr=0x0, sh-ldi=0x0]
  gateway array update type-time 1 Feb  4 22:46:29.730
 LDI Update time Feb  4 22:46:29.730
   via ::ffff:192.168.5.5, 3 dependencies, recursive [flags 0x6000]
    path-idx 0 NHID 0x0 [0xa176b0bc 0x0]
    recursion-via-/128
    next hop VRF - 'default', table - 0xe0000000
    next hop ::ffff:192.168.5.5 via ::ffff:192.168.5.5:0
     next hop 10.1.24.4/32 Gi0/0/0/1    labels imposed {19 23}
Egress platform showdata is not available.



   Load distribution: 0 (refcount 1)


   Hash  OK  Interface               Address
   0     Y   Unknown                 ::ffff:192.168.5.5:0
```

The traffic forwarding counters are verified using the **show mpls forwarding** command by looking at the Packets Switched or Bytes Switched counters, although it is hard to say that the interface is switching the correct packets or not, because in real deployments, there could be multiple VRFs that are routing across the same outgoing interface toward the core. Use the command **show mpls forwarding labels** *label-value* **hardware** [**ingress** | **egress**] [**location** *location-id*] to view the hardware forwarding counters on an IOS XR router.

Another method to verify the traffic forwarding counters is by using the command **show interface** *interface-name* **accounting**. This command displays the various protocols that are running on an interface and their respective input and output counters. Multiple iterations of the command should be collected while investigating traffic-forwarding issues on IOS XR.

Example 12-26 illustrates the use of the **show interface accounting** command to verify the forwarding counters. Notice the MPLS counters on the interface before and after the ping test is performed. Because five pings were successful, the input and output packets were increase by 5 each (5 for echo sent on output counters and 5 for echo-reply received on input counters). The counters are incrementing for MPLS because the VPNv6 traffic in the core is viewable only as MPLS traffic and not as regular IPv4 or IPv6 unicast traffic.

Example 12-26 *Verifying Interface Accounting Statistics*

```
RP/0/0/CPU0:PE2# show interface gigabitethernet0/0/0/1 accounting
GigabitEthernet0/0/0/1
  Protocol            Pkts In        Chars In      Pkts Out      Chars Out
  IPV4_UNICAST         261333       20337753         46929        2305821
  IPV6_UNICAST          21017        2062274         20995        1964348
  MPLS                     10           1180         14426         968553
  ARP                      84           5040            84           3528
  IPV6_ND               13296        1193736         10306         742016
```

```
RP/0/0/CPU0:PE2# ping vrf red 2001:db8::7
Type escape sequence to abort.
Sending 5, 100-byte ICMP Echos to 2001:db8::7, timeout is 2 seconds:
!!!!!
Success rate is 100 percent (5/5), round-trip min/avg/max = 9/15/19 ms
```

```
RP/0/0/CPU0:PE2# show interface gigabitethernet0/0/0/1 accounting
GigabitEthernet0/0/0/1
  Protocol            Pkts In        Chars In      Pkts Out      Chars Out
  IPV4_UNICAST         261334       20337829         46929        2305821
  IPV6_UNICAST          21017        2062274         20995        1964348
  MPLS                     15           1770         14431         969163
  ARP                      84           5040            84           3528
  IPV6_ND               13296        1193736         10306         742016
```

On NX-OS there are no CEF-related commands. The forwarding information on NX-OS is verified by using the command **show forwarding** [**vrf** *vrf-name*] **ipv6 route** *v6-route*. This command displays the next-hop value, outgoing interface, and MPLS labels (if any). Based on the MPLS labels, the forwarding information is further verified using the command **show mpls switching** *ip-address*. This command helps attain the local as well as the outgoing label for the MPLS packet.

Verify the hardware forwarding information for the VPNv6 prefix using the command **show system internal forwarding vrf** *vrf-name* **ipv6 route** *v6-address* [**module** *number*] [**detail**]. This command provides details about the hardware adjacency index and the egress interface. Both the values are in hex-format. Using the value received from the preceding command, verify the details of the hardware adjacency using the command **show system internal forwarding adjacency** *adj-value* [**module** *number*] [**detail**]. This command displays the egress interface information, which should match with the logical interface (LIF) value observed before. It also displays the packet forwarding count, which can be further used to troubleshoot any hardware-forwarding issues in 6VPE setup.

Example 12-27 demonstrates the 6VPE hardware forwarding verification on the NX-OS platform.

Example 12-27   *6VPE Forwarding Verification on NX-OS*

```
PE3# show forwarding vrf red ipv6 route 2001:db8::7
slot  2
=======
IPv6 routes for table red/base


*2001:db8::7/128
   10.1.34.4               Ethernet2/2          PUSH2  19 23


! Verify MPLS Forwarding Information
PE3# show mpls switching 192.168.5.5


Legend:
(P)=Protected, (F)=FRR active, (*)=more labels in stack.


In-Label   Out-Label  FEC name             Out-Interface     Next-Hop
21         19         192.168.5.5/32       Eth2/2            10.1.34.4


! Verify hardware forwarding information for the VPNv6 prefix
! Fetch the Adjacency Index and Egress Interface from this command
PE3# show system internal forwarding vrf red ipv6 route 2001:db8::7 module 2


Hardware IPv6 FIB entries for table red/base
```

```
2001:db8::7/128, Index:  0x1406
Dev: 1          Adj Index:  0xa020, Lif Base:   0, Egress Lif: 0x4003


! Using the adjacency information from above command, verify the hardware
! programming for the VPNv6 prefix. The below command displays the IGP and
! the VPN label received from remote peer
PE3# show system internal forwarding mpls adjacency 0xa020 module 2 detail
Device: 1   Index: 0xa020    dmac: 0022.5576.1283 smac: 0026.980c.8bc1
    PUSH TWO             Label0 19       Label1 23
    e-vpn: 1        egr_lif: 0x4003  packets: 0              bytes: 0
    DI: 0x1     CCC: 4     L2_FWD: NO FRR_TE: 0    FRR_NODE_ID: 0x0


! Use the below command to verify the adjacency information and also the
! packet forwarding counters
PE3# show system internal forwarding adjacency entry 0xa020 module 2 detail
Device: 1   Index: 0xa020    DMAC: 84a0.c009.a603 SMAC: 00f0.4000.4400
            LIF: 0x4003 (Ethernet2/2) DI: 0x1    ccc: 4   L2_FWD: NO  RDT: YES
            packets: 650   bytes: 81900   zone enforce: 1


! Verify Hardware forwarding information for the MPLS Label
! Label 21 is the locally assigned label for the the loopback of PE5
PE3# show system internal forwarding mpls label 21 detail
slot  2
=======


Table id = 0x1
------------------
----+--------+------------+----------+----------+-----------+--------+
Dev | Index  | In-label   | AdjIndex | LIF      | Out-label | Op
----+--------+------------+----------+----------+-----------+--------+
Device: 0    HW Index: 0x1655   In Label: 21        Valid: 1
        Vpn valid: 1 M: 0 Eos: 0 Lif or Label1: 0       Vpn or Table id: 1
        Adj Index: 0xa01d        Egr Lif: 0x4003
        Out Label: 19            SWAP ONE


! Use the below command to verify the MPLS hardware adjacency information and
! the MPLS packet forwarding counters
PE3# show system internal forwarding adjacency entry 0xa01d module 2 detail
Device: 1   Index: 0xa01d    DMAC: 84a0.c009.a603 SMAC: 00f0.4000.4400
            LIF: 0x4003 (Ethernet2/2) DI: 0x1    ccc: 4   L2_FWD: NO  RDT: YES
            packets: 650   bytes: 81900   zone enforce: 1
```

Summary

This chapter covered various IPv6 BGP concepts and features that are important for understanding and troubleshooting IPv6 BGP deployments in both enterprise and service provider environments. It explained how the IPv6 BGP next-hop value is calculated. The chapter discussed how IPv6 routes can be exchanged over IPv4 transport and how IPv4 routes can be exchanged over IPv6 transport and next-hop. With both the methods, the next-hop calculation method is different. The chapter then explored 6PE and 6VPE deployments and various commands to configure, verify, and troubleshoot these deployments.

References

RFC 2545, *BGP-4 Multiprotocol Extensions for IPv6 IDR*, P. Marques, F. Dupont, IETF, https://tools.ietf.org/html/rfc2545, March 1999.

RFC 5549, *Advertising IPv4 Network Layer Reachability Information with an IPv6 next Hop*, F. Le Faucheur, E. Rosen. IETF, http://tools.ietf.org/html/rfc5549, May 2009.

RFC 4798, *Connecting IPv6 Islands over IPv4 MPLS Using IPv6 Provider Edge Router (6PE)*, J. De Cleroq, D. Ooms, S. Prevost, F. Le Faucheur, IETF, https://tools.ietf.org/html/rfc4798, February 2007.

RFC 4659, *BGP-MPLS IP Virtual Private Network (VPN) Extension for IPv6 VPN*, J. De Cleroq, D. Ooms, M. Carugi, F. Le Faucheur, IETF, https://tools.ietf.org/html/rfc4659, September 2006.

RFC 4760, *Multiprotocol Extensions for BGP-4*, Y. Rekhter, T. Bates, R. Chandra, D. Katz, IETF, https://tools.ietf.org/html/rfc4760, January 2007.

RFC 3107, *Carrying Label Information in BGP-4*, Y. Rekhter, E. Rosen, IETF, https://tools.ietf.org/html/rfc3107, May 2001.

Cisco. IPv6 VPN over MPLS: 6PE and 6VPE—Configuration Guide, http://www.cisco.com,

Cisco. Implementing IPv6 over MPLS—6PE, http://www.cisco.com.

## Chapter 13

VxLAN BGP EVPN

The following topics are covered in this chapter:

- Understanding VxLAN
- Overview of VxLAN BGP EVPN
- Troubleshooting VxLAN BGP EVPN

For years, legacy switching has ruled the data center network. Spanning Tree Protocol (STP) and VLANs have been running in the data center for decades but with the rapidly growing need for virtualization, on-demand virtual machines and increasing customer base, 4K Virtual Local Area Networks (VLAN) (VLAN ID is a 12-bit field) are not sufficient. Also, because of the limitations of STP, such as link/path utilization, convergence issues, Media Access Control (MAC) address table size, and so on, some parts of the network were underutilized. Also, the modern day data centers look for plug-and-play mechanisms for the host virtual machines (VM) and flexibility to move the hosts anywhere in the data center without having to make any changes to the configuration, which is a big challenge with traditional data center designs.

To overcome the growing needs of the data center and the design challenge, Virtual Extensible LAN (VxLAN) is replacing the Spanning Tree Protocol in Layer 2 networks. Thus it becomes important to understand how VxLAN works and how the VxLAN Ethernet VPN (EVPN) solution can help scale VxLAN deployments.

Understanding VxLAN

VxLAN is a MAC-in-unit datagram protocol (UDP) encapsulation method used for extending a Layer 2 or Layer 3 overlay network over an existing Layer 3 infrastructure. The VxLAN encapsulation provides a virtual network identifier (VNI) that can be used to provide segmentation of Layer 2 and Layer 3 data traffic. A VNI is a unique 24-bit segment ID that is used to identify each VxLAN segment. Only hosts within the same VNI are allowed to communicate with each other.

To facilitate the discovery of these VNIs over the underlay Layer 3 network, virtual tunnel end points (VTEP) are used. VTEP is an entity that terminates VxLAN tunnels. It maps Layer 2 frames to a VNI to be used in the overlay network. Encapsulating customer Layer 2 and Layer 3 traffic in VNI over the physical Layer 3 network provides decoupling of overlay from the underlay network and provides flexible overlay topology that is independent of the physical network topology. Each VTEP has two interfaces.

- **Local LAN segment:** Provides a bridging function for local hosts connected to the VTEP. In other words, these are switchport interfaces on the LAN segment to support local endpoint communication through bridging.

- **IP interface:** The interface on the core network for VxLAN. The IP address on the IP interface helps in uniquely identifying a VTEP in the network. It is also used for VxLAN encapsulation and deencapsulation.

Figure 13-1 depicts the diagrammatical representation of VTEP. Figure 13-1 shows how end systems (hosts) are connected to the VTEP.

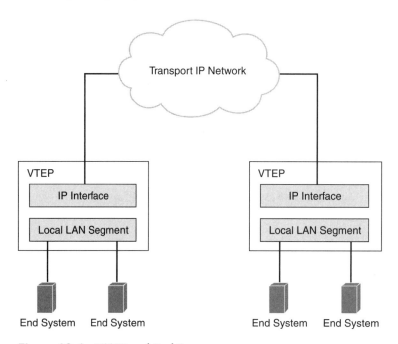

Figure 13-1   *VTEP and End Systems*

Note   IP intrasubnetwork traffic (bridged) or non-IP Layer 2 traffic is mapped to a VNI that is set aside for the VLAN or bridge domain. Routed traffic, on the other hand, is mapped to a VNI that is set aside for Layer 3 VRF.

Because of the Layer 3 underlay network, VxLANs are capable of performing equal cost multipath (ECMP), link aggregation, and other Layer 3 functionality. Also, because

Spanning Tree Protocol is not required anymore, there are no more blocked paths making the network underutilized. VxLANs provides a multi-tenant solution wherein the network traffic is isolated by a tenant and the same VLAN can be used by different tenants.

VxLAN Packet Structure

A VxLAN packet is nothing more than MAC-in-UDP encapsulated packet. The VxLAN header is added to the original Layer 2 frame and then placed in a UDP-IP packet. The VxLAN header is an 8-byte header that consists of 24-bit VxLAN Network Identifier (VNID) and a few reserved bits. The VxLAN header along with the Layer 2 Ethernet frame is then carried as a UDP payload. The VNID uniquely identifies the Layer 2 segments and helps in maintaining isolation among them. Because the VNID is a 24-bit field, VxLAN can support 16 million LAN segments.

Figure 13-2 examines the VxLAN packet format. The two primary fields in the VxLAN header are as follows:

- **Flags:** 8-bits in length, where the fifth bit (I flag) is set to 1 to indicate a valid VNI. The remaining 7 bits (R bits) are reserved fields and are set to zero.

- **VNI:** 24-bit value that provides a unique identifier for the individual VxLAN segment.

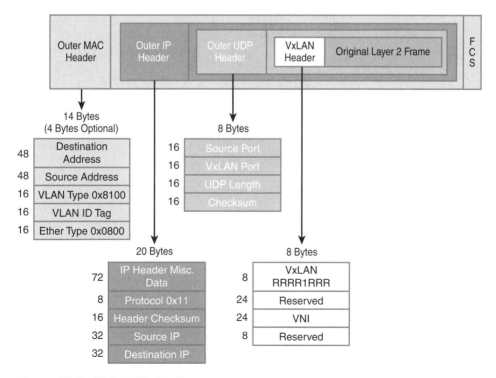

Figure 13-2 *VxLAN Packet Format*

The other fields shown in the Figure 13-2 are as follows:

■ **Outer UDP Header:** The source port in the outer UDP header is dynamically assigned by the originating VTEP. The source port is calculated based on the hash of inner Layer 2/Layer 3/Layer 4 headers of the original frame. The destination port is an Internet Assigned Numbers Authority (IANA) assigned UDP port 4789 or customer configured.

■ **Outer IP Header:** The source IP address in the outer IP header is the originating VTEP's IP interface. The IP address on the IP interface uniquely identifies a VTEP. The destination address of the outer IP header is the IP address of the destination VTEP's IP interface.

■ **Outer Ethernet/MAC Header:** The source MAC address is the source VTEP MAC address. The destination MAC address is the next-hop MAC address. The next-hop is the interface used to reach the destination or remote VTEP.

Figure 13-3 depicts the use of a VxLAN overlay between two VTEPs in a data center environment. The data center follows the spine-leaf architecture. The host in VTEP-A tries to communicate with the host in VTEP-B using VxLAN. Host1 and Host2 are VMs; they can also be a physical host, but the forwarding mechanism remains the same.

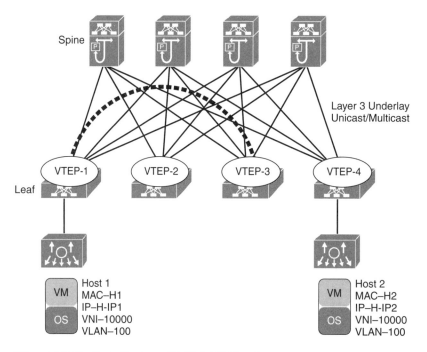

Figure 13-3 *Data Center with VxLAN Overlay*

VxLAN Gateway Types

Frame encapsulation and decapsulation is performed by a VTEP. A VTEP originates and terminates VxLAN tunnels. VxLAN gateway bridges traffic between a VxLAN segment and another physical or logical Layer 2 domain (such as a VLAN). There are two kinds of VxLAN gateways:

- **Layer 2 Gateway:** The Layer 2 gateway is required when the Layer 2 traffic (IEEE 802.1q tagged traffic) comes from VLAN into the VxLAN segment (encapsulation) or the ingress VxLAN packet egresses out an 802.1q tagged interface (decapsulation), where the packet is bridged to a new VLAN.

- **Layer 3 Gateway:** A Layer 3 gateway is used when there is a VxLAN to VxLAN routing; that is, when the egress VxLAN packet is routed to a new VxLAN segment. A Layer 3 gateway is also used when there is a VxLAN to VLAN routing; that is, the ingress packet is a VxLAN packet on a routed segment, but the packet egresses out on a tagged 802.1q interface and the packet is routed to a new VLAN.

VxLAN Overlay

The VxLAN overlay mechanism requires that the VTEPs peer with each other so that the data can be forwarded to the relevant destination. There are primarily three mechanisms for establishing VxLAN overlay:

- Flood and learn

- Ingress replication

- BGP EVPN

VxLAN Flood-and-Learn Mechanism

VxLAN RFC 7348 defines a multicast-based *flood-and-learn* mechanism for VxLAN overlay establishment. The flood-and-learn mechanism is a data plane learning technique for VxLAN, where a VNI is mapped to a multicast group on a VTEP. The underlay requires standard routing for VTEP connectivity and must be enabled for multicast. Because there is no control or signaling protocol defined, emulation of multidestination traffic is handled through the VxLAN IP underlay through the use of segment control multicast groups.

The host traffic is usually in broadcast, unknown unicast, or multicast (BUM) format. The BUM traffic is flooded to the multicast delivery group for the VNI that is sourcing the host packet. The remote VTEPs that are part of the multicast group learn the remote host MAC, VNI, and source VTEP IP information from the flooded traffic (just like Address Resolution Protocol (ARP) in traditional switched networks). Unicast packets to the host MAC are sent directly to the destination VTEP as a VxLAN packet.

> **Note**   Local MACs are learned over a VLAN (VNI) on a VTEP.

Figure 13-4 demonstrates the VxLAN overlay flood-and-learn mechanism packet flow with the help of an example. Host-A is connected to VTEP-1 with IP 192.168.1.1 and MAC address MAC-A; Host-B is connected to VTEP-2 with IP 192.168.2.2 and MAC address as MAC-B; and VTEP-3 has IP address 192.168.3.3 and MAC address as MAC-C. In this example, Host-A is having MAC address as MAC-A and IP address as IP A. Similarly, Host-B has a MAC address as MAC-B and IP address as IP B. In this example the core multicast group is 239.1.1.1.

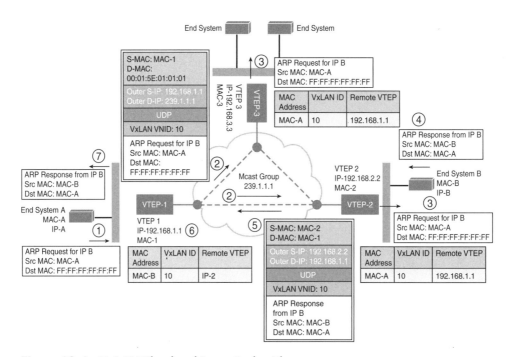

Figure 13-4   *VxLAN Flood-and-Learn Packet Flow*

The following steps describe the complete packet flow as shown in Figure 13-4.

Step 1.   The End System A with MAC-A and IP A sends an ARP request for host with IP B. The source MAC address of the ARP packet is MAC-A and the destination MAC address is FFFF.FFFF.FFFF. Suppose the host is in VLAN 10. This packet is sent toward VTEP-1. VTEP-1 has VNID 10 mapped to VLAN 10.

Step 2.   When the ARP request is received on VTEP-1, the packet is encapsulated and forwarded to the remote VTEP-2 and VTEP-3 with the source as 192.168.1.1 and the destination as 239.1.1.1 as a VxLAN packet. When the encapsulation is done, the VNID is set to 10, the source MAC of the packet is MAC-1, and the destination MAC is 0001.5E01.0101, which is the multicast MAC address for 239.1.1.1.

Step 3.   Both the VTEP-2 and VTEP-3 receive the VxLAN packet and deencapsulate it to forward it to the End Systems connected to the respective VTEPs. Note that at this point, both VTEP-2 and VTEP-3 update their MAC address table with the following information:

- MAC Address—MAC-A

- VxLAN ID—10

- Remote VTEP—192.168.1.1

In other words, both VTEP-2 and VTEP-3 now know that the MAC address MAC-A is behind VTEP-A and is learned over VNID 10.

Step 4.   After the ARP packet is forwarded to Host-B after deencapsulation, Host-B responds back with the ARP reply.

Step 5.   When the ARP reply reaches VTEP-2, VTEP-2 already knows that to reach MAC-A, it needs to go to VTEP-1. Thus, VTEP-2 forwards the ARP reply from Host-B as a unicast VxLAN packet.

Step 6.   When the VxLAN packet reaches VTEP-1, it then updates its MAC address table with the following information:

- MAC Address—MAC-B

- VxLAN ID—10

- Remote VTEP—192.168.2.2

Step 7.   After the MAC table is updated on VTEP-1, the ARP reply is forwarded to Host-A.

Note   In Step 2, only those VTEPs that have subscribed to that multicast group receive the multicast packet. The multicast group is configured to map to the VNI on each VTEP.

Configuration and Verification

To understand the packet flow and how VxLAN is set up, examine the topology as shown in Figure 13-5. Nexus 9500 is the spine, and Nexus 9300 is the leaf switches. Host-A and Host-B are attached to N9k-Leaf1 and N9k-Leaf2 switches, respectively.

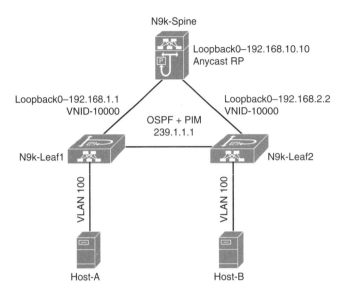

Figure 13-5   *VxLAN Flood-and-Learn Topology*

> **Note**   For the sake of simplicity, only one spine is being used, but in real production
> deployments, more than one Spine switch should be used. Anycast Rendezvous Point (RP)
> is configured across all Spine switches—that is, all the Spine switches have a loopback
> configured with same Anycast RP IP address.

For configuring VxLAN with the flood-and-learn mechanism, the spine-and-leaf switches
are configured with Protocol Independent Multicast (PIM) and Open Shortest Path First
(OSPF) for reachability and forwarding on the underlay network. The VTEP functionality is configured on the leaf switches. The following steps can be used to configure the
VxLAN segment:

Step 1.   Enable the VxLAN feature. To enable VxLAN on the leaf switches, two
features need to be enabled—*nv overlay* and *vn-segment-vlan-based*. The
command **feature nv overlay** enables VxLAN on the switch. The command
feature vn-segment-vlan-based enables the VLAN-based VN segment.

Step 2.   Configure the VLAN and map to VN segment. Create VLANs on the leaf
switch for connectivity to the host. To map the VLAN to VN-Segment, use
the command **vn-segment** *segment-id*, where the segment id value can range
from 4096 to 16773119. The *segment-id* is the VxLAN VNID.

Step 3.   Configure the network virtualization endpoint (NVE) Interface and Associate
VNIs. The NVE interface is the overlay interface that receives the VxLAN encapsulation traffic in the underlay on each VTEP. The NVE interface is configured
using the command **interface nve** *interface-number*. The VTEP IP is then configured by specifying the source-interface command. This is usually a loopback
interface. To associate the VNIs, use the command **member vni** *vni*. The *vni*
value is the VNID or the VN-Segment specified under the VLAN configuration.

Example 13-1 demonstrates the configuration of spine-and-leaf switches as shown in the topology in Figure 13-5. The leaf node does not support the *RP*. Thus, the RP is configured on the spine node. The PIM Anycast RP is used for redundancy and load-balancing purposes. Thus, if there are two or more spine nodes, all the nodes have Anycast RP configured on them.

Example 13-1 *VxLAN Overlay Configuration*

```
! Configuration on N9k-Spine
feature ospf
feature pim
!
interface loopback0
  ip address 192.168.10.10/32
  ip router ospf 100 area 0.0.0.0
  ip pim sparse-mode
!
ip pim bsr-candidate loopback0
ip pim rp-candidate loopback0 group-list 239.1.1.0/24 priority 100
ip pim anycast-rp 192.168.10.10 192.168.1.1
ip pim anycast-rp 192.168.10.10 192.168.2.2
ip pim bsr listen forward
! Configuration on N9k-Leaf1
feature ospf
feature pim
feature vn-segment-vlan-based
feature nv overlay
!
vlan 100
  vn-segment 10000
!
ip pim bsr listen forward
!
interface loopback0
  ip address 192.168.1.1/32
  ip router ospf 100 area 0.0.0.0
  ip pim sparse-mode
!
interface nve1
  source-interface loopback0
  no shutdown
  member vni 10000 mcast-group 239.1.1.1
! Configuration on N9k-Leaf2
feature ospf
feature pim
```

```
feature vn-segment-vlan-based
feature nv overlay
!
ip pim bsr listen forward
!
vlan 100
  vn-segment 10000
!
interface loopback0
  ip address 192.168.2.2/32
  ip router ospf 100 area 0.0.0.0
  ip pim sparse-mode
!
interface nve1
  source-interface loopback0
  no shutdown
  member vni 10000 mcast-group 239.1.1.1
```

After both the spine and the leaf nodes are configured, the forwarding plane is ready for the core. The NVE interface comes up after the nve1 interface is unshut using the **no shut** command. The command **show interface nve1** and the command **show nve interface** display the details and status of the NVE interface. Example 13-2 examines the output of the command **show interface nve1** and **show nve interface** command. The **show interface nve1** command displays the status of the nve1 interface, encapsulation and ingress (RX), and egress (TX) packet counters.

Example 13-2 *NVE Interface Details*

```
N9k-Leaf1# show interface nve1
nve1 is up
    Encapsulation VXLAN
    Last link flapped 02:45:32
    Last clearing of "show interface" counters never
    Load-Interval is 5 minute (300 seconds)
    RX
      0 unicast packets  0 multicast packets
      0 bytes  0 bits/sec  0 packets/sec
    TX
      0 unicast packets  0 multicast packets
      0 bytes  0 bits/sec  0 packets/sec

N9k-Leaf1# show nve interface
Interface: nve1   State: up      Encapsulation: VXLAN
  Source Interface: loopback0  (Primary: 192.168.1.1)
```

To view the platform-level information on the NVE interface, use the command **show nve internal platform interface** *interface-id* [**detail**], where *interface-id* is the NVE interface configured on the router. Example 13-3 examines the platform-level information of the NVE interface. Most of the information is similar to the commands shown in Example 13-2. One important field to notice in the following output is the SecIP field. The SecIP field will be 0.0.0.0 except for when VTEPs are configured for virtual port channel (VPC) and the host VLAN is across the VPC. This command also displays the peer VTEP details, such as the peer IP and its status. The NVE peers can also be viewed using the command **show nve peers**.

Example 13-3 *Platform Details of NVE Interface*

```
N9k-Leaf1# show nve internal platform interface nve1 detail
Printing Interface ifindex 0x22380001 detail
|======|=========================|===============|===============|=====|=====|
|Intf  |State                    |PriIP          |SecIP          |Vnis |Peers|
|======|=========================|===============|===============|=====|=====|
|nve1  |UP                       |192.168.1.1    |0.0.0.0        |2    |1    |
|======|=========================|---------------|===============|=====|=====|


SW_BD/VNIs of interface nve1:
=================================================
|======|======|=========================|======|
|Sw BD |Vni   |State                    |Intf  |
|======|======|=========================|======|
|100   |10000 |UP                       |nve1  |
|======|======|=========================|======|


Peers of interface nve1:
==========================================

peer_ip: 192.168.2.2, peer_id: 1, state: UP
active_swbds:
add_pending_swbds:
rem_pending_swbds:
```

> **Note** Unless frames are being sent between hosts over the VNI, the VTEP peers are not seen under the **show nve peers** command. As soon as the host traffic is initiated, the peering is established and the MAC address table is populated. This is the reason why this mechanism is known as the data plane learning mechanism.

Confirm the VNI details and ensure that the hardware is ready to do the forwarding. This is verified by using the command **show nve vni** *vnid* [**detail**]. This command displays the interface name, VNIs mapped to it, multicast-group for the segment, VNI state, and the Flags. If the Flags are set to add-complete, it represents that the hardware is ready to forward the VxLAN traffic. Example 13-4 examines the VNI details from the command **show nve vni** *vnid* **detail**.

Example 13-4 *Verifying VNI Status*

```
N9k-Leaf1# show nve vni 10000 detail
Interface        VNI        Multicast-group   VNI State   VNI Flags
---------------  --------   ---------------   ---------   --------
nve1             10000      239.1.1.1         up          add-complete [0x4]
```

Finally, confirm the MAC address table on the leaf nodes for the host VLAN. Example 13-5 verifies the MAC address table of VLAN 100 using the command **show mac address-table vlan** *vlan-id*. Notice that in the output, the MAC address 8c60.4f1b. e43c is learned from interface Eth1/12, which indicates that it is a MAC learned from the host that is locally attached to the VTEP. The other MAC address displays the port as **nve1** (*remote-vtep-ip*). This is the MAC address that is learned from the remote VTEP.

Example 13-5 *MAC Address Table on Leaf1*

```
N9k-Leaf1# show mac address-table vlan 100
Legend:
        * - primary entry, G - Gateway MAC, (R) - Routed MAC, O - Overlay MAC
        age - seconds since last seen,+ - primary entry using vPC Peer-Link,
        (T) - True, (F) - False
   VLAN     MAC Address     Type      age      Secure NTFY Ports
---------+---------------+--------+---------+------+----+-----------------
*  100      8c60.4f19.51fc  dynamic   0         F      F    nve1(192.168.2.2)
*  100      8c60.4f1b.e43c  dynamic   0         F      F    Eth1/12
```

Ingress Replication

The VxLAN flood-and-learn mechanism as defined in RFC 7348 requires an IP multicast enabled core to provide VxLAN overlay, but some network operators are not comfortable using multicast in their core. For such customers, the Ingress Replication (IR) method was developed. With IR, the BUM packets that are received from the host VLANs are replicated to all remote VTEPs in the VNI as unicast. The sending device has two options:

■ Use the individual IP address for replication.

■ Use the virtual VTEP IP (VIP) to send traffic to the remote VTEPs.

Using VIP is a preferred model because it is efficient and cuts down replication overhead on the sender, although replication using a regular IP address is also supported.

There are two methods for peer learning that are used in IR:

■ Static IR

■ BGP EVPN IR

On Nexus devices, a maximum of 16 static IR VTEPs is recommended. Both the multicast and IR configuration can co-exist on the same switch but on different VNIs. The main difference between the multicast core VTEP and static IR VTEP is that the static IR VTEP tunnel is alive as long as the route to the VTEP is available. In the case of multicast IP core-based VTEP, the tunnel is removed as soon as all the dynamically learned MAC addresses that are associated with the VTEP are aged out. To enable the static IR method, use the command **ingress-replication protocol static** under the vni configuration section of nve interface. Example 13-6 illustrates the sample configuration of IR method.

Example 13-6 *Ingress Replication Configuration*

```
! Configuration on Leaf Switch
interface nve1
member vni 16000
  ingress-replication protocol static
   peer-ip 192.168.2.2
   peer-ip 192.168.3.3
member vni 16001
  ingress-replication protocol static
   peer-ip 192.168.3.3
```

Note Nexus 3000 series switches provide support only for a single peer for ingress-replication.

Overview of VxLAN BGP EVPN

VxLAN overlay using the flood-and-learn mechanism is being used in quite a lot of data center deployments so far, but this method has its own challenges. Network operators are looking for following key requirements in their data center networks:

■ Flexible workload placement

■ Reduce flooding in the data center

■ Overlay setup using control plane that is independent of specific fabric controller

■ Layer 2 and Layer 3 traffic segmentation

The VxLAN overlay flood-and-learn mechanism does not meet these requirements.

RFC 7432 introduces a BGP MPLS-based Ethernet VPN (EVPN) solution that was developed to meet the limitations of the flood-and-learn mechanism. *Draft-ietf-bess-evpn-overlay* defines the network virtualization overlay solution using EVPN. This draft is based on RFC 5512 (for tunnel encapsulation) and discusses the encapsulation mechanism for VxLAN, Network Virtualization using Generic Routing Encapsulation (NVGRE), and Multiprotocol Label Switching (MPLS) over Generic Routing Encapsulation (GRE). With this solution, both the Layer 2 and Layer 3 VxLAN overlay networks are established using the BGP EVPN control plane. Thus, even if the MAC addresses in the VTEP times out, the overlay tunnel still remains up.

In the BGP EVPN solution for VxLAN overlay, a VLAN is mapped to a VNI for the Layer 2 services, and a VRF is mapped to a VNI for the Layer 3 services on a VTEP. An IBGP EVPN session is established between all the VTEPs or with the EVPN route reflector to provide the full-mesh connectivity required by IBGP peering rules. After the IBGP EVPN session is established, the VTEPs exchange MAC-VNI or MAC-IP bindings as part of the BGP network layer reachability information (NLRI) update. Before proceeding to understand the VxLAN BGP EVPN control plane, it is important to understand the distributed anycast gateway.

Distributed Anycast Gateway

Distributed anycast gateway refers to the use of anycast gateway addressing and an overlay network to provide a distributed control plane that governs the forwarding of frames within and across a Layer 3 core network. The distributed anycast gateway functionality facilitates transparent VM mobility and optimal east-west routing by configuring the leaf switches with same gateway IP and MAC address for each locally defined subnet. The main benefit of using the distributed anycast gateway is that the hosts or VMs will use the same default gateway IP and MAC address no matter which leaf they are connected to. Thus, all VTEPs have the same IP address and MAC address for the switched virtual interface (SVI) in the same VNI.

Within the spine-and-leaf topology, there can be various traffic forwarding combinations. Based on the forwarding type, the distributed anycast gateway plays its role in one of the following manners:

■ **Intra-subnet and non-IP traffic:** For the host-to-host communication that is intra-subnet or non-IP, the destination MAC address in the ingress frame is the target end host's MAC address. Thus, the traffic is bridged from VLAN to VNI on the ingress/egress VTEP.

■ **Inter-subnet IP traffic:** For host-to-host communication that is intersubnet, the destination MAC address in the ingress frame belongs to the default gateway's MAC address. Thus, the traffic gets routed. But on the egress switch, there can be two possible forwarding behaviors—it can either get routed or bridged.

If the inner destination MAC address belongs to the end host, then on the egress switch, after VxLAN decapsulation, the traffic is bridged. On the other hand, if the inner destination MAC address belongs to the egress switch, the traffic is routed.

To configure distributed anycast gateway, all the leaf switches or VTEPs are required to be configured with the global command **fabric forwarding anycast-gateway-mac** *mac-address*, where *mac-address* is the statically assigned address to be used across all switches by the anycast gateway. The next step is to assign the fabric forwarding mode to anycast gateway using the command **fabric forwarding mode anycast-gateway**. This is configured under the Layer 3 VNI—the SVI interface. Example 13-7 illustrates the configuration for enabling anycast gateway on the leaf switch.

Example 13-7   *Distributed Anycast Gateway Configuration*

```
fabric forwarding anycast-gateway-mac 0001.0001.0001
!
interface Vlan100
no shutdown
vrf context test-evpn-tenant
ip address 172.16.1.254/24
fabric forwarding mode anycast-gateway
```

ARP Suppression

ARP requests from a host is flooded in the VLAN. It is possible to optimize the flooding behavior by maintaining an ARP cache locally on the attached VTEP and generating an ARP response from the information available from the local cache. This is achieved using the ARP suppression feature. Using ARP suppression, network flooding due to host learning can be reduced by using Gratuitous ARP (G-ARP).

Typically, a host will send out a G-ARP message when it first comes online. When the local leaf VTEP receives the G-ARP, it creates an ARP cache entry and advertises to the remote leaf VTEP using BGP (Route Type 2—BGP EVPN MAC route advertisement). The remote leaf node puts the IP-MAC info into the remote ARP cache and suppresses incoming ARP requests to that particular IP. If a VTEP does not have a match for the IP address in its ARP cache table, it floods the ARP request to all other VTEPs in the VNI.

Figure 13-6 illustrates the ARP suppression feature on the overlay.

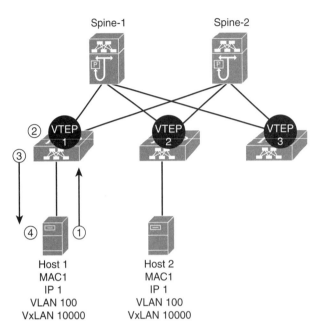

Figure 13-6   *ARP Suppression*

With the help of the ARP suppression cache, Host-1 and Leaf-1 go through the following steps to gain information regarding the Host-2 MAC address:

Step 1.   Host-1 in VLAN 100 sends an ARP request for Host-2 IP address.

Step 2.   VTEP-1 on Leaf-1 intercepts the ARP request. Rather than forwarding it toward the core, it checks in its ARP suppression cache table. It finds a match for Host-2 IP address in VLAN 100 in its ARP suppression cache. It is important to note that the BUM traffic is sent to other VTEPs.

Step 3.   VTEP-1 sends the ARP response back to Host-1 with the MAC address of Host-2, thus reducing the ARP flooding in the core network.

Step 4.   Host-1 gets the IP and MAC mapping for Host-2 and updates its ARP cache.

Integrated Route/Bridge (IRB) Modes

The IETF EVPN draft defines two integrated routing and bridging (IRB) mechanisms:

- Asymmetric IRB
- Symmetric IRB

Asymmetric IRB

In this method, it is required to configure the source VTEP with both the source and destination VNIs for both Layer 2 and Layer 3 forwarding. Asymmetric IRB uses different paths from the source to the destination and back.

Figure 13-7 shows the packet flow used in asymmetric IRB mode.

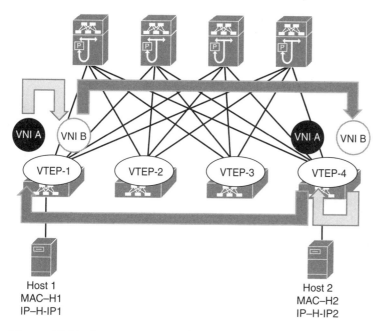

Figure 13-7 *Asymmetric IRB Flow*

The packet flow with asymmetric IRB occurs in the following sequence:

1. Host-1 in VNI-A sends a packet toward Host-2 with the source MAC address of Host-1 and the destination MAC address set to gateway MAC.

2. The ingress VTEP routes the packets from the source VNI to the destination VNI; that is, if the source packet was received in VNI-A, the packet is routed to the destination VTEP VNI-B. When the packet is sent, the source MAC of the inner packet is set to gateway MAC and the destination MAC as the Host-2 MAC address.

3. When the packet reaches the destination VTEP, the egress VTEP bridges the packets in the destination VNI.

4. The return packet also follows the same process.

Because the ingress VTEPs need to be configured with both the source and the destination VNIs, this creates a scalability problem, because all the VTEPs are required to be configured with all the VNIs in the network so that they can learn about all the hosts attached to those VNIs.

Symmetric IRB

The symmetric IRB is the more scalable and preferred option. The VTEPs here are not required to be configured with all the VNIs. The symmetric IRB uses the same path from the source to the destination and on the way back as well. In this method, the ingress VTEP routes packets from source VNI to L3 VNI where the destination MAC address in the inner header is rewritten to egress VTEP's router MAC address. On the egress side, the egress VTEP decapsulates the packet and looks at the inner packet header. Since the destination MAC address of the inner header is its own router MAC address, it performs Layer 3 routing lookup. Because the Layer 3 VNI (in the VxLAN header) provides the VRF context to lookup, the packets are routed to the destination VNI and VLAN.

Figure 13-8 walks through the packet flow with symmetric IRB.

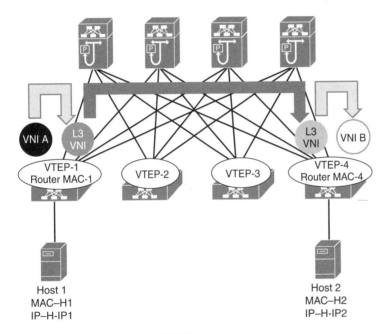

Figure 13-8   *Symmetric IRB Flow*

Multi-Protocol BGP

Various components are involved as part of the BGP EVPN control plane; these work together to implement the VxLAN functionality using control plane learning and the discovery mechanism.

Multi-protocol BGP (MP-BGP) plays an important role with the VxLAN BGP EVPN feature. The route distribution is carried out via multiprotocol internal BGP (MP-IBGP) update messages in the L2VPN EVPN address-family. There is a new address-family identifier (AFI)/subaddress-family identifier (SAFI) defined for the L2VPN EVPN address-family. The selected AFI/SAFI for the L2VPN EVPN address-family is AFI = 25 and SAFI = 70. The L2VPN EVPN NLRI is encoded in the message shown in Figure 13-9.

```
Route Type (1 Octet)

Length (1 Octet)

Route Type Specific (Variable)
```

Figure 13-9   *L2VPN EPVN NLRI*

RFC 7432 defines four route types:

- Ethernet Auto-Discovery (A-D) route

- MAC/IP advertisement route

- Inclusive Multicast Ethernet Tag route

- Ethernet Segment route

BGP uses route type 2 to advertise MAC and MAC+IP information of the hosts and route type 3 to carry VTEP information.

The BGP EVPN overlay specifies the distribution and discovery of VTEP using EVPN. The information is carried as EVPN Inclusive Multicast (IM) NLRI, which has the format shown in Figure 13-10.

```
RD (8 Octets)

Ethernet Tag ID (4 Octets)

IP Address Length (1 Octet)

Originating Router's IP Address
(4 or 16 Octets)
```

Figure 13-10   *EVPN Inclusive Multicast NLRI*

Encoding of the IM NLRI is based on "Single Virtual Identifier per EVI," wherein every VNI is mapped to a unique Ethernet VPN instance (EVI) as follows.

- **RD:** Route distinguisher for the EVPN instance, auto derived

- **Ethernet Tag ID:** VNI for the bridge domain

- **IP address length:** 1 byte

- **Originating Router's IP address:** VTEP IP address of the advertising endpoint.

Advertisement and learning of IP host addresses associated with a VTEP is accomplished via BGP EVPN MAC advertisement NLRI, specified in RFC 7432. The VTEP information is implicitly sent as the BGP next-hop associated with the IP host, and by also providing the VTEP gateway MAC address in the MAC advertisement NLRI, as shown in Figure 13-11.

```
┌─────────────────────────────────────────────────┐
│ RD (8 Octets)                                    │
├─────────────────────────────────────────────────┤
│ Ethernet Segment Identifier (10 Octets)          │
├─────────────────────────────────────────────────┤
│ Ethernet Tag ID (4 Octets)                       │
├─────────────────────────────────────────────────┤
│ MAC Address Length (1 Octet)                     │
├─────────────────────────────────────────────────┤
│ MAC Address (6 Octets)                           │
├─────────────────────────────────────────────────┤
│ IP Address Length (1 Octet)                      │
├─────────────────────────────────────────────────┤
│ IP Address (4 or 16 Octets)                      │
├─────────────────────────────────────────────────┤
│ MPLS Label (3 Octets)                            │
└─────────────────────────────────────────────────┘
```

Figure 13-11 *MAC Advertisement NLRI*

Encoding of the NLRI is as follows:

- RD: Route distinguisher (RD) for the EVI, auto derived

- Ethernet Segment Identifier

- Ethernet Tag ID: VNI for the VRF

- MAC Address Length: 6 bytes

- MAC Address: Router MAC

- IP Address Length: 1 byte

- IP Address: Host IP address

- MPLS Label: 0

The RT value is either manually configured or autogenerated, which is based on a 2-byte AS number and the VNI value. The route is imported into the correct VLAN or bridge domain based on the import route target configuration.

The design for the VxLAN deployment follows the spine-and-leaf architecture. With VxLAN BGP EVPN solution, the spine nodes are usually configured as the route reflectors and only require the **nv overlay** feature to be enabled along with BGP. The leaf nodes, on the other hand, require the **nv overlay** feature along with the **vn-segment-vlan-based** feature to be enabled. The **vn-segment-vlan-based** feature is required to map the VLAN to the VNI. The spine can be configured either on a Nexus 9500 or Nexus 7000 switch. The leaf can be configured on Nexus 9300 or on Nexus 7000 or 7700 with F3 and M3 modules.

During the course of this chapter, various components on Nexus 9000 architecture are used from time to time. Some of those components are as follows:

- **VxLAN Manager:** VxLAN Manager is the VxLAN control and management plane component that is responsible for VxLAN local tunnel endpoint configuration, remote endpoint learning, management of Address Resolution Protocol (ARP) suppression, and platform-dependent (PD) programming.

- **L2RIB:** The L2RIB component manages the Layer 2 routing information. The L2RIB component interacts with VxLAN Manager, BGP, Layer 2 Forwarding Manager (L2FM), ARP, and Multicast Forwarding Distribution Manager (MFDM).

- **MFIB:** Multicast Forwarding Information Base (MFIB) finds out all VxLAN VNIs that share multicast group and program encapsulation/decapsulation entries for each of the VNI when the VTEP interface is in outgoing interface list (OIL) for a group.

- **AM:** Adjacency Manager (AM) performs two tasks:

  - Hosts IP and MAC binding for locally learned hosts

  - Programs routing information base (RIB) and forwarding information base (FIB) for host route and adjacency binding, respectively

Configuring and Verifying VxLAN BGP EVPN

VxLAN BGP EVPN functionality is supported from the 7.0(3)I1(1) release on NX-OS. Both Nexus 9500 and Nexus 9300 switches support inter-VxLAN routing in hardware. For understanding the configuration and verification of VxLAN BGP EVPN solution, examine the topology shown in Figure 13-12. There is a single spine node that is a Nexus 9508 switch and four leaf nodes that are Nexus 9396 switches. There is a Nexus 5000 switch attached to the Leaf3 and Leaf4 node for VPC. Hosts are attached to Leaf1, Leaf2, and the Nexus 5000 switch. For demonstration purpose, only one spine is used. The other spine is used for RP redundancy with anycast RP.

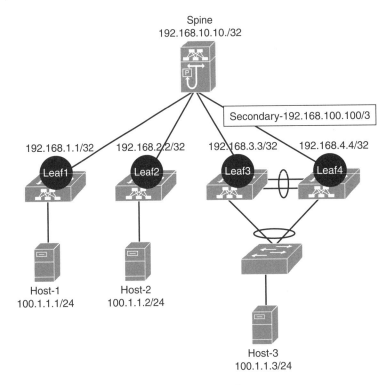

Figure 13-12 *VxLAN BGP EVPN Topology*

From the VxLAN EVPN control-plane overview, it is understood that the role of the spine switch is to provide connectivity between the leafs and also act as an EVPN RR. The VxLAN EVPN configuration for the spine switch is performed in a few simple steps:

Step 1.   Enable Features. Enable nv overlay and BGP feature on the spine switch. Because the spine provides connectivity for the leaf switches, and not actually for terminating VNIs, the vn-segment-vlan-based feature is not enabled. To enable EVPN AFI supported under BGP, use the command **nv overlay evpn**.

Step 2.   Configure BGP with EVPN AFI. Configure BGP with the appropriate AS number. Enable the l2vpn evpn address-family and then configure the BGP peering with the VTEPS; that is, the leaf switches. The leaf switches act as RR clients.

Note   Use the Interior Gateway Protocol (IGP) and PIM configuration from the VxLAN Flood-and-Learn demonstration because it is the same for the VxLAN BGP EVPN solution.

Example 13-8 demonstrates the configuration of the spine switch (running Nexus 9500).

Example 13-8 *EVPN RR Configuration on Nexus 9500 Spine Switch*

```
! Spine Switch
feature nv overlay
feature bgp
!
nv overlay evpn
!
router bgp 100
  router-id 192.168.10.10
  address-family l2vpn evpn
  neighbor 192.168.1.1
    remote-as 100
    update-source loopback0
    address-family l2vpn evpn
      send-community both
      route-reflector-client
  neighbor 192.168.2.2
    remote-as 100
    update-source loopback0
    address-family l2vpn evpn
      send-community both
      route-reflector-client
```

Now configure the leaf switches. Perform the following steps for configuring the leaf switches with Layer 2 VNI.

Step 1.   Enable Features. Enable nv overlay, vn-segment-vlan-based, and the BGP feature on the leaf switches. To enable EVPN AFI support under BGP, configure the command **nv overlay evpn**.

Step 2.   Create L2 VNI. Create a VLAN and assign VNID to the VLAN using the command **nv-segment** *vnid*.

Step 3.   Add the L2 VNI to the Overlay with BGP Control Plane and Enable Arp Suppression. Configure the NVE interface. The command **host-reachability protocol bgp** enables control-plane advertisement of the host IP/MAC address learned on the VNI via BGP EVPN. Under the member VNI, add the multicast group and configure the command **suppress-arp** to enable ARP suppression. The **suppress-arp** command is applicable only for L2 VNIs.

Step 4.   Configure EVPN with RT Import/Export for each VNI. Configure the EVPN section using the command **evpn**. Under each VNI, set the RD manually or for auto assignment. Use the command **route-target** [**import** | **export**] *rt-value* to configure the import and export RT statements.

Step 5.   Configure SVI for L2 VNI. Configure the SVIs for each L2 VNI. The SVIs must be part of proper VRF. Also configure the **anycast gateway mac-address** command on each leaf node. Note that the IP address configured for each L3 VNI should be the same on all VTEPs.

Step 6.   Configure BGP with the EVPN AFI. Configure BGP with the appropriate AS number. Enable the l2vpn evpn address-family and then configure the BGP peering with the spine switches that are acting as the RR routers. Under the BGP, also enable the VRF address-family that is configured for the L3 VNI.

Example 13-9 demonstrates the configuration of the leaf nodes Leaf1 and Leaf2, which are running on Nexus 9396 switches.

Example 13-9   *VxLAN EVPN Configuration on Leaf Nodes for L2 VNI*

```
Leaf1
feature bgp
feature interface-vlan
feature vn-segment-vlan-based
feature nv overlay
!
nv overlay evpn
!
vlan 100
  vn-segment 10000
!
vrf context EVPN-TENANT
!
evpn
  vni 10000 l2
    rd 10000:1
    route-target import 10000:1
    route-target export 10000:1
!
interface nve1
  no shutdown
  source-interface loopback0
  host-reachability protocol bgp
  member vni 10000
    mcast-group 239.1.1.1
    suppress-arp
!
fabric forwarding anycast-gateway-mac 0001.0001.0001
interface Vlan100
  no shutdown
  vrf member EVPN-TENANT
```

```
    ip address 100.1.1.254/24
    fabric forwarding mode anycast-gateway
!
router bgp 100
  router-id 192.168.1.1
  address-family l2vpn evpn
  neighbor 192.168.10.10
    description "Peering with Route Reflector"
    remote-as 100
    update-source loopback0
    address-family l2vpn evpn
      send-community extended
  vrf EVPN-TENANT
    address-family ipv4 unicast
      advertise l2vpn evpn
```

```
Leaf2
feature bgp
feature interface-vlan
feature vn-segment-vlan-based
feature nv overlay
!
nv overlay evpn
!
vlan 100
  vn-segment 10000
!
vrf context EVPN-TENANT
!
evpn
  vni 10000 l2
    rd 10000:1
    route-target import 10000:1
    route-target export 10000:1
!
interface nve1
  no shutdown
  source-interface loopback0
  host-reachability protocol bgp
  member vni 10000
    mcast-group 239.1.1.1
    suppress-arp
!
fabric forwarding anycast-gateway-mac 0002.0002.0002
```

```
! SVI for L2 VNI

interface Vlan100
  no shutdown
  vrf member EVPN-TENANT
  ip address 100.1.1.254/24
  fabric forwarding mode anycast-gateway
!
router bgp 100
  router-id 192.168.2.2
  address-family l2vpn evpn
  neighbor 192.168.10.10
    remote-as 100
    description "Peering with Route Reflector"
    update-source loopback0
    address-family l2vpn evpn
      send-community extended
  vrf EVPN-TENANT
    address-family ipv4 unicast
      advertise l2vpn evpn
```

Note   For the ARP Suppression functionality to work with BGP EVPN solution, it is required to carve out hardware ternary content-addressable memory (TCAM) resources for the ARP access control list (ACL) by using the command **hardware access-list tcam region arp-ether 256**. After configuring this command, a reload is required for the resources to be carved out and take effect.

After configuring the NVE interface and the SVI interface, verify the NVE interface status. Example 13-10 examines the status of the NVE interface created on both the leaf nodes.

Example 13-10   *NVE Interface Status*

```
Leaf1
Leaf1# show interface nve1
nve1 is up
admin state is up,  Hardware: NVE
  MTU 1500 bytes
  Encapsulation VXLAN
  Auto-mdix is turned off
  RX
    ucast: 0 pkts, 0 bytes - mcast: 0 pkts, 0 bytes
  TX
    ucast: 0 pkts, 0 bytes - mcast: 0 pkts, 0 bytes
```

```
Leaf1# show nve interface
Interface: nve1, State: Up, encapsulation: VXLAN
 VPC Capability: VPC-VIP-Only [not-notified]
 Local Router MAC: f40f.1b6f.926f
 Host Learning Mode: Control-Plane
 Source-Interface: loopback0 (primary: 192.168.1.1, secondary: 0.0.0.0)
```

```
Leaf2
Leaf1# show interface nve1
nve1 is up
admin state is up,  Hardware: NVE
  MTU 1500 bytes
  Encapsulation VXLAN
  Auto-mdix is turned off
  RX
    ucast: 0 pkts, 0 bytes - mcast: 0 pkts, 0 bytes
  TX
    ucast: 0 pkts, 0 bytes - mcast: 0 pkts, 0 bytes

Leaf2# show nve interface
Interface: nve1, State: Up, encapsulation: VXLAN
 VPC Capability: VPC-VIP-Only [not-notified]
 Local Router MAC: 88f0.312a.f2c1
 Host Learning Mode: Control-Plane
 Source-Interface: loopback0 (primary: 192.168.2.2, secondary: 0.0.0.0)
```

After the configuration is done, the BGP L2VPN EVPN session comes up. After the session comes up, no prefixes are exchanged unless the locally connected host sends G-ARP or tries to send traffic toward the remote host. This is when the MAC address and the ARP are learned from the host. To verify the BGP EVPN session, use the command **show bgp l2vpn evpn summary**. When the prefixes are exchanged, for every end host, two BGP NLRIs are exchanged: one NLRI for the MAC address of the host and the other for the MAC and IP address of the host.

Examine the output of the **show bgp l2vpn evpn summary** and the **show bgp l2vpn evpn** command in Example 13-11 to verify the EVPN session and prefixes. Use the command **show bgp l2vpn evpn vni-id** *vni-id* to view the prefixes in a particular VNI. In Example 13-11, there are two prefixes received from the Leaf2 node. The first highlighted prefix is the MAC address of the host. The second highlighted prefix along with the IP address shows the IP address of the remote host attached to Leaf2.

Example 13-11 *BGP L2VPN EVPN Session and Prefix Verification*

```
Leaf1
Leaf1# show bgp l2vpn evpn summary
BGP summary information for VRF default, address family L2VPN EVPN
BGP router identifier 192.168.1.1, local AS number 100
BGP table version is 11, L2VPN EVPN config peers 1, capable peers 1
4 network entries and 4 paths using 784 bytes of memory
BGP attribute entries [2/288], BGP AS path entries [0/0]
BGP community entries [0/0], BGP clusterlist entries [1/4]


Neighbor        V    AS MsgRcvd MsgSent   TblVer  InQ OutQ Up/Down  State/PfxRcd
192.168.10.10   4   100      69      68       11    0    0 00:58:11 2


! Verifying EVPN Prefixes
Leaf1# show bgp l2vpn evpn
BGP routing table information for VRF default, address family L2VPN EVPN
BGP table version is 11, local router ID is 192.168.1.1
Status: s-suppressed, x-deleted, S-stale, d-dampened, h-history, *-valid, >-best
Path type: i-internal, e-external, c-confed, l-local, a-aggregate, r-redist,
  I-injected
Origin codes: i - IGP, e - EGP, ? - incomplete, | - multipath, & - backup


   Network             Next Hop            Metric     LocPrf     Weight Path
Route Distinguisher: 10000:1    (L2VNI 10000)
*>i[2]:[0]:[0]:[48]:[8c60.4f19.51fc]:[0]:[0.0.0.0]/216
                     192.168.2.2                      100         0 i
*>l[2]:[0]:[0]:[48]:[8c60.4f1b.e43c]:[0]:[0.0.0.0]/216
                     192.168.1.1                      100     32768 i
*>i[2]:[0]:[0]:[48]:[8c60.4f19.51fc]:[32]:[100.1.1.2]/248
                     192.168.2.2                      100         0 i
*>l[2]:[0]:[0]:[48]:[8c60.4f1b.e43c]:[32]:[100.1.1.1]/248
                     192.168.1.1                      100     32768 i
```

The NVE peers are viewed using the command **show nve peers** [**detail**]. This command displays the NVE peer status, Peer's first VNI, the time when the peer came up, and the provision state (indicates that the hardware is programmed to forward the traffic). Example 13-12 displays the output of the command **show nve peers detail**.

Example 13-12 *NVE Peers*

```
Leaf1
Leaf1# show nve peers detail
Details of nve Peers:
----------------------------------------
Peer-Ip: 192.168.2.2
    NVE Interface         : nve1
    Peer State            : Up
    Peer Uptime           : 02:32:43
    Router-Mac            : n/a
    Peer First VNI        : 10000
    Time since Create     : 02:32:43
    Configured VNIs       : 10000
    Provision State       : add-complete
    Route-Update          : Yes
    Peer Flags            : DisableLearn
    Learnt CP VNIs        : 10000
    Peer-ifindex-resp     : Yes
----------------------------------------
```

The MAC address table can also be verified for the MAC address of both the hosts
that are part of the L2 VNI. The leaf nodes also learn the ARP information for the local
hosts attached in the VRF. Example 13-13 displays the MAC address table for VLAN
100 and the ARP table for VRF EVPN-TENANT. Notice that the first MAC address
8c60.4f19.51fc is learned over the NVE peer that is the node Leaf2. The MAC is learned
from L2FM, and the MAC-IP information is learned from ARP.

Example 13-13 *MAC Address Table for L2 VNI VLAN*

```
Leaf1
Leaf1# show mac address-table vlan 100
Legend:
        * - primary entry, G - Gateway MAC, (R) - Routed MAC, O - Overlay MAC
        age - seconds since last seen,+ - primary entry using vPC Peer-Link,
        (T) - True, (F) - False
   VLAN     MAC Address      Type      age     Secure NTFY Ports
---------+-----------------+--------+---------+------+----+------------------
*  100     8c60.4f19.51fc   dynamic  0          F     F    nve1(192.168.2.2)
*  100     8c60.4f1b.e43c   dynamic  0          F     F    Eth1/12
G  100     f40f.1b6f.926f   static   -          F     F    sup-eth1(R)
```

```
! ARP TABLE
Leaf1# show ip arp vrf EVPN-TENANT
IP ARP Table for context EVPN-TENANT
Total number of entries: 1
Address          Age       MAC Address      Interface
100.1.1.1        00:17:52  8c60.4f1b.e43c   Vlan100
```

After the MAC and MAC-IP information is learned, it gets downloaded into L2RIB. Verify the information by using the command **show l2route evpn [mac | mac-ip] evi** *vlan-id*. Example 13-14 displays the output of the two commands verifying whether the MAC and MAC-IP information is downloaded to L2RIB.

Example 13-14   *Installing MAC and MAC-IP into L2RIB*

```
Leaf1
! MAC Information into L2RIB
Leaf1# show l2route evpn mac evi 100
Mac Address     Prod    Next Hop (s)
--------------  ------  ---------------
8c60.4f19.51fc  BGP     192.168.2.2
8c60.4f1b.e43c  Local   Eth1/12


! MAC-IP Information into L2RIB
Leaf1# show l2route evpn mac-ip evi 100
Mac Address     Prod Host IP                                  Next Hop (s)
--------------  ---- --------------------------------------   ---------------
8c60.4f19.51fc  BGP  100.1.1.2                                192.168.2.2
8c60.4f1b.e43c  HMM  100.1.1.1                                N/A
```

```
Leaf2
Leaf2# show l2route evpn mac evi 100
Mac Address     Prod    Next Hop (s)
--------------  ------  ---------------
8c60.4f19.51fc  Local   Eth1/13
8c60.4f1b.e43c  BGP     192.168.1.1


Leaf2# show l2route evpn mac-ip evi 100
Mac Address     Prod Host IP                                  Next Hop (s)
--------------  ---- --------------------------------------   ---------------
8c60.4f19.51fc  HMM  100.1.1.2                                N/A
8c60.4f1b.e43c  BGP  100.1.1.1                                192.168.1.1
```

The internal platform-level information on the NVE interface can also be verified. Example 13-15 displays the output of the command **show nve internal platform interface nve [number] [detail]**. Along with the NVE information, the command also displays the VNI-related information. Notice that the type is set to CP, which means control plane. This command also displays the information about the NVE peers.

Example 13-15 *NVE Internal Platform Information*

```
Leaf1
Leaf1# show nve internal platform interface nve 1 detail
Printing Interface ifindex 0x49000001 detail
|======|=========================|===============|===============|=====|=====|
|Intf  |State                    |PriIP          |SecIP          |Vnis |Peers|
|======|=========================|===============|===============|=====|=====|
|nve1  |UP                       |192.168.1.1    |0.0.0.0        |1    |1    |
|======|=========================|===============|===============|=====|=====|


SW_BD/VNIs of interface nve1:
=============================================
|======|======|=========================|======|====|======|========
|Sw BD |Vni   |State                    |Intf  |Type|Vrf-ID|Notified
|======|======|=========================|======|====|======|========
|100   |10000 |UP                       |nve1  |CP  |0     |Yes
|======|======|=========================|======|====|======|========


Peers of interface nve1:
==========================================

Peer_ip: 192.168.2.2
  Peer-ID  : 1
  State    : UP
  Learning : Disabled
  TunnelID : 0x0
  MAC      : 0000.0000.0000
  Table-ID : 0x1
  Encap    : 0x1
```

Similar to the steps required for an L2 VNI, the L3 VNI can also be configured in a few simple steps:

Step 1. Create VLAN/VNI for L3. Similar to L2 VNI, configure a VLAN for L3 VNI using the command **vn-segment** under the VLAN configuration mode.

Step 2. Create L3 VRF and link to L2 VNI. Create a VRF and associate the L3 VNI with the tenant VRF routing instance.

Step 3.   Create SVI for the L3 VNI and associate it with the L3 VRF. Create an SVI for the L3 VNI with no IP address assigned to it. Associate the VRF created in Step 2.

Step 4.   Add L3 VNI to NVE. Add the L3 VNI as a member of the NVE interface using the command **member vni** *vni-id* **associate-vrf**.

Step 5.   Add VRF to BGP EVPN. Configure VRF under the BGP with IPv4 address-family and configure the command **advertise l2vpn evpn** to advertise the EVPN routes to remote peers.

Example 13-16 demonstrates the configuration of the L3 VNI on the Nexus 9300 leaf nodes.

Example 13-16   *Configuring L3 VNI on Leaf Nodes*

```
Leaf1
vlan 200
  vn-segment 20000
!
vrf context EVPN-TENANT
  vni 20000
  rd 20000:1
  address-family ipv4 unicast
    route-target import 20000:1
    route-target import 20000:1 evpn
    route-target export 20000:1
    route-target export 20000:1 evpn
!
interface Vlan200
  no shutdown
  vrf member EVPN-TENANT
  ip forward
!
interface nve1
  no shutdown
  source-interface loopback0
  host-reachability protocol bgp
  member vni 20000 associate-vrf
!
interface loopback200
  vrf member EVPN-TENANT
  ip address 200.1.1.1/32
!
```

```
router bgp 100
  vrf EVPN-TENANT
    address-family ipv4 unicast
      network 200.1.1.1/32
      advertise l2vpn evpn
```

```
Leaf2
vlan 200
  vn-segment 20000
!
vrf context EVPN-TENANT
  vni 20000
  rd 20000:1
  address-family ipv4 unicast
    route-target import 20000:1
    route-target import 20000:1 evpn
    route-target export 20000:1
    route-target export 20000:1 evpn
!
interface Vlan200
  no shutdown
  vrf member EVPN-TENANT
  ip forward
!
interface nve1
  no shutdown
  source-interface loopback0
  host-reachability protocol bgp
    member vni 20000 associate-vrf
!
interface loopback200
  vrf member EVPN-TENANT
  ip address 200.1.1.2/32
!
router bgp 100
  vrf EVPN-TENANT
    address-family ipv4 unicast
      network 200.1.1.2/32
      advertise l2vpn evpn
```

Because the symmetric IRB requires the introduction of a transit L3 VNI for L3 segmentation service per tenant, after the configuration of L3 VNI, the BGP table imports the host routes and network statement prefixes in the EVPN table as part of the L3 VNI routes. Example 13-17 displays the output of the BGP EVPN table with both the L2 VNI and the L3 VNI information.

Example 13-17   *L3 VNI Prefixes in BGP EVPN Table*

```
Leaf1
Leaf1# show bgp l2vpn evpn
BGP routing table information for VRF default, address family L2VPN EVPN
BGP table version is 18, local router ID is 192.168.1.1


   Network          Next Hop           Metric    LocPrf    Weight Path
Route Distinguisher: 10000:1    (L2VNI 10000)
*>i[2]:[0]:[0]:[48]:[8c60.4f19.51fc]:[0]:[0.0.0.0]/216
                    192.168.2.2                  100          0 i
*>l[2]:[0]:[0]:[48]:[8c60.4f1b.e43c]:[0]:[0.0.0.0]/216
                    192.168.1.1                  100      32768 i
*>i[2]:[0]:[0]:[48]:[8c60.4f19.51fc]:[32]:[100.1.1.2]/272
                    192.168.2.2                  100          0 i
*>l[2]:[0]:[0]:[48]:[8c60.4f1b.e43c]:[32]:[100.1.1.1]/272
                    192.168.1.1                  100      32768 i


Route Distinguisher: 20000:1
*>i[5]:[0]:[0]:[32]:[200.1.1.2]:[0.0.0.0]/224
                    192.168.2.2                  100          0 i


Route Distinguisher: 20000:1    (L3VNI 20000)
*>i[2]:[0]:[0]:[48]:[8c60.4f19.51fc]:[32]:[100.1.1.2]/272
                    192.168.2.2                  100          0 i
*>l[5]:[0]:[0]:[32]:[200.1.1.1]:[0.0.0.0]/224
                    192.168.1.1                  100      32768 i
*>i[5]:[0]:[0]:[32]:[200.1.1.2]:[0.0.0.0]/224
                    192.168.2.2                  100          0 i


Leaf2
Leaf2# show bgp l2vpn evpn
BGP routing table information for VRF default, address family L2VPN EVPN
BGP table version is 23, local router ID is 192.168.2.2


   Network          Next Hop           Metric    LocPrf    Weight Path
Route Distinguisher: 10000:1    (L2VNI 10000)
*>l[2]:[0]:[0]:[48]:[8c60.4f19.51fc]:[0]:[0.0.0.0]/216
                    192.168.2.2                  100      32768 i
*>i[2]:[0]:[0]:[48]:[8c60.4f1b.e43c]:[0]:[0.0.0.0]/216
                    192.168.1.1                  100          0 i
*>l[2]:[0]:[0]:[48]:[8c60.4f19.51fc]:[32]:[100.1.1.2]/272
                    192.168.2.2                  100      32768 i
*>i[2]:[0]:[0]:[48]:[8c60.4f1b.e43c]:[32]:[100.1.1.1]/272
                    192.168.1.1                  100          0 i
```

```
Route Distinguisher: 20000:1
*>i[5]:[0]:[0]:[32]:[200.1.1.1]:[0.0.0.0]/224
                     192.168.1.1                      100         0 i


Route Distinguisher: 20000:1    (L3VNI 20000)
*>i[2]:[0]:[0]:[48]:[8c60.4f1b.e43c]:[32]:[100.1.1.1]/272
                     192.168.1.1                      100         0 i
*>i[5]:[0]:[0]:[32]:[200.1.1.1]:[0.0.0.0]/224
                     192.168.1.1                      100         0 i
*>l[5]:[0]:[0]:[32]:[200.1.1.2]:[0.0.0.0]/224
                     192.168.2.2                      100     32768 i
```

The EVPN routes are also seen in the Tenant VRF. The routing table shows which routes have been locally learned and others that have been learned over EVPN with VxLAN encapsulation. Example 13-18 examines the Tenant VRF routing table. Note that the *tunnelid* is nothing but the remote VTEP IP. The hex value *0xc0a80202* represents 192.168.2.2 in decimal format.

Example 13-18 *Tenant VRF Routing Table*

```
Leaf1
Leaf1# show ip route vrf EVPN-TENANT
IP Route Table for VRF "EVPN-TENANT"
100.1.1.0/24, ubest/mbest: 1/0, attached
    *via 100.1.1.254, Vlan100, [0/0], 11:37:59, direct
100.1.1.1/32, ubest/mbest: 1/0, attached
    *via 100.1.1.1, Vlan100, [190/0], 11:21:00, hmm
100.1.1.2/32, ubest/mbest: 1/0
    *via 192.168.2.2%default, [200/0], 08:10:21, bgp-100, internal,
    tag 100 (evpn) segid: 20000 tunnelid: 0xc0a80202 encap: VXLAN

100.1.1.254/32, ubest/mbest: 1/0, attached
    *via 100.1.1.254, Vlan100, [0/0], 11:37:59, local
200.1.1.1/32, ubest/mbest: 2/0, attached
    *via 200.1.1.1, Lo200, [0/0], 07:54:28, local
    *via 200.1.1.1, Lo200, [0/0], 07:54:28, direct
200.1.1.2/32, ubest/mbest: 1/0
    *via 192.168.2.2%default, [200/0], 05:59:49, bgp-100, internal,
    tag 100 (evpn) segid: 20000 tunnelid: 0xc0a80202 encap: VXLAN
```

The command **show bgp l2vpn evpn** *ip-address*, where *ip-address* is the end host IP address, provides more detailed information about the prefix. In this command, there are two labels received for the prefix. The first label is the L2 VNI vni-id, and the second label is the L3 VNI vni-id. Also, as explained previously, the router MAC is sent as the destination MAC address for VxLAN encapsulation. This command output holds that information as well. Example 13.19 displays the output of the host prefix 100.1.1.2, which is connected to Leaf2 node.

Example 13-19   *EVPN Host Prefix*

```
Leaf1
Leaf1# show bgp l2vpn evpn 100.1.1.12
BGP routing table information for VRF default, address family L2VPN EVPN
Leaf1# show bgp l2vpn evpn 100.1.1.2
BGP routing table information for VRF default, address family L2VPN EVPN
Route Distinguisher: 10000:1    (L2VNI 10000)
BGP routing table entry for [2]:[0]:[0]:[48]:[8c60.4f19.51fc]:[32]:[100.1.1.2]
   /272, version 16
Paths: (1 available, best #1)
Flags: (0x00021a) on xmit-list, is in l2rib/evpn, is not in HW, , is locked

  Advertised path-id 1
  Path type: internal, path is valid, imported same remote RD, is best path,
 no labeled nexthop
  AS-Path: NONE, path sourced internal to AS
    192.168.2.2 (metric 5) from 192.168.10.10 (192.168.10.10)
      Origin IGP, MED not set, localpref 100, weight 0
      Received label 10000 20000
      Extcommunity:  RT:10000:1 RT:20000:1 ENCAP:8 Router MAC:88f0.312a.f2c1
      Originator: 192.168.2.2 Cluster list: 192.168.10.10


  Path-id 1 not advertised to any peer


Route Distinguisher: 20000:1    (L3VNI 20000)
BGP routing table entry for [2]:[0]:[0]:[48]:[8c60.4f19.51fc]:[32]:[100.1.1.2]
   /272, version 17
Paths: (1 available, best #1)
Flags: (0x00021a) on xmit-list, is in l2rib/evpn, is not in HW,

  Advertised path-id 1
  Path type: internal, path is valid, is best path, no labeled nexthop
            Imported from
10000:1:[2]:[0]:[0]:[48]:[8c60.4f19.51fc]:[32]:[100.1.1.2]/144 (VNI 10000)
  AS-Path: NONE, path sourced internal to AS
    192.168.2.2 (metric 5) from 192.168.10.10 (192.168.10.10)
      Origin IGP, MED not set, localpref 100, weight 0
      Received label 10000 20000
      Extcommunity:  RT:10000:1 RT:20000:1 ENCAP:8 Router MAC:88f0.312a.f2c1
      Originator: 192.168.2.2 Cluster list: 192.168.10.10


  Path-id 1 not advertised to any peer
```

After adding the L3VNI, the NVE internal platform information also shows the Tunnel Id and the Router MAC address. Also when viewing the **show nve peers** [**detail**] command, the peer flags are set to RmacL2Rib, TunnelPD, and DisableLearn, which was earlier set to just DisableLearn without the L2 VNI. Example 13-20 shows the NVE internal platform information for the NVE interface and the NVE peer information.

Example 13-20 *NVE Internal Platform Information and NVE Peers*

```
Leaf1
Leaf1# show nve internal platform interface nve 1 detail
Printing Interface ifindex 0x49000001 detail
|======|=========================|===============|===============|=====|=====|
|Intf  |State                    |PriIP          |SecIP          |Vnis |Peers|
|======|=========================|===============|===============|=====|=====|
|nve1  |UP                       |192.168.1.1    |0.0.0.0        |2    |1    |
|======|=========================|===============|===============|=====|=====|


SW_BD/VNIs of interface nve1:
===============================================
|======|======|=========================|======|====|======|========
|Sw BD |Vni   |State                    |Intf  |Type|Vrf-ID|Notified
|======|======|=========================|======|====|======|========
|100   |10000 |UP                       |nve1  |CP  |0     |Yes
|200   |20000 |UP                       |nve1  |CP  |3     |Yes
|======|======|=========================|======|====|======|========


Peers of interface nve1:
=============================================


Peer_ip: 192.168.2.2
  Peer-ID  : 1
  State    : UP
  Learning : Disabled
  TunnelID : 0xc0a80202
  MAC      : 88f0.312a.f2c1
  Table-ID : 0x1
  Encap    : 0x1


Leaf1# show nve peers detail
Details of nve Peers:
----------------------------------------
Peer-Ip: 192.168.2.2
    NVE Interface       : nve1
    Peer State          : Up
```

```
Peer Uptime          : 11:40:04
Router-Mac           : 88f0.312a.f2c1
Peer First VNI       : 10000
Time since Create    : 11:40:04
Configured VNIs      : 10000,20000
Provision State      : add-complete
Route-Update         : Yes
Peer Flags           : RmacL2Rib, TunnelPD, DisableLearn
Learnt CP VNIs       : 10000,20000
Peer-ifindex-resp    : Yes
```

Another scenario that is heavily seen in production deployment is when virtual port channel (VPC) is terminated on the leaf nodes and the host is attached across the VPC. In such situations there are few things that require special attention while configuring the VTEP.

A pair of VPC peers are seen as a single VTEP node to other peer VTEPs. A secondary IP is configured on the loopback address for the VPC running leaf nodes. The secondary IP address is same on both the primary VPC and the secondary VPC peer. Nexus 9000 uses the secondary IP to create a virtual VTEP. The rest of the configuration remains the same as the non-VPC examples. Example 13-21 illustrates the partial configuration on the leaf node Leaf3 and Leaf4 running VPC between them.

Example 13-21   *VxLAN EVPN Configuration on VPC Peers*

```
Leaf3
vlan 100
  vn-segment 10000
vlan 200
  vn-segment 20000
!
vrf context EVPN-TENANT
  vni 20000
  rd 20000:1
  address-family ipv4 unicast
    route-target import 20000:1
    route-target import 20000:1 evpn
    route-target export 20000:1
    route-target export 20000:1 evpn
!
evpn
  vni 10000 l2
    rd 10000:1
    route-target import 10000:1
    route-target export 10000:1
!
```

```
vpc domain 10
  peer-switch
  peer-keepalive destination 10.1.34.4 source 10.1.34.3
  delay restore 60
  peer-gateway
  ipv6 nd synchronize
  ip arp synchronize
!
interface loopback0
  ip address 192.168.3.3/32
  ip address 192.168.100.100/32 secondary
  ip router ospf 100 area 0.0.0.0
  ip pim sparse-mode
!
! Output omitted for brevity
!
router bgp 100
  router-id 192.168.3.3
  address-family ipv4 unicast
  address-family l2vpn evpn
  neighbor 192.168.10.10
    remote-as 100
    description Peering with Route Reflector
    update-source loopback0
    address-family l2vpn evpn
      send-community extended
  vrf EVPN-TENANT
    address-family ipv4 unicast
      advertise l2vpn evpn
```

```
Leaf4
vlan 100
  vn-segment 10000
vlan 200
  vn-segment 20000
!
vrf context EVPN-TENANT
  vni 20000
  rd 20000:1
  address-family ipv4 unicast
    route-target import 20000:1
    route-target import 20000:1 evpn
    route-target export 20000:1
    route-target export 20000:1 evpn
```

```
!
evpn
  vni 10000 l2
    rd 10000:1
    route-target import 10000:1
    route-target export 10000:1
!
vpc domain 10
  peer-switch
  peer-keepalive destination 10.1.34.3 source 10.1.34.4
  delay restore 60
  peer-gateway
  ipv6 nd synchronize
  ip arp synchronize
!
interface loopback0
  ip address 192.168.3.3/32
  ip address 192.168.100.100/32 secondary
  ip router ospf 100 area 0.0.0.0
  ip pim sparse-mode
!
! Output omitted for brevity
!
router bgp 100
  router-id 192.168.4.4
  address-family ipv4 unicast
  address-family l2vpn evpn
  neighbor 192.168.10.10
    remote-as 100
    description Peering with Route Reflector
    update-source loopback0
    address-family l2vpn evpn
      send-community extended
  vrf EVPN-TENANT
    address-family ipv4 unicast
      advertise l2vpn evpn
```

Note   Explanation on how VPC feature works is outside the scope of this book. Refer to Cisco documentation for understanding VPC.

After it is configured, the NVE internal platform information shows both the primary as well as the secondary IP. The remote VTEPs show the NVE peering formed over the secondary IP. Example 13-22 displays the NVE peers and the NVE internal platform information on the leaf node running VPC.

Example 13-22 *NVE Internal Platform Detail*

```
Leaf3
Leaf3# show nve internal platform interface nve1 detail
Printing Interface ifindex 0x49000001 detail
|======|========================|==============|===============|=====|=====|
|Intf  |State                   |PriIP         |SecIP          |Vnis |Peers|
|======|========================|==============|===============|=====|=====|
|nve1  |UP                      |192.168.3.3   |192.168.100.100|2    |2    |
|======|========================|==============|===============|=====|=====|


SW_BD/VNIs of interface nve1:
=================================================
|======|======|========================|======|====|======|========
|Sw BD |Vni   |State                   |Intf  |Type|Vrf-ID|Notified
|======|======|========================|======|====|======|========
|100   |10000 |UP                      |nve1  |CP  |0     |Yes
|200   |20000 |UP                      |nve1  |CP  |3     |Yes
|======|======|========================|======|====|======|========


Peers of interface nve1:
=========================================

Peer_ip: 192.168.1.1
  Peer-ID   : 2
  State     : UP
  Learning  : Disabled
  TunnelID  : 0xc0a80101
  MAC       : f40f.1b6f.926f
  Table-ID  : 0x1
  Encap     : 0x1


Peer_ip: 192.168.2.2
  Peer-ID   : 1
  State     : UP
  Learning  : Disabled
  TunnelID  : 0xc0a80202
  MAC       : 88f0.312a.f2c1
```

```
 Table-ID   : 0x1
  Encap     : 0x1

Leaf3# show nve peers detail
Details of nve Peers:
----------------------------------------
Peer-Ip: 192.168.1.1
    NVE Interface       : nve1
    Peer State          : Up
    Peer Uptime         : 01:37:25
    Router-Mac          : f40f.1b6f.926f
    Peer First VNI      : 20000
    Time since Create   : 01:37:25
    Configured VNIs     : 10000,20000
    Provision State     : add-complete
    Route-Update        : Yes
    Peer Flags          : RmacL2Rib, TunnelPD, DisableLearn
    Learnt CP VNIs      : 10000,20000
    Peer-ifindex-resp   : Yes
----------------------------------------
Peer-Ip: 192.168.2.2
    NVE Interface       : nve1
    Peer State          : Up
    Peer Uptime         : 01:37:25
    Router-Mac          : 88f0.312a.f2c1
    Peer First VNI      : 20000
    Time since Create   : 01:37:25
    Configured VNIs     : 10000,20000
    Provision State     : add-complete
    Route-Update        : Yes
    Peer Flags          : RmacL2Rib, TunnelPD, DisableLearn
    Learnt CP VNIs      : 20000
    Peer-ifindex-resp   : Yes
```

Leaf1
```
Leaf1# show nve peers detail
Details of nve Peers:
----------------------------------------
Peer-Ip: 192.168.2.2
    NVE Interface       : nve1
    Peer State          : Up
```

```
    Peer Uptime          : 1d06h
    Router-Mac           : 88f0.312a.f2c1
    Peer First VNI       : 10000
    Time since Create    : 1d06h
    Configured VNIs      : 10000,20000
    Provision State      : add-complete
    Route-Update         : Yes
    Peer Flags           : RmacL2Rib, TunnelPD, DisableLearn
    Learnt CP VNIs       : 20000
    Peer-ifindex-resp    : Yes
-----------------------------------------
Peer-Ip: 192.168.100.100
    NVE Interface        : nve1
    Peer State           : Up
    Peer Uptime          : 02:36:18
    Router-Mac           : 88f0.312b.9e4d
    Peer First VNI       : 10000
    Time since Create    : 02:36:18
    Configured VNIs      : 10000,20000
    Provision State      : add-complete
    Route-Update         : Yes
    Peer Flags           : RmacL2Rib, TunnelPD, DisableLearn
    Learnt CP VNIs       : 10000,20000
    Peer-ifindex-resp    : Yes
```

So far, all the previous examples are shown with BGP EVPN running with a multicast core. With BGP EVPN solution with multicast core, the peer discovery is done using the BGP Remote Next-Hop (BGP-RnH). BGP EVPN solution also supports unicast core with the IR method. As discussed earlier, there are two methods with IR:

- Static IR
- IR-based BGP-EVPN

With static ingress replication, the peers are statically configured, whereas with BGP EVPN with IR peer learning, the peer discovery is done using BGP inclusive multicast Ethernet tag (BGP-IMET) NLRI. Figure 13-13 examines the various host learning and peer-discovery mechanism and their respective configuration.

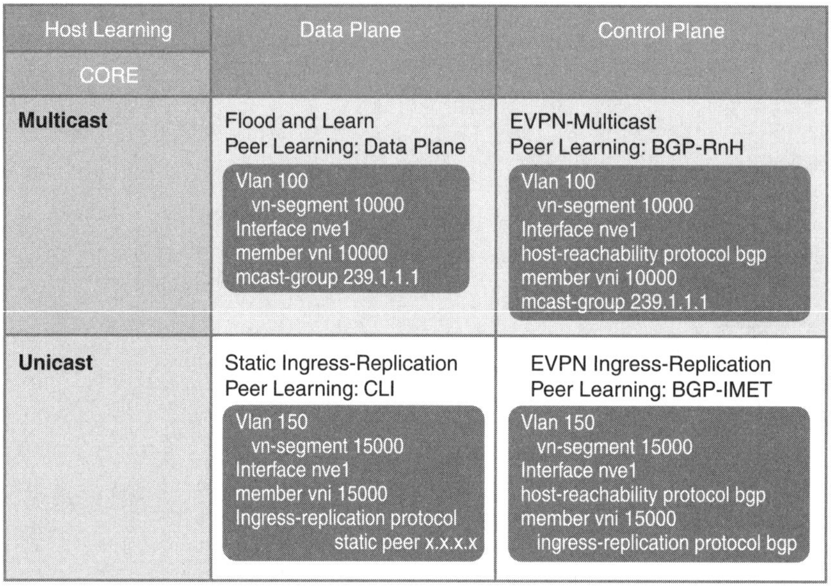

Host Learning	Data Plane	Control Plane
CORE		

Multicast	Flood and Learn
	Peer Learning: Data Plane
	
	Vlan 100
	    vn-segment 10000
	Interface nve1
	member vni 10000
	mcast-group 239.1.1.1
		EVPN-Multicast
		Peer Learning: BGP-RnH
		
		Vlan 100
		    vn-segment 10000
		Interface nve1
		host-reachability protocol bgp
		member vni 10000
		mcast-group 239.1.1.1

Unicast	Static Ingress-Replication
	Peer Learning: CLI
	
	Vlan 150
	    vn-segment 15000
	Interface nve1
	member vni 15000
	Ingress-replication protocol
	                    static peer x.x.x.x
		EVPN Ingress-Replication
		Peer Learning: BGP-IMET
		
		Vlan 150
		    vn-segment 15000
		Interface nve1
		host-reachability protocol bgp
		member vni 15000
		    ingress-replication protocol bgp

Figure 13-13 *Host Learning and Peer Discovery Configuration Options*

To further understand how the output differs for the BGP EVPN with IR method, examine the configuration shown in Example 13-23. Two VLANs are created: VLAN 150 mapped to VNI 15000 and VLAN 151 mapped to VNI 15001. The VNI 15000 is a L2 VNI, and VNI 15001 is an L3 VNI; both are part of tenant VRF EVPN-IR-TENANT. The IR is enabled using the command **ingress-replication protocol bgp** under the L2 VNI configuration.

Example 13-23 *BGP EVPN Configuration with IR Method*

```
Leaf1 and Leaf2
interface nve1
  no shutdown
  source-interface loopback0
  host-reachability protocol bgp
  member vni 15000
    ingress-replication protocol bgp
  member vni 15001 associate-vrf
```

When the EVPN prefixes are exchanged between the two peers, they not only share the host routes, but they also advertise VTEP IP into the BGP EVPN table as a Type 3 (IMET) route. Example 13-24 displays the BGP EVPN table for hosts in VLAN segment 150 along with the VTEP IP information. In the following example, notice that the VTEP-IP 192.168.2.2 is received as a Type 3 route. The prefix also shown the Tunnel type as *Ingress Replication*.

Example 13-24 *BGP EVPN Table with IR Method*

```
Leaf1
Leaf1# show bgp l2vpn evpn vni-id 15000
BGP routing table information for VRF default, address family L2VPN EVPN
BGP table version is 32, local router ID is 192.168.1.1
Status: s-suppressed, x-deleted, S-stale, d-dampened, h-history, *-valid, >-best
Path type: i-internal, e-external, c-confed, l-local, a-aggregate, r-redist,
  I-injected
Origin codes: i - IGP, e - EGP, ? - incomplete, | - multipath, & - backup


   Network           Next Hop            Metric      LocPrf      Weight Path
Route Distinguisher: 192.168.1.1:32917    (L2VNI 15000)
*>i[2]:[0]:[0]:[48]:[8c60.4f19.51fc]:[0]:[0.0.0.0]/216
                    192.168.2.2                       100            0 i
*>l[2]:[0]:[0]:[48]:[8c60.4f1b.e43c]:[0]:[0.0.0.0]/216
                    192.168.1.1                       100        32768 i
*>i[2]:[0]:[0]:[48]:[8c60.4f19.51fc]:[32]:[150.1.1.2]/272
                    192.168.2.2                       100            0 i
*>l[2]:[0]:[0]:[48]:[8c60.4f1b.e43c]:[32]:[150.1.1.1]/272
                    192.168.1.1                       100        32768 i
*>l[3]:[0]:[32]:[192.168.1.1]/88
                    192.168.1.1                       100        32768 i
*>i[3]:[0]:[32]:[192.168.2.2]/88
                    192.168.2.2                       100            0 i


Leaf2# show bgp l2vpn evpn 192.168.2.2
BGP routing table information for VRF default, address family L2VPN EVPN
Route Distinguisher: 192.168.2.2:32917    (L2VNI 15000)
BGP routing table entry for [3]:[0]:[32]:[192.168.2.2]/88, version 26
Paths: (1 available, best #1)
Flags: (0x00000a) on xmit-list, is not in l2rib/evpn


  Advertised path-id 1
  Path type: local, path is valid, is best path, no labeled nexthop
  AS-Path: NONE, path locally originated
    192.168.2.2 (metric 0) from 0.0.0.0 (192.168.2.2)
      Origin IGP, MED not set, localpref 100, weight 32768
      Extcommunity:  RT:100:15000
      PMSI Tunnel Attribute:
        flags: 0x00, Tunnel type: Ingress Replication
        Label: 15000, Tunnel Id: 192.168.2.2


  Path-id 1 advertised to peers:
    192.168.10.10
```

The IMET route can be seen in the L2RIB using the command **show l2route evpn imet evi** *VLAN-ID*. This command displays both the VTEP IPs: one that is of the local VTEP and the other of the remote VTEP. Also, when looking at the VNI 15000, notice that there is no multicast group listed for the VNI, and the host learning is done via *UnicastBGP*. This information is seen using the command **show nve vni** *vni-id*. Example 13-25 displays the IMET route and the VNI information using the preceding commands. Notice in the output, the NVI 15000 is running with a unicast core but the peer learning mode is again via BGP.

Example 13-25   *IMET Route and VNI Information*

```
Leaf1
Leaf1# show l2route evpn imet evi 1150
VNI          Prod  Originating Router IP Addr
-----------  ----- --------------------------------------

Leaf1# show l2route evpn imet evi 150
VNI          Prod  Originating Router IP Addr
-----------  ----- --------------------------------------
15000        BGP    192.168.2.2
15000        VXLAN  192.168.1.1


Leaf1# show nve vni 15000
Codes: CP - Control Plane         DP - Data Plane
       UC - Unconfigured          SA - Suppress ARP


Interface VNI      Multicast-group   State Mode Type [BD/VRF]      Flags
--------- -------- ----------------- ----- ---- ----------------- -----
nve1      15000    UnicastBGP        Up    CP   L2 [150]
```

The IMET route information can also be verified in the NVE event-history information, which is seen by using the command **show nve internal event-history event**. Example 13-26 shows that the IMET notification is received by the leaf node for the remote VTEP. The output of the command **show nve internal event-history event** is in reverse direction; that is, the more recent information is added on top of the output. In the following output, it is seen that the IMET notification is received for the remote VTEP IP for VLAN 150 and VNI 15000. Then the peer is added for the VNI. Finally, the hardware is programmed for the discovered peer when the state is set to *add-complete*. The VTEP IP is added to the VNI flood list (FL). The VNI FL can be viewed using the command **show l2route evpn fl all**.

Example 13-26 *NVE Event-History Information*

```
Leaf1
Leaf1# show nve internal event-history events | in IMET
    [102] [9403]: Adding FL 192.168.2.2 in position 0 to VNI 15000
    [102] [9403]: First Entry: Adding FL 192.168.2.2 for VNI 15000
    [102] [9403]: nve_pi_peer_discovered Processed peer 192.168.2.2
[State:add-complete] create-ts:00:10:18 add request on vni 15000 to PD
 on nve1 learn-type:[CP]->[CP] src IMET [mac-unchanged]
    [102] [9403]: XOS_EVT: nve_peer_vni_sdb_update: Add peer VNI node to SDB
ip:192.168.2.2 vni:15000 learn-src:IMET mac:0000.0000.0000
    [102] [9403]: XOS_EVT: nve_peer_vni_add: Add peer VNI node ip:192.168.2.2
vni:15000 learn-src:IMET mac:0000.0000.0000 on intf:0x49000001
    [102] [9403]: nve_pi_peer_discovered Peer 192.168.2.2 discovery notification
on VNI 15000 ready:Yes on intf nve1 src:IMET type:CP mac:0000.0000.0000
tunnel-id:0x0 peer ID:0 disable-learning: 1
    [102] [9403]: nve_vni_fl_peer_add_or_delete: ADD peer 192.168.2.2 for all
vni:15000-15000 [source:IMET]
    [102] [9403]: Got IMET notification 192.168.2.2 for BD 150 and vni 15000.
Operation: ADD
    [102] [9395]: IMET route for topo 150 [vni 15000] added to L2RIB
    [102] [9395]: IMET Registration for topo 150 added to L2RIB


! VNI Flood List
Leaf1# show l2route evpn fl all
Topology ID Peer-id     Flood List      Service Node
----------- ----------- --------------- ------------
150         1           192.168.2.2     no
Troubleshooting VxLAN BGP EVPN
```

Now that you have an understanding of how VxLAN BGP EVPN works and the list
of commands that can be used to verify whether VxLAN BGP EVPN is working fine,
troubleshooting VxLAN BGP EVPN becomes fairly simple on Nexus 9000. The Nexus
platforms running NX-OS code are designed to ease troubleshooting and debugging
using event-history data that is available for almost all the components and features
running on the system.

The troubleshooting of L2 VNI; that is, the MAC learning on both the local as well as
the remote VTEP, can be broken down into a few simple steps and can be verified using
various event-history commands on the leaf nodes. To troubleshoot the MAC address
advertisement via BGP EVPN and installation in the hardware, use the packet flow and
the steps that follow:

Step 1.   The host sends an ARP request for the remote host. The MAC address is
              learned on the VLAN for the local host. The MAC address information is sent
              to the Layer 2 Forwarding Manager (L2FM) component of the system. This

information can be viewed using the command **show system internal l2fm event-history debugs | include** *mac-address*. The mac-address variable is the MAC address of the locally attached host.

Step 2.   The L2FM component then sends a notification about the L2VNI and MAC address to the Layer 2 Routing Information Base (L2RIB). The information on the L2RIB that is received from L2FM is viewed by using the command **show system internal l2rib event-history mac | include** *mac-address*.

Step 3.   The L2RIB then sends the L2 VNI and MAC address information to BGP L2VPN component, which is then advertised to the remote VTEP. BGP builds the L2 NLRI information with the local host MAC received:

■ Prefix—0

■ MAC—Host MAC Address

■ Label1—0

■ Label2—L2 VNI-ID

■ BD-RT—Configured RT

■ NH—VTEP-IP

The Type 2 NLRI is then sent to the remote VTEP as part of the update.

Step 4.   On receiving the update, the remote VTEP stores the information in the L2VPN EVPN table. Apart from viewing the information on the BGP EVPN table, the route import on the remote VTEP is verified by using the command **show bgp internal event-history events | include** *mac-address*. The command is executed on the remote VTEP (Leaf2) and *mac-address* of the host attached to Leaf1 can be used as a filter option.

Step 5.   The BGP process on the remote VTEP sends Peer information and VNI notification to the VxLAN manager. This information is verified using the command **show nve internal bgp rnh database** and also from the event-history logs using the command **show nve internal event-history event**. It also adds VNI and the MAC address of the remote host learned from VTEP Leaf1 with the Next-Hop set to Leaf1.

Step 6.   The VxLAN manager then programs the hardware; that is, the data plane, and also allocates the Peer ID, which is then sent to L2RIB. The information from VxLAN Manager is sent to the Unicast RIB (URIB) / Unicast Forwarding Distribution Manager (UFDM) process which is used to program the FIB. The forwarding information can be viewed using the command **show forwarding nv3 l3 peers** and the command **show forwarding nve l3 adjacency tunnel** *tunnel-id*, where the *tunnel-id* is received from the first command. The L2RIB, on the other hand, adds the VNI and the MAC address information in the L2FM table, which contains an entry consisting of the MAC address and the next-hop Peer ID (Remote VTEP – Leaf1).

The previously mentioned steps make it easy to figure out which component on the system is causing a problem. The following steps can be used to troubleshoot the L3 VNI route advertisement and installation:

Step 1.   A host attached to a VTEP sends an ARP request. The VTEP receives the ARP request and updates its ARP table for the VLAN.

Step 2.   After the ARP table is updated, the information is passed onto an AM, which installs the adjacency for the local host. This is viewed by using the command **show forwarding vrf** *vrf-name* **adjacency.**

Step 3.   The AM then sends an adjacency notification to the Host Mobility Manager (HMM) with MAC+IP also known as the combo routes. Because the host MAC needs to be carried in a BGP update along with the host IP, HMM publishes the combo route into the L2RIB. Use the command **show system internal l2rib event-history mac-ip** to view the combo route in L2RIB.

Step 4.   The L2RIB then sends the combo route along with the L3 VNI to BGP. The BGP uses the information to prepare its L2 + L3 NLRI, which consists of the following fields:

- Prefix—Host-IP

- MAC—Host MAC

- Label1—L3VNI

- Label2—L2VNI

- VRF-RT

- BD-RT

- NH—VTEP-IP

- Remote Next-Hop (RNH)—Router MAC (RMAC)

The L2 + L3 NLRI is sent as an update to the remote VTEP.

Step 5.   The update received on the remote node is viewed by using the command **show bgp l2vpn evpn** *ip-address*; where the *ip-address* is of the host connected to Leaf1 node. The BGP update has the encapsulation as VxLAN; that is, of value 8. BGP, on receiving an update on remote VTEP, updates two components. First, it updates the URIB with VRF, Host-IP, L3 VNI, and VTEP-IP information. Second, it updates the VxLAN Manager with Peer information and VNI and RMAC notification.

Step 6.   The information in the URIB is used by UFDM along with the information from VxLAN manager, which programs the data plane with the encapsulation and decapsulation information for the L3 VNI. The VxLAN manager also sends RMAC to UFDM and allocates the Peer-ID.

Step 7.   VxLAN manager, on the other hand, sends the Peer-ID notification to the L2RIB. During this time, the VNI is set with the next-hop of the Peer-ID.

Step 8.   The L2RIB then updates the L2FM to update the MAC address table.

> **Note**   Data plane or platform troubleshooting for VxLAN EVPN is outside the scope of this book.

Summary

This chapter discussed how VxLAN works and plays a crucial role in the next-generation data centers. As defined in RFC 7348, this chapter described how VxLAN Flood-and-Learn mechanism works. This chapter also briefly talks about the IR method, which uses unicast core instead of multicast. To overcome the challenges faced because of both VxLAN flood-and-learn and IR mechanisms, the VxLAN BGP EVPN solution was developed. This chapter explains how the BGP EVPN solution is used to carry VxLAN Host routes across the VTEPs and provide scalability to VxLAN deployments. VxLAN BGP EVPN provides features such as the following:

- Less flooding required

- Dynamic peer VTEP discovery

- Stability (no timing out of BUM groups)

BGP EVPN primarily carries five types of routes:

- Route Type 1—Ethernet Auto-Discovery route

- Route Type 2—MAC advertisement route (carries L2 VNI MAC / MAC-IP)

- Route Type 3—Inclusive multicast route (EVPN IR and peer discovery)

- Route Type 4—Ethernet segment route

- Route Type 5—IP Prefix Route (L3 VNI route)

VxLAN EVPN supports both multicast as well as unicast underlay networks between the spine and leaf, but the peer discovery is done using BGP EVPN. This chapter discussed various configuration and verification commands that are used for troubleshooting VxLAN EVPN. Finally, the chapter examined the flow of packets across various components in VxLAN EVPN deployment.

References

RFC 7348, *Virtual eXtensible Local Area Network (VxLAN)*, M. Mahalingam, D. Dutt, K. Duda, P. Agarwal, L. Kreegar, T. Sridhar, M. Bursell, C. Wright, IETF, https://tools.ietf.org/html/rfc7348, August 2014.

RFC 7432, *BGP MPLS-Based Ethernet VPN*, A. Sajassi, R. Aggarwal, Arktan, N. Bitar, A. Isaac, J. Uttaro, J. Drake, W. Henderickx, IETF, https://tools.ietf.org/html/rfc7432, February 2015.

RFC 7209, *Requirements for Ethernet VPN (EVPN)*, A. Sajassi, R. Aggarwal, Arktan, N. Bitar, A. Isaac, J. Uttaro, W. Henderickx. IETF, https://tools.ietf.org/html/rfc7209, May 2014.

VxLAN Network with MP-BGP EVPN Control Plane Design Guide, Cisco, http://www.cisco.com/c/en/us/products/collateral/switches/nexus-9000-series-switches/guide-c07-734107.html.

## Chapter 14

BGP High Availability

The following topics are covered in this chapter:

- BGP Graceful-Restart
- BGP SSO and Nonstop Routing
- BFD
- Fast External Failover
- Route Dampening
- BGP Add-Path
- BGP Prefix-Independent Convergence

BGP Graceful-Restart

The BGP Graceful-Restart (GR) feature allows a BGP speaker to express its ability to preserve forwarding state during Border Gateway Protocol (BGP) restart or Route Processor (RP) switchover. In other words, it is the capability exchanged between the BGP speakers to indicate its ability to perform Nonstop Forwarding (NSF). This helps in minimizing the impact of services caused by BGP restart. Specially in large network deployments, where BGP carries large number of prefixes, a BGP restart, especially by a route-reflector (RR) router, can have a severe performance and service impact and can lead to major outages.

Examine the network topology shown in Figure 14-1. R1 is acting as the RR and its peering with multiple clients. If there is a BGP restart or RP switchover on R1, the peer detects the session flaps and propagate routing updates throughout the network. This can lead to increased CPU utilization if the RR is holding a large BGP table. The traffic destined to the prefixes that were removed are impacted.

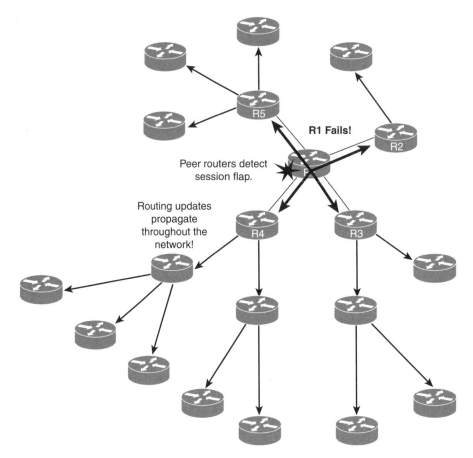

Figure 14-1   *Impact of Node Failure in a Network with BGP Route Reflectors*

RFC 4724 defines the GR mechanism for BGP. The BGP GR was developed with the following motivations:

- Avoid widespread routing changes.

- Decrease control plane overhead throughout the network.

- Enhance overall stability of routing.

A GR-capable device announces its ability to perform GR for the BGP peer. It also initiates the graceful-restart process when a RP switchover occurs and acts as a GR-aware device. A GR-aware device, also known GR helper mode, is capable of understanding that a peer router is transitioning and takes appropriate actions based on the configuration or default timers.

GR capability should always be enabled for all routing protocols, especially when the routers are running with dual route processors (RP) and perform a switchover in case of any failure instance. Because BGP runs on Transmission Control Protocol (TCP), GR should be enabled on both the peering devices. After GR is configured or enabled on both peering devices, reset the BGP session to exchange the capability and activate the GR feature.

> **Note** GR is always on by default for non-TCP–based protocols such as Interior Gateway Protocol (IGPs). These protocols start operating in GR mode as soon as the other side is configured with GR capability.

BGP GR is an optional feature and is not enabled by default. BGP peers announce GR capability in the BGP OPEN message. Within the OPEN message, the following information is negotiated:

- **Restart Flag:** This bit indicates if a peer sending the GR capability has just restarted. This is used to prevent deadlocks if both peers restart at the same time.

- **Restart Time:** Indicates the length of time that the sender of the GR capability requires to complete a restart. The restart timer also helps in speeding up convergence in the event the peer never comes back up after a restart.

- **Address-Family Identifier (AFI)/Subaddress-Family Identifier (SAFI):** Address-family for which GR is supported.

- **AFI Flags:** It contains a *Forwarding State* bit. This bit indicates whether the peer sending the GR capability has preserved forwarding during the previous restart.

Peers can include GR capability without including any address-families. This implies GR awareness (nonrestarting support for GR) without the ability to perform a GR.

When a BGP restart happens on the peer router or when RP switchover occurs, the routes currently held in the forwarding table; that is, hardware, are marked as stable. This way, the forwarding state is preserved as the control plane and the forwarding plane operate independently. On the restarting peer (where the switchover occurred), BGP on the newly active RP starts to establish sessions with all the configured peers. BGP on the other side, the nonrestarting side, sees new connection requests coming in while BGP already is in established state. Such an event is an indication for the nonrestarting peer that the peer has restarted. At this point, the restarting peer sends the GR capability with *Restart State* bit set to 1 and *Forwarding State* bit set to 1 for the AFI/SAFIs.

The nonrestarting peer at this point cleans up old (dead) BGP sessions and marks all the routes in the BGP table that are received from the restarting peer as **stale**. If the restarting peer never reestablishes the BGP session, the nonrestarting peer purges all stale routes after the *Restart Time* expires. The nonrestarting peer sends an initial routing table update, followed by an End-of-RIB (EoR) marker. Restarting peer delays best-path calculation for an AFI until after receiving EoR from all peers except for those that are not GR capable or for the ones that have *Restart State* bit set.

The restarting peer finally generates updates for its peers and sends the EoR marker for each AFI after the initial table is sent. The nonrestarting peers receive the routing updates from the restarting peer and remove stale marking for any refreshed route. It purges any remaining stale routes after EoR is received from the restarting peer or the *Stale Path Timer* expires.

GR can be configured both globally or on a per neighbor basis. Use the command **bgp graceful-restart** to enable GR globally. Example 14-1 demonstrates the global configuration of GR on Cisco IOS, IOS XR, and NX-OS platforms. Use the command **bgp graceful-restart restart-time** *value* to set the GR restart timer and the command **bgp graceful-restart stalepath-time** *value* to set the maximum time for which the router will maintain the stale path entries in case it does not receives an EoR from the restarting peer. In IOS XR, the command **bgp graceful-restart stalepath-timer** sets the maximum time to wait for restart of GR capable peers and a new command is introduced to take care of purging the stale paths from the peer—**bgp graceful-restart purge-time** *value*.

Example 14-1   *Global Configuration for Graceful-Restart*

```
! Configuration on Cisco IOS
R1(config)# router bgp 100
R1(config-router)# bgp graceful-restart
R1(config-router)# bgp graceful-restart restart-time 300
R1(config-router)# bgp graceful-restart stalepath-time 400


! Configuration on IOS XR
RP/0/0/CPU0:R2(config-line)# router bgp 100
RP/0/0/CPU0:R2(config-bgp)# bgp graceful-restart
RP/0/0/CPU0:R2(config-bgp)# bgp graceful-restart restart-time 300
RP/0/0/CPU0:R2(config-bgp)# bgp graceful-restart stalepath-time 400
RP/0/0/CPU0:R2(config-bgp)# bgp graceful-restart purge-time 400
RP/0/0/CPU0:R2(config-bgp)# commit


! Configuration on NX-OS
R3(config)# router bgp 100
R3(config-router)# graceful-restart
R3(config-router)# graceful-restart restart-time 300
R3(config-router)# graceful-restart stalepath-time 400
```

If the BGP session is already in established state before GR configuration, the BGP sessions are required to be reset in order to exchange the GR capability. The GR capability is verified by using the command **show bgp** *afi safi* **neighbors** *ip-address*. Examine the output of **show bgp ipv4 unicast neighbors** *ip-address* in Example 14-2. Notice that in the command output, the GR capability is in advertised and received state. If either the advertised or received state is missing, it means that one of the peers is not having GR configured or the GR was configured after the session came up.

Example 14-2   *Verifying GR Capability for BGP Neighbor*

```
! Command Output on Cisco IOS
R1# show bgp ipv4 unicast neighbors 192.168.2.2
BGP neighbor is 192.168.2.2,  remote AS 100, internal link
  BGP version 4, remote router ID 192.168.2.2
  BGP state = Established, up for 01:10:35
  Last read 00:00:30, last write 00:00:29, hold time is 180, keepalive interval is
    60 seconds
  Neighbor sessions:
    1 active, is not multisession capable (disabled)
  Neighbor capabilities:
    Route refresh: advertised and received(new)
    Four-octets ASN Capability: advertised and received
    Address family IPv4 Unicast: advertised and received
    Graceful Restart Capability: advertised and received
      Remote Restart timer is 300 seconds
      Address families advertised by peer:
        IPv4 Unicast (was not preserved
    Enhanced Refresh Capability: advertised
! Output omitted for brevity
```

```
! Command Output on IOS XR
RP/0/0/CPU0:R2# show bgp ipv4 unicast neighbors 192.168.1.1
BGP neighbor is 192.168.1.1
 Remote AS 100, local AS 100, internal link
 Remote router ID 192.168.1.1
 Cluster ID 192.168.2.2
  BGP state = Established, up for 01:11:37
  NSR State: None
  Last read 00:00:41, Last read before reset 01:11:39
  Hold time is 180, keepalive interval is 60 seconds
  Configured hold time: 180, keepalive: 60, min acceptable hold time: 3
  Last write 00:00:31, attempted 19, written 19
  Second last write 00:01:31, attempted 19, written 19
  Last write before reset 01:11:39, attempted 82, written 82
  Second last write before reset 01:11:46, attempted 19, written 19
  Last write pulse rcvd  May 12 05:12:40.534 last full not set pulse count 267
  Last write pulse rcvd before reset 01:11:39
  Socket not armed for io, armed for read, armed for write
  Last write thread event before reset 01:11:39, second last 01:11:39
  Last KA expiry before reset 00:00:00, second last 00:00:00
  Last KA error before reset 00:00:00, KA not sent 00:00:00
  Last KA start before reset 00:00:00, second last 00:00:00
```

```
    Precedence: internet
    Non-stop routing is enabled
    Graceful restart is enabled
    Restart time is 300 seconds
    Stale path timeout time is 400 seconds
    Multi-protocol capability received
    Neighbor capabilities:
       Route refresh: advertised (old + new) and received (old + new)
       Graceful Restart (GR Awareness): received
       4-byte AS: advertised and received
       Address family IPv4 Unicast: advertised and received
    Received 140 messages, 1 notifications, 0 in queue
    Sent 126 messages, 1 notifications, 0 in queue
    Minimum time between advertisement runs is 0 secs
    Inbound message logging enabled, 3 messages buffered
    Outbound message logging enabled, 3 messages buffered

  For Address Family: IPv4 Unicast
   BGP neighbor version 2
   Update group: 0.3 Filter-group: 0.4  No Refresh request being processed
   Route-Reflector Client
   AF-dependent capabilities:
      Graceful Restart capability advertised
         Local restart time is 300, RIB purge time is 400 seconds
         Maximum stalepath time is 400 seconds
! Output omitted for brevity
```

```
! Command Output on NX-OS
R3# show bgp ipv4 unicast neighbors 192.168.2.2
BGP neighbor is 192.168.2.2,  remote AS 100, ibgp link, Peer index 1
  BGP version 4, remote router ID 192.168.2.2
  BGP state = Established, up for 02:03:32
  Using loopback0 as update source for this peer
  Last read 00:00:22, hold time = 180, keepalive interval is 60 seconds
  Last written 00:00:29, keepalive timer expiry due 00:00:30
  Received 172 messages, 1 notifications, 0 bytes in queue
  Sent 173 messages, 0 notifications, 0 bytes in queue
  Connections established 2, dropped 1
  Last reset by peer 02:03:43, due to session cleared
  Last reset by us never, due to No error

  Neighbor capabilities:
  Dynamic capability: advertised (mp, refresh, gr)
```

```
Dynamic capability (old): advertised
Route refresh capability (new): advertised received
Route refresh capability (old): advertised received
4-Byte AS capability: advertised received
Address family IPv4 Unicast: advertised received
Graceful Restart capability: advertised received

Graceful Restart Parameters:
Address families advertised to peer:
  IPv4 Unicast
Address families received from peer:
  IPv4 Unicast
Forwarding state preserved by peer for:
Restart time advertised to peer: 300 seconds
Stale time for routes advertised by peer: 400 seconds
Restart time advertised by peer: 300 seconds
! Output omitted for brevity
```

Sometimes, not all peers are GR capable and are not required to be GR capable as well.
GR can also be configured on a per-neighbor basis and having the GR globally disabled.
This helps in exchanging GR capability with only those neighbors for which forwarding
should not be impacted or be least impacted. GR is enabled for an individual neighbor
using the command **neighbor** *ip-address* **graceful-restart** on both Cisco IOS XR and
NX-OS and using the command **neighbor** *ip-address* **ha-mode graceful-restart** on Cisco
IOS software. Example 14-3 demonstrates the configuration of GR on a per-neighbor
basis.

Example 14-3 *Per-Neighbor Graceful-Restart Configuration*

```
! Configuration on Cisco IOS
R1(config)# router bgp 100
R1(config-router)# neighbor 192.168.2.2 ha-mode graceful-restart


! Configuration on IOS XR
RP/0/0/CPU0:R2(config)# router bgp 100
RP/0/0/CPU0:R2(config-bgp)# neighbor 192.168.1.1
RP/0/0/CPU0:R2(config-bgp-nbr)# graceful-restart


! Configuration on NX-OS
R3(config)# router bgp 100
R3(config-router)# neighbor 192.168.2.2
R3(config-router-neighbor)# graceful-restart
```

The NX-OS software also supports for GR-aware feature configuration; that is, the router does not perform full GR functionality but can have peers that are GR capable and is capable of sending EoR to restarting peers. This feature can also be configured on NX-OS either globally or on a per-neighbor basis. To enable GR aware configuration, use the global BGP command **graceful-restart-helper** or use the neighbor command **neighbor** *ip-address* **graceful-restart-helper**.

Cisco's implementation of GR assumes NSF is enabled and tells the peers: "If I ever drop this session, it is because I am failing over from primary RP to secondary RP and will keep forwarding packets." This makes the peer think that it needs to keep sending the packets. This scenario works as long as there is no reload or reboot on the router. If the router goes down, the neighbor router keeps sending the packets to this router, instead of forwarding the traffic to a working path, assuming the router that restarted is performing a switchover and it has its Forwarding Information Base (FIB) updated. This causes the traffic to black hole and causes an outage.

The problem is not with the feature itself but with the understanding between GR and NSF. GR does not mean that NSF is enabled but only assumes that NSF is enabled on the router. NSF is not configurable but is enabled by default when the router is running in Stateful Switchover (SSO) mode. NSF can also be defined as a function to checkpoint the FIB on the standby router.

The GR Restart Timer, which defaults to 120 seconds, takes care of clearing the stale path entries in case the BGP peer does not comes up within this time period.

> **Note**   Before moving to the next topic, it is important to understand routers' and switches' different high-availability operating modes with dual RPs.
>
> ■ **Stateful Switchover (SSO):** Failover from the active RP (crashing or reloading) to the standby RP (which takes over as the active role) where state is preserved and the router was in hot-standby mode before the switchover.
>
> ■ **RPR+:** RP redundancy mode where standby RP is partially initialized, but there is no synchronization of state.
>
> It is required to have SSO state for features like NSF, Nonstop Routing (NSR), or GR.

BGP Nonstop Routing

High-availability features like GR are really useful in critical network environments, where traffic loss even for few seconds can cost a lot to the organization, whether it is a service provider network or an enterprise. But GR is not really a feasible solution in all deployments. Think about a service provider network. It is easy to deploy a GR feature everywhere in the service provider core and edge, but the service provider cannot expect to have the customers enable GR or be GR capable. There might be customer environments where the customer premises equipment (CPE) might be running a platform or software that does not support GR or might be running the CPE with just a single RP. In such situations, GR is not feasible for the customers.

An RP switchover should be transparent to the customer, and this was the primary motivation behind NSR. NSR is a feature where routing protocols explicitly checkpoint state from active RP to the standby RP to maintain routing information across a switchover. Thus, NSR sessions are in established state on the standby RP prior to switchover and remain established even after the switchover. The main benefit of using NSR is it is transparent to the remote speaker; that is, the remote does not need to be NSR capable for the feature to work.

There are three phases in NSR operation. Each phase performs certain actions, and based on these phases, it becomes easier to identify any problem with BGP NSR.

- **Synchronization:** During this state, the task of session state mirroring happens between the active and the standby RP. The TCP stack is first synchronized, followed by the application stacks—in this case, BGP.

- **NSR-ready:** The active and standby stacks operate independently, but the incoming packets or updates are replicated to both the RPs. The outgoing segments or updates are sent out via the standby RP or active RP depending on the underlying platform. On IOS/IOS XE, the active RP sends the update to the peers, but on IOS XR, the update is sent out via the standby RP. Note that the system uses asynchronous inter-process communication (IPC) between the active and standby RPs to replicate the information. In this state, the active RP sends prefix/best-path information to the standby.

- **Switchover:** When the switchover occurs, TCP activates the sockets based on the application trigger and restores keepalive functionality to maintain the session states. In other words, the new active RP (previously acting standby RP) continues from where the active RP left.

Figure 14-2 depicts the BGP NSR architecture with the various functions occurring between the active and the standby RP on Cisco IOS/IOS XE platform.

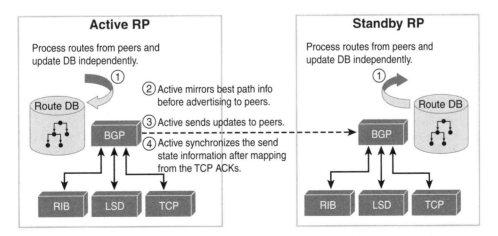

Figure 14-2 *BGP NSR Architecture on Cisco IOS*

The BGP NSR feature is supported on IOS/IOS XE and IOS XR platforms. To enable BGP NSR on Cisco IOS, use the command **neighbor** *ip-address* **ha-mode sso**. On IOS XR, NSR is not supported on a per-neighbor basis and can only be enabled globally for all address families using the command **nsr** under the **router bgp** configuration mode. Example 14-4 demonstrates the configurations of BGP NSR on both Cisco IOS and IOS XR platforms. NSR is enabled globally on Cisco IOS by using the command **bgp sso route-refresh-enable**. This command only allows BGP NSR to be enabled to peers that are Route Refresh capable.

Example 14-4   *BGP NSR Configuration*

```
! Configuration on Cisco IOS
R1(config)# router bgp 100
R1(config-router)# bgp sso route-refresh-enable
R1(config-router)# neighbor 192.168.2.2 ha-mode sso


! Configuration on IOS XR
RP/0/0/CPU0:R2(config)# router bgp 100
RP/0/0/CPU0:R2(config-bgp)# nsr
RP/0/0/CPU0:R2(config-bgp)# commit
```

The BGP NSR related information is found for each peer by using the command **show bgp** *afi safi* **neighbor** *ip-address*. Example 14-5 displays the output of the command **show bgp ipv4 unicast neighbors** *ip-address* to verify the BGP NSR status. On IOS XR, another command to verify if NSR is enabled for the BGP process is the command **show bgp process**. This command displays the information related to the BGP process, such as Router ID, default timers, NSR information, and other generic information.

Example 14-5   *BGP NSR Verification*

```
IOS
R1# show bgp ipv4 unicast neighbors 192.168.2.2
BGP neighbor is 192.168.2.2,  remote AS 100, internal link
  BGP version 4, remote router ID 192.168.2.2
  BGP state = Established, up for 08:13:01
  Last read 00:00:00, last write 00:00:11, hold time is 180, keepalive interval is
   60 seconds
  Neighbor sessions:
    1 active, is not multisession capable (disabled)
  Neighbor capabilities:
    Route refresh: advertised and received(new)
    Four-octets ASN Capability: advertised and received
    Address family IPv4 Unicast: advertised and received
    Enhanced Refresh Capability: advertised
    Multisession Capability:
    Stateful switchover support enabled: NO for session 1
```

```
! Output omitted for brevity


IOS XR
RP/0/0/CPU0:R2# show bgp ipv4 unicast neighbors 192.168.1.1
BGP neighbor is 192.168.1.1
 Remote AS 100, local AS 100, internal link
 Remote router ID 192.168.1.1
 Cluster ID 192.168.2.2
  BGP state = Established, up for 08:26:48
  NSR State: None
  Last read 00:00:37, Last read before reset 00:00:00
  Hold time is 180, keepalive interval is 60 seconds
  Configured hold time: 180, keepalive: 60, min acceptable hold time: 3
  Last write 00:00:40, attempted 19, written 19
  Second last write 00:01:40, attempted 19, written 19
  Last write before reset 00:00:00, attempted 0, written 0
  Second last write before reset 00:00:00, attempted 0, written 0
  Last write pulse rcvd  May 15 11:52:27.695 last full not set pulse count 1074
  Last write pulse rcvd before reset 00:00:00
  Socket not armed for io, armed for read, armed for write
  Last write thread event before reset 00:00:00, second last 00:00:00
  Last KA expiry before reset 00:00:00, second last 00:00:00
  Last KA error before reset 00:00:00, KA not sent 00:00:00
  Last KA start before reset 00:00:00, second last 00:00:00
  Precedence: internet
  Non-stop routing is enabled
  Multi-protocol capability received
  Neighbor capabilities:
    Route refresh: advertised (old + new) and received (old + new)
! Output omitted for brevity


RP/0/0/CPU0:R2# show bgp process
BGP Process Information:
BGP is operating in STANDALONE mode
Autonomous System number format: ASPLAIN
Autonomous System: 100
Router ID: 192.168.2.2 (manually configured)
Default Cluster ID: 192.168.2.2
Active Cluster IDs:  192.168.2.2
Fast external fallover enabled
Neighbor logging is enabled
Enforce first AS enabled
Default local preference: 100
Default keepalive: 60
```

```
Non-stop routing is enabled
Update delay: 120
Generic scan interval: 60

Address family: IPv4 Unicast
Dampening is not enabled
! Output omitted for brevity
```

In IOS XR, there are instances when a process crashes because of various reasons. So, if a TCP or BGP process starts on the active RP, the system can force the active RP to failover to standby RP as a recovery action in such situations. But this is not done automatically. To enable this behavior, configure the command **nsr process-failures switchover**. Note that if a process restarts on the standby RP, only the NSR functionality is lost until the time the process comes up again, but there is not any other service impact.

From the command-line perspective, there isn't much information that can be viewed on the Cisco IOS or IOS XE platforms, but on IOS XR, a lot of information is available for BGP NSR. The BGP NSR goes through various states. Figure 14-3 examines the finite state machine (FSM) that BGP NSR goes through at different stages.

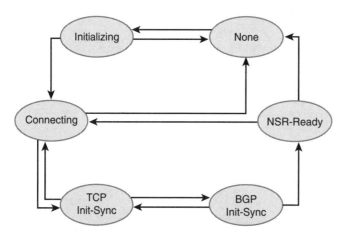

Figure 14-3   *BGP NSR Finite State Machine*

The following describes the different states of the BGP NSR finite state machine:

- **None:** NSR is disabled (not configured).

- **Initializing:** Basic initialization in progress. This is done after the first time NSR is configured.

- **Connecting:** Attempting to connect to peer (ACTV/STDBY) process.

- **TCP Init-Sync:** Synchronization of TCP sessions in progress.

■ **BGP Init-Sync:** Synchronization of BGP database in progress.

■ **NSR-Ready:** Ready to perform NSR-enabled switchover.

Note that in Example 14-5, the NSR state is None. This is because there is not a standby RP present in the system. In an ideal situation with dual RPs, the NSR state should be NSR-Ready. To view the NSR state on a dual RP system, use the command **show redundancy**. This command displays the active and the standby RP redundancy states.

Example 14-6 displays the output of the command **show redundancy** from another node running on dual RPs. Also the command **show bgp ipv4 unicast neighbor** *ip-address* command displays the NSR state as *NSR-Ready*.

Example 14-6 *Redundancy Status*

```
RP/0/RSP0/CPU0:R2# show redundancy
Redundancy information for node 0/RSP0/CPU0:
==========================================
Node 0/RSP0/CPU0 is in ACTIVE role
Node Redundancy Partner (0/RSP0/CPU0) is in STANDBY role
Standby node in 0/RSP1/CPU0 is ready
Standby node in 0/RSP1/CPU0 is NSR-ready
Node 0/RSP0/CPU0 is in process group PRIMARY role
Process Redundancy Partner (0/RSP1/CPU0) is in BACKUP role
Backup node in 0/RSP1/CPU0 is ready
Backup node in 0/RSP1/CPU0 is NSR-ready

Group            Primary        Backup         Status
---------        ---------      ---------      ---------
dsc              0/RSP0/CPU0    0/RSP1/CPU0    Ready
dlrsc            0/RSP0/CPU0    0/RSP1/CPU0    Ready
central-services 0/RSP0/CPU0    0/RSP1/CPU0    Ready
v4-routing       0/RSP0/CPU0    0/RSP1/CPU0    Ready
netmgmt          0/RSP0/CPU0    0/RSP1/CPU0    Ready
mcast-routing    0/RSP0/CPU0    0/RSP1/CPU0    Ready
v6-routing       0/RSP0/CPU0    0/RSP1/CPU0    Ready
Group_10_bgp2    0/RSP0/CPU0    0/RSP1/CPU0    Ready
Group_5_bgp3     0/RSP0/CPU0    0/RSP1/CPU0    Ready


RP/0/RSP0/CPU0:R2# show bgp ipv4 unicast neighbors 192.168.1.1
BGP neighbor is 192.168.1.1
 Remote AS 100, local AS 100, internal link
 Remote router ID 192.168.1.1
 Speaker ID 1
  BGP state = Established, up for 1d04h
  NSR State: NSR Ready
  Last read 00:00:03, Last read before reset 1d04h
! Output omitted for brevity
```

Use the command **show bgp afi safi** [*prefix* | **summary**] [**standby**] to view the BGP session state and the BGP table for an AFI/SAFI on the standby RP.

Note   If a manual switchover is required for maintenance purposes, ensure that the redundancy state is Standby hot and also the standby is in NSR-Ready state. This ensures seamless activity without any service impact.

After a switchover, the standby RP goes through all the NSR states as previously mentioned. This information is viewed by using the command **show bgp summary nsr** or **show bgp nsr**. These commands display all the various modes that the standby goes through after it moves to a standby ready state along with the timeline. It also shows the state of the BGP neighbor along with the NSR state. To view the NSR states and the neighbor state on the standby RP, use the command **show bgp summary nsr standby**. Example 14-7 displays the command output of the **show bgp summary nsr** command.

Example 14-7   show bgp summary nsr *Command Output*

```
RP/0/RSP0/CPU0:R2# show bgp summary nsr
BGP router identifier 192.168.2.2, local AS number 100
BGP generic scan interval 60 secs
Non-stop routing is enabled
BGP table state: Active
Table ID: 0xe0000000   RD version: 37
BGP main routing table version 37
BGP NSR Initial initsync version 3 (Reached)
BGP scan interval 60 secs


BGP is operating in STANDALONE mode.



node0_RSP0_CPU0      Speaker

Entered mode  Standby Ready                : May 15 15:35:05
Entered mode  TCP NSR Setup                : May 15 15:35:05
Entered mode  TCP NSR Setup Done           : May 15 15:35:05
Entered mode  TCP Initial Sync             : May 15 15:35:05
Entered mode  TCP Initial Sync Phase Two   : May 15 15:35:06
Entered mode  TCP Initial Sync Done        : May 15 15:35:07
Entered mode  FPBSN processing done        : May 15 15:35:07
Entered mode  Update processing done       : May 15 15:35:07
Entered mode  BGP Initial Sync             : May 15 15:35:07
Entered mode  BGP Initial Sync done        : May 15 15:35:07
Entered mode  NSR Ready                    : May 15 15:35:07

Current BGP NSR state - NSR Ready achieved at: May 15 15:35:07
```

```
NSR State READY notified to Rmf at: May 15 15:35:07


Process   RcvTblVer   bRIB/RIB   LabelVer   ImportVer   SendTblVer   StandbyVer
Speaker          37         37         37          37           37           37


Neighbor        Spk    AS    TblVer   SyncVer    AckVer NBRState      NSRState
192.168.1.1       1   100        37        37        37 Established   NSR Ready
RP/0/RSP0/CPU0:R2# show bgp summary nsr standby
Mon May 16 06:44:38.868 UTC
BGP router identifier 192.168.2.2, local AS number 100
BGP generic scan interval 60 secs
Non-stop routing is enabled
BGP table state: Active
Table ID: 0xe0000000   RD version: 37
BGP main routing table version 37
BGP NSR Initial initsync version 1 (Not Reached)
BGP tunnel nexthop version 1
BGP scan interval 60 secs


BGP is operating in STANDALONE mode.



node0_RSP1_CPU0      Speaker

Entered mode  None                    : May 15 15:34:05
Entered mode  Standby Ready           : May 15 15:35:05
Entered mode  TCP Replication         : May 15 15:35:05
Entered mode  TCP Init Sync Done      : May 15 15:35:07
Entered mode  NSR Ready               : May 15 15:35:07


Process   RcvTblVer   bRIB/RIB   LabelVer   ImportVer   SendTblVer   StandbyVer
Speaker          37          1         37          37            1            0


Neighbor        Spk    AS    TblVer   SyncVer    AckVer NBRState      NSRState
192.168.1.1       1   100        37         0         1 Established   NSR Ready
```

A cumulative view of all the session states, that is, Neighbor State and NSR State, is viewed by using the command **show bgp sessions**. If there are sessions that are not NSR ready, such sessions are viewed by using the command **show bgp sessions [not-nsr-ready]**. Example 14-8 displays the BGP sessions that are not NSR ready. The output indicates the NSRState field as None because it was captured when the IOS XR router R2 was running on single RP.

Example 14-8   *Not-NSR-Ready BGP Sessions*

```
RP/0/RSP0/CPU0:R2# show bgp sessions not-nsr-ready
Neighbor        VRF          Spk   AS    InQ  OutQ  NBRState     NSRState
192.168.1.1     default       0   100     0     0  Established  None
```

Because the TCP state is required to be synchronized between the active RP and the
standby RP, it is vital to verify how many sessions an application (in this case BGP)
ask TCP to synchronize and how many have actually synchronized. To verify this
information, use the command **show tcp nsr session-set brief**. Examine the output of
this command in Example 14-9. The IPv4 AFI has total of one session to sync, and the
output shows that it has been synced on the standby.

Example 14-9   *TCP NSR Sync Information*

```
RP/0/RSP0/CPU0:R2# show tcp nsr session-set brief
------------------------------------------------------------
                    Node: 0/RSP0/CPU0
------------------------------------------------------------

  SSCB        Client     LocalAPP Set-Id Family State  Protect-Node Total/Synced
0x10272978    581993       bgp#1     1    IPv4 Ac YN   0/RSP1/CPU0      1/1
0x1017f338    581993       bgp#1     2    IPv6 Ac YN   0/RSP1/CPU0      0/0
```

While troubleshooting BGP NSR issues, ensure that the TCP session related to BGP is
synched with the standby or is NSR ready. This is verified by using the command **show
tcp nsr brief**. In this command, look for the same protocol control block (PCB) value
that is achieved from the command **show tcp brief** and ensure that the NSR state is Up.
Example 14-10 illustrates how to verify if the TCP session is NSR ready.

Example 14-10   *Verifying TCP NSR State*

```
RP/0/0/CPU0:R2# show tcp brief
PCB          VRF-ID      Recv-Q Send-Q Local Address        Foreign Address       State
0x10161660 0x60000000        0      0  192.168.2.2:646      192.168.10.1:25070    ESTAB
0x101698b0 0x60000000        0      0  192.168.2.2:646      192.168.3.3:23158     ESTAB
0x102311b4 0x60000000        0      0  192.168.2.2:179      192.168.1.1:41318     ESTAB

RP/0/RSP0/CPU0:R2# show tcp nsr brief
Tue May 17 05:18:15.908 UTC
------------------------------------------------------------
                    Node: 0/RSP0/CPU0
------------------------------------------------------------

  PCB        VRF-ID    Local Address       Foreign Address        NSR
0x102311b4 0x60000000 192.168.2.2:179      192.168.1.1:41318      Up
```

The command **show tcp nsr detail pcb** *pcb-value* displays how much time was taken to perform the initial sync for the TCP connection. Example 14-11 shows the output of the command **show tcp nsr detail pcb** *pcb-value* of the previously stated TCP connection.

Example 14-11   *TCP NSR Session Detail*

```
RP/0/RSP0/CPU0:R2# show tcp nsr detail pcb 0x102311b4
Tue May 17 05:22:34.573 UTC
------------------------------------------------------------
                       Node: 0/RSP0/CPU0
------------------------------------------------------------


============================================================
PCB 0x102311b4, VRF Id 0x60000000, Client PID: 56177002
Local host: 192.168.2.2, Local port: 179
Foreign host: 192.168.1.1, Foreign port: 41318
SSCB 0x102316d4, Client PID 56177002
Node Role: Active, Protected by: 0/RSP1/CPU0, Cookie: 0x00000000

NSR State: Up
Replicated to standby: Yes
Synchronized with standby: Yes
FSSN: 1823391429, FSSN Offset: 0

ID of the last or current initial sync: 2077858654
Initial sync done in two phases: yes
Initial sync started at: Sun May 15 15:35:05 2016
Initial sync ended    at: Sun May 15 15:35:07 2016

Number of incoming packets currently held: 0

Number of iACKS currently held: 0
```

If there is a delay noticed between the sync, the TCP packet can be traced within the system to examine what action is being taken for a particular packet along with the packet details, such as sequence number, ack, length, window size, and so on. Use the command **show tcp packet-trace** *pcb-value* to trace the TCP packet. Example 14-12 examines the packet for the TCP session established by the BGP session between 192.168.2.2 and 192.168.1.1.

Example 14-12 *TCP Packet Trace*

```
RP/0/RSP0/CPU0:R2# show tcp packet-trace 0x102311b4


===============================================================
Packet traces for: PCB 0x102311b4, 192.168.2.2:179 <-> 192.168.1.1:41318,
    VRF 0x60000000


May 17 04:56:58.757>S (app write)
           snduna 3633157372 sndnxt 3633157372 sndmax 3633157372 sndwnd 32198
           rcvnxt 1823434377 rcvadv 1823466820 rcvwnd 32443


May 17 04:56:58.757>s --A-P- SEQ 3633157372 ACK 1823434377 LEN   19 WIN 47998 (pak:
    0x0, line: 733)
           snduna 3633157372 sndnxt 3633157391 sndmax 3633157391 sndwnd 32198
           rcvnxt 1823434377 rcvadv 1823466820 rcvwnd 32443


May 17 04:56:58.960>R --A--- SEQ 1823434377 ACK 3633157391 LEN    0 WIN 32179 (pak:
    0xb196c50b, line: 3603)
           snduna 3633157372 sndnxt 3633157391 sndmax 3633157391 sndwnd 32198
           rcvnxt 1823434377 rcvadv 1823466820 rcvwnd 32443


May 17 04:56:58.960>D --A--- SEQ 1823434377 ACK 3633157391 LEN    0 WIN 32179 (pak:
    0xb196c50b, line: 893)
           snduna 3633157391 sndnxt 3633157391 sndmax 3633157391 sndwnd 32179
           rcvnxt 1823434377 rcvadv 1823466820 rcvwnd 32443


May 17 04:57:47.569>R --A-P- SEQ 1823434377 ACK 3633157391 LEN   19 WIN 32179 (pak:
    0xb1971453, line: 3603)
           snduna 3633157391 sndnxt 3633157391 sndmax 3633157391 sndwnd 32179
           rcvnxt 1823434377 rcvadv 1823466820 rcvwnd 32443


May 17 04:57:47.569>R (app read)
           snduna 3633157391 sndnxt 3633157391 sndmax 3633157391 sndwnd 32179
           rcvnxt 1823434396 rcvadv 1823466820 rcvwnd 32424
! Output omitted for brevity
```

If the TCP data related to TCP packet flow, the socket state for session that is already closed, and so on is required for investigating what happened to the TCP session, use the command **show tcp dump-file** *filename*. The *filename* for the peer is found using the command **show tcp dump-file list** *ip-address*.

The **show bgp trace sync** command is also very useful to view the timelines of various state changes. This command is useful if there is a delay in the BGP NSR sync.

Example 14-13 displays the output of the command **show bgp trace sync** [**reverse**]. The *reverse* keyword is used to view the output in reversed form so that you don't have to scroll down to the end to view the latest logs. The unfiltered command gives more details on what is happening during the sync process, but filtering the output for just *NSR state* can help identify where the actual delay occurred, and further logs can be reviewed around the same timeline.

Example 14-13 *BGP Sync Trace*

```
RP/0/RSP0/CPU0:R2# show bgp trace sync reverse | inc "NSR state"
15:35:07.737 default-bgp/spkr-tr2-sync 0/RSP0/CPU0 t16 [SYNC]:4831: Active
 NSR state trans, event 'Stdby NSR ack', state 'BGP Initial Sync done'
 -> 'NSR Ready'
15:35:07.734 default-bgp/spkr-tr2-sync 0/RSP0/CPU0 t16 [SYNC]:4831: Active
NSR state trans, event 'BGP Initial sync done', state 'BGP Initial Sync'
 -> 'BGP Initial Sync done'
15:35:07.733 default-bgp/spkr-tr2-sync 0/RSP0/CPU0 t16 [SYNC]:4831: Active
 NSR state trans, event 'Standby ready for BGP sync message', state
  'Update processing done' -> 'BGP Initial Sync'
15:35:07.732 default-bgp/spkr-tr2-sync 0/RSP0/CPU0 t16 [SYNC]:4831: Active NSR state
  trans, event 'Update Processing Done', state 'FPBSN processing done' -> 'Update
 processing done'
15:35:07.732 default-bgp/spkr-tr2-sync 0/RSP0/CPU0 t16 [SYNC]:4831: Active
 NSR state trans, event 'FPBSN Processing done', state 'TCP Initial Sync Done'
 -> 'FPBSN processing done'
15:35:07.732 default-bgp/spkr-tr2-sync 0/RSP0/CPU0 t16 [SYNC]:4831: Active
 NSR state trans, event 'TCP initial sync done', state 'TCP Initial Sync' ->
 'TCP Initial Sync Done'
15:35:05.725 default-bgp/spkr-tr2-sync 0/RSP0/CPU0 t16 [SYNC]:4831: Active
 NSR state trans, event 'End of Convergence', state 'TCP NSR Setup Done' ->
 'TCP Initial Sync'
15:35:05.725 default-bgp/spkr-tr2-sync 0/RSP0/CPU0 t16 [SYNC]:4831: Active
 NSR state trans, event 'TCP NSR setup done', state 'TCP NSR Setup' ->
  'TCP NSR Setup Done'
15:35:05.724 default-bgp/spkr-tr2-sync 0/RSP0/CPU0 t16 [SYNC]:4831: Active
 NSR state trans, event 'End of read-only', state 'Standby Ready' ->
 'TCP NSR Setup'
15:35:05.724 default-bgp/spkr-tr2-sync 0/RSP0/CPU0 t16 [SYNC]:4831: Active
 NSR state trans, event 'Standby ready message', state 'None' ->
 'Standby Ready'
15:34:04.258 default-bgp/spkr-tr2-sync 0/RSP0/CPU0 t8  [SYNC]:8274: Trigger
 to Init rmf with bgp NSR state 0 Client type 0
! Output omitted for brevity
```

There are a few debug commands that can be used for debugging BGP NSR sync issues:

■ **debug bgp sync:** General interaction between active and standby

■ **debug bgp commlib:** Details of message encoding or decoding happening between active and standby or speaker and BGP routing information base (RIB)

■ **debug tcp nsr:** TCP NSR related debug

A collective set of commands and traces are found in **show tech-support bgp** and **show tech-support tcp nsr**. These commands are useful while investigating an outage event and are really helpful for root cause analysis.

Bidirectional Forwarding Detection

Bidirectional forwarding detection (BFD) is a simple, fixed-length hello protocol that is used for faster detection of failures. BFD provides a low-overhead, short-duration mechanism for detection of failures in the path between adjacent forwarding engines. Defined in RFC 5880 through RFC 5884, BFD supports adaptive detection times and a three-way handshake that ensures both systems are aware of any changes. BFD control packets contains the desired transmit (tx) and receive (rx) intervals by the sender. For example, if a node cannot handle a high rate of BFD packets, you can specify a large desired rx interval. This way its neighbor(s) cannot send packets at a smaller interval. The following features of BFD make it a most desirable protocol for failure detection:

■ Subsecond failure detection

■ Media independent (Ethernet, Packet over Sonet (POS), Serial, and so on).

■ Runs over User Datagram Protocol (UDP), data protocol independent (IPv4, IPv6, LSP).

■ Application independent: Interior Gateway Protocol (IGP), Tunnel liveliness, Fast Re-route (FRR) trigger, and so on

When an application (BGP, OSPF, and the like) creates or modifies a BFD session, it provides the following information:

■ Interface handle (single-hop session)

■ Address of the neighbor

■ Local address

■ Desired interval

■ Multiplier

The product of the desired interval and multiplier indicates the *desired failure detection interval*. The operational workflow of BFD for BGP or any other application is as follows:

■ User configured BFD for a BGP neighbor (usually internal BGP (IBGP) / external BGP (EBGP) on physical interface).

■ BGP initiates creation of BFD session.

- After the BFD session is created, timers are negotiated.

- BFD sends periodic control packets to its peer.

- If a link failure occurs, BFD detects the failure in the desired failure detection interval (desired interval * multiplier) and informs the peer of the failure as well as informing the local BFD client (for example, BGP).

- The BGP session goes down immediately rather than waiting for the hold timer to expire.

BFD runs on two modes:

- Asynchronous mode

- Demand mode

Note Demand mode is not supported on Cisco platforms. In demand mode, no control packets are exchanged after the session is established. In this mode, BFD assumes that there is another way to verify connectivity between the two endpoints. Either host may still send control packets if needed, but they are not generally exchanged.

Asynchronous Mode

Asynchronous mode is the primary mode of operation and is mandatory for BFD to function. In this mode, each system periodically sends BFD control packets to one another. For example, packets send by router R1 have a source address of R1 and a destination address of router R2, as shown in Figure 14-4.

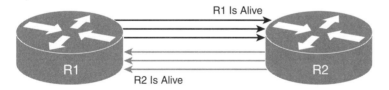

Figure 14-4 *BFD Asynchronous Mode*

Each stream of BFD control packets is independent and does not follow a request response cycle. If a number of packets in a row are not received by the other system, then the session is declared down. An adaptive failure detection time is used to prevent false failures if a neighbor is sending packets slower than what it is advertising.

BFD Async packets are sent on UDP port 3784. The BFD source port must be in the range of 49152 through 65535. The BFD control packets contain the following fields:

- **Version:** Version of BFD control header. XR runs version 1 as default, but legacy sessions can run version 0 as well.

- **Diag:** A diagnostic code specifying the local system's reason for the last change in session state, detection time expired, echo failed, and so on.

- **State:** The current BFD session state as seen by the transmitting system.

- **P:** Poll bit, if set, the transmitting system is requesting verification of connectivity, or of a parameter change, and is expecting a packet with the Final (F) bit in reply.

- **F:** Final bit, if set, the transmitting system is responding to a received BFD Control packet that had the Poll (P) bit set.

- **Detect Multiplier:** Detection time multiplier. The negotiated transmit interval, multiplied by this value, provides the detection time for the transmitting system in Asynchronous mode.

- **My Discriminator:** A unique, nonzero discriminator value generated by the transmitting system, used to de-multiplex multiple BFD sessions between the same pair of systems.

- **Your Discriminator:** The discriminator received from the corresponding remote system. This field reflects back the received value of My Discriminator, or is zero if that value is unknown.

- **Desired Min TX Interval:** This is the minimum interval, in microseconds, that the local system would like to use when transmitting BFD Control packets.

- **Desired Min RX Interval:** This is the minimum interval, in microseconds, between received BFD control packets that this system is capable of supporting.

- **Required Min Echo RX Interval:** This is the minimum interval, in microseconds, between received BFD Echo packets that this system is capable of supporting.

The BFD control packets as defined by IETF is shown in Figure 14-5.

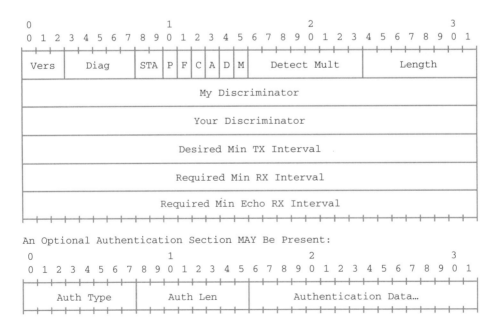

Figure 14-5 *BFD Control Plane Format*

> **Note**   BFD authentication is not supported on all platforms. BFD single-hop authentication is supported on IOS XE and NX-OS platforms.

Asynchronous Mode with Echo Function

Asynchronous mode with echo function is designed to test only the forwarding path and not the host stack on the remote system. It is enabled only after the session is enabled. BFD echo packets are sent in such a way that the other end just loops them back through its forwarding path. For example, a packet sent by router R1 could be sent with both the source and destination address belonging to R1 as shown in Figure 14-6.

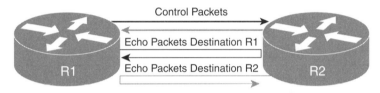

Figure 14-6   *BFD Asynchronous Mode with Echo Function*

Because echo packets do not require application or host stack processing on the remote end, it can be used for aggressive detection timers. Another benefit of using the echo function is that the sender has complete control of the response time. In order for the echo function to work, the remote node should also be capable of echo function. The BFD control packets with echo function enabled are sent as UDP packets with source and destination port 3785. Also, the interfaces running BFD with the echo function should be configured with the command **no ip redirects**.

Configuration and Verification

BFD is usually configured on a per-interface basis for the routing protocols that support BFD. BFD is enabled using the configuration **bfd interval** *interval* **min_rx** *min_rx_ interval* **multiplier** *multiplier*. The variable *interval* is the transmit interval between BFD packets, whereas *min_rx_interval* is the minimum receive interval capability.

BFD can be enabled for BGP peer on Cisco IOS using the command **neighbor ip-address fall-over bfd**. On IOS XR, the command **bfd fast-detect** is part of the neighbor configuration. BFD for BGP can be enabled on NX-OS using the command **bfd** under the neighbor configuration. To be able to configure BFD, the **feature bfd** command should be configured to enable the BFD feature. To understand the BFD feature for BGP, examine the topology as shown in Figure 14-7. Router R1 has an EBGP peering with IOS XR router R2 and NX-OS router R3.

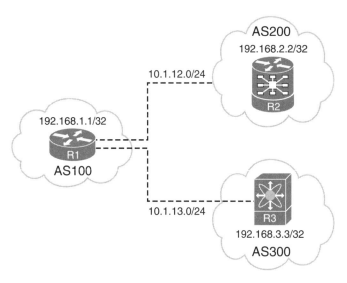

Figure 14-7   *EBGP Peering with BFD*

Example 14-14 demonstrates the configuration of BFD for BGP on all three Cisco operating systems. The asynchronous mode configuration is shown without the echo function, which was disabled manually. Some of the platforms have echo function enabled by default and thus require manual configuration to disable the echo function.

Example 14-14   *BFD for BGP Configuration*

```
R1
interface GigabitEthernet2/0/3
 ip address 10.1.13.1 255.255.255.0
 ip ospf 100 area 0
 no ip redirects
 bfd interval 300 min_rx 300 multiplier 3
 no bfd echo
 !
 interface TenGigabitEthernet2/1/0
 ip address 10.1.12.1 255.255.255.0
 ip ospf 100 area 0
 no ip redirects
 bfd interval 300 min_rx 300 multiplier 3
 no bfd echo
 !
 router bgp 100
 bgp router-id 192.168.1.1
 bgp log-neighbor-changes
```

```
 no bgp default ipv4-unicast
 neighbor 10.1.12.2 remote-as 200
 neighbor 10.1.12.2 fall-over bfd
 neighbor 10.1.13.3 remote-as 300
 neighbor 10.1.13.3 fall-over bfd
 !
 address-family ipv4
  neighbor 10.1.12.2 activate
  neighbor 10.1.13.3 activate
 exit-address-family
R2
interface TenGigE0/0/2/0
 ipv4 address 10.1.12.2 255.255.255.0
!
bfd
 interface TenGigE0/0/2/0
  !
  echo disable
  !
router bgp 200
 bgp router-id 192.168.2.2
 address-family ipv4 unicast
  !
 neighbor 10.1.12.1
  remote-as 100
  bfd fast-detect
  bfd multiplier 3
  bfd minimum-interval 300
  address-family ipv4 unicast
R3
feature bfd
feature bgp
!
interface Ethernet3/2
  mpls ip
  bfd interval 300 min_rx 300 multiplier 3
  no bfd echo
  no ip redirects
  ip address 10.1.13.3/24
  ip router ospf 100 area 0.0.0.0
  no shutdown
```

```
!
router bgp 300
  router-id 192.168.3.3
  address-family ipv4 unicast
  neighbor 10.1.13.2
    bfd
    remote-as 100
    address-family ipv4 unicast
```

After the BGP session is up, the BFD session is also established. The BFD session is viewed using the command **show bfd neighbors [details]** on both Cisco IOS and NX-OS platforms. On IOS XR, use the command **show bfd session [detail]**. The detail command option displays more information on which client applications are using BFD and other details on the packets sent and received, and so on.

Example 14-15 examines the output of the command **show bfd neighbors [detail]** and **show bfd session [detail]**. In the output, notice that the BFD client is BGP. The BFD on all three platforms runs on version 1 by default. The BFD command output with **detail** keyword displays all the fields that are part of the BFD control packet. These fields can be very useful for debugging purposes and to understand whether there is a mismatch between the peers that could possibly cause BFD session to flap. Ensure that the State bit is set to *Up* rather than *AdminDown*. The output also shows that the echo function has been disabled, and the echo function interval value is 0.

Example 14-15   *Verifying BFD Session*

```
IOS
R1# show bfd neighbors
IPv4 Sessions
NeighAddr                    LD/RD            RH/RS    State    Int
10.1.12.2                    4097/2148073473 Up       Up       Te2/1/0
10.1.13.3                    4098/1090519041 Up       Up       Gi2/0/3


R1# show bfd neighbors details
IPv4 Sessions
NeighAddr                    LD/RD            RH/RS    State    Int
10.1.12.2                    4097/2148073473 Up       Up       Te2/1/0
Session state is UP and not using echo function.
Session Host: Hardware
OurAddr: 10.1.12.1
Handle: 1
Local Diag: 0, Demand mode: 0, Poll bit: 0
MinTxInt: 300000, MinRxInt: 300000, Multiplier: 3
Received MinRxInt: 300000, Received Multiplier: 3
Holddown (hits): 677(0), Hello (hits): 300(62318)
Rx Count: 59338, Rx Interval (ms) min/max/avg: 5/312/277 last: 223 ms ago
```

```
Tx Count: 62317, Tx Interval (ms) min/max/avg: 5/304/264 last: 30 ms ago
Elapsed time watermarks: 0 0 (last: 0)
Registered protocols: BGP CEF
Uptime: 04:33:56
Last packet: Version: 1              - Diagnostic: 0
             State bit: Up           - Demand bit: 0
             Poll bit: 0             - Final bit: 0
             C bit: 1
             Multiplier: 3           - Length: 24
             My Discr.: 2148073473   - Your Discr.: 4097
             Min tx interval: 300000 - Min rx interval: 300000
             Min Echo interval: 0


IPv4 Sessions
NeighAddr                LD/RD          RH/RS     State     Int
10.1.13.3                4098/1090519041 Up        Up        Gi2/0/3
Session state is UP and not using echo function.
Session Host: Hardware
OurAddr: 10.1.13.1
Handle: 2
Local Diag: 0, Demand mode: 0, Poll bit: 0
MinTxInt: 300000, MinRxInt: 300000, Multiplier: 3
Received MinRxInt: 300000, Received Multiplier: 3
Holddown (hits): 891(0), Hello (hits): 300(3452)
Rx Count: 3029, Rx Interval (ms) min/max/avg: 296/304/300 last: 9 ms ago
Tx Count: 3451, Tx Interval (ms) min/max/avg: 1/302/264 last: 192 ms ago
Elapsed time watermarks: 0 0 (last: 0)
Registered protocols: BGP CEF
Uptime: 00:15:11
Last packet: Version: 1              - Diagnostic: 0
             State bit: Up           - Demand bit: 0
             Poll bit: 0             - Final bit: 0
             C bit: 0
             Multiplier: 3           - Length: 24
             My Discr.: 1090519041   - Your Discr.: 4098
             Min tx interval: 300000 - Min rx interval: 300000
             Min Echo interval: 50000
IOS XR
RP/0/RSP0/CPU0:R2# show bfd session
Interface       Dest Addr        Local det time(int*mult)      State
                                 Echo            Async    H/W   NPU
--------------- ---------------- ---------------- ---------------- ----------
Te0/0/2/0       10.1.12.1        0s(0s*0)         900ms(300ms*3)   UP
                                                           No    n/a
```

```
RP/0/RSP0/CPU0:R2# show bfd session detail
I/f: TenGigE0/0/2/0, Location: 0/0/CPU0
Dest: 10.1.12.1
Src: 10.1.12.2
 State: UP for 0d:4h:41m:27s, number of times UP: 1
 Session type: PR/V4/SH
Received parameters:
 Version: 1, desired tx interval: 300 ms, required rx interval: 300 ms
 Required echo rx interval: 300 ms, multiplier: 3, diag: None
 My discr: 4097, your discr: 2148073473, state UP, D/F/P/C/A: 0/0/0/0/0
Transmitted parameters:
 Version: 1, desired tx interval: 300 ms, required rx interval: 300 ms
 Required echo rx interval: 0 ms, multiplier: 3, diag: None
 My discr: 2148073473, your discr: 4097, state UP, D/F/P/C/A: 0/0/0/1/0
Timer Values:
 Local negotiated async tx interval: 300 ms
 Remote negotiated async tx interval: 300 ms
 Desired echo tx interval: 0 s, local negotiated echo tx interval: 0 ms
 Echo detection time: 0 ms(0 ms*3), async detection time: 900 ms(300 ms*3)
Local Stats:
 Intervals between async packets:
   Tx: Number of intervals=100, min=1 ms, max=302 ms, avg=139 ms
       Last packet transmitted 103 ms ago
   Rx: Number of intervals=100, min=225 ms, max=300 ms, avg=264 ms
       Last packet received 61 ms ago
 Intervals between echo packets:
   Tx: Number of intervals=0, min=0 s, max=0 s, avg=0 s
       Last packet transmitted 0 s ago
   Rx: Number of intervals=0, min=0 s, max=0 s, avg=0 s
       Last packet received 0 s ago
 Latency of echo packets (time between tx and rx):
   Number of packets: 0, min=0 ms, max=0 ms, avg=0 ms
Session owner information:
                        Desired              Adjusted
  Client        Interval  Multiplier Interval  Multiplier
  ------------------- -------------------- --------------------
  bgp-default     300 ms      3        300 ms      3


NX-OS
R3# show bfd neighbors

OurAddr    NeighAddr   LD/RD           RH/RS  Holdown(mult)  State  Int     Vrf
10.1.13.3  10.1.13.1   1090519041/4098  Up     689(3)        Up    Eth3/2  default
```

```
R3# show bfd neighbors details
OurAddr     NeighAddr    LD/RD            RH/RS    Holdown(mult)    State    Int    Vrf
10.1.13.3   10.1.13.1    1090519041/4098  Up       689(3)           Up       Eth3/2 default


Session state is Up and not using echo function
Local Diag: 0, Demand mode: 0, Poll bit: 0, Authentication: None
MinTxInt: 300000 us, MinRxInt: 300000 us, Multiplier: 3
Received MinRxInt: 300000 us, Received Multiplier: 3
Holdown (hits): 900 ms (0), Hello (hits): 300 ms (12449)
Rx Count: 14153, Rx Interval (ms) min/max/avg: 0/21232/265 last: 200 ms ago
Tx Count: 12449, Tx Interval (ms) min/max/avg: 296/296/296 last: 234 ms ago
Registered protocols:  bgp
Uptime: 0 days 1 hrs 2 mins 12 secs
Last packet: Version: 1              - Diagnostic: 0
             State bit: Up           - Demand bit: 0
             Poll bit: 0             - Final bit: 0
             Multiplier: 3           - Length: 24
             My Discr.: 4098         - Your Discr.: 1090519041
             Min tx interval: 300000 - Min rx interval: 300000
             Min Echo interval: 0    - Authentication bit: 0
Hosting LC: 3, Down reason: None, Reason not-hosted: None, Offloaded: No
```

Note   Although BFD can be enabled for IBGP sessions as well, it is better to have BFD implemented for IGP than for IBGP sessions. This is because the IBGP is typically established using routes learned from the IGP and is not typically configured between the directly connected neighbors.

An important thing to notice in R1's BFD neighbors' detail output is that the session host is Hardware. When the echo function is disabled, BFD is offloaded to hardware. Because BFD is a forwarding path failure detection protocol, it requires sending the BFD echo packets as low as 50 ms in order to reduce overall network convergence time. With multiple BFD sessions, it is hard to process such aggressive timers by the software. Thus, the BFD session gets offloaded to hardware and manages aggressive timers as low as 50ms. It is important to note that the echo function should be disabled in order to offload BFD into hardware. On Cisco IOS and IOS XE platforms, hardware offloaded BFD sessions are verified by using the **show bfd neighbors details** command or by using the **show bfd neighbors hardware details** command. If the echo function is enabled, BFD is not hardware offloaded and is processed by CPU (software).

On IOS XR, when the BFD hardware offload is enabled, the async control packets are not generated and received by the line card (LC) CPU but by the Network Processor (NP) on the line card, thus increasing the BFD scale. To enable hardware offload for BFD on ASR9k, use the command **hw-module bfd-hw-offload enable location** *rack/slot/cpu* from the admin config mode. After the command is configured, the line card previously mentioned is required to be reloaded before BFD hardware offload is enabled.

> **Note**   BFD is offloaded onto LC by default on NX-OS platforms.

The BFD echo function is enabled by default on most of the Cisco platforms. To enable the echo function (if its disabled), use the command **bfd echo** on both Cisco IOS and NX-OS software under the interface configuration mode and use the command **no echo disable** to enable the echo mode globally or under the interface on IOS XR. When the session is configured with the echo function, the BFD session starts off in asynchronous mode using a slow interval of 2 seconds. After the session is up, and if the interval specified by the client is less than 2 seconds, the echo function gets activated (assuming the echo function is enabled on the remote peer as well).

Example 14-16 shows the command output for BFD neighbors when the echo function is enabled. In the output on router R1, the minimum echo interval shows the value of 1 ms. This is because this value is hard-coded to 1 ms, and if the echo function is supported on both ends, the actual echo tx interval for a session is maximum of the following:

1. Local desired echo tx interval.

2. Remote required minimum echo rx interval. (This value is obtained from incoming control packets.)

Example 14-16   *BFD Neighbors with Echo Function*

```
IOS
R1# show bfd neighbors details


IPv4 Sessions
NeighAddr                    LD/RD          RH/RS      State      Int
10.1.12.2                    4098/2148073473 Up         Up         Te2/1/0
Session state is UP and using echo function with 300 ms interval.
Session Host: Software
OurAddr: 10.1.12.1
Handle: 2
Local Diag: 0, Demand mode: 0, Poll bit: 0
MinTxInt: 1000000, MinRxInt: 1000000, Multiplier: 3
Received MinRxInt: 2000000, Received Multiplier: 3
Holddown (hits): 0(0), Hello (hits): 2000(4)
Rx Count: 7, Rx Interval (ms) min/max/avg: 5/1951/1293 last: 798 ms ago
Tx Count: 5, Tx Interval (ms) min/max/avg: 1525/1941/1733 last: 1625 ms ago
Elapsed time watermarks: 0 0 (last: 0)
Registered protocols: BGP CEF
```

```
Uptime: 00:00:08
Last packet: Version: 1          - Diagnostic: 0
              State bit: Up       - Demand bit: 0
              Poll bit: 0         - Final bit: 0
              C bit: 1
              Multiplier: 3       - Length: 24
              My Discr.: 2148073473  - Your Discr.: 4098
              Min tx interval: 2000000  - Min rx interval: 2000000
              Min Echo interval: 1000
! Output omitted for brevity
```

```
IOS XR
RP/0/RSP0/CPU0:R2# show bfd session detail
I/f: TenGigE0/0/2/0, Location: 0/0/CPU0
Dest: 10.1.12.1
Src: 10.1.12.2
 State: UP for 0d:0h:2m:12s, number of times UP: 6
 Session type: PR/V4/SH
Received parameters:
 Version: 1, desired tx interval: 1 s, required rx interval: 1 s
 Required echo rx interval: 300 ms, multiplier: 3, diag: None
 My discr: 4098, your discr: 2148073473, state UP, D/F/P/C/A: 0/0/0/0/0
Transmitted parameters:
 Version: 1, desired tx interval: 2 s, required rx interval: 2 s
 Required echo rx interval: 1 ms, multiplier: 3, diag: None
 My discr: 2148073473, your discr: 4098, state UP, D/F/P/C/A: 0/0/0/1/0
Timer Values:
 Local negotiated async tx interval: 2 s
 Remote negotiated async tx interval: 2 s
 Desired echo tx interval: 300 ms, local negotiated echo tx interval: 300 ms
 Echo detection time: 900 ms(300 ms*3), async detection time: 6 s(2 s*3)
! Output omitted for brevity
```

```
NX-OS
R3# show bfd neighbors details
OurAddr    NeighAddr   LD/RD         RH/RS  Holdown(mult)  State   Int    Vrf
10.1.13.3  10.1.13.1   1090519041/4098  Up     689(3)         Up      Eth3/2 default

Session state is Up and using echo function with 300 ms interval
Local Diag: 0, Demand mode: 0, Poll bit: 0, Authentication: None
MinTxInt: 300000 us, MinRxInt: 2000000 us, Multiplier: 3
Received MinRxInt: 1000000 us, Received Multiplier: 3
Holdown (hits): 6000 ms (5), Hello (hits): 1000 ms (332494)
Rx Count: 320684, Rx Interval (ms) min/max/avg: 0/10634/269 last: 1370 ms ago
Tx Count: 332494, Tx Interval (ms) min/max/avg: 756/756/756 last: 190 ms ago
```

```
Registered protocols:  bgp
Uptime: 0 days 0 hrs 1 mins 52 secs
Last packet: Version: 1            - Diagnostic: 0
             State bit: Up         - Demand bit: 0
             Poll bit: 0           - Final bit: 0
             Multiplier: 3         - Length: 24
             My Discr.: 4097       - Your Discr.: 1090519042
             Min tx interval: 1000000  - Min rx interval: 1000000
             Min Echo interval: 300000 - Authentication bit: 0
Hosting LC: 3, Down reason: None, Reason not-hosted: None, Offloaded: No
```

IOS XR has support for viewing the packet counters in a detailed manner at the line card level using the command **show bfd counters packet private detail location** *rack/slot/cpu*. Example 14-17 displays the counters for BFD control packets on IOS XR.

Example 14-17 *BFD Packet Counters*

```
IOS XR
RP/0/RSP0/CPU0:R2# show bfd counters packet private detail location 0/0/CPU0
TenGigE0/0/2/0           Recv        Rx Invalid    Xmit     Delta
   Async:                406384      0             387357
   Echo:                 15030       0             15030    0
```

Troubleshooting BFD Issues

Issues with BFD can cause convergence issues; thus, this section discusses some of the most common issues seen with BFD.

BFD Session Not Coming Up

Perform the following steps to verify why the BFD session is not coming up:

Step 1.   Verify the application that created the BFD. If the application is BGP, ensure that BFD is properly configured with the same interval and multiplier value on both sides.

Step 2.   Verify there is reachability to the remote with which the BFD session is being established. Ensure there is proper adjacency and reachability between the two peering devices.

Step 3.   If the reachability is there, but the BFD session is not coming up, verify the received and sent counters on each side of the BFD neighbors and continue with the following:

   ■ Ensure there is no ACL that is blocking the BFD packets, that is, UDP ports 3784 and 3785.

- Verify if the line card supports the aggressive timers (if configured) and also that the line card and the RP are not hitting any resource limitation. For this, refer to the hardware data sheet on Cisco.com.

- On IOS XR, check which NP corresponds to which interface and if the NP is receiving BFD packets or not. This can be done using the following commands:

```
show controllers np ports all location rack/slot/cpu
show controllers np counters np location rack/slot/cpu | include
 "Rate|BFD"
show uidb data location rack/slot/cpu interface ingress
show uidb location rack/slot/cpu interface ing-extension
```

- On NX-OS, verify the event-history for any events or errors.

```
show system internal bfd event-history [all | error | session]
```

- On IOS XR, verify the BFD traces for any errors or events.

```
show bfd trace [event | error]
```

- Verify if there is any CoPP policy dropping BFD packets. Ensure that BFD packets are treated in a separate class-map under the CoPP policy.

- On IOS XR, verify that the BFD packets are not exceeding the LPTS limit for BFD control packets.

BFD Session Flapping

Perform the following steps to troubleshoot BFD issues if the BFD session is flapping:

Step 1. Ensure that the link is not getting congested or oversubscribed.

Step 2. Ensure that BFD is part of the priority queue in QoS configs, and proper resource allocation is given to the BFD class.

Step 3. Ensure that the BFD adjacency is stable. This is usually seen in scenarios after RP switchovers.

Step 4. On IOS XR, ensure that the *bfd_agent* process is not respawning.

Step 5. Ensure the BFD packets are hardware switched on NX-OS—not software switched and thus getting delayed or dropped. This can be due to hardware misprogramming as well. Also, ensure **no ip redirects** command is configured under the interfaces.

Step 6. Ensure there is no control plane congestion and there is no configuration that remarks BFD packets from the default IP precedence value of 6, because this will affect the Rx handling of control packets. Verify the queueing policies on the egress to ensure that BFD is not delayed or dropped.

For BFD-related issues, the following outputs can be collected during the problematic state:

- On IOS XR

    - **show tech routing bfd**

- On NX-OS

    - **show tech bfd**

BGP Fast-External-Fallover

Historically, when the fast-external-fallover feature was not available and a link went down, the EBGP session remained up until the hold-down timer expired. This situation used to cause a traffic black hole situation and service impact. To overcome this problem, **bgp fast-external-fallover** command was introduced. With this command configured, the EBGP session terminates immediately if the link goes down. This command is enabled by default on recent IOS releases, and IOS XR and NX-OS releases.

This feature is enabled by default for EBGP sessions but disabled for IBGP sessions. The feature can also be enabled at the interface level using the command **ip bgp fast-external-fallover** on Cisco IOS software.

Although the command **bgp fast-external-fallover** improves on convergence time, it is good to disable the command if the EBGP link is flapping continuously. By disabling fast-fallover, the instability caused by neighbors continually transitioning between idle and established states and the routing churn caused by the flood of ADVERTISE and WITHDRAW messages can be avoided. Use the **no bgp fast-external-fallover** command to disable this feature on both Cisco IOS and NX-OS, and use the command **bgp fast-external-fallover disable** command to disable this feature on IOS XR.

BGP Add-Path

In BGP, only one best path is advertised by a BGP router or a BGP RR. The BGP speaker accepts only one path for a given prefix from a given peer. If a BGP speaker receives multiple paths for the same prefix, then because of BGP's implicit withdraw semantics, the latest announcement of the prefix replaces the previous announcements. Even when multipath is configured, BGP RR does not advertise multiple paths but only the best path. This prevents the efficient use of the BGP multipath feature. Also, because of this behavior there could be other side effects, such as Multi-Exit Discriminator (MED) oscillations, suboptimal hot potato routing, and the like.

To understand the default behavior of BGP with multiple paths, examine the topology shown in Figure 14-8. It will be used for all future examples. RR1 is an RR running Cisco IOS, RR2 is running IOS XR, and RR3 is running NX-OS. All the other routers are running Cisco IOS software.

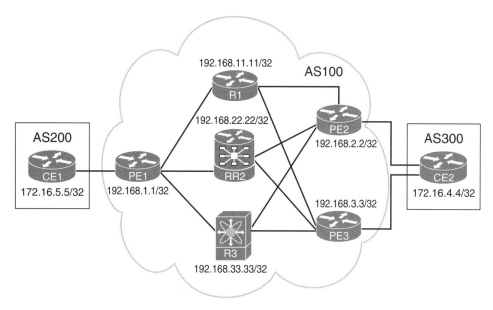

Figure 14-8   *Topology with Route Reflector*

In Figure 14-8, the prefix 172.16.4.4/32 is being advertised by CE2, which is in AS-300. The prefix is learned in AS-100 via two paths: one via PE2 and the other via PE3. Although there are two paths for the prefix, only the best path is advertised to the RR. Even if the RR has multiple paths, it hides all but the best path. Thus the ingress routers most often know about one exit point. When that path fails, traffic loss is proportional to control-plane convergence.

The solution to such issues is having a diverse path available to the ingress router, so that the convergence time is not high. Some of the BGP diverse path features were discussed in Chapter 6, "Troubleshooting Platform Issues Due to BGP." One of the other features to achieve the diverse path is the BGP add-path feature. The BGP add-path feature signals not only the primary and backup path but the diverse paths ranging from 2 to n or all paths available for the prefix. To implement BGP add-path feature, both the RRs and the edge BGP router should have add-path feature support.

The BGP add-path features provides a lot of benefits to the network as a whole. A few of the benefits are as follows:

■ **Fast Convergence:** Because the ingress routers now have visibility to more paths, they can switch to backup paths faster after the primary path fails.

■ **Load Balancing:** Because there is more visibility for the paths to the ingress routers, they can do equal cost multipath (ECMP) on multiple paths to achieve load balancing. This requires either the advertisement of backup paths or all paths to be advertised.

■ **Churn Reduction:** Withdraws can be suppressed because of available alternate paths.

■ **Route Oscillation Prevention:** Route oscillation scenarios are covered in RFC 3345. The scenarios presented in the RFC can be overcome by advertising group best paths (in some cases all paths).

The BGP add-path feature is defined in RFC 7911. The RFC proposes an extension to the Network Layer Reachability Information (NLRI) by including path-ID, so that multiple paths for the same prefix can be advertised. Path-IDs are unique to a peering session and are generated for each network. The encodings specified in RFC 4271 and RFC 4760 are extended, as shown in Figure 14-9.

| Path Identifier (4 Octets) |
| Length (1 Octet) |
| Prefix (Variable) |

Figure 14-9 *Extended Encodings for BGP Add-Path*

For carrying labeled prefixes, the encoding specified in RFC 3107 is modified for the add-path feature, as shown in Figure 14-10.

| Path Identifier (4 Octets) |
| Length (1 Octet) |
| Label (3 Octets) |
| ... |
| Prefix (Variable) |

Figure 14-10 *Modified Encoding for Carrying Labeled Prefixes*

The add-path feature is negotiated as a capability on a per AFI/SAFI basis and done separately for both Send and Receive direction. The per AFI and per neighbor configuration triggers capability exchange with the peers. For exchanging add-path capability between two routers—for instance, router A and router B, both A and B should configure the add-path capability to send, receive, or both.

For router A to send add-paths to router B, router A should enable send capability and router B should enable receive capability. Similarly, for router A to receive add-paths from router B, router A should be configured with receive capability and router B with the send capability. Any configuration changes will take effect only during the next session establishment.

The add-path capability is configured in two ways. It can either be configured globally under the address-family or on a per-neighbor basis. To enable the BGP add-path capability, use the command **bgp additional-paths** [send | receive] under the address-family. Cisco IOS routers reset the session as soon as the command is configured, but it is manually required on IOS XR and NX-OS to clear the BGP session to exchange add-path capability.

Example 14-18 illustrates the configuration to exchange BGP add-path capability on all three platforms. In this example, all the RR routers are configured to both send and receive add-path capability. The PE1 router is globally configured to both send and receive add-path capability but configured to receive add-path only from the RR1 router.

Example 14-18 *BGP Add-Path Capability Configuration*

```
RR1
RR1(config)# router bgp 100
RR1(config-router)# address-family ipv4 unicast
RR1(config-router-af)# bgp additional-paths send receive
```

```
RR2
RP/0/0/CPU0:RR2(config)# router bgp 100
RP/0/0/CPU0:RR2(config-bgp)# address-family ipv4 unicast
RP/0/0/CPU0:RR2(config-bgp-af)# additional-paths send
RP/0/0/CPU0:RR2(config-bgp-af)# additional-paths receive
RP/0/0/CPU0:RR2(config-bgp-af)# commit
```

```
RR3
RR3(config)# router bgp 100
RR3(config-router)# address-family ipv4 unicast
RR3(config-router-af)# additional-paths send
RR3(config-router-af)# additional-paths receive
```

```
PE1
PE1(config)# router bgp 100
PE1(config-router)# address-family ipv4 unicast
PE1(config-router-af)# bgp additional-paths send receive
PE1(config-router-af)# neighbor 192.168.11.11 additional-paths receive
```

After the BGP session is reset, the add-path capability is negotiated and is viewed under the command **show bgp** *afi safi* **neighbor** *ip-address*. Example 14-19 displays the add-path capability negotiated on all the RR routers and PE1 router. The output shows that PE1 is exchanging only receive capability with RR1 and both send and receive capability with RR2 and RR3 (based on the configuration under the AFI).

Example 14-19   *Verifying BGP Add-Path Capability*

```
RR1
RR1# show bgp ipv4 unicast neighbors 192.168.1.1
BGP neighbor is 192.168.1.1,  remote AS 100, internal link
  BGP version 4, remote router ID 192.168.1.1
  BGP state = Established, up for 00:07:05
  Last read 00:00:49, last write 00:00:34, hold time is 180, keepalive interval is
  60 seconds
  Neighbor sessions:
    1 active, is not multisession capable (disabled)
  Neighbor capabilities:
    Route refresh: advertised and received(new)
    Four-octets ASN Capability: advertised and received
    Address family IPv4 Unicast: advertised and received
    Enhanced Refresh Capability: advertised and received
    Multisession Capability:
    Stateful switchover support enabled: NO for session 1
. . .
. . .
For address family: IPv4 Unicast
  Additional Paths send capability: advertised
  Additional Paths receive capability: advertised and received
  Session: 192.168.1.1
  BGP table version 8, neighbor version 8/0
! Output omitted for brevity


RR2
RP/0/0/CPU0:RR2# show bgp ipv4 unicast neighbors 192.168.1.1
Fri May 20 03:23:58.765 UTC

BGP neighbor is 192.168.1.1
 Remote AS 100, local AS 100, internal link
 Remote router ID 192.168.1.1
 Cluster ID 192.168.22.22
  BGP state = Established, up for 00:07:07
  NSR State: None
. . .
. . .
For Address Family: IPv4 Unicast
  BGP neighbor version 8
  Update group: 0.1 Filter-group: 0.2  No Refresh request being processed
  Route-Reflector Client
  AF-dependent capabilities:
    Additional-paths Send: advertised and received
    Additional-paths Receive: advertised and received
```

```
! Output omitted for brevity
```

RR3
```
RR3# show bgp ipv4 unicast neighbors 192.168.1.1
BGP neighbor is 192.168.1.1,  remote AS 100, ibgp link, Peer index 1
  BGP version 4, remote router ID 192.168.1.1
  BGP state = Established, up for 00:01:28
  Using loopback0 as update source for this peer
  Last read 00:00:32, hold time = 180, keepalive interval is 60 seconds
  Last written 00:00:27, keepalive timer expiry due 00:00:32
  Received 661 messages, 1 notifications, 0 bytes in queue
  Sent 613 messages, 0 notifications, 0 bytes in queue
  Connections established 4, dropped 3
  Last reset by peer 00:01:36, due to session closed
  Last reset by us never, due to No error

  Neighbor capabilities:
  Dynamic capability: advertised (mp, refresh, gr)
  Dynamic capability (old): advertised
  . . .
  . . .
  Additional Paths capability: advertised received
  Additional Paths Capability Parameters:
  Send capability advertised to Peer for AF:
     IPv4 Unicast
  Receive capability advertised to Peer for AF:
     IPv4 Unicast
  Send capability received from Peer for AF:
     IPv4 Unicast
  Receive capability received from Peer for AF:
     IPv4 Unicast
! Output omitted for brevity
```

PE1
```
PE1# show bgp ipv4 unicast neighbors 192.168.11.11
BGP neighbor is 192.168.11.11,  remote AS 100, internal link
  BGP version 4, remote router ID 192.168.11.11
  BGP state = Established, up for 00:28:35
  . . .
  . . .
 For address family: IPv4 Unicast
  Additional Paths send capability: received
  Additional Paths receive capability: advertised and received
! Output omitted for brevity
```

Because RR receives multiple paths from the border or edge routers, the RR router performs the best-path computation for 2 to N paths or all paths and sends the N or all paths to the border routers. The number N is limited to 2 for IOS XR and up to 3 on Cisco IOS to preserve CPU and improved convergence. If there is multipath configured, the RR router performs the best path and send all the multipaths to the border routers.

Note   If the add-path policy is defined under the vpnv4 address-family, the policy applies to all the VRFs unless it is overridden at individual VRFs.

Now, to advertise the backup paths or additional paths from the RR, two steps should be followed:

Step 1.   Make a selection of additional paths on the RR.

Step 2.   Install the additional paths on the border router.

For making a selection of additional paths, use the command **bgp additional-paths select [all | backup | best | group-best]** on Cisco IOS. On IOS XR and NX-OS, use the **additional-paths selection** command under the address-family with a route policy or a route-map. Under the policy, all the options are available for advertising the backup or all paths for the prefix and also installing them locally. The Table 14-1 lists the purpose of the available options with the path selection.

Table 14-1   *BGP Add-Path Selection Options*

all	Select all available paths
backup	Select backup path
best	Select best N paths, where N is based on the platform
group-best	Select best path in the group

Example 14-20 illustrates the configuration on all three RRs to make the path selection for advertising it toward the border router PE1. Even though the RR routers are advertising the backup or additional paths, PE1 only installs the backup paths when the **bgp additional-paths install** command is configured under the address-family.

Example 14-20   *Additional Path Selection Configuration on RRs*

```
RR1
RR1(config)# router bgp 100
RR1(config-router)# address-family ipv4 unicast
RR1(config-router-af)# bgp additional-paths select ?
  all           Select all available paths
  backup        Select backup path
```

```
     best          Select best N paths
     best-external Select best-external path
     group-best    Select group-best path
RR1(config-router-af)# bgp additional-paths select best 2
```

```
RR2
RP/0/0/CPU0:RR2(config)# router bgp 100
RP/0/0/CPU0:RR2(config-bgp)# address-family ipv4 unicast
RP/0/0/CPU0:RR2(config-bgp-af)# additional-paths selection route-policy ADD_PATH
RP/0/0/CPU0:RR2(config-bgp-af)# exit
RP/0/0/CPU0:RR2(config-bgp)# exit
RP/0/0/CPU0:RR2(config)# route-policy ADD_PATH
RP/0/0/CPU0:RR2(config-rpl)# if destination in (172.16.4.4/32) then
RP/0/0/CPU0:RR2(config-rpl-if)# set path-selection backup 1 advertise
RP/0/0/CPU0:RR2(config-rpl-if)# endif
RP/0/0/CPU0:RR2(config-rpl)# end-policy
RP/0/0/CPU0:RR2(config)# commit
```

```
RR3
RR3(config)# router bgp 100
RR3(config-router)# address-family ipv4 unicast
RR3(config-router-af)# additional-paths selection route-map ADD_PATH
RR3(config-router-af)# additional-paths install backup
RR3(config-router-af)# exit
RR3(config-router)# route-map ADD_PATH permit 10
RR3(config-route-map)# match ip address prefix-list fromCE2
RR3(config-route-map)# set path-selection all advertise
```

```
PE1
PE1(config)# router bgp 100
PE1(config-router)# address-family ipv4 unicast
PE1(config-router-af)# bgp additional-paths install
```

Note   The command **bgp additional-paths install** on Cisco IOS and the command **option additional-paths install** on IOS XR and NX-OS are only for demonstration purposes here. These are not part of the BGP Add-Path feature but are used in the BGP Prefix-Independent Convergence feature discussed later in this chapter.

After PE1 is configured to install the additional paths, PE1 receives a total of six paths from the three RRs. Of the six paths, one path is selected as best, and one is selected as the backup/repair path. Example 14-21 displays the output showing multiple paths received on the PE1 router from all the RRs.

Example 14-21 *BGP Table on PE1*

```
PE1# show bgp ipv4 unicast 172.16.4.4
BGP routing table entry for 172.16.4.4/32, version 7
Paths: (6 available, best #6, table default)
  Additional-path-install
  Not advertised to any peer
  Refresh Epoch 1
  300
    192.168.3.3 (metric 3) from 192.168.22.22 (192.168.22.22)
      Origin IGP, metric 0, localpref 100, valid, internal
      Originator: 192.168.3.3, Cluster list: 192.168.22.22
      rx pathid: 0x2, tx pathid: 0
  Refresh Epoch 1
  300
    192.168.3.3 (metric 3) from 192.168.33.33 (192.168.33.33)
      Origin IGP, metric 0, localpref 100, valid, internal
      Originator: 192.168.3.3, Cluster list: 192.168.33.33
      rx pathid: 0x2, tx pathid: 0
  Refresh Epoch 3
  300
    192.168.3.3 (metric 3) from 192.168.11.11 (192.168.11.11)
      Origin IGP, metric 0, localpref 100, valid, internal, backup/repair
      Originator: 192.168.3.3, Cluster list: 192.168.11.11
      rx pathid: 0x1, tx pathid: 0
  Refresh Epoch 1
  300
    192.168.2.2 (metric 3) from 192.168.22.22 (192.168.22.22)
      Origin IGP, metric 0, localpref 100, valid, internal
      Originator: 192.168.2.2, Cluster list: 192.168.22.22
      rx pathid: 0x1, tx pathid: 0
  Refresh Epoch 1
  300
    192.168.2.2 (metric 3) from 192.168.33.33 (192.168.33.33)
      Origin IGP, metric 0, localpref 100, valid, internal
      Originator: 192.168.2.2, Cluster list: 192.168.33.33
      rx pathid: 0x1, tx pathid: 0
  Refresh Epoch 3
  300
    192.168.2.2 (metric 3) from 192.168.11.11 (192.168.11.11)
      Origin IGP, metric 0, localpref 100, valid, internal, best
      Originator: 192.168.2.2, Cluster list: 192.168.11.11
      rx pathid: 0x0, tx pathid: 0x0
```

On the RR routers, BGP selects a best path and second-best path and installs in the BGP table and RIB. Example 14-22 displays the prefix information on all the RR routers. Because the route policy is configured to advertise the additional path on RR1, RR2, and RR3 routers, all the RRs don't just advertise the best path but also advertise additional paths. On RR1, the prefix 172.16.4.4 is advertised as the best as well as the additional path learned from another PE router. Both RR2 and RR3 show both the paths being advertised to the neighbors or route reflector-client router PE1: 192.168.1.1.

Example 14-22 *Prefix Information*

```
RR1
RR1# show bgp ipv4 unicast 172.16.4.4
BGP routing table entry for 172.16.4.4/32, version 14
Paths: (2 available, best #1, table default)
  Path advertised to update-groups:
     2          6
  Refresh Epoch 2
  300, (Received from a RR-client)
    192.168.2.2 (metric 2) from 192.168.2.2 (192.168.2.2)
      Origin IGP, metric 0, localpref 100, valid, internal, best
      rx pathid: 0, tx pathid: 0x0
  Path advertised to update-groups:
     6
  Refresh Epoch 2
  300, (Received from a RR-client)
    192.168.3.3 (metric 2) from 192.168.3.3 (192.168.3.3)
      Origin IGP, metric 0, localpref 100, valid, internal, best2
      rx pathid: 0, tx pathid: 0x1


RR1# show bgp ipv4 unicast neighbors 192.168.1.1 advertised-routes
BGP table version is 88, local router ID is 192.168.11.11
Status codes: s suppressed, d damped, h history, * valid, > best, i - internal,
              r RIB-failure, S Stale, m multipath, b backup-path, f RT-Filter,
              x best-external, a additional-path, c RIB-compressed,
Origin codes: i - IGP, e - EGP, ? - incomplete
RPKI validation codes: V valid, I invalid, N Not found


     Network          Next Hop          Metric LocPrf Weight Path
 *>i 172.16.4.4/32    192.168.2.2            0    100      0 300 i
 *  ia172.16.4.4/32   192.168.3.3            0    100      0 300 i

Total number of prefixes 2
```

```
RR2
RP/0/0/CPU0:RR2# show bgp ipv4 unicast 172.16.4.4
```

```
BGP routing table entry for 172.16.4.4/32
Versions:
  Process           bRIB/RIB  SendTblVer
  Speaker              11         11
Last Modified: May 20 07:51:28.941 for 00:53:25
Paths: (2 available, best #1)
  Advertised to update-groups (with more than one peer):
    0.2
  Advertised to peers (in unique update groups):
    192.168.1.1
  Path #1: Received by speaker 0
  Advertised to update-groups (with more than one peer):
    0.2
  Advertised to peers (in unique update groups):
    192.168.1.1
  300, (Received from a RR-client)
    192.168.2.2 (metric 2) from 192.168.2.2 (192.168.2.2)
      Origin IGP, metric 0, localpref 100, valid, internal, best, group-best
      Received Path ID 0, Local Path ID 1, version 11
  Path #2: Received by speaker 0
  Advertised to peers (in unique update groups):
    192.168.1.1
  300, (Received from a RR-client)
    192.168.3.3 (metric 2) from 192.168.3.3 (192.168.3.3)
      Origin IGP, metric 0, localpref 100, valid, internal, backup, add-path
      Received Path ID 0, Local Path ID 2, version 11
```

```
RR3
RR3# show bgp ipv4 unicast 172.16.4.4
BGP routing table information for VRF default, address family IPv4 Unicast
BGP routing table entry for 172.16.4.4/32, version 78
Paths: (2 available, best #2)
Flags: (0x08001a) on xmit-list, is in urib, is best urib route, is in HW,

  Advertised path-id 2
  Path type: internal, path is valid, not best reason: Router Id
  AS-Path: 300 , path sourced external to AS
    192.168.3.3 (metric 41) from 192.168.3.3 (192.168.3.3)
      Origin IGP, MED 0, localpref 100, weight 0

  Advertised path-id 1
  Path type: internal, path is valid, is best path
```

```
AS-Path: 300 , path sourced external to AS
  192.168.2.2 (metric 41) from 192.168.2.2 (192.168.2.2)
    Origin IGP, MED 0, localpref 100, weight 0

Path-id 1 advertised to peers:
  192.168.1.1        192.168.3.3
Path-id 2 advertised to peers:
  192.168.1.1
```

If for some reason, either one of the RRs goes down or if the **bgp additional-paths select best** command is removed from RR1 router, PE1 selects the backup path learned via other RR. Example 14-23 demonstrates a negative testing by removing the command **bgp additional-paths select best** from RR1 router. PE1 router selects the backup path from RR2 router while the primary path is still being learned from RR1.

Example 14-23 *BGP Additional-Path Select Command Testing*

```
RR1
RR1(config)# router bgp 100
RR1(config-router)# address-family ipv4 unicast
RR1(config-router-af)# no bgp additional-paths select best 2
```

```
PE1
PE1# show bgp ipv4 unicast 172.16.4.4
BGP routing table entry for 172.16.4.4/32, version 13
Paths: (5 available, best #5, table default)
Multipath: eBGP
  Additional-path-install
  Not advertised to any peer
  Refresh Epoch 1
  300
    192.168.3.3 (metric 3) from 192.168.22.22 (192.168.22.22)
      Origin IGP, metric 0, localpref 100, valid, internal, backup/repair
      Originator: 192.168.3.3, Cluster list: 192.168.22.22
      rx pathid: 0x2, tx pathid: 0
  Refresh Epoch 1
  300
    192.168.3.3 (metric 3) from 192.168.33.33 (192.168.33.33)
      Origin IGP, metric 0, localpref 100, valid, internal
      Originator: 192.168.3.3, Cluster list: 192.168.33.33
      rx pathid: 0x2, tx pathid: 0
  Refresh Epoch 1
  300
    192.168.2.2 (metric 3) from 192.168.22.22 (192.168.22.22)
```

```
        Origin IGP, metric 0, localpref 100, valid, internal
        Originator: 192.168.2.2, Cluster list: 192.168.22.22
        rx pathid: 0x1, tx pathid: 0
Refresh Epoch 1
300
    192.168.2.2 (metric 3) from 192.168.33.33 (192.168.33.33)
        Origin IGP, metric 0, localpref 100, valid, internal
        Originator: 192.168.2.2, Cluster list: 192.168.33.33
        rx pathid: 0x1, tx pathid: 0
Refresh Epoch 4
300
    192.168.2.2 (metric 3) from 192.168.11.11 (192.168.11.11)
        Origin IGP, metric 0, localpref 100, valid, internal, best
        Originator: 192.168.2.2, Cluster list: 192.168.11.11
        rx pathid: 0x0, tx pathid: 0x0
```

BGP best-external

After examining the topology shown in Figure 14-8 and looking at all the outputs from the add-path examples, PE2 was chosen as the best path because of its lowest router-id. With the add-path feature on the RR routers, both the primary and backup paths are being advertised via RR. Both PE2 and PE3 select the best path that it learns directly from their peering with CE2.

But what happens if the default BGP routing policy is modified? For example, if the path from PE2 is set with a local preference of 200, PE3 instead of having the best path learned via CE2, it will have the best path learned via PE2. So, even if the RR advertises the primary and the backup paths to the remote border router, there is actually a single path via the PE2 router.

After examining the BGP table for the prefix 172.16.4.4, notice that the best path on PE3 is also being learned from PE2 and not from the direct link between CE2 and PE3. Example 14-24 displays the BGP table for the prefix 172.16.4.4/32 on both PE2 and PE3 routers.

Example 14-24   *BGP Table Output*

```
PE2
PE2# show bgp ipv4 unicast 172.16.4.4
BGP routing table entry for 172.16.4.4/32, version 9
Paths: (1 available, best #1, table default)
  Advertised to update-groups:
      3
  Refresh Epoch 3
  300
    172.16.24.4 from 172.16.24.4 (172.16.4.4)
```

```
    Origin IGP, metric 0, localpref 200, valid, external, best
    rx pathid: 0, tx pathid: 0x0
```

```
PE3
PE3# show bgp ipv4 unicast 172.16.4.4
BGP routing table entry for 172.16.4.4/32, version 10
Paths: (4 available, best #1, table default)
  Advertised to update-groups:
     2
  Refresh Epoch 2
  300
    192.168.2.2 (metric 3) from 192.168.11.11 (192.168.11.11)
      Origin IGP, metric 0, localpref 200, valid, internal, best
      Originator: 192.168.2.2, Cluster list: 192.168.11.11
      rx pathid: 0, tx pathid: 0x0
  Refresh Epoch 1
  300
    192.168.2.2 (metric 3) from 192.168.33.33 (192.168.33.33)
      Origin IGP, metric 0, localpref 200, valid, internal
      Originator: 192.168.2.2, Cluster list: 192.168.33.33
      rx pathid: 0, tx pathid: 0
  Refresh Epoch 1
  300
    192.168.2.2 (metric 3) from 192.168.22.22 (192.168.22.22)
      Origin IGP, metric 0, localpref 200, valid, internal
      Originator: 192.168.2.2, Cluster list: 192.168.22.22
      rx pathid: 0, tx pathid: 0
  Refresh Epoch 6
  300
    172.16.34.4 from 172.16.34.4 (172.16.4.4)
      Origin IGP, metric 0, localpref 100, valid, external
      rx pathid: 0, tx pathid: 0
```

To overcome this behavior, the BGP best-external feature was introduced. The BGP best-external functionality is defined in IETF draft *draft-ietf-idr-best-external*. Using this feature, the backup PE router propagates its own best external route—the path directly learned from CE, and not via another PE, to the RRs or IBGP peers. The BGP table on the backup PE still shows the best path via another PE but also shows the external path as the backup/repair path.

To enable the BGP best-external feature, use the command **bgp advertise-best-external** on the backup PE router. This command enables BGP to treat an external route as the best backup path, install the best external as a backup path, and advertise that using BGP updates. It is not needed to configure or enable the **bgp additional-paths** command to enable BGP best-external functionality, because the installation of backup path functionality is rolled into the **bgp advertise-best-external** command.

Example 14-25 demonstrates the configuration of the BGP best-external feature on both IOS and IOS XR platforms.

Example 14-25   *BGP Best-External Configuration*

```
IOS
PE3(config)# router bgp 100
PE3(config-router)# address-family ipv4 unicast
PE3(config-router-af)# bgp advertise-best-external
```

```
IOS XR
PE3(config)# router bgp 100
PE3(config-bgp)# address-family ipv4 unicast
PE3(config-bgp-af)# advertise-best-external
```

After PE3 is configured to advertise the best-external path, RRs receive the primary path via PE2 and the backup/repair path via PE3 that is the best-external path. Examine the output of the BGP table for the prefix 172.16.4.4 on the PE3 router in Example 14-26. Prefix 172.16.4.4 on PE3 has the best path via PE2; the external path via CE2 is marked as backup/repair and advertise-best-external. Also, the command **show bgp ipv4 unicast neighbors** *ip-address* **advertised-routes** displays the advertised prefix, which is marked as *b* and *x*, where *b* represents the backup path and *x* represents the best-external path.

Example 14-26   *Verifying BGP Best-External Path*

```
PE3# show bgp ipv4 unicast 172.16.4.4
BGP routing table entry for 172.16.4.4/32, version 12
Paths: (4 available, best #1, table default)
  Advertise-best-external
  Advertised to update-groups:
     1         2
  Refresh Epoch 3
  300
    192.168.2.2 (metric 3) from 192.168.11.11 (192.168.11.11)
      Origin IGP, metric 0, localpref 200, valid, internal, best
      Originator: 192.168.2.2, Cluster list: 192.168.11.11
      rx pathid: 0, tx pathid: 0x0
  Refresh Epoch 1
  300
    192.168.2.2 (metric 3) from 192.168.33.33 (192.168.33.33)
      Origin IGP, metric 0, localpref 200, valid, internal
      Originator: 192.168.2.2, Cluster list: 192.168.33.33
      rx pathid: 0, tx pathid: 0
  Refresh Epoch 1
```

```
300
   192.168.2.2 (metric 3) from 192.168.22.22 (192.168.22.22)
      Origin IGP, metric 0, localpref 200, valid, internal
      Originator: 192.168.2.2, Cluster list: 192.168.22.22
      rx pathid: 0, tx pathid: 0
Refresh Epoch 7
300
   172.16.34.4 from 172.16.34.4 (172.16.4.4)
      Origin IGP, metric 0, localpref 100, valid, external, backup/repair,
         advertise-best-external , recursive-via-connected
      rx pathid: 0, tx pathid: 0

! The below output shows the advertised path to RR1 router


PE3# show bgp ipv4 unicast neighbors 192.168.11.11 advertised-routes
BGP table version is 12, local router ID is 192.168.3.3
Status codes: s suppressed, d damped, h history, * valid, > best, i - internal,
              r RIB-failure, S Stale, m multipath, b backup-path, f RT-Filter,
              x best-external, a additional-path, c RIB-compressed,
Origin codes: i - IGP, e - EGP, ? - incomplete
RPKI validation codes: V valid, I invalid, N Not found


     Network          Next Hop            Metric LocPrf Weight Path
 *b x172.16.4.4/32    172.16.34.4              0          0 300 i
```

Note Both BGP Prefix Independent Convergence (PIC) and BGP best-external are
mutually exclusive to each other. Also, the BGP Best-External feature is required only
when there are policies configured, such as setting of local-preference to influence the
routing. This feature should not be configured when there are no such attributes set on the
PE routers.

BGP FRR and Prefix-Independent Convergence

Routing protocols convergence have certain well-known limitations and can take from
a few milliseconds to a few seconds in some cases to compute the current state of the
network. BGP has been widely deployed for both interdomain or intradomain routing
exchanges. BGP computes a best path for each prefix at regular intervals and installs the
next-hop for each network entry in the routing and forwarding table to forward the data
packets toward the final destination of a packet.

When the BGP table holds routing for multiple customers, a single event such as route flap or link flap can cause the BGP session to go down, BGP needs to update about it to other peers immediately, so that a best path can be recalculated for a prefix. When there are large number of prefixes involved in the BGP table and RIB table, it might happen that the withdraws from the BGP peer can take few seconds to arrive at the remote peer, especially in cases when RR is involved to reflect the updates to the remote peers. This may result in traffic loss until the time the whole network is converged.

With a large number of prefixes that share the same next-hop, it would be ideal to precompute a backup path in BGP beforehand and update the same in the RIB and the FIB. BGP FRR allows backup path computation, which not only gets updating in the RIB but is also installed in the FIB on the line cards. It is called BGP FRR because BGP does the precomputation of the backup path, and since the FIB already knows about the backup path, it knows where to reroute the traffic in case the next-hop or the link to the next-hop goes down. With BGP FRR enabled, the pointers exist to the next-hop interfaces or next-hop IP addresses in the FIB. The BGP next-hop is also stored as a pointer in the FIB and points to the primary next-hop pointer. When the current path goes away, only the BGP next-hop pointer needs to be updated instead of programming all the routes in the RIB with a new next-hop. In case of failure, the FIB is quickly able to switch the traffic to the other precomputed path by repairing the path adjacency. Thus the FIB or CEF can achieve the PIC.

BGP FRR solution works but doesn't provide subsecond convergence and low packet loss unless FIB supports PIC with a shared object and precomputed backup path. There are various scenarios where BGP PIC can reduce the convergence time and traffic loss to a great extent. The two flavors of BGP PIC that provide maximum convergence are as follows:

- BGP PIC core
- BGP PIC edge

BGP PIC Core

The BGP PIC core feature takes care of node or link failure in the provider core network toward the BGP prefix next-hop. Examine the topology in Figure 14-11. For PE1 to reach the PE3 prefix, the core follows the path via router P1. If there is a failure even in the core network, such that a core link or the core router P1 itself goes down, with PIC core feature, the traffic quickly converges to the backup path via the P2 router.

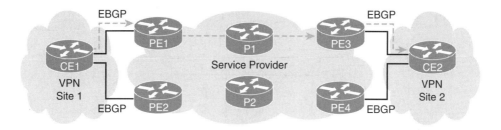

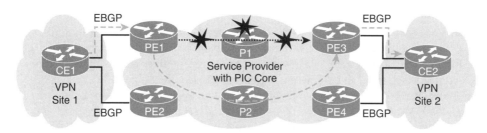

Figure 14-11   *BGP PIC Core*

BGP PIC core completely depends on how quick the IGP can converge. Traditionally, the Cisco IOS platforms supported flat FIB tables. With flat FIB, each prefix has its own forwarding information directly associated with an outgoing interface as one-to-one mapping. Figure 14-12 displays how the BGP prefixes are mapped in a flat FIB table.

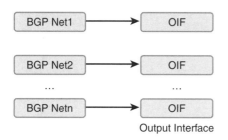

Figure 14-12   *Flat FIB Architecture*

Thus, examining the topology in Figure 14-8, the flat FIB has the forwarding table mapped as shown in Figure 14-13. Figure 14-13 displays the forwarding table from the PE1 perspective. If multiple prefixes are being learned from the CE2 router—for example, 172.16.4.4, 172.16.x.x, … and 172.16.z.z with some prefixes being learned in AS100 via RR1 and some via RR2—then there is a one-to-one mapping in the FIB pointing to the adjacency for the outgoing interface toward RR1 or RR2. And because all the prefixes are being learned via PE2 (assumed as a best path), and PE1 learns about PE2 via RR1, RR2, and RR3, there are three individual mappings for the next-hops to reach RR1, RR2, and RR3, respectively.

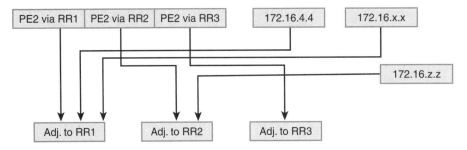

Figure 14-13   *Flattened FIB on PE1*

BGP PIC core uses hierarchical FIB to achieve faster convergence. In hierarchical FIB, a path-list is assigned to all IGP or BGP prefixes. A path-list is a data structure that lists all paths that can be used to reach a destination prefix. IGP prefixes get a path-list of type next-hop, which mean all information is available to select the outgoing interface. BGP prefixes, on the other hand, gets a path-list of type recursive, which points to another path-list type of next-hop. Figure 14-14 displays the hierarchical FIB architecture with both single path and multipath. The difference with multipath is only that the other path is learned from a different next-hop and could possibly be learned from a same or a different outgoing interface.

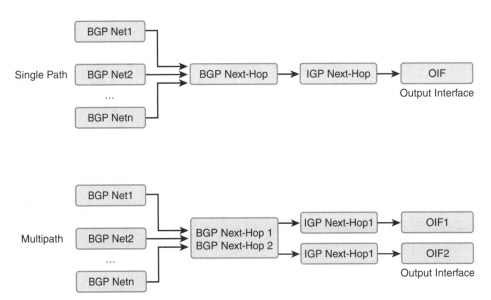

Figure 14-14   *Hierarchical FIB Architecture*

Cisco IOS platforms works on flat FIB by default but can be manipulated to support hier-archical FIB using the command **cef table output-chain build favor convergence-speed**. This command is a global command and should be configured during a maintenance win-dow because it might cause some traffic loss while the FIB is being updated in the new hierarchical structure. There is no command to enable on IOS XR or NX-OS because it functions on hierarchical FIB by default.

BGP PIC Edge

BGP PIC core deals with failure in the provider core network. But what if there is a link failure on the edge toward the CE, or what if the edge router itself goes down? The reconvergence of traffic from the primary Provider Edge (PE) router to backup PE router can cost a lot to the service providers, and there can be major outages as a single PE might be terminating 100s or 1000s of customers. To overcome the convergence issues, BGP installs the backup path in the RIB, FIB, and Label Forwarding Information Base (LFIB) (in case of MPLS Virtual Private Networks (VPNs)).

The BGP PIC solution can be implemented with a few simple commands in BGP that are AFI specific, as well as a few additional commands, such as the following:

■ **Backup path calculation and installation: bgp additional-paths install** on Cisco IOS, the command **additional-paths selection route-policy** *route-policy-name* on both IOS XR and NX-OS, along with the command **additional-paths install** on NX-OS.

■ **Best-External knob: bgp advertise-best-external**.

Note   In NX-OS, there is no route policy configuration but route-map.

To better understand the BGP PIC edge solution, let's examine various scenarios.

Scenario 1—IP PE-CE Link/Node Protection on CE Side

Examine the topology shown in Figure 14-15. CE1 has a dual-homed connection to PE1 and PE2. Another customer router, CE2, is also having a dual-homed connection with PE3 and PE4. Both the CE1 and CE2 routers are establishing EBGP peer with their con-nected PE routers, respectively. To reach the CE2 router, CE1 takes the path from PE1 via RR and then to PE3 (following the dotted arrow line).

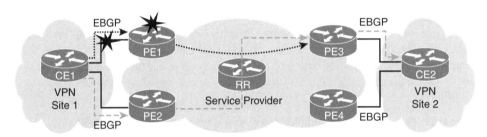

Figure 14-15 *BGP PIC for PE-CE Link/Node Protection on CE Side*

Now, when the PE1-CE1 link goes down, BGP detects the link-flaps (using BFD or fast-external–fallover), CE1 re-computes the best path via PE2 and then installs the best path in the RIB and programs the FIB. This causes traffic loss for the time CE1 recomputes the forwarding path. With BGP PIC, this is avoided by having the backup path installed in the FIB.

To further understand this concept, consider the topology shown in Figure 14-8. CE1 is advertising the prefix 172.16.5.5. For CE2 to reach CE1 (172.16.5.5), there are two paths. One via PE2 and other via PE3. To implement BGP PIC, for high availability from the CE node perspective, configure the command **bgp additional-paths install**. This command allows the router to install the backup path in the FIB. Example 14-27 demonstrates the BGP and the FIB table before and after the PIC implementation.

Example 14-27 *BGP PIC on CE Node*

```
CE2# show bgp ipv4 unicast 172.16.5.5
BGP routing table entry for 172.16.5.5/32, version 3
Paths: (2 available, best #2, table default)
  Advertised to update-groups:
    1
  Refresh Epoch 3
  100 200
    172.16.24.2 from 172.16.24.2 (192.168.2.2)
      Origin IGP, localpref 100, valid, external
      rx pathid: 0, tx pathid: 0
  Refresh Epoch 5
```

```
   100 200
     172.16.34.3 from 172.16.34.3 (192.168.3.3)
        Origin IGP, localpref 100, valid, external, best
        rx pathid: 0, tx pathid: 0x0


CE2# show ip cef 172.16.5.5 detail
172.16.5.5/32, epoch 0, flags [rib only nolabel, rib defined all labels]
  recursive via 172.16.34.3
    attached to GigabitEthernet0/2
```

```
CE2(config)# router bgp 300
CE2(config-router)# address-family ipv4 unicast
CE2(config-router-af)# bgp additional-paths install
```

```
CE2# show bgp ipv4 unicast 172.16.5.5
BGP routing table entry for 172.16.5.5/32, version 5
Paths: (2 available, best #2, table default)
  Additional-path-install
  Advertised to update-groups:
     1
  Refresh Epoch 3
  100 200
    172.16.24.2 from 172.16.24.2 (192.168.2.2)
       Origin IGP, localpref 100, valid, external, backup/repair ,
                   recursive-via-connected
      rx pathid: 0, tx pathid: 0
  Refresh Epoch 5
  100 200
    172.16.34.3 from 172.16.34.3 (192.168.3.3)
       Origin IGP, localpref 100, valid, external, best , recursive-via-connected
      rx pathid: 0, tx pathid: 0x0

CE2# show ip cef 172.16.5.5 detail
172.16.5.5/32, epoch 0, flags [rib only nolabel, rib defined all labels]
  recursive via 172.16.34.3
    attached to GigabitEthernet0/2
  recursive via 172.16.24.2, repair
    attached to GigabitEthernet0/1
```

In the output, notice that there is an additional flag set for the prefixes: *recursive-via-connected*. Recursive-resolution for connected prefixes for routes from directly connected peers are automatically set with *recursive-via-host* flag.

Scenario 2—IP MPLS PE-CE Link/Node Protection for Primary/Backup

Examine the topology in Figure 14-16. The service provider is running IP MPLS and providing MPLS VPN services to the customers. Customer router CE2 follows the path via PE3 toward PE1 to reach CE1. While inside the MPLS cloud, the traffic is flowing from PE3 through RR toward PE1, in which at each hop it is performing MPLS operations.

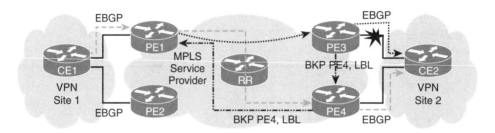

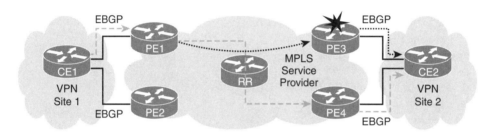

Figure 14-16 *BGP PIC with PE-CE Link Protection in MPLS VPN Network*

There are two failure scenarios in the MPLS VPN deployment from the provider standpoint:

- PE-CE link failure

- PE node failure

PE-CE Link Failure

When a PE-CE link goes down—for example, the link between PE3 and CE2—PE3 detects the link flaps (using BFD or fast-external-fallover) and recomputes the best path via PE4. After the best path is computed, the RIB and the FIB are updated. On the PE1 router, there is certain delay in calculating the best path again after a withdraw is received from PE3 for the failure event. The process of updating the RIB and the FIB again on PE1 can lead to a few seconds of traffic loss along with some more delay while PE4 is updating its RIB and FIB for the MPLS VPN customer.

With BGP FRR/PIC, one PE can act as primary and the other can act as backup. To achieve a higher rate of convergence and have the PEs act as primary and backup, configuring all the PE routers—PE1, PE2, PE3, and PE4—with the command **bgp additional-paths install** provides high availability in case of any PE-CE link failure event. This command is configured under vpnv4 address-family or under individual VRF address-families. If there are policies configured between PE3 and PE4 (similarly between PE1 and PE2), use the command **bgp advertise-best-external** instead of **bgp additional-paths-install** command.

So with BGP FRR, when CEF detects a link failure on the PE-CE link, CEF does in-place modification of the forwarding object to the backup node PE4 that is already existing in FIB without the need of routing protocols to update the RIB for the best path to be installed into FIB. Traffic is rerouted because of local fast convergence in CEF or FIB using the backup label switching path (LSP), which was already calculated when the FIB was populated with the backup path.

Later on PE1, when it receives a withdraw from RR for the PE3-CE2 path, BGP recomputes best-path calculations and computes and installs PE4 as the best path with a new label into FIB.

To further understand the behavior with the help of an example, consider the topology shown in Figure 14-8 with the difference that the service provider is now running the MPLS backbone. The PEs are having vpnv4 neighbor relationships with all the RRs. The customer-facing interfaces are part of VRF ABC on all three PE routers with a unique RD value. Example 14-28 displays the BGP table for the VRF ABC on all three PE routers. The command **bgp additional-paths install** is configured under the VRF address-family on all the PE routers. With BGP PIC enabled, both the PE routers learn the backup path for the customer prefix 172.16.4.4/32 via each other.

On PE2 router, the VPN label allocated for prefix 172.16.4.4/32 is 30, whereas on PE3 it is 28. This information is seen in the **show ip cef vrf** *vrf-name ip-address* [**detail**] output. Similar information is seen on PE3 as well. The labels beside the next-hop fields in the CEF output point toward the IGP labels received from the RR routers, respectively. PE1 shows the primary path via PE2 and the backup path via PE,3 but also has its FIB populated because of BGP PIC enabled.

Example 14-28 *BGP and FIB Table on All PE Routers*

```
PE2
PE2# show bgp vpnv4 unicast vrf ABC
     Network          Next Hop          Metric LocPrf Weight Path
Route Distinguisher: 100:2 (default for vrf ABC)
 *>  172.16.4.4/32    172.16.24.4            0               0 300 i
 *bi                  192.168.3.3           0    100        0 300 i
 *>i 172.16.5.5/32    192.168.1.1           0    100        0 200 i
 *>i 172.16.15.0/24   192.168.1.1           0    100        0 ?
 *>  172.16.24.0/24   0.0.0.0               0           32768 ?
 *>i 172.16.34.0/24   192.168.3.3           0    100        0 ?


PE2# show ip cef vrf ABC 172.16.4.4 detail
172.16.4.4/32, epoch 0, flags [rib defined all labels]
  dflt local label info: other/30 [0x2]
  recursive via 172.16.24.4
```

```
        attached to GigabitEthernet0/4
    recursive via 192.168.3.3 label 28(), repair
      nexthop 10.1.112.11 GigabitEthernet0/1 label 24()
      nexthop 10.1.222.22 GigabitEthernet0/2 label 24003()
```

PE3

PE3# **show bgp vpnv4 unicast vrf ABC**

Network	Next Hop	Metric	LocPrf	Weight	Path
Route Distinguisher: 100:3 (default for vrf ABC)					
*bi 172.16.4.4/32	192.168.2.2	0	100	0	300 i
*>	172.16.34.4	0		0	300 i
*>i 172.16.5.5/32	192.168.1.1	0	100	0	200 i
*>i 172.16.15.0/24	192.168.1.1	0	100	0	?
*>i 172.16.24.0/24	192.168.2.2	0	100	0	?
*> 172.16.34.0/24	0.0.0.0	0		32768	?

PE3# **show ip cef vrf ABC 172.16.4.4 detail**

```
172.16.4.4/32, epoch 0, flags [rib defined all labels]
  dflt local label info: other/28 [0x2]
  recursive via 172.16.34.4
    attached to GigabitEthernet0/4
  recursive via 192.168.2.2 label 30(), repair
    nexthop 10.1.113.11 GigabitEthernet0/1 label 23()
    nexthop 10.1.223.22 GigabitEthernet0/2 label 24006()
```

PE1

PE1# **show bgp vpnv4 unicast vrf ABC**

Route Distinguisher: 100:1 (default for vrf ABC)					
*>i 172.16.4.4/32	192.168.2.2	0	100	0	300 i
*bi	192.168.3.3	0	100	0	300 i
*> 172.16.5.5/32	172.16.15.5	0		0	200 i
*> 172.16.15.0/24	0.0.0.0	0		32768	?
*>i 172.16.24.0/24	192.168.2.2	0	100	0	?
*>i 172.16.34.0/24	192.168.3.3	0	100	0	?

PE1# **show ip cef vrf ABC 172.16.4.4 detail**

```
172.16.4.4/32, epoch 0, flags [rib defined all labels]
  recursive via 192.168.2.2 label 30()
    nexthop 10.1.111.11 GigabitEthernet0/2 label 23()
    nexthop 10.1.122.22 GigabitEthernet0/1 label 24006()
  recursive via 192.168.3.3 label 28(), repair
    nexthop 10.1.111.11 GigabitEthernet0/2 label 24()
    nexthop 10.1.122.22 GigabitEthernet0/1 label 24003()
```

The repair paths are viewed in the RIB by using the command **show ip route [vrf** *vrf-name*] **repair-paths** *ip-address* on Cisco IOS and the command **show route [vrf** *vrf-name*] on IOS XR and NX-OS platforms. Example 14-29 displays the repair paths in the VRF routing table.

Example 14-29 *Repair Paths in Routing Table*

```
PE2
PE2# show ip route vrf ABC repair-paths 172.16.4.4

Routing Table: ABC
Routing entry for 172.16.4.4/32
  Known via "bgp 100", distance 20, metric 0
  Tag 300, type external
  Last update from 172.16.24.4 00:02:52 ago
  Routing Descriptor Blocks:
  * 172.16.24.4, from 172.16.24.4, 00:02:52 ago, recursive-via-conn
      Route metric is 0, traffic share count is 1
      AS Hops 1
      Route tag 300
      MPLS label: none
    [RPR]192.168.3.3 (default), from 192.168.11.11, 00:02:52 ago, recursive-via-host
      Route metric is 0, traffic share count is 1
      AS Hops 1
      Route tag 300
      MPLS label: 28
      MPLS Flags: MPLS Required, No Global
```

When the PE2-CE2 link goes down, the FIB changes itself to point toward PE4. Example 14-30 displays the FIB table on router PE1.

Example 14-30 *FIB Verification on PE1*

```
PE1
PE1# show ip cef vrf ABC 172.16.4.4 detail
172.16.4.4/32, epoch 0, flags [rib defined all labels]
  recursive via 192.168.3.3 label 28()
    nexthop 10.1.111.11 GigabitEthernet0/2 label 24()
    nexthop 10.1.122.22 GigabitEthernet0/1 label 24003()
```

Enabling the debug command **debug bgp vpnv4 unicast addpath** shows that the best path is selected via other path even before the update is received from the RR. Example 14-31 displays the output of the **debug** command **debug bgp vpnv4 unicast addpath** on router PE2 when the link between PE2 and CE2 goes down. During this event, notice that the best path is bumped from the PE2-CE2 interface to back up the path learned via 192.168.3.3.

Example 14-31   debug *Command Output*

```
PE2
%BGP-5-NBR_RESET: Neighbor 172.16.24.4 reset (Interface flap)
BGP(4): Calculating bestpath (bump) for 100:2:172.16.4.4/32 :path_count:- 1/0,
 best-path =192.168.3.3, bestpath runtime :- 0 ms(or 453 usec) for net 172.16.4.4

BGP(4): compare_member_policy regarding best-external for nbr 172.16.24.4
  (nbr:F|group_policy:F)

BGP(4): compare_member_policy regarding best-external for nbr 172.16.24.4
  (nbr:F|group_policy:F)

%BGP-5-ADJCHANGE: neighbor 172.16.24.4 vpn vrf ABC Down Interface flap
%BGP_SESSION-5-ADJCHANGE: neighbor 172.16.24.4 IPv4 Unicast vpn vrf ABC
   topology base removed from session  Interface flapd
BGP(4): Calculating bestpath (bump) for 100:2:172.16.24.0/24 :path_count:- 0/0,
 best-path =0.0.0.0, bestpath runtime :- 1 ms(or 450 usec) for net 172.16.24.0

BGP(4): 192.168.11.11 rcv UPDATE about 100:2:172.16.4.4/32 -- withdrawn, label
   524288
```

PE Node Failure

Now consider the second scenario, as shown in Figure 14-14, where the PE3 node fails. When PE3 goes down, PE1 is aware of the removal of the /32 host prefix (that PE3 originally installed, and the prefix got populated by IGP earlier) by IGPs in subseconds (IGP convergence), and it recomputes the best path, chooses PE4 as the best path, and installs the routes into RIB and FIB. On PE1, there is certain delay in calculating the best path again after a withdraw is received from IGPs and installing the routes into RIB and programming FIB with the new forwarding adjacencies. Normally some traffic loss can occur for a few seconds during the time when BGP is recomputing best paths and installing them into RIB and FIB on PE1.

With BGP FRR/PIC enabled on the PE routers using the command **bgp additional-paths install**, PE1 installs both the primary path via PE3 and the backup path via PE4 in the FIB. Thus, when PE3 goes down and when the /32 host route failure is detected, FIB very quickly updates its forwarding object to PE4, in turn minimizing the traffic loss.

Later, when PE1 detects that the /32 route is gone, BGP recomputes best-path calculations and installs PE4 as the best path with a different label into FIB.

BGP Recursion Host

As part of the hierarchical FIB, BGP prefixes are marked as recursive. Recursion is the capability of the FIB to find the next longest matching path when the primary path fails. This feature is useful when BGP PIC is not enabled, when the next-hop is multiple hops away, and there are multiple paths to reach the next-hop.

In an ASBR node failure case, where ASBR's /32 loopback prefix is BGP next-hop (next-hop-self), black holing may happen if it could still be resolved via a less-specific or default route. The command **bgp recursion host** makes BGP only resolve recursive paths via the /32 host route. This command is automatically enabled when PIC edge is configured with **bgp additional-paths install** or **bgp advertise-best-external**.

Thus, this command is useful when implementing BGP PIC node protection but is not required when BGP PIC is implemented for PE-CE link protection. To disable CEF recursion, use the command **no bgp recursion host** on Cisco IOS and use the command **no nexthop resolution prefix-length minimum 32** on IOS XR.

Summary

BGP, being a highly scalable and robust protocol, is massively deployed across the Internet. With today's networking demands, it becomes crucial that BGP is also made highly available in the service provider as well as the enterprise networks. This chapter discussed various high-availability mechanisms that make BGP highly available and provide faster convergence.

BGP Graceful-Restart and BGP NSR prevent the traffic forwarding and BGP session flap during failure conditions. BGP graceful-restart indicates that the router is NSF capable, whereas BGP NSR ensures that the BGP sessions remain intact even during process failure or switchover conditions. This chapter also covered the BGP fast-external-fallover feature, which brings down the BGP session as soon as the link fails, thus helping with faster rerouting of traffic.

The chapter also covered features such as BGP Add-Path, BGP best-external, and BGP PIC, which provide not only faster, but also predictable linear convergence independent of the number of prefixes in the network. The command **bgp additional-paths select** allows the user to advertise additional paths along with the best-path by the route reflector. The command **bgp advertise-best-external** and **bgp additional-paths install** helps in providing prefix-independent convergence, thus ensuring minimum traffic disruption when the primary path fails.

References

RFC 4724, *Graceful Restart Mechanism for BGP*, S. Sangli, E. Chen, R. Fernando, J. Scudder, Y. Rekhter, IETF, http://tools.ietf.org/html/rfc4724, January 2007.

RFC 5880, *Bidirectional Forwarding Detection*, D. Katz, D. Ward, IETF, http://tools.ietf.org/html/rfc5880, June 2010.

RFC 5881, *Bidirectional Forwarding Detection for IPv4 and IPv6 (Single Hop)*, D. Katz, D. Ward, IETF, http://tools.ietf.org/html/rfc5881, June 2010.

RFC 5882, *Generic application of Bidirectional Forwarding Detection*, D. Katz, D. Ward, IETF, http://tools.ietf.org/html/rfc5882, June 2010.

RFC 5883, *Bidirectional Forwarding Detection for Multihop Paths*, D. Katz, D. Ward, IETF, http://tools.ietf.org/html/rfc5883, June 2010.

RFC 5884, *Bidirectional Forwarding Detection for MPLS Label Switched Paths*, R. Aggarwal, K. Kompella, T. Nadeau, G. Swallow, IETF, http://tools.ietf.org/html/rfc5884, June 2010.

RFC 7911, *Advertisements of Multiple Paths in BGP*, D. Walton, A. Retana, E. Chen, J. Scudder, IETF, https://tools.ietf.org/html/rfc7911, July 2016.

draft-rtgwg-bgp-pic, *BGP Prefix Independent Convergence*, A. Bashandy, C. Filsfils, P. Mohapatra, IETF, https://tools.ietf.org/html/draft-rtgwg-bgp-pic-02, September 2012.

Chapter 15

Enhancements in BGP

The following topics are covered in this chapter:

- Link-State Distribution using Border Gateway Protocol (BGP)
- BGP for Tunnel setup
- Provider Backbone Bridging with Ethernet VPN (PBB-EVPN)

This chapter serves as an introduction to some of the new features and enhancements that have been developed in recent years in BGP. During the course of this book, you have seen how BGP can be used in various environments, such as enterprise, service providers, and even data centers. Some new features developed in BGP extended the capability of BGP in the SDN world and also provides the organizations with the capability to use BGP for overlay-based features. This chapter provides an introduction to such features and helps direct the future of networking and possibilities with BGP.

Link-State Distribution Using BGP

Over the past few decades, there has been a massive change on how networks behave and how organizations manage the networks. The networking industry has seen a change from process switching of packets to hardware switching. With new developments happening across the networking industry, the focus has now turned to software defined networks (SDN), where the network can be programmatically controlled by a centralized controller.

Resource Reservation Protocol for Traffic Engineering (RSVP-TE) has been used for path computation purposes, but it has its own limitations. RSVP-TE does not provide optimal path computation and faces the bin-packing problem with Multi-Area or Multi-AS TE. The bin-packing problem is a classic problem, which deals with the distribution of traffic along available paths so that the available paths are efficiently utilized. The TE head-end router has limited visibility only in its domain—that is, the local Interior Gateway Protocol (IGP) area or local autonomous system (AS). To overcome such challenges, it makes more sense to move the label switch path (LSP) path computation control over to a central controller, which has visibility to the entire domain. This further allows for more efficient path calculation.

Because of the previously stated challenges, there has been a growing interest in providing an abstracted view of networks that enables higher-level applications to provide useful functionalities to businesses and users. The Application Layer Traffic Optimization (ALTO) servers, defined in RFC 5693, and Path Computation Elements (PCE), defined in RFC 4655, are examples of such components that provide network abstractions. An ALTO server hosts the ALTO service, which directs the resource consumer on which resource provider to select to optimize performance while improving resource consumption. PCE is an entity that is capable of computing paths in a network based on a network graph by applying computational constraints during computation, such as in case of TE LSP. These components, while external to the network, require network state information on a real-time basis. Specifically, they require link-state database information of each IGP node (Open Shortest Path First (OSPF) or Intermediate System to Intermediate System (IS-IS)) from the entire network.

Even in Segment Routing, a centralized path controller can prevent traffic steering problems. This is done by calculating the paths at the controller and then signaling it to the head-end node.

An ALTO server needs to have L3 topology, BGP or IGP, to compute the network distance between various endpoints. Likewise, the PCE server needs similar information for computing traffic engineering tunnels. Although topology information may be acquired by peering with both BGP and IGP, the IGP feed may not be viable in practice because of different administration control of the network operation, and IGP peering may not provide full visibility into all areas of the IGP.

Figure 15-1 displays a topology with PCE as a central controller. The PCE is being used to calculate optimal paths for TE in an Inter-Area TE deployment. For PCE to calculate optimal paths, PCE requires the complete topology and resource information database, usually known as Traffic Engineering Database (TED). The TED requires the topology from each domain along with the resources such as bandwidth, available bandwidth, link metric, TE metric, and so on from each domain.

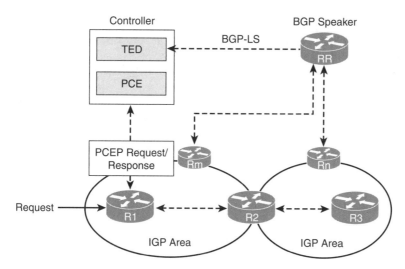

Figure 15-1   *Topology with PCE as a Central Controller*

Now, if the method of passively peering the PCE/ALTO controller with a node using IGP is chosen, the following problems could be faced:

■ IGP can be very chatty. This can cause the controller to consume a lot of resources and time to process those chatty updates.

■ In a distributed network environment, where the network is spanned across geographical boundaries, it becomes a challenge on where to place the controller.

RFC 7752 describes another mechanism via BGP, a.k.a. BGP for Link-State Distribution (BGP-LS), to distribute the IGP topology information to other BGP speakers using a BGP network layer reachability information (NLRI). In this method, the link-state data (and other related IGP states) are encoded into BGP NLRI to disseminate link-state information using BGP. The aforementioned application servers may then peer with BGP to collect both IGP and BGP topology information.

Figure 15-2 describes a typical deployment scenario of a network that utilizes BGP LS. The IGP network consists of many IGP nodes. The IGP network is divided into three areas. Each node receives the full link-state of every other node within its own area. To provide connectivity between different areas, there are nodes called the Area Border Routers (ABR) that belong to multiple areas. ABRs summarize the link-state information of a given area and send the summary to the node in the rest of the areas.

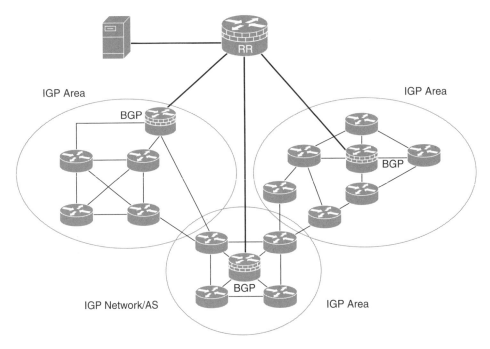

Figure 15-2 *Topology with BGP-LS Deployment*

BGP is configured on at least one node in each IGP area. The IGP running on that node provides the link-state of *all nodes* that it knows of (within its own area) to BGP. This way, there is at least one BGP speaker that learns the link-state of all nodes of a given area.

The BGP speakers are in the same AS. For providing the required connectivity between the BGP speakers, all the BGP speakers connect to a route reflector (RR) and each sends its own information to the RR. Therefore, the RR accumulates the link-state information from the entire network. The external element, such as PCE, then simply connects to the RR and extracts the required link-state information.

Before getting into the details of BGP-LS NLRI, it is necessary to understand the difference between IGP and BGP. IGP updates are sent using BGP and thus a conversion mechanism takes place to achieve the task. IGP provides a hop-by-hop connectivity between a relatively small number of nodes in the network, typically within an AS, including nodes that run BGP. It is designed to instantaneously react to underlying network topology changes to minimize data loss. The focus of an IGP is fast convergence during network changes and loop-free routing. BGP, on the other hand, provides connectivity between the ASs, thereby connecting the entire network. Therefore, BGP is optimized to transport massive routing state.

IGP and BGP use different routing algorithms. IGP (IS-IS and OSPF) uses link-state routing where each node constantly floods its one-hop connectivity information (the "link-state") to all nodes in an area as link-state advertisements (LSA) or LSPs. With link-state routing protocols, every node learns the one-hop connectivity information of every other node within the area and independently constructs the full network topology of the area by running the Dijkstra Algorithm. The LSAs are flooded after a network event to provide fast convergence, and each node may receive a very large number of LSAs in a short time.

In contrast, BGP is oblivious to physical links and receives from its immediate neighbors (although the neighbors could be multiple hops away) the prefixes each of them can "reach." BGP computes the best path (information from a neighbor) for each prefix, and then advertises that prefix as reachable. The BGP best-path algorithm scales linearly with the number of prefixes. Moreover, BGP uses various throttling mechanisms to improve scalability or decrease CPU usage.

> **Note**   In this chapter, the word IGP is used exclusively in context to link-state routing protocols (OSPF or IS-IS).

The IGP primarily contains two pieces of information: localized network topology and reachability information.

To convert this information or send the information over to BGP, RFC 7752 defines two new components for BGP: BGP-LS NLRI and BGP-LS Path Attributes.

To exchange the BGP-LS information among the BGP peers, a new address-family was introduced named **link-state**. This address-family is used to form the peering with BGP speakers in different IGP areas and also with the PCE/ALTO servers.

BGP-LS NLRI

There are four BGP-LS NLRIs defined in RFC 7752:

- Type 1: Node NLRI
- Type 2: Link NLRI
- Type 3: IPv4 Topology Prefix NLRI
- Type 4: IPv6 Topology Prefix NLRI

Thus, BGP-LS carries information for three primary objects: Nodes, Links and IP Prefix (which is used for IP reachability information). BGP uses AFI 16388 and SAFI 71 for all non-VPN link, node, and prefix information and uses AFI 16388 and SAFI 72 for VPN-based link, node, and prefix information.

The Node NLRI (Type 1) consists of Node Identifier and Node Descriptor fields. Typically, the OSPF Router ID or IS-IS System ID is carried in the Node Description field. Figure 15-3 displays the BGP-LS Node NLRI.

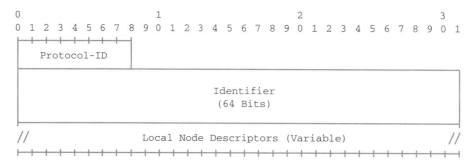

Figure 15-3 *Type - Node NLRI*

The Link NLRI (Type 2) is used to uniquely identify a link in the network. The link NLRI consists of the following:

- **Link Identifier**

- **Local Node Descriptor:** Used to identify the local end of the link

- **Remote Node Descriptor:** Used to identify the remote end of the link

- **Link Descriptor:** A set of Type/Length/Value (TLV) triplets used to uniquely identify a link among multiple parallel links.

Figure 15-4 displays the BGP-LS Link NLRI.

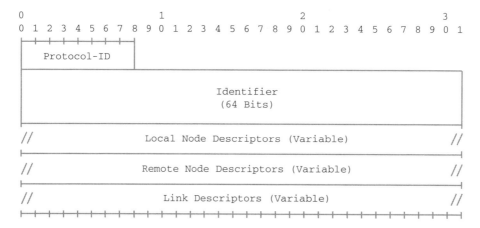

Figure 15-4 *Type 2—Link NLRI*

> **Note** Both the Local and Remote Node Descriptors contain three fields: Type, Length, and Node Descriptor Sub-TLVs. The Node Descriptor Sub-TLVs consists of various code points as follows:
>
> - Autonomous System: 4 bytes
> - BGP-LS Identifier: 4 bytes
> - OSPF Area-Id: 4 bytes
> - OSPF Router-Id: Variable length

IP Topology Prefix NLRI (Type 3) consists of three major fields: Identifier, Local Node Descriptor, and Prefix Descriptor. The Prefix Descriptor field is also a set of Type/Length/Value (TLV) triplets. The Prefix Descriptor TLVs uniquely identifies an IPv4 originated by a node. Figure 15-5 displays the BGP-LS Prefix NLRI.

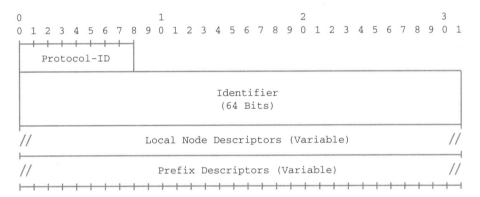

Figure 15-5 *Type 3 and Type 4—Prefix NLRI*

The IPv6 topology prefix NLRI (Type 4) consists of three major fields: Identifier, Local Node Descriptor, and Prefix Descriptor. The Prefix Descriptor field is also a set of Type/Length/Value (TLV) triplets. The Prefix Descriptor TLVs uniquely identifies the IPv6 prefix originated by a node. The format of the TLV is the same as IP Topology Prefix NLRI, as shown in Figure 15-5.

BGP-LS Path Attributes

The BGP-LS Path attribute is an optional, nontransitive BGP attribute used to carry necessary attributes to characterize the link, node, and prefix parameters and attributes. The BPG-LS Path attributes are categorized into two categories:

- **Node Attributes:** Encoded with a Node NLRI. The following Node Attribute TLVs are defined:

  - Multi-Topology Id

  - Node Flag Bits

  - Opaque Node Attribute

  - Node Name

  - IS-IS Area Id

  - IPv4 Router-Id (local node)

  - IPv6 Router-Id (local node)

- **Link Attributes:** Encoded with Link NLRI. The TLVs can carry information sourced from any of the extensions for the IGP (IS-IS or OSPF). The following Link Attributes are defined:

  - IPv4/IPv6 Router-Id (local as well as remote node)

  - IGP metric

  - Administrative group

  - Maximum link bandwidth

  - Maximum reservable bandwidth

  - Unreserved bandwidth

  - TE default metric

  - Link protection type

  - MPLS protocol mask

  - Shared risk link group

  - Opaque link attribute

  - Link name

BGP-LS Configuration

At the time of this writing, BGP-LS is supported only on the IOS XR platform starting with the 5.1.1 release. Configuring BGP-LS is a simple two-step process.

Step 1.   Enable IGP to distribute information to BGP-LS.

Step 2.   Configure BGP to form peering over link-state address-family with BGP speakers.

IGP Distribution

Configure IGP to distribute link-state information to BGP-LS by using the command **distribute bgp-ls** [**throttle** *time-in-seconds*] for OSPF or the command **distribute bgp-ls** [**level** *1-2*] [**throttle** *time-in-seconds*] for IS-IS. The throttle command is used to set the timer during successive LSA updates.

BGP Link-State Session Initiation

To configure BGP to exchange BGP-LS information with PCE/ALTO servers or other BGP speakers in other IGP domains (areas), the link-state address-family is enabled using the command **address-family link-state link-state**. After the address-family is enabled, the BGP peers can then be configured for the link-state address-family to exchange BGP-LS information.

Figure 15-6 is used to explain the BGP-LS functionality further. In this topology, there are four routers in an IS-IS Level-2 domain. R2 is peering with PCE, which is installed on Cisco's Open SDN Controller (OSC).

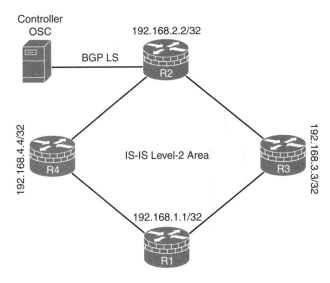

Figure 15-6   *Topology*

Example 15-1 illustrates the configuration of router R2 for IS-IS and BGP-LS. The IS-IS is enabled for distributing IGP information to BGP-LS. Under the BGP configuration, address-family link-state is enabled first and then the neighbor is configured for that address-family.

Example 15-1 *BGP-LS Configuration*

```
R2
router isis SDN
 is-type level-2-only
 net 49.0100.0000.0000.0002.00
 distribute bgp-ls level 2
 address-family ipv4 unicast
  !
 interface Loopback0
  address-family ipv4 unicast
   !
  !
 interface GigabitEthernet0/0/0/0
  point-to-point
  address-family ipv4 unicast
   !
  !
 interface GigabitEthernet0/0/0/1
  point-to-point
  address-family ipv4 unicast
   !
 !
router bgp 100
 bgp router-id 192.168.2.2
 address-family link-state link-state
  !
neighbor 172.16.1.150
  remote-as 100
  address-family link-state link-state
```

After the configuration is done, the BGP peering is not established unless the Cisco OSC is configured to peer with router R2. Example 15-2 illustrates the configuration to enable BGP and configuring BGP peering with R2 on OSC.

Example 15-2 *BGP Configuration on OSC*

```
! Configuration on OSC to define the local IP address and the Local AS Number
! to be used by BGP-LS

<module xmlns="urn:opendaylight:params:xml:ns:yang:controller:config">
  <type
  xmlns:x="urn:opendaylight:params:xml:ns:yang:controller:bgp:rib:impl">x:rib-impl
 </type>
  <name>example-bgp-rib</name>
  <bgp-rib-id
```

```
xmlns="urn:opendaylight:params:xml:ns:yang:controller:bgp:rib:impl">172.16.1.150
 </bgp-rib-id>
  <local-as
  xmlns="urn:opendaylight:params:xml:ns:yang:controller:bgp:rib:impl">100
  </local-as>
</module>
! The below config module is used to define the settings of a BGP peer.
<module xmlns="urn:opendaylight:params:xml:ns:yang:controller:config">
 <type xmlns:x="urn:opendaylight:params:xml:ns:yang:controller:bgp:rib:impl">
  x:bgp-peer</type>
 <name>example-bgp-peer</name>
 <host xmlns="urn:opendaylight:params:xml:ns:yang:controller:bgp:rib:impl">
 172.16.1.100
 </host>
 <holdtimer
 xmlns="urn:opendaylight:params:xml:ns:yang:controller:bgp:rib:impl">180
 </holdtimer>
 <rib xmlns="urn:opendaylight:params:xml:ns:yang:controller:bgp:rib:impl">
  <type xmlns:x="urn:opendaylight:params:xml:ns:yang:controller:bgp:rib:cfg">
  x:rib</type>
  <name>example-bgp-rib</name>
 </rib>
 <peer-registry
  xmlns="urn:opendaylight:params:xml:ns:yang:controller:bgp:rib:impl">
  <type xmlns:x="urn:opendaylight:params:xml:ns:yang:controller:bgp:rib:impl">
  x:bgp-peer-registry</type>
  <name>global-bgp-peer-registry</name>
 </peer-registry>
 <advertized-table
 xmlns="urn:opendaylight:params:xml:ns:yang:controller:bgp:rib:impl">
  <type
 xmlns:x="urn:opendaylight:params:xml:ns:yang:controller:bgp:rib:impl">
 x:bgp-table-type</type>
  <name>ipv4-unicast</name>
 </advertized-table>
 <advertized-table
 xmlns="urn:opendaylight:params:xml:ns:yang:controller:bgp:rib:impl">
  <type
 xmlns:x="urn:opendaylight:params:xml:ns:yang:controller:bgp:rib:impl">
  x:bgp-table-type</type>
  <name>linkstate</name>
 </advertized-table>
</module>
```

> **Note**   The modules in Example 15-2 can be configured on the OSC using a REST client like POSTMAN.

After the configuration has been done on the OSC, the BGP session is established between the OSC and R2. The BGP session is viewed using the command **show bgp link-state link-state summary**. Example 15-3 displays the output of the BGP-LS session between XR2 and OSC. Notice that there are 0 prefixes received. This is because the OSC is not advertising any link-state prefixes.

Example 15-3   *Verifying BGP-LS Session*

```
RP/0/0/CPU0:R2# show bgp link-state link-state summary
BGP router identifier 192.168.2.2, local AS number 100
BGP generic scan interval 60 secs
Non-stop routing is enabled
BGP table state: Active
Table ID: 0x0   RD version: 244
BGP main routing table version 244
BGP NSR Initial initsync version 66 (Reached)
BGP NSR/ISSU Sync-Group versions 0/0
BGP scan interval 60 secs


BGP is operating in STANDALONE mode.


Process        RcvTblVer    bRIB/RIB   LabelVer   ImportVer   SendTblVer   StandbyVer
Speaker              244         244        244         244          244            0


Neighbor       Spk     AS MsgRcvd MsgSent    TblVer  InQ OutQ  Up/Down   St/PfxRcd
172.16.1.150     0    100     992    1006       244    0    0 16:30:15           0
```

Although R2 has not received prefixes from the OSC server, the BGP-LS table is populated locally on R2 from the information learned from IGP. To view the local IGP information in the BGP-LS table, use the command **show bgp link-state link-state**. This command displays three sets of IGP information in the form of routes: node attribute routes, link attribute routes, and prefixes attribute routes. Example 15-4 displays the BGP-LS prefixes on R2. The output [V] denotes the Node Descriptor, [E] denotes the Link Descriptor, and [T] denotes the Prefix Descriptor.

Example 15-4 *BGP-LS Table*

```
RP/0/0/CPU0:R2# show bgp link-state link-state
Status codes: s suppressed, d damped, h history, * valid, > best
              i - internal, r RIB-failure, S stale, N Nexthop-discard
Origin codes: i - IGP, e - EGP, ? - incomplete
Prefix codes: E link, V node, T IP reacheable route, u/U unknown
              I Identifier, N local node, R remote node, L link, P prefix
              L1/L2 ISIS level-1/level-2, O OSPF, D direct, S static
              a area-ID, l link-ID, t topology-ID, s ISO-ID,
              c confed-ID/ASN, b bgp-identifier, r router-ID,
              i if-address, n nbr-address, o OSPF Route-type, p IP-prefix
              d designated router address
   Network            Next Hop            Metric LocPrf Weight Path
*> [V] [L2] [I0x0] [N[c100] [b192.168.2.2] [s0000.0000.0001.00]]/328
                     0.0.0.0                               0 i
*> [V] [L2] [I0x0] [N[c100] [b192.168.2.2] [s0000.0000.0002.00]]/328
                     0.0.0.0                               0 i
*> [V] [L2] [I0x0] [N[c100] [b192.168.2.2] [s0000.0000.0003.00]]/328
                     0.0.0.0                               0 i
*> [V] [L2] [I0x0] [N[c100] [b192.168.2.2] [s0000.0000.0004.00]]/328
                     0.0.0.0                               0 i
*> [E] [L2] [I0x0] [N[c100] [b192.168.2.2] [s0000.0000.0001.00]] [R[c100] [b192.168.2.2]
[s0000.0000.0003.00]] [L[i10.1.13.1] [n10.1.13.3]]/696
                     0.0.0.0                               0 i
*> [E] [L2] [I0x0] [N[c100] [b192.168.2.2] [s0000.0000.0001.00]] [R[c100] [b192.168.2.2]
[s0000.0000.0004.00]] [L[i10.1.14.1] [n10.1.14.4]]/696
                     0.0.0.0                               0 i
*> [E] [L2] [I0x0] [N[c100] [b192.168.2.2] [s0000.0000.0002.00]] [R[c100] [b192.168.2.2]
[s0000.0000.0003.00]] [L[i10.1.23.2] [n10.1.23.3]]/696
                     0.0.0.0                               0 i
*> [E] [L2] [I0x0] [N[c100] [b192.168.2.2] [s0000.0000.0002.00]] [R[c100] [b192.168.2.2]
[s0000.0000.0004.00]] [L[i10.1.24.2] [n10.1.24.4]]/696
                     0.0.0.0                               0 i
! Output omitted for brevity

*> [T] [L2] [I0x0] [N[c100] [b192.168.2.2] [s0000.0000.0003.00]] [P[p10.1.23.0/24]]/392
                     0.0.0.0                               0 i
*> [T] [L2] [I0x0] [N[c100] [b192.168.2.2] [s0000.0000.0004.00]] [P[p10.1.14.0/24]]/392
                     0.0.0.0                               0 i
*> [T] [L2] [I0x0] [N[c100] [b192.168.2.2] [s0000.0000.0004.00]] [P[p10.1.24.0/24]]/392
                     0.0.0.0                               0 i
```

Along with PCE-P, OSC server also has a BGP-LS Manager feature installed. OSC uses the preceding BGP-LS table to build a link-state topology in the BGPLS Manager. Figure 15-7 displays the BGP-LS Manager view of the IGP topology. Notice that the exact topology is displayed in the OSC's BGPLS Manager, which was being used for this example. If any of the four nodes are clicked, the OSC can display more information about the node and the links on the nodes.

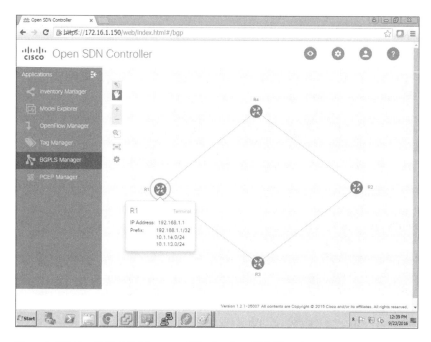

Figure 15-7 *BGP-LS Manager Displaying IGP Topology*

After examining Example 15-4, it is easy to determine which prefixes are node attributes, link attributes, and prefix attributes based on the prefix codes denoted at the beginning of each route. What cannot be figured from the preceding output is what the other field means. The other piece of information is actually the link-state information from each node, link, and prefix in the IGP domain.

Examine the output in Example 15-5 for the Node Descriptor route. The output shows that the Node-name is R1, the IS-IS area is 49.0100, and the local TE Router-ID is 192.168.1.1.

Example 15-5 *Node Descriptor Prefix*

```
RP/0/0/CPU0:R2# show bgp link-state link-state
[V] [L2] [I0x0] [N[c100] [b192.168.2.2] [s0000.0000.0001.00]]/328
BGP routing table entry for
[V] [L2] [I0x0] [N[c100] [b192.168.2.2] [s0000.0000.0001.00]]/328
Versions:
  Process              bRIB/RIB  SendTblVer
  Speaker                  159         159
Last Modified: Apr 14 17:58:40.068 for 1d18h
Paths: (1 available, best #1)
  Advertised to update-groups (with more than one peer):
    0.2
  Path #1: Received by speaker 0
  Advertised to update-groups (with more than one peer):
    0.2
  Local
    0.0.0.0 from 0.0.0.0 (192.168.2.2)
      Origin IGP, localpref 100, valid, redistributed, best, group-best
      Received Path ID 0, Local Path ID 1, version 159
      Link-state: Node-name: XR1, ISIS area: 49.01.00, Local TE Router-ID:
                  192.168.1.1
```

The prefix also contains a lot of information that is very useful. Following is the break-down of the Node Descriptor prefix.

- **[V]**: Node Descriptor route

- **[L2]**: IS-IS Level-2 node

- **[s0000.0000.0001.00]**: ISO System ID is 0000.0000.0001.00

Now, let's examine the Link Descriptor prefix. Example 15-6 displays the details of the Link Descriptor prefix. The Link Descriptor prefix gives more details about the link and TE attributes, such as local TE router-id, max. link bandwidth, max. reserved link bandwidth, max. unreserved link bandwidth, and TE default metric.

Example 15-6 *Link Descriptor Prefix*

```
RP/0/0/CPU0:R2# show bgp link-state link-state
[E] [L2] [I0x0] [N[c100] [b192.168.2.2] [s0000.0000.0001.00]] [R[c100] [b192.168.2.2]
 [s0000.0000.0004.00]] [L[i10.1.14.4] [n10.1.14.1]]/696
BGP routing table entry for [E] [L2] [I0x0] [N[c100] [b192.168.2.2] [s0000.0000.0001.00]]
  [R[c100] [b192.168.2.2]
 [s0000.0000.0004.00]] [L[i10.1.14.4] [n10.1.14.1]]/696
```

```
Versions:
  Process            bRIB/RIB  SendTblVer
  Speaker                 382         382
Last Modified: Apr 16 15:09:26.068 for 00:07:17
Paths: (1 available, best #1)
  Advertised to peers (in unique update groups):
    172.16.1.150
  Path #1: Received by speaker 0
  Advertised to peers (in unique update groups):
    172.16.1.100
  Local
    0.0.0.0 from 0.0.0.0 (192.168.2.2)
      Origin IGP, localpref 100, valid, redistributed, best, group-best
      Received Path ID 0, Local Path ID 1, version 382
      Link-state: Local TE Router-ID: 192.168.1.1, Remote TE Router-ID:
          192.168.4.4 admin-group: 0x00000000, max-link-bw (kbits/sec): 1000000
          max-reserv-link-bw (kbits/sec): 0, max-unreserv-link-bw (kbits/sec):
          0 0 0 0 0 0 0 0 TE-default-metric: 10, metric: 10
```

The Link Descriptor prefix also contains other information, such as the following:

- **[E]:** Link Descriptor route

- **[s0000.0000.0001.00]][R[c100][b192.168.2.2][s0000.0000.0004.00]]:** Describes half-link between ISO node 0000.0000.0001, which is the local node, and 0000.0000.0004.00, which is the remote node.

- **[L[i10.1.14.1][n10.1.14.4]]:** Describes that the local link address is 10.1.14.1 and the remote end IP is 10.1.14.4.

The command **show bgp link-state link-state** *bgp-ls-prefix* can be run for other Link Descriptor prefixes in the table to fetch the information on other side of the link.

For understanding the Prefix Descriptor route, examine the output of Example 15-7. The output primarily displays the metric of the IGP prefix, in this case 10.

Example 15-7 *Prefix Descriptor Route in BGP-LS Table*

```
RP/0/0/CPU0:R2# show bgp link-state link-state
[T] [L2] [I0x0] [N[c100] [b192.168.2.2] [s0000.0000.0003.00]] [P[p10.1.23.0/24]]/392
BGP routing table entry for
[T] [L2] [I0x0] [N[c100] [b192.168.2.2] [s0000.0000.0003.00]] [P[p10.1.23.0/24]]/392
Versions:
  Process            bRIB/RIB  SendTblVer    .
  Speaker                 393         393
```

```
Last Modified: Apr 16 15:09:26.068 for 1d06h
Paths: (1 available, best #1)
  Advertised to peers (in unique update groups):
    172.16.1.150
  Path #1: Received by speaker 0
  Advertised to peers (in unique update groups):
    172.16.1.100
  Local
    0.0.0.0 from 0.0.0.0 (192.168.2.2)
      Origin IGP, localpref 100, valid, redistributed, best, group-best
      Received Path ID 0, Local Path ID 1, version 393
      Link-state: Metric: 10
```

But otherwise, the Prefix Descriptor prefix in itself, contains more information as listed.

■ **[T]:** Prefix Descriptor route

■ **[s0000.0000.0003.00]][P[p10.1.23.0/24]]:** Tells that the prefix 10.1.23.0/24 is being advertised by a node with ISO ID 0000.0000.0003.00 with IGP metric 10.

By evaluating all the prefixes in the BGP-LS table, a complete IGP topology can be built. Based on the IGP topology and the TE related information, PCE-P can be used to build LSPs on the fly from the OSC server web portal.

BGP for Tunnel Setup

The networking industry is getting transformed very rapidly with the newer technologies and features being innovated every day. The current focus is directed at cloud technologies; most of the newer features being innovated are dependent on tunneling of packets. Tunneling allows for packets to transit an underlay network by adding network headers strictly for the purpose of forwarding packets on the underlay network. In essence, the encapsulated packets are transported on an overlay network.

Packet encapsulation occurs by one transport edge device and is decapsulated at the remote transport edge device. This is similar to the existing tunneling mechanism such as GRE.

RFC 5512 defines a mechanism for using BGP to signal tunnel encapsulation information between the BGP speakers. Using BGP provides an opportunity for development and innovation of various new overlay mechanisms for existing, as well as future technologies. BGP tunnels can be used as alternatives for MPLS service based on BGP, such as MPLS L2VPN, and so on, because BGP is scalable and proven for control plane signaling. The BGP tunneling mechanism helps in cost optimization by getting rid of the following:

■ Core MPLS control plane

■ Internet and customer prefixes from ISP core

Under the BGP tunneling mechanism, the BGP database carries tunnel endpoints and identifiers. This helps BGP-based dynamic tunneling mechanism work on both Intra-domain as well as Inter-domain. The BGP tunnels could provide convergence below 100 ms.

The tunnel encapsulation is carried out with an address-family identifier (AFI) value of 1 or 2 based on IPv4 or IPv6 and SAFI value of 7, which is also known as the encapsulation subaddress family identifier (SAFI). The BGP NLRI consists of the IP address of the originator of the update. The encapsulation information is carried out in a new attribute called the BGP tunnel encapsulation attribute. The BGP tunnel encapsulation attribute contains the encapsulation protocol as well as any additional information that is required by the specified encapsulation protocol. Figure 15-8 displays the format of the BGP tunnel encapsulation attribute. The Tunnel Type field specifies the type of tunnel encapsulation to be carried over in the BGP NLRI. The value field actually comprises multiple sub-TLVs. Each sub-TLV consists of three fields: 1-octet type, 1-octet length, and zero or more octets of value.

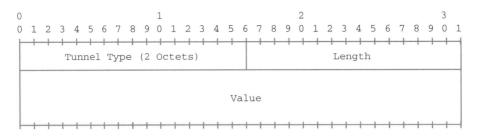

Figure 15-8 *BGP Tunnel Encapsulation Attribute*

Table 15-1 lists the protocols that have been defined under various RFCs that can be specified under the BGP tunnel encapsulation attribute.

Table 15-1 *BGP Tunnel Encapsulation Attribute Tunnel Types*

Value	Name	RFC/Draft
0	Reserved	RFC 5512
1	L2TPv3 over IP	RFC 5512
2	GRE	RFC 5512
3	Transmit tunnel endpoint	RFC 5566
4	IPsec in Tunnel-mode	RFC 5566
5	IP in IP tunnel with IPsec transport mode	RFC 5566
6	MPLS-in-IP tunnel with IPsec transport mode	RFC 5566
7	IP in IP	RFC 5512

Value	Name	RFC/Draft
8	VXLAN Encapsulation	draft-ietf-bess-evpn-overlay
9	NVGRE Encapsulation	draft-ietf-bess-evpn-overlay
10	MPLS Encapsulation	draft-ietf-bess-evpn-overlay
11	MPLS in Generic Routing Encapsulation (GRE) Encapsulation	draft-ietf-bess-evpn-overlay
12	VxLAN GPE Encapsulation	draft-ietf-bess-evpn-overlay
13	MPLS in UDP Encapsulation	RFC 7510
14	IPv6 Tunnel	
15-65535	Unassigned	

Table 15-2 lists the BGP tunnel encapsulation attribute sub-TLVs.

Table 15-2 *BGP Tunnel Encapsulation Attribute Sub-TLVs*

Value	Name	RFC/Draft
0	Reserved	RFC 5512
1	Encapsulation	RFC 5512
2	Protocol Type	RFC 5512
3	IPsec Tunnel Authenticator	RFC 5566
4	Color	RFC 5512
5	Load-Balancing Block	RFC 5640
6-255	Unassigned	

Provider Backbone Bridging: Ethernet VPN (PBB-EVPN)

Virtual Private Wire Service (VPWS) is used to build a topology of point-to-point connections that connect end customer sites over an IP/Multiprotocol Label Switching (MPLS) network. VPWS enables the sharing of a provider's core network infrastructure between IP and Layer 2 VPN services, reducing the cost of providing those services. Virtual Private LAN Service (VPLS) as defined in RFC 4664, 4761, and 4762, is a proven and widely deployed technology by service providers. However, the existing solution has a number of challenges when it comes to redundancy and multicast optimization.

A limitation of current implementations is that VPLS can only support multihoming with active/standby resiliency model, for example, as described in *draft-ietf-bess-vpls-multihoming*. Flexible multihoming with all-active attachment circuits (ACs) cannot be supported without adding considerable complexity to the data plane.

In the area of multicast optimization, *draft-ietf-l2vpn-vpls-mcast*, describes how Label Switched Multicast (LSM) Distribution Trees (MDTs) can be used in conjunction with VPLS. However, this solution is limited to point-to-multipoint (P2MP) MDTs, because there's no easy way for leveraging multipoint-to-multipoint (MP2MP) MDTs with VPLS. The lack of MP2MP support may create scalability issues for multicast-intensive applications.

The current solution for VPLS, as defined in RFC 4664, relies on establishing a full mesh of pseudowires (PWs) among participating provider edges (PE), and data-plane learning for the purpose of building the media access control (MAC) forwarding tables. This learning is performed on traffic received over both the attachment circuits as well as the PWs. Supporting an all-active multihoming solution with current VPLS is subject to three fundamental problems:

- Formation of forwarding loops

- Duplicate delivery of flooded frames

- MAC Forwarding Table instability

Customers are looking for an L2VPN solution that can deliver the following:

- PE node redundancy with load-balancing based on L2/L3/L4 flows from customer edge (CE) to PE.

- Flow-based multipathing of traffic from PE to core, and vice versa.

- Geo-redundant PE nodes with optimum unicast forwarding.

- Flexible Redundancy grouping (PE1 and PE2 can be used for dual-homing one set of CEs, and PE2 and PE3 can be used for dual-homing different set of CEs, thus PE2 supporting multiple redundancy groups).

Ethernet VPN (EVPN) is a next-generation solution for Ethernet services. It relies on BGP control plane for segment/MAC learning reachability among PEs. It uses simple principles such as that of L3VPNs. The EVPN solution provides services for both point-to-point as well as point-to-multiple L2VPN deployments. Figure 15-9 depicts the EVPN solution architecture. EVPN-VPWS provides E-LINE (point-to-point) services, whereas EVPN and Provider Backbone Bridging EVPN (PBB-EVPN) provide E-LAN services.

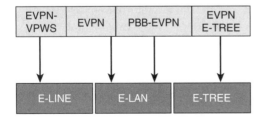

Figure 15-9 *EVPN Solution Architecture*

EVPN, in simple terms, can be described as treating customer MACs as routable addresses and distributing them in BGP over MPLS core, thereby avoiding any data-plane MAC learning over MPLS core. The MAC addresses are distributed over MPLS core using BGP with a label identifying the service instance. Receiving PE devices inject these routable MAC addresses into their L2 routing information base (RIBs) and forwarding information base (FIBs) along with their associated adjacencies.

Distributing of MAC address over BGP results in following benefits:

■ Ability to associate a MAC address with Equal Cost Paths to multiple PE devices, even though the IGP paths to these PE devices are not Equal Cost

■ Ability to use BGP policy routing to prefer one path over another for a given MAC in case of Active/Standby multihoming scenarios

■ Ability to use BGP policy routing to have the same preference among multiple paths for a given MAC in case of Active/Active multihoming scenarios

■ Ability to do optimum forwarding of L2 unicast packets for both single-homed and multihomed devices of a given customer simultaneously

■ Ability to represent a single customer by a single MPLS label in contrast to using a set of N labels (N PWs)

Note This section primarily focuses on the PBB-EVPN solution.

In the case of PBB-EVPN, the PE devices receive 802.1Q frames from the attachment circuit (AC), encapsulation them into PBB header and forward the frames over IP/MPLS core. On the egress PE, the PBB header is removed following the MPLS disposition, and the original 802.1Q frame is delivered to the customer device.

The PE nodes perform the following functions:

■ Learn customer MAC (C-MAC) addresses over the attachment circuits in the data plane, per normal bridge operation.

■ Learn remote C-MAC to backbone MAC (B-MAC) bindings in the data plane from traffic ingress from the core.

■ Advertise local B-MAC address reachability information in BGP to all other PE nodes in the same set of service instances. Note that every PE has a set of local B-MAC addresses that uniquely identify the device.

■ Build a forwarding table from remote BGP advertisements received associating remote B-MAC addresses with remote PE IP addresses.

EVPN NLRI and Routes

EVPN defines a new BGP NLRI, which is used to advertise different types of routes. EVPN also defines the new route attributes. The EVPN BGP NLRI is carried in BGP with an AFI value of 25 and a SAFI value of 70. Before two devices can exchange EVPN NLRIs, they must signal their capability to do so by using BGP capabilities advertisement.

The PBB-EVPN NLRI consists of three fields:

- Route Type (1 byte)

- Length (1 byte)

- Route Type Specific (variable length)

The value of the Route Type field can be one of the following:

- **0x01:** Ethernet Auto-Discovery Route

- **0x02:** MAC Advertisement Route

- **0x03:** Inclusive Multicast Route

- **0x04:** Ethernet Segment Route

- **0x05:** Selective Multicast Auto-Discovery Route

- **0x06:** Leaf Auto-Discovery Route

The various Route Types fields and their usage are described next:

- **Ethernet Auto-Discovery Route:** Used for MAC mass-withdraw, aliasing, split-horizon filtering.

- **MAC Advertisement Route:** Used for advertising MAC address reachability and IP/MAC bindings.

- **Inclusive Multicast Route:** Used for multicast tunnel endpoint discovery.

- **Ethernet Segment Route:** Used for redundancy group discovery and Designated Forwarder (DF) election.

Along with the BGP NLRI, EVPN also involves E-VPN Route Distinguisher (RD). Two different BGP RDs are required for an EVPN solution: VPN RD and Segment RD.

Note   Presently, Route Type 0x05 and 0x06 are not supported on Cisco platforms. BGP drops unsupported Route Types and does not propagate it to neighbors.

Two different BGP RDs are required for EVPN: VPN RD and Segment RD.

- **VPN RD:** VPN RD is the RD assigned to each EVPN instance on a PE. The RD is unique across all EVPN instances supported on the PE. This is achieved using Type 1 RD defined in RFC 4364. The value field is composed of the IP address of the PE followed by a unique number. The number may be generated by the PE or in the default single VLAN EVPN case, may be the 12-bit VLAN Id, with the remaining 4 bits set to 0.

- **Segment RD:** The segment RD uniquely identifies the PE and does not change on a per EVPN instance basis. The value is achieved by again using Type 1 RD in which the value field is composed of an IP address of the PE with the remaining bits all set to 0.

The EVPN instance route target (RT) can either be configured manually or derived automatically.

EVPN Extended Community

There are four different extended communities for the EVPN routes:

- Ethernet Segment Identifier (ESI) MPLS Label Extended Community
- Ethernet Segment (ES)-Import Extended Community
- MAC Mobility Extended Community
- Default Gateway Extended Community

ESI MPLS Label Extended Community is a new transitive extended community which is advertised along with Ethernet autodiscovery route. This extended community carries properties associated with Ethernet Segment Identifier (ESI). The purpose of this extended community is to encode split-horizon label for Ethernet segment and indicate redundancy mode (Single-Active vs. All-Active).

ES-Import Extended Community is a new transitive extended community that includes all PEs in a redundancy group. This extended community is advertised along with Ethernet Segment route. It is used to limit the scope of Ethernet segment routes.

MAC Mobility Extended Community is a new transitive extended community that is advertised with MAC advertisement routes. It indicates that a MAC address has moved from one segment to another across PEs. In other words, the MAC address that was previously advertised by another PE has moved and is now reachable via the advertising PE.

Default Gateway Extended Community is a new transitive extended community advertised with MAC advertisement routes, used to indicate the MAC/IP bindings of a gateway.

EVPN Configuration and Verification

The Cisco EVPN and PBB-EVPN solution is presently supported on the ASR9000 platform and on the ASR1000 series router running IOS XE as a route reflector for L2VPN EVPN address-family.

Examine the topology in Figure 15-10. There are two PE routers, PE1 and PE2, connected via router RR-P. The PE routers are running IGP (OSPF/IS-IS) and MPLS within the core.

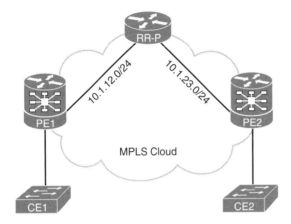

Figure 15-10   *PBB-EVPN Topology*

Example 15-8 illustrates the basic minimal configuration to provision a PBB-EVPN circuit between two PE routers. Notice that there are two bridge-domains created: one bridge-domain for the core and one bridge-domain for the edge. The edge bridge-domain named PBB-EDGE-1001 is the one associated with the attachment circuit. The command **pbb edge i-sid** *service-id* **core-bridge** *core-bridge-name* configures the bridge domain as PBB edge with the service identifier and the assigned core bridge domain. This completes the basic configuration for EVPN.

Next, establish BGP peering with the remote PE device or with the route reflector over **address-family l2vpn evpn**, which is used for exchanging EVPN routes via BGP. The **address-family l2vpn evpn** is used both for autodiscovery and the signaling mechanism for EVPN.

Example 15-8   *L2VPN EVPN Configuration on IOS XR*

```
! EVPN Configuration on PE1
interface Loopback0
 ipv4 address 192.168.1.1 255.255.255.255
!
interface GigabitEthernet0/0/0/0
!
```

```
interface GigabitEthernet0/0/0/0.2 l2transport
 encapsulation dot1q 2
!
interface GigabitEthernet0/0/0/1
 ipv4 address 10.1.14.1 255.255.255.0
!
l2vpn
 router-id 192.168.1.1
 bridge group 1
  bridge-domain PBB-CORE-1001
   pbb core
    evpn evi 1001
    !
   !
  bridge-domain PBB-EDGE-1001
   interface GigabitEthernet0/0/0/0.2
    !
   pbb edge i-sid 1001 core-bridge PBB-CORE-1001
!
mpls ldp
 router-id 192.168.1.1
 address-family ipv4
  neighbor 192.168.2.2 targeted
  !
 interface GigabitEthernet0/0/0/1
!
router bgp 100
 bgp router-id 192.168.1.1
 address-family ipv4 unicast
  network 101.101.101.101/32
  !
 address-family l2vpn evpn
 !
 neighbor 192.168.2.2
  remote-as 100
  update-source Loopback0
  address-family l2vpn evpn
```

Similar configuration is performed on the PE2 router with AC connected toward the CE2. After the configuration is done, the BGP L2VPN EVPN session is established and the EVPN routers are exchanged. Because there are four types of routes in EVPN, each route is represented in a different format. The four formats are as follows:

- **Ethernet Auto-Discovery Route:** [Type][ESI][ETag]

- **MAC Advertisement Route:** [Type][ESI][ETag][MAC Addr Len][MAC Addr] [IP Addr Len][IP Addr]

- **Inclusive Multicast Route:** [Type][ETag][Router IP Addr Len][Router IP Addr]

- **Ethernet Segment Route:** [Type][ESI]

Use the command **show bgp l2vpn evpn summary** to view the L2VPN EVPN peerings on the router. Use the command **show bgp l2vpn evpn** to view the locally originated as well as remotely learned EVPN routes. Example 15-9 displays the established BGP session for L2VPN EVPN address-family and also displays the local as well as EVPN routes exchanged from the remote PE router. Notice that the RD for all the prefixes has been automatically assigned in *ip-address:ESI* format. In the output, the local RD is 192.168.1.1:1001, whereas the RD learned from the remote PE router is 192.168.2.2:1001.

Example 15-9   *BGP L2VPN EVPN Table*

```
IOS XR
! L2VPN EVPN BGP Session Output
RP/0/RSP0/CPU0:PE1# show bgp l2vpn evpn summary

Process        RcvTblVer   bRIB/RIB   LabelVer   ImportVer   SendTblVer   StandbyVer
Speaker               45         45         45          45           45            0

Neighbor       Spk    AS MsgRcvd MsgSent    TblVer   InQ OutQ  Up/Down   St/PfxRcd
192.168.2.2      0   100   35373    1001        45     0    0 15:29:31           2
! PBB-EVPN Prefixes
RP/0/RSP0/CPU0:PE1# show bgp l2vpn evpn

Status codes: s suppressed, d damped, h history, * valid, > best
              i - internal, r RIB-failure, S stale, N Nexthop-discard
Origin codes: i - IGP, e - EGP, ? - incomplete
  Network           Next Hop         Metric LocPrf Weight Path
Route Distinguisher: 192.168.1.1:1001 (default for vrf PBB-CORE-1001)
*>i[2][0][48][5087.891c.30a7][0]/104
                   192.168.2.2                    100      0 i
*> [2][0][48][5087.8968.266f][0]/104
                   0.0.0.0                                 0 i
```

```
*> [3][1001][32][192.168.1.1]/80
                        0.0.0.0                                      0 i
*>i[3][1001][32][192.168.2.2]/80
                        192.168.2.2                      100         0 i
Route Distinguisher: 192.168.2.2:1001
*>i[2][0][48][5087.891c.30a7][0]/104
                        192.168.2.2                      100       0 i
*>i[3][1001][32][192.168.2.2]/80
                        192.168.2.2                      100       0 i

Processed 6 prefixes, 6 paths
```

For the forwarding to work properly, ensure that both the core as well as the edge bridge domains are up, and the PBB is showing in up status. This is verified by using the command **show l2vpn bridge-domain [detail]**. The **show l2vpn bridge-domain** displays both the core as well as the edge bridge domain status, the status of PBBs, and the AC attached to the bridge domain (edge) along with its status. This command also lists the ACs that are part of the edge bridge domain.

The command **show l2vpn bridge-domain detail** displays more detailed information related to both the core and the edge bridge domain, such as the packet counters for both imposition and disposition, PBB lists, and more detailed information of the ACs. The detail command output is useful when performing troubleshooting related to traffic forwarding issues. The output can be used to match the counters of the packets with that of the controller counters for the AC. Example 15-10 displays the output of the command **show l2vpn bridge-domain [detail]**.

Example 15-10   show l2vpn bridge-domain *Command Output*

```
IOS XR
RP/0/RSP0/CPU0:PE1# show l2vpn bridge-domain
Legend: pp = Partially Programmed.
Bridge group: 1, bridge-domain: PBB-CORE-1001, id: 0, state: up, ShgId: 0, MSTi: 0
  Type: pbb-core
  Number of associated pbb-edge BDs: 1
  Aging: 300 s, MAC limit: 4000, Action: none, Notification: syslog
  Filter MAC addresses: 0
  ACs: 0 (0 up), VFIs: 0, PWs: 0 (0 up), PBBs: 1 (1 up)
  List of PBBs:
    PBB Core, state: up
  List of ACs:
  List of Access PWs:
  List of VFIs:
```

```
Bridge group: 1, bridge-domain: PBB-EDGE-1001, id: 1, state: up, ShgId: 0, MSTi: 0
  Type: pbb-edge, I-SID: 1001
  Aging: 300 s, MAC limit: 4000, Action: none, Notification: syslog
  Filter MAC addresses: 0
  ACs: 1 (1 up), VFIs: 0, PWs: 0 (0 up), PBBs: 1 (1 up)
  List of PBBs:
    PBB Edge, state: up, Static MAC addresses: 0
  List of ACs:
    Gi0/0/0/0.2, state: up, Static MAC addresses: 0
  List of Access PWs:
  List of VFIs:
! Detailed Output
RP/0/RSP0/CPU0:PE1# show l2vpn bridge-domain detail
Legend: pp = Partially Programmed.
Bridge group: 1, bridge-domain: PBB-CORE-1001, id: 0, state: up, ShgId: 0, MSTi: 0
  Coupled state: disabled
  Type: pbb-core
  Number of associated pbb-edge BDs: 1
  EVPN:
    EVI: 1001
    Route Distinguisher: (auto) 192.168.1.1:1001
    Imposition Statistics:
      Packet Count: 40320109
      Byte Count  : 5467529444
    Disposition Statistics:
      Packet Count: 40000053
      Byte Count  : 5440004624
    AS Number: 100
  MAC learning: enabled
  MAC withdraw: enabled
    MAC withdraw for Access PW: enabled
    MAC withdraw sent on: bridge port up
    MAC withdraw relaying (access to access): disabled
  Flooding:
    Broadcast & Multicast: enabled
    Unknown unicast: enabled
  MAC aging time: 300 s, Type: inactivity
  MAC limit: 4000, Action: none, Notification: syslog
  MAC limit reached: no
  MAC port down flush: enabled
  MAC Secure: disabled, Logging: disabled
  Split Horizon Group: none
  Dynamic ARP Inspection: disabled, Logging: disabled
  IP Source Guard: disabled, Logging: disabled
```

```
DHCPv4 snooping: disabled
IGMP Snooping: enabled
IGMP Snooping profile: none
MLD Snooping profile: none
Storm Control: disabled
Bridge MTU: 1500
MIB cvplsConfigIndex: 1
Filter MAC addresses:
P2MP PW: disabled
Create time: 22/04/2016 17:10:13 (1w0d ago)
No status change since creation
ACs: 0 (0 up), VFIs: 0, PWs: 0 (0 up), PBBs: 1 (1 up)
List of PBBs:
  PBB Core, state is up
    XC ID 0x80000001
    MAC learning: enabled
    Flooding:
      Broadcast & Multicast: enabled
      Unknown unicast: enabled
    MAC aging time: 300 s, Type: inactivity
    MAC limit: 4000, Action: none, Notification: syslog
    MAC limit reached: no
    MAC port down flush: enabled
    Split Horizon Group: none
    DHCPv4 snooping: disabled
    IGMP Snooping: enabled
    IGMP Snooping profile: none
    MLD Snooping profile: none
    MMRP Flood Optimization: disabled
    Storm Control: bridge-domain policer
  List of ACs:
  List of Access PWs:
  List of VFIs:
Bridge group: 1, bridge-domain: PBB-EDGE-1001, id: 1, state: up, ShgId: 0, MSTi: 0
  Coupled state: disabled
  Type: pbb-edge, I-SID: 1001
  Core-bridge: PBB-CORE-1001 (State: Bridge Up)
  MIRP-lite: supported, enabled
    Format: MVRP PDU with Vlan 0
  MAC learning: enabled
  MAC withdraw: enabled
    MAC withdraw for Access PW: enabled
    MAC withdraw sent on: bridge port up
    MAC withdraw relaying (access to access): disabled
```

```
Flooding:
  Broadcast & Multicast: enabled
  Unknown unicast: enabled
MAC aging time: 300 s, Type: inactivity
MAC limit: 4000, Action: none, Notification: syslog
MAC limit reached: no
MAC port down flush: enabled
MAC Secure: disabled, Logging: disabled
Split Horizon Group: none
Dynamic ARP Inspection: disabled, Logging: disabled
IP Source Guard: disabled, Logging: disabled
DHCPv4 snooping: disabled
IGMP Snooping: enabled
IGMP Snooping profile: none
MLD Snooping profile: none
Storm Control: disabled
Bridge MTU: 1500
MIB cvplsConfigIndex: 2
Filter MAC addresses:
P2MP PW: disabled
Create time: 22/04/2016 17:10:13 (1w0d ago)
No status change since creation
ACs: 1 (1 up), VFIs: 0, PWs: 0 (0 up), PBBs: 1 (1 up)
List of PBBs:
  PBB Edge, state is up
    XC ID 0x80000002
    MAC learning: enabled
    Flooding:
      Broadcast & Multicast: enabled
      Unknown unicast: enabled
    MAC aging time: 300 s, Type: inactivity
    MAC limit: 4000, Action: none, Notification: syslog
    MAC limit reached: no
    MAC port down flush: enabled
    MAC Secure: disabled, Logging: disabled, Accept-Shutdown: disabled
    Split Horizon Group: none
    DHCPv4 snooping: disabled
    IGMP Snooping: enabled
    IGMP Snooping profile: none
    MLD Snooping profile: none
    Storm Control: bridge-domain policer
  Statistics:
    packets: received 40000053 (unicast 40000047), sent 40320130
    bytes: received 4720003670 (unicast 4720003170), sent 4741768910
    MAC move: 0
```

```
    List of ACs:
      AC: GigabitEthernet0/0/0/0.2, state is up
        Type VLAN; Num Ranges: 1
        VLAN ranges: [2, 2]
        MTU 1504; XC ID 0x1080001; interworking none
        MAC learning: enabled
        Flooding:
          Broadcast & Multicast: enabled
          Unknown unicast: enabled
        MAC aging time: 300 s, Type: inactivity
        MAC limit: 4000, Action: none, Notification: syslog
        MAC limit reached: no
        MAC port down flush: enabled
        MAC Secure: disabled, Logging: disabled
        Split Horizon Group: none
        Dynamic ARP Inspection: disabled, Logging: disabled
        IP Source Guard: disabled, Logging: disabled
        DHCPv4 snooping: disabled
        IGMP Snooping: enabled
        IGMP Snooping profile: none
        MLD Snooping profile: none
        Storm Control: bridge-domain policer
        Static MAC addresses:
        Statistics:
          packets: received 40345017 (multicast 344833, broadcast 36,
              unknown unicast 36, unicast 40000117), sent 40000156
          bytes: received 4743466070 (multicast 23448644, broadcast 2304,
              unknown unicast 2304, unicast 4720013158), sent 4720015662
          MAC move: 0
        Storm control drop counters:
          packets: broadcast 0, multicast 0, unknown unicast 0
          bytes: broadcast 0, multicast 0, unknown unicast 0
        Dynamic ARP inspection drop counters:
          packets: 0, bytes: 0
        IP source guard drop counters:
          packets: 0, bytes: 0
    List of Access PWs:
    List of VFIs:
```

The PBB-EVPN solution relies on two MAC addresses: B-MAC and C-MAC. The B-MAC on each PE is viewed by using the command **show l2vpn pbb backbone-source-mac**. This command displays the chassis MAC and the backbone MAC address. When the packet from the AC is supposed to be forwarded, it is encapsulated into B-MAC and forwarded across the MPLS backbone. To view the customer MAC address learned across

the MPLS cloud, use the command **show l2vpn forwarding bridge-domain mac-address**
[location *rack/slot/cpu*]. This command displays the MAC address of the source as well
as the destination. It also displays the BMAC and S-BMAC as well as the MAC address of
the source and the destination CE router.

Example 15-11 displays both the B-MAC and the customer learned MAC. The MAC
5087.891c.30a7 is the backbone MAC of PE2, whereas 5087.8968.266f is the backbone
MAC of PE1. The MAC address 001c.577f.7f01 is the MAC address of the interface connecting the PE1 on the CE1 router. The MAC address 001c.577f.7f42 belongs to VLAN 2
on PE1, and the MAC address 001e.f78d.49c1 belongs to VLAN 2 on CE2 learned across
the PBB-EVPN circuit.

Example 15-11   *EVPN MAC Addresses*

```
! Output from PE1 (EVPN Backbone MAC)
RP/0/RSP0/CPU0:PE1# show l2vpn pbb backbone-source-mac
Backbone Source MAC: 5087.8968.266f
Chassis MAC        : 5087.8968.266f


! EVPN Customer MAC
RP/0/RSP0/CPU0:PE1# show l2vpn forwarding bridge-domain mac-address loc 0/0/CPU0
To Resynchronize MAC table from the Network Processors, use the command...

    l2vpn resynchronize forwarding mac-address-table location <r/s/i>


Mac Address    Type    Learned from/Filtered on  LC learned Resync Age   Mapped to
--------------------------------------------------------------------------------
5087.891c.30a7 BMAC    BD id: 0                   N/A        N/A          N/A
5087.8968.266f S-BMAC  BD id: 0                   N/A        N/A          N/A
001c.577f.7f01 dynamic Gi0/0/0/0.2               0/0/CPU0   0d 0h 0m 16s   N/A
001c.577f.7f42 dynamic Gi0/0/0/0.2               0/0/CPU0   0d 0h 0m 17s   N/A
001e.f78d.49c1 dynamic BD id: 1                  0/0/CPU0   0d 0h 0m 17s 5087.891c.30a7

! Output from PE2 (EVPN Backbone MAC)
RP/0/RSP0/CPU0:PE2# show l2vpn pbb backbone-source-mac
Backbone Source MAC: 5087.891c.30a7
Chassis MAC        : 5087.891c.30a7
```

The PBB core allocates two labels for forwarding across the MPLS core. One label is for
unicast and the other for multicast. The two labels are viewed by using the command
show evpn evi [detail]. This command not only displays the label information but other
EVPN related information, such as RD and RT. Example 15-12 displays the output of
the command **show evpn evi detail**. In the output, label 24013 is the unicast label, and
24014 is the multicast label.

Example 15-12   *Verifying EVPN EVI and Label Information*

```
RP/0/RSP0/CPU0:PE1# show evpn evi detail
EVI        Bridge Domain              Type
---------- -------------------------- -------
1001       PBB-CORE-1001              PBB
   Unicast Label  : 24013
   Multicast Label: 24014
   Flow Label: N
   RD Config: none
   RD Auto   : (auto) 192.168.1.1:1001
   RT Auto   : 100:1001
   Route Targets in Use       Type
   -------------------------- -------
   100:1001                   Import
   100:1001                   Export

65535      ES:GLOBAL                  BD
   Unicast Label  : 0
   Multicast Label: 0
   Flow Label: N
   RD Config: none
   RD Auto   : (auto) 192.168.1.1:0
   RT Auto   : none
   Route Targets in Use       Type
   -------------------------- -------
```

After the labeling information is received, the forwarding counters are verified using the command **show mpls forwarding**. This command displays the packets forwarded beside a particular Forwarding Equivalence Class (FEC), which in this case is the unicast and the multicast labels allocated for the PBB core. Example 15-13 displays the output of the command **show mpls forwarding**.

Example 15-13   *Verifying Labels in MPLS Forwarding Table*

```
RP/0/RSP0/CPU0:PE1# show mpls forwarding | include BD
24013   Pop      No ID           BD=0 PE      point2point    3230574768
24014   Pop      No ID           BD=0 PEIM    point2point    606
```

Summary

BGP is a mature protocol and has been in the field for a very long time. But over the years, the scope of BGP has expanded due to its capability to extend its flexibility to the development of new features.

This chapter examined various features that rely on BGP for their functioning. It discussed BGP for link-state distribution. Using BGP-LS, modern day SDN controllers can use the information to build the IGP topology on the fly and help the network administrators to manage their network and make deployment of features like Traffic Engineering (TE) easier.

The chapter then explained how BGP is used for tunnel signaling and its role in solutions such as Virtual Extensible LAN (VxLAN) BGP EVPN and other solutions that require tunnel functionality. Finally, the chapter covered provider backbone bridging for the Ethernet VPN (PBB-EVPN) solution. This solution provides many benefits, such as the following:

- PE node redundancy with load-balancing based on L2/L3/L4 flows.

- Flow-based multipathing of traffic from PE to core, and vice versa.

- Geo-redundant PE nodes with optimum unicast forwarding.

PBB-EVPN works across the MPLS core with the edge router running BGP and exchanging EVPN routes.

Additional functionality will continue to be added to BGP in the future, reinforcing the concepts and initial architecture of BGP when first developed.

References

RFC 7752, *North-Bound distribution of Link-State and TE information using BGP*, H. Gredler, Ed., J. Medved, S. Previdi, A. Farrel, S. Ray , IETF, https://tools.ietf.org/html/rfc7752, March 2016.

RFC 5693, *ALTO Problem Statement*, J. Seedorf, E. Burger, IETF, https://tools.ietf.org/html/rfc5693, October 2009.

RFC 4655, *PCE Based Architecture*, A. Farrel, J.P. Vasseur, IETF, https://tools.ietf.org/html/rfc4655, August 2006.

RFC 5512, *The BGP Encapsulation SAFI and the BGP Tunnel Encapsulation Attribute*, P. Mohapatra, E. Rosen. IETF, https://tools.ietf.org/html/rfc5512, April 2009.

Cisco. Cisco IOS Software Configuration Guides. http://www.cisco.com

Index

Numbers

A